TRADITION IN A TURBULENT AGE

Tradition in a Turbulent Age

Whitman College

1925 – 1975

G. THOMAS EDWARDS

Whitman College
Walla Walla, Washington

ISBN 0-9632955-4-3

Library of Congress Control Number 2001093911

Copyright © 2001 by the Board of Trustees of Whitman College.

Manufactured in the United States of America.

Dedication

This book is dedicated to the Whitman professors who have maintained the liberal arts dike against the rising sea of career education.

Note from the President

Professor of History Emeritus G. Thomas Edwards provides us a well-researched, gracefully written second volume on the history of Whitman College. It covers the era from 1925 through 1975, a fifty-year period in which a struggling liberal arts college on the frontier becomes one of the best liberal arts colleges in the West and one of the top liberal arts colleges in America.

The genius of Whitman College over the years, as Professor Edwards ably explains, has been its gifted faculty members, who so often went "above and beyond" in their dedication to students. Tom Edwards, who taught at Whitman College for thirty-four years, was one of the best of those teachers. He did it all: superb teaching, inspired advising, splendid service to his colleagues, leadership in community and professional associations, and excellent scholarship.

Great teachers not only "know their stuff" and have a passion for learning, they also say and do things that unlock our energies, imagination, and creative impulses. Exceptional ones, like Tom Edwards, convince us that we can work a lot harder and be more disciplined, and that we should always be trying. They challenge us to question conventional wisdom and to confront our own prejudices.

Great teachers "bring their subject home." They are somehow able to relate abstract ideas and theories to the realities of everyday life. They often understand, as Thomas Jefferson did, that a liberal education is a training ground for citizenship and a means to acquire discernment, tolerance, and judgment.

Edwards' first volume, *The Triumph of Tradition*, placed today's college in its historical context. *The Triumph of Tradition* was a poignant story of struggle, sacrifice, and survival. This theme continues into the second volume as the college grows from about five hundred students and virtually no endowment to a college of about eleven hundred and an endowment of nearly $28,000,000. The faculty grows also, from a couple of dozen to nearly eighty regular faculty members. (Whitman today has about fourteen hundred students and endowment and trust funds of nearly $350,000,000.)

Tom Edwards offers an objective and sometimes even grainy interpretation of the evolution of Whitman College, one of the most detailed and thoroughly researched studies of any college or university in the Northwest. This history draws on knowledge gained from his having taught Pacific Northwest and Western history and by his extensive scholarship on this region, and is thus nicely grounded in both the history of the region and the history of higher education in America.

Whitman College is a very special place of learning. It is a place that celebrates the joy of learning and inspired teaching, and that encourages every student to discover essential values that free the mind and nourish the spirit. It is a place dedicated to scholarship and the education of character, courage, and personal responsibility. Yet, as this volume attests, it is always a work in progress, always in the process of becoming and of trying to live up to its aspirations.

Professor Edwards and I wish to acknowledge a generous gift to this history of the college by DeLos Ransom, a 1935 Whitman graduate. A native Northwesterner, Mr. Ransom has long been a keen student of this region and its rich history. His gift helped underwrite a good portion of the research that made the publication of *Tradition in a Turbulent Age* possible.

Thomas E. Cronin
President, Whitman College
March, 2001

Contents

Foreword

A dramatic theme emerges from the story of establishing Whitman College, beginning in 1859. The first volume of this history, published in 1992, told of heroic pioneers sacrificing eastern comforts to endure frontier hardships as they brought formal higher education westward. Above all others, President Stephen Penrose dominated the action between 1894 and 1924, when the first volume ends. The reader thinks of Penrose battling a variety of deprivations, ranging from a lack of money to his loss of sight.

By 1924 academic standards had been recognized by the formation of a Phi Beta Kappa chapter, and able graduates had begun to mark their imprint on the world. Whitman was a success, and Penrose, hailed as a great educational leader, considered resigning his presidency after three decades and continuing only to teach. Sentimental—and properly appreciative—board members prevailed upon him to remain as president.

Tom Edwards concludes the first volume by expressing Chester Maxey's 1925 perspective that Penrose should have retired in 1924. Maxey, a 1912 graduate and newly returned to campus as a professor, argued that the president's achievements had crested, financial conditions were still precarious, and the campus physically was deteriorating. Penrose, going blind, literally could not see the deterioration. After three decades, Penrose felt he had the information in his head that he needed to run the school, but Maxey thought he was becoming inattentive, and necessarily delegated too much to others.

It was the view of Professor Maxey that Whitman's Great Depression came to the campus prematurely in the 1920s, which only made more difficult the arrival of the 1930s.

The second volume of this history opens in 1925, and continues through a dramatic half-century of change. The title of the first volume, *The Triumph of Tradition*, captured the theme of creating a Williams College or a Knox College in a new place. *Tradition in a Turbulent Age* captures the theme of this second volume equally well. The campus drama of these years was indeed turbulent, as contesting groups battled for influence in determining the future of Whitman. The story of these tensions and sometimes open conflicts lays unusually bare what went on during the fifty years. This is not college catalogue copy or public relations promotional material. All colleges, in truth, have these histories, to one degree or another—campus life is not actually as it is portrayed in student recruitment videos—but the stories are seldom told.

No other western small college has received two such fat volumes of its history written by a professional scholar. Tom Edwards has made a unique contribution to the study of higher education in the Pacific Northwest, and to those interested in Whitman. The effort is justified by the importance of Whitman in the region combined with the richness of existing historical source material. The result will be appreciated by readers, who will note that the collegiate lily has not been gilded by the author.

It is a suggestive fact concerning the difficulties inherent in campus leadership that during the near-century of college presidencies chronicled in these two volumes down to 1975 only Walter Bratton, Chester Maxey, and Louis Perry resigned voluntarily. Alexander Jay Anderson, James Eaton, Stephen Penrose, and Rudolph Clemen, the first four leaders, were forced to resign; Winslow Anderson and Donald Sheehan died in office. Thus, prior to 1975, two-thirds of Whitman's nine presidents resigned involuntarily, or died.

Trustees similarly had a difficult role to play during the years covered by Edwards' histories. Accused of being provincial, parsimonious, and occasionally self-serving, no truly significant trustee leadership appears in these pages prior to that of Donald Sherwood in the 1950s, and Sherwood was in some respects as much a part of the story of alumni activity and the board of overseers as that of the board of trustees. It is not until the juxtaposition of Chester Maxey's presidency with Don Sherwood's trusteeship that these two potential sources of leadership flowed relatively congruently and thus with more concerted results than ever before. Management, fund raising and faculty support did not proceed productively until a foundation had been built by the Maxey-Sherwood years. Because they were such lean and acrimonious years, particularly from the faculty perspective, it is mainly in retrospect that this era seems a most beneficial foundation for the future.

Edwards makes clear that the Whitman faculty was the glory of the place from the first. He also makes clear that the lot of a professor was difficult. Poorly paid, ill-housed professionally, overworked pedagogically, starved in scholarly nurture, the faculty for decades had as its worldly reward earnest students and their appreciation for good teaching.

Ever-resilient students loom large in Edwards's two volumes, for he never forgets the purpose for which the campus exists, the recipients of the faculty's and staff's service. The most meaningful vignettes in these books are those of youngsters from remote rural backgrounds, who find at Whitman the human and intellectual resources to assist them to live productively in the great world to which they graduate.

How are we to understand the ultimate meanings of the turbulence described by Edwards in the second volume? What are the shifting constellations in the Whitman cosmos? Against what background should Whitman constituents interpret what happened in the past, and what happens today?

At the highest and most general level, Whitman is to be understood as one of many regional versions of the national evolution over the last century or so of mainstream residential undergraduate arts and science colleges. Of greater interest to us is the precise nature of the dialectic by which Whitman evolved. Apart from overall national trends, which obviously influenced faculty and student development, there is a specific historical dynamic. It is best characterized as the interaction between the Penrose principle and the Maxey-Sherwood principle. The former provided the initiative between the turn of the last century and the Great Depression; the latter from the 1950s to the 1970s, if not later.

The shorthand Penrose principle is meant to indicate his idealistic aspiration in all things, which drew wide parameters within which all later Whitman activities would fall. Economic realities continually ate away at the foundations of Penrose's dreams and threatened their destruction. The Maxey-Sherwood principle did not argue with the aspiration, but rather applied the brakes to what it alleged was a college on a run-away course. Debts were mounting, mismanagement could be detected, fiduciary inattention had to be corrected, and vows of frugality needed to be taken. Practical implications of the Maxey-Sherwood principle down-sized the faculty during the 1950s, converted cash to endowment, and embraced disciplinary policies for management to follow. Turbulence in the earlier Penrose era followed the institutional struggle for existence. Turbulence in the Maxey era followed conscious self-denial policies of both the president and the trustees, policies designed to secure a future which would be Depression-proof. It worked. Edwards tells how the Perry and Sheehan years saw institutional progress in all areas, and paved the way for the easier achievements of the last twenty-five years of the twentieth century.

Stephen Penrose, Chester Maxey, and Donald Sherwood are the three most important figures in Whitman's history. The first was virtually the founder, extending his influence over half a century. The second was an exemplary student, teacher, scholar, president, and Walla Walla leader for most of the twentieth century. The third, who had the most problematic role, was active for most of the century in Walla Walla as student, businessman, community citizen. His period of significant influence on campus extended almost six decades. Chester Maxey left the presidency in 1959, returning as acting president during 1966–1967, and then resuming retirement. Sherwood remained influential for three decades after that.

The reason Sherwood's influence may be judged problematic is that, long after the financial crises of the 1930s and 1940s were surmounted, he influenced Whitman policies to be self-denying in ways reasonable people can debate today. In light of Whitman's present success, the onus of the debate may fall to the critic of the policies that were followed. But, one may ask, would Whitman be even more successful if it had not followed such rigid principles of frugality for so long? (Baker Ferguson, who graduated in 1939, and who chaired the board of trustees from 1972 to 1983, has suggested that Don Sherwood himself was more pragmatic than rigid, and that Sherwood's followers may have been less flexible than Sherwood himself.)

Whitman incurred virtually no external debt, granted virtually no non-need financial aid, and placed as much unrestricted cash as possible into the endowment between the 1940s and 1970s. Stated differently, in that period, Whitman expanded as little as possible, improved physical plant less than it might, provided few financial incentives to diversify the applicant pool, and generally saved rather than spent its money.

So ingrained are the habits of the Sherwood policies that until recently most Whitman people did not realize that these policies represented choices. Tom Edwards nicely ends his historical account before the emergence of the contemporary day. Now, new policies are practiced. For quite a few years, Whitman has complemented its historic no-need financial aid practice with an energetic attempt to attract the "best and brightest" with no-need financial awards. At a historic trustee meeting in the spring of 1999 the unanimous decision was made to borrow $25,000,000 million for capital construction. Today, unrestricted cash frequently is applied to discretionary projects to improve the quality of the student experience rather than being applied to the endowment. Because of favorable financial market conditions, fund raising, and the employment of a five-percent maximum take-out rate for income yield, the endowment has grown steadily despite these policies, which would have been considered improvident in earlier times.

One might say that the Penrose principle began the dialectic during the first third of the twentieth century; that the Maxey-Sherwood principle countered it during the second third and more of the century; that a synthesis of the two prevailed by the end of the century. To put it sympathetically, Maxey and Sherwood struggled to preserve what Penrose had created. Those of us who followed were the beneficiaries.

As Tom Edwards has finished Whitman's historical prologue up through 1975, the next quarter-century has drawn to a close, and the new century has begun. A majority of living Whitman alumni have graduated since 1975. Three more presidents have served, Tom

Cronin being the twelfth. Whitman has maintained its relative superiority in overall institutional health compared to the other independent colleges of the Northwest (except for Reed College, which now matches its traditional academic strength with financial security as well). Indeed, it is pleasing to be able to observe that probably all of the surviving Northwest colleges—there have been failures—are healthier today in every respect than they were in 1975. That is remarkable, in view of the widespread gloomy predictions of the 1970s that American private colleges faced decline and extinction. The story of that successful most recent quarter-century of collegiate history will have to await the historian who will one day write the third volume of Whitman history.

Robert Allen Skotheim
President,
   The Huntington Library, Art Collections, and Botanical Gardens
January, 2001

Preface

The word "turbulence" in the title of this book may be surprising to some, given Whitman's present serenity. A person strolling across the campus is delighted with the buildings (especially the older ones), the manicured lawns, the large trees, the fountain, the stream, and the lake. Conversations with students and faculty are almost always positive. Individuals may be harried or stressed, but rarely do they voice criticism of the institution's boards, administration, faculty, students, or alumni. These positive circumstances have generally characterized the college since the mid-1970s. This is not to say that every student and faculty member is currently satisfied with conditions—no school can perpetually satisfy every constituent. College-age students and faculty members of all ages are by nature critical. Students of every generation complain about costs, ineffective teachers, and uninspiring classmates. Faculty members also express dissatisfaction, pointing to unmotivated students, inappropriate salaries, and inept administrators and colleagues.

But the current high retention rate of professors and students reflects a remarkable degree of satisfaction with their campus. It is fair to say that, at the end of the twentieth century, Whitman is a highly successful institution. Its present academic standing is owing to dozens of dedicated women and men. Their contributions are chronicled in the *Triumph of Tradition* and in this sequel.

The question could be posed: Why should a small school's history be recounted in two large volumes? The first book, *The Triumph*

of Tradition, begins with the college's founding as Whitman Seminary and relates how it survived difficult growing pains and by 1925
had become a highly respected institution. The history demonstrated that societal problems and successes impacted even this remote
campus; colleges do not live in cocoons, although a few professors
would prefer to.

This second book covers fifty years in which the college struggled
even more with the pressures of external forces: from the Great Depression through the disruptions attendant upon the Vietnam War,
Whitman experienced considerable turbulence. Not every year, of
course, was difficult, but the groups composing the college community suffered stressful conditions in these decades. This period is crucial to an understanding of the present college.

Fortunately, college records are available for a close study of
Whitman. President Stephen Penrose kept hundreds of letters and
other documents; other leaders also stored valuable records, including the official records of trustees, overseers, and the faculty. All
of these primary documents have been carefully preserved by librarian Ruth Reynolds and, later, by archivist Larry Dodd. Alumni publications recount the personal and professional successes of graduates.
The *Pioneer* and other student publications—until the early 1970s—
provided coverage of campus events. In addition, oral histories were
taken by Professor Donald King's classes, Professor Robert Whitner taped a few individuals, the board of overseers sponsored an
extensive oral history program, and I have conducted many interviews. The scores of transcripts should be useful to a variety of individuals. Whitman is fortunate to have such rich college archives.

A detailed history provides an opportunity to explore controversial issues that are fuzzy in the minds of the Whitman community, including fund raising in the 1920s, the actions of the boards
in the early 1930s, the troubled Rudolf Clemen presidency, the tenure
issue, the faculty's gaining power in the 1960s, and the student activists of the 1960s and early 1970s. Furthermore, Whitman's story
deserves to be told because the college has had a tremendous impact upon the region and nation. This present history does not include a detailed record of its alumni. Penrose often asserted the
truism that, "While teachers make a college, its alumni make its reputation." The accomplishments of alumni explain the need for a

study of the school that prepared them for significant contributions to their occupations, families, neighborhoods, regions, and nation.

All of the colleges in the Pacific Northwest have made similar contributions to the area's political, social, cultural, and economic life. Unfortunately, thorough histories of the University of Oregon, Oregon State University, the University of Washington, smaller universities, and private schools have not yet appeared. When more of these histories are published, it will be possible for scholars to compare these institutions. But before such an analytical study can be undertaken, it is fair to assume that all the schools had similar experiences in the period from 1925 to 1975, including the financial problems of the 1930s; major adjustments to the Second World War, the Korean War, the Cold War, and the Vietnam War; the yeasty civil rights movement and the rebirth of the women's rights movement; and the emerging grade inflation of the 1970s, the excesses of athletic programs, and the rise of womens' athletics.

Collegiate history is often uncritical. It is difficult for scholars to be objective when writing about their institutions and colleagues. It is tempting to gloss over difficulties and miscalculations, and to praise people and programs. Aware of this problem of objectivity, I have made every effort to be fair. Despite the size of this book, there are many important stories that are not included; I hope that these accounts will be recorded and added to the college archives and eventually become a part of new institutional studies.

Finally, a note about nostalgia is in order. In 1935, a Whitman pamphlet defined nostalgia as "an irresistible desire to walk again with friends, to hear again remembered voices" and assured alumni that such a longing could be cured by attending Homecoming. I hope that alumni, who have expressed pangs of nostalgia in interviews or in informal conversations, will find in these pages accounts that will remind them of their happy undergraduate experiences. Numerous senior alumni have often stated that their college years were among the happiest of their lives. They and younger individuals emphasize that several classmates and some professors became their good friends, and they keenly anticipate meeting them at Homecoming or class reunions. The author hopes that alumni from other schools will read about individuals and events similar to those important in their own undergraduate lives.

The illustrations have been selected on the basis of their importance to student generations. Students and alumni know buildings and professors better than they know earlier or later classes, and thus photographs of administrators, faculty members, and buildings have been given more space than student groups or activities. An attempt has been made to find appropriate illustrations for various time periods and to cover a range of activities. Those interested in further perusing campus photographs should contact the college archives.

During seven years of researching and writing this history, I have become obliged to numerous individuals, including those who read chapters and lent encouragement. Former president Robert Skotheim, who encouraged me to write *The Triumph of Tradition*, insisted that there should be a sequel. Because of his interest, he has read all of the chapters more than once and has generously given me advice and support. President Thomas Cronin, who has also been consistently interested in this history, has read chapters and provided ideas and perspective. Former treasurer Pete Reid has served as a researcher and consultant, particularly for those sections dealing with the college's financial matters. For nearly sixty years Reid has been connected with Whitman. Although he is devoted to his alma mater, he recognizes the shortcomings of individuals and groups. He—and everyone I consulted—wanted a fair history, not a promotional piece.

My colleagues David Schmitz, David Deal, Pat Keef, and David Stevens, as well as former student John Bogley, have carefully read chapters and made valuable suggestions. I have also profited from conversation with many professors and staff members. Colleagues Donald King, Frederick Breit, David Deal, Walter Weingart, James Pengra, David Frasco, and Craig Gunsul were particularly helpful.

Librarians have been extremely useful. Archivist Larry Dodd frequently and cheerfully provided me space in his crowded archives and located boxes of material that provided the book's foundation. Even during the stressful move of the archives, he took time to dig out documents. Librarian Marilyn Sparks was as helpful as always. Other librarians at other institutions provided assistance, especially my former student, Arlene Weible, at Willamette University and my daughter, Stephanie Plowman, at Gonzaga University.

Again I have relied upon talented Whitman students to carry out research activities and to duplicate hundreds of primary documents.

Derek Michael spent a summer researching the Whitman College *Pioneer* under a Louis Perry research grant. Sarah Munson, Jason Lindenberger, and Eric Odegard were other valuable student researchers.

I have conducted dozens of oral histories in both the East and the West, and I appreciate the willingness of alumni to share their experiences. Many of these sources are cited in the endnotes. Louis Perry, Kenyon Knopf, Donald Sherwood, Baker Ferguson, Larry Beaulaurier, Pete Reid, Gordon Scribner, David Stevens, Arthur and Lucille Rempel, Roy Hoover, John Haigh, Katherine Sheehan, Richard Stuart, and Peggy Metastasio answered numerous questions.

Several eagle-eyed editors, who have provided friendship and encouragement, have carefully read the manuscript. Michael Wyatt Smith, who was a resourceful researcher and editor for *The Triumph of Tradition*, assisted with this manuscript until he became director of the alumni association. Professor Margo Scribner made valuable editorial contributions, including helping to organize the narrative. John Laursen handled this book as skillfully as he did *The Triumph of Tradition*. An outstanding editor and designer who has diligently attended to myriad details, he has been determined to make this a clear and accurate retelling of the college story as well as a handsome one. Alumna Ellen Watts Lodine was wonderfully helpful in reviewing and revising the text and painstakingly proofreading the manuscript. Skilled and patient typists Robbie Skiles, Shirley Muse, Cora Heid, and Donna Jones worked on several drafts of each chapter.

My wife, Nannette, has been thoughtful and patient. As a faculty wife for more than three decades she has a keen awareness of the college, and I have profited from her insights. Not only has Nannette allowed my research to interfere with our vacations, she has listened to me discuss each chapter and sharpened my prose. My devoted children, Randall and Stephanie, share their parents' enthusiasm for the liberal arts, and have provided consistent encouragement.

My deep gratitude goes to all of these people who sustained me as I worked to relate the history of a significant Northwest institution, important to us and to thousands of others.

G. Thomas Edwards
Whitman College
July, 2001

Tradition in a Turbulent Age

Prologue:
Two Freshman Years
1925–1926 and 1933–1934

Freshman years have many similarities; in any fall the apprehensive freshman comes to campus with some familiarity with the college catalog, explores the facilities, and receives a considerable amount of official and unofficial advice. But there would be vast differences between the experience of a young man or woman entering Whitman College in 1925 — President Stephen Penrose's thirty-first school year — and that of such a person enrolling in 1933 — the leader's fortieth and final school year. As the mood of the United States had changed from the optimistic 1920s to the gloomy early 1930s, so too had the mood of the campus.

In any decade, freshmen heard Penrose in chapel, in class, or on the sidewalk relate the college's dreadful conditions when he took the helm in 1894. At that time the school had faced many woes — a tiny enrollment, unmanageable debt, an unpaid faculty, and a lack of prestige and friends. The 1925 freshman would conclude that Penrose told an unfamiliar though powerful story, but the 1933 freshman would surmise that conditions of the early 1930s were all too similar to those of the early 1890s. In 1933, as in 1894, the college staggered under a pressing debt; its supporters, many of whom had their own financial problems, could not help Whitman resolve its money crisis, and the faculty went unpaid. In 1925 Penrose was an inspiring leader, predicting that the college faced a brilliant future; in his last year he was circumspect. A few observers predicted the school's economic collapse and feared that, after forty years of heroic service — Penrose had reportedly gone blind from the stress of his office—trustees would tell him that the school must temporarily be padlocked.

In 1925, however, there was no hint of such a disaster. Whitman had just completed what appeared to be a very successful financial campaign, and its enrollment exceeded six hundred for the very first time. The catalog published in the spring of 1925 described an impressive regional institution. The college operated eight buildings on thirty acres, which were "well laid out with lawns and trees," and a stream and a small lake were campus landmarks. There were two athletic fields: Baker for women, bordering Mill Creek; and Ankeny for men, in the quad. A 1925 freshman would be told that the school was planning to acquire eighteen additional acres for athletics and that there were even exciting plans to build a grandstand to seat fifteen thousand. Freshman women learned that crowded Reynolds Hall would close, and a spacious new dormitory, Prentiss Hall, would open in 1926.

Faculty and students pose in front of the Whitman Memorial Building in 1925.
The women, some of whom wear the latest hair fashions, sit in front, and the men,

Students learned that women lived in Reynolds Hall, Langdon House, or Green Cottage. Freshman men took rooms in Lyman Hall (commonly called Lyman House), a handsome new dormitory. Many upperclassmen resided in fraternity houses. Students filled every nook and corner of the residence halls. Penrose complained that, because of the over-enrollment, he "would like to drop 50 or 75 at Christmas time."[1] The 1925 catalog did not list two prominent campus buildings: the president's attractive home and the unattractive library shack. Freshmen learned that the library—part of which was in the Whitman Memorial Building—included about thirty-seven thousand bound volumes, subscribed to 250 periodicals, and housed a valuable collection of United States government documents.

A freshman arriving on the campus in 1925 would be most impressed with the Whitman Memorial Building (commonly called Memorial Hall). Completed in 1899, this three-story building was constructed of yellow pressed brick and sported a red roof. It con-

nearly all of whom are wearing ties, stand to the rear. President Stephen Penrose is seated with the faculty. Professor Walter Bratton is to his left.

tained recitation rooms, a chapel seating five hundred, and administrative offices. Across the street, the three-story Conservatory of Music (now called the Hall of Music), dedicated in 1910 and designed by architect Ellis Lawrence (who had also designed Lyman House), featured a concert hall. The gymnasium, erected in 1905, included a swimming tank and modern exercise equipment. Billings Hall, built at the same time as Memorial Hall, housed the physics, chemistry, and biology departments. New students investigated its laboratories, drafting room, and three-inch telescope, as well as its museum, where exhibits included a natural history section, a plant collection, "an industrial exhibit showing noxious and beneficial plants and animals," a mineral collection, tables and cases of fossils, ethnological materials "illustrating the life of the Indians of the Puget Sound region," and considerable material relating to Marcus Whitman and the missionary period.

In talks to freshmen, Penrose explained the college's purpose and history. He stated that Whitman was "modern and scientific, endeavoring to give students a knowledge of the world in which they live according to the best scientific insight," and that it was trying "to make them good citizens and Christians."[2] The college catalog contained a brief history, emphasizing institutional accomplishments since Whitman Seminary opened in 1866 in a wood-frame structure fronting Boyer Avenue. Penrose elaborated on this remarkable history and reported general financial figures to new students. The school had just conducted a successful fund-raising campaign, it had property worth more than half a million dollars, and its endowment exceeded a million dollars. While students knew something about scholarships, prizes, and loans, they were less acquainted with endowed professorships and the Phi Beta Kappa chapter. They would come to understand their importance.

School officers bluntly told freshmen to take advantage of their impressive educational opportunities, especially the rewarding liberal arts classes taught by an able faculty. They were also informed in 1925 that the $50-a-term tuition fee was low. In fact, the charge even included two weeks of free hospital service. Annual dormitory fees were only $75 for women and $100 for men; board cost $6 a week. To those who worried that they could not pay these fees—estimated at about $350 a year—the college deans gave assurances that there were many local jobs available. Almost every student worked part-time, but Penrose warned that this outside work must not detract from scholarship or participation in "student activities, which constitute a large part of the enriching enjoyment of college life."[3] The faculty fully shared these sentiments.

Whitman's catalogs reflected its financial status. Freshmen arriving in 1933 consulted a slimmer version, one that did not describe the buildings. But in the spring of 1934 a more impressive catalog appeared, including a new section on the college's aims. The college sought to provide an education "that enables a student . . . to discover himself and to choose that life work for which his abilities best fit him. . . ." Whitman also thought it necessary to list its several advantages over competitors, including its location. Walla Walla was "large enough to furnish the support and advantages of urban life without the distractions of the large city." Penrose informed students that a Californian had predicted that "it was the destiny of the Pacific Northwest to be the conscience of the Pacific Coast." This individual "feared the undermining influences of the California climate, wealth, and luxury." Walla Walla's mild climate, Penrose concluded, meant that it had "enough winter to invigorate the blood and strengthen the moral fibers."[4] The institution boasted that the ratio of one professor for each twelve students ensured "the opportunity of close, vital contact with friendly advisers."

The school assured parents that college fees were "relatively low"; in fact, the tuition was less "than half the actual cost to the college of the students' education." Students might have been surprised to read in the catalog that tuition—$100 each semester—was higher during the Great Depression, but board costs had been reduced to $5 a week. Freshmen learned that the combined costs prevented dozens of qualified women and men from joining them. Penrose stressed that, "We have more completed applications than ever before," but the institution lacked the financial resources to help these applicants.[5]

At the start of the 1933 school year, freshmen as usual took part in a traditional orientation, went through Greek rush, and mingled with upperclassmen. On September 22, 1933, however, the *Pioneer* stressed that this school year would be unusual in that Penrose would retire and that a new man would be chosen "to guide the destinies" of Whitman.

Subsequent articles in the *Pioneer* reflected concern about the regional economy. Freshmen learned that the price of wheat influenced the size of the student body, faculty salaries, and more. Bursar George Marquis wrote in the college newspaper that, if wheat (which had hovered around forty cents per bushel the previous season) should climb to $1 a bushel, then more students would enroll and the school's farm mortgages would generate some income. He summarized: "So goeth the price of wheat, so goeth Whitman."[6] Some faculty members urged students to appreciate the positive influence of the New Deal, because its programs could mean campus jobs and increased wheat prices.

In 1933–1934 the school was much less confident about the students' chances of finding work on campus or in town than it had been in 1925. Penrose worried that students could rarely earn more than $100 a year; thus, the school emphasized: "No student should enter College who has not funds sufficient to cover at least the first semester of the freshman year." To aid its hard-pressed young people, Whitman operated a bureau of appointments, an office designed to assist alumni and seniors in finding "desirable professional and business positions."

Another change reflecting economic realities was the college's emphasis upon a practical curriculum. In 1934 the school concluded that, "At the present time the professions are crowded and the best professional schools have more applicants than they can receive." But the catalog went on to boast that Whitman graduates had a better chance than those of other colleges of getting into graduate schools and succeeding. The curriculum prepared students for law, medicine, engineering, theology, business, public service (a field becoming "increasingly important and attractive to women"), teaching, journalism, dramatics, music, and physical education.

In the college's weakened condition, the catalog no longer listed the value of the buildings, grounds, and endowment. On the other hand, although the Great Depression brought painful problems, at least enrollments had not fallen to drastic levels. Penrose assured readers that, although the student body was only two-thirds what it had been ten years earlier, the drop in enrollments had been halted, and conditions were improving. Privately, however, he expressed grave doubts about the institution's future.

Walla Walla's mood had also changed, but the city, unlike its college, did not brag about growth. In 1925 Walla Walla had a population estimated at 15,700; in fact, in the decade between 1920 and 1930 its population grew by only three percent. This meant that Walla Walla fell to the rank of Washington's seventh largest city. Older residents remembered that, when the college started in 1882, Walla Walla had boasted about being the territory's largest city. Freshmen from eastern Washington knew that Walla Walla's sluggish growth typified the region. The state's impressive new growth occurred west of the Cascades where cities attracted youth seeking adventure and jobs.

A 1925 freshman strolling the streets of Walla Walla encountered townspeople who preferred to talk about the quality of their lives rather than the quantity of their numbers. Residents boasted about their mild and seasonal climate, broad streets, shade trees, pure water, and fashionable homes. Some citizens called the place the "City of Beautiful Homes," and Penrose told students that the town was "characterized by a love of music and an appreciation of things intellectual and artistic."[7] Walla Wallans also took pride in the fact that their city enjoyed more culture than other agricultural centers: it had two colleges, two schools of music, the state's oldest symphony orchestra, an opera house, and libraries.

A freshman knew or soon discovered that the city was the site of the state penitentiary and veterans hospital; there was some manufacturing—farm machines, bricks, cement pipe, lumber—and there were iron works, canneries, and flour mills, but as an editor pointed out, emphasizing the role of the penitentiary, veterans hospital, courthouse, city hall, and public schools, the city's "largest payrolls were governmental."[8] Still, it was primarily farming that drew people to the region, and it was diversified farming that drove Walla Walla's economy. This valley, the largest in Washington, produced fruit, vegetables, alfalfa, sheep, livestock, cows, and, especially, wheat.

Post-war economic adjustments had retarded Walla Walla's development, but in 1925 its prospects improved. An editor boasted that the city's "wealth and resources, its future, are not mean but are very substantial." Speaking for many, one businessman assured townspeople: "I believe we have passed through the bad times and are now on the verge of the best times the Northwest has ever seen."[9]

But a freshman visiting business houses in 1933 would hear a more guarded assessment of the city's and the state's economic future. Townspeople would inform a student that, during the past year, hundreds of transients—boys and men—had slept on the YMCA's floor. It was also possible to hear Walla Wallans argue over the proposed repeal of the Eighteenth Amendment, including fears that a long row of disreputable saloons would reappear on Main Street. Although citizens worried about financial matters, they expressed pride in new structures, especially the Marcus Whitman Hotel and the Congregational Church. Walla Wallans boasted that the streetcar tracks had been torn out of Main Street and that the Liberty Theater presented "talkies." At least a dozen New Deal programs passed in the first hundred days of the administration of Franklin D. Roosevelt shaped the thinking of residents, but in the fall of 1933 two seemed particularly important—the National Recovery Administration (NRA) and the Agricultural Adjustment Act (AAA).

In November 1933, freshmen participated in a memorable city parade supporting the NRA, a New Deal economic measure designed to revitalize the sluggish economy. The parade—called the greatest in Walla Walla's history by a local newspaper because its line of march stretched for twelve miles—included President Penrose, who held grave doubts about both the NRA and its administrator, Hugh Johnson. Although Penrose disliked Johnson's "vituperative language" and predicted that he would "be thrown to the dogs," the educator realized that his office required him to participate in this public display in support of a managed economy.[10] Accompanied by student body president Russ McNeill, the blind and dubious Penrose led his students and faculty and received the crowd's ovation. The enthusiastic students wore the school's or the nation's colors; some impersonated characters, including "statuesque Dick Buell and ravishing Bill Fifield, [who] vied for honors as Mae West."[11]

This great parade, with its thousands of marchers, and the NRA's blue eagle symbol, placed in many Walla Walla shop windows, encouraged residents. And so did the AAA, a program that won the support of men in coveralls and suits because it was increasing wheat prices. After many struggles, by 1933 both the community and its college were slowly turning the economic corner. The college had survived its most turbulent period since the First World War.

I

Fading Optimism

1925–1930

President Stephen Beasley Linnard Penrose was as important to Whitman in 1925 as he had been in 1894 when he assumed office. This remarkable leader had taken a nearly moribund institution and led it through difficult times to its respected position. In 1927 he assured friends that the school enjoyed "rapidly improving prospects"[1] and that it had greater financial strength than Williams College had possessed when he attended in the early 1880s; furthermore, it was as strong as Yale had been in 1850.[2]

Penrose's many admirers, including faculty members, alumni, townspeople, and regional educators and leaders, cited his impressive accomplishments. Many women and men could recite portions of the college's history, especially how Penrose had replaced wooden buildings with brick ones, established an endowment, employed an outstanding faculty, enrolled bright students, personally influenced the lives of hundreds of young people, and brought prestige to Walla Walla through the college's academic prowess as well as through its activities, including music, debate, dramatics, and athletics.

A man of energy, vision, morality, and intelligence, Penrose was a memorable teacher. A young professor described Penrose as "a person of very considerable elegance and eloquence, and [one who] used both. . . . He struck the fear of something into you."[3] The college's students and alumni praised his stimulating courses in philosophy and his concern for the well-being of students. In fact, alumni, recalling his friendship, often brought their spouses and children

to meet him. Although he was blind, he had the capacity to deal simultaneously with an enormous number of issues that came to his
desk. Faculty members, board members, alumni, townspeople, and
others approached him in person or by mail, seeking advice, information, reactions, or solutions. An effective speaker on various issues, he received frequent calls for lectures. Pacific Northwest residents considered him to be among the pre-eminent college presidents.
He was an intellectual force in Walla Walla and far beyond.

In 1925 Penrose started his thirty-first year as the college's president, maintaining his strong leadership style. According to a young
faculty member, the blind Penrose sat at the rear in faculty meetings and occasionally would pound his cane on the floor. The angry
president thought that the faculty "got fatuous and would tongue
lash them."[4] Whitman was clearly his school; he was firm but not
authoritarian. Although he exercised great power in selecting new
faculty members, in making faculty committee assignments, in chair-
ing faculty meetings, and in setting the college's direction, he allowed
professors considerable voice in shaping the curriculum and in teaching what they considered to be important. The faculty controlled the
curriculum, calendar, student life, and more. Penrose defended academic freedom, a policy that contributed to faculty morale. The governing boards generally followed the president's leadership but rejected some of his proposals. The students, who rarely challenged
his authority, greatly respected his high standards, his concern for
their well-being, and his positive approach to life.

An ordained minister in the Congregational Church, Penrose
sometimes preached in regional churches. He also brought his Christian faith into the classroom and into student conferences. A man
of high moral standards, he urged that all Whitman students serve
society. Two investigators of the college summarized: "The Penrose
administration was paternalistic in character. Penrose, a clergyman
of forceful and colorful personality, regarded himself as a benevo-
lent father to the small college. . . . This benign paternalism was
undoubtedly responsible in large part for certain marked individual traits that characterize Whitman," including a liberal Christian
orientation.[5]

During the 1920s journalists, alumni, and others asked college
leaders about social, athletic, and intellectual conditions on the na-

tion's campuses. Penrose defended students against "the accusations of wildness being hurled at them in general." He pushed for "serious study," because the nation's "public life is determined by the qualities developed in our colleges and universities." He insisted that the faculty, not the students, should determine the curriculum. "The question in the modern college should not be 'what does the student want,' but 'what ought the student to have.' Treating boys and girls as though they were mature men and women flatters their vanity but does not develop their best intellectual effort. Students need guidance and inspiration as well as opportunity."[6]

The president, like other intellectuals, had mixed feelings about the 1920s. He appreciated the fact that the college was in a stronger position. It had escaped the shackles of debt, it enjoyed a respectable endowment, it employed a talented faculty, and it attracted solid students. The school boasted about its successful financial campaign of 1924–1925, and it publicized its achievements in constructing a women's dormitory, acquiring an athletic field, and receiving a foundation grant. These accomplishments and record-breaking enrollments fueled Penrose's optimism, but the president sometimes experienced problems with the governing boards. Trustees voiced more guarded views about the school's future, reluctant to increase either tuition or faculty salaries. Furthermore, few of them, and few overseers, worked to increase the college's endowment, a fund that Penrose feared was inadequately invested.

Tall, portly, and dignified, Penrose had become blind, a disability that he openly discussed. In 1916 he lost the sight in one eye, he stated, "by a displacement of the retina"; eight years later "the other eye suffered a similar, though not a complete, displacement of the retina."[7] Indoors he saw bright lights; outdoors he recognized objects as if they were in a dense smoke. But he walked to the campus unaided, assuring friends that he "guarded myself against all jolts or strains."[8] His awareness of his whereabouts on campus, on roads, and in neighborhoods often surprised his companions. To those amazed by his knowledge of city streets, he explained: "I knew my blindness was coming, so I prepared for it."[9] Penrose judged that it was better to be blind than deaf, "for I have found that the human voice is the bridge over which souls pass in communion rather than the eyes"; furthermore, "The deaf person becomes suspicious as he sees people talking around him and oftentimes imagines morosely that they are talking about him."[10] The leader complained that a major handicap was his inability to read, but he confided to friends that he was now freed from another responsibility: "I always hated like blazes to go out and raise money or try to get people to give money to the College. Now I am absolved from the necessity of doing this, and can sit back and enjoy life, doing things that I want to do."[11]

His daily schedule put teaching first. Penrose confided: "If I could not teach, I would resign at once."[12] He taught nine hours a week, offering such courses as the philosophy of religion and the history of philosophy. The educator had taught these courses so many times that he did not need notes, but he required a student to read certain passages. Like all professors, he wanted diligent students, and once told the registrar that a logic class was "open to all bright students; no dullards need apply."[13] The president also taught a unique, required freshman class dealing with the history of higher education, in which he emphasized the similarities between Whitman and colleges in New England and urged his students to prepare themselves for lives of public service.[14] By 1929 he modified this class, inviting professors from various disciplines to participate by explaining the nature of their academic departments.

Besides teaching, Penrose conducted chapel twice a week and performed administrative duties until late afternoon. He had learned to touch-type on a slightly modified machine; his competent secretaries helped with his correspondence and other administrative responsibilities. Late in the afternoon, freshmen escorted him for a walk that covered three to six miles. This gave him a chance to become acquainted with his guides and to exercise. Penrose boasted: "Usually my escorts are more tired than I."[15] Upon his return home, his wife or students read to him for four or more hours. While Penrose enjoyed magazines such as the *Atlantic Monthly* and *Foreign Affairs*, he preferred books. He told friends not to pity him and assured them that his total loss of sight had "not lessened my interest in the larger world of men and things."[16] Maintaining that his disability had not reduced his effectiveness, he sometimes admitted, however, that it was "harder to keep posted in regard to persons and things."[17] His friends praised him for his ability to over-

come his blindness, especially for learning to touch-type, but they
worried about him upon hearing in 1927 that he had broken two
ribs in a fall at the Portland Hotel. This injury limited his travel for
the college.

Penrose's blindness prompted him to question whether he should
remain as president. He assured everyone that he could handle the
school's internal matters but worried that his inability to travel, especially as a fund raiser, weakened the institution. Although his personal efforts in the 1924–1925 campaign were responsible for its
reported success, in 1925, and again in 1929, he submitted his resignation, largely because of his inability to serve again as the prime
fund raiser. He confessed to a friend that blindness had made him
"a prisoner to a considerable degree."[18]

Mary Penrose, the president's intelligent and dedicated wife, had
been his major assistant since 1896. As interested as her husband
in the college's well-being, she played many roles, including friend,
consultant, chaperon, and hostess. Mary was as familiar a figure
on the campus as her husband. In the late 1920s she put considerable time and energy into various community pursuits, and assisted her husband by describing buildings and people, by spending long
hours reading to him, by hosting dinners, and, most important, by
encouraging him. In 1930 he summarized that she was "really a
rather remarkable person with a brain as big as her heart and with
great capacities for personal friendship."[19] Stephen Penrose joked
that because his helpmate shouldered so many responsibilities he had
concluded "that a man had better be a Mohammedan and have four
wives, one for every kind of need as, for instance, publicity work,
attending conventions, etc."[20]

The Two-Board System

When recruiting overseers and answering inquires, Penrose often explained the college's unique two-board system. The nine trustees,
who were "necessarily local,"[21] enjoyed legal control, but they cooperated with the board of overseers, a group of sixty-four regional leaders. The college's charter gave the trustees "ultimate authority in the [school's] management," but they took the role of an
executive committee for the overseers. At their monthly meetings the

trustees handled administrative details and sent their minutes to overseers. Penrose, in seeking new overseers, assured them that there was no "necessity of frequent attendance at the college."[22] Bankers, business executives, physicians, lawyers, ministers, wheat growers, publishers, and other professional men served as overseers; in 1930 the membership list included three homemakers. Penrose assumed that these women brought different and important perspectives to the overseers, but he thought it was unnecessary to appoint a woman trustee "because there have been enough influential and devoted men for the purpose." He asserted, however, that "a co-educational college cannot reasonably justify a governing organization made up wholly of men." In appointing women as overseers, Penrose considered their "character, influence, social standing, wealth, possible service, and the like."[23] Overseers established permanent committees with specific responsibilities, including buildings and grounds, the Conservatory of Music, finances, and athletics.

The president praised the quality of the overseers: "No other small college" had been so successful "in drawing into its administration so many representative and influential men."[24] Undoubtedly their local prestige aided the overseers as they raised funds, recruited students, and brought recognition to the college.

The Faculty

Like the governing boards, the faculty also had a unique organization. Penrose boasted that it was "so well organized that the work of administration goes very well without much attention from me."[25] While many institutions had created the position of dean of men, Penrose vigorously opposed appointing one. He preferred Whitman's unique system: a board of three deans—each a faculty member— to carry out duties traditionally given to a dean of men. Each dean had a particular responsibility. Thus, in 1925 Latin professor Edward E. Ruby chaired the academic group, English professor William Davis chaired the internal life group, and mathematics professor Walter A. Bratton chaired the external relations group. Each leader conducted meetings of faculty members in his group but spent even more time advising freshman men. Assigned one-third of the members of the class, each dean sometimes assembled them for a general meeting; but the deans spent more time meeting individually with freshman advisees and discussing academic matters or disciplining rule breakers. After a student declared a major field of study at the end of his freshman year, the chairman of that academic department then replaced the dean as a student's advisor.

While Penrose disliked the traditional position of dean of men, he championed having a talented individual in the traditional role of dean of women. This administrator, who enjoyed considerable power and authority, served as the academic and personal advisor of all the freshman women. In 1925, she also had the responsibility for improving living conditions in the dormitories, guiding female students, and guarding the health of all students. This dean sometimes taught a class in her specialty. Indeed, next to the president, she was the most over-worked administrator.

In Penrose's unique system of faculty governance, every professor assumed some administrative duties. Ever since the energetic and persuasive dean Archer Hendrick had resigned in 1911, Penrose had warned against powerful deans and favored distributing power among the faculty. Each professor chaired a special committee responsible for an administrative matter such as the school calendar, the college catalog, student religious life, or student health, and each served on at least one other committee. Besides putting the faculty in closer touch with students, Penrose asserted that dividing responsibility and delegating authority made faculty members feel more involved. In 1925 he defended the system as accomplishing "a more effective and deep-reaching method of administration by throwing responsibility upon many men and women rather than by concentrating power in the hands of one or two."[26]

Professors were able to exercise considerable authority because of their leader's belief in faculty governance: "Though the trustees are given all power by the charter, and are the legal administrative body, the faculty . . . has exercised many functions not therein expressly provided, and has for many years been the actual governing body, with responsibility for almost all matters apart from finances. This has been by the sufferance of the trustees and with their approval."[27]

Issues of Presidential Leadership

During the college's expansion in the late 1920s Penrose expressed delight with the ability, attitude, composition, and size of the student body. Although applications increased at Whitman, as they did at other schools, Penrose convinced overseers to limit the college enrollment to five hundred, including three hundred men. Operating what it called a selective admissions program unique in the region, Whitman announced that it chose students "on the basis of health, character, scholarship, special talents and general promise."[28] Children of alumni received preference.[29] In some years the college accepted sixty percent of the applicants; in one year it took only thirty percent of the women applicants.[30] Penrose explained to an alumnus that these admissions procedures provided "an unusually fine body of students with standards of scholarship and conduct and character which are in vivid contrast with those which you found here in 1881."[31] Because of an increasing number of qualified applicants, the school also admitted more than the maximum figure; for example, in 1929 it enrolled 589 students.

However, the school consistently found it difficult to enroll three hundred men. Penrose explained the difficulty of attracting males: "The boys of the northwest are not yet developed to the point of appreciating an institution like Whitman College which does not seek fame by exaggerating the importance of athletics and prefers remaining small for the sake of its individual students."[32] According to the college records, most of the students were "native born of native born Americans. The exceptions were mainly of North European stocks with occasional Italian, Japanese, Chinese, and Pacific Island students." Of one of these exceptions, Grace Y. Lee, Penrose boasted in 1924: "She is the first Chinese girl in the Pacific Northwest who has graduated from college anywhere and she shows not the slightest trace of her Chinese ancestry, except to some extent in her features." Whitman maintained that it did not discriminate, and explained: "The prevailing character of the student body in this respect reflects the status of the population of the region."[33]

In 1929 the school enrolled 429 students from Washington, eighty-six from Oregon, thirty-six from Idaho, and a scattering from ten other states. The Conservatory of Music enrolled 259 women and only seventy men; about 150 of these music students also took some college classes. By serving the three states carved out of the old Oregon Territory, Penrose boasted that Whitman was "the one institution in the northwest which has escaped from the provincialism of state boundaries."[34]

This enrollment pattern did not trouble Penrose, but he expressed concern because twenty-six percent of the students were Walla Wallans, and he feared that this percentage might increase. The president warned overseers that the college must "think of itself as truly a national institution and not one that is merely local."[35] Thus, the deans joined the president in proposing that the 1925 freshman class would accept eighty women, and only twenty could be from Walla Walla. Pressure from Walla Wallans and others to double Whitman's student population wearied Penrose. He often tried to explain the advantages of a small student body, in particular that it provided students with an opportunity to know their teachers.

But in the 1920s American society generalized that big was better than small. Thus, in his 1927 report the exasperated president offered a facetious proposal. Knowing that some parents and their sons were opposed to coeducation, he suggested that, with their support, he would be able to start another college for just $2,500,000. He would build this college for five hundred men; with a second campus, the number of female students on the original campus could then be increased to five hundred. Penrose was not serious about this proposal, but he hoped that even the most obtuse citizen or board member would see that the college could not double the size of the student body.

In his concern about admission procedures, Penrose wanted the school to examine an applicant's high school record "to find the personal qualities of mind and heart and body, the experience in school activities, the development of self reliance, the range of social expertise, and the development of the moral character." The president did not want to limit admissions to the top high school students. He was especially interested in attracting "promising boys" who had not yet reached their potential, and he hoped that the college "will never become an institution whose membership will be made up solely of those who stand at the top of their classes in high school."

Penrose frankly stated that Whitman, like other schools, admitted "many idlers" and those seeking "pleasures and social advantages" rather than "intellectual training or spiritual enrichment." But he did not blame young people for their attitude: "I wish that American college students had higher ideals in the fields of the intellect and the spirit, but, of course, they are the products of their up-bringing and environment. To form their ideals seems to me to be the subtlest, most appealing, and most needed undertaking for education."[36] The president charged that "the elimination of the unfit is a present problem . . . in college education" but a complicated problem because the "hanger-ons" who seemed "totally incapable or asleep" often surprised the faculty by succeeding in their post-college years.

Penrose proposed an innovative solution to improve the quality of the college degree: a lower college for freshmen and sophomores and an upper college for juniors and seniors. The four hundred students in the two lower classes would attend large lecture classes in basic subjects. After two years they would be examined over all of their classwork, and, upon passing, they would receive a certificate. A maximum of 150 students holding these certificates would be admitted to the upper college, where they would receive specialized courses and enjoy very close personal contact with professors. Each student in the upper college, Penrose elaborated, "would be encouraged in every way to think for himself, to read widely, to develop his powers, and to prepare himself for the highest sort of trained service so far as the college could afford it." The educator declared that those who earned a bachelor's degree in his proposed program would win national distinction.

Realistically, Penrose did not anticipate that the boards would adopt what he called a "radical" proposal, but he wanted it to be discussed. To make board members aware of the need to maintain standards, Penrose asserted: "Many a boy or girl would live a happier life if dropped from college early before they were filled with false ambitions or encouraged to think themselves capable of careers for which they could never have the requisite ability."[37]

Penrose also proposed a change in the scholarship program. Believing that most freshmen could pay the full $150 tuition figure, he argued that the honors scholarship program—one that gave a free scholarship to regional valedictorians and salutatorians—attracted solid students but was too expensive. In 1924 the program yielded about fifty men and women, but each scholarship cost the school $135. In 1925 Penrose proposed reducing the number of honors scholarships to five for women and to about forty for men. Instead of awarding numerous scholarships, the college could encourage freshmen to compete for cash prizes. The president also proposed reducing other types of scholarships and increasing tuition by $50 a year. While trustees agreed to slash the costly scholarship program, they refused until 1928–1929 to increase tuition to $200 a year. Penrose and the underpaid faculty considered this delay to be a serious mistake because the school immediately needed this additional income to increase inadequate salaries.

Enrollment figures for the school year 1926–1927 provided a test for the school's altered scholarship program. Attendance declined from 608 to 559. It remained easy to recruit women, for about three hundred competed for eighty admission slots, but it became more difficult to attract men. The school actually enrolled fifty fewer men in 1926 than the preceding year. Penrose explained that boys had a "different spirit from girls" and still needed to be recruited.[38] In 1927 he charged that men were more likely to be "infatuated by bigness and by athletic prominence."[39] The school had made a great effort to recruit men: in the spring, professor and registrar Edward Ruby had turned his Latin classes over to a substitute, and, accompanied by a student driver, traveled forty-two hundred miles in Oregon, Washington, and Idaho. But when this energetic recruiting effort failed to find many new applicants, the trustees reinstituted a revised version of the popular but costly scholarship programs; perhaps it was to cover the cost of these generous scholarships that they finally raised tuition in 1929.

A variety of other administrative matters crowded the president's desk. In 1926 Penrose became embroiled in a dispute after the Associated Press erroneously reported that Whitman had brought suit against Judge Thomas Burke's estate for a subscription that he had made to the college. Penrose cried out indignantly that the story was "a malicious attempt to manufacture news at the expense of Whitman" and that it "was printed all over the northwest . . . with headlines representing Whitman College in the very unenviable position of suing the estate of one of its chief benefactors."[40] The angry educator informed the Associated Press that the writer had "fabricated [the article] out of whole cloth" and that the college could "not be compensated for the damage which has been done."[41] Although the Associated Press subsequently attempted to placate Penrose, he responded: "I do not see how any profession can justify such a code of ethics."[42]

Many small problems also proved irksome; for example, in 1928 a printer published the college catalog on the wrong paper. Penrose wrote several letters to correct the difficulty. Members of the Whitman community must have complained that the president should be relieved from such administrative chores, but there was no employee who could handle these responsibilities.

The Whitman Conservatory of Music sometimes embroiled Penrose. The institution operated under its own administration and employed its own teaching staff. He explained that the conservatory had "its own separate life and requirements,"[43] but Penrose sometimes participated in its management. Howard E. Pratt, a talented musician and experienced administrator, served as the conservatory's director. His institution had a two-year certification program, requiring study in English, psychology, education, teaching methods, ear training, harmony, history of music, and, especially, applied music. Although it differed from the college in that it enrolled many townspeople and children, Penrose insisted that the conservatory maintained "high standards of musicianship" just as the college established high standards of scholarship.[44] The institution claimed to be well-equipped, but it had to borrow a victrola and records from local music dealers.

The conservatory helped to increase female college enrollments when women who had been denied college admission learned that they would receive preference if they reapplied from the music program. Several women followed this procedure, enrolling in the conservatory, taking college courses, and then transferring to the college.

In the late 1920s Penrose dealt with three major issues in the conservatory. First, he complained that there was a shortage of able music teachers and that it was unwise "to entrust all teaching of music in the public schools to just one kind of teacher; namely those prepared in normal schools."[45] He proposed that conservatory students who took additional courses in the college's education department should qualify to be public school music teachers. The state department of education rejected the proposal.

A second problem had to do with the allocation of the proceeds from Glee Club concerts. Director Pratt, who insisted that it was an old problem, stated that Glee Club members did not think they should pay their own travel costs. On the other hand, Coach Vincent "Nig" Borleske, in his other position as graduate manager (watchdog over student finances and general advisor to student government), warned that the associated students' budget could not cover these bills. Penrose devised a plan whereby members of the Glee Club would not have to pay for their traveling costs, and some of the student opera profits would transfer to the associated students to keep them out of debt. He made this decision fully aware that Pratt had generously used some of the profits from student musical performances to wallpaper Green Cottage and to calcimine the music building. Although Penrose called the dispute "a tempest in a teapot," he sought to prevent trouble between the programs and personalities of a popular coach and an equally popular director.[46]

The other problem in the conservatory was its secretary, Rosella H. Woodward. Penrose accused her of keeping improper student records, of criticizing conservatory teachers, and of opposing admission procedures. Penrose warned her: "You will understand that it is not practicable to have an officer of the conservatory criticizing the regulations made by the trustees."[47] Apparently the secretary became more efficient and discreet, because she held her position for another five years.

Prentiss Hall

By 1926 there were two significant additions to the physical campus: Lyman House—officially named Lyman Hall, for the late history professor William D. Lyman—was built in 1923 to house freshman men; and in 1926 the school dedicated Prentiss Hall, a three-story brick dormitory housing 150 women. Whitman now operated two attractive, modern dormitories.

Penrose confided to trustees that the dormitories at Whitman were "overcrowded and unsanitary," words that were never used in the college catalogs to describe these buildings. In his 1925 report

Penrose had advised readers that, because so many women sought admission, the school should ask the older ones to find city housing so that freshmen women could live in the dormitories. The leader assumed that the college could rent houses nearby for upperclass women. Whitman, he ruled, must be concerned about student living conditions: "It cannot afford to let its girls live in private houses scattered about the town without the safeguards and supervisions which are properly involved in the responsibilities of such a college."[48]

The construction of Prentiss Hall, following the blueprints of the accomplished architect Ellis F. Lawrence, was a major campus event. In 1925 Penrose, the building committee, and the trustees spent long hours pondering the dormitory's financial cost. Dean of women R. Louise Fitch and others ignored funding limitations and emphasized the need for beauty, convenience, and landscaping. Fitch's fears about noisy dining rooms and the lack of fire-proof construction irritated Penrose, who informed her that the building could not have every desirable facility. He added an admonishment: "Wisdom in this world consists in cutting your coat according to your cloth and not in wishing you might have more cloth."[49] But Fitch responded with concerns about the need for sewing and pressing rooms and kitchenettes, "where the girls can do their toast and tea and fudge."[50]

Built in 1926 and shown here in 1929, Prentiss Hall is a three-story brick dormitory housing both independent and sorority women. For many years the bonds

Apparently architect Lawrence incorporated some such suggestions, but plans for a cupola proved to be too expensive.

The original Prentiss Hall had fronted Park Street. Constructed in the 1880s as Ladies' Hall, it had served as a dormitory and as a sorority chapter room, but was demolished to make space for the carriage entrance to the new dormitory. In September 1925 workmen started construction on the Baker Field site: "With amazing rapidity under the able superintendency of O. D. Keen, our unrivalled contractor and builder," Penrose boasted, it was completed within a year.[51] The *Pioneer* described the new dormitory, emphasizing the library room, which meant that women would not need to use the congested library reading room, and the small dining tables seating six, which would make it "much easier to practice the art of conversation."[52]

The president wrote that the dormitory was "by common consent one of the most beautiful and beautifully equipped dormitories in the country."[53] Mrs. Penrose chose attractive furnishings; friends of the college, including four sisters who donated $3,000, paid for them.[54] When this impressive dormitory opened in 1926, nobody anticipated that its costs would create serious problems for decades.

that financed the building burdened college leaders, but thousands of women have enjoyed their college careers in this attractive structure.

The Stadium and the Athletic Fields

Planning to erect a convenient stadium for high school, college, and community activities, Walla Walla boosters had optioned the Dacres Field site in 1922. In March 1926 the school purchased from Mary Dacres its eighteen acres of the forty-four-acre tract and a one-third interest in the eight-acre stadium grounds for $10,500. The college laid out four intramural football fields and made plans for twelve tennis courts, a quarter-mile track, three baseball diamonds, and a putting green.

The stadium board, representing the college and other owners, spent $45,000 on grading, seeding, fencing, and constructing the first unit of the grandstand, including dressing rooms. Future plans (never realized) proposed seating for fifteen thousand, with a total project cost of $100,000.

Pleased with these developments, Penrose admitted that "for fifteen years I have entertained the hope that this particular piece of ground might become available as an athletic field for Whitman. For ten years I breathed that hope to no one for fear that the suggestion might defeat the hope."[55]

The college dedicated the stadium on October 30, 1926, at a football game with the University of Washington, the first meeting between the schools in Walla Walla in nineteen years. The students publicized the contest by placing posters in Walla Walla shop windows and stickers on automobiles. Businesses and even local golf courses closed for the game. The week prior to the contest, the city fell victim to football fever, and the *Walla Walla Bulletin* judged that it was to be "the greatest athletic event in this old city's history." With a crowd estimated at five thousand, "The Washington team came on the field, a rocket bomb was sent up, bursting and allowing the Washington colors to descend via parachute. The same thing greeted the Whitman players."[56] A parade of dignitaries and a solemn flag raising preceded the kickoff. These impressive ceremonies were more gratifying than the game's outcome: the visitors won by a score of forty-four to nothing. Stadium Field would be renamed Borleske Field in 1940 in celebration of Coach Borleske's twenty-five years of service to Whitman.

The Anderson Mansion

In 1927 Penrose tried but failed to acquire the Louis F. Anderson mansion adjacent to the campus. Professor Anderson offered his home, one of the city's finest, and its three acres for $25,000, about $40,000 less than its value, stipulating that the college must use the mansion for an institute of fine arts and establish an endowment to maintain the institute. In addition, Anderson offered to donate paintings, statuary, and books to make it an attractive art center. The trustees favored using the house temporarily as the college library, assuring Anderson that this use would not detract from the building's artistic beauty. As soon as money was raised, the house would then be converted into an institute for the fine arts.

Penrose approved this plan, because it would mean that the "unsightly" library shack would be torn down and two rooms in Memorial Hall then being used for library purposes could be freed for other uses. He asserted that the proposed art institute would enrich Whitman's curriculum by adding drawing, painting, and eventually even architecture and sculpture, and confessed, "The education which Whitman . . . has given in the past has been lacking on the artistic side. It will now be enriched and ennobled."[57] But Anderson heatedly opposed the use of his house as a library, even temporarily, and withdrew his offer. The college would not acquire it until 1956.

Continuing Building Needs

From 1926 until he left office in 1934, Penrose argued that the college's most pressing need was a modern fire-proof library building. He compared the library "to the heart supplying blood to all the limbs."[58] In 1926 he stated that a good college "cannot be imagined without a library and reading rooms." He was aware that the University of Washington had opened the beautiful Suzzallo Library; meanwhile Whitman's library was a temporary wooden shack—an eyesore abutting Memorial Hall—which housed a reading and reference room. Thirty-eight thousand more valuable books were in Memorial's ill-lit and inconvenient basement. Students could neither browse the shelves nor find a library seat. Penrose groused that books crammed the shelves and that professors complained about their inability to instruct advanced students in the confined reading room. The educator outlined the new teaching methods: in the past a student recited from a textbook, but "nowadays he is obliged to consult many reference books, and these can be obtained only in the library."[59] Professors unsuccessfully petitioned the board to increase the size of the shack to provide small study rooms for seniors. Some faculty members and others wanted to remodel Reynolds Hall as a library, but Penrose and the trustees rejected the proposal because it would delay a new library building, which they prayed a benefactor would agree to finance. Reynolds, in fact, came to house the college museum; its conversion to a library was delayed until 1934.

The president also pushed other campus needs. In 1929, for example, he urged the overseers to develop the amphitheater. After grading and terracing, the school would have "a perfect amphitheater for out of door spectacles." As Penrose looked toward the college's seventy-fifth anniversary, he hoped several ambitious plans might be realized, especially the construction of a library, science laboratories, a chemistry building, a women's gymnasium ("for the proper daily training and exercises of the girls"), an auditorium, and a museum to honor the contributions of pioneers. "There is still an abundance of [pioneer] material which," Penrose insisted, "together with rich stores of Indian life and customs would fill a large museum and constitute a valuable educational exhibit."[60]

The Quest for Stability

While Penrose sought money, publicity, and buildings for the college, he simultaneously tried to employ a suitable dean of women and to improve his faculty. A passionate defender of *in loco parentis*, the president sought ways for the college to carry out this responsibility. He wanted his students, especially women, to be healthy and safe from the entrapments besetting the young in the 1920s. One of his basic problems was to find a dean of women who would be strict but fair. He sought one who would be "a friend and helper of each individual girl . . . and a promoter of the most wholesome and rational life."[61] It proved to be difficult to hire and retain an individ-

ual possessing the energy and patience to handle so many demanding responsibilities.

In 1924 the school hired the highly qualified Miss R. Louise Fitch
of Eugene. According to Penrose, she was more than "a glorified matron or housekeeper." He later described Fitch as "a very well balanced and able woman" who won the admiration of her charges and
whose "influence over them is unbounded." [62] Fitch carried an enormous workload, including office responsibilities and the teaching
of a household economics class required of all Whitman women. The
dean's lectures on home management covered such subjects as housing, clothing, food, management of domestics, nursing, the care of
children, and the family as a social unit. Overburdened, she complained to Penrose that the women's self-government structure had
failed, and that she spent too much of her time as a nurse and as a
housekeeper. By 1926 the president reported that she suffered from
the trials of her position and was "on the edge of nervous prostra-
tion." After only two demanding years she resigned and took an impressive position at Cornell, with the rank of professor, a salary of
$5,000, a house, and other benefits. Penrose congratulated Fitch,
confiding that he had not expected her to "remain permanently because you are fitted for larger things." [63]

Ruth Wenstrom, a graduate of Carleton College and a dean of
girls at Walla Walla High School, replaced Fitch. Penrose praised the
newcomer for quickly winning "the respect and affection of both students and faculty," but he voiced a criticism: "The only thing against
her is her youth and good looks. She has only been out of college for
twelve years and gives the impression of being about twenty-seven
years old." [64] Her youthfulness, however, did not explain her short
tenure. The strain of her work, especially housing women in the new
dormitory, became "exceptionally trying, as many new problems
arose and novel adjustments had to be made." Her physician and
her president both recommended that she resign. "I am sorry," Penrose wrote her, "that the wear and tear of the position are too much
for your nervous system." [65] He replaced her with a third capable individual, Miss Louise Bloomquist, who soon resigned to marry.

The fourth person to receive the appointment remained several
years and had an important impact upon college women. Hired in
1930, Thelma Mills had received degrees at Willamette University

and at Columbia University, where she studied to become a college dean of women. Mills had also earned an advanced degree in history, which she taught at Whitman.

Penrose cared about finding a suitable dean of women and even more about the quality of his faculty, the group that he argued made the college. Many of the best professors had been hired prior to the First World War, including Walter A. Bratton (mathematics), Benjamin H. Brown (physics), Howard S. Brode (biology), William Bleakney (Greek), William R. Davis (English), Nig Borleske (physical education), and Frank Haigh (chemistry). Two men added in the early 1920s—Eli T. Allen (Biblical literature) and Russell Blankenship (English)—were significant campus figures. Although this outstanding group was aging, and despite the fact that it was suffering from low salaries, only two professors departed in the 1920s.

It was the president's responsibility to maintain a high-quality faculty. Penrose informed an eastern friend that Whitman employed "some really great teachers. . . . Somehow they have been willing to stay here for very modest salaries. I suppose because they have liked the freedom and the opportunity to teach the active-minded students whom they have found."[66] In his last years, he lacked funds to hire good young faculty members to join the dedicated veterans who had remained in harness for decades.

Penrose believed that there were advantages for young professors at Whitman. He told one young professor thinking of returning to Williams College that his professional advancement would be furthered "in the isolation and freedom of the West." He added that Whitman "gives you the chance to think for yourself and get on your own feet, whereas, in the East you would be obliged to conform to precedent and to wait upon your masters. . . . Education is the process of becoming free, and I believe that you would gain in permanent freedom by staying longer in the wilderness."[67] Because of faculty stability, freshmen could count upon their teachers being present through their senior year. Few professors could afford a leave of absence, and the college had no money for a sabbatical program.

Penrose also supported faculty development. He did not foster the publish-or-perish stricture, but he favored faculty publications, listing in his reports the names of those who had published. In 1926 Penrose proposed that the *Whitman College Quarterly* should be revived as an outlet for the professors' essays and informed overseers that one of their duties was the stimulation of faculty scholarship. "The impulse toward creative activity," he urged, "needs to be quickened and encouraged. Without it teachers tend to become mechanical and dry as dust."[68] The president wrote to foundations, graduate schools, summer schools, and publishers on behalf of faculty members striving to further their professional careers.

Meanwhile, despite Penrose's efforts, faculty salaries and faculty numbers remained low. The president told overseers that a small raise given to them in 1925 was neither adequate nor final. He consistently asked overseers to improve salaries, arguing that teachers were more important than books, equipment, or buildings.

> It is the teachers who make a college and its peculiarly true that Whitman College has been made by its teachers. The reputation which this institution has gained, quite extraordinary and inexplicable when its buildings and equipment are considered, has been made not by its trustees or overseers but by its faculty. . . . Because of our graduates who have made so unusual a record in post-graduate work, Harvard, Yale, Columbia, and Johns Hopkins hold Whitman in unusual regard and credit its undergraduate work as equal to their own.

Penrose cautioned that there was a shortage of effective teachers and that "teachers must not be coming and going"; to retain them, conditions and salaries needed improvement. "No longer," he warned, "can a college expect to keep permanently a tried and successful faculty because of their spirit of self sacrifice."[69]

Penrose often used Professor Bratton's career to demonstrate the deplorable salary situation. A highly reputable mathematician, Bratton came to the college at a salary of $1,000. After thirty-two years of loyal and solid service, his salary had increased to just $3,600. Penrose reminded trustees that the faculty had been assured that the 1924–1925 fund-raising campaign would improve their salaries. When this improvement did not occur, the president had to explain that the construction and maintenance costs of Lyman and Prentiss dormitories resulted in greater costs than anticipated and "constitute a reason for making no increases of salary to the faculty regardless of their term of service." In 1928 the leader urged over-

seers to increase the maximum salaries to $4,000.[70] To show that
Whitman was not spending enough money on instruction, Penrose
prepared a chart comparing it with other liberal arts colleges dependent upon tuition income and endowment earnings. Whitman
put only thirty-seven percent of its expenditures into teaching; other
liberal arts colleges spent well over fifty percent.

In general, the college had invested in buildings, equipment, and
maintenance rather than faculty salaries. As Penrose pointed out,
Whitman was actually borrowing money from its professors. He reasoned that it owed Bratton $25,000 in back pay for the long serv-
ice he had rendered. The president cautioned overseers that the faculty, whose low salaries already demoralized them, voiced another
serious problem: they complained that large classes fatigued them.

Penrose thought that a college like Whitman should have a faculty-student ratio of one to ten. It actually stood at one to 15.4 and
compared poorly to Reed College's one to 10.6. Improving this un-
favorable ratio required the addition of twenty faculty members, but
Penrose did not provide a plan to add this number.[71] He understood
that it was "hard for businessmen to realize the necessity of maintaining proper proportions between the number of teachers and the
number of those taught," but he warned that, unless there was a
reduction of class sizes, the school's reputation for effective teaching
would diminish.[72] In 1926 Penrose complained that the college had
more than thirty-five classes that enrolled more than thirty students;
a few of the largest were Penrose's required freshmen education class
with 213, Brode's introduction to biology class with 132, and Chester
Maxey's basic political science class with sixty-four. Despite these
pleadings, there was no significant reduction in class sizes.

Thus, in the age of expansion, the trustees denied the faculty both
adequate salaries and smaller classes. Even in this period of increased
enrollments, the faculty went underpaid just as they had in the earlier times of retrenchment. In a 1929 report, Penrose deplored the
statement by an overseer who opposed increasing the salaries of
those professors who had served fifteen or more years. The overseer calculated that: "They have reached an age when they cannot
get a position anywhere else; therefore, [they] will be obliged to stay
where they are regardless of the salary given them. We have them
over a barrel."[73]

Fund Raising in the Field

Undoubtedly, fund raising and financial matters consumed far more of Penrose's administrative time than did any other responsibility. In the 1924–1925 school year Whitman seemed to be in an improved financial condition. In the fall of 1925 the president announced that the college would soon be out of debt, that the recently conducted financial campaign had brought in $250,000, and that the General Education Board—which awarded John D. Rockefeller's money—would soon provide a $125,000 matching grant.

Unfortunately, the financial campaign exhausted Penrose and contributed to his blindness, a disability that limited his travel. Conducted by the eastern firm of Tamblyn and Brown, the stressful financial campaign had demonstrated the need for the president and a financial agent to travel extensively. Fortunately, Mildred Winship, who had demonstrated considerable skills in this campaign, agreed to remain at Whitman for another year, and Tamblyn and Brown generously paid her salary. A graduate of Mount Holyoke College with a winning personality, this gifted fund raiser became deeply committed to the Penrose family and Whitman College. Penrose described her as "a brilliant and resourceful young woman of marked personal attractiveness."[74]

Winship and the president realized that she must travel alone and make calls. Her New York employers, however, disapproved of this practice, arguing that Penrose should travel with their employee. Besides working alone, Winship faced the additional challenge of trying to raise money immediately after concluding a major financial campaign. The limited options open to her were another major problem. It was obvious that alumni were neither wealthy enough nor numerous enough to provide major contributions; furthermore, they had already contributed generously to the 1924–1925 campaign. With pangs of envy Penrose learned that his two old schools, Williams College and Yale University, received large sums from their well-heeled alumni. Friends recommended to Penrose that Whitman turn for help to Congregational churches and organizations at the state and national level. He responded that this was hopeless because the church lacked the resources to assist the struggling colleges that it had founded. Thus, in the mid-1920s Whitman must turn to the only regional source of money—those wealthy Pacific Northwest residents who appreciated a quality liberal arts education and the positive impact Whitman had upon regional society. Winship must tell these influential leaders that the college was important and sell it even to those who had little interest in private education.

Penrose handed Winship a short list of potential donors, and overseers in their cities lengthened it. Most of the men and women she visited had already received ardent pleas for contributions from schools, churches, museums, associations, hospitals, societies, charities, and other hard-pressed organizations. In short, philanthropists were few, and fund raisers were many. What Winship found on the West Coast in the 1920s was what Penrose had discovered on the East Coast in the 1890s. She wrote: "In this day and age a man of wealth is hounded to death and they almost have to put on a wall of protection."[75] Moreover, Penrose, who understood the region's economy, emphasized to her that it was difficult to borrow money and nearly impossible to receive large financial gifts from those unfamiliar with the college. He also recognized that the philanthropic tradition was much stronger in the East than in the West.

Nevertheless, full of hope, Winship traveled to Spokane, launching a five-month campaign that would take her to the West Coast's major cities. She demonstrated her ability to get Whitman's name and needs before potential donors, reciting both the college's accomplishments and its many needs—a library, a women's gymnasium, a science building, an art institute, and endowment money to assist a faculty living in poverty. Penrose assured her that, "even if you do not get a dollar," the trustees believed that she was doing valuable work in preparing the way for future gifts.[76] She responded that the 1924–1925 campaign had spread the school's fame and that its faculty should be informed "that the public is gradually getting it through its head that they come from the finest college of the Northwest."[77]

From Seattle, Winship sent Penrose remarkable letters about the vicissitudes of her work. H. F. Ostrander, she reported, "glowered at me and thrust forward his bull-dog jaw and demanded, 'What do you want?'" She disarmed him by remarking, "You know this isn't my idea of a good time." A cultured woman, she expressed surprise with the assertions of Ostrander and several others who grumbled: "I have very definite opinions regarding education. If a boy hasn't the guts to get through a big university there is no sense in bothering with him. I am for public education." (Ostrander was aware of Whitworth College, where, he noted, "The boys who were pious in college and attended all the devotionals were not half as successful as those who didn't.") A. B. Steward argued with the fund raiser, generalizing that the state had "plenty of schools—Bellingham, Annie Wright, Pullman, and the University of Washington."[78] Winship reported that "W. E. Boeing sent word that I must talk with his manager and the little shrimp made quick work of me." She reported going to a slaughterhouse and meeting Charles H. Frye, who furthered her "liberal education" by drinking milk from a bottle. Winship recalled making her point that Frye would approve of Whitman's faculty and students, when suddenly, "He stopped me, his terrifying eyes piercing through me, and said, 'Don't believe they have jazz students there. Don't believe the girls smoke.' Whereupon I assured him that Whitman had that sort of girls who wouldn't even want to smoke!" William Calvert argued that the University of Washington "was pouring boys out by the thousands that didn't know how to do a day's work and didn't want to, and the businessmen didn't know what to do with them." He admitted that he would send his own children to college, "but he wasn't certain it was for the best." After meeting with several women, Winship reported that she would prefer working with opinionated men. "I would rather try to tackle a half dozen men than one woman."[79] A telegram to Penrose from Portland supported this sentiment: "Had long session with Mrs. [Caroline Gray] Kamm today and want to spend one more day with her. She says I wear my dresses too short so I am frantically having them lengthened."[80]

Although Winship expressed disappointment because of her inability to do much more than bring the college to the attention of wealthy West Coast residents, Penrose consistently reassured her that she was doing all that he anticipated. He credited her, moreover, with convincing Reginald Parsons and his wife to make a timely donation. The president feared that Winship would not stay another year as his assistant and confided to her: "If I am to be without an assistant in my state of blindness, unable to visit the leading people of the Northwest and cultivate friendly relations with them which may be productive of aid . . . in the future, I would think it better to resign and let the college have a president who could devote himself to that task."[81] Penrose tried to get Winship's eastern employers to release her for a year so that she could follow her promising leads. He described his situation: "Since the loss of my eyesight I have depended entirely upon her for cultivating relations with the outside world."[82] Winship was torn by her desire to aid both the disabled president in the West and her sick mother in the East. Late in the summer of 1925 she finally decided to play the role of the dutiful daughter. Penrose sympathized with her decision but expressed his disappointment: "My heart sinks at the thought of your work being allowed to drop when no one is in sight to take it up. Alas! I fear that it will be as water spilled upon a rock."[83]

Unfortunately, the college failed to find her successor that fall, and Penrose described himself as being "like a farmer whose corn has started to grow in the rows but is being choked by weeds which he cannot get out to hoe. Heaven help us if we cannot get you to return in the spring or get some one to follow feebly in your footsteps. No man could do what you have done or gain in three years time what you now know about this field. Moreover, no man could get the approach to people that you have."[84]

Winship departed for a position at Radcliffe College, reporting that she was "buried in the deepest of New England culture and conservatism. I find myself worrying constantly over my 'shalls' and 'wills.'"[85] For years she continued her interest in the Penroses and their college, and they may have felt she was irreplaceable. Penrose lamented that nobody else at Whitman thought "about cultivating relationships with the outside world" and that he alone had always done this work.[86] Even so, overseer Thomas Burke insisted that some other person than the president should carry out this responsibility: "Looking up persons who are supposed to be friendly to education, interviewing or soliciting funds for a college is, as a rule nerve wracking work. It is unfair to look to you for it. You are doing enough for the college as it is."[87]

Penrose's insistence that the college find a fund raiser led to the appointment of Colonel Robert A. Burton, Whitman's most controversial administrator since Dean Archer Hendrick. But Burton was not hired until the spring of 1927. Between the resignation of Winship and Burton's hiring, the president and board members disagreed about the shape of the administration. Penrose's annual report for 1925 explained to board members how well he had functioned with his handicap. He was positive, explaining that he had taught 336 students a week, conducted chapels, and handled administrative duties. His major difficulty, he reported, was his inability to promote the college through regional travel. The leader emphasized that this was an essential task: "The future of the college depends in large measure upon establishing itself in the confidence, respect, and even affection of the people of influence and wealth in the Northwest especially and this can only be done by having some person give thoughtful attention to it throughout the year." To resolve the problem brought about by his inability to travel, the president gave overseers three options. A new president could be selected, or a new president might be chosen for external administration—providing Penrose with time to teach and handle the school's internal affairs—or he could remain in office and a replacement for Mildred Winship could be hired. After explaining the three choices, Penrose submitted his resignation, re-emphasizing that "Nothing would be more short-sighted than to abandon the cultivation of the outside world." [88]

Regretting that their leader's physical condition required some action, overseers rejected his administrative options and created the office of vice president. This administrator would carry a limited teaching load and would handle the field work. The board used as its model the role of the vice president in the business world but acknowledged that it would be difficult to find "a broad gauge" man who could match Penrose's talent in promoting the college.

The board failed to find a suitable vice president. Although Penrose privately opposed the creation of this office, he openly argued for the need to hire a competent individual to handle external relations and told a friend: "Heaven has not sent such an angel." [89]

In his 1926 report to overseers, Penrose again discussed his health and the board's attempt to find a vice president. "I think you received an impression that my general health was in a precarious condition and believed that I must soon give up my work." The president assured his listeners that there was no reason for such fear and that, except for his blindness, he enjoyed good health. He boasted that

he daily walked long distances and that he carried a full teaching
load, handled the school's general correspondence, and had addressed about twenty-five regional audiences. Penrose hoped to complete forty years as president and saw no need to employ a vice president to "go into training for the presidency." But he again asserted
the real need for the appointment of a financial agent "to cultivate
the external field" and warned: "If such a work of cultivation be
neglected longer as it has been for the past year, you may be sure
that the college will suffer great loss and will miss the opportunity
now afforded it of impressing people of wealth with the special
claims which it has upon their consideration." The president recommended that treasurer Dorsey Hill assume this vital position as financial agent.

Hill rejected the offer, and in the 1926–1927 school year the institution again lacked a field representative. In the spring 1927 report to overseers, Penrose begged them to appoint someone who
would spend his full time increasing the school's "financial resources." The new individual, working harmoniously with alumni
and overseers, should seek donors, especially for scholarships.

This new money seemed important because Penrose again sought
a way to terminate the expensive honors scholarship program and
replace it with a new type. If the field agent could secure a $5,000
fund in a community, the interest from this sum could go to a local
scholarship winner. A committee composed of the mayor, the high
school principal, and other leading townspeople would select the recipient. The president wanted a hundred such scholarships established within three years to help the school attain its goal of enrolling
three hundred men. Penrose also proposed that the field representative seek funds for graduate assistants, visiting lectureships, library
endowment, professorships, buildings, and a new department of fine
arts. At the same time, the new person should also recruit in high
schools, especially for promising men.

After considerable discussion, in the spring of 1927 the govern-
ing boards shelved their plans to employ a vice president and grudg-
ingly accepted Penrose's request for a field agent. They hired Colonel
Burton, who had been investigated in Lexington, Kentucky, by Hugh
Elmer "Hez" Brown, a respected alumnus. Penrose admitted that
Burton, who had won Brown's endorsement, remained a stranger.[90]

He was chosen from several candidates because of what Penrose considered to be impressive credentials. Burton had graduated from the University of Kentucky, earned an M.A. at the University of Virginia, served as a colonel in the First World War, struggled as the president of a small and failing college, and traveled as a college representative. His appointment was a notable departure: in 1925 Whitman College sent a New England woman into the field; in 1927 it employed a Southern colonel.

Burton arrived on campus in September, receiving assurances from Penrose that the college would support him in his "difficult and trying task" and that he would be neither "a high-powered salesman nor a beggar," but his major task, like that assigned to Winship, was to publicize the college.[91] The new administrator met with faculty members, students, and trustees, absorbing the school's history, traditions, and goals. Burton chose the title of counselor, a term that Penrose liked because of its ambiguity. The president did not want the title to imply that he sought only money; Penrose insisted that publicity was Burton's chief responsibility. Trustees and overseers, however, candidly stated that the counselor sought donations and students.[92] In any case, publicity was an important consideration, because the general populace was often either unaware of Whitman or else likely to identify it as a Presbyterian or Seventh-Day-Adventist institution; and "Missionaries," the nickname for the college's athletic teams, led some uninformed sports fans to conclude that the college was a theological seminary.

In the fall of 1927 Penrose took Burton to cities in the region, introducing him to board members and prominent citizens. The president often praised the fund raiser: "He is a quiet, delightful Southern gentleman with good manners, a kindly disposition, and an ability to meet people easily. . . . He and I get along beautifully together, and I believe that he will prove to be the man we have been looking for."[93]

Burton plunged into his work, traveling to major cities for meetings, speeches, and interviews. He learned that Spokane was much more interested in the college than Portland, observing that Portlanders were interested only in Oregon. He commented: "If John C. Calhoun were living the Oregonians would certainly advocate him for president on account of State Rights."[94] Delighted with the counselor's energy, Penrose boasted that he had established "most important contacts . . . and that the future will find rich rewards for his efforts."[95] In his annual report of 1928, Penrose boasted that Burton had accomplished much more than the introduction of the college to wealthy residents, having received some promises from potential donors, whose names must be held in confidence. But Penrose assured the Whitman community that: "Never before in the thirty-four years of my presidency have I felt so comfortable a sense of helpfulness concerning the outlook of the college."[96]

Dubious about their leader's enthusiastic support of Burton, some administrators, faculty members, and trustees expressed reservations. Treasurer Hill, whom Penrose identified as Burton's leading critic, faulted him to students, the faculty, and trustees. Undoubtedly Hill informed the poorly paid faculty that Burton had received a $500 moving expense, was paid a $3,500 annual salary (this was as much as Whitman's most senior professor made after thirty years of strenuous service), and enjoyed a generous traveling account. Penrose deduced that Hill's criticism turned trustees against Burton and that they had not "sought his acquaintance, invited him to lunch or dinner, or voluntarily given him any advice and help." Furthermore, trustee Allen Reynolds suggested to the president that the school should "send out an investigating committee to follow on Colonel Burton's track and find out what he was doing."[97] Close friends of Penrose warned him that the counselor undermined college morale, but he discounted such concerns, reminding them that there was always "considerable criticism . . . when new people appear on a college campus."[98]

But by the fall of 1928 the president also worried about the counselor. He had heard from eastern creditors that Burton had debts resulting from losses in the Florida land boom. Penrose had signed a $200 note for Burton, and creditors in Spokane and Seattle asked him to help them collect Burton's bills for clothing, jewelry, and groceries.

While Penrose pondered these troubling debts, Burton complained of ill health; Penrose described the Kentuckian as being in a "wretched nervous condition . . . on the edge of collapse."[99] Burton took treatment in an Idaho sanitarium and then disappeared. After about a month, he sent a letter postmarked from Fort Worth: "I am making the fight of my life for restoration of health and strength."[100] On October 19 he explained: "I must absolutely remain inactive."[101] Hill wrote to Burton that the trustees had voted to dispense with his services until he returned and to hold his salary until he straightened out his expense accounts. Penrose wanted to believe in his counselor's integrity and accepted his excuse that his nervous condition resulting from unfortunate financial conditions prompted his move to a Texas hospital. The president wrote the counselor: "So many inquiries have come to me concerning your unsettled accounts, promises to pay, and unpaid bills that I suspect you are harassed by financial difficulties. . . .You have been garnisheed once in the year you have been here, and I understand that one or more legal firms are ready to institute garnishee proceedings against you."[102] Penrose advised him to resign before he was fired. In late November, Burton responded, elaborating on his financial problems and resigning.

A year later, Penrose wrote him asking if he actually personified the ideals associated with a Southern gentleman. He charged the Kentuckian with creating fictional donors, with falsely reporting that Spokanite Adolph Galland (one of the trustees of the Julius Galland estate) would make a major donation, and with failing to pay Penrose's $200 note and numerous other debts. In a bitter letter, Penrose complained: "Let me compliment you, and I suppose Mrs. Burton as your helper, upon the skill with which you have created characters for my entertainment. I imagine that you must have felt a good deal of amusement in inventing such characters for the entertainment of a blind man."[103] The Burtons heatedly denied the accusations; apparently Penrose accepted Mrs. Burton's plea of innocence and rejected her husband's. In 1930 the disgusted president abandoned his attempts to reform Colonel Burton, for he faced more serious business. But for years the underpaid faculty criticized Burton for taking money and hurting Whitman's reputation by leaving widely scattered debts. And they criticized Penrose for being hoodwinked.

The next field representative, William Worthington, had worked his way through Whitman, graduating as valedictorian in 1900. He had briefly taught economics at his alma mater and served as a fund raiser for a regional charity at the time of his appointment in 1928. Penrose confided to Worthington that the trustees "feel that they rather burned their fingers on Burton . . . and in consequence feel somewhat shy about filling the place with anyone."[104] The president sympathized with the fund raiser's task: "The Pacific Northwest is materialistically minded because it is still in the throes of a great material development, and I suppose that it will take a long time yet before having developed its body it finds its soul." [105]

One of Worthington's first responsibilities was to write what Penrose called "Heart Throbs," accounts of current Whitman men and women struggling to work their way through the college. Worthington's pamphlet, "Working Their Way," met the president's requirements: it included touching stories of young people in adverse situations battling for a college degree, and, of course, it appealed for money that would be distributed as either scholarships or loans to these worthy "strugglers." Professors realized that these funds would help poor students meet the recent tuition increase, which in turn would upgrade their salaries.

Penrose urged Worthington to confer with wealthy Pacific Northwest residents: "There may be some grains of wheat in a bushel of chaff." [106] The special representative faithfully carried out this responsibility. Then the president proposed another plan: Worthington should shift his work to New York City, where large sums of money—much of it accumulated during the great bull market of the 1920s—were available and controlled by people "accustomed to give as they are not accustomed out here." [107] However, New Yorkers quickly informed Penrose that these efforts would be wasted because the market had been checked. Furthermore, the cultured residents who might help Whitman "are not the ones who have made spectacular profits in the market." [108] Thus, Worthington must solicit regionally, especially in creating an alumni fund. He acknowledged that for several years it would be "a poor man's fund although I would not proclaim it as such." The fund raiser thought that the school's future depended upon the generous alumnus. Thus, there was a need to cultivate him "while he is still poor, otherwise he might not give to us when he is rich." [109] Penrose worried about the timing of this new effort: launching an alumni fund drive could conflict with a proposed campaign to raise $500,000 "for the Diamond Jubilee and the fortieth anniversary of the presidency of myself and Mrs. Penrose." [110]

In 1929 Penrose again offered his resignation, a decision that surprised trustees and overseers. He explained that he had served thirty-five years and reflected: "The only consideration for you or for me is the good of Whitman. If you think that the college would be better served by accepting my resignation and electing a successor, you ought now to be free to do so."[111] Many who read of Penrose's proposed resignation urged him to remain. John L. Rand, an Oregon Supreme Court judge who had once taught at Whitman for a brief time, wrote him: "I have never yet talked with anyone who did not give you the entire credit of having built up Whitman College from a small institution to its present recognized position as the leading, if not the very best, of all the small colleges on the Pacific Coast. I believe that nothing could be more injurious to the . . . college than for you to sever your connection with it."[112] Overseers insisted that he remain in office, but perhaps a thorough study of the resignation offer was impossible, because his report reminded them that in 1934 the school would be celebrating its seventy-fifth anniversary and he would be finishing his fortieth year as president. Overseers agreed that 1934 was the year to appoint his successor.

After his decision to remain, Penrose wrote on December 14, 1929, a reflective summary of his career to an old friend and ally, former overseer Wayne Darlington:

> We cannot tell what we are getting into when we begin a thing, but I know well enough that in 1894 I did not think that I had permanently turned my back upon the East whence I had come and was identifying myself permanently with the Pacific Northwest. In my youthful greenness I imagined that with a slight and brief effort I could bring Whitman College into prosperity and then leave it to undertake something else in the East.
>
> Probably it is a good thing that I could not carry out this optimistic program, but I never imagined that the job would be so long, so trying, and yet so pleasant. I suppose that being a college president in an institution like this requires more of the virtue of patience than anything else. Perhaps it would have been better if I had not developed patience but had pushed harder to achieve immediate results. I have been an opportunist who accommodated himself to conditions and only tried to [change] them little by little. Perhaps a strong man would have been less contented and have brought about a more rapid progress.

Fund Raising from Boyer Avenue

While Penrose sent three different fund raisers into the field between 1924 and 1930, he also conducted considerable fund raising from his Boyer Avenue office. He appealed to several individuals and foundations and sometimes included his own publications with his letters. In 1927 he sent his "Education at Less Than Cost," a synopsis of the college's needs. This convenient publication revealed that Whitman and every college spent "far more money on the education of its students than it received from them."[113] Whitman charged a low tuition because it paid its devoted faculty a small salary and practiced a rigid economy.

Seeking the names of potential donors, Penrose accumulated regional city directories and other lists. He sent dozens of letters to the wealthy and probably wrote more to Portlander Caroline Gray Kamm than to any other prospect. He wanted her to build a badly needed library at a cost of about $250,000 and to name it after her father, William H. Gray, a colleague of Dr. Marcus Whitman, the missionary in honor of whom the college had been named. Penrose frequently informed her of Gray's historical importance and the need to memorialize him. Kamm's unwillingness to contribute such a large donation led the exasperated president to remind the daughter that, not only was her father significant, but her mother "was, I suspect, the finest grained and best bred women of all the early settlers in old Oregon." He admonished her: "The main question for you is whether you think highly enough of your father and mother to want to build a worthy memorial to them. If you do not estimate their character and service very highly, an ordinary, common place memorial will do."[114]

Penrose must have thought his bluntness had succeeded with Kamm when he learned that her will provided funds for a library. To his astonishment, however, when her will was executed in 1932 it made no mention of Whitman. Penrose complained: "For twenty-five years I had worked on her . . . and had been given positive assurance that she had made a will about seven years ago containing a bequest to the college . . . it looks to me as if undue influence had been exerted upon her by members of her family to change it to give up all bequests."[115] Lawyers discouraged him from contesting her will.

Penrose urged another potential benefactor, Genevieve Vollmer Bonner, to make a major donation so that the new women's dormitory would be called Vollmer House to honor "the foremost woman of Idaho." He also tried to get from her a gift for the science department or for the remodeling of Reynolds Hall.[116] She rejected all these appeals, but donated a sundial. Penrose then asked for other modest gifts, including library books and scholarships. In 1934 the college, honoring Mrs. Bonner's service as an overseer, named the courtyard south of Prentiss Hall for her mother, Mrs. John Phillip Vollmer, one of the first women to be selected as an overseer.

Penrose also became involved in an interesting effort to receive support from the trustees of the Galland estate. Spokanite Julius Galland had left $400,000 to groups that promoted Jewish welfare. Penrose proposed that money be given to Whitman to provide professorships of Hebrew and Hebrew literature as well as scholarships, and he met with the estate's trustees, explaining that, while only a few Jewish students had attended Whitman, they had excelled. The school had employed Jewish instructors, including Mignon Borleske; furthermore, a Jew, Jack Gurian, had been student body president, and another had been a commencement speaker. At first, the estate's trustees rejected the proposal, but Penrose got Rabbi Samuel Koch of Seattle to endorse it, as did the Jews of Walla Walla. They wrote that if a rabbi came to Whitman, it would assist the community as well as the college and that Whitman, a tolerant and solid institution, would attract more Jewish boys and girls. Armed with this support, Penrose again appeared before the Galland trustees and learned from lawyers that, because his school was not a Jewish institution, his proposal was denied.[117]

Then the leader introduced yet another money-raising proposal, one he argued with enthusiasm. Aware that eastern universities had used a life-insurance plan to increase their endowments, Penrose and the trustees sought to emulate it. Starting with the class of 1928, the college implemented a two-part program that provided endowment money from the annual policy dividends and also from beneficiary payments. But it proved difficult to get participating alumni and friends to pay their annual premiums, and although Penrose labored through letters and interviews to promote the system, it failed to increase the college's endowment.

The president also wrote to many individuals seeking money for scholarships, buildings, professorships, and fellowships. In 1928 he sought to establish funds for "something new in the field of college education," a fellowship for Whitman's most promising graduate entering a medical school. He asked Portlander Robert C. Coffey, a physician who had begun his distinguished career in eastern Washington, to fund an annual $500 fellowship program. Penrose believed that such a fellowship offered several benefits: it would attract excellent students, place Whitman into close relations with the best medical schools, and assist deserving students. The leader also hoped to establish similar fellowships in the fields of law, engineering, and religion. After lengthy negotiations, Coffey chose not to fund the program. Astonished with the physician's change of mind, Penrose dropped all the proposed fellowship programs.

He still thought that eastern foundations were promising sources of support for the sciences, and asked Rockefeller's General Education Board for money to remodel Billings and Reynolds halls for science departments and to provide scientific equipment. After receiving a rejection, Penrose complained, "I think it would be very unfortunate for American education if the idea should prevail that research laboratories in universities are the only places where important education discoveries can be made."[118] The foundation, however, did provide $125,000 in matching money for the endowment. In 1926 Seattle overseer Reginald Parsons donated $25,000 to secure this grant. The foundation provided only interest until the college fulfilled the grant's requirements; in 1928 Penrose urged a principal payment, or the school would "end the year disastrously." He explained that the trustees had not increased tuition because an unusual cold spell damaged the wheat crop, and "this disaster has set back this country and made business conditions more difficult."[119]

While Penrose sought money from the General Education Board for the school's science program, he turned to the Carnegie Corporation for other kinds of help, asking, at different times, for a library, for a significant memorial (a professorship of fine arts honoring Judge Burke), for an art collection, for musical concerts, and for library books. Only this last request won approval. After a disappointing delay, Carnegie in 1932 awarded $15,000 for books.

Frustrated with the vexing problem of fund raising, the president sometimes vented his feelings. Yale University, for example, asked Whitman to join with other regional colleges in donating $15,000 for a Walter Camp memorial. Although Penrose knew Camp and called him "the patron saint of football," he found no reason why the college should help the university with its athletic fields while it struggled to establish its own.[120] There was a different local irritation. Mine owner August Paulsen of Spokane had died, leaving a large estate without a single bequest to a charity. Penrose grumbled: "It is singular that a foreign born citizen who made a great fortune out of the rocks of his adopted country should have no sense of gratitude or obligation to the country of his adoption."[121]

The Life of a Leader

Although the president put tremendous energy into the promotion of his college, he pursued many other interests. His family ranked first. In the late 1920s the Penroses remained a close family, experiencing gratifying changes and painful separations. Most of Penrose's personal letters have been lost, but his official correspondence contained reports of his family's impressive accomplishments. His wife, Mary, lived a very active life, and admirers boasted of her as the state's most prominent woman. She served on the national boards of the YWCA and the Congregational Church, responsibilities which required her annually to make two long eastern trips, where she attended board meetings, lectured, and visited with family and friends. Explaining that his handicap made it uncomfortable for him to accompany his wife, Stephen joked that presently "a husband is not much of an encumbrance for women who go their own way," and that he was "accustomed to be thought of as Mary Shipman's husband."[122] He understood that Mary's involvement "with great public causes" pleased her and publicized Whitman, and he told alumni that he and his wife "are one."[123]

Maysie, the oldest daughter, married architect Paul Copeland, lived in Longview, Washington, and in 1929 made Mary and Stephen grandparents. Another daughter, Frances, received more attention in her father's business letters because she graduated from the Prince

School in Boston, concurrently earning an M.A. at Harvard. In 1925 this talented daughter took a position in Seattle as educational director at Frederick and Nelson's, training the department store's salespeople.[124] Her father boasted that Frances had attained an important position at a young age and observed that: "Many people . . . regard her as the flower of our family. Whether she is or not, she is a very lively and interesting person."[125]

The twins followed business careers: Clement joined an insurance company in Los Angeles and Nathaniel became a Seattle banker. Both married. Clement fathered Clement Biddle Penrose, called "Tim"—short for Septimus—because he was the seventh male in the family. Penrose observed: "The novelty of realizing that one is a grandfather does not immediately wear off."[126]

The lives of the twins, however, received less of their father's attention than did that of his youngest son, Stephen B. L. "Binks" Penrose. Like all of his brothers and sisters, Binks graduated from Whitman, but he alone prepared to follow in his father's footsteps by becoming either a college administrator or a minister. He compiled an enviable college record similar to his father's. During his five years as an undergraduate, Binks completed a double major in chemistry and Greek, was a member of Phi Beta Kappa, captained the tennis team, served as student body president, and sang in the college Glee Club and the conservatory opera. He graduated at the young age of twenty, whereupon his admiring father wrote a letter recommending him for an instructorship in physics at the American University of Beirut: "He holds a rather unique place in people's regard not merely because he does so many things easily and well but because of his personality."[127] Binks signed a three-year contract with the university to teach physics, and Stephen Penrose rejoiced: "He is the first missionary of my children and I am greatly pleased."[128]

Virginia Penrose, the youngest daughter, surprised her parents by moving to New York City and by sailing alone to Paris.[129] After several months abroad, she had improved her conversational French and returned home. In 1930 she assisted her father by taking attendance and grading papers, and she taught French at Whitman.

Stephen Penrose's official letters, of course, gave more space to the subjects of education, religion, politics, and history than to his family. In the 1920s Americans expressed interest in education, dis-

Stephen B. L. Penrose, the third president of Whitman College, served from 1894 to 1934. The 1926 Waiilatpu noted that he had successfully made Whitman "the Friendly College." He was the most influential person in the college's history, though his last years were troubled by blindness and the Great Depression.

cussing schooling from kindergarten through higher education and the teaching profession. Because of his learning and reputation, educators and editors turned to Penrose for his thoughts. He often voiced them because, he explained, "I have studied the history of education and educational problems with unwavering interest, endeavoring to consider every question with disinterested scientific mindedness." [130] Penrose insisted that society should "meet two educational problems, the determination of differences between individuals as to their capacities for education, and the elimination of the unfit."[131]

Perhaps the best summary of his educational thoughts appeared in February 1926 in the *Washington Education Journal*. He rejected the "American superstition" that children were all alike and needed the same schooling and instead emphasized their differences — some children were brighter and more ambitious than others. The writer stressed: "I do not believe that all boys and girls who graduate from high school ought to go to college nor that all boys and girls who graduate from the grade schools should go to high school." Penrose insisted that young people needed "adequate ability and ambition" to advance in education and that college "ought to be confined to those who are capable of receiving it." He argued that society should be concerned about the health of school children and about opportunities for poor children to attend college, and warned: "The danger of a public school system is the cultivation of mediocrity. To discover the unusual child and to encourage him to go far beyond his fellows ought to be the object of every wise teacher. Perhaps democracy can never get away from mediocrity but unless it does, I think that democracy will perish."

In another essay, Penrose complained that public education did not train "boys and girls in honesty, truthfulness, respect for property, or respect for law." He reasoned: "The condition of swiftly increasing lawlessness is due to a fundamental defect in American education. As the state has taken over education it has deliberately professed to leave morals and religion to the church." But these institutions, the educator reminded readers, no longer attracted most children into their Sunday schools, institutions that instilled "moral ideals." Thus, he insisted that the state of Washington's great need was the selection of teachers "primarily chosen for their power of moral inspiration."[132]

Penrose expressed other opinions about education. He doubted that kindergartens "sufficiently develop the self-reliance and initiative of children"; he opposed junior colleges because their emphasis upon vocational subjects threatened "cultural education"; and he fought proposals to turn the state's normal schools into colleges.[133] He suggested ways to strengthen the public schools. He wanted more male teachers because of the particular way that they handled and instructed boys but qualified his generalization: "I want to see no pale-faced, anemic old maids in trousers going doggedly through the routine of high school, but rather vigorous red-blooded, warm-hearted men who are not ashamed to be teachers but glory in their work."[134] Penrose believed that married women should not be barred from teaching and that motherhood prepared women for teaching. He accused the public of being too interested in handsome school buildings and modern equipment while being indifferent to the teachers' qualities.

Constantly defending academic standards in universities as well as in high schools, Penrose argued that neither the University of Idaho nor Washington State College merited a Phi Beta Kappa chapter. He warned that Idaho's politicians threatened to weaken the university by moving some programs to a more populated area; thus, a decision on the honorary should be delayed until the school's future seemed secure. Whitman's leader even more strongly opposed Washington State College's bid. He confided to a professor that his "New England bred soul shudders at the thought of establishing a chapter . . . in an agricultural college"; furthermore, he feared that Washington State had remained unrepentant "for earlier sins of low scholarship."[135] Both schools pressured Penrose to support applications for membership in Phi Beta Kappa; in fact, a professor at Idaho threatened to use his influence to prevent a local Whitman fraternity from receiving a charter from Phi Gamma Delta if the college did not support Idaho's bid. Because these applications could not be blocked, the Whitman chapter voted for each school's admission into the society. Whitman's Phi Betes must have been amused by the fact that the new Idaho chapter refused to vote for Washington State's application.

Penrose adamantly opposed church control of colleges, a system he called medieval: "I have come to believe that it is wiser to entrust the management of a college to laymen than to ministers."[136] He complained that Willamette University and Linfield College suffered from denominational control. They were simply not "adapted to present day educational conditions but represent a survival from a time when interdenominational co-operation had not developed. . . . The interdenominational college like Whitman is the college of the future."[137] Penrose was particularly critical of Whitworth, whose "management," he explained, "had been dictated by a hand-ful of Presbyterian ministers at whose head stood Dr. [Mark A.] Matthews." Penrose saw that the wealthy men of Spokane refused to aid Whitworth because of its sectarianism. Penrose added that, while he was brought up as a Presbyterian, the church was now too often dominated by fundamentalists, particularly the Reverend Matthews, a powerful Seattle figure.[138] He boasted that "Congregationalists long since adopted the policy of leaving the educational institutions which they founded free from legal restriction. . . . Whitman in its present freedom from legal denominational control . . . is in precisely the same situation as Oberlin, Beloit, Grinnell, Carleton, and Pomona."[139]

Penrose was a liberal Congregationalist in his religious views. He explained that the college was Christian but that it was not denominational. Chester Maxey recalled that the school made "no effort to impose any religion upon anybody and there was no evangelism on the campus at all." For graduation, students must attend chapel (until 1933 there were three religious services a week), take a course in the Bible (taught by a retired missionary), and complete Penrose's philosophy of religion class, which included discussions of the nature of religion and descriptions of the world's great religions. In this class, Penrose insisted that there "was a lot of mythology in the Bible."[140] According to Maxey, Penrose, who granted the faculty freedom of speech, tolerated a wide spectrum of religious beliefs and defended the liberalism of Professor Howard Brode, as well as that of Professor Benjamin Brown, who shocked students by making fun of Christianity.

The president consistently argued that those seeking admission into the professions should first be educated in the liberal arts. For example, he praised the Harvard and Johns Hopkins medical schools for requiring such training. If physicians lacked broad culture, he warned, then the medical profession will be in "the ranks of the bread and butter winning trades." But he feared that few men would follow his advice: "The trouble with most Americans is that they are in so much of a rush that they will not prepare thoroughly to do the work in the best possible way."[141]

In addition to emphasizing liberal arts, Penrose promoted religion because of its importance in building a moral society: "The in-

fluences which determine the moral character of a people are . . .
mainly religion and education."[142] The president maintained that:
"The excessive individualism of our American life has brought about
the disintegration of family religion."[143] Yet he also criticized poorly informed and mechanical ministers: "We have suffered in the Pacific Northwest enough, God knows, from uneducated and half-
baked ministers."[144] Penrose lamented that only fourteen Whitman
men "of different denominations [were] headed for the ministry,"
and that most of them were second rate. "The first rate men," he
warned, "have little use for the ministry."[145] Still, Penrose insisted
that church conditions could be improved and used as an example
the successful efforts of the Reverend Theodore Vogler, who had
rebuilt the congregation of Walla Walla's Congregational church;
Penrose noted that even the "old malcontents" rejoined his church
and helped construct a beautiful new building.

To improve the quality of preaching, Penrose pushed on two
fronts. He urged his old friend, state superintendent of the Congregational churches Lucius Baird, to revitalize church councils and to
enlist only first-rate ministers. He also sponsored an interdenominational ministerial conference to which he invited all the ministers
within a hundred-mile radius of Whitman. At his twelfth annual conference, held in 1927, even Whitman faculty members participated:
historian Melvin Jacobs explained the religious factor of the American Revolution and political scientist Maxey gave a stereopticon lecture on Geneva and the League of Nations. Although only about half
of the ministers invited to his conferences attended, Penrose continued to sponsor them because he feared that: "Ministers are apt to
get technical and dry as dust. They need to water the dry gardens
of their souls with freshening showers of great writers and students
of life."[146]

Parallel to his interest in moral and religious issues was Penrose's
abiding interest in domestic and international politics. He identified himself as "a life long Republican, but I believe that at the present time we need someone to declare again for a salutary doctrine of
states' rights."[147] Thus, he heartily endorsed James M. Beck's *The
Vanishing Rights of the States*. Penrose's fear of "centralization and
bureaucracy" explained his opposition to the creation of a federal
department of education with cabinet rank. He cautioned: "A chief

peril of democracy is the tendency towards uniformity in education."
In his, mind forty-eight state educational programs were more likely
to advance public education than a single one emanating from Washington, D.C.[148] Because of his states' rights position, the educator
also opposed the passage of a federal amendment that would ban
children under the age of eighteen from working. In a speech delivered to the state legislature, he reaffirmed that the states—not the
federal government—should write the child labor laws and insisted
that most teenagers should work. "I do not like to picture . . . the
boys from fifteen to eighteen years of age in this state standing in
idleness upon the street corners because Congress had forbidden
them to work."[149]

A close observer of and commentator on federal elections, Penrose in 1928 expressed pleasure that so many southern states had rejected Democrat Al Smith and endorsed Republican Herbert Hoover.
He effused, "Was there ever in American politics such a Waterloo
as this?"[150]

Having lived in the state of Washington for forty years, Penrose
declared that he was "keenly interested in its development and
watchful over the progress which it was making."[151] Aware of his
interests and also of his influence, politicians, editors, businessmen,
and friends sought his opinions. In talks and letters, Penrose addressed a variety of issues: he criticized the legislature for passing
bills after the expiration of its session; he supported Josephine Corliss
Preston's election as state superintendent of public instruction; and
he pressured Governor Roland Hartley to oppose an effort to turn
normal schools into colleges. But Penrose brought even more attention to himself and his college by proposing that the Pacific Northwest senators and representatives form a bloc to promote regional
development. Numerous editors, politicians, business leaders, and
others debated the ramifications of this idea. Perhaps most writers—
many of whom feared economic stagnation—agreed that the under-
developed and underpopulated Pacific Northwest needed to form a
political bloc. A December 6, 1924, editorial in the *Portland Oregonian*, voicing reservations about political blocs, acknowledged
Penrose in a thoughtful and widely quoted consideration of the issue.

Penrose gradually became involved in another controversy, the
effort to win a pardon for Eugene Barnett, who had been among

those found guilty of murdering American Legionnaires in the Centralia Massacre of 1919 (and the case against whom, according to a recent authority, "was very weak.")[152] The prisoner's mother visited Penrose, pleading with him to help win her son's release from the state penitentiary. He investigated and wrote the parole board about Barnett, admitting that he was not well enough informed to ask for clemency. He added: "I think that the pardoning power has been much abused of late and that in consequence a spirit of sentimentality has grown up in regard to prisoners serving just sentences."[153] A few years later, Penrose reversed himself, writing the parole board and the governor that Barnett should be pardoned "as a matter of public policy, as well as private mercy."[154] An historian has recently concluded that Penrose was among a distinguished group that influenced the governor to parole Barnett in 1931.[155]

On a better-known issue of the time, the president supported state and federal prohibition laws, ruling that they should "be enforced vigorously until both drinking and drunkenness have been banished permanently from American life." His long-time friend, William Cowles, publisher of the *Spokane Spokesman-Review*, eagerly opened his newspaper's columns to Penrose's defense of prohibition. In 1926 the educator recalled that Walla Walla "used to be a rather lawless town with a saloon row in which drunkenness, gambling, and all kinds of vice went on and were winked at by the city authorities"; now students no longer passed saloons on Main Street and rarely brought alcoholic beverages to campus. Penrose asserted that prohibition greatly improved conditions: "The moral life of the college community is cleaner, more wholesome, and more law abiding than it used to be."[156]

In 1928 Penrose participated in another regional controversy, forest conservation. The president clashed with Pennsylvania governor Gifford Pinchot over Washington's logging practices. An early, famous, and persistent conservationist, Pinchot blamed forest fires on the axe; Penrose disagreed, insisting that lightning caused ninety percent of regional fires. The educator agreed with the governor that forests should be protected and that reforestation was often desirable, but, Penrose insisted, "The suggestion that all forests must be preserved is sentimentality which does not appeal to the scientific minded." Penrose reminded Pinchot that the forest problem was complicated, but that the resource must be utilized. The president accused the conservationist of concluding that "all people living in the region of forests and all owners of forest lands are either fools or knaves," to which Pinchot angrily retorted that the state's great timber companies rarely engaged in reforestation and that, unless the nation protected its forests, it would have to import wood. Pinchot urged the Walla Wallan to assume his responsibility to the state and nation.[157]

Penrose also took a keen interest in international relations and studied the subject, especially in *Foreign Affairs*, which he told Elihu Root he considered the nation's foremost magazine because it cultivated internationalism.[158] In 1928 he attended an institute of international relations in Seattle sponsored by the Carnegie Endowment for International Peace, and promised that he would work "to develop international mindedness." Such efforts were necessary, he explained, because, "We have little or no foreign element here and are inclined to be provincial."[159] However, Penrose opposed American entry into the League of Nations, fearing that American power wielded in the organization would arouse "jealousy, suspicion, and hatred" among the members.[160] While he hailed the fact that the United States remained out of the League, in letters to the state's two senators he deplored the fact that the nation failed to join the World Court. Penrose blamed the "unscrupulous Hearst newspapers for leaving no stone unturned" in its fight to prevent America from joining the organization.[161] Maintaining that he closely studied the Soviet Union, he denounced its economic system and hostility to Christianity. He considered this nation to be a world problem but felt certain that the educated American work force would ignore "Soviet teachings."[162] At the same time, he sympathized with Japan because of "the discourteous way in which congress" refused to grant her a quota in the 1924 immigration law. He hoped that this "unfortunate blunder affecting international good will" would be rectified.[163]

History was extremely important to Penrose, especially regional history and the role of Marcus Whitman. For more than three decades he had been relating the heroic story of the ill-fated missionary, and he admitted that he had told "some questionable tales."[164] The president published an account of Whitman in the *New York Times*, and in 1930 wrote a more comprehensive essay, "Master Surgeons of America." Considering Whitman to be a selfless patriot as well as a worthy missionary, Penrose insisted that the primary reason that Whitman had gone east in 1842 was to urge the Tyler administration not to trade Oregon to Great Britain. While scholars declared that the missionary made his perilous journey for religious reasons, Penrose disagreed, stating that politics was the prime motivation. Thus, he pushed the Whitman-saved-Oregon interpretation in the late 1920s, as he had in the late 1890s. The essay that appeared in 1930 was unusual, however, in that Penrose did not specifically blame the Cayuse tribe for the Whitman massacre; and he now wrote that the Whitmans had been scalped.

Penrose, who still asserted that Myron Eells had authored the best Whitman biography, anticipated that a trained historian would write a better one based upon new material. To support such a study, he assisted Professor Archer Hulburt in collecting Whitman letters for publication. Penrose hailed W. J. Ghent's *The Road to Oregon* because the author considered the missionary to be a great man, but he criticized the fictional portrayal of Whitman in Honore Wilson Morrow's *We Must March*. Penrose eagerly collected Whitman materials for the school's archives and read manuscripts about the missionary. He concluded that the portrait of Narcissa Whitman given to Prentiss Hall in 1927 by the Daughters of the American Revolution was idealized, but appropriate because, "The artist has caught delightfully the idealism and devotion of Mrs. Whitman." [165] The president repeatedly told the missionaries' story to his students, and he also related it to influential citizens like Clara Crane, whose brother had underwritten Robert Peary's expedition to the North Pole. Penrose requested money to maintain Marcus Whitman's burial site, reasoning that the Whitman expedition "was more daring than Peary's, and in a nobler cause." [166]

Besides interpreting the lives of the controversial missionaries, Penrose attracted publicity—and simultaneously involved the college in a historical dispute—by erecting a campus memorial to Chief Lawyer, a controversial Nez Perce leader. In 1926 the Washington State Historical Society prompted the president's action by asking if the college, which it believed to be on the site of a famous 1855 treaty council with the Indians, would erect a monument to "Chief Lawyer, who befriended Governor [Isaac I.] Stevens." [167] During the strained negotiations, Stevens had pressured several eastern Washington tribes to sign treaties selling their lands. Biographer Hazard Stevens maintained that the Cayuse became so angry with the governor that they plotted to murder him and other whites. After learning of this treachery, Lawyer protected Stevens by moving his tipi into the governor's camp. Some authorities believe that Lawyer actually relocated because Indian foes threatened his own life. Historian Alvin Josephy correctly concluded that: "What happened among the Indians that evening will probably never be clear." [168] But Penrose, possessing a romantic view of history, insisted that Lawyer's movement of his family to the Stevens camp was "an act of heroic friendship." [169] The state's historical society agreed that "Lawyer averted an intended attack by an unfriendly tribe." [170]

Beginning in the fall of 1929, Penrose spent considerable time arranging the memorial celebration to be held in early June, the seventy-fifth anniversary of Lawyer's disputed action. During the preparations, Penrose, who maintained that any commemoration of an Indian by whites was unusual, also honored Lawyer for his role as a Christian leader among reservation Nez Perce.

Penrose issued hundreds of invitations, including those to Governor Hartley and Corbett Lawyer, a grandson of the headman. Idaho's Potlatch Timber Company agreed to deliver an appropriate boulder for the bronze tablet honoring Lawyer. Railroad companies cooperated by shipping the boulder free of charge and by reducing passenger fares for the celebrants. Penrose arranged for Whitman's graduating seniors to donate the bronze tablet and publicized the event in the *Congregationalist*, the *New York Times*, and other outlets.

He encountered numerous difficulties. The enormous boulder split when blasted. A second boulder—described by a Potlatch official as "somewhat the shape of a big round potato cut in half"—required considerable paperwork and physical labor in its movement from Elk River to Walla Walla. [171] More irksome to Penrose than obtaining a suitable boulder were the criticisms and confusion about the ceremony. Many Nez Perce opposed celebrating Lawyer because he had surrendered land. Corbett Lawyer cautioned Penrose that the Nez Perce were a "very sensitive people and hard to please." [172] James E. Babb, a Whitman overseer from Idaho with knowledge of the Nez Perce, warned Penrose that, by celebrating Lawyer, "You may be

wading into waters yet unfathomed," and that an ambitious journalist would try to make "a sensational scoop" out of the matter.[173]
Umatilla Indians voiced their opposition to the press, arguing that
Lawyer moved his tent to protect himself, that Cayuse Indians had
not plotted the governor's death, and that the college should honor
the elder Chief Joseph, not Lawyer.

Penrose responded to critics by generalizing that Lawyer, like such
famous leaders as Washington and Jefferson, had been subject to "all
sorts of base insinuations."[174] The president reasoned that Stevens
and the badly outnumbered whites could not have protected Lawyer
from an attack by hundreds of tribesmen. To his way of thinking,
the Nez Perce leader was a hero, not a coward. Thus, the president
would not include in the program some elderly Indian women who
disagreed with his interpretation, but he would allow them an opportunity to speak at its conclusion. Penrose explained that he had
more confidence in Stevens' written account than in a seventy-five-
year-old Cayuse oral account. The regional press became involved
in the controversy. The *Seattle Times* joked that the Cayuse and other
tribes had engaged in a war of words with "Big Chief" Penrose, who
led the Nez Perce.[175]

Besides controversy with the tribes, Penrose also had to untangle
some confusion about the celebration's intent. An Indian agent, for
example, thought that its purpose was to acknowledge an important
treaty in which several tribes sold large sections of land. Penrose corrected him, stating that the college sought only to "recognize the
great qualities of mind and heart of Chief Lawyer" and that the college's seniors should be praised for erecting a tablet to a heroic chief
who had "uplifted his people and was friendly with whites."[176]
While journalists, historians, editors, and others debated Lawyer's
career, workmen set the boulder in concrete, and Penrose expressed
pleasure that the rock looked "as if it had always been there."[177]

The ceremony took place on June 3, 1930. A procession went
from the Marcus Whitman Hotel to the memorial rock, where Corbett Lawyer gave the college some documents written by Governor
Stevens; N. W. Durham, a Spokane journalist and regional historian, delivered his lecture praising Lawyer for signing a treaty rather
than making war; and the senior class president presented the monument to Governor Hartley, who accepted it for the state and turned

it over to the college trustees for safekeeping. A journalist noted that, at the end of the ceremonies, "Two venerable [Cayuse] squaws . . . cast aspersions upon Chief Lawyer."[178] At a banquet, Hartley praised the college for honoring Lawyer and added: "This monument will do the Indians good and will be good for the coming generation . . . to draw inspiration from the plaque." Penrose observed that white men rarely honored a man of a different race because, "We on the coast have not yet developed to a point where we can see virtue in a red man or a yellow man."[179]

Penrose made an effort to enlighten Washingtonians about a variety of issues, including racial ones; he had wide-ranging interests, and he spoke about them to diverse Pacific Northwest audiences, always publicizing the college. A 1925 lecture in Seattle attracted "a large and influential group, and there seemed to be unanimous enthusiasm over his talk." A college fund raiser thought that the address would "be a great help in our efforts to revive local interest in Whitman."[180] Undoubtedly the high point of his lecturing was in 1930, on the two-thousandth anniversary of Virgil's birth, traveling to eastern Washington towns under the auspices of Phi Beta Kappa. His address in Wenatchee attracted eight hundred listeners; in Ellensburg he drew around twelve hundred. He reported that his "Virgilian pilgrimage" to four scattered lecture sites drew nearly three thousand listeners.[181]

The president was offered a lecture contract, which he refused because, as he said, he had "no desire to augment my income by lectures nor to bind myself to a schedule."[182] He occasionally rejected opportunities to preach or speak because of exhaustion, but he once explained to a friend why he did not wish to make an address: "The impression which one can make on an audience of businessmen during the twenty minutes of their digesting their luncheon is not profound or lasting. I don't believe that Whitman College needs me to do that sort of publicity stunt any longer."[183] Meanwhile, he did considerable writing about his school.

In the late 1920s Penrose continued to write the college's history, but he was unsuccessful at getting a major publishing house to bring out the book in 1934, his fortieth anniversary as president. Meanwhile, he published a lengthy, entertaining newspaper account of his first years in Dayton, Washington. In the community of Walla Walla,

Penrose was a founding member of Rotary, enjoying its fellowship. His membership was important to the college, he explained, because local businessmen found him "to be quite as human as they."[184] He also participated in the Inquiry Club, which he and a few others founded in the 1890s. Its fifteen members met regularly to deliver thoughtful papers and engage in spirited discussions on a wide range of topics. The bylaws fostered these exchanges with the rule: "To encourage the utmost freedom of discussion, it is declared that the lady of the house is not expected to be present. . . ."[185]

While obviously devoted to Whitman, Penrose maintained a lively interest in Williams College (an old classmate, Harry A. Garfield, was its long-time president) and in his class of 1885. Although unable to attend class reunions, Penrose sent letters and poetry to be read at these emotional gatherings. The western educator expressed a desire to visit with his distant classmates living in a different society, and to be nostalgic about their happy undergraduate years. Thoughts of class reunions aroused pangs of loneliness that resulted from his living "off on the edge of the world."[186]

From his edge of the world Penrose evaluated the popular culture of the late 1920s. When asked about the influence of motion pictures and the radio, he eagerly faulted both forms of popular entertainment. He judged that "lighter and wholly entertaining pictures" were harmless but denounced those featuring a triangle love plot because they capitalized on sex and served no good purpose. Penrose complained that high school and college students wasted their time at the movies and—in a reversal of his politics—favored national rather than state censorship of films. As a critic he urged the industry to produce "pictures of a higher standard" and thought that the movies, including those on historic themes, had improved.[187] The Penrose family purchased a radio, but after two months returned it to the dealer, because it "seemed such a waste of time" and because "I cannot let the printed word of serious thinkers be displaced by the jazz of the air."[188] The *Saturday Evening Post* he read only as a diversion at summer camp.

Penrose also evaluated the character of Pacific Northwest cities. He believed that, if Seattle aimed to be one of the nation's largest cities, then it must be more concerned about economic development of its rich eastern Washington hinterland and the Great Northern's proposed Cascade tunnel link. He also instructed Seattleites that, if they wanted to be a great city, then they must be concerned about culture, education, and spiritual values. He thought Portland was more broad-minded and international-minded than most western cities, but he complained that Portlanders thought "that the world ends with the city limits,"[189] and would only aid Oregon institutions, although its men should be "tall enough to look over Oregon's boundaries" into eastern Washington, a historic and valuable part of the region.[190] He recognized great changes in Pendleton. When he first had seen the town in the 1890s it was a "wild and woolly" railroad town, and its saloons "thronged with men and women whose hard faces suggested . . . those of beasts of prey." To him the Pendleton Roundup meant that the city had moved from "savage individualism . . . to a display of community spirit." And a performance of Haydn's *Creation* by sixty of its residents was proof of "a new epoch in Pendleton's evolution."[191]

One of Penrose's greatest loves was his remote camp, about which he enthused: "A summer on Puget Sound is the best preparation for heaven."[192] For many summers the family came to this beautiful spot, where they could not be bothered by telephones or telegrams. Penrose explained that the family and their guests—on some weekends a dozen joined them—lived "in tents scattered among the trees near the tip of the point and have only a shingle roof over our dining room and kitchen to protect us from rain." Penrose confessed that, in his tranquility, he "forgot all about the college . . . and let its burdens be carried by . . . the faculty and administrative force."[193]

2

President Penrose Battles Financial Crisis During the Great Depression

1931–1934

During his last four years in office, Stephen Penrose waged a painful, losing battle against the effects of the Great Depression, a struggle which consumed his days as his writing on education and other subjects diminished. He intermittently labored on his college history but wrote fewer provocative essays on the issues that still mattered to him. Instead of joyously concluding a long and illustrious career, the educator spent his energy trying to keep his beloved college afloat in a rising pool of red ink. Penrose had long anticipated that in the 1930s the college could launch a major campaign to expand its physical plant in commemoration of two anniversaries—the school's seventy-fifth and his fortieth as president. The year 1934 was to be a great celebration, but it turned out to be one of the college's most difficult years. The distinguished leader sadly concluded:

> It has been a great grief to me that during the ten years of my blindness the college should have entered into a period of difficulty and privation from which I could not rescue it. It is financially sound, but its assets are frozen and it has only been able to keep going by borrowing from the faculty the amount of their unpaid salaries . . . the present poverty is pressing and I must go out of office with a heavy weight of disappointment . . . because I could not relieve the situation.[1]

Today, when concerned individuals look back at Whitman's conservative fiscal policies—especially the sacred balanced budget—they invoke the devastating 1930s, a time when they believe the college nearly closed. The lesson they learn is simple, though difficult to follow: avoid debt. It would seem that such a profound operating principle would be based on solid research and writing on the period from 1925 to 1934, but, in fact, few have sought the reasons for the college's financial chaos and attempted solutions.

This little-understood episode is one of the most confusing in Whitman's history, but it is also one of the most interesting, and important. To comprehend the college's history in the late 1920s and the 1930s it is necessary to understand the financial crisis, for it touched the life of every Whitman constituent. Although it is impossible to reclaim the full financial story because of missing and confusing documents and the deaths of college leaders, even limited research into the numerous Penrose letters reveals that the college's financial crisis did not suddenly emerge with the stock market crash in late 1929 and the ensuing Great Depression.

The nation's economic troubles of the early 1930s obviously increased Whitman's woes, but the college faced painful financial conditions—especially bond indebtedness—prior to the economic downturn of 1930. Whitman's ship washed into the financial shoals faster than other academic vessels. The University of Washington and Washington State College both endured hardships, especially in the early 1930s after the legislature slashed their budgets, but Pacific and Willamette universities weathered the economic storm because they, unlike Whitman, had avoided crippling debt in the late 1920s and had maintained an adequate income.[2]

Chester Maxey lived through these troubled times and wrote briefly and talked extensively about the experience. His autobiography, *The World I Lived In*, provides the conventional summary: "From 1924 onward the financial condition of Whitman College grew worse every day. Even in the hectic prosperity which lasted until October 1929, Whitman College went down the skids instead of up."[3] He emphasized three factors that contributed to the school's economic decline: the trustees' poor money management over an extended period; a small endowment, which the 1924–1925 Tamblyn and Brown campaign drive increased by less than $200,000 (Maxey remembered that Whitman had sought about eight times as much); and, especially, the payments on a bond debt totaling $495,000. This crushing debt, he explained, resulted from construction of the heating plant, Lyman House, and Prentiss Hall, and from the payment of old debts. The three buildings had been required in order to house an expanding student body, and the boards had optimistically assumed that dormitory fees, along with increased tuition revenues, would retire the bonds. Thus, in 1923 the college's alumni, following the example of Carleton College, created the Whitman Building Corporation, a subsidiary of Whitman College, and from 1923 to 1926 sold bonds at six-percent interest to build the three buildings.[4]

Penrose argued that the only way to provide these vital structures was for the college "to pay a yearly rental for the use of the buildings sufficient to cover the interest and retire the bonds in twenty years."[5] Maxey explained that the structures "were supposed to be self-liquidating, but they never were." He added: "To meet the scheduled payments of principal and interest, income from tuition fees and endowment earnings was diverted to the service of the bonded debt; which was robbing Peter to pay Paul."[6]

Penrose's account, *Whitman: An Unfinished Story*, lacks an explanation of the financial troubles of the late 1920s, and the trustee minutes are also sketchy. The president's correspondence, however, offers a much fuller treatment of those difficult years and a much different explanation from Maxey's writings. The difficulty in the late 1920s began with the trustees' decision to issue bonds for $320,000, of which $150,000 was used for the construction of Prentiss Hall, "and the balance," Penrose explained, "was given to the college for endowment and current needs."[7] Only a few Walla Wallans knew that $105,000 of the bond money was actually used to pay old operating debts—apparently from the expensive scholarship program—and that Prentiss cost at least $23,000 more than anticipated. Trustees and Penrose defended the bond issue because dormitory fees, together with more than $200,000 in subscription notes from the 1924–1925 campaign, would cover the bond payments. In 1930, when this repayment system had clearly failed, Penrose, unlike Maxey, insisted that it did not result "from carelessness, extravagance, or unbusinesslike methods but is a temporary condition for which a relief must speedily be found, as the college cannot borrow more money locally to meet the emergency."[8]

Instead of explaining the debt by invoking the failure of the dormitories to be self-supporting and their unanticipated maintenance costs, Penrose in the late 1920s gave potential donors a different reason. In the financial campaign of 1924–1925, he explained, Whitman received about $600,000 in subscriptions; thus, the trustees confidently floated a bond issue and built Prentiss Hall. Initially the subscriptions covered the bonds; however, in 1930: "The principal and interest on the bond issue has been fully met up to this year by subscriptions due and paid. But this year the delinquent subscriptions have obliged us to draw heavily on the college's current expense fund, causing great inconvenience and embarrassment in the payment of salaries and current bills."[9] The president identified those

Members of the Delta Gamma chapter pose in front of their section of the brand-new Prentiss Hall during the winter of 1926–1927.

who had not paid $100,000 in subscriptions as the younger alumni, but assured doubters that they would eventually honor their commitments. Thus, Penrose's explanation for the financial distress on the eve of the Great Depression played down the decision to sell bonds, and instead blamed those who neglected their subscriptions. Maxey, however, faulted the decision to issue such a large number of bonds and ignored the issue of the subscription notes. Neither explanation for the mounting financial crisis is complete or convincing.

Both writers' interpretations of the financial history of 1924 to 1930 failed to mention Penrose's futile efforts to halt the school's financial slide. He wanted to terminate an expensive scholarship program, to raise tuition and dormitory fees, to enhance endowment earnings, and to refinance the debt. Apparently Penrose found it too painful to recount his ineffective actions, and Maxey had no interest in researching the college records or placing the crisis into a fuller historical perspective. However, Maxey did emphasize the fact that for years Penrose expected Whitman to surmount its economic difficulties as it grew. In his 1928 report, the president summarized his financial policy, one that the trustees also endorsed: "A growing college must occasionally run into debt if it is not to be arrested in its development."[10] He related how his impressive college—a daughter of Williams College in Massachusetts—had triumphed under such a policy. He could have added that, had the institution found another generous individual like Dr. Daniel "D. K." Pearsons (Whitman's chief benefactor from 1894 until his death in 1912),[11] it might have built buildings without issuing bonds. Basically, the school could not grow unless it borrowed money. Its history proved that progress and debt went hand in hand, a view that was certainly not unique to Whitman's leaders, as Maxey acknowledged. In fact, Americans mortgaged their futures for a wide variety of purposes, including the great bull market of the 1920s. As late as 1928 Penrose defended this policy of controlled deficits and frequently assured regional businessmen of the college's stability.

In 1926 he stated that Whitman had "never been in so excellent a financial condition";[12] two years later he proclaimed that it had "passed beyond the danger point and is so firmly established that its future is not in doubt. I think that it is safe to say . . . that a thousand years from now the college will be here."[13] The next year he again

assured overseers that the school had no large debt. He still expected
field agents to find new money for an expansion of buildings and
scholarships, but in 1929 he asked William Worthington to seek
money only for operating costs, a sure sign of financial stress. As late
as 1930 Penrose did not fully realize—and perhaps neither did Maxey
—the seriousness of the financial problem. Like other private institutions, Whitman had been in and out of debt for almost its entire history. Moreover, it was actually far stronger during the late 1920s than
it had been during the 1890s or in the 1912 economic crisis that followed the failure of the ambitious plan for a "Greater Whitman."[14]

By 1930, however, Whitman was in another one of its precarious predicaments. In fact, college leaders incorrectly maintained that
the books balanced until the 1931–1932 school year.[15] (These positive budget figures were at odds with Maxey's interpretation, the
Russell report of 1934, and the ten-year audit done in 1936.) At the
1930 commencement perhaps only a few in the Whitman family recognized anything unique about their rickety financial house, since
board members, students, and the faculty had long lived with a persistent financial crisis that was as much a part of Whitman as intercollegiate football or low faculty salaries.

During the late 1920s Penrose, joined by some trustees and overseers, raised significant concerns at trustee meetings about the college's financial practices. His correspondence raised meaningful questions about the board's investment policies. As early as 1925 the
president questioned the trustees' decision to invest most of the college's endowment in farm mortgages because of the "disturbance
of agricultural conditions since the war."[16] Overseers agreed, urging
investments in municipal bonds. Penrose privately blamed trustee
Frank Baker, the influential chairman of the college's finance committee and president of the Baker-Boyer Bank, for acquiring farm
mortgages. According to Penrose, this crucial committee had "a radical distrust of all bonds and investments outside of the Walla Walla
Valley. This provincialism," he predicted, "will be hard to cure."[17]
Penrose pleaded with out-of-town overseers to provide an alternative investment plan because, "It is a great disadvantage to be in a
small country town where few of the people have connections outside of it."[18] Trustee William Cowles of Spokane endorsed this view,
insisting that the endowment should be put into bonds. In 1927 he

correctly warned: "If we do not do this promptly, we are neglecting our obligation and will lay ourselves open to serious criticism."[19]

Penrose questioned another policy of the Baker-led committee: the college deposited its funds only in Baker's bank, which paid fourpercent interest. He thought they "might obtain 5 1/2 or 6%" in some other institution, and an overseer committee agreed.[20]

Penrose also had disagreements with Whitman's treasurer, Dorsey Hill. The president charged that Hill—who owned a farm and sided with Baker's finance committee—was "completely taken with the idea that only farm mortgages in the Walla Walla Valley are possible as a source of college investment despite the experience of innumerable other colleges that local investments alone are not safe for an educational institution."[21] The president complained to the treasurer that the committee seemed satisfied to receive four percent at the Baker-Boyer Bank when Whitman could receive six percent in Spokane. "We are losing," Penrose pointed out, "about $4,000 a year by letting this money stand on certificate of deposit in the Baker-Boyer Bank."[22] The leader doubted the "wisdom of doing all the college financing with one bank when there are five banks in the community," and challenged the policy of "keeping a large amount of money at 4% in the savings department of the one bank with little or no effort to find more lucrative investments in the outside."[23] Hill disagreed, arguing that the bank was not "desirous of holding this money and paying 4% to us, but I consider that they are doing the college a great favor in keeping it safe and paying this rate of interest."[24]

Penrose wanted to revise institutional banking policies; he also proposed a tuition increase in 1926 to boost income. From 1925 to 1928 the trustees ignored his requests for a $50 increase in tuition, and merely raised the annual dormitory fees from $100 to $125 for the 1928–1929 school year. Growing debt and continued annual deficits did not stir the trustees to accept fiscal recommendations advocated by Penrose and the overseers. The president charitably interpreted the trustees' negative decision when "an almost unheard of disaster" fell on the area. "An extraordinary spell of cold weather caught the fall wheat in just the stage when it was most susceptible to freezing." The banks paid for the reseeding, and it "made business conditions more difficult."[25] Penrose must have thought back to the panic of 1893, when bitter weather had devastated local farmers and a collapsed economy nearly crushed the emerging college. In those troubled times, however, he had not been at odds with the trustees.

Thus, the school's financial dilemma in the late 1920s resulted from a combination of factors: the bond issue, the failure to collect subscriptions, generous scholarships, low tuition and dormitory charges, poor investments of the endowment funds, loans from the Baker-Boyer Bank, and an unwillingness to hire a fund raiser from 1925 to 1927. To cover these resultant shortfalls, the trustees borrowed in 1925 and again in 1927, using Liberty Bonds as collateral. In 1928 and 1929 they borrowed again, a total of $105,000 to pay operating costs and the principal and interest on the bonds. In 1930 Penrose noted with chagrin that the delinquent subscriptions forced the college to draw about $40,000 from the current expense fund.[26]

Responding to Penrose's concerns about Whitman's investments, the overseers created a special college finance committee, which made significant recommendations in 1928. It preferred investing in "interest bearing securities" and cautioned against acquiring farms, "which are subject to excessive costs for upkeep and the proceeds of which depends so largely on a degree of intelligent management that is not often to be had in tenant farmers." The committee also vigorously opposed the purchase of real estate and again advocated investing in municipal bonds.[27] Penrose predicted that the findings of this special committee would teach trustees that a college was "a different sort of enterprise from an ordinary business and that the investment of college endowment funds presented peculiar problems."[28]

While the finance committee sought ways to enhance investments, Penrose, who was deeply troubled by the fact that Whitman was paying a steep six percent on its bonds, recommended to overseers that the current debt be covered by a new bond issue at five percent. Penrose himself investigated the bond market, asking to borrow around $100,000 at five percent, but the novice failed. Meanwhile, he had tried to "increase the college's resources" through the life-insurance program adopted by the class of 1928.[29] This attempt failed too.

Because of its grave financial crisis, the college should have been more aggressive in its solicitations. To locate donors, Penrose unsuccessfully proposed in 1928 that the school employ a second field representative. Although the boards disagreed, Worthington, Penrose, Cowles, and others were able to raise $40,000 during the 1929–1930 school year.

In 1929, on the eve of the Great Depression, Whitman's financial matters worsened. Faced with growing deficits and the inability to borrow at a lower interest rate, Penrose desperately tried to collect the delinquent 1924–1925 subscriptions. Directed by both governing boards, Penrose wrote tactfully to alumni, informing them that, if they paid, "the college would be in a satisfactory condition, but without their payment the situation is serious."[30] Penrose asked young alumni Harper Joy and Paul Garrett to help collect unpaid subscriptions, emphasizing that he and some faculty members had not received salaries. He reasoned: "It does not seem to me right or fair that the college should make this forced borrowing from the faculty because so many subscribers have failed to keep their promises."[31] But these personal appeals to subscribers failed. In late 1929 Penrose, unable to overcome what he called his "financial embarrassment," lamented: "The college is likely to go along in poverty under my administration."[32]

Personalities as well as differences about investment strategies brought additional problems. Treasurer Dorsey Hill and bursar George Marquis disliked each other, so Hill moved his office from the campus to downtown, making it more difficult for the president to conduct business with the treasurer. Early in 1930 Hill became Walla Walla's mayor; surely the responsibilities of this office during a depression reduced his effectiveness as Whitman's treasurer.

While Hill sought to resolve civic as well as college financial problems, Penrose still attempted to collect subscriptions and to raise $20,000 to cover current expenses. He recommended that this be done by finding two hundred people who would each donate $100. Meanwhile, trustee William Cowles initiated a grander plan. He proposed giving $5,000 if seven others would also donate $5,000 each. In an exhaustive attempt to find these donors, Penrose wrote sixty-seven letters and many telegrams to a variety of individuals scattered from Maine to California, and Worthington sent about sixty additional appeals. They could find only six individuals willing to give $5,000; none were Walla Wallans. The solicitors located seventeen persons who donated $500 or more; ten of them lived on the East Coast and two were Walla Wallans. Unimpressed with these results,

Cowles insisted that Penrose find all seven donors. The trustee at first sent only $2,000 of his pledge, in an effort to goad the president into meeting his requirement. In June 1931 the defeated educator wrote to the publisher: "I think," he explained, "it is the first time I have failed to do what I undertook. . . . There is not a person I know capable of giving such a sum, whom I have not asked to give. I feel that there is nothing more which I can do."[33] Cowles reluctantly fulfilled his pledge, and his proposal resulted in the college raising approximately $50,000, some of which the trustees placed in the endowment.

In 1930 Penrose and Worthington established an organization to promote the Whitman Alumni Fund in order "to lighten the burden of the college trustees." When Penrose wrote about the organization's appeals to the alumni, he insisted that "the college needs help, desperately needs it," and emphasized: "It is not the size of the gift that counts so much as its regularity of recurrence."[34] Already feeling the pinch of the Great Depression, alumni could provide only limited financial assistance.

While the embattled president wrote dozens of letters to raise money, he again tried to obtain a loan at less than five percent to restructure the college debt. His 1930 report ignored his failure but emphasized that recent donations prevented "a threatened deficit . . . due to the delay in the payment of [1924–1925] subscriptions." Penrose knew that an annual appeal for covering the operating budget was a risky policy because donors would become annoyed with annual requests, but he had no alternative. Meanwhile, the college turned again to the bank and borrowed more money at a stiff six percent, raising the total to about $110,000.

The two-board system had not served the college well in Penrose's last decade. Local trustees and outside overseers had disagreed about farm mortgages, municipal bonds, tuition, and fund raising, and the trustees prevailed because they wielded their authorized power. Now debts owed to bondholders and bankers put the college at risk. Unfortunately, the college had not resolved its economic crisis prior to the Great Depression. With deep debt, and with discord between board members, the institution plunged into the outgoing tide of 1931. This situation, as Maxey observed, demoralized poor professors as well as their poor countrymen.

The President's Annual Reports on the Fiscal Crisis

The Great Depression meant heartache and hardship for the Whitman faculty, as it did for so many Americans. During those years Professor Maxey and others thought the college might collapse because of mismanagement. Fortunately, President Penrose left a considerable paper trail that provides insight into this very difficult period in the college's history.

The president's annual reports to the overseers from 1931 to 1934 —the worst years of the Depression—are a less satisfactory account of Whitman's terrible economic crisis than are his numerous letters. If he were too frank in his official statements, he might lose public support. As the president confidentially told a dedicated supporter, Harper Joy, "We are having such difficulty with meeting our monthly bills that it might be injurious to advertise our financial situation."[35] Frustrated by numerous difficulties, including debt, blindness, and the inability to attract support, Penrose could be impatient and sarcastic. In letters to friends and potential donors, he provided more specifics about Whitman's finances and his extensive and generally futile efforts to relieve the financial pressure. Despite their limitations, however, the reports, which covered many topics other than financial issues, still provided the college's many friends with a useful summary of its financial distress.

In his 1931 and 1932 reports, the president provided some favorable news: "Despite the depressed financial situation the attendance of the college has been surprisingly good." Meanwhile, field representative Worthington was successfully "cultivating individuals for bequests." Penrose informed his audience that, when all the alumni and overseers provided for the college in their wills, then many wealthy outsiders would do the same. He again praised alumni and friends for rallying to the college's standard.

But negative financial news, of course, dominated his assessment of his final years; in fact, the conditions were sometimes so discouraging that they were kept from the public. Although Penrose made his reports to the boards annually, in some years they were not released. He privately explained later: "On account of hard times the annual reports were not published in 1932 and 1933, which I

think was unfortunate. The constituency of the college is entitled
to know the financial situation of the institution as presented in the
budget and the Treasurer's report."[36]

In 1931 the president mentioned the cancellation of major plans
to strengthen the college by 1934. Furthermore, Penrose stated that
he had discarded the word "campaign" because of "its questionable
associations." He advised, however, that planning for college improvements should proceed during this period of "business gloom."
In 1932 Penrose discussed balanced budgets with a revised perspective: "No economic principle has appealed more strongly to the
American people within the last six months than that of a balanced
budget. . . . It is generally recognized that the principle of a balanced
budget is indispensable to the security and continuance of a nation,
a municipality, or an institution. The principle involves the careful
planning of next year's expenditure based on this year's income." He
explained that a college could not be certain of its expenditures;
therefore, the overseers should agree with the trustees, who had cut
the budget. Penrose then discussed the current deficit and assured
readers that it would be met. The leader cautioned overseers that
there could be another annual debt because of "the unexampled fall
in the price of wheat and the failure of interest payments." The decline in the college's earnings—primarily from farm mortgages—resulted in the trustees slashing faculty salaries by twenty percent and
greatly reducing departmental and library budgets.

Penrose generalized about the impact of donations: "Too great
reliance upon gifts and bequests may lead to an exaggerated optimism which will imperil the future of a college and on the other hand
too great pessimism may result from disregard of this source of income and may paralyze or unduly retard its growth." He then summarized Whitman's financial history since the 1890s; his purpose was
to demonstrate that its income could not be predicted because gifts
and bequests could come at any time. The president bluntly told
board members: "If you let yourselves be paralyzed by this year's
deficit, forgetful of past history, you will be foolish, and, if on the
other hand, you throw caution to the winds and fail to cut down expenses you will be foolhardy."

In this report, Penrose was also mildly critical of Walla Wallans
for not providing more assistance to the beleaguered institution.

Again he employed history to prod donors. According to his calculations, since 1894 the college and its students had spent $8,000,000 in the city, and Walla Wallans had given only about $250,000 of the $2,000,000 that the college had raised. While Penrose appreciated this contribution, he charged that townspeople had, in effect, hampered the school's effort to meet the current $91,000 deficit, reasoning that the appeals to alumni and friends were "weakened because I could not say that the community had taken the lead in providing its share of the amount needed."[37] After this admonishment, the president again praised Walla Wallans for past assistance. But he knew it was difficult to raise local money since townpeople "are apt to see and to remember the mistakes which the college has made . . . and not to see [its] progress."[38]

The most discouraging news appeared at the end of the 1932 report: "The dwindling resources of men of wealth and the deepening gloom of the financial depression have made it impossible to obtain the gifts for current expenses which the college sorely needed." The school simply could not raise enough money despite the help of the "generous hearted" and the field agent's "keen-eyed intelligence" in securing bequests.

His 1933 report was the most pessimistic delivered during the Great Depression. Several factors were responsible for Whitman operating without adequate income. Because it had been making desperate appeals since the late 1920s, the college had exhausted its donors. The shallow well had run dry. Thus, Worthington was instructed not even to ask for money; apparently all appeals to delinquent subscribers ended. Another financial problem was that the school's investments in farm mortgages brought only meager returns. Penrose informed a confidant of the reasons for the financial crisis. Whitman's endowment funds were "invested largely in farm mortgages, regarded as gilt edged and always heretofore reliable, safe, and productive." But the low price of wheat had consistently been below the cost of production; thus, farmers had been "unable to pay their interest."[39] Yet the college had to stick with the farmers because it would do no good to foreclose, and Whitman's immediate need was money, not land. Furthermore, tuition income was low because student enrollment had dropped. The president added that even the students who remained could not pay their accounts. At the same time, the school owed payments to bondholders and bankers.

As a result of this miserable financial situation, Penrose explained: "The faculty had to endure privation and want. . . . The only alleviation to [their] distress was their knowledge that so many other people were in similar circumstances." The president said that Worthington, who had abandoned the "impossible task of securing financial aid for the college, had . . . transferred his efforts to the cultivation of relations with the high schools." This effort to recruit students, Penrose emphasized, was necessary because enrollments had decreased by sixteen percent from the 1929–1930 school year. Penrose tried to put a gloss on this news by assuring his audience that many families wanted their children to attend Whitman. An improved enrollment would occur, he reasoned, "as soon as the tide of prosperity turns and begins to flow back again into the wheat and lumber business of the Northwest, our basic industries." Because some graduating seniors would be unable to find employment, Penrose recommended that they be allowed to remain in school without paying tuition. Worthington successfully recruited students and in some cases even used his own funds to find them, but in 1933 the distressed institution told even this loyal alumnus that it could no longer afford his services.

Penrose also reminded readers of this 1933 report that he had twice offered to resign because, "My blindness seriously interfered with the effectiveness of administration."[40] This stark admission sharply contrasted with the assurances that had accompanied his previous resignation offers. In 1924, and again in 1929, he had provided evidence of his effectiveness. Clearly the lengthy, exhausting, and losing struggle against the economic crisis had defeated him. Therefore, he again submitted his resignation to take effect in either 1933 or 1934. For reasons of public relations, the weary leader thought it wiser to use the latter date.

Penrose's last report, made in 1934, was more optimistic. It included a brief autobiography, relating the economic problems he had battled in the 1890s. Then he presented some hopeful news: "The tide of student attendance which has been ebbing steadily since the beginning of the depression turned last summer and has shown signs of increasing. The change has not been marked so much by an actual increase in attendance as by the cessation of the decrease."

The report's most unique part made reference to government aid. The federal Civil Works Administration and the state's own agency, the Washington Emergency Relief Administration, both employed a few needy students who worked in campus buildings or on the grounds. Their wages kept them in school. Whitman had also submitted a proposal to the federal Public Works Administration for a grant or a loan to build a sorely needed library. In truth, Penrose, who had opposed Franklin D. Roosevelt's election in 1932, had not seen the federal government play such a useful role in his institution since the First World War. He stepped into office in a great depression under a Democratic president; he stepped out in the Great Depression under another Democratic president.

Penrose concluded his report with warm thoughts about his successor, Dr. Rudolf Clemen. The departing leader observed: "It took courage and determination on his part to accept the presidency of an institution which had suffered severely from the financial depression." As a faculty member, Penrose promised to do all he could to help his successor battle the economic forces that had crushed him.

Penrose's Continuing Efforts

In evaluating these years, Chester Maxey bluntly wrote that by 1930 the school badly needed a new leader. In these "tragic and pathetic" years, he insisted, Penrose was inefficient in campus meetings and in out-of-town business meetings; moreover, he "could not begin to keep abreast of the memoranda, reports, and other papers which must be read every day if he was going to keep up with what was going on."[41] Maxey may be right about Penrose's reading, but the president's correspondence did not lag. The reports to the governing boards partly demonstrate Penrose's efforts to meet the financial crisis. His personal appeals tell the rest of the story as the president sought the resolution of financial difficulties through his voluminous correspondence.

To educate others in the subject of college finance, in 1931 Penrose reprinted and distributed two thoughtful and timely essays by Julius Rosenwald that had appeared in the *Atlantic Monthly*. In one cover letter, Penrose admitted that D. K. Pearsons' insistence "on the sacredness of endowment funds as perpetual trusts" had shaped his own thinking; Rosenwald's two essays challenged such an interpretation in arguing that those who donated to a college endowment should allow "the use of part of the principal . . . as needs arise."[42] He added that such a system put "confidence in living trustees and prevents control by the dead hand." While few responded to Penrose about Rosenwald's controversial ideas, they had relevance in the Great Depression. Trustee Donald Sherwood later explained that in 1934 and 1935 the college transferred $108,000 from the endowment to pay "various indebtedness."[43]

Penrose's letters, including those regarding faculty salaries, provide a more comprehensive account of difficulties than do his official reports. In a 1931 request for money to his friend, trustee William Cowles, he confided, "I have not known financial conditions to be so bad or the payment of faculty salaries so uncertain. We practically force the faculty to lend money to the college for its running by obliging them to go for months at a time without their salaries." Penrose refused a salary until the teachers had been paid in full and tried to raise enough money "to give the faculty a Christmas present in the shape of a partial payment on their salaries."[44]

Although his 1931 report indicated that the school would not launch a campaign drive, the president was actually corresponding with easterners about this and other help. He remembered that easterners had come to the school's assistance in the depression of the 1890s and hoped they might do so again. He wrote to alumnus Paul Garrett, a journalist in New York City, about finding an easterner who would "conduct a quiet personal campaign among the wealthy."[45] Garrett, who emphasized that the failure of Wall Street made it impossible to launch an eastern financial campaign, urged the president to ignore the East and concentrate on the Far West. Penrose, however, explored other avenues through renewed correspondence with Tamblyn and Brown—the New York City fund raisers who had directed the 1924–1925 campaign. Penrose thought that these New Yorkers did not understand that the Pacific Northwest's sad financial condition made it impossible for overseers or alumni to make substantial gifts. But at the same time he sought their opinion about a campaign to raise $4,000,000 to celebrate the two 1934 anniversaries. He complained to George Tamblyn that the trustees had few ideas about such an extensive drive: "They do not see the need of organization and outside help but apparently expect miracles to happen."[46] Later Penrose elaborated on the problem: "The local trustees would always like to have the president go thousands of miles away and not try and raise money in the Pacific Northwest where the burden would fall naturally upon Walla Walla."[47] Penrose also informed Tamblyn that Whitman's trustees were "faint hearted."[48] He explained that the overseers and trustees waited for eastern assistance: "Some of the overseers innocently imagine that the great wealth of the East can be tapped if only one knew how to do so. . . . One of the trustees hopefully remarked that there must be some foundation in New York City where such relief could be attained, but that seemed to me a pipe dream."[49]

In seeking specific information from these noted fund raisers about launching a more modest two-year campaign for $200,000, the president stated: "My heart is heavy . . . when the faculty are delayed in receiving their salaries and the college cannot promptly pay its bills."[50] Despite Penrose's fears, Tamblyn boasted that his firm was successfully raising money for colleges, assured him that they could do the same for Whitman, and proposed tactics.[51] Overseers, trustees, and the faculty's department chairmen were then polled about the wisdom of launching a campaign recommended by Tamblyn. The overseers narrowly opposed it, the trustees overwhelmingly voted no, and the financially distressed faculty chairmen, including Maxey, favored it. Professors added an interesting proviso. They insisted that the "personality and reputation of President Penrose are so necessary to any appeal for funds . . . that we fear that ill success would attend any campaign to which his time and energies could not be fully devoted."[52] Thus, the already overworked faculty was willing to assume their leader's duties so that he might participate in a new campaign the way he had in 1924–1925.

Although the president did not head a new campaign, he placed more paper irons into the financial furnace. In his last two years he wrote even more letters—to John D. Rockefeller for debt relief, to relatives for operating or endowment funds, and to others for a $50,000 maintenance budget. Some letters played on history. For example, he reminded one potential donor that Cushing Eells had made financial sacrifices for Whitman and that the donor might do the same. He sought to convince some businessmen that farm mortgages held by the college were safer than other types of investments would be (though privately he had his doubts); he informed various correspondents in 1932 that this was the worst year he had ever experienced as president; and he confided to many friends that, unless there were positive responses, the college would lose its hard-won prestige, gained through years of diligent devotion.

Penrose enjoyed good connections with the Carnegie Corporation's leadership, especially with its former president, Henry Pritchett, and with the current head of the Carnegie Foundation for the Advancement of Teaching, Henry Suzzallo (who was also a member of the corporation's executive committee). Penrose made a greater effort to seek help from this organization than from any other, attempting to obtain assistance for a library and emergency funds from the corporation's new president, F. P. Keppel. For years, the educator had endeavored to get a library building from the Carnegie Corporation. In 1926 he had written, "The Library is the very heart of a college. . . . I would like before the darkness shuts in entirely upon me . . . to see a library building on the campus."[53] The corporation, however, responded that in 1917 it had practically ceased funding college libraries. Unable to get the new building he wanted, Penrose then tried to get the corporation to pay for remodeling Reynolds Hall as a library, explaining that he had not earlier asked them for it because he expected Mrs. Caroline Gray Kamm to fund it. The inadequate library shack was neither weather-tight nor fire-proof, and by the early 1930s the president wanted to replace it with Reynolds remodeled as a library, at a cost of about $45,000. He emphasized to the Carnegie Corporation that Whitman would hire a large number of unemployed men to remodel the old dormitory; by supporting this effort, the organization would help to relieve the depression in "this wheat growing region."[54] Penrose stressed that Whitman's professors required directed reading, but, in order to carry out "this unusual method of directed education," they needed better facilities.[55] The leader preferred a new building but realized that he must be content with remodeling an existing building.

Penrose mobilized support for the request. His son Binks Penrose made Whitman's case to the corporation, while trustees and others wrote or telegrammed their support. Henry Suzzallo, a former president of the University of Washington and a friend of Stephen Penrose, understood the validity of Whitman's request and personally argued it before the executive board. He failed, but the Carnegie Corporation awarded the college $15,000 for library books, a gift that made the administration scramble to find space.[56]

While Penrose awaited the answer from the Carnegie board, he suffered injuries in an automobile accident, which, he reported to friends, was "due to a blow-out from a tire which had been described by the garage man as . . . good for two years."[57] Soon after, Penrose suffered another blow: the Democrats won the national and state elections. He wrote a friend that he did not know what the Democrats might do, and complained, "I do not feel like making any plans for 1934 or 1936 in view of the uncertainty."[58]

But these difficulties failed to discourage him. In 1933 and 1934 he pushed on two fronts: he tried to get the Public Works Administration (PWA), a New Deal federal agency, to fund a library, and he asked the Carnegie Corporation for an emergency grant. Desperately hoping to have a library by the time of his retirement, Penrose joined hundreds of others who plunged into the PWA bureaucratic pool. The president wrote frequently to politicians and administrators in both Olympia and Washington, D.C., including Secretary of the Interior Harold Ickes. Among his main arguments was that the construction of a library would provide jobs for unemployed local workmen and a facility for townspeople as well as students. Denied, he blamed bureaucrats for his inability to get federal funds.

Meanwhile, Penrose stressed to the Carnegie Corporation that an emergency grant would assist "an honest institution striving to do first class work."[59] Desperate for a grant to tide the school through the difficult fall of 1933—a period that both Maxey and Penrose considered to be the financial nadir of Whitman College in the twentieth century—Penrose pleaded with the corporation: did its leaders know of any other excellent college "which is in the emergency caused by the retirement of a president who has held office for forty years, during the last ten of which he has been totally blind?"[60] Whitman trustees asked the corporation for money to pay Penrose's successor, who must travel away from the campus to seek new donors. They explained: "The blindness of President Penrose during the last ten years has prevented him from devoting himself to the indispensable work of financial upbuilding."[61] The corporation denied the request.[62] Fearing that Whitman was "ripe for bankruptcy," Maxey agreed that trustees or some other group must take action and judged that the 1933–1934 school year was the most critical in the college's history.[63]

In effect, the trustees now acknowledged that for ten years an incapacitated leader had not been engaged in the critical work of fund raising out of Walla Walla. If Hez Brown, whom Penrose favored as his successor, had been appointed in the late 1920s, he would have had time to acquire the experience and reputation needed to wage a more active struggle than that of the handicapped leader. Although in 1931 Penrose and a few others journeyed to Carleton College, where they listened to its president explain successful fund-raising techniques, perhaps the major difficulty was his inability to travel in search of regional assistance, a problem neither he nor the trustees officially acknowledged until 1933. As the crisis worsened, the trustees had failed to appoint another president or assume fund-raising duties themselves. The Carnegie Corporation, the faculty, and the alumni concluded that the trustees had allowed the college's financial condition to deteriorate.

While Penrose sought funds from various sources, he sometimes expressed relief over the fact that the college's money was in "gilt-edged" farm mortgages, but he more often emphasized that the school's investments were not lost, but instead frozen. The overseers, who lived in urban centers and possessed financial expertise, "expressed surprise and deep gratification" that the school's "financial foundations were sound and secure."[64] Some board members still believed, however, that Whitman would have increased its endowment earnings in the 1920s if it had diversified its investments.

In the middle of his financial woes, Penrose grasped at an opportunity to improve the college and raise morale by obtaining as much as $100,000 for a chair in geology. The death of a rich relative, first cousin Dr. Richard Penrose, provided a great opportunity to improve conditions. According to President Penrose, his cousin had discussed funding a chair but died prior to taking action. His cousin willed over $4,000,000 to the American Philosophical Society and the Geological Society of America; in 1932 Penrose prompted his relatives and others to write these institutions that they should fund a chair at Whitman. These correspondents agreed that a Penrose chair was a fitting memorial, some of them asserting that the college was well-located for geological research because the faculty and students would have abundant opportunity to conduct meaningful research at Grand Coulee, the Wallowa Uplift, and the John Day fossil beds. Once again, despite a flurry of supportive letters, the institutions denied Penrose's request.

While the leader failed to raise the money the college needed, he succeeded in reversing the slide in admissions. Early in the Great Depression fewer students sought entrance, in part because Whitman had the highest tuition in the Pacific Northwest. To counter this dangerous situation, Penrose wrote many letters to high school seniors, and he sent carefully coached faculty members and seniors as recruiters into high schools. He urged alumni to serve as recruiters and pushed the trustees to award as much scholarship money as possible to incoming freshmen. Professor Maxey reported on his recruiting experience: he encountered professors from different colleges simultaneously visiting a high school, where they "were all singing the same song and selling the same piece of goods almost."[65] For the first time in its history Whitman sought high school students graduating at mid-semester and put more effort into recruiting in the urban high schools. It was the college's experience that students from Portland, Seattle, Tacoma, and Spokane were better trained than those from rural schools and took less of the faculty's time. Penrose planned, "to lick [them] into shape"; furthermore, the graduates of the bigger high schools did more to enhance Whitman's reputation. Penrose's vigorous recruitment effort was a major reason why the admissions picture began to brighten by the mid-1930s.[66]

In the gloomy year of 1933 treasurer Dorsey Hill and trustee Allen Reynolds presented a paper on the school's finances, stating that the college's bookkeeping was the same as that employed by Stanford University and that Whitman was "in straitened circumstances . . . because the interest of many of its farm mortgages has not been paid owing to the financial depression and the prevailing low price of wheat." This grain cost fifty cents a bushel to produce and sold for about thirty cents. The committee maintained that the school had no funded indebtedness, supporting this controversial generalization with the statement: "It rents two dormitories from the Whitman Building Corporation on a rental basis sufficient to amortize the bonds." Whitman had made these rental payments, covering principal and interest, until early 1933, when it paid only the interest and deferred payment on the principal, "on account of prevailing economic conditions." The signers acknowledged an accumulated floating indebtedness of about $221,000, "which represents unpaid salaries to faculty and money borrowed for yearly deficits."[67] The document noted the receipt of bequests and informed readers that a campaign would be launched to end the indebtedness.

Faculty members probably criticized this report. German professor Fredric Santler, for example, pointed out that neither bursar Marquis nor treasurer Hill was a professional: in fact, the school lacked an accountant and a bookkeeper. Santler and Maxey charged that both of these individuals borrowed money from the college and used their farms as security. While the professors went unpaid, these administrators borrowed college money that should have gone to the faculty.[68]

In 1933 Penrose informed his friend and former Whitman fund raiser Mildred Winship: "We are poor but proud. The college is going on because of the devotion of the faculty. They endure the hardship of not getting their salary and live in hope that the time may come when they will receive what is due them from the past and an increased compensation for the future."[69] The president took enormous pride in the faculty's willingness to support the institution. But he questioned his own record: "I do not think that my administration has been particularly successful."[70]

The trustees, who had the ultimate authority in financial decisions, listened to the president and the overseers and made some significant financial decisions, most of which won Penrose's endorsement. Some actions pertained to students: to keep men in Lyman House the trustees granted them tuition remissions, and they, as well as women in Prentiss Hall, agreed not to leave the dormitories for alternative housing without permission. To offset this unpopular rule, the trustees cut room and board costs. To provide money for poor students, the school employed them as janitors and faculty assistants. In other significant actions, the board borrowed funds from the Miles C. Moore Professorship of Political Science to cover current expenses, froze and then reduced faculty salaries, terminated some professors' contracts, slashed the library and departmental budgets, defaulted on the principal of the building bonds, borrowed money when possible, and ended Worthington's employment.

At their last meeting under Penrose's leadership, the overseers investigated the school's finances. They complained about a shortage of records and time to digest them, but they found no major faults. Board members still urged that in the future the college's investments might be diversified, but they honestly admitted: "These are particularly difficult times in which to judge just what to do or which way to turn. All directions show obstacles, confusion, and doubt."[71] Surely Penrose nodded agreement as he left office; it would now be his successor's responsibility to grapple with the problems of the Great Depression.

Early in his retirement, Penrose published his college history, which practically ignored the terrible economic problems that beset his administration in the 1930s. He chose to dwell on the positive and happy side of his long presidency. Although the energetic leader ignored this unpleasant story, he saved his papers so that a future historian could tell it and interpret its complexities.

Thinking Beyond Money: Penrose's Diverse Interests

Although the Great Depression occupied most of Penrose's time during the last years of his presidency, he still pushed other interests, especially some ambitious proposals for 1936, the hundredth anniversary of the arrival of Marcus and Narcissa Whitman in the Walla Walla Valley. As early as 1929 he voiced two objectives: the federal government should provide a museum stressing the importance of pioneer women, and the state should construct a park at Waiilatpu, where the Whitman Mission had been. In seeking support he stressed that Narcissa Whitman and Eliza Spalding were the first American homemakers in the Pacific Northwest, an important event because, Penrose insisted, "Civilization cannot be said properly to begin until woman appears and a home is made."

Penrose realized that Governor Roland Hartley was "strongly antagonistic" to state parks, so this proposal had to be delayed.[72] While waiting for a sympathetic state leader, Penrose prepared an elaborate plan for Waiilatpu: a mission station constructed of concrete, the appointment of a curator to guard the property and "sell postcards and refreshments to the thousands of pilgrims who would throng to visit the historical spot," and the filling of the old Walla Walla River bed with water.[73]

The president put even more effort into his other proposal, a museum on the college campus. He endeavored to get the federal government to give $250,000 to Walla Walla, which, in turn, would construct the building on the college campus. To get the appropriation, Penrose wrote to a congressman, but he also tried to enlist the assistance of the National Council of Women in New York City. He asked its president to support a federally funded museum and a second project, a privately funded bronze statue of Marcus and Narcissa Whitman and their daughter Alice, also to be erected on campus. Penrose, who declared that both of these proposals were "now dearest to my heart," also stated that: "What woman asks for and insists on having man eventually grants."[74] The leader also asked the Seattle Women's Club to assist in financing the statue. While Penrose proposed that these two women's groups and others, including the Daughters of the American Revolution, would pay part of the costs, he tried to get Dr. William Mayo to take charge of a committee raising money from physicians for a statue of Dr. Marcus Whitman, the pioneer physician. In this appeal, Penrose, who had met the Mayo Clinic's famous leader in Walla Walla, wrote: "Whatever opinion one may have concerning the service of Dr. Whitman to his country and to science, there can be no question that the home which he and Mrs. Whitman established here was the real beginning of American civilization west of the Rocky Mountains." While each appeal won sympathy, none attracted a financial commitment.

Telling his friends that he still hoped that his dreams could be realized, the president blazed ahead, advancing his proposals in Portland and Seattle and exhibiting a sketch of the group statue. Many citizens supported his plans to honor the Whitmans, but he found it impossible to raise money for historical monuments during the Great Depression. Much of what Penrose advocated would be accomplished long after the 1936 celebration. The federal government now operates the Whitman Mission National Historic Site, historical markers there and elsewhere honor the missionary family, and Marcus Whitman's statue stands near the campus. But a major regional pioneer women's museum—perhaps Penrose's most interesting idea—has not yet been realized. The president also unsuccessfully sought support for another production of his pageant, *How the West Was Won.* Some fondly recalled the excitement it had aroused in the mid-1920s, but they also remembered that it had lost money. Nobody offered to underwrite the play.

In 1932, however, the president had more success promoting the college during the George Washington Bicentennial. Penrose took the lead in arranging a local celebration; the college played a major role, especially in the performance of a suitable pageant directed by Edith Merrell Davis, head of the dramatics department. Penrose missed the ceremonies because he was in Seattle at the invitation of the state bicentennial commission, speaking at two important occasions; both speeches were broadcast to a Northwest audience. He spoke at the opening of the George Washington Memorial Bridge on Lake Union, an address that was cut short when, he explained, Governor Hartley "injected himself into the program and claimed an unexpected ten minutes."[75] But the leader thought that his abbreviated talk had publicized the college. His featured address in Seattle's Civic Auditorium was more satisfying, as he spoke for fifty minutes to fifteen hundred people on "Washington and the Fundamentals of Our Government as Originally Founded." Penrose, who had carefully prepared for "the big occasion," tried to make it "the best speech in my life."[76] The speaker admired Washington for his "real ability and character, which some people like to disparage." Many applauded the message; one radio listener declared that it was the best address he had ever heard.[77]

Penrose continued to be active in the region. In 1931 he gave a major address in Spokane as part of that city's fiftieth anniversary celebration. He recognized the current problems of unemployment and crime, which, he maintained, were "an indication of our failure to rationalize our economic efforts." He stressed that the United States was "the most lawless of any civilized nation because we have left out the ethical element from our system of education. . . . You expect boys and girls to grow up into reliable and law abiding citizens when they have never been taught the fundamentals of law and order. . . . [and] the home has shown that it cannot be depended on for this function." The speaker insisted that "the breakup of the American home through divorce and irresponsibility of innumerable parents meant a decline in ethical life."[78]

The educator continued to study and speak on various issues. He maintained his interest in East Asia. He continued to support collegiate education in China and tried to comprehend the war between China and Japan. To this end he invited Kiyoshi Uchiyama, the consul for Japan residing in Seattle, to address Whitman students. Penrose consistently opposed the United States joining the League of Nations, because Americans were "so self-satisfied, if not arrogant, that the tranquility of the League might have been shattered and the nations of Europe driven to violent opposition to the United States." He worried about education, objected to emphasizing vocational education over the liberal arts, complained that teachers were too dependent upon textbooks (as though the books "were the voice of God"), and lamented the fact that parents and newspapers favored colleges that emphasized fraternity life and athletics.[79] Dedicated to the advancement of the Congregational Church, Penrose continued to promote its interests at the local and regional level. He still considered the movies to be an unresolved problem: "Lovers of amusement are not apt to think of their amusement's effect on youth and as a result the unregulated moving picture has become a serious influence for evil on young people."[80] The president confessed that the way the country had "treated the Indians" made him "hang my head in shame."[81]

As Penrose watched national politics in 1931, he thought that President Herbert Hoover "towers above the level of petty politics and personal animosities, retaining always his clearness of vision and steadfastness of character."[82] He grudgingly acknowledged, however, the economic improvements resulting from the early New Deal. He granted that the Democrats were responsible for improving Walla Walla's economy early in 1933, but he did not understand New Deal economics. "It runs counter to everything I have believed in all my life, yet the results of the last four years have been such as to shake my belief and to bring me almost to the desperate point of trying anything once. It looks as if we could dispense with Congress, for Roosevelt is willing to take all power and all responsibility for their successful enterprise. . . . Perhaps I am too much of an ingrained Republican to feel complete confidence in so plausible and attractive a Democrat as Franklin Delano Roosevelt."[83]

In the summer he again acknowledged signs of economic improvement and hoped it would continue "even though all my past economic creed is trampled upon."[84] In August 1933 he congratulated Senator Clarence Dill, a Democrat from Spokane, for getting the Coulee Dam project supported.

While he praised some actions by Democrats, Penrose had difficulty with those who proposed ending prohibition in 1933. He wrote a friend: "A life long Republican like me [and] believer in the Eighteenth Amendment . . . has a dazed sort of feeling in not knowing on what side of his head he will be struck next."[85] Penrose ridiculed the federal government's permitting the brewing of beer, and participated in the struggle to maintain the Eighteenth Amendment. He asked a friend: "Do you not think that it would be a good idea for us to serve beer instead of milk at Lyman House and Prentiss Hall?"[86] But he battled against hard liquor. The moral leader directed the city's publicity campaign against repeal and was a "dry" candidate seeking election as a delegate to a state convention considering repeal of the amendment. Penrose argued that "the sale of liquor . . . is a traffic in narcotics accompanied by enormous profits and followed by pernicious consequences."[87] Although he failed to be elected, Penrose continued to support his dry views; for example, he distributed pamphlets to the students and offered a $10 prize for the best essay on prohibition. But his efforts failed. In August 1933 more than 698,000 Washingtonians voted for delegates to a convention considering repeal; the crucial presidential election of 1932 had attracted only 614,000 voters. The convention's delegates voted ninety-four to four for repeal.[88] Penrose accepted defeat; concluding that prohibition was still desirable but impossible, he advocated placing the liquor business under state control.[89]

Throughout the Great Depression, the president would not allow the college's agonizing economic situation to narrow his breadth of vision. In his last years in office, as in his first years, he took a lively interest in the conditions of his adopted state and its institutions. He still maintained that minds honed by the liberal arts should be utilized in the resolution of social problems and in the advancement of culture.

3

Two Brief Presidencies:
Rudolf A. Clemen and Walter A. Bratton
1934–1942

Following Stephen Penrose's remarkable presidency, the college's greatest challenge was to find effective leadership. It would be difficult to replace the man whom many hailed as an institution. Any successor would be measured by this legendary figure. While being compared with a beloved president, the new man would also have to grapple with debt, initiate changes, and win the confidence of others — especially that of the entrenched trustees. These factors would overwhelm Dr. Rudolf A. Clemen, and, combined with his personal shortcomings, would cause his administration to last just two years and to be filled with controversy.

From the time Penrose announced his resignation in 1933 until he departed the following year, he spent considerable energy seeking a successor. The president, not the trustees, led the initial search. His first choice was Hez Brown. Born in 1881 in Dayton, Washington, Brown was, Penrose judged, Whitman's most well-rounded student: a brilliant scholar, an excellent athlete, and the only undefeated debater. He had graduated from Yale Divinity School and was a Congregational minister, building a solid reputation in Evanston, Illinois. In 1924 Whitman had awarded him an honorary doctorate, because his impressive career had brought honor to his alma mater.

Penrose explained to confidants how he came to choose Brown. He rejected the idea of elevating a faculty member, because the selection would prompt some others to resign. He opposed hiring an outsider, especially if that individual were "a professional educator with definite opinions on the solution of all educational problems."[1] The president wanted someone who loved the school, so he scrutinized the alumni list for an individual who "can address the public effectively and develop outside relations rather than direct the minutiae of internal educational development." What the college needed, the experienced leader argued, was "a large visioned, vigorous, red-blooded human . . . who can inspire confidence and give new heart to what has become of late under my blind administration a somewhat discouraged clientele." Mary Penrose and trusted alumni agreed with his selection of Brown. With this support Penrose informed the minister that "you are the only alumnus fitted for the job who can lift the college to a higher level." In asking Brown to be president, Penrose—who had not polled the boards or the faculty —enthusiastically described the position: "It gives you freedom to live your largest and best life and to render the finest sort of service to the surrounding civilization. . . . The presidency provides a platform from which a man can speak to the entire country."[2]

Amazed by his old mentor's invitation, Brown requested information about Whitman's financial condition. He joked: "How far ahead of the Sheriff are the President and Treasurer?"[3] Brown wanted $6,000 a year salary and a house, since he currently received $7,500 plus ministerial fees. He described his current economic commitments, including the college education of two sons.

Delighted with Brown's response, Penrose provided him with details about the school's finances. The aging leader assured Brown that his alma mater was not in any "danger of going under" although it was "mighty hard up."[4] He added that it enjoyed good relations with eastern foundations, calculated that Walla Walla's living costs were much less than Chicago's, and boasted that many considered Whitman to be a premier West Coast college.

Willing to take a significant cut in salary, Brown scrutinized the financial records sent to him, calculated the depth of the college's financial crisis, and agreed to serve if his personal financial needs were met. Brown emphasized to Penrose that he was a novice: "My knowledge of college internals is as deep as a Walla Walla dust storm."[5] To help him with his unfamiliar tasks, he wanted to hire a dean. Penrose reassured Brown, reminding him that he, too, had come to office inexperienced.

In the fall of 1933, convinced that his choice was willing to succeed him, the president won support from trustees and overseers and
prepared an official announcement. But there was a delay owing to
the fact that Penrose could not raise $15,000 to pay the salaries of
both a president and a dean for three years. He desperately tried to
fund Brown's presidency, but received negative replies from eastern
foundations, wealthy individuals, and the Congregational Education
Society.

In his rejection, Henry Pritchett of the Carnegie Foundation informed Penrose that the trustees, "who are influential and men of
property, and who know the sources from which Whitman College
has drawn support, ought themselves to take over the load of finding support for the next ten years."[6] He advised him that, in emer-
gencies, the trustees should shoulder responsibilities. Penrose quickly
responded: "Your suggestion that in this emergency they ought to
assume the responsibility for tiding the college over its time of need
seems to be sane and irrefutable."[7]

Using Pritchett's letter, Penrose reminded the trustees that they
had fiscal responsibilities, urged them to provide the $15,000, and
gave them three choices—guarantee Brown's salary, find a candidate
who would not need financial guarantees, or appoint a temporary
president. But he clearly favored the first alternative, for it "would
be far the best thing for the college."[8]

In January 1934 Penrose thought that the trustees—after frustrating delay—were deciding to meet Brown's financial requirements,
but to the president's chagrin, Brown withdrew his name. The distinguished alumnus explained, "I am increasingly dubious about my
possible value to the college and increasingly dubious about the wisdom of leaving the pastorate . . . and increasingly certain that Whitman cannot afford me on my terms." Brown understood the feelings
of an unpaid faculty about the appointment of a new president with
a $6,000 salary.[9] The writer suggested that either Penrose's son Binks
or Rudolf Clemen should be considered for the office. Thus, it was
Brown who brought Clemen to the college's attention.

The failure to appoint Penrose's choice had grave ramifications.
Brown had many attributes necessary for success, including energy,
temperament, personality, and connections in the church and in higher education. The minister was appealing to college students, had

lectured impressively at many campuses, and had won acclaim from his wealthy Evanston parishioners. His reputation in the Midwest equaled that of Penrose in the Pacific Northwest. Furthermore, he had regional roots, and expressed love and gratitude for Penrose and his alma mater. The failure of the trustees to raise the $15,000 caused the institution to lose momentum and created internal dissension. The trustees had done little to resolve the financial crises of 1928 through 1933, and they failed to find the money to meet Brown's modest financial requirements. Thus, they rejected a capable and well-known candidate and turned to another individual whom they did not know well, at about the same salary that Brown had requested. Rarely had their inaction had such a negative impact upon the institution. It resulted in the realization of Penrose's fear that the appointment of a man who did not know Whitman's history "would be hazardous in the extreme."[10]

The Selection of Rudolf Clemen

In less than two months after Brown's refusal, Whitman appointed a new president from an unknown number of candidates. Dean Bruce Baxter of the University of Southern California was one, but Penrose vigorously opposed his selection. He charged that the Fisk Teachers Agency pushed Baxter because it wanted a commission from his salary, and he provided an even more telling objection: "I cannot see the slightest reason why he, a Methodist minister . . . without any experience in raising money should be considered seriously as the president of Whitman."[11] While Whitman did not investigate Baxter, Willamette University did. He became its president in 1934 and would become one of its great builders.

After Whitman trustees studied Rudolf Clemen's background and recommendations, they quickly brought him to campus. The forty-one-year-old native of Nova Scotia held a Ph.D. from Harvard in economics and history and had taught those subjects at Northwestern University and the University of Chicago. He had published respected books on agricultural economics, served as an economic adviser for Armour and Company, and then left academics and business for the ministry. The president of the Chicago Theological Seminary, who appreciated Clemen's diverse background, praised him for having "deliberately turned his back on the business world" and for taking the pulpit in a small church.[12]

Clemen came to Whitman in mid-February 1934, lived a week with the Penroses, and won their hearty support because of his social tact, business skills, and intellectual attainments. Faculty members, trustees, and others also endorsed him. Penrose thought he would "bring vigor, business experience, and practical good sense to college affairs,"[13] and that he would cooperate with trustees. The president wrote close friends that Clemen "was a man of independent means and a scholar of recognized standing in the joint worlds of education and business. He will take hold of the college with vigor and ability."[14] Chester Maxey thought the candidate displayed energy, adding that, although "I would venture no prophecy as to what he will do, I feel certain that we are in for some sweeping changes. I hope we may measure up to the opportunities before us. That, of course, is on the knees of the gods."[15]

During his busy campus visit, Clemen indicated that he had rejected other college presidencies and that he must consult with his wife prior to accepting an offer.[16] Penrose rushed a solicitous letter to a Whitman alumna: "Whether he will accept . . . will depend largely upon his wife. . . . Would you be willing to call upon her and tell her something about the college and Walla Walla, the healthfulness of the climate and other matters?"[17]

After leaving the campus, Clemen visited and impressed board members from Salem to Seattle. Thus, on February 28, 1934, the trustees unanimously voted to call him as president at a salary of $5,000 a year—subject to a twenty-percent reduction like the faculty—with the use of the President's House. Prior to acceptance, Clemen asked about a contract. Penrose replied that neither he nor the professors signed one: "The faculty have felt secure in their tenure, knowing that as long as they did their work loyally and effectively nobody would disturb them." Because Whitman's president was also a member of the board of trustees in that era, Penrose had not felt that he needed a contract; rather, he held the view that the president was "not an official employed by [the trustees] but rather one of them, and as long as he and they work together in sympathy and common understanding I do not see that anything could be gained by a formal contract."[18]

Because the Clemen administration ended in controversy, Whit-manites argued for years over who was to blame for his appointment. Maxey insisted that the trustees "were inclined to let [Penrose] pick his own successor" and that the departing president "did not care too much about the particular man, provided he were a Congregational minister and also had some stature as a scholar."[19] But Penrose's correspondence presents another point of view: that it was necessary to consider hiring a minister, who would have "a spirit of devotion and self-sacrifice which are not readily found in other professions." He feared, however, the appointment of a "sanctimonious minister" and would not recommend "either a minister or an alumnus for my successor unless I thought that he were genuinely fitted for the place."[20]

Penrose also maintained that he did not appoint the new president. "I have turned over completely to the trustees the responsibility for finding my successor. Nevertheless, I am, of course, greatly interested in the matter."[21] The evidence indicates that, while Penrose indeed did support Clemen, the overseers and trustees did not defer to him as they had in the Brown appointment. They expressed the same enthusiasm for Clemen as did Penrose. Furthermore, Penrose's list of presidential requirements was longer than Maxey reported: he wanted a man who had energy, personality, and business experience.

From the time he accepted the appointment in early March until his inauguration as president at the June commencement, Clemen plunged into his work. In several letters to Penrose, he indicated the shape of his forthcoming administration. He sought to prepare for the position by reading books on education, by consulting with college presidents and faculty members from Carleton to Princeton, and by meeting with foundation heads and Whitman alumni. The new leader tried to raise money from the Billings family for the rehabilitation of Billings Hall, from the Johns-Mansville Corporation for a science building, and even from Mary and Stephen Penrose's own families. He hoped that Spencer Penrose, whom the president had once identified as the richest Coloradan, worth $20,000,000, would fund a Whitman library. Clemen, however, came to the sad conclusion that Spencer and other relatives would not aid Whitman and that, "The East will not do anything for a western college. The constituency was not kept warmed up and nothing can be done now. . . . The Pacific Northwest must do its part."[22]

While becoming informed about eastern collegiate education and attempting to raise money, Clemen was asking his predecessor for information about the faculty, the governing boards, and the budget. This correspondence revealed his agenda, starting with the rehabilitation of the campus buildings and grounds. "I am," Clemen insisted, "a stickler on such matters," but the critic did not blame the blind president for the physical plant's unattractive condition.[23] Disturbed by the appearance of Billings and Reynolds halls, he wanted to know the cost of repairing them and converting Reynolds into a library. Indifferent to the college's history, he suggested re-naming the two buildings for those who paid the reconstruction costs.

Clemen wanted to construct a bridge to the faculty, for they had complained to him of their financial plight and their reduced departmental budgets. Thus, he proposed asking them to write "dream letters" about what they would like.[24] Penrose warned his successor that he too had tried this approach and received little faculty cooperation. Fearful of antagonizing professors, the new president discarded his idea but speculated about ways to pay and to improve the faculty.

More important than his initial thoughts about the faculty were his plans to reform the governing boards. Penrose must have told Clemen during the latter's first visit to Walla Walla that he and the Carnegie Foundation's Pritchett had concluded that the trustees must assume more responsibility. Clemen privately informed Penrose: "I intend to make the trustees and overseers work or contribute to the college or get off the respective boards. They will do it if diplomatically handled, and I intend to be tactful."[25] Penrose sympathized with his approach and confided: "It is easy to fall in the habit of saying, 'let George do it.' It will be a good thing . . . if pressure is brought to bear on those connected with [the college] to share a fair part of the burden, in proportionate ability. You have my joyous consent to bring pressure on them all to carry their share of the load."[26]

Because of the financial crisis, the new leader wanted to increase the size of the student body. Penrose, who still considered this to be a sensitive issue, responded that the school should add more paying students and more students from Walla Walla, but, he cautioned, "It needs always to be remembered that the downtown businessmen want a big institution regardless of quality and would like to have everybody taken in that can be induced to come." The old leader feared that such a policy would make the college a local institution rather than a regional one. He wanted Whitman to "win respect and prestige" by maintaining high standards and by not "allowing itself to be democratized."[27] Clemen responded that he also wanted to maintain high standards, adding that he wanted Whitman "to be a desirable place to go to like Amherst or Williams or Carleton. I want it to stand out in the Pacific Northwest as much as possible, building on the fine foundations that you and your older colleagues have laid."[28]

Clemen warned the trustees that he would not make the types of personal financial sacrifices that had been made by the Penroses. "I am going to put all the ability and energy into this work, but I am expecting to be paid for that effort, and I am not going to make any contributions other than that. I do not wish the fact that my wife has a little money . . . to be taken advantage of, as it was in the case of the church work I have done."[29]

During this transitional period, Penrose not only supplied Clemen with information, he also asked him to seek funding from the American Medical Association for a "heroic bronze statue" of Marcus, Narcissa, and Alice Whitman, which he hoped would be unveiled in 1936.[30] The outgoing president also hoped that his replacement might find money for a college library, for he wanted to announce its plans as his last presidential act.

Penrose often praised Clemen. "I cannot tell you," he once wrote, "what a load has rolled off my shoulders with your election as my successor and with what thankfulness I have discovered increasingly your sagacity, foresight, and balance."[31] Clearly, Penrose anticipated a successful Clemen presidency. Others agreed.

The Celebration of Stephen Penrose's Retirement

For several years Penrose had anticipated his retirement at the 1934 commencement. Thus, in his last school year, 1933–1934, he considered his own career after retirement, hoping that the trustees would ask him to teach philosophy. He told friends that his "greatest satisfaction is teaching. I know that if I should give that up and be left with nothing to do I would become miserable and useless."

If he did not continue as a professor, he thought about a move to Seattle to be near his children. But he confessed that Seattle had few attractions and that he "would be like a cat in a strange garret."[32] In February 1934 the trustees asked him to be a professor emeritus and to live in Green Cottage. Enthusiastic about this offer, Penrose informed a friend, "I want to make the department of philosophy famous," and he told another individual, "I think that philosophy is needed to supply sanity in present day confusion of thought, and I have, therefore, a mission to serve."[33] A friend, warning him against looking over the shoulder of his successor, observed that the new president would be in about the "same position as the second wife whose husband told her how his first wife used to do."[34]

With his teaching position secured, Penrose sought to improve his personal finances. He asked an old friend, trustee Park Weed Willis, to request a pension for him from the Carnegie Foundation. He told Willis to base his case upon the facts that Penrose had served forty years and that he was blind and lived in poverty. The president stated that his salary had been $5,000, but it had been reduced by twenty percent; furthermore, for two years he had given the college $1,000. The foundation refused the plea and recommended that Whitman give him a pension, an idea which he rejected.[35]

While Penrose prepared for a change in responsibilities, he was probably unaware—at least initially—that in the spring of 1933 some faculty members, including the deans (Chester Maxey, Frank Haigh, and Walter Bratton), were urging the trustees to force his retirement.[36] Meanwhile, Penrose was explaining to everyone that he was departing because of blindness and that "in these troubled days when a college president needs to be active for the financial strengthening of his institution a blind man is at so serious a disadvantage that he ought to give the place to a man possessed of all his faculties."[37] Apparently, Penrose had denied the effects that his limitations had upon the college until it was nearly too late.

At the same time that Maxey exerted pressure to remove Penrose, he also chaired the committee that planned the president's retirement celebration. The four-day event, which attracted scores of alumni and townspeople, also honored Mary Penrose. About four hundred women attended an American Association of University Women luncheon in her honor and heard speakers praise her leadership in the Congregational Church and the YWCA, her role as "College Mother," and her assistance to faculty wives.[38] Mary Penrose had served in nearly every city club dedicated to schools, playgrounds, art, and the preservation of local history.

A pageant, written by alumna Annie Rue Robinson and with a cast of Whitman students and alumni, related Whitman's history, with scenes of Cushing Eells' pledge to found a school and Penrose's first meeting with benefactor D. K. Pearsons. Some of the casting proved interesting: Nig Borleske was Marcus Whitman, Maysie Penrose was Myra Eells, Virginia Penrose was Mary Penrose, Clem Penrose was Stephen Penrose, and future Oregon congressman Al Ullman was a member of the "Yale band" of Congregational missionaries that had come to eastern Washington in the 1890s.

One evening another crowd, including regional educators, packed the Keylor Grand Theater for exercises honoring Penrose. Among those on the program was Professor Bratton, speaking for the faculty. The mathematician stated that Penrose was an able leader "due to his ability to ask for opinions, his recognition of the worth-whileness of the work, and the values he places on opposition." Speakers stressed his character traits, including faith, energy, sympathy, vision, and intelligence. Some applauded Penrose for advancing culture in the Pacific Northwest. Greetings were read from several college presidents, including Norman Coleman of Reed College, who had once taught at Whitman.

Episcopal bishop Edward M. Cross delivered the baccalaureate sermon. He must have won Penrose's approval when he concluded that: "The messes we are making of national and family life are due to our taking responsibility and throwing it on the shoulders of Atlas." When Penrose spoke, he informed the seniors that, by attending college during a great depression, they had endured "a sobering experience" and had been freed from illusions. Later, the crowd proceeded to Prentiss Hall, where alumnus Robert Ringer presented oil portraits of Dr. and "Mother" Penrose, the works of another alumnus, Ernest Norling. Speaking for the alumni, Ringer stated that the group appreciated the couple for their "nobility, culture, sincerity, and devotion."[39] At the commemorative services at the Whitman grave site, Russell Whitman of Chicago praised the missionary and his wife.

On graduation day, an audience watched senior Isabelle Welty's *Dust, Shadow, and Life,* a production featuring music, drama, and dance. In the afternoon sixty seniors received degrees, and eleven individuals, including publisher William Cowles, received honorary degrees. Then the school inaugurated its new president. Clemen recognized that he had been entrusted with a "sacred mission" and acknowledged that "a college president has to serve as a coordinating agency, a harmonizing influence, and an energizing stimulus." He evaluated the art of teaching: "Men and women who have a genius for teaching are few. . . . The best teacher is the leader of an exploring party, not the conductor of a tour. . . . A college president in pursuing his mission of service for youth must look for quality in his faculty and not numbers." The new leader denounced practical "cash value" courses and wanted the college to develop "the habit of learning." He described Whitman as "a lighthouse [that] has for its mission the diffusion of the beneficent light of ideas."[40]

Between the featured events of the celebration, Maxey had scheduled music, athletics, and oratory. Meanwhile, Walla Walla celebrated its diamond jubilee with a pioneer parade, a street carnival, horse racing, and a style show.

The entire celebration was a great success. It was a way to escape the hardships of the Great Depression and to honor a significant era in the college's history. Decades later, Robert Skotheim, by then a former president of Whitman, correctly judged that "it was survival rather than prosperity which was being celebrated."[41] Clemen came to the same conclusion. He referred to the college as "Bleak House," but said that he had "Great Expectations." Rarely has a new president had more warm wishers than Clemen had as he embarked upon his demanding tasks.

Rudolf Clemen's Controversy-Filled Presidency

Stephen Penrose's unusually long presidency was followed by Rudolf Clemen's unusually short one. Clemen submitted his resignation after only sixteen months, withdrew it, and then, under pressure, resubmitted it.

But Clemen began his short term energetically. Perhaps his zeal made Penrose consider that he himself had stayed in office too long.

"I suppose," he pondered, "that it may be because I am getting old or because I have been blind for the last ten years that I have not realized that there are men who can go out and do things which are impossible for me now."[42]

Prior to his arrival in Walla Walla, Clemen sought information from treasurer Dorsey Hill so that he could immediately tackle the school's financial problems. He requested details about faculty salaries, and, at the same time, guessed that some professors were "worth no more than they receive." The president requested figures about the amounts donated by board members. He also told Hill that he desired to "get the jump on the new man at Reed College and that includes going after new students!"[43] The busy new leader assured the faculty that his "conception of a college president's job is to help the members of the faculty to carry on their work effectively."[44] He assured students that the campus was being rehabilitated in order that "you will enjoy your classes so much that we will find it hard to get you out of them at the end of the hour!" He urged students to help recruit other young people because, "We want to make the campus a thrilling place, the more the merrier!"[45]

Clemen immediately pushed curriculum reform. He explained to professors that he would like the school to reach "a point where we would be giving an educational prescription to each individual student and not the same bottle of intellectual medicine to everyone." Thus, he arranged with Professor Eli T. Allen to make his Biblical literature course an elective and with Professor Penrose to do the same with his philosophy class. Penrose's course on college life, in which he traced the history of liberal arts education, was dropped.[46]

Impressed with Clemen's energetic administration, the eagle-eyed Maxey explained to an alumnus: "We are head[ing] for a remarkable rise in the world or a complete collapse. I am gambling on the former."

In July 1934, in the midst of these sweeping changes, the new president reported to the trustees. He revealed that he "faced . . . an acute psychological problem" in that he needed "to inspire confidence in trustees, overseers, alumni, faculty, students, and the public generally."[47] While seeking to restore college morale, Clemen had set about the task of rehabilitating the buildings and grounds, arguing that "the competition is too keen for students these days, and the

Rudolf Clemen was the fourth college president, serving from 1934 to 1936. Clemen arrived with both academic and business experience and effected some sound changes during his time at Whitman, but he soon tangled with the trustees, faculty members, and students.

college which does not have sufficient pride to maintain its plant is going to close its doors." In fact, one evening he and his wife assessed the school's gloomy physical condition and "almost ordered our freight cars turned back to Chicago." He employed workmen to clean, paint, calcimine, and replaster rooms in almost every building and to prepare for the conversion of Reynolds Hall into a library, a significant move. The president thought that this old dormitory would make an adequate library, and advised against asking friends or the government for a $150,000 library building during a depression. Although Clemen's predecessor had been hostile to the New Deal, Penrose had jumped at the chance to obtain a Public Works Administration loan for a library, since he considered Reynolds to be an inadequate building (and, in fact, Penrose had never abandoned appeals for funding a library, whether made to private donors or to the federal government). But Clemen moralized: "My own position is that asking for a government loan is unethical, something that a college for educating young people must never do."[48] Besides, the school lacked the ability to repay any loan.

Clemen made staff appointments, traveled to meetings with overseers and alumni, gave speeches, made arrangements for a financial
survey—resulting in the Russell report of 1934—which some of the
overseers agreed to underwrite, and formulated plans to raise
$25,000 to meet the current operating debt.

By September the president had arranged to increase faculty
salaries by ten percent. Maxey praised him for launching a policy
designed "to cease defaulting faculty salaries and to start making
payments on arrears. The governing boards, in order to avoid defaulting payments of principal and interest on the building bonds,
had elected to default faculty salaries." But Clemen quickly ended
this practice and made a drastic change. He discovered that Whitman was paying annually about $30,000 on the three bond issues.
"This was," he ruled, "a colossal interest amount" and made it impossible to balance the books. "Therefore, on my own authority,"
he boasted, "I declared a moratorium"; the savings covered faculty
salaries for three months.[49] While the long-suffering faculty hailed
his action, Walla Walla bondholders denounced him.

The new president appointed a few local people to the faculty.
They received no pay and offered practical courses: attorney Herbert
Ringhoffer taught business law, editor H. Sherman Mitchell of the
Walla Walla Union-Bulletin taught journalism, and local doctors
John C. Lyman and Alfred E. Lange taught health courses.

Then Clemen made a significant change in administrative structure: he created the office of college dean and appointed Walter Bratton to the post. This new office, with responsibility for educational
and internal administration, was one that Penrose had steadfastly opposed. The president also made faculty additions; the most interesting were the appointment of John Ackley as a speech professor, William Martin as a track coach, and Binks Penrose as an instructor in
philosophy and psychology and an assistant to his father. He enticed
retired scientist Benjamin Brown to return, a move that strengthened
both the curriculum and alumni support. Clemen assured the trustees
that these additional faculty members received low salaries.

While this financial austerity pleased trustees, they must have
been uncomfortable with $19,000 in bills for rehabilitating and re-
furbishing buildings, including the women's restroom in Memorial
Hall, re-done in an early-American style. Clemen explained the need

for this improvement: "We are . . . in many ways, like a manager of a hotel in our public relations."[50] Although they paid the bills, the trustees, Maxey recalled, disliked it when the new president referred to the dilapidated campus as "the Roman ruins."[51] To cover these new expenses and old debts, trustees accepted Clemen's call for "a dignified campaign to obtain funds for the next year."[52]

Early in his administration the newcomer had engaged John Dale Russell of the University of Chicago Graduate School of Education, an expert who had surveyed 150 colleges, to make a similar study of Whitman. The overseers who funded this report wanted a close examination of the school's financial status. Clemen probably wanted Russell to write a broad condemnation of the school's previous practices and an endorsement of his reforms. Undoubtedly he voiced such hopes to Russell, who investigated campus conditions during a week's stay in September 1934 and recommended many changes.

Many of the policies Clemen advocated from 1934 to 1936 came from his own experiences or from the Russell report. This comprehensive study of the college, one of the most thorough in its history, included sixty-six recommendations for change. Naturally, its criticisms of the college practices, as well as its controversial proposals, offended many readers. But Maxey and others in the Whitman community championed much of the report.

The sixty-six recommendations covered various subjects, including the need for new bylaws, a limitation on the number of local board members, more commitment from overseers, a reorganization of the administrative structure, changes in the preparation of budgets, a single hall for coeducational dining, a new investment policy emphasizing bonds and stocks rather than real estate mortgages, removal of enrollment limits, and the encouragement of unrestricted rather than restricted giving.

In responding to Whitman's limits on the enrollment of women, Russell generalized: "There is nothing to fear from 'overfeminization.' The immediate need of the college is for an increased enrollment rather than for a snobbish limitation." The expert also denounced the practice of loading the board of trustees with Walla Wallans. He doubted that a city of sixteen thousand "would yield seven men of satisfactory caliber for service as trustees of a college with a national reputation." Russell warned that, when local residents dominated a board, "the community generally will tend to look upon the situation as something upon which it may feed; something conducted for its local benefit, rather than as an expression of service on a wide basis to society at large." The investigator demonstrated that the overseers had made insignificant cash donations: in 1932 the average amount given by each overseer was $28.30; in 1933 it was a paltry $1.33. Russell criticized trustees for believing that payments to bondholders "were more sacred obligations than the salaries of faculty members. . . . The faculty have thus been forced to become the bankers for the college and to provide it the capital necessary for its operation." The investment policy received his further censure: "The fact that the board [of trustees] has chosen to limit its investments to farm mortgages because 'this is the game they know' is the strongest possible evidence of the need for some new blood on the Board."[53]

Chester Maxey's autobiography, *The World I Lived In*, provides a colorful telling of the college's reaction to the Russell report. He read the report with Clemen, and the political scientist warned the president: "It's loaded with dynamite." But Clemen expressed delight with the report and responded that it was exactly what he wanted because it would help him remove trustee roadblocks. Maxey wrote that the president was secretive about the report, hoping to arouse public interest. The professor also related that leading Walla Wallans believed that Russell had libeled them, but Maxey disagreed: "It paraded the simple facts so clearly and effectively that its pages shouted to the world that Whitman College had been grossly mismanaged" by trustees who "had displayed gross incompetence."[54] Alumnus Donald Sherwood, looking back with the perspective of having been a longtime trustee himself, agreed with this assessment: "They were a bunch of 'do-nothings.' . . . They were names, prominent people, but they didn't raise money for Whitman."[55]

According to Maxey's interpretation, Clemen favored adoption of all the sixty-six recommendations but failed to adopt any, while over later years the college enacted fifty-seven of them. Actually, Clemen's administration soon adopted several recommendations, including a revision of the school's constitution and bylaws. Russell had stressed that the school in effect had two executives because the treasurer, not the president, handled the budget. The revised bylaws made the president responsible for preparing and reporting on the budget.

Endorsing most of Russell's recommendations, Maxey nonetheless accused Clemen of being "reckless" in pushing their adoption.[56] Penrose must have expressed views about the report similar to those of Maxey, for he had voiced some similar criticisms of the boards, but, of course, he had not publically denounced their members. The former president must have appreciated the fact that Russell was much more critical of the boards' performance than of his own. But both the president and the trustees came under criticism. Russell stated that Penrose's administration had allowed the school "to live beyond its income. This policy is chiefly responsible for the present state of the finances of the college. It is surprising that the board . . . would allow such a policy to be maintained year after year."[57]

Although Penrose did not receive a copy of the Russell report until late 1936, overseers and trustees must have conveyed its contents to him. Penrose expressed exception to much of the report, but his letter listing his points of disagreement has not survived.[58] Surely his previously stated views on admissions conflicted with those of Russell. Penrose had expressed to Clemen in April 1934: "I think that in the United States we are too much inclined to listen to the voice of the uneducated or half educated public and to let our standards down to fit the common demand." He admonished the University of Washington for admitting all high school graduates and concluded that Whitman would win prestige by insisting upon higher standards "rather than by allowing itself to be democratized."[59]

President Clemen's November 1934 report, influenced by the Russell report, offended several trustees and some overseers. There were, however, aspects that they endorsed, especially his opposition to the enrollment limit of five hundred and his willingness to register more Walla Wallans. (The board had opposed Penrose's policies on enrollment numbers but had not blocked him.) Clemen's fundraising plans also seemed desirable. But his harsh words for board members contrasted with Penrose's carefully couched sentences. Clemen charged that Whitman did not expect to receive much money this year: "Naturally one does not expect to achieve great results, especially since the overseers have for years contributed practically nothing." He bluntly said to all the board members who would not render financial assistance that they would "find it an easy thing to resign."[60] He informed trustees that it was impossible to raise money for indebtedness, but he thought that Walla Wallans would be willing to pay $15,000 for recent repairs on the buildings. He instructed them that it was not his responsibility to secure all the subscriptions and that the bursar, treasurer, and trustees must become fund raisers. He promised that a fund drive would make Whitman the best private school in the Pacific Northwest. Trustees must have resented such an evaluation, because Penrose had always told them that Whitman already was one of the Far West's best.

Clemen also complained that the school had been purchasing at retail; if it had purchased at wholesale, then the savings could have been used to maintain the physical plant. The implication was that the trustees had not safeguarded the school's financial interests. Clemen predicted that trustees would reject some parts of the Russell report but he also voiced the belief that, if most of the report's recommendations were followed, Whitman would then be operating more like other American colleges.

In January 1935 Clemen issued a second comprehensive report that reflected less of Russell's influence. It was more optimistic about finances, boasting that much had been accomplished for only a slight increase in liabilities. He included his personal experiences in order to assure trustees that he would conduct the college's business in a reputable manner: "Since the time I was twenty I have never owed anything that I could not pay with a turn of the hand. Even through this depression I owe no man anything and have added to my savings." He maintained that the college's finances were presently in good enough shape for him to seek money and that "it would have been unwise to have attempted this before." Aware that the alumni had repeatedly been solicited for money, Clemen said he would ask them to help find students, not donations.

To publicize the college, Whitman would award an honorary doctorate to Basil Cameron, conductor of the Seattle Symphony, and distribute a promotional booklet written by noted journalist and alumnus Nard Jones. Clemen defended the publication's cost: "The lack of knowledge of Whitman in this Pacific Northwest is simply appalling to me."

Not only was Whitman about to raise money, it would also cut its expenses. Clemen told local creditors that they "must deal with the college not as a normal relation of creditors to a commercial debtor but as creditors in relation to the best cultural and business asset of this city and in a public spirited way."

Looking ahead to the 1936 anniversary of the arrival of the Whitman family in the region, Clemen offered his thoughts about the college's namesake: "Whatever the merits of the two sides of the controversy concerning [Marcus] Whitman's contribution to American history by bringing the Oregon country into the United States, he was an important enough figure simply as a pioneer of settlement and religion to warrant all the honor that can be given him." This equivocal portrayal was in sharp contrast with Penrose's oft-repeated claim that the missionary had been a heroic martyr.

Clemen listed building needs. He emphasized the desirability of a center that would teach arts and crafts, noting somewhat condescendingly that regional residents were "ready for the aesthetic in life." The easterner added: "You gentlemen live in homes of culture which reflect this spirit and a desire for lovely and beautiful things. Most of the people of this countryside, however, know very little about this phase of life and therefore have no great desire to raise the standard of living in this particular." He thought that the popular taste could be elevated and that the college could help by offering courses for Walla Wallans as well as students. Besides courses in design and painting, handicrafts such as wood carving, ceramics, and pottery would be taught. "The girls would be developing skills of use to them in home making and the boys would be preparing for future hobbies which would make their lives happier."[61]

At various times throughout his first year, Clemen reported other changes, including campus beautification. Workmen pruned the college's 380 neglected trees, widened sidewalks, and improved the amphitheater with a Works Progress Administration grant of $2,200.[62] An committee of overseers investigated the rehabilitation of the grounds and supported the new president: "Prospective students viewing the campus and buildings comparing them with the buildings and grounds of competing [regional] colleges . . . must have been struck with the inadequate equipment at Whitman."[63] Clemen complained that, through neglect, Whitman had wasted $25,000 in fuel bills, so he hired an expert to tend the heating plant and to serve as purchasing agent.

Clemen sought to improve the faculty as well as the physical campus. Proud of his own doctorate, he sought to increase the faculty's reputation and ability by hiring more professors with Ph.D.s. To attract them, the president insisted that the school needed $500,000 in new endowment, its earnings to pay faculty salaries; thus: "The reputation of Whitman College will be the reputation of its faculty."[64] While Penrose would have agreed about the importance of professors, he would have disagreed about the significance of their having Ph.D.s.

Seeking a regional reputation, Clemen gave several addresses while he worked zealously to carry out his reforms. Unlike Penrose, he was not an authority on regional issues, but, like his predecessor, he often lectured on education and moral values. Soon after his arrival, he gave a speech in Spokane about higher education and Whitman's role in the resolution of economic, political, and social problems. He proposed, for example, that the college conduct a study of penal institutions, helping to discover the correct method—"punishment or reclamation of human beings."[65] In a convocation address he wisely told students that the college sought "to develop a habit of mind rather than to impart a given content of knowledge. Its concern is far greater with how men shall think, than what they shall think."[66] At another occasion the president stressed: "To avoid the shifting restlessness typical of the American public, a young person whose major task is to learn, should not surrender too much of his or her vitality to social and entertaining activities."[67] And on Armistice Day Clemen instructed students that the World Court and the League of Nations were agencies of peace. He summarized: "The warmakers are not patriotic. . . . The peacemakers are the patriots. This is one of the most radical changes that ever took place in human history."[68]

The *Walla Walla Union-Bulletin* reported that he impressed his audiences as a "virile force." With his growing regional reputation and a list of campus improvements, it would seem that Clemen's administration was winning applause.[69] But such was not the case. There were two major problems: the Russell report's criticisms—especially of the trustees—and the president's own actions and attitudes. Early in 1935 overseer William "W. W." Baker, a veteran member of the college's policy-shaping finance committee, heatedly

resigned because the report "carried abundant unfounded objectionable accusations of incompetence against the finance committee."
Furthermore, it contained "many untrue statements that have a
strong tendency to destroy confidence in the ability of the college
to care for its endowment funds, and it is also unfair to those who
have given their services to the college."[70] A special overseer committee, however, studied the report and, to Clemen's pleasure, concurred with almost all of its recommendations.

When the two boards gathered in June 1935, the Russell report
prompted periods of acrimonious debate that went unreported in the
official minutes. Overseers seemed willing to accept the report, apparently indifferent to Baker's resignation. However, the chairman
of the board of trustees, Allen Reynolds, complained that the survey contained "certain harsh criticisms," unjustified by the "records
of the College or of its Boards, or by the facts." But he conceded that
Clemen should bring some of Russell's recommendations to the
board for action. On the other hand, Park Weed Willis of Seattle,
another long-time trustee, concurred with all but five of the sixty-
six recommendations and judged that the report "as a whole is most
excellent."

Undoubtedly Clemen's enthusiasm for the report angered several
board members, and his June report to the boards fueled the political fire. There he charged that the school had drifted for a decade;
that he had acted as a businessman "rehabilitating a business"; and
that he would reorganize Whitman "educationally and on the business side along the lines of the Russell report." He admonished the
boards that the school's position was more precarious than they realized: "The competition from other privately endowed colleges is
keener. And frankly, Whitman is in a position of financial vulnera-
bility compared with other institutions of equal academic rank. For
example, Willamette University and Reed College have each doubled
the endowment of Whitman. They are debt free, or practically so.
The College of Puget Sound, while sometimes considered on an inferior level, has nevertheless about a quarter of a million more endowment than Whitman, and I am told, no debt." He warned that
colleges could not live on their traditions. "The only thing that will
save a college is the creation of new traditions, and that right early."
He proposed making Whitman a "democratic school with a new

type of loyalty to the college rather than to the fraternity, and [with] the main interest of the students [being in the] getting of an education." He even introduced the radical idea of having the state take over the college to save it. But Clemen assured readers that such drastic action would be unnecessary. By organizing "the governing boards, the alumni, and the staff for the purpose of raising additional endowment," Whitman could then "function as Pomona or Swarthmore colleges."[71] However, he insisted that, if the school were to be saved, the boards must commit to his leadership.

Clemen later admitted to making "inevitable mistakes in revamping the college in an extreme emergency."[72] Surely he blundered with his sweeping support of the Russell report, and with his own 1935 report. He had bluntly told the boards that the college was no better than its competitors, that the fraternity system was detrimental, that the school might have to be converted into a state institution, and, more important, that they had mismanaged Whitman.

In the fall of 1935 the president and the Walla Walla trustees waged a bitter battle for control. Clemen found allies among the overseers, who, in turn, contested with the trustees. Only Maxey provided a history of this significant struggle, and, as a political scientist, he must have enjoyed observing and writing about it. One of the basic disagreements stemmed from the fact that Clemen tried to get the overseers—most of whom lived outside of Walla Walla—more involved in the school's management. Thus, some of them allied with him against the local trustees. But it seemed at first to be a short fight, because the president surrendered to his Walla Walla foes by resigning in late October. He wrote to trustee Reynolds: "I have reluctantly come to the conclusion that you and the other board members residing in Walla Walla have such a different attitude of mind from mine regarding the proper policies and personnel in reorganizing and rehabilitating the institution, that my services cannot achieve success."[73]

Two faculty members expressed sympathy with Clemen's criticism of the trustees. Professor of German Fredric Santler described the local trustees as being from old Walla Walla families and likeable. But, he recalled, they were "not particularly interested in education." Santler believed that the school's poverty resulted from their inaction: they simply agreed with the school's president and treasurer.[74] Maxey described the trustees as "self-satisfied, inert, local businessmen. And they didn't have any conception of how to run a college . . . or any conception of education." He accused them of "gross mismanagement," and argued that trustee Reynolds should have been replaced. At the same time, however, Maxey blamed Clemen for his arrogance: "He regarded himself as absolutely secure and indispensable and entrenched."

The trustees delayed acting upon Clemen's resignation until 1936, when they could meet with the overseers. Meanwhile, the president reversed himself and sought to remain in office. As he wished to recall his resignation, he needed the support of the overseers. That group, he hoped, could pressure the trustees into rejecting his resignation, or they could overrule the trustees.[75] Clemen campaigned among the overseers and the out-of-town trustees, prevailing upon them to attend and support him at a special April meeting of both boards. In his attempt to regain his position, he reminded board members that, when he assumed office, the physical plant was a disgrace, the finances were a tangled mess, and the demoralized faculty had lost its effectiveness. Apparently Clemen impressed the board of overseers. Seventeen of its forty-seven members wrote to the trustees, urging that no action be taken on his resignation.

Dismayed by the support the president had won from the overseers, the local trustees presented their side of the dispute to both boards. The trustees insisted that they had not blocked the president's actions; in fact, they had allowed him "practically a clear field in the management of the college." They reported to the other board that the college's deans and faculty predicted that, unless Clemen departed, the campus could "blow up." The faculty complained that the president talked to them in a "slighting manner" and that he predicted "the inevitable destruction of the college unless he personally directed it." Professors had initially embraced Clemen; now they opposed him. The trustees also resented Clemen's assertion that he would either run the college, "wreck it, or put it in the hands of a receiver."[76] They desired his resignation, but wanted overseer support prior to accepting it.

The struggle spilled into the student body. Some students learned from faculty members about the internal struggle. Phil Ashby, who, later on, in Princeton, New Jersey, came to admire Clemen, recalled that the president had upset the Whitman community. Ashby aptly described Clemen as a "rather difficult man with big ideas, but not a man who knew how to get along very well with people."[77]

At a joint meeting on April 4, the trustees voted four to three to refuse Clemen's withdrawal of his resignation. The president and two trustees from outside Walla Walla cast the three votes for allowing him to continue. To placate the overseers, the trustees now agreed to accept Dorsey Hill's resignation also, since overseers had long complained that the treasurer had not provided complete financial records, and counted him as one of Clemen's ardent foes. But this concession did not satisfy the overseers: they voted seventeen to four to allow the president to withdraw his resignation. The trustees retired from the room, debated, and exercising their ultimate authority, accepted Clemen's resignation. But in an attempt to win support among the overseers, the trustees agreed to replace two Walla Walla trustees with outsiders. While many overseers appreciated this significant change, some argued that they, not the trustees, had the authority to determine Clemen's fate.

Soon after this crucial meeting, the college deans and several faculty members petitioned the trustees, requesting that they immediately terminate Clemen. On April 14 the president publicly resigned again, not because of the faculty action, but because he did not want to be fired in June. Some board members resented the victory of the local trustees; for example, trustee Reginald Parsons of Seattle—a good friend of the college—telegraphed Allen Reynolds that he protested "this unwise inconsiderate uncalled for and possibly illegal action. . . . It is a sad day for Whitman that you would sacrifice your savior on the altar of unfair prejudice and greed."[78] Reynolds responded that there had been no personal attack on the president and explained the acceptance of the resignation: "Clemen, after having closed so many doors behind him and placed himself in a position of almost universal opposition to the people in the college, and the city, which must, after all, be the substantial support of Whitman," could not be retained.[79]

The *Pioneer*, in its April Fool's issue of 1936, presented two revealing headlines: "Rudy Given Boot in Grand Style . . . Board Jerks Prexy Because of Dissension," and "Goody, Goody, Clem's Leaving." After he had actually resigned, a tepid editorial credited him with increasing the enrollment, rehabilitating the campus, and publicizing the college.[80] On the other hand, the city's two dailies thought Clemen had made significant contributions.

But the alumni read a much different assessment in a long letter explaining "the abrupt change recently made in the executive headship of Whitman." Three prominent alumni—trustees Allen Reynolds and Virgil Bennington and Professor Chester Maxey—presented the case against the president, arguing that Clemen had increased the college debt. The writers reported that the faculty had loyally supported all of the president's policies, but then became concerned "that both their jobs and their back salaries were in jeopardy."

On campus, the faculty charged Clemen with gossiping about them, with failing to follow accepted administrative procedures, and with favoring those professors he had appointed. Students were courted by the president and some of them supported him at first, but as time went by many students opposed him. Criticism appeared in the *Pioneer*, and an anonymous student publication contained "scathing and scurrilous denunciations" of Clemen.[81] The authors denied rumors that Penrose had led Clemen's critics and that Clemen had turned back his Whitman salary and generously donated to the college. (It must have irritated faculty members that they were not being paid and that the president—who claimed to have wealth—received a salary.) The leader had also lost support in Walla Walla by attempting to force college creditors to reduce their financial claims, and by remaining aloof from the life of the community.

The alumni also joined the dispute. In June 1935, after Clemen's first year, the alumni association, headed by Virgil Bennington, had informed him that it appreciated his "constructive leadership" and pledged the group's "unswerving loyalty" in his attempt "to further expand the rich and useful program of the institution which we love and revere."[82] In 1936, angered by the firing of Clemen, Nard Jones resigned as president of the alumni association. He maintained that he had discussed Whitman's internal problems in "hundreds of discussions" with alumni, who concluded that the college had long been "grossly mismanaged" by a small Walla Walla faction and that the Russell report's recommendations were sensible. Jones, who enthusiastically accepted the report, judged that Whitman had a dim "future as long as it is dominated by the Baker policies and their various ramifications. There's a saying in those parts that everybody is related to the Bakers or owes them money. That means death to Whitman, starvation for the faculty."[83]

Penrose's own involvement in the administrative struggle is unknown. An overseer wrote him, "I feel the dismissal of Clemen, without consulting the overseers was not only an act of bad faith but what is even worse, under the circumstances it was stupid."[84] Penrose responded that the original resignation in October, which Clemen had revealed to faculty members, students, and townspeople, reduced his influence. He added that the controversial president "gave the decided impression that he wanted to get out of living in so small a town where there was so little social life."[85] Penrose defended the trustees for removing Hill, for appointing out-of-town trustees, and for delaying action on Clemen's resignation.

Chester Maxey's assessment of Clemen was that he, "like James F. Eaton, bears no luster in Whitman College"; moreover, he "was as great a paradox as I ever knew." Maxey described Clemen as being opinionated, energetic, political, profane, boastful, and anxious to use Whitman as a stepping-stone to an Ivy League institution. The political scientist judged that trustees and the outgoing president had thought that Clemen would be another Penrose, but "what they got was a bull in the china shop." Clemen was certain that he knew how "to get Whitman back on its feet, and he immediately set about doing that job—with all the finesse of a man putting out a fire. . . . If he had been a smoother politician," Maxey ruled, "and not been in such a tearing hurry, he might have accomplished a great deal more."[86]

In 1937 Walter Bratton, then acting president, wrote another critical assessment. He judged that Clemen, whom he thought self-centered, first came into conflict with the trustees because he "expended nearly $25,000 in fairly effective but quite expensive [campus] repairs," which was $15,000 more than they had allocated. Then Clemen had accused overseer W. W. Baker "of exploiting the college for the benefit of the bank." He also had angered the faculty by attempting to remove two deans without consulting anyone. Bratton concluded that the ousted leader had faced "huge difficulties . . . both from persons and from conditions, still I cannot but feel that his troubles were largely due to his own personality."[87]

Alumni would long express strong feelings about Clemen. Phil Ashby stated that it was a vast change to go from a "warm feeling about Penrose, who was really interested in individuals," to a stern leader. Ashby recalled that it was the new president's arrogance and the hiring of some unsuitable instructors that upset students and added that "there was never a student rebellion, but there was student anger."[88] Keith Soper recalled that he and other scholarship athletes revolted against Clemen's treatment of them "and burnt crosses on Clemen's porch." For about six months, this group did everything they could "to cause misery or upset." Soper judged that Clemen "was the most hated man I have ever known because he came to the school with his fancy dress and his little glasses like Teddy Roosevelt. He just didn't fit."[89] Other alumni recalled that students called him "The Chicago Butcher."

Concerning the president's wife, Bratton called Margaret Clemen "a charming woman,"[90] but Ashby compared her unfavorably with Mary Penrose. "Mrs. Penrose was active, sweet, but her own lady. . . . Mrs. Clemen was quiet as a mouse, never said a word, she might upset her husband."[91] During this controversial period, Mrs. Clemen wrote some doggerel verse about her husband's difficulties:

> With cap and gown he soon entrained
> Stopping off, to be ordained
> For Whitman's gray and gloomy walls
> Where ancients taught in crumbling halls.
>
> They greeted him with senile smirks
> In private—sharpened up their dirks
> With which to stab him in the back
> Ere he got wise—gave them the sack.
>
> Fierce raged the fight—now here, now there
> Back biting, knifing, pulling hair
> Until the campus reeked of gore
> And foemen tired—could fight no more.
>
> So while they rested at their ease
> The fight went on between trustees,
> And overseers taking sides
> Tore madly at each others hides.[92]

While the political storm swirled around their father, the young Clemen sons—Art and Rudolf, Jr.—thoroughly enjoyed Walla Walla, including trout fishing behind the President's House. Rudolf recalled: "Our Walla Walla years sparked major interests in my brother and me, his in aviation, mine in sports. Art became an aero engineer for General Dynamics and helped design the B-58 . . . after starting to build model airplanes in Walla Walla. I played catch with the Whitman team on the field across the brook from our house and later pitched a no-hitter for Princeton vs. Cornell in 1946 and struck out a Yale first baseman named George Bush the same year!"[93]

The Clemen family rarely talked about his failed presidency, but for years the campus community debated its impact. In the spring of 1936 the college struggled with debt and division. Maxey was one of the few who acknowledged Clemen's contributions. He gave the newcomer high marks for identifying problems, but charged that "he was inordinately ambitious and was not averse to Machiavellian means."[94] In truth, Clemen had initiated some important changes. He rehabilitated the buildings and the grounds, moved the library to Reynolds Hall from the unsuitable shack, paid the faculty part of its back salaries, appointed John Dale Russell to study the college, declared a moratorium on the bond issues, and extended the life of the bonds.[95] Clemen encouraged the revision of the college's constitution and bylaws, cut fuel costs, improved the purchasing system, and devised a more efficient administrative system. He strengthened the board of trustees by pushing for more members from out of town, which eventually led to a more responsive board. Unlike Penrose, he did not vacation in the summer, but labored at his heavy responsibilities.

This is an impressive list of accomplishments, especially considering the college's pressing financial problems during Clemen's twenty-two months in office. Initially everyone supported him; eventually the campus community opposed him. When he left in April, however, he still counted supporters. Some board members stood by Clemen, including overseer John G. Kelly, the publisher of the *Walla Walla Union-Bulletin*, who applauded Clemen's administrative record and disliked the way he was dismissed. Kelly, who called himself one of Clemen's many friends, believed that his resignation was "not justified by facts, reason, or equity."[96] But there was no way that the controversial administrator could remain. Almost all of the faculty signed the petition against him. It was bad enough to be poor —this was typical—but to be unappreciated and to be compared unfavorably with Reed's faculty by their president was demoralizing.[97] The student body, too, expressed its displeasure with his officious behavior, and students spread stories that some of them would transfer if the arrogant president stayed. Maxey generalized that, if Clemen had remained, then "the fight would go on indefinitely, and that would destroy the college, probably."[98]

To anyone acquainted with Whitman's administrative history, there are clear similarities between the resignations of James Eaton, the college's second president, and Clemen, the fourth one. Both executives, who were unfamiliar with the college and the Pacific Northwest, counted many well-wishers when they took office, but Eaton, in 1894, and Clemen, in 1935, created powerful opponents. These easterners identified significant problems and energetically sought to resolve them, but both ignored the institution's accomplishments and dwelled on its faults. Their personalities and manners created conditions that forced their resignations. Penrose wrote of Eaton that most of the campus community initially accepted "the judgments of this wise man of the East who had come from the realms of light into the twilight dawn of the West."[99] His superior attitude—and a similar one expressed by Clemen—rankled the college and the community. Both Eaton and Clemen were ill-suited to the job of college president. A collegiate environment requires listening, compromise, and patience; neither man demonstrated these crucial skills. By belittling faculty members, trustees, and townspeople, they drove these groups into determined opposition to their troubled presidencies. Eaton lasted four years, and Clemen served less than half that time. Surely, there are some lessons from this administrative history; perhaps the most obvious one is the need to have a good understanding of a presidential candidate prior to his appointment. Neither man's elitism and arrogance should have been a surprise. And, in the case of Clemen, the trustees were at fault for not hiring Hez Brown. He had the prerequisite skills and a love for his alma mater; surely his administration would not have resulted in such heartache in a time of hardship.

Acting President Walter Bratton Calms the Waters

Walter A. Bratton was appointed acting president in April 1936, became president two years later, and served until 1942. He did not apply for the position. The president of the board of trustees telephoned him late one night instructing him to assume presidential responsibilities the next morning. With some trepidation, Bratton confronted his demanding duties. Maxey, who had harsh words for the trustees for mismanaging the college, praised them for elevating Bratton from dean to the position of acting president. This action demonstrated, Maxey judged, "a good understanding of the needs of the situation."[100] Bratton, a talented administrator, immediately harmonized the boards, faculty, students, and townspeople as the Whitman community had hoped.

Popular in the city as well as on the campus, the sixty-two-year-old mathematician had served at Whitman since 1895, the same year that he graduated from Williams College. A dedicated student who had earned a Phi Beta Kappa key, he had ignored most extracurricular activities except tennis and debate. His major professor enthusiastically recommended him to Penrose, and, soon after graduation, the two sons of Williams journeyed to Walla Walla. The long rail trip gave Penrose an opportunity to relate heroic stories about the missionaries and to explain his ambitious plans for the college. Bratton, a Vermont native who had never before been west, was, like so many eastern educators, planning only a brief western teaching career. Through community involvement he met members of many of Walla Walla's pioneer families, and they informed the young professor that they wanted to advance local civilization through the college. Bratton related that he "came to feel that I too could have a part in the doing of something very wonderfully worthwhile."[101] He immediately established himself as a thorough teacher with high standards. His concern for students and for Whitman won him considerable respect during the forty-one years he served as a teacher, advisor, and administrator. He worked with Professor Benjamin Brown to develop the mathematics-physics program that, Penrose boasted, "became the sturdy foundation for many brilliant careers in the sciences."[102] Bratton was a clear speaker and writer, and his colleagues remembered his apt descriptions: Boyer Avenue was "a sea of dust" and the local wheat fields were the "checkerboard of the Gods." [103]

In 1901 he married Clarice Colton, who had come to Walla Walla to teach voice at the Whitman Conservatory of Music. (A South Carolinian, she insisted that Bratton place a picture of Virginian Woodrow Wilson in his office.) [104] The Brattons had two children and housed two Whitman coeds to assist with meals and housework. The faculty couple was socially active: the community praised Mrs. Bratton's dinners, especially for new faculty members, and her support of the Walla Walla Symphony. [105]

During his long career at Whitman, Bratton pursued the study of mathematics at the University of Berlin and at Columbia University, received an honorary doctorate from his alma mater (Penrose had urged Williams to honor its talented son), and served the community in various ways. An avid tennis player, he sometimes coached the Whitman team. Bratton diligently attended athletic contests, musicals, and recitals. His popularity with students had an interesting result; he wrote in 1928: "It has come to be true that no commencement season is complete for me without giving away at least one bride." [106] He had been a key supporter of Penrose and knew his struggles and accomplishments, and an affectionate bond had developed between the two leaders. In 1935 the trustees wrote resolutions honoring Bratton's forty years of service. They acknowledged his enthusiasm, optimism, and "efficient labors" and asserted: "Few men have so endeared themselves to so many generations of students or have become so well known as the accurate and inspiring and noteworthy teacher in that difficult field of mathematics." [107]

With his long experience as an administrator, including service as dean of the college during Clemen's presidency, Bratton was a logical choice to be acting president. In his new office office, he delivered a thoughtful report in June 1936; its structure and content were similar to those of the reports authored by Penrose. The acting president reminded board members that Whitman's role was to serve a vast region, that it should have higher standards than the public universities, and that student advising was critical to the college's success. He proposed a balanced budget, as he had experienced the institutional problems that had come with continuous and debilitating

Walter Bratton had been recruited as a professor of mathematics in 1895 by President Penrose. He built an outstanding reputation as a teacher, tennis coach, and administrator. Following the difficult presidency of Rudolf Clemen, Bratton became president in 1936 and served until 1942. He restored morale and won praise for his fair-minded leadership.

debt. At some point, the school must stop running deficits, a view that alumnus Donald Sherwood and other businessmen enthusiastically endorsed.

Bratton's report pointed out that too many students transferred at the end of their sophomore year. This meant a loss of income and a reduction of important upper-division offerings. Responding to student demand, the faculty proposed teaching secretarial courses, which they assured the Whitman community would be more demanding than those offered at vocational schools. This was not the first time that the school had offered practical courses designed to attract and retain students.

The acting president reported that a field representative would seek annual gifts rather than endowment funds. Bratton wanted regional residents to learn that Whitman needed money "for progressive improvement." He urged the trustees to restore the twenty percent previously cut from faculty salaries, because other schools were starting to pay higher salaries. "We cannot," he cautioned, "hope to keep the members of our faculty on a low salary scale and continue to keep the standard of the faculty where it must be if we are to

serve significantly." The leader acknowledged that Whitman's reputation for high academic standards had been "due to merit awards,"
but he, like Penrose, argued that these expensive scholarships must
be cut.[108]

Bratton's lengthy report identified the need for campus maintenance, for enriching the curriculum, and for new buildings. His list
of desirable buildings was similar to Penrose's, including a gym for
women, a science building, and an auditorium and theater. Bratton
boasted that the school's enrollment of 640 was the highest in its history, but there were only eighty-four seniors compared to 262 freshmen. Despite a less stringent admissions policy, he saw no decline
in student quality. The acting president assured his readers that the
faculty morale was high, and he wanted a professor as well as an
alumnus to be on the presidential search committee. Obviously, the
process by which Rudolf Clemen had been chosen—and the result
of that choice—led Bratton to seek a broader committee.

The overseers responded carefully to Bratton's report. Concerned
about the loss of upper-division students, members wondered if
Whitman could ever offer enough advanced courses to prevent students from transferring to large universities. The board wanted the
faculty to discover why so many students left after their sophomore
year. Overseers supported adoption of secretarial courses, but
warned they should not be given "undue publicity." The board
agreed with Bratton that the school's future depended upon more
financial aid, but it disagreed with him as to where the money should
be found. "It is the sense of this board that Walla Walla and Whitman are inseparably linked and cannot be divorced; that the cir-
cumstance involves obligations of loyalty and financial support upon
the part of the Walla Walla people which are not incumbent upon
any other section or community of the Northwest."

Overseers agreed about the need for a more inclusive presidential search committee, but, chastened by the Clemen experience, emphasized that there was no hurry to find a new leader: "It is easy
to act in haste and repent at leisure."[109] Bratton had set a clear agenda for the boards; the Russell report recommendations would have
to wait for a less emotional time.

Bratton's reports did not mention the assistance he sought from
the Walla Walla Chamber of Commerce. According to Donald Sher-

wood, the president came to him seeking "advice and assistance on the urgent financial problems of the college." The two had been well-acquainted for about eighteen years; Bratton had taught Sherwood and coached him in tennis. The mathematician appreciated Sherwood's leadership in the alumni organization and identified him as "one of the most promising young businessmen in this section." An officer of the Chamber of Commerce, Sherwood, along with Virgil Bennington, a Whitman trustee and the chamber's president, told Bratton that their organization wanted to understand Whitman's problems. The leader welcomed the chamber's help; it responded by appointing a special committee, with Sherwood as its secretary, to assist Bratton. Working with bursar George Marquis, Sherwood did an extensive audit of the college's finances and complained, as had others, that it was difficult to find accurate numbers. Nevertheless, Sherwood prepared a comprehensive report that won the special committee's approval and went to the college trustees in mid-June 1936.

The report acknowledged that Whitman was "unquestionably [Walla Walla's] greatest single asset." It calculated that Whitman had a debt of about $185,000, and that between 1930 and 1935 the trustees had transferred more than $108,000 from the endowment to pay debts. The committee, however, believed that more endowment money should be utilized to eliminate the debt, because donors "would be very reluctant to give funds to pay off indebtedness already incurred." The committee believed that creditors would willingly give the college substantial discounts and that citizens would donate funds to cover the debt. To assure donors that the school was stable, the committee recommended that a president should soon be appointed, but they opposed elevating a faculty member. Perhaps the report's major point was its insistence that the trustees adopt the balanced-budget principle.

Sherwood wrote that the trustees responded defensively to the report. One stated: "It is a damn outrage and business people had no right to dictate policy decisions such as required balanced budgets to the board. A college could not be operated in the same manner as a business."

By December, however, the trustees had embraced the special committee report, including "a binding resolution providing for bal-

anced budgets in future years." Sherwood, who believed that Whitman had not balanced its books for about twenty years, agreed to
serve on a special financial campaign committee that would seek
money for unpaid salaries and debts. In January 1937 Sherwood
found that the total indebtedness was $120,110, and sought to pay
it off within ten years.[110]

While Sherwood's assistance was very helpful, the departure of
Seattle trustee Reginald Parsons was a setback. Committed to the
college, Parsons had sharply disagreed with the Walla Walla trustees,
who reminded him of the United States Senate obstructionists identified by President Woodrow Wilson as a "handful of willful men."[111]
Concluding that the trustees were indifferent to the recommendations of the Russell report and, in fact, were opposing Clemen
because of his efforts to enact them, Parsons resigned from the board
of trustees in late 1936. According to Sherwood, his departure was
a significant loss, for Parsons had a better understanding of the college than did the local trustees.

Starting in 1937, Whitman entered a new financial era. Not only
would the college balance its budgets, it had also won the devotion
of Sherwood. He and other younger alumni would do much for their
alma mater.

President Bratton Leads the Rebuilding Process

Bratton realized that he must rebuild the college financially as well
as internally. He quickly achieved the second goal, ending the stress
between the two boards and between the administration and the faculty. In 1937 an overseer credited Bratton with "exercising a degree
of wisdom and diligence which has called forth an amazing response
in faculty, students, and officers for which we should be thankful."[112]
The Whitman community respected Bratton's dedication, fairness,
and energy, approving the trustees' decision to make him president
rather than to risk another outsider. The search committee concluded
that Bratton had demonstrated "such conspicuous ability in the crisis of April 1936, and in the year following, and had so successfully met the various problems which confronted the institution, with
such an admirable temper of mingled tact, sympathy, and impar-
tiality that he had won their respect and admiration."[113] The fears

of promoting a faculty member to the presidency had obviously been unwarranted. Surely some Whitmanites must have recognized that, in 1934, such a narrow sentiment had prevented Bratton from succeeding Penrose.

According to his family, Bratton constantly worried about Whitman's finances. The new leader found it more difficult to achieve all of his financial goals than to harmonize all of his constituencies. By careful management, however, he balanced the annual budget once the overseers made personal donations to avoid red ink. He and the boards also raised $124,000 to cover the existing debt. Speaking for the board of trustees, John C. Lyman later recalled: "Only by a superhuman effort under the leadership of President Bratton was the College able to overcome an accumulated deficit through a campaign."[114] Walla Wallans responded to the appeals and by 1938 pledged enough money to eliminate a debt described by Bratton as "a strangling handicap."[115] Although there was some delay in collecting each pledge, townspeople once again covered a college debt, as they had done in 1913, 1919, and 1924.[116]

Bratton and the boards pondered a major campaign drive to increase the endowment and to construct buildings. The president wanted to increase the endowment from $1,000,000 to at least $3,000,000.[117] He went east in 1938, seeking the advice of Tamblyn and Brown and college leaders about the wisdom of launching a major campaign in a recession. The college's two boards heard his report and concluded that a major campaign based on the theme of a tribute to Mary and Stephen Penrose would fail. Thus, they voted to conduct a very modest regional solicitation. Bratton, who admitted that the school's experience with fund raisers was generally not "a happy one," did not personally canvass funds.[118] He limited his activities to appeals through the mails, in particular to alumni in 1938. With the uncertainty following the outbreak of the Second World War in 1939, school leaders again delayed a major financial campaign.

While board members thought it unwise to conduct a substantial fund-raising drive in the late 1930s, they did provide for more professional management of the college's financial resources. The revitalized finance committee, led by Harper Joy, played a crucial role. Assisted by other astute businessmen, including George Yancey of

Spokane and Donald Sherwood of Walla Walla, this committee shrewdly invested the endowment in profitable stocks and bonds, disposed of properties that generated small returns, and refinanced the old dormitory bonds at a low four-percent interest rate. Both boards praised this committee for its financial management; these were the most competent money managers in Whitman's history to that time.

During Bratton's administration, assistance came in old and new ways. The school received some substantial gifts, including donations from Agnes Healy Anderson for scholarships and buildings; from the estate of alumnus Edward D. "Ned" Baldwin for the library; from the president of the Carnation Company, E. A. Stuart, for the promotion of the college's religious life; and from the Sigmund and Rose Schwabacher family for the establishment of a loan fund. The Alumni Loyalty Fund was re-established; its modest contributions went to meeting the current operating debt. In 1936 parents formed the Puget Sound Mothers' Club; four other such clubs followed. The clubs hosted college speakers, publicized the school, and paid for small redecoration projects in the dormitories. In 1938 the Whitman Guild was created; this group assisted at social functions and redecorated rooms.

The president's thorough reports listed several financial needs, most of which were unattainable without a major capital campaign. Like Penrose before him, he asked for money to increase faculty salaries and to hire additional professors. The English, history, sociology, psychology, business, and physical education departments all sought more faculty members, but the school made only a few additions—mostly in the social sciences—in response to increasing student enrollments. By 1938 the faculty received its back pay (dating from 1932) but thereafter received only modest pay increases. In both his 1936 and 1942 reports, Bratton urged the boards to increase salaries.

Bratton's reports also listed many old and new needs: to develop the art program, to relieve the overcrowding in Billings Hall by constructing a chemistry building, to increase the dining and housing capacity of Prentiss Hall, and to add a women's gymnasium. To this list he added a request for a student union, which he and the dean of women argued would enliven the students' social life (the overseers rejected such a structure and favored a chemistry building). Unlike Penrose, Bratton often budgeted for significant remodeling projects, making certain that such expenditures would not lead to an unbalanced budget. From 1938 to 1942 the school had the funds to finance various maintenance projects, including $12,000 in extensive repairs to Billings Hall (Bratton said it was now no longer necessary to apologize for it) and the construction of small classrooms and faculty offices in Memorial Hall.

Whitman's scholarship program received considerable attention from the president and both boards. In 1938 the college established forty new pre-professional scholarships of $500 each, whose purpose was, Bratton explained, "to impress on the minds of schoolmen . . . high school students and their parents the fact that the courses offered . . . constitute the soundest approach to professional education."[119] Restricted to male applicants, this scholarship program attracted excellent students, fostered the liberal arts, and garnered considerable attention.

The college also recruited extensively during these years. "A Planned Approach to College," a booklet by registrar Douglas Mc-Clane, appeared in 1940 and stimulated considerable interest. Total enrollment figures pleased everyone. In 1940 Bratton announced an enrollment of 627, the highest in the college's history. He also assured readers that student quality and retention had improved during his presidency. The administration emphasized the need for certain types of students: those from Walla Walla, from small towns, and from out of state. It also discarded the old ratio of three men students to two women students and accepted a more realistic five-to-four ratio. On the eve of the Second World War, the college contemplated the time when women students would outnumber men.

The Bratton administration steadily reduced the amount of money spent on student aid because the National Youth Administration paid for student employment on campus and students found jobs in an improving local economy.

Bratton's successful administration resulted, in part, from his ability to identify and maintain the school's mission. He praised Penrose for keeping Whitman "on the narrow path of scholarly discipline and wholesome campus life . . . at a time when educational fads were rife. We have chosen a limited field of service and have undertaken to do quality work within it. To this policy I believe we owe much of the great reputation we have."[120]

The president often reminded overseers that the school needed their commitment, their financial assistance, and the submission of names of potential donors and students. At their annual meetings they made useful reports on financial matters. Members studied the need for increased faculty salaries, student recruitment, and scholarships; the potential threat of junior colleges; the implications of the Second World War; and much more. One overseer reminded other members that the restoration of faculty salaries was "simple justice" because professors had supported Whitman "in what amounts to forced contributions."[121] The board also considered the college's mission; in 1937 one member emphasized: "Education is a life long process; it begins when a great and inspiring teacher throws open the doors to achievement, to appreciation, and to intelligent living."[122] In 1940 another overseer concluded that Whitman was a unique regional school devoted to "the twin ideals of high character and of high scholarship."[123] The minutes demonstrated that this board, responding to the president's pleas, was of more assistance than it had been in Penrose's last years. Similarly, the trustees improved their attendance and the range of their discussion. Both boards were doing much more for the college in the late 1930s than they had done in the previous decade.

Working harmoniously with the boards, Bratton appointed some younger men, including Harper Joy and Herbert Ringhoffer, as trustees. Two long-time board members, trustee Allen Reynolds and overseer Mack F. Gose, died in the winter of 1941–1942. While the majority of the nine trustees were Walla Wallans, only ten of the forty-five overseers were local men. Two well-known overseers were Supreme Court Justice William O. Douglas, a 1920 graduate of the college, and President Emeritus Penrose. With the death of overseer Genevieve Vollmer Bonner of Lewiston in 1940, all the board members were male, despite some modest presidential efforts to find prominent Northwest women.

One of Bratton's earliest administrative difficulties arose in late 1937, when the Association of American Universities investigated Whitman. An association committee expressed concern that professors gave eighty-seven percent of grades at the level of "C" or bet-

ter and that the teaching loads were excessive. Bratton, who wanted to remain in the association's good standing, responded that the
higher grades resulted from the school's selective admission program
and from an advising program that encouraged students to withdraw
from classes when they were not doing well. He added that faculty
members, who were conscious of appropriate grading, officially met
and compared grading standards. The president explained that the
faculty, teaching as many as nineteen hours, actually had small student enrollments. When the committee asked whether the college
awarded Ph.D.s, Bratton assured the association that the college had
never granted one. In late 1938 the committee reported that Whitman had improved its grading practices, but it questioned the college catalog assertion that Whitman offered "a unique opportunity
in the Pacific Northwest."[124]

The Second World War put far more pressure on the college's administration than did the association's criticisms of grade inflation
and catalog copy. In 1939 Bratton reported that the army and navy
wanted the Civil Aeronautics Authority to train college men as pilots. Students and the Chamber of Commerce wanted the college
to apply for the program. By the spring of 1941 sixty-eight Whitman
men had completed the civilian pilot training program.[125]

Because Bratton resigned in June of 1942, the war's impact upon
the college would create far greater problems for his successor than
it did for him. Whitman's fifth president departed at a time of solid
enrollments, although the small size of the junior and senior classes still created worry. He and older members of the Whitman community feared that the Second World War would have as devastating an impact on enrollments as the First World War had.

Bratton, who had mourned the death of his wife in 1939, announced in 1941 that he would retire at the age of sixty-eight. Honors came to him in his last semester: he was chosen as Walla Walla's
first citizen, and in May 1942 he was feted at a recognition dinner
celebrating his forty-seven productive years as a Whitman professor,
dean, and president. Various individuals praised his character, sincerity, and wisdom. Stephen Penrose applauded his scholarship, high
classroom standards, impact upon students, and leadership. Perhaps
the most unusual tribute came from Otto A. Harbach, who, as Otto
Hauerbach, had served on the faculty with Bratton at the turn of the

century. He had gone on to become a noted librettist and lyricist; the *New York Times* reported that his contributions to such musical hits as *No, No, Nanette*, *Rose Marie*, and *Sunny* earned him $15,000 a week.[126] Despite his accomplishments, he fondly recalled his years teaching English at Whitman, and claimed to envy Bratton's collegiate accomplishments.

Unfortunately, although many well-wishers hoped that Bratton would enjoy a long and richly deserved retirement, he died just seventeen months later. Again there was a round of tributes, including one from Edith Hinkley Quimby, a 1912 graduate who had gone on to become a distinguished radiologist at Columbia University. Bratton, she reported, supported her by "insisting on admission to physics classes whose doors had never before opened to a girl," and he also urged that she should overcome her shyness by participating in extracurricular activities. The scientist concluded: "Truly he dedicated his life to all of us. He was one of that little group of remarkable men whose vision and untiring effort have made our college a unique institution."[127]

William O. Douglas praised Bratton for teaching "subject matter, mental discipline and precision, . . . the way of perseverance and the worth of devotion to an ideal, and the art of teaching."[128] He also acknowledged Bratton's skill as a counselor and his "great patience and vision" as president.

While Bratton handled the college's internal affairs with considerable skill, he could not compare with Penrose in the conduct of external affairs. Bratton did not receive the attention of editors, ministers, businessmen, and civic leaders as had his predecessor (although, as a Democrat, Bratton was chosen in 1938 to greet Eleanor Roosevelt at the local airport). Despite the fact that the school lost some of its regional prestige, Bratton repaired both buildings and constituencies. Thus, in 1941, when Whitman College plunged into the wartime maelstrom, it was stronger than it had been when it was battling the Great Depression. Sadly, until the opening of the Bratton Tennis Center in 1996, there was slight recognition of the conscientious Bratton as a significant builder of Whitman.

4

The Faculty in the Age of Hardship
1925–1942

The lives of Whitman professors were, of course, intertwined with administrative problems and politics. But they led lives that were different from those of the presidents, and, in many ways, their efforts and concerns remained the same regardless of who occupied the presidency: they taught heavy loads, served on various committees, advised students, and, with their families, fought to survive during the Great Depression. Understandably, faculty members at Whitman, like those at other schools, were unhappy about certain professional conditions, including inadequate facilities and irregularly paid salaries.

Late in the nineteenth century, James Bryce, who had investigated American colleges, had judged that, despite small salaries, "men of intellectual tastes prefer a life of letters with poverty to success in business or at the bar."[1] Whitman professors had always faced this choice, but the difficulties of their financial situation were exacerbated during the 1920s and 1930s. From the time they were hired until their resignations or retirements, faculty members suffered from economic hardship. Experienced teachers struggled, year after year, to support their families; younger individuals joining the faculty understood from the president—whether Stephen Penrose, Rudolf Clemen, or Walter Bratton—that salaries were low, but would improve. Each president dominated the hiring process. For over thirty years, Penrose insisted that "the selection of a faculty member [was] so important I would place it as perhaps the chief prerequisite for a successful college president."[2] In 1933 three professors agreed with that assessment: "The highest duty of a college president is to secure and retain a faculty made up of men and women who add to fine scholarship the rare gift of teaching."[3]

Penrose preferred to make an appointment only after conferring with senior members of the faculty or with an alumnus. Once, he favored hiring an alumnus "rather than a stranger unaccustomed to our ways," but, most often, he found individuals through graduate departments or teachers' agencies.[4] On one occasion, the leader sought "a dependable, warmhearted, adaptable genuine Christian, who will win people by his attractive personality and inspire students with ambition."[5] Because the college was "on the western edge of the continent" and in poverty, it did not bring candidates to campus. Although this hiring system, with its dependence upon letters rather than personal interviews, appeared to be unprofessional, Penrose boasted that "unbiased judges" thought that it resulted in excellent faculty additions.[6]

Penrose authored interesting recruitment and appointment letters. For example, he informed Louis A. Parsons that he was being hired to replace the legendary professor Benjamin Brown, but because of Parsons' age, Penrose cautioned: "It is much harder for a man of fifty to move from the Atlantic to the Pacific than for a younger man."[7] Choosing Rowena Ludwig as a teacher of music theory and organ, Penrose confided that, in appointing her to such an important post, "I know that I shall be criticized by some people for not appointing a man."[8]

The president often evaluated the importance of a Ph.D. and the relationship between research and teaching. Although he had sometimes required the Ph.D., he had doubts about the need for it. He ruled that many college presidents made too much of the doctorate: "I always look upon it with some suspicion because I feel that it may have made its possessor too technical and likely to have lost his zeal for teaching; it is teachers I am looking for, rather than Ph.D.s," who, he observed, could "be as stupid in class as a boiled owl."[9] Penrose wanted to maintain a science faculty committed to teaching, not research, but acknowledged: "It is frequently necessary to keep a little fire of research burning on the individual professor's hearth lest he lose his ardor and become merely a hack teacher."[10] The problem for Whitman and other institutions—then and now—has been to keep the professor's little fire of research from becoming an all-consuming inferno. Perhaps Penrose's fullest statement on the relationship between teaching and research came in a letter to a Stanford professor:

> This is not an institution for research, but primarily for teaching, and I want on our faculty men who have the teaching gift, and who are not always turning their hearts toward research as their primary purpose. If a man on the Whitman faculty can do both, I rejoice, and whenever I find a person carrying on a piece of private investigation or research, I do all that I can to encourage him, but I am sure that the quality of teaching is by far the most important desideratum, and I lay stress on it above all else.[11]

Whitman faculty members were troubled by the lack of research opportunities. Many of them wanted to engage in some degree of research, but most lacked either the time or energy for such scholarship. English professor William R. Davis emphasized the need for research because, "It is poor college policy to develop a faculty of Jacks of all trades." Political scientist Chester Maxey admitted that he found time for research "by stealing from teaching"; Professor Walter Eells conducted research "at the expense of health and sleep"; a few others squeezed time for research out of their vacations.[12]

From the surviving evidence, it appears that the faculty often lacked contracts, promotional guidelines, or terms of tenure. In letters, Penrose confessed he did not know what contracts should include: "It is impossible to define in advance all the things which a faculty member may be asked to do, and I have found it far better to engage them with the general understanding that they will serve the institution to the best of their ability."[13] Most new professors served a two-year probationary period. Some learned that, to be promoted, they must earn an advanced degree (solid teachers, such as professor of English Russell Blankenship, received advancement on the basis of winning an M.A.) and that they must show "more than an ordinary devotion to their work and responsibilities." Penrose added: "The mere teaching of classes, however faithfully . . . is not a sufficient ground for promotion because we want to have in all the higher ranks . . . men who are more than teachers. They must be interested in the development of the college, interested in their students outside of classes, and desirous of cultivating those friendly personal relationships which are essential to the successful operation of a college of this sort."

During their probationary period, newcomers came under the scrutiny of senior professors, especially the deans, who submitted their informal evaluations to the president. Penrose explained to inexperienced faculty members that, because of the school's small size, the trustees kept "closely posted upon the contribution of each professor" and participated in promotional discussions as well as salary decisions.[14]

A few teachers did not meet the school's high standards. Penrose explained that if an individual "did not have his heart in his work, he was quickly got rid of," but the new additions received administrative assurance that they "were not subject to surveillance nor regarded with suspicion."[15] In a dismissal letter, he bluntly told professor of German Dr. Mary Bausch that the trustees wanted her resignation but that he would furnish her a recommendation.[16] In 1928 Penrose informed Assistant Professor John P. Miller that he would not be retained; the German teacher angrily charged that he was being released because he was a Roman Catholic. He appealed to the American Association of University Professors and the Carnegie Foundation. Penrose explained to them that he and other faculty members found Miller's personality egotistical and teaching methods inappropriate, which led to the dismissal. Arguing that he was the victim of religious persecution, Miller threatened to publish student letters "in reference to immoral conditions prevailing at Whitman," which would "undoubtedly" cause many parents to "withdraw their sons and daughters."[17] Both the association and the foundation inquired into Miller's case and rejected his claims.

The faculty worked under an irregular promotion system; Penrose and his two successors recommended to the trustees the advancement of successful professors. Penrose interpreted successful teaching for the benefit of young teachers: "Popularity is not the measure of success, but rather the stirring of pupils' minds and the awakening of that intellectual curiosity and wonder and reverence . . . [which] mark the genuine scholar."[18] During the Great Depression, the president offered Markham Harris, an inexperienced teacher, the choice of either a promotion to assistant professor or a $200 annual salary increase. Harris chose the promotion.[19]

After a year's experience, professors could participate in Whitman's pension program. The Carnegie Foundation for the Advancement of Teaching gave the college money for this plan, the forerunner of the present Teachers Insurance and Annuity Association program. Faculty members put five percent of their salary into the program; the college matched it with another five percent. But during the Great Depression less than a third of the faculty could afford to enroll in the retirement plan.

Whitman could not underwrite a sabbatical program but offered a stringent leave policy. This system paid the professor his full pay but required him to cover his replacement's salary. Few of the faculty could afford to participate; thus, they labored year after year without the opportunity for research, study, writing, travel, or rest.

Many faculty members urged Penrose to inaugurate a sabbatical program. But after they and the college became mired in the Great Depression, professors did not push for such a program from either Clemen or Bratton. Because of their low salaries, teachers continued to enjoy tuition remission for their children. Some board members, however, opposed this benefit.[20]

Occasionally professors submitted reform proposals after making comparisons with other schools. In 1926 Professor Eells, for example, tried to convince the administration that the faculty should be larger and that professors should teach fewer classes.[21] He demonstrated that the faculty-student ratio of one to 15.4 was one of the worst for quality liberal arts colleges; furthermore, he reported that half of his colleagues carried more than the standard load of twelve teaching hours a week. Penrose supported the professor's request; the tight-fisted trustees did not.

While Penrose correctly generalized that the faculty was "a quiet body who do not make news and, therefore, escape publicity," it was not passive.[22] A questionnaire from the administration to the faculty was completed by fourteen professors—about half of the faculty— and provided significant information about conditions in January 1930, early in the Great Depression.[23] Even before this stressful period, professors had lacked adequate salaries, and their responses to the questionnaire emphasized the need for better pay. The plea for improved compensation came as no surprise to Penrose, who stated that the average Whitman professor made slightly less than $3,000, which was about half of what faculty members at Williams College earned.[24] In 1929 the school had faced a $100,000 deficit, and the president had informed teachers that the anxious trustees opposed salary improvements.[25] Penrose had admitted in 1928 that the college borrowed money from faculty members to cover operating costs, adding that "all improvements made and all increases in maintenance costs have been possible only through keeping down faculty salaries."[26]

In a petition summarizing faculty complaints, director of physical education Nig Borleske warned that each year his colleagues become more restless because of low salaries. Chemist Frank Haigh, who consistently argued that the college's most acute problem was inadequate faculty compensation, complained that, after fourteen years of service, he had failed to improve his financial condition. He and his colleagues had been assured that the fund-raising campaign of 1924–1925 would increase salaries up to a $4,000 maximum for department chairmen. The continuing delay of the pay increase lowered faculty morale, which he currently found to be lower "than at any time since I have been connected with the college." A newcomer resented Walla Walla's high cost of living and Whitman's uncertain paydays. Unless the administration improved compensation, older faculty members warned that competent young teachers could not be hired, and that seasoned professors would continue to fear the specter of old age.

In response to a question about the staffing needs of the departments, a few writers requested additions. Historian Melvin Jacobs lamented: "The attempt of the present teacher to teach all subjects in history represents an existence, not a living." Haigh disagreed, opposing any additional faculty until salaries improved. Howard Brode proposed increasing the student body to 750; the resulting tuition revenue would go to the professors. The respondents uniformly opposed adding any new departments until the existing ones received needed additions.

The faculty wrote extensively about their buildings and equipment. Borleske argued that the basketball floor was too small and reminded the committee that the women needed their own gymnasium. Bratton stressed the need for library books and building repairs, but insisted that faculty salaries and teaching equipment were more important than any new building. Every scientist found fault with Billings Hall. Brode described it as ill-lit but cautioned, "If the windows were enlarged or rearranged the building would probably fall." Haigh acknowledged the need for a new science building but stressed again that increased salaries deserved priority. Physicist Louis Parsons bluntly requested a science building "to replace the old barn and fire trap known as Billings Hall." He judged that new facilities would help attract students and benefactors. Several faculty members urged the construction of a new library and repairs on Memorial Hall, the walls of which were stained from leaks in the roof. This and other unattractive features of major buildings made a poor impression on visitors, but Professor Reginald Green emphasized: "A first class faculty is of much more importance to Whitman than buildings."

In response to a call for general recommendations, the faculty supplied various ideas. A new education professor concluded that Whitman seemed "to be asleep or without any defined ideas as to what it is about." Borleske thought that the school needed a person on the road recruiting students and seeking positions for alumni. Brode advised the college to raise a large endowment because, he correctly prophesied, "conditions are liable to change at any time." Green emphasized the popularity of Whitman's economics and business classes and predicted that an enrichment of this curriculum would make it easier to recruit men. Professors Haigh, Parsons, and William Leonard favored a sabbatical system. Economist Leonard advanced many other proposals: the conversion of the old Beta Theta Pi house into a faculty club; a clearer message about Whitman's purpose; and additional pre-professional courses for women, "suited to their new status." Parsons expressed a provocative idea: Whitman should admit that the 1924–1925 campaign had raised less than half of the amount it sought. He explained the importance of this admission: "From all that I hear on the outside it seems to be the general impression that the college raised all their endowment and has all the money" it needs.[27]

This 1930 questionnaire demonstrated that the faculty advanced legitimate institutional concerns. Chester Maxey did not respond to the questionnaire, but his autobiography later touched on issues similar to those raised by his colleagues. Referring to the last ten years of the Penrose administration as "an era of callous neglect," Maxey recalled the low faculty morale of that time: "To a man they were discouraged, dispirited, and anxiety-ridden. Not only had they largely lost faith in the future of Whitman College, most of them were fearful of calamities to come. . . . In vain they had hoped and hoped for adequate salaries, for lighter teaching loads, for money to buy library books and laboratory equipment, and most of all for any dependable evidence that they could look forward to something better in their remaining years at Whitman." The political scientist insisted that every colleague acknowledged that Whitman "was desperately in need of dynamic executive leadership"; indeed, it "was sailing without a pilot."[28]

Although faculty members would not, of course, evaluate their president on a form that was mailed back to him, it seems highly plausible that many of Maxey's colleagues agreed with him. But they were even more critical of the trustees. In 1928 the trustees, because of a $25,000 budget deficit, refused the president's request to increase faculty salaries. Professors unsuccessfully appealed this decision to the overseers, emphasizing that the building program was taking money from their salaries. The trustees had also angered the faculty by delaying salaries, by allowing the college to fall into a precarious financial position, by opposing a tuition increase, by failing to maintain buildings or buy equipment, and—according to professors Maxey and Fredric Santler—by lacking a knowledge of college purposes and conditions. Physicist Benjamin Brown stated in 1925 that he had little "use for the trustees."[29] He and his colleagues learned that there was little hope for an immediate salary increase because, as Penrose explained to them, "the conservative trustees" would not raise tuition "oftener than once in four years so that no one generation of undergraduates may have to stand a double increase above that which was in effect when they started in as freshmen."[30] The Russell report of 1934 was much more critical of trustees than of the president for the "era of callous neglect."

Income and morale were both low when the Great Depression hit in the early 1930s. Faculty members and townspeople felt that even the weather turned against them. During the great spring flood of 1931, biologist Howard Brode stated that Mill Creek expanded its banks and "ran down all the principal business streets, washing out the pavement in some cases and piling up rock three feet deep, covering lawns and filling basements with mud." Water surrounded his house; thus, "When the report came that there was another cloudburst in the mountains, we thought we would feel more comfortable to sleep elsewhere, so we left the house for two nights."[31]

In the spring of 1931 Markham Harris, now a promising assistant professor, decided to leave Whitman. Upon presenting him his last check, bursar George Marquis commented: "You are one of the lucky ones; those who are staying will not receive checks."[32] During that fall, professors did not receive regular salary payments; in November, Penrose gave only a brief verbal statement about the college's financial condition and predicted better times. The president wrote a friend that the teachers suffered from irregular payments, and if they had "acted like street car employees, a general strike would have been ordered long ago."[33]

Although the faculty did not strike, it did act. In February 1932, alarmed by their own deteriorating financial position and that of the college, professors chose a committee of Brode, Bratton, and Maxey to present their concerns to the governing boards. Their letter to the boards described a "threatening condition," and acknowledged that board members were the college's business leaders. The delay in salary payments, the three men warned, was a serious problem: "The inevitable loss of morale and of effectiveness in work which already is beginning to appear in both students and faculty, and which will surely accelerate unless halted, mean the wiping out of a half-century of hard, consistent, successful efforts to build a really great higher education institution." The professors concluded that they could not believe that Whitman would "be allowed to die, but it is our opinion that immediate and vigorous action is necessary to keep it safe."[34]

This letter led to a meeting between professors and trustees. President Penrose reported that the faculty "proposed and cheerfully accepted a salary cut of twenty percent . . . not because they thought it was either desirable or just but because they saw it was necessary if the college was to be maintained." Apparently all groups agreed with Penrose's new assertion that, "No institution can long continue unless it can balance its budget."[35]

From 1931 through 1937 the professors would have twenty percent of their salary held back, but they would receive five percent interest on this money. During these years their payments included limited amounts of cash and notes. In December 1936 the college owed the faculty $42,300, including $2,700 to Professor Haigh and $3,100 to Professor Bratton. Records indicate that Chester and Elnora Maxey were fortunate enough to receive salaries, not notes.[36]

Maxey presented a fuller account of the agreement to reduce faculty salaries by twenty percent. He described a meeting where two trustees and the faculty committee discussed the salary crisis. The political scientist thought that his colleagues should have "forced an immediate showdown and possibly a liquidation of enough of the assets of the college to pay all the arrears." But insisting that they could not make "immediate payment of salaries in arrears," trustees promised to pay all current salaries in full if the teachers agreed to a twenty-percent pay cut. The trustees agreed to "give any faculty member requesting it a promissory note for all or any part of his unpaid salary."[37] According to Maxey, the trustees subsequently violated this agreement, because they made "no effort whatever to raise money for current salaries," and they even tried "to discourage the taking of notes for unpaid salaries." So the meeting accomplished very little: the faculty accepted a twenty-percent salary reduction, endured the frustration of irregular payments, and continued their complaints about a five-year delay in overdue salaries. It would take several years before the trustees fully paid current and past salaries.

Whitman professors knew that the faculty situations at the University of Washington and Washington State College were also grim. In 1932 and 1933 budget cuts meant slashes in faculty salaries similar to those at Whitman. But the state institutions, unlike Whitman, did not fail to meet payrolls. On the other hand, both of the state schools reduced their faculties, thereby increasing class sizes; fortunately, the private school did not resort to such a stern measure.

In December 1932 the Whitman faculty requested that the trustees supply information about the endowment, indebtedness, income, and their actions to meet the deficit.[38] This letter brought a written response from treasurer Dorsey Hill and an oral one from Stephen Penrose.

Penrose had been personally affected by the economic crisis. He had turned over his 1931–1932 salary to the faculty, borrowed $1,500 for personal expenses, resigned his membership in Rotary and all clubs requiring membership fees, and cancelled his traditional summer vacation. Early in 1933 he addressed the dispirited faculty about the financial crisis and admitted that the professors should have been more fully informed. He frankly confessed that the college was "in the clutch of a desperate financial situation, for which no one is responsible, and from which there does not seem to be any present likelihood of immediate escape." The institution's financial paralysis resulted, he explained, from its inability to collect student tuition or money on farm mortgages and from its payment on dormitory bonds. These conditions forced the school to cut faculty salaries and to delay payments to local merchants. Until the price of wheat increased, the president feared, the college would continue to be "involved in this great disaster."[39]

Professors heard little that was new in this section of their leader's address, and took more interest in his explanation of what the administration had done to alleviate economic pain. In the depression's early years it raised about $70,000 for current operations, but in 1932 "the springs of plenty . . . dried up." The alumni, struggling with their own financial predicaments, turned deaf ears to the college's solicitations. Although Penrose did not relate this information to his audience, he became so discouraged about the alumni's inability to contribute that he considered resigning.[40]

The president did tell the faculty that he had contemplated going east to seek donations but that the Carnegie Corporation had dissuaded him, predicting that he would fail as had the numerous other beleaguered college presidents knocking on doors in New York City. Because of this situation, the overseers instructed the president and the trustees to seek funds in Walla Walla. But this effort soon failed, Penrose explained, because "money has practically retired from current business," and he reminded his listeners that local physicians even accepted vegetables as payment. The most encouragement the president could give his rapt audience was the news that the trustees had recently defaulted on the dormitory bonds, which meant that money could be switched from bondholders to professors.

At this point the president summarized and evaluated the three options that the trustees had considered. They could temporarily close the college, dismiss all the professors, and reopen it when prosperity returned, saving the college but hurting its prestige. Second, the trustees could dismiss all lower-ranking professors and thereby cut the curriculum, although such a measure would be cruel to younger teachers, and the reduction of classes would make it difficult to recruit freshmen. Third, the school could continue its arduous struggle, requiring the faculty to continue its financial sacrifice. The trustees easily selected this third option.

Penrose informed the faculty that he had again considered resigning because it might help Whitman overcome the arduous economic struggle. But he rejected the idea because such action would be interpreted "in the light of the saying that 'rats desert a sinking ship.'" He was uncertain whether the faculty agreed with his interpretation, but he informed them that the trustees thought that his resignation would "be an unfortunate blow to the college." If he were replaced, the school would have to spend more money on administration (including an expensive fund raiser) and on a philosophy teacher.

Penrose made some interesting economic points. The school's sluggish growth during the past two decades had resulted from its inability to find a major donor, but it would not collapse, because it had about $2,000,000 in assets. The speaker reminded his listeners that the college had survived other economic crises, and he promised that salaries would be paid, but he could not predict when.

He concluded by offering advice: the faculty should maintain a positive attitude, which would impress students and townspeople. He feared that Walla Wallans who believed that the college would collapse were hearing it from the lips of discouraged professors. Penrose reasoned that any individual who actually anticipated the school's collapse should have already resigned.

The president acknowledged that the school's enrollment in 1933 was about twenty percent below the 1931 figure, but he assured his solemn audience that students would be attracted by stimulating teaching. He advised everyone to help with the institutional plans for the 1936 centennial celebration of the Whitman family's arrival in the region. Such action would demonstrate confidence: "I believe that evidences of looking ahead on the part of the faculty will constitute a very effective antidote to the wide spread belief that we are defeated and about to quit."[41]

Unfortunately, little is known about the faculty's response to this address. Most professors must have anticipated that the trustees would continue to operate the college and that their own sacrifices must continue. They fully agreed with Penrose that "even a poor position is better than none at all."[42] But a member of the modern languages department resigned, anticipating reductions in the teaching staff and in salaries, and reasoning that his department could accommodate his departure and he could save Penrose the embarrassment of cutting his position. To reduce costs, the trustees terminated assistant athletic coach Roger Folgate, but the president confided to his successor that the real reason for this action was the coach's exclusive interest in track.

In May 1933 Penrose assured professors that their salaries would not be reduced. The next month he announced that he would resign at the next commencement. According to Maxey, the faculty forced his resignation. The deans—Maxey, along with Haigh and Bratton—had met and sent a statement to the trustees "saying in effect that we would not continue in the service of the college if . . . Penrose's retirement were not forthcoming in the near future." The department heads also signed the letter, which was, Maxey said, an ultimatum, "which simply stated that if Dr. Penrose's resignation were not promptly obtained, the entire faculty would resign in a body. This was no idle threat, because the total amount of unpaid faculty salaries was so great that a mass resignation of the faculty could have thrown the college into bankruptcy."[43] Fredric Santler remembered the situation differently. He recalled that about twenty faculty members supported the petition to ask for Penrose's resignation and that some students, prompted by faculty members, allied with them.[44] Although no evidence exists, the trustees probably informed Penrose of the deans' ultimatum, convincing him to take the step he had so long considered. In any event, the boards now accepted his resignation and chose to celebrate both his long service and the college's seventy-fifth anniversary in 1934.

Thus, the faculty took action against Stephen Penrose, as it had against Alexander Jay Anderson and James Eaton and as it would against Rudolf Clemen just a few years later; of the first five presidents of Whitman College, only Walter Bratton did not have his colleagues request his resignation. Maxey did not publicize the faculty's action against Penrose, but he bluntly described the college's financial difficulties. He wrote that 1934 "may well decide whether it is to survive or go under. The buffetings of the depression have left the college in a desperate financial situation." The resulting debt could be ruinous because, "The faculty have reached the limit of their ability to carry the college, and so have the merchants and bankers. Forced liquidation can scarcely be avoided if substantial relief cannot be secured."[45]

President Penrose's last year brought the faculty no economic relief; in fact, he lamented to old friends that by borrowing from professors "without their consent we tide the institution along" and that they struggled to "pay their grocery bills."[46] The trustees gave the faculty notes drawing six-percent interest instead of salary payments, and, as Professor Santler would later recall in his 1984 Founder's Day address, the method of payment was unusual. The treasurer occasionally came to his office and revealed, "There's a little check upstairs. Don't tell anybody." The board awarded Santler a small salary increase to $1,200 a year, denied French professor Louis Curcio's request for an increase of his $500 salary, and informed the faculty that the whole question of salaries would be delayed until Clemen became president.

According to young professor Harris, the faculty respected but disliked Penrose. Undoubtedly the majority, discouraged with conditions, welcomed a presidential change. Professors had chatted with Clemen during campus interviews, and, like other groups, they thought he would be an excellent leader because he had been a professor, college president, and businessman. After his appointment, Clemen wanted to send a message to the faculty, but Penrose dissuaded him: "Whatever you say will be listened to attentively and criticized keenly. The academic mind is exceedingly quick to raise objections, to find flaws, and to misinterpret."[47]

Nevertheless, Clemen's first months in office pleased the faculty, especially when he paid them ten percent of their back salary. Maxey recalled: "One of the first, and best things President Clemen did was to force the trustees and overseers to cease defaulting faculty salaries and to start making payments on arrears."[48] The new president told board members that it was wrong to default on these salaries, and he convinced them to default again on the building bonds and to refinance them. Maxey and an unknown number of his colleagues applauded Clemen's expenditures for the repair of the buildings and grounds, but some must have insisted, as they had in 1930, that improved salaries should rank higher than maintenance projects. A majority supported Clemen's removal of the five-hundred-student limit on the basis that more students would increase the school's income.

In August Clemen boasted to overseers that his actions had improved faculty morale, which had been low when he arrived. Some professors had their loads reduced, and he added four local experts—who received no compensation—to teach such courses as journalism, business law, and sex education, which would, he stated, appeal to "a lot of grateful parents."[49] More important, he appointed a few new men to the faculty, including Dr. Peter F. Palmer in economics. Clemen explained why Palmer appealed to him: "I think it more important to have a sound economist than a brilliant one . . . [who] may change the way of economic thinking for generations to come, but . . . may decidedly upset the generation at present." Palmer's salary was in part funded by the reduction in Professor Eli Allen's teaching load and pay, which occurred when Biblical literature was made an elective. Clemen made another deal with Professor Howard Brode and his son Malcolm, who had taught biology at Beloit before returning to Walla Walla. Commenting that Malcolm "prefers this part of the country to live in, indeed, he has a rather unusual affection for this region, something not common in America," Clemen persuaded the Brodes to share a low salary, which strengthened the biology department for less money. The president joked of his deals that he could "be accused of a certain amount of horse trading."[50]

For years, some faculty members associated the Clemen administration with Dr. John Dale Russell's careful study of the college. Russell had interviewed professors, but his final report received a limited circulation; most members of the faculty heard only parts of it, unofficially from Maxey or officially from Clemen. Nevertheless, as Maxey asserted: "Measured by long-range results, this report marks the beginning of a new era at Whitman."[51]

Russell's assessment of the curriculum must have stirred faculty controversy. He concluded that, by offering fifteen different majors, the school wrongly emphasized specialization. To meet this problem, he recommended the combination of departments; for example, history, political science, economics, and business should be combined into a department of social studies; and French, German, and Spanish could be made into a department of modern foreign languages. Russell further asserted that many departments offered too many courses. "It is . . . astounding to find that the college has apparently made no effort in these [past five years of financial stress] to reduce the total offerings of courses and, in fact, has even been extending its offerings."[52] He generalized: "It seems to be the universal experience of American colleges of liberal arts that the course offerings, unless carefully controlled, tend always to expand faster than the resources of the institution."

The investigator made some controversial comments about faculty rank and pay. He pointed out that fifteen of Whitman's thirty-four teachers enjoyed the rank of full professor and advised: "A more economical organization may be obtained by a less generous use of the rank of full professor." The educator also recommended that each addition to the top rank of faculty should possess a doctorate.

Russell found inequalities in teaching loads; some professors had many more students than others. Philosophy, history, and political science were especially popular, while there were low enrollments in sociology, Latin, Greek, and physics. He reminded administrators that nationally a standard load was twelve hours, a standard that the college routinely ignored. The evaluator also believed that there should be no faculty additions until the student body was increased in size.

While professors argued over the recommendations about professional rank, class size, and departments, they also disputed Russell's assertion that Whitman had employed "more faculty members than has been absolutely necessary, and as a result the average salary has been lower than it might otherwise have been." His view countered the faculty's and Penrose's argument that a lower student-faculty ratio would enhance learning. But all teachers would applaud some of Russell's generalizations: "A superior faculty can be assembled only when adequate salaries are paid"; and, "The basic salaries of faculty members . . . are considerably below the average for institutions of similar rank." Russell asserted that a professor's salary should be based on two considerations: "his scholarliness and

ability as a teacher [and] the demand for similarly qualified persons."
He praised the college for paying teachers according to their worth
rather than attempting "to develop a uniform salary scale." But Russell opposed a faculty committee that was studying salaries because
of its bias, writing, "If there is inequality and injustice in the present assignment of salaries, that is a matter with which the administration of the college should deal."[53]

Russell endorsed the retirement plan, urged more teachers to be
enrolled, thought that the retirement age should be set at sixty-five
years of age (he noted that several Whitman faculty members were
older than that), and recommended that two persons from the same
family should not be employed as administrators and teachers. The
administration agreed with Russell and soon set the retirement age
at sixty-five with employment after that on a yearly basis, but the
college continued to employ multiple members of the same family.

Although some aspects of the Russell report irritated faculty
members, the actions of President Clemen were much more trou-
blesome. He displayed decreasing interest in faculty prerogatives.
Professors had enjoyed Penrose's deference to them in curriculum
matters and teaching assignments. Maxey judged that he had "never
known a president . . . who defended [faculty] freedom more val-
iantly," and Russell Blankenship wrote that he enjoyed teaching
under Penrose because of "the absolute freedom that you give your
faculty."[54] Clemen, however, made sweeping curriculum and personnel changes and proposed others, violating the faculty's traditional prerogatives, and riling the mild-mannered Frank Haigh. At
a faculty meeting Clemen announced that he would arrange departments into divisions—a plan advocated in the Russell report—
whether his listeners liked it or not. In a voice that sounded, Professor Santler recalled, like it came "from the bowels of the earth,"
Haigh bluntly informed the president: "I challenge your authority."[55]
The dean's courage won his colleagues' lasting admiration.

Although Maxey felt that most professors accepted the president's
leadership, the faculty played a secondary but significant role in forcing Clemen's resignation. The political scientist explained that department heads met at his house and considered "some sort of action for the protection of the faculty." This group unanimously
favored a resignation because, Maxey explained, "It was not so

much that we had grievances against Clemen and wanted to get rid of him as we felt sure, if he were restored to office, the fight would go on, maybe for years, and we would be its helpless victims."[56]

With Bratton as president, the faculty had as a leader someone who had suffered extended economic hardship along with them. Just prior to accepting the presidency, he had joined his colleagues in reminding the trustees that faculty members were creditors of the college and should receive their back salaries and restoration of the salary schedule that existed prior to the twenty-percent reduction of 1932. Soon after assuming the presidency, Bratton announced that an overseer committee would consider a plan to meet these faculty requests. He emphasized the need to resolve these problems, for with its low pay scale the school could not retain professors, expect them to maintain high standards, or compete for young teachers. The president noted that other colleges were increasing their salaries; Whitman must do the same.

In 1937 he informed the overseers: "The greatest need of the college has to do with salaries of the faculty." He reminded them that professors had not received restoration of any part of the twenty-percent pay cut and that this worked a continuing hardship on older individuals. Faculty members rejoiced when Bratton wrote, in words reminiscent of Stephen Penrose, that their salaries had "priority over much needed repairs to foundations, roofs, floors, and painting. . . . It is my own belief that the foundation of values which the college presents is to be found in the quality of its faculty rather than in the excellence of its buildings, grounds, or equipment."[57] In 1938 Bratton pleased his weary colleagues by reporting that a local committee had raised or borrowed money to pay them their unpaid salaries, but some expressed dismay that the president solicited them to donate a large part of this money to a debt-lifting fund.[58] For years professors would have to be satisfied with kind words, rather than receiving adequate pay. Bursar Marquis joined others in praising "a faculty that never faltered in unselfish and unwavering devotion [to the college] in its time of financial trial."[59]

Thus, starting in the late 1930s, the faculty received its pay on time, with small increases. The salary of chemist Frank Haigh, for example, had been slashed by twenty percent to $2,400 in 1932; by 1941 it had been gradually increased to $3,000. In other words,

The social science faculty in 1939 included Reginald Green, Chester Maxey, Melvin Jacobs, and Goldie Taggart. Standing are Paul Glick, Charles Howard, and Lyman Bothwell.

Haigh earned the same salary in 1941 that he had made ten years earlier.[60] In 1942, fearing that low salaries made Whitman uncompetitive in attracting "teachers of the required caliber," Bratton must have alarmed unsympathetic board members by proposing that the college temporarily resort to unbalanced budgets.[61]

While the faculty's financial hardship gradually eased, teaching loads for some professors, especially those in the increasingly popular social sciences, remained arduous. A 1937 study found that, in one semester, historian Jacobs taught five semester classes with 205 students, economist Green taught four classes with 148 students, and political scientist Maxey taught four classes with 128 students.

In 1939 Maxey reported that half the student body majored in social sciences, and noted that this led to two significant problems for his division: overwhelming teaching loads and the employment of some inadequate professors. He frankly stated that the two men in economics carried heavy burdens, adding, "They are not the best men obtainable but they are probably the best we can get for the money paid." In history, the dean summarized, "One part of the teaching is well done, and part of it is poorly done."[62] To strengthen his division, Maxey proposed that seven new social scientists be hired between 1939 and 1943.

Members of Whitman's faculty desiring time for research or a sabbatical program remained frustrated; working conditions in all the divisions improved only marginally. The science faculty contended with inadequate equipment and Billings Hall's miserable physical conditions, but in 1940 teaching conditions improved with remodeling of the building. Professors must have envied their colleagues at Willamette University, who enjoyed a new library completed in 1938, and a new science hall finished three years later.

Reforms, Recognitions, Retirements, and Replacements

Although the faculty labored under extremely difficult working conditions, it consistently sought to make educational improvements by reorganizations or reforms. Faculty members met twice a month, discussing routine administrative matters at one meeting and pedagogy, curriculum, and other relevant issues at the other. Discussions became more heated when they debated changes. For example, in 1926 the faculty—with student support—terminated the ten-year-old honor grading system because it had been abused. Students would neither report nor punish cheaters. In 1928, concluding that an experimental term system fragmented subject matter, left scant time for student research or reflection, and required too few thorough final examinations, the faculty narrowly voted a return to the semester system.[63] As president, Penrose did not dominate the faculty in curricular matters: in 1928 he made sweeping proposals that it rejected as being too expensive and too time-consuming.

Professors voted in 1930 to give only the Bachelor of Arts degree, dropping the Bachelor of Science degree. They next removed the Latin requirement for graduation, causing Latin enrollments to plummet. Although the faculty required two years of a foreign language, some graduates evaded the requirement. In 1931 professors renumbered classes to clarify the sequential arrangement of departmental courses; and in 1933 they changed the grading system from numerical grades to letter grades: "A" through "D," "F," and "I" (for incomplete). In an attempt to curb grade inflation, they recommended that departments not award more than fifty percent of their grades at the "A"and "B" levels. The faculty placed students on probation or dropped them for failing to earn a minimum number of "C" or better grades. In the continuing quest to improve the grading system, teachers debated moving to a simple pass-fail system. According to the *Pioneer* of January 11, 1935, Maxey advocated abolishing all grades and credits, but Bratton defended the letter-grade system because of its national usage. The various academic departments frequently altered the format of senior comprehensive examinations, but each required an oral part. In 1933 a few departments worked out arrangements to have outside professors submit written questions, but this attempted reform proved to be unwieldy.

The faculty agreed with Penrose that Whitman sought to be "a first class college of pure science and liberal arts carrying out the New England idea of education in the far Northwest."[64] They opposed becoming a university that would offer practical courses or

The humanities faculty in 1939 included Fredric Santler, Edith Davis, William Davis, Paule Ravasse, and Melvin Jacobs. Standing are Thomas Howells, John Ackley, Paul Jackson, Procope Costas, Douglas McClane, and William Hart. (Historian Jacobs was pictured with both the social sciences and the humanities.)

graduate degrees. The Master of Arts degree could be obtained by those preparing for secondary teaching and "in a few departments whose teaching staff and equipment warrant."[65] Proposals for degrees in engineering and forestry had died long ago, when the plans for "Greater Whitman" went into the dustbin. Penrose explained the school's limited mission: "This is a cultural college, which does not undertake to prepare its students for definite lines of life work immediately, except in the field of teaching, where many of our graduates find it practically valuable if they can teach for a few years."[66]

While the faculty recognized the need to prepare teachers— women were especially encouraged to take education courses— Whitman offered a bare-bones education curriculum, seeking only to meet the state's requirements for high school teachers. But even this limited operation proved to be a problem, because of misunderstandings with the state board of education and because Whitman employed only Charles W. Howard in its department of education and psychology. Howard offered a vast array of subjects; for example, in the fall of 1936 he taught 103 students in seven different classes. Two years later Dean Maxey admitted that the department was so weak that he advised students seeking a psychology major to transfer.[67]

The faculty spent more time evaluating the roles of intramural and intercollegiate sports than it did in overseeing the teacher certification program. In 1933 a faculty committee asserted that Whitman "did not go to the extreme of abandoning intercollegiate athletics," but maintained a harmonious relationship between intramural and intercollegiate sports. It also praised Nig Borleske, an alumnus "whose sane loyalty to the educational ideals has kept [the college] free from the degenerative influences often found in intercollegiate athletics."[68] In 1940, after an unsuccessful season and a student argument that football lost money that could be used for better purposes, the faculty participated with other groups in a discussion about dropping intercollegiate football. The discussion resulted in a better game schedule and more efficient recruitment of players.[69]

Despite the faculty's displeasure with some of Clemen's attitudes and actions, it welcomed his administrative reorganization, which included a faculty dean and three divisional deans, positions found on most campuses. First, in a popular move, he appointed Bratton

The science faculty in 1939 included Louise Pope, Frank Haigh, Arthur Rempel, and Carroll Zimmerman. Standing are Philip Pope, Alfred Lange, and Leo Humphrey.

as dean of the college, arguing that this was a critical position. Next, working with a faculty committee, Clemen led a reorganization based upon the curriculum. (The new president disliked his predecessor's unique organization, which had divided the faculty not into academic divisions but into three groups, each with its specific area of administrative responsibility: academic, internal life, and external relations.) The three new divisions—replacing the old groups—were social sciences, letters and arts, and sciences. Each division was led by a dean, and these deans joined with the president, the dean of faculty, and the dean of women—as well as, later, the dean of men—to form the board of deans. Maxey, who served as dean of the division of social sciences, described his duties: to preside at divisional faculty meetings; to participate in matters of appointments, promotions, and salaries; to advise all freshmen interested in a major within the division; and to serve on the academic committee.

In the fall of 1934 the faculty assigned its members into ranks: professors, associate professors, assistant professors, and instructors.[70] The lowest rank could attend faculty meetings but could not vote. Oddly, Stephen Penrose, who had built the college and who taught a full load of classes in his retirement, received only the rank of instructor, with its limited authority. Penrose also soon discovered that Clemen did not want his advice; thus, within months, the most influential person on campus had quickly become one of the least powerful.

Another new administrative position, the dean of men, was established in 1938. Chemist Leo Humphrey, who had served on several committees working with college men, received the appointment, requiring him to expand the administration's contacts with men. His administrative duties reduced his work in the chemistry department, a fact that upset his fellow chemist, Dean Frank Haigh. Humphrey was remembered by Lawrence P. Murphy as "a patient instructor who was . . . interested in his students. I appreciated his many kindness as dean of men . . . [to] a bewildered freshman."[71]

An important addition to the staff in 1931 was alumnus Douglas McClane. Over time, he held various positions, including secretary of the faculty, registrar, instructor in business English, and director of admissions. Two women received appointments to positions that would strengthen the college: Ruth Reynolds became head librarian in 1932, and Elnora Maxey, the wife of Chester Maxey, became the director of the Glee Club in 1937.

When Bratton became president, he made new appointments in the Conservatory of Music because, he explained, it had suffered "most severely during the depression. Music lessons were regarded as a luxury . . . with consequent serious lowering of income to the conservatory teachers and to the college." The conservatory had also lost momentum in 1936 with the extended illness and death of Howard Pratt, who received Bratton's praise for his talent and "rich personality."[72] Esther Bienfang, who taught piano and music theory, filled in for Pratt and then won appointment as director in 1937. Despite her numerous duties and competence, she held only the rank of instructor.

But far more important to President Bratton than staff changes in the conservatory were other transitions in the college's faculty. In 1940 he noted that veteran professors, who had established Whitman's "truly great reputation," had either retired or reduced their teaching loads, but they had been "succeeded by a fine group of young teachers who seem willing and able to maintain the highest

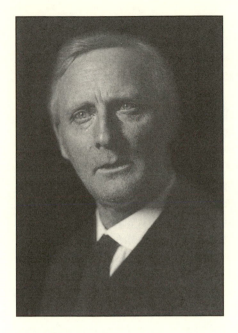

Considered by many Whitman alumni to have been the college's greatest teacher, Benjamin Brown taught a variety of science classes and led popular bicycle field trips. Suffering from poor health and personal problems, and worried about his teaching effectiveness, Brown resigned in 1930, but returned to the classroom a few years later.

standards."[73] Among the important retirements were professors Benjamin Brown (1930 and 1936), Walter Eells (1927), Edward Ruby (1931), Russell Blankenship (1933), Howard Brode (1935), William Bleakney (1939), and Stephen Penrose (1941). Retirements of long-time faculty members were important and emotional occasions. A banquet, oral and published tributes, gifts, and a book of letters from alumni and friends were traditional parts of the celebration.

While each of these retirements weakened the institution, the loss of three professors—Brown, Brode, and Blankenship—seemed particularly significant. The highly respected Benjamin Brown first sought to resign in 1926, after thirty-one years of devoted teaching. In a letter of resignation, the physicist explained that he had remained at the college because his wife enjoyed her Walla Walla friends. After his wife's death and his own illness, Brown had decided that he should leave. He also told then-president Penrose that he wanted to resign because of conflict with a colleague over the conduct of the physics department, because of his lack of respect for the college trustees, and because his "interest in Whitman has grown less and less and less." He further warned that he was "failing in mental acumen," a condition that had resulted from long hours over many years of service.[74] Penrose tried to change Brown's mind: "I am dismayed and disheartened by your letter, and hope that you will not consider it a final . . . determination. You are the most distinguished teacher whom Whitman College has had, and are in the full tide of a career of usefulness and splendid service, unexampled in American college life. I take more pride in your work and influence than anything else connected with the institution."[75] Penrose added that he expected the trustees to grant the faculty a pay increase. In seeking a pension for the sixty-one-year-old Brown, Penrose wrote: "He is an extraordinarily able teacher, having developed the Department of Physics by a real genius for devising and making apparatus, and inspiring his students with a genuine scientific spirit."[76] Additional attempts to placate Brown failed; early in 1926 he insisted that he be allowed to retire after commencement. The president advised the professor to remain in harness because he would soon receive a salary increase and because he was ineligible for a Carnegie pension until he was sixty-five. Brown compromised by reducing his teaching load: he would no longer teach physics, but he would offer annually one course in geology and another in astronomy. The professor frankly informed the president that he was not "holding up the standard of the past."[77] In 1930 ill health forced his retirement, but a few years later he returned to the classroom.

Howard Brode, one of the earliest Ph.D.s on the faculty, had built the biology program into one of the most popular departments. In 1929 half the student body of about five hundred took biology classes. Brode also developed the college museum and served the community by lecturing to farmers about new advances in biology, and he "pioneered in instituting country and school visiting nurses and full-time health officers."[78] Maxey, who had been a student of the skilled biologist, praised Brode for making certain "that his students were thoroughly instructed in the Darwinian theory of evolution."[79]

Although he had served a much shorter tenure than the two scientists, Russell Blankenship's departure also jolted the college community. After teaching civics at Walla Walla High School, he had joined the Whitman faculty in 1923. A skilled teacher, Blankenship earned an advanced degree and published a respected book. He resigned in 1933, and then began a distinguished career at the University of Washington, which he described to Penrose as "certainly

*One of the fine professors who made Whit-
man's reputation in science, Howard Brode
took a keen interest in building the college's
museum. Some made much of the fact that
the diligent and well-respected Brode, one
of the few faculty members of the time to
hold a Ph.D., was the father of triplets, each
of whom also earned a doctorate in science.*

the largest industrial plant I ever saw. Huge crowds are run through
certain processes that may or may not be educational."[80]

In addition to the loss of these able men, others limited their
teaching. Professor Eli Allen in Biblical literature taught fewer classes after his subject became an elective rather than a requirement.
In 1932 professor of English William Davis, an able teacher and administrator, had his teaching load reduced and was given work recruiting in the high schools after being severely injured.

Despite these changes, the reputation of the faculty was maintained by the hiring of some able teachers, including Chester Maxey
(1925) in political science, Melvin Jacobs (1926) in history, Fredric
Santler (1932) in German, Paul Jackson (1935) and Thomas Howells
(1938) in English, and Arthur Rempel (1938) in biology. Two women,
Yvonne Ravasse (1924) and her sister Paule (1930) in French, up-
graded the modern languages department.

An interesting aspect of the faculty story was the brief return of
a few professors' children, who taught during the Great Depression.
Virginia Penrose and her brother, Binks, taught for meager salaries.
She taught French and the history of art and assisted her father; Binks
Penrose, who had earned a Ph.D., offered a variety of courses, in-

cluding a philosophy course with his father. His wife, Margaret, was hired to teach Spanish. Dr. Malcolm Brode taught with his father in the biology department. However, these temporary additions did not provide much relief for the overburdened faculty.

Despite enormous demands on their time, remoteness from research libraries, and the lack of a sabbatical program, faculty members kept abreast of their fields by personal study, and a few even found the energy to publish. The school's most notable authors were Walter Eells in education, Chester Maxey in political science, and Russell Blankenship in literature. In 1931 Blankenship published *American Literature as an Expression of the National Mind*, and won a favorable review from the famous critic, H. L. Mencken, who called Whitman a "modest filling-station . . . in far-away Walla Walla" and praised Blankenship as an "enlightened man" who intelligently discussed "the racial make-up of the American people and the influence of the national geography upon them."[81]

While professors spent long hours laboring in their demanding positions, they also maintained families. Information on these families is limited, but some patterns of their lives can be summarized. Because of their small incomes, most of them lived restricted lives. During the Great Depression they requested credit at grocery stores, medical offices, and department stores. Faculty wives rarely worked to supplement their families' incomes, but they supported and sympathized with each other as they encountered difficulties in their family lives. Chester and Elnora Maxey lived better than most of their colleagues because both enjoyed employment, and because he earned good royalties from his political science books. The Bratton family provided room and board for Whitman students in return for domestic services.

Newcomers to the teaching staff learned from the veterans that, although the school was non-sectarian, the faculty "felt strongly the responsibility for guiding the moral and spiritual life of its students."[82] While some professors, such as Chester Maxey, were distant and reserved, others, such as the Penroses, Brodes, Popes, and Davises, brought colleagues into their homes. Faculty friendships often had a divisional basis: Professor Rempel recalled that the scientists generally met together socially. But there was no faculty lounge or club providing opportunities for divisional conversation, and apparently only President Clemen arranged faculty luncheons.

Occasionally, professors taught summer school in western institutions; more frequently they studied at home or at a major library. Whitman did not offer a summer program, but faculty members preferred to eke out a living on low salaries rather than take part-time jobs. There is little evidence that professors in the 1930s—other than Fredric Santler—worked in the canneries during the summer as their successors would in the years after the Second World War. The professors tried to maintain the dignity of a respected profession.

Some faculty families, following a summertime Walla Walla custom of escaping the heat of the valley floor, moved into small cabins on Mill Creek; a few packed camping gear and took automobile vacations. During the Great Depression seven faculty members somehow found the money to attend the Chicago World's Fair; about sixteen male students saved on transportation to the fair by riding sheep trains.[83]

The Walla Walla community knew and recognized the importance of the faculty from newspaper articles and from their participation in churches and various social groups. Townspeople heard Penrose and others state that the teachers endured a hand-to-mouth existence, and they consistently offered kindness and friendship. In the mid-1930s appreciative local families, responding to the appeal of the Chamber of Commerce, donated money for faculty salaries. Meanwhile, faculty families found ways to cope with low and infrequent payments. Jake Jacobs, the son of Whitman historian Melvin Jacobs, recalled that four professors hunted jackrabbits; he explained: "During those times we used to bring one home and mother would cook it because there wasn't too much meat on the table."[84] Several faculty families raised and canned fruits and vegetables. Chemist Frank Haigh formulated his own wintergreen shaving cream in his laboratory.[85]

Perhaps Maxey was correct in his assessment that the Whitman faculty of his student days, from 1908 to 1912, was stronger than that of the period from 1925 to 1942. If so, it was probably owing to the fact that an aging faculty wore down under persistent adversity. The earlier faculty was young and optimistic; the later one feared an old age without economic resources. But even if the faculty had declined in quality, it still remained Whitman's greatest strength.

5

Students in the Age of Hardship
1925–1942

Students attended Whitman for a variety of reasons, including its reputation, academic offerings, scholarship program, athletics, and music; some came because of the influence of parents and alumni, or as the result of contact with admissions recruiters; some attended because of the school's location (a factor important to townspeople); and some came because of the opportunities for employment in Walla Walla while attending college. Although many men and women selected the college without ever encountering its recruiters, the school thought it necessary to keep at least one such individual in the field seeking capable students, especially men. In the late 1920s Whitman's registrar, Edward Ruby, traveled across the Pacific Northwest, arriving at high schools or homes in an inexpensive, college-owned 1929 Ford.

Before the Great Depression reduced enrollment, the college annually sought a freshman class of two hundred, including a minimum of sixty women and 110 men from out of town and thirty Walla Wallans. Ruby reported that it was extremely difficult to recruit men; in 1925 he joked that he was "stalking them first in gum shoes and then . . . dragging them in by the hair."[1] In his experience, men had greater financial needs than women; furthermore, the 1928 increase in tuition to $200 a year—making Whitman the region's most expensive college—required a greater recruiting effort to fill the male quota.

In presenting Whitman's advantages, recruiters boasted about an unusually selective admission policy, a studious and cohesive student body, a small freshmen enrollment in "bonehead" English, and a limited academic probation list.[2] They also emphasized that those who wanted to live in the West should be educated in the region, that the college offered opportunities to lead, and that the University of Washington—a major competitor—was too impersonal and enrolled too many fun-seekers. Surprisingly, during the Great Depression, Whitman recruiter Douglas McClane reported far more applicants than in the 1920s; unfortunately, the college lacked the money to assist many worthy high school graduates.

In the mid-1920s Whitman abandoned the attractive merit scholarship program that rewarded high school valedictorians, salutatorians, and other scholars. Apparently this decision resulted largely from the perception that high school principals improperly awarded these merit scholarships. Stephen Penrose, who had come to favor need-based scholarships over ones based on merit, bristled: "We do not want this to be thought of as a college for rich men's sons and daughters, and [we] take pride in the large number of students who are earning their own way through college."[3] Recruiter Ruby disagreed with Penrose, arguing that the school had never completely abandoned its merit scholarship program, that these awards enhanced Whitman's reputation, and that principals had chosen capable seniors who went on to compile solid college records.

In 1928—and throughout the Great Depression—the college community, including students, debated the issue of need-based or merit-based scholarships. According to catalogs published in the late 1920s, the school offered honor scholarships only to those applicants providing "satisfactory evidence of financial need," but the college actually considered the applicant's character and promise.[4] The number of freshman scholarships jumped from twenty in 1927 to sixty the following year, because of higher tuition fees.[5] To retain a scholarship the recipient had to maintain an eighty-point scholastic average (on a hundred-point scale) and had to be free from "expensive habits."[6] In some years, only freshmen were eligible for scholarships, because the college could not fund others.

College leaders also wrestled with the tuition remission program. Some families who could afford most of the $200 tuition—if not all of it—nevertheless requested a remission. Because Whitman could ill afford the reputation of being an "easy mark," its recruiters and scholarship committee spent many hours making crucial decisions about who deserved a remission and in what amount.[7]

In 1929 the college sharply revised its scholarship policy. A college committee, accepting the individuals recommended by Ruby, awarded twenty-two honor scholarships and gave remission of tuition (apparently based on need) ranging from $25 to $100 a semester to nineteen others. The committee also awarded full or partial scholarships to thirteen men recommended by Coach Nig Borleske. The committee gave scholarships in other categories to fifteen men and nineteen women currently enrolled, and to seven faculty children. The total number of scholarship holders was ninety-eight men and forty-six women; thus, nearly twenty-five percent of the student body received scholarships, costing the college about $14,300.[8]

To meet the crisis of the Great Depression, Whitman again revised its scholarship program. Instead of reducing the $200 tuition, the college searched for students able to pay it; at the same time it sought to help the majority who could not. In a worsening economy, the catalog explained the new assistance programs: Whitman in 1933 awarded honor scholarships worth $200 "to one graduate each year from each of the leading Pacific Northwest high schools."[9] A high school principal would submit the names of three outstanding seniors, and the college would select the winners. The college also established a program it called "grants": the "Freshman Fund" provided partial tuition remission to deserving freshmen; more advanced students were eligible for a remission based on need; and the school offered loans to upperclassmen.

This grant program underwent modifications after the college, in the early 1930s, had to reject dozens of capable applicants who were unable to finance their freshmen year.[10] Thus, the 1937 catalog presented a revamped program, listing four methods for helping students to afford the cost of a college education: employment, assistance from the National Youth Administration, the Freshman Fund and scholarships, and loans. In 1937 high school seniors in Seattle became more aware of these methods when recruiter McClane established an office in their city, one which would operate for years.

Freshmen receiving honor scholarships paid no tuition the first semester, and none the second if their first-semester scholastic average equaled the average for all students.[11] After completing the freshman year, students often inquired into Whitman's loan policy. For decades, the college had been loaning money at low interest to students; Penrose encouraged them to borrow about $200 annually "rather than to devote a disproportionate amount of time earning one's way."[12] Students heard him and their advisors say that it was better to borrow and enjoy college life than to work long hours and be unable to participate in the extracurricular activities.

Upperclassmen found it difficult to win scholarships because the college preferred that they take out loans. Penrose explained that "the indiscreet granting of scholarship aid is apt to develop in the student the idea that the world owes him a living, or that he can obtain something for which he has not worked. We think it wiser to develop the ambition to be self-supporting."[13] Applicants for loans found that, to encourage them to make prompt payments, they must pay four-percent interest; the school sought to encourage them further by informing them that those who had borrowed from the college in earlier years had rarely defaulted. Many young people declined loans because they did not want to mortgage their futures, preferring to work longer hours to cover college bills. Some dropped out because of an unwillingness to borrow. Bernard Peach said that his mother's Scottish beliefs held that borrowing was "basically sinful"; thus, he left after his freshman year.[14]

In 1939 the college launched a pre-professional scholarship program. Each year, ten men or women who aimed to enter a profession such as law, medicine, education, or public service would receive a $500 scholarship to cover the full cost of the first year's tuition; these students would receive $100 towards tuition charges for the next three years, which helped to retain them.

Even before the economic crisis of the 1930s, about eighty percent of the men and about fifty percent of the women needed jobs to pay for their education; in 1931 nearly ninety percent of the men and sixty percent of the women were in that situation. Penrose spoke for his colleagues when he evaluated these figures: "Perhaps one reason for the earnestness and faithfulness of Whitman students is their poverty. . . . They cannot afford to be foolish or extravagant."[15]

The economic crisis did not fully strike students until the 1930–1931 school year; job-seekers seemed successful prior to that year. Margo Collins Hoth remembered graduating in 1930, when students could pay their bills: "Everything was hunky-dory."[16] But after graduating she experienced frustration in seeking a job.

Soon after arrival in Walla Walla, the majority of students sought jobs on or off the campus. Searching for work was nearly as important as registering for classes. Herbert Armstrong chose Whitman over Washington State College because Walla Walla provided more job opportunities, and it was impossible to find work in "a little town [with] a big campus."[17] William Harris stated that he chose Whitman "not necessarily for its academic excellence. It was the opportunity to get employment."[18] He calculated that it would be unwise to attend Oregon State College because it would be hard to find a job in Corvallis. In 1936 freshman John Richards arrived in town in the afternoon, dashed to campus for a job lead, and began washing dishes at the Book Nook that very day.

Numerous Whitmanites worked downtown or in neighborhoods, but, in the depths of the Great Depression, townspeople could not employ as many. Al Ullman arose daily at 2:30 AM to clean a confectionary shop until 7:00 AM.[19] Bernard Peach, like other collegians, arose at 5:00 AM to fire neighborhood furnaces; once he caught a cold in freezing weather, and the college nurse confined him to the Lyman House infirmary.[20] Men washed windows and performed yardwork in exchange for room and board. Women worked downtown as waitresses and secretaries, and in private homes as cooks and baby-sitters. There was no stigma associated with working. Margo Collins Hoth, who did not need a job, remembered that she had believed that there "but for the grace of God go I."[21] A 1935 *Pioneer* editorial, "Children of the Depression," identified students "with serious faces and lean pocket books and the willingness to tackle any kind of a job that pays money." These individuals became valuable members of the student body, and Whitman was deemed "outstanding for its generous efforts in aiding students to find employment and for its kindly avoidance of any social discrimination between those who work and those who do not."[22]

The college employed job-seekers as student assistants, as library and office workers, as groundskeepers, as waiters and kitchen helpers in the dormitories, and as temporary laborers. Some of these positions were taxing: freshman Tom McNeill, for example, peeled two hundred pounds of potatoes at Lyman House every morning.[23] After

1930 Whitman replaced janitors and other employees with eager college men, including Jim Beer, whose job paid half of his tuition.

Prior to the New Deal programs, Whitman struggled to find work for needy students. Education professor Charles Howard, who had charge of the student employment service, appealed to Walla Wallans through the radio, the newspaper, and service clubs, urging them to hire collegians. The request brought some success, but many unemployed young people had to return home. Soon, however, New Deal programs provided funds for students to work on campus. In the spring and fall semesters of 1934 Professor Howard coordinated student work under the program of the Federal Emergency Relief Administration (FERA). In both semesters, Howard assigned Whitman's quota of fifty jobs to needy applicants who worked on the grounds, in the library, and in the various academic departments. Both men and women received these positions, earning a maximum of thirty-five cents per hour and up to twenty dollars a month.[24]

The National Youth Administration (NYA), enacted in 1935, had a greater impact on the campus than the FERA did, because it lasted longer. Designed to keep young people in school, the NYA was successful in doing so at Whitman. To receive this federal assistance, applicants had to demonstrate need, scholarship, and character. The school's quota of positions depended upon its enrollment. For example, in 1935 it offered sixty-five jobs with the same income limits as those imposed by the FERA. Most recipients worked on campus, but others labored in off-campus jobs, with the Boy Scouts, the Girl Scouts, the YMCA, the YWCA, and the public schools.[25] In 1936 the *Pioneer* stated that "one out of every eight students draw monthly pay checks financed by the NYA," and praised the government for developing "its richest resource, youth."[26]

With the local economy improving, the 1935 catalog carried an optimistic message: Walla Wallans wanted to aid Whitmanites; there were "relatively numerous opportunities for student employment"; and the proximity of the college to the city meant that employees did not waste time getting to jobs.[27]

Students struggling with college debts consulted with bursar George Marquis. Remembered as a somewhat brusque individual or as a cowboy philosopher, he had a local reputation as a western novelist enjoying a large British audience (many members of the Whit-

Bursar George Marquis, who in his official duties both received student's payments and helped those struggling with financial hardship, was noted on campus as a storyteller and as an author of cowboy novels.

man community knew his character Bat Jennison). Marquis sympathized with hardship cases and frequently found scholarships, loans, or jobs—many of them off campus—for women and men. He won a reputation for being the man who not only collected college bills but also found ways to pay them, including the arrangement of small loans from Mrs. Penrose. The bursar personally sized up those asking for financial help; he did not require detailed information about a family's financial status. He even allowed students to register for a second semester when they could not put money down.[28] Many left the college owing what seemed to be large debts, but Marquis usually got his money without writing dunning letters. However, not everyone received help. A few students ran afoul of the marriage rule that was not repealed until 1948: "If a student marries while an undergraduate he thereby severs his connection with the college."[29] When Janette Moses Armstrong, a senior who had recently married without seeking the required permission from the college, asked for a renewal of financial help, Marquis bluntly responded, "No, we're not going to help you. . . . Why don't you ask your father?" She also remembered that President Walter Bratton's negative criticism contributed to her decision to leave the college. Her husband had graduated from Whitman, but following this brutal denial she left after "three wonderful years."[30]

Sometimes students worked too many hours, and their grades or social life suffered. William Harris worked thirty-five hours a week as a doorman in local theaters, which limited his time for school activities.[31] Herbert Armstrong admitted that "I cheated myself out of a lot of things just working."[32] John Richards worked downtown, played in a dance band, and enjoyed an NYA job on campus. In his sophomore year, he took French and German classes, failing them both because he lacked time to study. He received a letter from the college suggesting that he "rusticate" for a semester.[33] Richards heartily approved of the college's suggestion and sat out a semester, living in Professor Howard's home and continuing to direct the college band.

The Physical Environment

New students soon became familiar with the compact campus, and, like upperclassmen, they sometimes described a need for landscaping and building repairs. But, in a time of economic hardship, they did not concern themselves very much with these matters, although they agreed with President Rudolf Clemen that the library shack, the wooden building abutting the west side of Memorial Hall, was an inconvenient eyesore. Iris Little Myers recalled: "It's just unbelievable to think of the library being housed in a place like that."[34] Others agreed, stating that they found it crowded, poorly lit, and highly flammable. One wag called the building "a replica of Marcus Whitman's original home."[35] Moving the library into Reynolds Hall improved conditions greatly. In both buildings, library patrons praised the efficiency and the discipline of librarian Ruth Reynolds. Frankie Ladley Wakefield recalled that: "When you went there to study you studied. . . . You wouldn't whisper or talk." She added, however, that Whitmanites often made dates at the library.

Women and men were enthusiastic about the new dormitories; the accommodations and furnishings were as good as or better than the homes that some students had grown up in. Science majors—

On the following pages is a student's-eye-view of Whitman, drawn in 1931 by Dorothy Robinson. The original is in color.

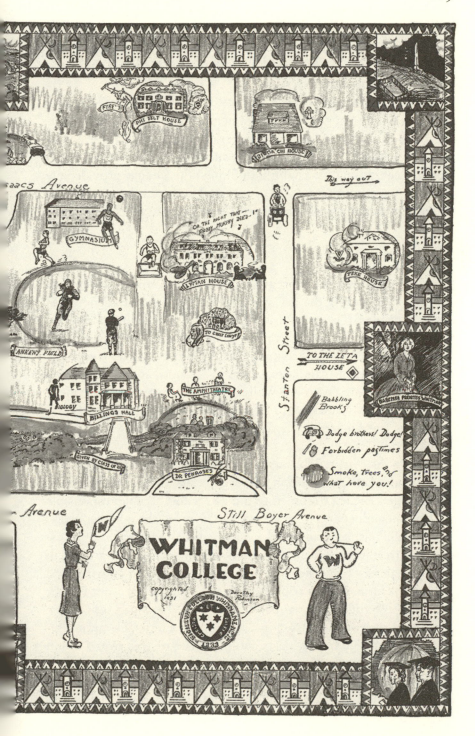

influenced, in part, by the faculty—grumbled about the inadequacies of Billings Hall, but they appreciated that most offices and classrooms were conveniently located in Memorial Hall and thus provided opportunities to socialize.

The bridges across College Creek—the one in front of Prentiss Hall was fondly known as "Last-Clinch Bridge"[36]—and the amphitheater were favorite campus features. Workmen from the Works Progress Administration enlarged the amphitheater for the 1936 centennial celebration of the Whitman family; this change provided attractive space for community events and college celebrations, including the May Fete and graduation ceremonies.

Academics

Over the years Whitman's regulations and procedures have often changed, but, during the last years of the Penrose presidency, tradition prevailed. The orientation program, for example, remained fairly consistent. For five days prior to the college's opening, the administration scheduled "Freshman Days," a time when newcomers registered and learned about regulations, customs, and traditions. At one point, Penrose described Walla Walla as an appropriate college site because of its "quietness . . . its aloofness from main lines of travel, and its freedom from the distractions which the big city offers to modern youth."[37]

During the orientation, freshmen took a written English examination; those failing enrolled in a remedial class at their own expense. The college assigned freshmen to a dean, who "became responsible for [their] conduct and improvement."[38] During the opening week, Walla Walla businessmen furnished about fifty automobiles to transport the freshmen to Waiilatpu (the Whitman Mission grounds), where Penrose or another speaker told the story of Marcus and Narcissa Whitman. This trip was called a "pilgrimage" until 1934, when it was termed an "excursion." A faculty-freshman supper, the pre-school rush week (started in 1935), and the annual sophomore-freshman "grudge battle," especially the tug-of-war over Lakum Duckum, excited participants and the whole college community.

The college's liberal arts curriculum provided "a broad general culture."[39] To achieve this goal, students had to take "definitely prescribed" courses, a major field, and electives. For many years, freshmen enrolled in either a year-long or semester course entitled "College Life," a class in public speaking, and a year of physical education. Prior to graduation, students took assigned work in English, Biblical literature, philosophy, foreign language, and laboratory science. To acquire a broad and meaningful education, the faculty required them to complete seventeen hours in each of the three divisions: philosophy and social sciences, language and literature, and mathematics and science.

For many years freshmen and sophomores engaged in tugs-of-war over Lakum Duckum. Fraternity men also dunked their pledges, a practice called "laking."

During the second semester, the freshman chose one of the fifteen majors and became an advisee of his or her major professor. Underclassmen expressed their career goals to their advisors, who often responded that they should not restrict themselves to a particular objective. While advising remained constant, President Clemen, who opposed requirements, reduced them by changing to electives all of Penrose's courses in education and philosophy, as well as Eli Allen's Biblical literature course. But he and the faculty added a required hygiene class for freshmen (taught by local physicians providing "indispensable information as to individual health and salutary social relations"[40]), instituted a traditional orientation program into the English survey courses, and greatly modified the foreign language requirement so that some students could omit it. Another change reduced the requirement for hours that majors must complete within their division by the end of their sophomore year from seventeen to fourteen. Clemen, influenced by the Russell report, also introduced a general major requiring fifty hours completed in one division; this major was discontinued when Clemen departed.

Catalogs listing courses and instructors simply could not convey the quality of the school's liberal arts curriculum, the best measure of which comes from alumni reflecting back upon their experiences as students. Most of them would agree with a *Pioneer* editorial that described Whitman as being "a college of great ideals and great personalities."[41]

Over sixty alumni interviewed in the college's oral history project have expressed their opinions about the teaching ability of the faculty serving between 1925 and 1942. They prefer to relate their happy experiences with their professors rather than to criticize them for uninspired teaching, but mild criticism was aimed at some of the older members of the faculty, who, wearied by their heavy work loads, had lost their effectiveness. Alumni frequently praised the entire group and acknowledged Penrose's ability to hire so many excellent professors. In 1938 William O. Douglas applauded the Whitman faculty for emphasizing teaching rather than research. He stated that, "Whitman gave us the best teaching I have either experienced or observed anywhere."[42] Dwelley Jones noted that many members of the faculty were "approaching their seventies, but they were . . . inspirational teachers."[43] Ken Garner agreed, noting their experience and dedication, and the respect with which they were regarded by students.[44] Herbert Armstrong recalled that "the faculty were delightful people."[45] Frankie Ladley Wakefield concluded: "One of the great things about Whitman [was] the teachers." Professors encouraged students "to do independent thinking, not just to learn what was in the books . . . and repeat it back in an exam."[46] Jake Jacobs deemed that the excellent Whitman education "prepared you for anything."[47]

Many alumni remembered Stephen Penrose better than any of their other professors, because he taught as many as four required courses, serving both as Whitman's chief professor and as its chief administrator. Hundreds of students found his education and philosophy courses fascinating and challenging. Penrose's required year-long freshman course called "College Life" originated from his conviction that he must prepare students for a four-year intellectual feast. Concluding that the Pacific Northwest's high schools improperly prepared students, the educator based his freshman course on the proposition that those seated in front of him needed to learn "the art of study." Like his colleagues, he readily accepted the responsibility "for helping freshmen to get on their feet intellectually."[48]

The president emphasized that he did not conduct orientation courses designed to "give the freshman a bird's eye view of the universe in order that they may be ready at once to attack any problem they may meet in college."[49] Rather, Penrose considered his lectures to be more practical. His wide-ranging approach stressed the dedication and accomplishments of Marcus and Narcissa Whitman; the history of higher education, and especially Whitman's place in it; the societal obligations of educated people; the contributions of music and art; the techniques of reading a book and studying; and even fatherhood and motherhood. He addressed the men on fatherhood, while his wife spoke to the women on motherhood. Mary Penrose's talk included instruction about proper dress—she explained that the color red excited men—and the need to wear a hat and gloves when going downtown. This advice proved embarrassing to Alice Hogue True, who had brought "a new five-piece dark red suit just for college."[50] Iris Little Myers remembered that Mrs. Penrose "touched upon the subject of sex in the delicate but . . . practical fashion of an era just emerging from the Victorian age." Her impeccable standards meant that coeds long remembered the momentous day when Mrs. Penrose had her hair bobbed by the barber at Shepherd's Smoke Shop.[51]

Juniors enrolled in the president's required philosophy courses—"The Problems of Philosophy" and "Comparative Religions"—and in both courses they heard lectures on ethics and morality, and a challenge to conservative religion. Graduates of the class recalled that Stephen Penrose taught a scholarly type of comparative religion, in contradiction to what they had heard at home. Speaking for many alumni, Almira Quinn remembered that Penrose "talked about the great religions, and our minds were broadened with new concepts and ideas."[52] Students admired his intellect and character, and as alumni they still held him in high regard, agreeing with Dorothy Robinson West that he gave "Whitman its fine name."[53] William Harris described him as "just head and shoulders above anything that any of us had ever experienced in our lives."[54] One alumna remembered that she successfully petitioned to be excused from Penrose's philosophy classes and then regretted her action because she could not talk with classmates who were enthusiastic about this course when she was twenty, and she remained unable to talk about it with alumni sixty years later.

But not everyone, of course, appreciated these required classes, which included material that would be published in Penrose's book, *Philosophy for Lowbrows By One of Them.* A few students played bridge during class, using hand signals to bid. Occasionally students slipped out of the classroom; alerted to this situation, Mary Penrose confronted the class and scolded it for taking advantage of a blind man. A junior, Clyde Bridger, complained to Penrose about his lecture method and his harsh grading. The professor responded that most students appreciated his teaching, and proposed a solution to the charge of unfair grading: "I invite you to join with me in asking a committee of three good students from the class to mark your papers henceforth."[55]

Scores of alumni recalled their walks with Penrose, which were so popular that frequently students had to schedule them. Walking about three miles along different routes with students—freshmen in particular—provided Penrose an opportunity to discover what was happening on a city block (he always amazed walkers by pointing out the trees, gardens, and buildings that they passed), and to learn something about his companion. Many related that their stimulating conversations about religion and philosophy added to their education. One reported afternoon walk started with a conversation about baseball as the pair left the campus and concluded with philosophy. The president revealed to Helen Barrett Woodroofe that, "When I get to heaven, I'm going to spend the first one thousand years studying mathematics."[56] Joe Davis wrote that Penrose gently challenged young walkers, even deliberately disagreeing with them, in order to make them defend their views.[57]

Students also came to the Penrose home and read to him. He asked them to help him keep up with current events by reading stories in the *New York Times*, the *Christian Science Monitor*, the *Atlantic Monthly*, and weekly magazines. Mary Johnson Koch struggled to read Aristotle and scholarly periodicals to him, and wondered "if he wasn't trying to broaden my mind."[58] Students living in the Penrose household read about two hours a day to the educator, who sometimes wore a smoking jacket and smoked a pipe or a cigar.

Many alumni recalled being invited to the Penrose home for dinner and being served artichokes. Dorothy Robinson West had a typical experience. "We were served artichokes, and I had never seen an artichoke before. I just watched what Mrs. Penrose did . . . so I ate my artichoke in this way."[59] Apparently the hostess wanted young people to know how to eat this vegetable so that they would not be embarrassed when they encountered it elsewhere.

Although Penrose was clearly the most remembered professor, he was certainly not the only effective one. Alumni also stressed the skill of his colleagues, especially those most important to them; they fondly remembered professors of both sexes, of various ages, and of diverse personalities.

In the social sciences, the towering figure was Chester Maxey. From the time he arrived in 1925, the political scientist enjoyed a reputation for being well-informed and challenging. Alumni remembered assignments from his required textbooks, but most emphasized his factual and interpretive lectures. Ken Garner, one of Maxey's first political science majors, praised him for his effective teaching of international law and constitutional law.[60] Iris Little Myers stated that she was the only woman in her class to major in political science and that Maxey's courses provided excellent background for her career in journalism.[61] Ralph Edgerton, who praised Maxey for being able to integrate current politics into his well-organized lectures, was one of several lawyers and judges who emphasized that the professor's courses were of great value.[62] Richard Eells said that Maxey's political philosophy course was superior to his constitutional law course. Although Eells noted that the professor "didn't light up the classroom with electric vibrations . . . the same way as others," he concluded that Maxey had a great influence on him after graduation, for he used the political scientist's writings in his own books.[63] Lucile Lomen praised his clear lectures, but noted that "he was a little distant until you graduated."[64]

Historian Melvin Jacobs, who shared Penrose's interest in Pacific Northwest history, was lively and scholarly. Students enjoyed his lectures on such divergent subjects as Henry VIII and art history. As a result of deafness his voice became soft, and his classes strained to hear him. As an adviser, Jacobs told one coed: "Majoring in history . . . doesn't prepare [you] for anything specific. [You] can take a civil service exam . . . and get a good job that way. . . . That's a good thing for girls to do."[65] An ordained Presbyterian minister, Jacobs preached in Umapine, Oregon, while lecturing at Whitman.

Fondly identified as a campus character, Professor Reginald Green taught accounting, marketing, and other subjects. One alumna recalled him as being "distinctive in that he was sort of like Ichabod Crane. He was tall and his hair kind of stood up."[66] Bert Edwards said that Green was popular and demonstrated great powers of concentration.[67] Merlin Young said that the lanky professor read as he strode across the campus and sometimes fell or ran into something.[68]

Some students most remembered the English department's professors. Professor William R. Davis uniformly received high praise for his teaching, his love of Whitman, and his interest in students. Herbert Armstrong concluded: "I adored Dean Davis. He was absolutely out of this world."[69] Almira Quinn stated that Davis taught a wonderful Shakespeare class and that she consulted his notes while teaching high school.[70] Dorothy Robinson West recalled that she told him that after graduation she would be married and raise a family. Davis responded: "No, not today in this day and age. You must use your education for practical reasons. You must be able to earn a

William and Edith Davis were popular and effective professors; both taught at Whitman for more than a quarter of a century.

livelihood."[71] His wife, Edith Davis, taught a required freshman course in public speaking and directed the school's plays. One observer thought that Mrs. Davis carried a very heavy load "because she was teaching English and drama and doing all the theater stuff and making the costumes, and raising four children, one of whom was disabled."[72] Rodney Alexander agreed with this assessment, and added: "A funnier woman never lived, and she was so helpful."[73]

During Professor Russell Blankenship's ten years at Whitman he made a tremendous impact in the English department. One student recalled that he sat on a front table and talked; a "demonstrative person," he acted out his presentation.[74] Another student recollected that he "fearlessly recommended" frank novels and made sure that the library allowed them to circulate.[75]

The foreign languages included a variety of strong teachers. Hattie Gordon Fry called Professor Edward Ruby "a great Latin teacher"; another alumna rated him "the best teacher that I have ever had,"[76] and added that students enjoyed being with him while "Mother Ruby" served them a Sunday supper. Recent additions to the department attracted considerable attention. Yvonne and Paule Ravasse were vital French teachers who seemed always to be teaching whether they were in the classroom or not; Ruth Baker Kimball was amused by the inability of the sisters "to pronounce the English language" and their objections "if you didn't pronounce French properly."[77] Paule Ravasse earned a B.A. at Whitman while teaching French.

German professor Fredric Santler was one of the college's most remarkable teachers. A native of Austria, he came to Whitman as a student, joined Sigma Chi, received a B.A. in 1941, and won a reputation for vitality. Students discovered that he could be diverted from German instruction and could speak meaningfully about music, history, Europe, and American slang.

Another teacher, Procope S. Costas, also brought his European background into the classroom. A stylish and lively classics professor, he lectured on his native Greece, attracted impressive enrollments, denounced the Nazis, and disagreed with Santler over the merits of German civilization.

The most influential professor in mathematics and science was Walter Bratton. Zelma Conway Williams observed that, "Bratton obviously loved his students, and he was loved by them."[78] They appreciated the mathematician's gentle manners, his optimism, and his ability to explain his subject. Although he was later busy as dean and then president, there was no diminution of his teaching ability.

In the 1930s the college educated the public through its museum, managed by Howard Brode. The biologist collected and displayed a variety of historical and scientific materials. School children, teachers, scholars, and others observed Indian artifacts, historical documents, old coins, and many other items. Unfortunately, Brode's recommendation that "someone trained in museum work" and able to teach either anthropology or geology should be employed to expand and protect the college's valuable collections was not heeded.[79]

Distinguished physics professor Benjamin Brown, whom Penrose identified as the school's most outstanding professor, sometimes taught astronomy and geology. His field trips combined fun and education. Margo Collins Hoth declared: "Everybody just revered him. He was wonderful. I . . . took one course, astronomy, from him because it meant that we would go out in the evening with boys and we could study the stars, and [also] get a taste of what Brown was."[80] Geology students remembered his Columbia River field trips, in which he discussed rock layers and provided doughnuts. William

Kelly recalled that Brown "possessed a great ability to communicate with his audience, both with facial expressions and words of wisdom . . . his humor, his honesty, his humility, and his warm earnest smile could disarm even the most doubtful and hostile student." He did not need to use theatrics in his "spellbinding" classes.[81]

In the late 1930s the physics department returned to the prominence it had enjoyed under Brown in the 1920s. Professor Ivar Highberg graduated from Whitman in 1932 and returned in 1936 with a Ph.D. earned at the California Institute of Technology. Professor Carroll Zimmerman joined the physics department the following year. Both scholars enjoyed solid teaching reputations. Ash O'Donnell declared that Highberg "was the theoretical physicist. He emphasized the abstract, mathematical side of physics." Zimmerman "loved to get in the lab, set up the experiments, and improvise to prove a certain principle."[82]

Chemist Frank Haigh's outstanding reputation came from his organized presentation of his material and his concern for students. One of his majors recalled that the county paid Haigh to analyze confiscated liquor and concluded that "most of the liquors that were causing people to have hallucinations . . . were caused by dirty stills. . . . They got some of the metallic stuff in their system. It was not poor alcohol."[83]

Student's appreciated Frank Haigh's dedicated teaching and his concern for their progress. The faculty appreciated his advocacy of improved professional conditions, and expressed great enthusiasm when the college awarded Haigh an honorary doctorate.

Dr. Philip Pope and his wife, Louise Pope, taught in the biology department. He offered the more advanced courses because he lacked the outgoing disposition of his wife. Many students met the science requirements by taking one of Mrs. Pope's classes. Both biologists took a great interest in students: besides leading specimen-gathering field trips to the mountains, coast, and desert, they hosted picnics for those who did not participate in Greek rush, and held other get-togethers in their home.

The conservatory professors also enjoyed solid reputations, especially the directors. Georgia Mae Wilkins Gallivan praised Howard Pratt for his "boundless energy."[84] Russ McNeill remembered him as being a disciplinarian, but one with a good sense of humor.[85] After Pratt's death in 1936, Esther Bienfang, who had a delightful personality and enjoyed a warm relationship with everyone, directed the conservatory and taught piano.

The college hired Paul Jackson, Leon Ellis, Thomas Howells, John Ackley, and Arthur Rempel in the 1930s, professors who students rightly believed would continue the school's remarkable teaching tradition. Their careers would help shape the institution.

Conservatory director Howard Pratt joined with President Penrose to establish the popular choral contest in 1926. Music teacher Esther Bienfang became the director after Pratt's death.

Whitman students have long been encouraged to mix academic activities with non-academic ones. One good example was Gordon Wright, who was class valedictorian and a member of Phi Beta Kappa, as well as being student body president, a member of Tau Kappa Epsilon, a campus journalist, and a varsity tennis player. He became a professor of history at Stanford and served as president of the American Historical Association.

Evaluating the Students

Whitmanites, of course, evaluated each other. Students often got acquainted on their long train rides from Seattle or Portland to Walla Walla. Their singing and noise making (sometimes as a result of beer drinking) occasionally upset the conductors. They recognized that most of their classmates had done well in high school and that many had chosen Whitman in preparation for professional careers. Looking back, alumni often stressed the motivation and competence of their classmates; for example, Tom McNeill recalled: "Everybody I knew seemed to work like the devil. . . . Hangers-on didn't last. They just flunked out. Many times the load was too much. You couldn't do it all, so you just had to let something go." He stressed the ability of his fraternity brother, Gordon Wright, to concentrate: "Everybody could be just raising hell around him in the room and he would be there studying."[86] Although Wright was exceptional, students generally took their classes seriously. Bernard Peach's assessment coincided with other recollections—"Nearly everybody was a reasonably serious student"—but he also told of a friend who did not want grades so high that he would not be allowed to sit by his girl at graduation.[87] Betty "Bunt" Johnson wrote her mother: "For once in my life I really like my studies and I do hope I get some good grades . . . but gosh—its hard to settle down 'cause everything is so much fun."[88] Some alumni conceded that they only studied enough to pass; a smattering admitted that Greek life was more important than their classwork.

But the faculty made the most crucial evaluation of students. Most classes required solid work and gave students a demanding final examination week with numerous traditional and inexpensive bluebooks. Probably most professors reasoned that the examinations were, as Penrose advocated, "a useful preparation for the tests of life." He informed a student that, "Not less but more examinations, longer, harder, more searching, is what I would recommend as one of the remedies for the carelessness, slackness, and acknowledged inefficiency of some high school students."[89] If Penrose spoke for the professors, then surely Ruth McBirney responded for most students. In the middle of final examinations, she wrote her parents: "I wanna go home! I am tired of taking tests. I feel as if I had been run through a grist mill."[90]

Until it adopted the letter-grade system, the college published semester grades in what students called "The Scandal Sheet." The record included the number grade for each class; the total of all classes was divided to give an overall average. According to Lola Sims Snyder, the fact that the grades were published meant that everyone knew who was failing, and this information was a basis for both reflection and conversation.[91] The published grades demonstrated that a "C" level was often awarded, that grading was uniform across the divisions, and that many Greek pledges could not earn the required "C+" average.

Seniors often dreaded the comprehensive major examinations, calling them "orgies of torture" or worse, and alumni long remembered the oral component. Many found it unnerving to sit before three professors who questioned them over their major fields. Almira Quinn recalled her nervousness, her examiners, and that a concerned professor searched for her afterwards to tell her that she had passed. Quinn said that one of her classmates fainted in front of her startled committee.[92] Bert Edwards recalled that the questions asked of him were fair and made him think.[93]

Professors believed that they had a responsibility to help the students succeed; at the same time, they accepted the college's high attrition rate. The typical freshman class numbered two hundred, and the senior class counted around ninety. Penrose explained these figures: the school had high standards that prevented "poorly prepared and unambitious boys" from graduating.[94] During the Great Depression, senior classes shrunk to as few as sixty-seven members (in 1934), a result of students being unable to pay bills, not of their inability to pass examinations.

Chapel

Penrose and the faculty long believed that required chapel had educational and social benefits. In the 1920s chapel monitors took roll at the daily thirty-minute chapels. Three chapels were religious services; the other two were under the control of the students, who scheduled speakers and musicians. The religious chapels often featured a short sermon by Eli Allen, professor of Biblical literature, and various musical numbers. Some students enjoyed Allen's accounts of his missionary work in Persia, but, of course, many grumbled about the requirement. Penrose explained that he supported a required religious service because it helped counter "the excessive individualism of our American life [that] has brought about the disintegration of family religion."[95]

School leaders scheduled many interesting chapel speakers, especially representatives of the various professions and national dignitaries such as historian William Durant, but both Penrose and the students in charge of the programs had difficulty finding twenty speakers a month. The president complained that, because the college was not on a transcontinental railway, it was difficult to secure lecturers and musicians.[96] In 1928 he contemplated bringing the leader of an anti-narcotics group as a chapel speaker but rejected the opportunity, explaining: "I talked with a number of thoughtful men about it and they all agreed that it would be wiser not to put into the heads of young people . . . ideas which might culminate in the desire to experiment with the drugs whose influence was described as so harmful." He thought mature people "might react sanely" to information about drugs but feared that "boys and girls are apt to have the spirit of wanting to try everything once and when they learn about things which are said to be dreadful in their consequence they do not have the sense to let them alone."[97] But Penrose applauded

Dr. Eugene Swan's chapel address on sex and social hygiene, because of both its practical content and the speaker's "charm, delicacy, and impressiveness."[98]

In 1926 Penrose assured a fellow college president that Whitman was "not suffering from any rebelliousness against chapel."[99] But student pranks in chapel, including alarm clocks and other distractions, were undermining this long-standing requirement. Tom McNeill recounted an occasion when some men who had timed the services caused a phonograph record to render the song, "Yes Sir, That's My Baby, No, Sir, I Don't Mean Maybe," just as Professor Allen started his sermon; the audience roared, and Allen hollered, "Amen." Wearied with these pranks, which he called "childish exhibitions," Penrose easily convinced the faculty to require only a weekly one-hour chapel that combined a religious observance and a student body meeting. (The *Pioneer* had editorialized: "Where are the faculty members at chapel time five days of each week? Certainly a very small percent are at chapel for the rows of benches on the platform are usually nearly vacant.")[100] Penrose admitted that the revision was necessary because the daily chapel was "often disorderly and a waste of time."[101]

Clemen terminated the required program altogether and permitted men and women to sit in the same section. Some alumni remembered that very few students attended the subsequent voluntary chapel, but Pete Hanson recalled that about fifty percent of the student body attended at the end of the 1930s.[102] Classmate Gordon Scribner agreed, stating that entertainment and student body business drew large numbers;[103] these meetings generally included a religious component, music, student and faculty speakers, fraternity skits, and other forms of entertainment.

Some students preferred to discuss religion in professor's homes rather than in a required chapel setting. One of the most interesting of these informal gatherings was hosted by Binks Penrose. Up to seventy-five Whitmanites came to his home on Sunday mornings to discuss his classes, religion, campus problems, and other topics. After the student-led discussion, many participants went to church. Professor Zimmerman carried on this Sunday program after Binks Penrose left.

In Loco Parentis

In 1930 Whitman advertised that it was "not a highbrow institu-tion," but one that maintained "a wholesome and well-balanced life in which the intellectual, the social, and the physical are equally en-couraged."[104] While the institution stressed academics, it also en-couraged students to participate in the social side of collegiate life. The faculty, acting like wise parents, realized that oppressive regu-lations would be ineffective. But, like parents, professors regulated the social lives of the young adults, especially the women. As Iris Lit-tle Myers declared, "You were looked after almost as carefully as you were at home."[105]

From campus publications and from faculty talks, students learned that a varied and rich social life would lead to long-lasting friendships, and these connections began in the dormitories. The small institution correctly described itself as a friendly college. Ruth McBirney's experience was typical: she had been on campus only a month when she observed that "one thing nice about Whitman, [is that] everyone speaks to everyone else."[106] Alumni fondly remem-bered the friendly atmosphere and treasured lifelong friendships.

To build loyalty to the institution and to establish meaningful friendships between freshmen, Whitman insisted that they all live in a dormitory, where, Penrose predicted, they would "wear off each other's corners."[107] Women were required to reside in Prentiss Hall, with sororities having their own sections and independent women having theirs; one of the positive results of this residence requirement was that occupants became well acquainted with both sorority women and independents. Although sorority rivalry added excite-ment in Prentiss, there was little snobbishness. Men also enjoyed equality; Tom McNeill stated that: "Everybody was in the same boat . . . trying to get along. I didn't ever run into anybody that tried to lord it over me because they had a little money."[108]

Newcomers in opening week heard not only that the campus was friendly, but also that Walla Wallans enjoyed Whitmanites and would make their acquaintance. Freshmen learned about traditions that ap-plied to them: for example, they could enter Memorial Hall only through the lower stairs, and "Girls [would] wear the traditional

green hair-ribbons, boys the green 'dinks' [beanies]"[109] until Homecoming, when the freshmen tossed these badges of low status into
the bonfire.

Rules, especially those regulating the dormitories, were more imposing than freshman traditions. The deans, assuming that most
freshmen men were mature, adopted a student self-government system in Lyman House. Its inhabitants generally responded well; Roger
Folgate and other Lyman managers tried to avoid being monitors.
But, of course, there were problems; for example, in 1927 Penrose
wrote that many parents complained to him and others about the
dormitory's disorder.[110]

While there was far more rowdiness in Lyman House than in
Prentiss Hall, the administration closely regulated Prentiss because
parents wanted their daughters to have a home-like atmosphere.
Rules for freshmen women came from upperclass women as well
as from the deans. Faculty committees, the three academic deans, the
dean of women, and coed leaders cooperated in establishing the
Women's Self-Governing (WSG) organization. The dean of women
explained that her role was "to keep an even norm between work
and play,"[111] and, with her assistance, upperclass women wrote rules
that applied to women during their college lives. Each coed received
a handbook, which often included Greek rush rules, the constitution
of the women's student organization, and a code of conduct.

In the 1920s the women's code advised that a "true Whitman
woman" would not loiter on street corners, eat on the streets, or
work or drive downtown alone at night. Furthermore, a woman
would be "very thoughtful and courteous to Mrs. Penrose, the Dean,
and Housemother" and would rise when any of these women entered the room. Students found that the rules shaped their lives.
Working with the authorities, the WSG took responsibility "for the
life and conduct" of Whitman women. The organization's executive board, made up of representatives from each section of Prentiss Hall, worked to regulate social life and promote scholarship.
Its rules required residents to be in their dormitory at 10:15 every
night, except Saturday when they might stay out until 11:45. Lights
had to be out at 10:30, but they could burn longer twelve times each
semester. To regulate social activities, there was a suggestion that
no Sunday picnics start until noon and a rule that dormitory women

must not attend public dances. But some individuals broke the rule and enjoyed the downtown dances at the Edgewater and other popular establishments.

An executive committee of the WSG, working with the dean of women, "campused" rule breakers, which meant that the woman must not leave the campus; moreover, on campus she could not attend a dance, have male callers, "or have any extended conversation with men."[112] (It was a tradition that a male responsible for his date being campused would send her a box of candy.) If the WSG could not curb a member's behavior, then the board of deans intervened. Georgia Mae Wilkins Gallivan and other "townies" escaped the rules; these local families would often have women into their homes overnight so that they could avoid the closing-hour rule.[113]

No doubt some of the women found the regulations somewhat confining. In December 1936 Prentiss Hall residents sang enthusiastically at dinner:

> Glory, Glory, and Salvation
> Sixteen days until Vacation
> When we leave the Whitman Station
> For the land of civilization.[114]

Over time the WSG changed, but its mission remained the same. Dormitory residents cooperated with the dean of women, the housemother, and the nurse living in Prentiss Hall to devise a system of governance. Many alumnae report that the women in these three positions eagerly enforced the rules. Margo Collins Hoth remembered that nurse Rachel Highley roomed near the carriage entrance and kept "track of everybody, and if you came in late, boy, she was right there. You got campused."[115] Highley had no power to discipline students, but Stephen Penrose explained that "she assumes a disciplinary attitude towards girls who do not fully live up to her standards."[116] Although most coeds accepted their situation in an age when their social life was closely monitored by their parents, almost everyone had an opinion about the rules regulating Whitman women. According to the *Waiilatpu*, the WSG leaders—sometimes called "tattle-tales" by critics—willingly punished rule breakers. Hoth judged that the rules "were not too oppressive," but some men thought that the rule makers sought to operate a cloister.[117] Every-

Although dean of women Thelma Mills had numerous and pressing responsibilities, she always had time for troubled students. Her concern for their wellbeing made her one of the most popular individuals ever to hold that difficult office.

one understood that Whitman was practicing *in loco parentis*; furthermore, they also knew that, through careful planning, Prentiss rules could be broken. The occupants and their male friends were aware that the lower windows permitted access after hours. Gordon Scribner, a student employed as a night watchman, later recalled boosting women through windows.[118]

On the other hand, the various deans of women were far more than disciplinarians and went beyond their official duties in dealing with students. Dean Thelma Mills, an athletic Scandinavian, even assisted a tardy girl through the window, mildly chided her, and sent the rule breaker to her bedroom.[119] John Richards recalled that Mills once asked him to escort a girl to a big dance because she had a limited social life. The dean bought the corsage and arranged for transportation.[120]

Men in Lyman House did not live under as strict a regimen as the women did in Prentiss Hall, but the campus community still scrutinized their behavior. President Penrose, for example, asked the tennis players to wear shirts.[121] The board of deans wrote rules for the dormitory against liquor, gambling, and disorderly conduct. In some years, the authorities required that beds and rooms had to be ready for a noon inspection. A resident professor or a manager maintained order and monitored quiet hours. Jasper Morrison served as manager for several years, while his wife operated the kitchen and acted as a housemother, providing "motherly care of the boys."[122] A professional checkers player, Morrison supported Whitman athletics, driving players to games on other campuses.

Regulation of students' automobiles began in 1932. Although only a few students had Fords or other small cars, the faculty concluded that it had to take action because the unrestricted use of automobiles detracted from academic work. Out-of-town students had to gain the permission of the board of deans before registering vehicles. Drivers with low grades or with a record of unsatisfactory conduct had to dispose of their vehicles. The *Pioneer*, reminding the deans that they lived in the automobile age, denounced the rules because they discriminated against out-of-town drivers, and because the "college fathers" must realize that the regulations would be ineffective, since "prodigal youth will fritter away so much of its time, vehicle or no vehicle."[123] Cars added to campus fun; Ed McMillan recalled: "Three of us had an old 1926 Chrysler roadster with a jump seat. We got our girlfriends to help finance the cost of a couple of tires and some gasoline, and we would go up to Kooskooskie and have picnics."[124]

Students' health was a greater concern than automobiles. A nurse examined those who claimed they were too ill to attend classes. One nurse observed that many girls reported an illness on Mondays, "most probably due to the heavy social program of the weekend."[125] The nurse also examined sick students in the various living groups when men or women were ill, and sometimes placed them in dormitory sick rooms or sent them to local hospitals.

During this period students suffered from several severe diseases. In 1926–1927 the nurse reported ten cases of the mumps and scores of students ill with influenza. In 1927 one student suffered from smallpox; county officials isolated him at the county farm and vaccinated the 116 residents of Lyman House.[126] For several years thereafter, the college required smallpox vaccinations, but the requirement ended when a few families objected.[127] In 1936, however, after a report of smallpox on the campus and in the area, college leaders cooperated with health officials in requiring inoculation: 512 students received vaccinations, and twenty-six others, who refused shots, were suspended from classes.[128]

Whitmanites wrote home about diseases, including mumps, influenza, and typhoid. The *Pioneer* reported on March 9, 1928, that, because of a mumps epidemic, the college physician had ordered all dances and other social functions postponed, and had turned Reynolds Hall into an infirmary for thirty-five patients. The women occupied the second floor and the men the third; recovered patients celebrated, played cards, and drew the envy of classmates. In April two men came down with typhoid; authorities unsuccessfully sought the cause of the disease.

The Greek System

The faculty and board members who had supported Penrose in the struggle to establish sororities and fraternities just prior to the First World War had reason to be pleased with their decision. These organizations assisted the faculty in advancing scholarship and provided a campus social life. Perhaps eighty percent of the students joined a sorority or fraternity, as V. Purdy Cornelison asserted, "because of the social life. There wasn't any place to go if you didn't belong. You had to be a real strong character to remain independent." [129] Some individuals, such as Lola Sims Snyder, did not become Greeks because of parental opposition or because of the costs. While independents enjoyed a small measure of campus social life, the very few married students had comparatively little.

The faculty insisted that the fraternities, like the sororities, also promote scholarship and exercise a degree of social control. Thus, many men and women recalled efforts to improve grades, including quiet hours, study tables, and a system whereby good students aided weaker ones. Vivian Cochran Garner remembered that there was "dead silence in [my] sorority's study hall." [130] The Greeks also taught social behavior, especially at dinner, and often forbade the consumption of alcoholic beverages in their section or house. Fraternity men punished members who made too much noise, and the older men talked with younger brothers about inappropriate class or campus behavior. At one time the Inter-Fraternity Council promoted the social graces by encouraging men to attend an afternoon tea with the dean of women.

The fraternities provided residences for non-freshmen men. Although students were hardly aware of it, the fraternity houses were serving Whitman's economic purpose by providing housing. Because of the operation of four or five fraternity houses, the college only needed to build a single male dormitory. College leaders well remembered their negative experience in housing upperclassmen in Billings Hall prior to the First World War. It was less expensive to administer a fraternity system than it was to operate dormitories like Lyman House; furthermore, the fraternities in the 1930s were more adept at controlling their members than the college had been at controlling the residents of Billings Hall.

The sororities, occupying sections of Prentiss Hall, also played crucial social and academic roles. The school tried to restrict all of the out-of-town women to Prentiss Hall or annexes (nearby residences, including the President's House during the Bratton presidency), and it rebuffed anyone asking for the installation of sorority houses. Most women enjoyed life in Prentiss Hall and did not request off-campus housing. Each sorority had its own section of Prentiss, and operated under both its own rules and those of the WSG. Sorority women, like fraternity men, enjoyed fireside gatherings, serenades, teas, dinners, and dances. Special dinners, a dress-up code, and singing made for a pleasant atmosphere that alumnae would remember with great fondness.

To provide a maximum number of students with opportunities for fraternal experiences, the school needed several Greek groups. In 1925 the school had three national fraternities—Phi Delta Theta, Beta Theta Pi, and Sigma Chi. It also had two local fraternities—Zeta Phi Epsilon and Alpha Omicron Kappa—which both came under pressure to acquire national affiliation. The national sororities were Phi Mu, Delta Gamma, Kappa Kappa Gamma, and Delta Delta Delta. Theta Chi Theta was a local. Although these Greek organizations were fairly stable, they underwent a few changes over the years. In 1928 Theta Chi Theta affiliated with Alpha Chi Omega; in 1931 Alpha Omicron Kappa—after unsuccessful negotiations with Sigma Alpha Epsilon—became Tau Kappa Epsilon. In 1933 Zeta Phi Epsilon, a local fraternity, disbanded, a victim of economic conditions. Three fraternities found homes along Isaacs Avenue: in 1927 Beta Theta Pi acquired the John Langdon House; in 1938 Sigma Chi constructed a house; and in 1941 Tau Kappa Epsilon purchased a house.

In 1930 the school welcomed the Phrateres (a national organization similar in many ways to a sorority) because the group admitted both sorority and non-sorority women. Ruth McBirney correctly summarized it as a club "for girls who don't want to, can't afford to, or just can't go into a sorority." The dean of women realized that every year some women failed to get into a sorority; thus —sometimes with the aid of the Phrateres—she held what one participant called "a consolation party" at the end of sorority rush.[131]

Some alumnae would long continue to feel uncomfortable with the fact that their sororities, which often chose pledges on the basis of popularity, caused pain and tears. An anonymous freshman published a biting account of the rush process, emphasizing the stress it placed on both the "prospects" and the sorority rushers. The prospect found, in every group, "the same pretty girls, the same rich foods, and the perfection in every detail." She added, "The sorority girls must be tired, terribly so, and yet they walk about in an animated manner, upon their high heels, upon their poor swelled feet, and smile their brilliant smiles."[132]

The Greeks dominated campus politics and intramural athletics, as well as social life. They competed for student body offices, leadership positions in various organizations, and editorships. Because student body officers enjoyed influence and prestige, heated elections for these positions featured orations, bands, posters, and fireworks. Coalitions of Greeks campaigned to win these spirited elections, and many participants evaluated the returns. An editor observed: "Holding grudges because someone double-crossed someone else, which is the usual talk after elections, will only show the smallness of the gripers."[133]

Intramural athletics attracted a large percentage of fraternity men; women competed also, but in fewer numbers. Students strove to win championships and trophies in football, tennis, baseball, basketball, track, and such minor sports as ping-pong and horseshoes. The football teams attracted nearly all of the fraternity men, and sometimes their spirited games resulted in injuries. Sometimes Coach Borleske scrimmaged these intramural teams with the varsity. Women competed in basketball, tennis, and field hockey—an activity, one onlooker noted, that "teaches some of the elements of the manly art of self-defense."[134]

The annual choral contest was an important tradition. In 1934 the trophy was won by the Beta Theta Pi chorus, led by voice instructor Elnora Maxey, center right.

Established in the mid-1920s, the choral contest for women's and men's groups was a major campus event, with considerable competition for the coveted cups and frequent complaints of unfair judging. The fraternity attracting Elnora Maxey's assistance usually won. At times, controversy arose over the great amount of time and effort required to prepare for the contest. But in an October 17, 1940, editorial, the *Pioneer* reminded the campus of the importance of the group singing tradition: "The choral contest . . . has always had splendid support from the student body and the townspeople."

The leading social activities sponsored by the Greeks, according to alumni, were their dances and parties. For example, in 1937 each organization held four dances, including a formal dinner dance. Every year, students busily engaged in preparing for dances because each group wanted the honor of hosting the best one. The student body association also sponsored dances, including the popular Saturday-night all-campus, no-date dances held in Prentiss Hall or the gymnasium. One of the popular bands in the 1930s was the Whitmaniacs, a group of college musicians.

In the mid-1920s the faculty, realizing that there was no way to prevent dancing, and acknowledging that dances provided exercise and entertainment, had voted to regulate them. While students were allowed to hold dances in town, President Penrose preferred gymnasium dances to dance halls where "there is no supervision and where individual impulses can run wild."[135] Thus, dance sponsors had to be concerned about scheduling, location (formal dances were held downtown), and chaperoning. A 1926 committee on social life ruled that informal dances must conclude at 10:00 PM and formal dances at 11:45 PM.[136] Over the years the rules became more liberal, but the question of expense remained. In an age of economic hardship, men found it expensive to cover the costs of formal dances —such as the Varsity Ball or the Miami Triad Ball—held at the Arcadia Ball Room or the Marcus Whitman Hotel. Tickets, corsages, rented tuxedos, and favors were expensive, but the *Pioneer* contended that popular, expensive formals could not be replaced by "spelling bees and taffy pulling for entertainment."[137]

The Greek system served to develop fellowship, social life, scholarship, and social control. Although the fraternities lacked housemothers, they did have faculty advisers, and they conformed fairly well to their own rules and those of the college. But there was a negative side. The houses sometimes allowed their scholarship to lag, and they overemphasized athletics and activities. To improve scholarship, the college in 1931 established a cup for the group earning the best grades.

Of the approximately eighty percent of all students who joined Greek organizations, some dropped out because they disliked fraternal living, and some could not afford dues and board and room charges. In 1936 sorority membership and a pin could cost a stiff $50. The houses had difficulty in holding upperclassmen, many of whom preferred living in less expensive apartments or had wearied of communal living.

Fraternity activity sometimes brought complaints, but the administration rarely had to admonish a group. Occasionally, some men and parents complained to the college about "hell week," the period of fraternity initiation, with its hack paddles, twenty-mile one-way rides, cold showers, and other assorted indignities. In 1925 Beta Theta Pi's initiation brought considerable negative publicity to Whitman when members forced pledges to eat raw pork sausage, instead of the traditional raw hamburger. Nine men became ill with trichinosis, were hospitalized, and missed classes. The college came under criticism, and Stephen Penrose, who heard from the governor concerning the episode, instructed the fraternity's national president to end such practices.[138]

In the late 1920s a chapter of Theta Nu Epsilon (TNE) infiltrated the Greek system. Bernard Molohon, a 1929 graduate, provides an account of TNE at Whitman in his book *Sons of Marcus Whitman*, although others expressed some different interpretations.[139] Appearing on many campuses nationwide, TNE recruited members from other fraternities. A national fraternity officer explained to Penrose that TNE created "discord in fraternity chapters" and led "young, impressionable fellows into drinking and immorality."[140] At Whitman the outlaw group became involved in campus politics and distributed mimeographed papers, the first of which was called "The One Sheet." These publications appeared irregularly from 1928 to 1933; one, in sophomoric language, urged that Penrose and registrar Ruby resign, faulted the Greek organizations, and criticized fellow students. In 1930 TNE kidnapped critic Kenneth Davis, a prominent campus politician and member of Phi Delta Theta, and drove him up into Kooskooskie. This event attracted considerable attention. The faculty, like those in other colleges, unsuccessfully tried to root out TNE. Since it was commonly believed that two men in each fraternity belonged to TNE, the deans summoned Greek leaders and questioned them about the unsanctioned organization. After a considerable amount of excitement, TNE faded out in 1933.

Perhaps the Greek system created more excitement at Halloween in 1939 than it had at any time since the TNE kidnapping. The *Pioneer* joked that this event demonstrated "the most spirit . . . in the musty halls since the memorable massacre." It started when men dressed as women crashed an all-woman party; meanwhile several women were caught at a men's "smoker." Prentiss residents attacked two fraternities, throwing mud and leaves on the floor, tearing fraternity emblems from the walls, and ripping cushions and mattresses. Men retaliated by trashing (then called stacking) some sorority rooms. The harried dean of women called the police, who threatened about a hundred milling males with their nightsticks. Police arrested some rioters, while some collegians let the air out of the tires of their patrol cars. President Bratton praised the police for acting with restraint, and the *Walla Walla Union-Bulletin* groused that the collegians had "reverted to childhood tactics."[141]

But the TNE difficulties and the Halloween "riot" were highly unusual. The board of deans and each fraternity faculty adviser spent much effort, especially in the 1920s, working with the groups in enforcing the rules against drinking, particularly in their houses. Penrose thought that the violations were rare, and the *Pioneer* proudly agreed in 1930: "There is a minimum of drinking at Whitman."[142] Although students consumed alcoholic beverages, the minutes of the board of deans rarely mention an infraction of the rules, and alumni such as Dwelley Jones remembered that alcoholic beverages caused few problems. But most alumni could recall instances of inebriated men, including one who walked the rain gutters of Lyman House. Generally the fraternities effectively policed themselves. Hattie Gordon Fry remembered that a Phi Delta Theta came to a dance "slightly under the influence of alcohol. His horrified brothers put his date in a taxi and sent her home."[143]

Students suspected of drinking appeared before the board of deans. Dean Thelma Mills, for example, charged Tom McNeill, saying that she had smelled liquor on his breath; he successfully defended himself before the board.[144] Sometimes the deans notified parents that their sons were drinking and made the guilty individual schedule appointments with a professor in which he reported his abstention.[145] In 1930 Jim, a drunken student on probation, used the Lyman House fire hose against a sleeping resident and did considerable water damage. The deans expelled him; two years later they cancelled a Glee Club tour because some of its members had been drinking alcohol on a recent tour.

After prohibition ended in 1933, Whitman men, like men nationally, consumed more alcohol. An improved economy meant that Whitmanites could afford beer in downtown taverns, and some fraternities frequented special ones. To make sure that coeds did not enter taverns or other undesirable places, the WSG ruled that women "shall not enter places of public resort where their presence will bring discredit upon themselves or upon the college."[146] The minutes of the board of deans record few fraternity violations of the alcohol policy; in fact, these rule enforcers took less interest in limiting liquor consumption at about the same time that more of it appeared in the fraternity houses. Indeed, school records indicate only a few alcohol-related problems. In 1942 the administration was lenient with Phi Delta Theta for drinking at a formal house dance because the chapter had a good record.[147]

Cigarette smoking was a long-standing issue, and some who were opposed to it complained that the *Pioneer* and the *Blue Moon* carried large tobacco advertisements and that many students smoked. A concerned mother wrote Penrose that she feared the dormitory rule against smoking would be dropped, and reminded him that, "We mothers have been feeling very safe in sending our daughters to Whitman just for the reason that we thought they would be perfectly safe on account of the strict ruling to keep all things of an objectionable nature out of Prentiss."[148] At times, women smokers going through rush had "a black mark against them." At other times, the cost of smoking was likely to shape behavior, as one coed wrote her mother: "You'll be so proud of me—I have stopped smoking. . . . I just couldn't afford to keep buying" cigarettes.[149] Professors and deans advised students not to smoke, and sometimes the deans ruled against smoking; for example, in 1935 they forbade smoking in the buildings. But, from long experience, the faculty understood that any ruling against tobacco could not be enforced. Tobacco usage could be limited to certain areas, but it could not be eradicated. Carlin Aden remembered: "Some of the finest conversations on campus were back of the library (the Shack) where George Marquis and Russell Blankenship went for their hourly smoke. It was an advanced course in practically everything."[150]

Student Pursuits

The school continued to host a variety of organizations, including such respected honorary societies as Phi Beta Kappa, Mortar Board, the Order of Waiilatpu, and Mu Phi Epsilon. Professors urged able students to earn good grades to qualify for Phi Beta Kappa, which carefully limited its membership. Penrose sometimes grumbled that most candidates would be girls, "since the men at Whitman seem generally to prefer student activities to scholastic activities, thinking that if they have held an office in some campus organization or fraternity, they will be better entitled to fame and future success in the world than if they had made a record on the college books for high endeavor."[151]

Some organizations protected the interests of students—the Women's League, the Panhellenic Council, and the Inter-Fraternity Council. There were numerous clubs attracting students interested in foreign languages, journalism, international relations, and much more. To prevent students from excessive numbers of activities and to distribute leadership positions, the faculty continued to assign points—a maximum of fifteen was traditional—for participation in organizations and athletics. Penrose favored giving the students considerable freedom; for example, when the printers of the 1932 *Waiilatpu* yearbook asked him to help them collect money from students who had signed a contract with them, he refused: "I am very much opposed to consistent faculty control of student affairs and believe that in business they should be taught to stand upon their own feet without relying upon faculty guidance or support."[152]

Students in the small school had the advantage of being able to participate in a variety of activities. Jim Hill observed that the extracurricular side of Whitman life provided individuals with a chance to "learn a lot about people, handling people, and working with people that you don't get in the big schools."[153]

Students enjoyed the swing music of Benny Goodman and others on the radio, but they also enjoyed their own vocal and instrumental efforts. Students sang at dinner, fraternity men serenaded Prentiss women, singers gathered on the steps of Memorial Hall for renditions of popular numbers, and musicians performed on local radio station KUJ, which sometimes broadcast college programs from the conservatory. In 1939 the Beta Theta Pi choral group drove across America, singing in various places and attending the New York World's Fair. Individuals and groups performed for service clubs, for churches, and at the state penitentiary. One Whitman soprano appeared before inattentive inmates, and later found out that they "were quite sullen and blue" because the guards "had tightened down on them."[154]

The college Glee Club enjoyed great prestige, and many auditioned for membership. Both the conservatory and the college used the Glee Club to promote their programs. Often accompanied by the college orchestra, the Glee Club traveled for as long as two weeks across the region. Appearing in high schools, churches, and halls, the group under either Professor Howard Pratt or Elnora Maxey performed appealing programs. Penrose praised the thirty-eight-member group in 1928: "I have never heard a Glee Club which was its superior and few, if any which were its equal."[155] The *Pioneer* commended the same group and judged that Whitmanites "spend more time on musical activities than on any other in the extra-curricular program."[156] In many years, editors and others praised the successful Glee Club programs. Ruth McBirney penned a detailed account of the 1937 tour across eastern Washington, evaluating the crowded bus, the quality of the performances (Mrs. Maxey said she still liked her group despite their careless effort before a listless Cle Elum audience), the hotels (many were dirty), and the meals. McBirney concluded that her travels made her "appreciate our dorm meals."[157]

Walla Wallans not only applauded the college's Glee Club, they also praised the conservatory's performances of operas and operettas, and recitals by students and professors. They followed the careers of talented musicians, including vocalist Joyce Nye, who, in her senior year, won second place in a prestigious San Francisco music audition, and Rod Alexander, who, in his senior year, composed the popular and delightful *Mother Goose Cantata*. The community praised college musicians for enriching the city's cultural life.

Singers added much to the college's chapel also. According to a few alumnae, the conductor of the choir once asked a music major why the students moaned when she announced the page of a hymn. The senior replied that they had bought numbers for five cents each, and lost the pot when the conductor had not picked their number.

The theater's popularity was primarily due to a remarkable faculty member, Edith Davis. An able instructor of dramatics, she successfully directed numerous plays. She oversaw the annual sophomore play, a play by the dramatics club, and various one-act plays, including those produced for such special campus events as Visitors' Weekend. Most plays, including those directed by students, were performed in the chapel, but major productions were presented in the Keylor Grand Theater, where the community applauded both comedies and tragedies. One of Professor Davis's most successful productions was *Elijah*, performed in 1931 at Borleske Stadium with a large chorus, the local symphony, and many student soloists before an audience estimated at five thousand; another was *Stage Door*, presented in 1939 with a cast of thirty-one.

In the late 1920s Whitman's limited debate program included a memorable debate in 1927 with a witty team from Cambridge University, and produced able debaters, including Albert Garretson and Kenneth Davis. The men argued such questions as, "Resolved, that the English indictment of American education is justified." Whitman's women varsity debaters took the affirmative side of the question, "Resolved, that the modern diversion of women from the home to the . . . business occupations is detrimental to society."

The debate program vastly improved because of able coaches, particularly John Ackley, who took over in 1936. Like other vital Whitman professors, Ackley aroused interest in his subject; the number of varsity debaters greatly increased, and so did the victories, especially in 1938, when the team won the Pacific Coast championship. The *Waiilatpu* soon hailed Ackley as "the best debate coach that any school could have." [158] Whitman debaters succeeded in California tournaments as well as in the annual tri-school competition with the University of Idaho and Washington State College. There were several able male debaters, including Ross Reid, Jed King, Baker Ferguson, Jack Edwards, and Ed Adams. Ackley also coached several skilled female debaters, including Helen Rasmussen, Marian Klobucher, Betty Jean Dykstra, and Ruth VanPatten. Richard Eells and others found debating to be intellectually stimulating and judged that Ackley helped participants realize their potential. Gordon Scribner stated that Ackley drew him into debate, which was "challenging and fun." [159] Baker Ferguson praised Ackley for taking the touring debate team to hear evangelist Aimee Semple McPherson in the Church of the Foursquare Gospel. The coach also developed an outstanding intramural debate program, and the Inter-Fraternity Council established the Ackley Trophy.

Campus journalism maintained a high quality. The journalists producing the *Pioneer*, like their counterparts responsible for the *Willamette Collegian* and the *Pacific Index*, set high standards. Each journal carried campus news, editorials, and a wide variety of features. The Whitman community carefully read their informative weekly, and so did many townspeople and alumni. The newspaper was seen in distant places; for example, in 1931 the *Seattle Times* charged that the *Pioneer* advocated the end of prohibition. In response, the campus paper accused the *Times* of the "imbecility characteristic of the modern daily press"; the *Pioneer* asserted that it opposed harsh punishment of students who drank and would maintain its neutrality on a vital public issue that deserved a thoughtful discussion rather than an emotional one.[160] Generally the paper editorialized on campus issues, including the fact that for a time students cutting classes prior to and after vacations had to pay a fine of a dollar for each class missed.

The *Blue Moon*, the students' magazine, continued publication until it fell into the economic fires of 1933. Its editorials, features (some of them written by alumnus Nard Jones), poetry, and humor attracted a solid readership. In a thoughtful and humorous editorial, the *Blue Moon* reflected on the Great Depression:

> Hark, Hark, the dogs do bark
> The alumni are coming to town
> Some in rags, some in tags,
> And some in last year's gowns.

The writer added: "Depression has hit everything but our spirits, and prohibition is trying hard to quell those." Nonetheless, the editor urged readers not to be "activity hounds," but to study, because once they graduated they would "never again have the time and inspiration for leisurely study that is afforded [them] in school."[161] As with the *Pioneer*, cigarette advertising helped sustain the magazine.

Yeast, a modest successor of the *Blue Moon*, lasted about two years. Students did not launch another magazine until 1938, with the publication of *Clock Tower*. Similar to the *Blue Moon*, the new publication featured articles, essays, poetry, and jokes and contained more woodcuts and photographs. College humor seemed consistent, and the following joke was representative:

> "Will you marry me?"
> "No, but I'll always admire your good taste."[162]

Clock Tower was the most impressive magazine ever published by Whitman students; it would continue publication until 1955. All of these publications provided space for talented writers, including Nard Jones, Edward P. Morgan, and Richard Eells.

While journalism and other activities proved enjoyable, students needed a place to relax. There was no student union building, but the *Pioneer* in 1928 described the Midway Café as "the favorite lounging place for college students," and the café advertised that it served "the wicked chapel cutters." [163] Men took their dates to the Jensen Tea Room, and college groups held banquets there or at the Marcus Whitman Hotel. For a few years the most popular café was the Cabin, located on lower Boyer Avenue next to the White Temple Baptist Church, and originally owned by Frank LeRoux and Allen Newman, two young 1931 Whitman graduates who fully understood the need for a student "hang-out." Collegians flocked to this "Coke and smoke" place, playing its jukebox and pinball machines. Dorothy Robinson West called it a "den of iniquity because we wasted so much time there. . . . You couldn't smoke on campus but smoking was allowed there." She recalled that Dean Mills assembled the women, informed them that she was trying to close the Cabin, and then shocked everyone by naming a sorority woman who became involved with a man at the place. He "had gotten her pregnant and took her to have a criminal abortion." [164] Probably President Bratton's call for the construction of a student center came less because of student complaints that other schools had such facilities than because a campus recreation center could be regulated.

Athletics

Intercollegiate athletics made the college visible in regional sports pages, helped recruit and retain men, promoted student unity and loyalty, and attracted alumni and Walla Walla fans, some of whom became interested in particular players and in the college in general.

Celebrating his twenty-fifth year at Whitman in 1940, the colorful and emotional coach Nig Borleske, was, according to Nard Jones, a "renaissance man": he could write an informative account of his teams for the *Whitman Alumnus*, deliver a cogent speech to a service club, play a solid role in the college theater, and contribute to Rotary and other community organizations. [165] Many hailed Borleske; in 1925 a student writer enthused, "Nig and Whitman are synonymous—he is as much a part of Whitman as Memorial Hall." [166] Because he had been at Whitman since the First World War, Borleske enjoyed the admiration of regional coaches and sports writers; next to Stephen Penrose he was the most noted and quoted member of the Whitman community.

In the December 1925 *Whitman Alumnus*, Borleske outlined his familiar concerns to alumni and students. He regretted that the University of Washington and other schools in the Pacific Coast Conference had abandoned the smaller schools, forcing six of them to create the Northwest Conference. The coach also reiterated some persistent problems: Whitman's high entrance requirements made it difficult to recruit athletes; he needed at least one assistant coach; and Walla Wallans did not attend football games in large enough numbers to make the games profitable. If the football program made money, Borleske reasoned, then the school could employ a recruiter specializing in athletics.

He appreciated some changes in the late 1920s: the construction of the new stadium athletic complex; the increased seating in the gymnasium; and the employment of assistant athletic coach Roger Folgate, who oversaw the popular intramural program. The school annually allotted Borleske about ten athletic scholarships, which he awarded to freshmen. His players secured jobs on campus or from Walla Walla businessmen, who were often sports fans.

Nearly all of his recruits could handle Whitman's academic requirements. A 1928 study of the scholarship of the college's male athletes demonstrated their competence. They had a grade point average of "C+" compared to the non-athletes' "B–," but the percentage of athletes who graduated was twice that of non-athletes, and athletes were also less likely to be placed on academic probation.[167]

Alumni, who along with Penrose were critical of the professionalization of college sports, appreciated this proof that their alma mater did not often recruit athletes unable to do academic work. A visiting Los Angeles journalist wrote in 1940: "Studies are taken seriously, athletic teams are made up of strictly students."[168] Alumni did not accuse Borleske of trying to protect his team members from taking demanding courses, and they understood that good athletes, wanting to have more time for their classes or for their jobs, often preferred intramural to intercollegiate participation.[169]

Borleske coached three major sports: football, basketball, and baseball. Folgate assisted in football and coached track until he was replaced by William Martin in 1935. There were several tennis coaches, including short tenures by Walter Bratton, Binks Penrose, and Paul Jackson.

Between 1925 and 1942 Whitman dominated in track, winning thirteen conference championships. The Missionaries were champions in basketball, football, and baseball several times before 1936. Championships were rare after the mid-1930s, but in 1941 the baseball team and the tennis squad won them.

Biographer Jack Hewins, in *Borleske: Never Far From Hope*, relates the fortunes of the teams, but a more incisive athletic history was the coach's column published in the *Whitman Alumnus*. Borleske's accounts provided readers with a frank assessment of his teams: in evaluating his 1925 baseball team, for example, he complained that, "In all my coaching experience I have never seen such poor outfield work." He wrote readable descriptions of his teams and games; fans unable to attend basketball games in 1932—as the Missionaries went undefeated in conference play—could enjoy his entertaining summaries of each contest.

Of course, a powerful personality like Borleske's created detractors as well as defenders. He impressed his players with his high standards, his morality, and his strictures, including one that girl friends were a distraction. Critics charged that he was opinionated and too severe with his players. In 1940 senior fullback Jim Morrill, an able athlete, wrote an account of his gridiron experiences, "I'm Glad It's All Over." He complained that the student body did not support the team, that the students and faculty called the players "muscle bound," and that practices and games in all types of weather did not necessarily develop character any more than other activities did.[170]

There were many excellent athletes at Whitman. Worth Oswald was an outstanding tennis player who, as a junior, went east to play in tournaments. Friends of Whitman paid expenses and much of his senior year's tuition in 1930. Oswald's supporters must have been pleased to learn that he had worked his way through college and to be assured that he would not become "a tennis tramp."[171] Two outstanding football players were quarterback John "Bud" Applegate and lineman Walfred "Wally" Holmgren, who was an end in the 1929 Shrine game in San Francisco. In the late 1920s and early

1930s they spearheaded Whitman to conference championships.

In the spring of 1941 Whitmanites went beyond Morrill's negative assessment of football and energetically debated the question
of retaining the sport. Opponents of football emphasized the team's
inability to win a championship after 1931, its lopsided losses (especially the seventy-five-to-nothing defeat by arch-rival Willamette University in 1934), doubts about Borleske's ability to adapt to changes
in the game, and student apathy. But the *Pioneer*'s editorial of April
10, 1941, stressed that the real problem with football was financial.
Unimpressive teams failed to attract fans; thus, students annually
had to cover a $1,500 football deficit. Fearing that recruiting male
students would be even harder if the sport were terminated, trustees
took the matter out of the hands of students and voted to retain the
football program.

Other male sports created no major difficulties. Borleske's favorite
game was baseball, and his rivalry with Coach Arthur "Buck" Bailey
of Washington State College created considerable interest. Biographer Hewins concluded that Borleske's 1936 team, which won forty-
three games and lost twelve, was one of his best. The team's outstanding player was outfielder Tony Criscola, but, even after Criscola
departed to become a major-leaguer, the Borleske squads continued
to compile impressive records. Alumni judged that Borleske was less
effective as a basketball coach than he was coaching other sports,
but he won championships with such able players as Kenneth Hove
and Fred West.

Personable and talented track coaches Roger Folgate and William
Martin—the latter was also a competent trainer—developed a track
dynasty. Folgate came from Lake Forest College, and Martin, who
had attended Whitman with Borleske, earned a degree at Notre
Dame. According to Baker Ferguson, Martin had the ability to spot
and develop talent. The outstanding trackman was sprinter Robert
Graham, but a pulled hamstring prevented him from representing
the United States in the 1936 Olympics.[172]

Intercollegiate athletics for women failed to expand. Although
the basketball program continued, the tennis program was inconsistent until 1935. It was hard to develop because many regional
colleges did not support women's tennis teams. Women varsity tennis players, coached by Mignon Borleske, could compete in intra-

mural tennis, but they could not earn coveted varsity letters.

The sports program achieved its various social and economic purposes. Although there were problems with football, the administration might have strengthened the program had the Second World War not intervened. There was no such enthusiasm to improve women's athletics. While women held many campus leadership positions, especially editorships, the march to athletic equality was no more than a crawl, a fact that troubled only a few.

Moving into the Wider World

Commencement weekend, which was under the faculty's control, was the highlight of any college year. On Saturday the senior class sponsored "Class Day Exercises"—often a pageant or a skit—in the amphitheater. On Sunday the college community marched in academic regalia to a church—usually the White Temple Baptist Church —and heard the baccalaureate sermon. Sometimes the celebrants proceeded to Waiilatpu to honor the memory of the Whitman family.

Commencement was held on Monday. Seniors wanted to graduate in the amphitheater because of its rustic beauty, but poor weather sometimes drove the celebrants into a church. For many years, three seniors spoke at the exercises—the faculty chose two, and the seniors chose one—because, as Penrose explained, the "public [was] more interested in hearing representatives of the graduating class than an outside speaker, however distinguished."[173] In the 1930s the custom changed, and the ceremony featured an outside speaker.

The varied accomplishments of alumni who graduated in the years from 1926 to 1942 have been recorded over the years in the *Whitman Alumnus*. A small traditional liberal arts college had prepared women and men for influential professional careers. The faculty could see that their sacrifices had affected the lives of many young people, who, in turn, would make societal contributions, especially to the Pacific Northwest.

6

Issues of War and Peace
1942–1948

A Stranger is Chosen over a Son

President Walter Bratton had served admirably, but in 1940 his deteriorating health led the trustees to consider employing an assistant for him, or, if necessary, to seek a replacement. While pondering a new president, the board was painfully aware of the unpleasant difficulties of the Clemen period, and thought about appointing a familiar figure such as Chester Maxey or Binks Penrose.

Maxey's recollections and the official records provide considerable detail about the selection of Bratton's replacement. The political scientist recalled that he had had no interest in the position, but had gladly served on the search committee so as "to prevent . . . the choice of another Clemen."[1] Binks Penrose, however, considered the office. Several months before the 1941 search for a successor, Frank Baker, president of the board of trustees, unofficially informed Penrose about the prospective vacancy and suggested that many in the Whitman community thought that he and his wife, Margaret, would form an effective administrative team similar to that of Stephen and Mary Penrose. Baker, who hoped that Binks Penrose would someday be his "father's worthy successor," asked him if he would like to serve as Bratton's assistant, a new position that was an obvious stepping stone to the presidency.[2] Penrose rejected the offer.

In 1941 Binks Penrose and his parents corresponded about the possibility of his returning to Whitman from New York City, where he was an administrator in higher education. Stephen and Mary Penrose urged Binks to return as vice president or else as his father's replacement in the philosophy department, hoping that either position would lead to the college presidency. But he was considering a deanship at Cornell and would make no commitment. In November, the elder Penrose expressed his sentiments to his son: "It gave me infinite pleasure to think that the college would go on under an administration which would be in complete sympathy with the ideas which I had stood for during the last half century." Trustees suddenly squelched his hope by selecting Winslow S. Anderson, a dean at Rollins College, as president. The old man groused that he hoped that Anderson would "not be another Dr. Clemen," and concluded: "I must resign myself to seeing a stranger in my place instead of my beloved son."[3]

The new president, like Clemen, had furnished impressive credentials to the search committee. A native of Maine, he had graduated from Bates College, earned an M.S. at Minnesota, and received an honorary doctorate. Anderson had taught chemistry at Bates and at large universities, and he had long service as a dean at Rollins College. He wore a Phi Beta Kappa key, had authored some articles, and was a member of professional organizations. Anderson, like the controversial Rudolf Clemen, impressed his interviewers in Walla Walla. Maxey later explained that he did so well that the selection committee decided to appoint him immediately, thereby saving money by not interviewing the other finalists.

While Stephen Penrose bitterly accepted the board's decision, his son informed trustee Baker that, although the decision had caught him by surprise, he thought it appropriate. Because Anderson was only forty-three years of age, Binks Penrose believed it would be unwise for him to put his own life on hold in hopes of ascending to the Whitman presidency, waiting out Anderson's term "in a state of hesitant indecision." But, like his father, he worried about the new appointment, concluding: "God forbid that we ever get into another Clemen situation."[4]

In the fall of 1941, while the trustees searched for a president, thoughtful students became more concerned about international events. In 1927 Stephen Penrose had complained that, "Europe is in such ferment and here life goes on so placidly. . . . People seem . . . like well fed cows in a rich pasture, only they do not chew the cud of reflection."[5] Six years later, history professor Melvin Jacobs agreed. Although he feared European instability and Japanese control of Asian markets, he judged that only a few in the student body expressed an interest in international affairs.

Until 1936 foreign affairs were less important to Whitmanites than domestic politics. In the 1930s excitable Americans expressed fear that radicals, including communists, were influencing the nation's colleges. This charge may have seemed reasonable when, in the presidential election of 1932, Maxey and some students supported the election of socialist Norman Thomas. But in 1934 Penrose saw no reason for this worry and favored student discussion of all radical political positions. He complained, however, that only a few took "an active interest in public affairs."[6] The *Pioneer* identified some campus radicals, explaining that their views were "the natural outgrowth of the present unsettled [economic] conditions."[7] Some Whitmanites advocated Huey Long's radical economic views, but the *Pioneer* cautioned that the Kingfish's tactics in Louisiana were similar to those of Adolph Hitler in Germany.[8]

Worsening conditions in Europe promoted greater student reaction, but it was not always serious. In March 1936 some Whitman students established a chapter of the "Veterans of Future Wars." A scholar concluded: "Since the VFW was created tongue in cheek, many local chapters followed up in the same vein. . . . At Whitman the chapter was named the Foc'sle Vets and was one of the few in the nation that took a naval theme and assumed that its members would be future veterans of the navy."[9] Whitman women formed the "Nurses of the Black and Blue Cross," adopting a humorous slogan: "Better Bandages—We Roll Our Own." Some Whitmanites formed a chapter of the "Profiteers of Future Wars." But students could also be serious: in April 1936, at a peace demonstration sponsored by the American Student Union, two hundred of them listened to classmates denounce war's steep costs and gruesome casualties.[10]

With the outbreak of the European war in 1939, the campus community took a greater interest in international affairs. Professors such as Fredric Santler denounced the Nazis, but cautioned that the United States should remain neutral. During the campus-wide discussion of international relations, the faculty debated the Neutrality Act and interpreted the First World War's legacy; meanwhile, the *Pioneer* often quoted newspapers of other colleges on their reactions to the conflict. Visiting speakers on foreign affairs attracted thoughtful campus audiences. In 1940 historian Will Durant argued that a prolonged European war would inevitably involve the United States in the conflict; commentator Harry Elmer Barnes charged that the eastern press was actually advocating American involvement in the war. The *Pioneer*, alert to such opinions, criticized students for not reading a daily newspaper or listening to radio news. "It is likely that the girls," the editor asserted, "are worse offenders in this respect than the men although it is true too many men are also totally oblivious to the affairs of the world."[11] In early 1941 Whitman men, like their counterparts nationally, worried that the peacetime selective service would terminate their collegiate careers. The International Relations Club became more prominent, and so did the classes and speeches of history professor Walter Riley, a capable teacher who, alumni recalled, lectured on the implications of the European war.

The Navy's Role in the College and Its Financial Health

Many in the Whitman community feared that American entry into the war would wreak havoc with the college's finances in the same way that it had in 1917–1918. But such was not the case. Whitman's involvement in naval programs enabled it to maintain its standing as a good liberal arts college, to enjoy full enrollments, and to improve its financial stability.

These benefits were not obvious when the Japanese bombed Pearl Harbor in December 1941. The surprise attack angered Whitmanites, altering their convictions. Speaking for classmates, a student concluded that all the complaints about the school's administration, including its narrow attitude about drinking, had become insignificant "in an all out war."[12]

By the spring of 1942 Whitman students learned how to combat incendiary bombs, purchased war bonds, followed the war news, and pondered the future. The *Pioneer* raised some wartime concerns, including an editorial entitled "Hatred in War" that criticized Americans for their hatred of naturalized citizens and warned that such sentiments would poison post-war international relations.[13] When a student asked Professor Maxey if the Japanese might bomb the

West Coast, he replied that it was possible, adding, "Why get upset about it? If a bomb comes with your name on it, why worry? Go to a movie just the same."[14] According to the *Portland Oregonian*, Whitman College was one of several interior schools "that offered to take American-born Japanese students" who had been ordered to evacuate from the University of Washington in May.[15]

But the major wartime topic was the future of Whitman men. Because the draft was set at twenty years of age, most students did not yet face it. Taking the advice of their professors and others, they preferred to complete the semester rather than to enlist. The *Pioneer* observed that a typical male wondered "how much longer he would be able to remain in college and . . . what he can do in the way of advance preparation to benefit both himself and his country." The editor advised men to "stay in school as long as possible, investigate the opportunities at hand, and make decisions carefully taking into consideration as much as possible personal plans for the future."[16]

Winslow Anderson, who gave similar advice, became president of Whitman in the midst of a war crisis, just as Rudolf Clemen had come in during a financial crisis. Neither man had the opportunity to lead the college during a "normal" period. Anderson's first priority was to retain male students, which had also been Clemen's task in 1934. The New Deal measures, especially the National Youth Administration, had helped Clemen keep men at Whitman during the Depression, and even as late as the 1942–1943 school year thirty needy students earned significant funds from this agency. But the college required some type of military program to help it retain its men during wartime.

Whitman shared this basic need with scores of other colleges and universities that also feared that the departure of male students would create new economic hardships. Some college administrators, urging the government to mobilize their schools, predicted that, if the government failed to act, many would have to close. Whitman professors joined the negative chorus, pointing to the First World War, when men left the classroom for the recruiting office, slicing enrollments and bringing financial privation. The overseers worried about the federal government taking control of the college, and about a deficit resulting from wartime conditions, but they preferred these negative circumstances to a military defeat at the hands of "the madmen of Germany, Italy, and Japan."[17]

However, there was no enrollment crisis in the fall of 1942, for several reasons. Recruiter Douglas McClane's diligent work, including form letters to men and women emphasizing that "Uncle Sam needs you in college," had produced a large freshman class.[18] The faculty assisted him by revamping the curriculum so that students might complete a B.A. in three years, a program that was particularly attractive to males desiring a degree prior to military service. Enrollment also remained high because only a few men took war industry jobs, enlisted, or were drafted.

An expanded aviation program even increased the male enrollment figures. In the summer of 1940 Whitman offered the Civilian Pilot Training Program, chose qualified students for it, and received payment for offering ground-school instruction. This program became the Civil Aeronautics Authority War Training Service. Thus, fifty army, army glider, or navy reservists took ground-school training on the campus and flying lessons at nearby Martin Field. In the fall of 1942 President Anderson reported that this pilot-training program had been shifted to the navy's control; later its members wore uniforms. In this accelerated V-5 program, aviation cadets came from active duty to Whitman. For eight weeks these midshipmen took a prescribed curriculum (Whitman faculty members taught only two of the required classes), lived in the dormitory or a fraternity house, and participated in college activities. In the spring of 1943 the college's quota jumped to 110 cadets, most of whom would now stay for twelve weeks.[19]

Aware that the war was likely to be lengthy and that the draft would shortly dip down to eighteen-year-olds, President Anderson and many of the students reasoned that the reserves were the most promising way for men to remain in school and, at the same time, to prepare for military service. In late October 1942, as the president warned men assembled in the chapel that soon they would be subjected to the draft, they listened closely to officers representing the navy, army, and marines.

The uniformed speakers stressed that the armed forces expected the colleges to furnish officer candidates, outlined the various reserve programs, and encouraged their listeners to join them. The navy offered a V-1 program to lower classmen. After completing the soph-

omore year and passing an examination, a reservist might enter the
V-5 or V-7 unit. The V-5 prepared cadets for naval aviation; the
V-7 graduates would attend officers' training schools. The army offered two reserve programs, the Enlisted Reserve Corps and the
Army Air Corps Reserve, and the marines offered the Marine Reserve Corps. In November more than a hundred Whitman men chose
among these units, recognizing that they could be called into the service at any time.[20]

Anderson feared that, if the government summoned large numbers of these reserves to active duty, many women would transfer.
According to the *Pioneer*, women dreaded the prospects of a "male
shortage," and a freshman lamented that, for her, this would be "a
calamity beyond all imagination."[21]

Like his fellow college presidents, Anderson worried about a severe loss of enrollment while politicians deliberated on military programs that would allow the colleges to train their men as officers.
The government's delay exasperated educators. Soon after Pearl Harbor, college presidents had met and urged the federal government
to mobilize their institutions. Anderson actively participated in this
attempt to shape a federal program. He attended several meetings in
Washington, D.C., and used the connections of Supreme Court Justice William O. Douglas, the college's most influential contact. In a
letter to the jurist, the president declared: "There is no question but
that the college manpower of the country must be mobilized to the
task of winning the war, but at the same time we must see to it that
our colleges are not destroyed in the process." Anderson opposed
a revival of the Student Army Training Corps, a program launched
late in the First World War, because "the entire program was administered by army men who . . . knew nothing about colleges."[22]
The educator emphasized that colleges were "potential officer training schools."[23] Douglas, who had studied at Whitman during the First
World War, agreed with Anderson's assessments and forwarded them
to Paul V. McNutt, the chairman of the War Manpower Commission.

In December 1942 Anderson journeyed to Washington, D.C.,
compared the newly created military programs, and selected the navy
V-12 program for Whitman. He explained to former president Walter Bratton that this navy program appeared "to be best . . . for the
men will be regularly enrolled students in the college and will pur-

sue a regular liberal arts course with emphasis on mathematics and physics."[24] During the spring semester naval authorities inspected the college's facilities, accepted Whitman among the 130 institutions to participate in the program, and informed the college that 215 trainees would arrive in July 1943. The navy, however, warned Anderson that the school's V-5 program would soon be terminated; but, fortunately, it lasted until August 1944.

The Whitman community applauded Anderson's bringing in the navy V-12 program, and now the college hosted two valuable naval units. Anderson assured Douglas that, "with 325 boys in uniform on the campus, we should not need to worry about girls either."[25] The jurist predicted that the V-12 program would "be a fine thing for the college."[26] Thus, the federal government, in the 1940s as in the 1930s, helped resolve Whitman's enrollment problems during a difficult period.

Prior to the arrival of V-12 trainees, 128 Whitman men entered the armed forces, including forty-six men called up to the Enlisted Reserve Corps. Despite these losses in the spring semester of 1943, the president reported to the boards that the total enrollment was similar to that of 1942. The expanded V-5 program was the major reason for this positive situation. Some old-timers favorably compared the 1942–1943 school year with that of 1917–1918, a war year when only one male had graduated.

The V-12 program was more important to Whitman than the V-5 program, which Anderson emphasized was not "a regular part of the college." The new naval program brought more trainees, who generally remained for four trimesters, rather than for only eight weeks. They enrolled in both traditional liberal arts courses and those required by the navy. Anderson boasted that it was "the evident desire of the Navy to cause as little change from the institution's normal procedure as possible."[27]

In July 1943 Whitman's V-1 and V-7 reserves were ordered to report for active duty in the new Whitman unit of the navy V-12 college training program. Additional V-12 trainees arrived from high schools, other colleges (thirty-eight were represented), and the fleet. The presence of numerous uniformed men and the absence of any women students until late September gave the college an unusual appearance.

Charles J. Armstrong was director of the V-12 program and a professor of classics; he would also serve the college as dean of the faculty and as vice president. When he tried to discipline returning veterans as he had the members of the V-12 program, many men resented him.

Anderson selected Dr. Charles J. Armstrong, from Brown University, to direct the program. A graduate of the University of British Columbia with a Ph.D. from Harvard, Armstrong taught the classics at Whitman and played a large role in the college's V-12 program. Lieutenant Edward J. Liston commanded the V-12 unit with the assistance of a staff of eight, including a medical officer. Later, Lieutenant J. L. Bostwick, an experienced educator, replaced Liston, and other staff changes followed.

The navy required the college to operate on a twelve-month schedule with three sixteen-week sessions. In the first two trimesters (often called terms), the basic program included courses in mathematics, English, and the historical background of the war, as well as physical training. In the third and fourth trimesters, the deck officer candidate's curriculum required electrical engineering, calculus, naval history and strategy, and psychology. The pre-medical and pre-dental candidates took a similar set of courses. Civilians could also enroll in these classes, which generally required fifty to sixty hours of weekly preparation. After completing the four-term V-12 curriculum, the trainees advanced to the reserve midshipmen's schools for sixteen weeks of additional training.

Whitman reported that the V-12 program placed greater emphasis upon academic success than military training, and that the demanding scientific curriculum was "more stringent than a normal college course."[28] Trainees took seventeen credit hours per trimester and underwent rigorous physical training. The college assured the public that the faculty, director Armstrong, and the naval officers did everything they could to assist the trainees, including extra teaching sessions and conferences. In 1944 Armstrong wrote that most of his time had been "devoted to personal conferences with navy trainees, to help them with their academic work and with their plans for the future."[29] To remain in the program, a cadet had to earn at least a 2.0 (C) average; an academic review board dropped twelve percent of the men in the first term and about ten percent in the second. The grade-point average rose from 2.3 in the first term to 2.5 in the third term. Armstrong reported that many trainees had little interest or background in the sciences and "found it very hard to adapt . . . to the Deck curriculum, which is the practical equivalent of a mathematics or science major."

The Whitman community found the trainees highly motivated; according to Armstrong, this motivation was "largely determined by a sense of patriotic duty, a desire to win commissions, and a desire to increase educational development for the post-war future."[30] The seriousness of the sailors, especially the large number of them coming from the fleet, inspired everyone.

Implementing the training program involved some rough sailing, of course. Civilians had difficulty accepting naval discipline; some enlisted men from the fleet had trouble with accelerated college classes. These enlisted men, however, helped the officers "bring the unit quickly to a state of military efficiency and smartness." Furthermore, the fleet men generally had greater motivation than other trainees. Armstong approved the "gradually evolved policy of restricting V-12 assignments to those with previous Navy experience."[31]

Whitman's professors maintained their teaching styles and adamantly opposed changing their liberal arts college to a technical school. As a college publication explained: "In time of war as well as in time of peace there is value in a well rounded education which includes, in addition to academic activities, experiences in social, extracurricular, and religious activities."[32]

After about two years of operation, the V-5 program terminated in 1944. It had been one of the nation's largest programs, training about five hundred naval aviators. These midshipmen had received some academic credit for the classes completed at Whitman, and had heard the college urge them to return and complete their degrees. Many did.

In May 1944 Whitman released some unique enrollment figures: an all-time high total enrollment of 746, with 399 men, 327 of them V-12 trainees. (The 315 V-5 naval aviation cadets, studying at the campus for only eight-week periods, were not counted.) The total included 347 women, 148 freshmen, and sixty-five seniors, only eighteen of them men. Most of the V-12 trainees came from the Pacific Northwest, but trainees from the South and East brought a wider geographical distribution to the college's population than ever before.[33] By 1945 the total enrollment dropped to 688 students, including 271 V-12 trainees. Women slightly outnumbered the male students in total enrollment, with only seven men in a small senior class of forty-eight.

While the college did not offer a military program for women, it actively recruited them as students. Early in the war, some high school girls joined the boys in rushing into the war industries. Whitman and other schools tried to attract them by reminding them that attending college "was also a patriotic duty."[34] To this end the college published "Career Planning for Whitman Women." In this April 1943 booklet, director of admissions Douglas McClane acknowledged that women were needed in industry and in "the WACs [Women's Army Corps] and the WAVES [Women Accepted for Voluntary Emergency Service with the navy] and other military units for women," but he emphasized that the nation also needed college-educated women in wartime and the post-war years. The booklet listed a few timely careers "which have particular value in war time, either in war industry or in government service"; among them were public service, social work, religious work, accounting, secretarial work, and merchandising. But one of the most interesting fields offered was "Reconstruction and Rehabilitation Work," an important opportunity because, "Women proficient in a foreign language . . . are needed for essential welfare work in countries devastated by the war."[35]

Perhaps this booklet helped to recruit women, as did some additional courses in the economics department. The faculty approved three courses entitled "War Secretarial Training," to be offered by the Walla Walla Business College. They would carry Whitman credit, but would not meet either departmental or divisional requirements. The college benefited from its recruitment of women because, as Chester Maxey judged, they were "of high quality."[36]

During the war years, as Anderson struggled to maintain enrollment, he had less trouble retaining his faculty. In the 1942–1943 school year some men departed for military service or government work, but others, such as John Ackley, received deferments. Probably the major losses were William Hart in foreign languages and Carroll Zimmerman in physics. The physicist became involved in war work at the Massachusetts Institute of Technology, but soon expressed a desire to return to Whitman. Among the important faculty additions were Dr. William L. Hutchings in mathematics, his wife, Dr. Phyllis H. Hutchings, in astronomy and mathematics, Dr. Ronald V. Sires in history, Glenn J. Woodward in chemistry, Jerry Fogarty in education, Kenneth Schilling in music, and Charles Armstrong, director of the V-12 program, in classics. The Hutchingses and Armstrong had all taught for a time at Rollins College, Anderson's old school. Another significant addition was alumnus Frederick "Fritz" Wilson, who joined the bursar's office and was responsible for the V-12 program's financial operation.

The naval programs not only brought the school needed income, they also helped pay for alterations in the Lyman House kitchen and dining room. The naval contracts paid for construction projects, including flooring in the gymnasium, a new roof for the library, a sound-proofed classroom in the conservatory, and even locks on all of the dormitory rooms in Prentiss Hall. The fraternities, enjoying better income because of contracts with the college, improved their houses for the navy tenants. The V-5 trainees intermittently utilized most of the Greek houses; the V-12 men lived in the Sigma Chi house.

Anderson reported in June 1945 that Whitman's V-12 program was one of the nation's smallest, but he evaluated it as one of the best. The president described the wartime college: "In a large sense Whitman has suffered but little due to the demands of war. We have maintained our enrollment, and our V-12 men have been assimilated into our student body as regularly registered students; our faculty has not been hit hard by Selective Service; and financially our budget has been in balance."[37] Professor Maxey agreed that the liberal arts did not suffer in the V-12 program, "for the Navy wanted its officer candidates to have as much of the liberal arts . . . as they can get."[38]

The president pointed out to alumni that their alma mater was "certainly one of the very few colleges that has been able to maintain its peacetime enrollment . . . and [it was] in a sound financial condition when most colleges were facing deficits."[39] The *New York Times* noted that Williams College had seen its student body reduced from 850 to 108, and was suffering a financial loss.[40] Anderson's evaluation of the effects of the Second World War contrasted starkly with Stephen Penrose's assessment of the impact of the First World War, when: "The effect of the war upon the college was financially disastrous. . . . The war worked havoc with its plans and its property. Its student body was depleted and its income from tuitions reduced; its expenses were increased, and a deficit of $10,000 a year was unavoidable."[41]

Maxey praised Anderson for having contracted for the naval units: "He not only handled all of the complex dealings, financial and other, with the Department of the Navy and the commanding officers on the campus but he also at the end of the war, effected the final settlements on terms which left Whitman College thousands of dollars to the good. Not all colleges were similarly successful in their dealings with . . . the Navy."[42]

Dean Frank Haigh agreed, emphasizing that the president's "far-seeing wisdom" during the war years resulted in Whitman's financial soundness and "unimpaired educational standards."[43] Board members emphasized that the endowment increased by $160,000 between 1941 and 1946, reaching a total of $1,335,000.

From one coast to the other, liberal arts colleges that sponsored V-12 programs had about the same positive experience as Whitman did. At Willamette University, President G. Herbert Smith received "the credit for securing the unit and thus saving Willamette from a perilous situation"; and at Colorado College, the unit "had enabled the college to maintain its enrollment and operate on a balanced budget . . . at the same time maintaining its high academic standards and liberal arts tradition."[44]

College Life in Wartime

The faculty had to adjust to the unusual wartime procedures. The navy's bureaucracy created extra paperwork: professors had to issue textbooks, fill out daily absence forms, and keep abreast of a variety of mimeographed official papers dealing with everything from mail to laundry service. They found it difficult to use such naval terms as "USS Lyman" and "USS Sigma Chi"; or to use the term "deck" rather than floor, "billet" rather than room, and "mess hall" rather than dining room, in the dormitory. It seemed odd to read that, "The Navy mess is served aboard the USS Lyman."[45]

While the faculty worked to learn the navy's vocabulary, it also adjusted to a different type of student. Until the faculty stopped the

In front of the "USS Lyman," battalion commander Francis Murphy reads the orders of the day to company commander Norman Jensen and platoons of V-12 cadets standing at parade rest.

practice, the trainees rose when a professor entered a classroom. When a few of the V-12 trainees failed to meet the school's admission standards, instructors spent more time dealing with their probation and dismissal cases than they did with civilian students. Because the seamen did not pursue majors, many professors taught more of a general curriculum. On the other hand, the pre-medical and pre-dental trainees enrolled longer than those in the deck program, and took a more specialized biology program than the civilian students in the same class.[46]

Professors reported that V-12 trainees were better motivated than pre-war students had been, and, as Professor Leo Humphrey said, he and his colleagues were aware of the fact that they were "making a substantial contribution to the war effort." But the faculty reported serious problems: the science department repeated the old complaint that Billings Hall needed repairs; the understaffed social science department labored under heavy teaching loads. Historian Ronald Sires observed that the navy program did not "encourage extensive and thoughtful reading," and English professor Paul Jackson, along with others, judged that, "by comparison with civilian students, the average V-12 trainee is woefully deficient in his knowledge and use of grammar," but teachers praised the navy for emphasizing writing.[47]

Under the navy program the faculty taught a longer year and thus received better salaries. In the fall of 1943 they offered a short inter-session to place civilians on the same schedule as the trainees, who had registered in July. Professor Arthur Rempel recalled his colleagues' amusement when a freshman woman, in registering for the inter-session, informed a professor that she wanted to register for the "intercourse."

Wartime conditions had other effects on faculty lives. In 1943 Professor Sires, with his wife and two children, arrived in Walla Walla from Muncie, Indiana, after a five-day automobile trip made possible by gasoline stamps allotted because he was going to teach servicemen. Because of a housing shortage—the army air base and McCaw (military) Hospital had brought thousands of servicemen and civilians to the city—the college permitted the Sires family to live in Prentiss Hall until they found a home. There had not been so many newcomers and excitement in Walla Walla since the gold rush of the 1860s. The wartime conditions also altered faculty family life. The Sireses and the Rempels rented rooms to the wives of servicemen. Whitman families shared meals of chili or waffles. Ada Howells and Maxine Sires stated that the close-knit faculty felt it "was all in this wartime together" and that an organization of faculty and staff wives helped families cope with stress and shortages.[48]

The war had brought black soldiers, both male and female, to the air base. Maxine Sires lunched with a black woman from the air base, who was denied service. Soon after this event, Dr. Horatio C. Wood, a psychiatrist at the air base, came to the Sireses' home and expressed his concern that black troops—men and women—had reported themselves sick "because of loneliness and exclusion from all of Walla Walla's restaurants, hotels, movies, and other public meeting places."[49] Outraged by this situation and by signs in store windows refusing service to blacks, the Sireses invited the Howellses and six others to meet at their house and formed an interracial organization. On October 16, 1945, the group became formalized as the Walla Walla Interracial Committee. Its constitution explained that the organization sought "to secure the basic American democratic rights of justice, equality of economic opportunity, equal access to adequate educational facilities, proper living conditions, protection and improvement of health, and the freedoms of the Bill of Rights and the Atlantic Charter, for all individuals of this community and area, irrespective of their race."[50]

Some Whitman students showed similar concern. In 1945 Bill Ballard pointed out that black servicemen could not find places in Walla Walla to eat or live. He added: "There is the specific example of a Whitman graduate war veteran Nisei whose family has been prevented from buying a home in Walla Walla."[51] Meanwhile, the Walla Walla Interracial Committee brought the noted black poet Langston Hughes to town for a performance in a city theater. This event increased the committee's growth; it counted fifty-five members in January 1946. Whitman faculty families continued to play a major role in this organization. Members of the group, including some blacks from the air base, went to restaurants asking that they not refuse service to blacks. While there was no immediate change in exclusion policies, this was an early step in the long climb toward the end of open discrimination.

While the faculty took the lead in improving social conditions, it also played a major role in improving the cultural environment. Under the leadership of Paul Jackson, professors were the prime movers in establishing the Walla Walla Little Theater. Jackson directed local actors in a comedy, *Yes, My Darling Daughter*, presented to soldiers at the army air base and to patients at McCaw Hospital. In May 1945 members of the Whitman community took the lead in incorporating the Little Theater (it had several purposes, including "the advancement of the community culture") and producing plays in the upstairs of a downtown business building.[52] The group also produced a play on campus, and in 1948 it purchased a building for a permanent site.

Gradually student life changed even more dramatically than faculty life. Prior to the arrival of the V-12 trainees in mid-1943 Whitman students were only marginally affected by wartime conditions, but the appearance of more than two hundred sailors radically altered the composition of the student body. In the first eighteen months of the war, students experienced a wartime climate but not a dominant military presence. The first obvious wartime change was that of the V-5 cadets living in fraternity houses, even though these uniformed men had their own separate curriculum and were not at the college long enough to influence student activities. In 1942 reservists did not wear uniforms or enroll in special classes, but these men, and the coeds as well, worried about when they might be called from the classroom for basic training.

The war influenced student life in several ways. Early in 1942 there were practice blackouts with student wardens; college women took instruction in first aid; Greeks conducted "V for Victory" dances; and collegians repeated such phrases as "Get in the scrap to lick the Jap."[53] Spring vacation was cancelled so that students could have a longer summer to work in war industries. At chapel and in classrooms, visitors joined professors in discussing the war and the peace that would follow. Professor Zimmerman stated that science would be crucial to the war effort, arguing that "the men in the laboratory are as essential to victory as those on the front."[54] Professor Maxey predicted an American victory because of the fighting ability of its men and added: "We are better fighters today than we were in World War I." President Emeritus Penrose wisely warned that, in the post-war world, citizens must guard against " 'Ameri-canitis' in offering solutions to world problems." [55]

Again prodding the conscience of readers, the *Pioneer* sometimes complained that readers expressed little interest in the war. One writer charged that most of her classmates were very involved in spring social activities and "blissfully unaware" of the war. She attributed this indifference to the fact that students were "buried in Walla Walla"; another journalist complained that some students "were concerned only with the high price of Scotch." [56] The administration took less interest in Scotch than in food stamps. During registration, students had to surrender their ration books to the college. Male students enrolling in the fall of 1942 carefully considered the implications of the war. Thus, German language enrollments increased, in sharp contrast to the years of the First World War when the number of students taking such classes plummeted. Heavy enrollments in mathematics and the sciences resulted in large classes. Irwin Stewart, the head of the mathematics department, estimated that sixty percent of the men were taking a mathematics class because they recognized the importance math would have when they were called into the service. To meet the heavy enrollments, Stewart hired Mrs. Henrietta Baker Kennedy, a 1914 Whitman graduate, as a full-time instructor; she would be a lively department member.

In 1942 campus life changed only slightly. Although the *Pioneer*, like many other college newspapers, was reduced to tabloid size, its coverage of music, debate, Greek life, and athletics was similar to what it had been in pre-war years. Students maintained traditions, including the requirement that freshman wear green until Thanksgiving. But there were some notable changes. For example, Whitman's athletes played against military teams from Walla Walla or Pasco; and there was endless speculation about when the enlisted reservists would be inducted. An explosion in a chemistry lab in which a student lost his hand saddened the wartime campus.

By the spring semester of 1943 military programs greatly altered the lives of Whitman men. In April the college announced that it had been chosen to sponsor the V-12 unit; this happy news meant that many in the V-1 and V-7 programs would remain at Whitman. The men in these two programs learned that in July they would be called to active duty or assigned to the new V-12 program. While men adjusted to this exciting news, about fifty enlisted reservists received a call to active duty. They attended a "kiss the boys goodbye" student assembly, and, accompanied by classmates and professors, went to the railroad station for an emotional farewell.

From the arrival of the V-12 unit in July 1943 until its termination twenty-eight months later, Whitman took on a distinctly military flavor. The president of the University of California asserted that his school was "no longer an academic main tent with military sideshows. It is a military tent with academic sideshows."[57] The same was true at Whitman, where trainees responded to bugle calls, stood in formation, marched to class, participated in vigorous physical exercise, and kept the USS Lyman shipshape. The dormitory was now "immaculate" and its condition no longer worried administrators.[58] The sailors, director Armstrong reported, became deeply involved in "extracurricular activities such as fraternities, student clubs and organizations . . . and played on college teams and joined the college

After an unofficial farewell party and an official special assembly in mid-March 1943, faculty and students bid farewell to members of the Enlisted Reserve Corps. They traveled by special Pullman car to Fort Lewis and then to other duty stations.

choir, band, or orchestra."[59] They pledged fraternities, formed a "stray fraternity" for Greeks who did not have a Whitman chapter, filled all the positions on the 1943 varsity football team (and suffered a disastrous 1944 season that included two losses to the University of Washington by scores of sixty-five to six and seventy-one to nothing), played bruising intramural sports, formed a navy chorus, joined the Glee Club, worked on the *Pioneer*, and sponsored dances. The cadets also helped Whitman women and faculty members raise money to open the Cabin as a student center. Controlled by students, who closed it during student body meetings, the popular hangout served the same function as when it was privately owned.

In their recollections, the trainees often stated that they had tried to become a part of the college community. Donald Pickering had been sent from the fleet for the start of the V-12 program and remained at Whitman studying pre-med. He remembered that the members of his unit "attempted to become part of the college," and appreciated the educational opportunity.[60]

In 1945 Ellen Heath, president of the student body, reviewed the contributions of the V-12 trainees, especially to the school's social life, and concluded: "You've been as much a part of the school as the rest of us, and we are going to hate to see you go."[61] The sailors had become attached to the college; one wrote, "We'll miss ol' Whitty like the very deuce,"[62] and another explained: "I was completely impressed with Whitman. It was what I had dreamed of. . . . The small campus and very sophisticated small classroom and excellence of the teaching staff . . . [were] very obvious from the beginning."[63]

The Walla Walla Valley was far enough inland that its Japanese residents were not interned, and a few of the V-12 veterans recalled that the college hired cooks of Japanese ancestry; according to President Anderson, the college did this because they were "better . . . and more economical [to employ] than white women."[64] The pleasant personality of one young Japanese woman helped counter the racial prejudice of some of the trainees.[65]

Although a limited budget forced the *Pioneer* to cut its size to four pages, it continued to provide information about traditional college activities. The paper made no attempt to follow the war news, but gave details about the war's impact upon the campus. The *Pioneer* carried stories about students in the service; the efforts of the

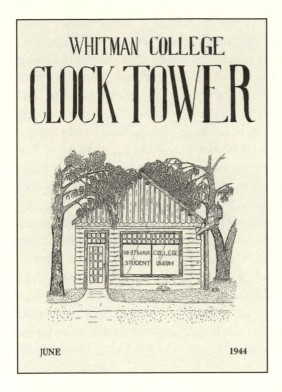

Appearing here on the cover of Clock Tower *in 1944, the Cabin was a popular hangout for Whitmanites seeking refreshments, a smoke, or conversation.*

"Minute Maids" (women selling savings stamps); the coeds who entertained servicemen at McCaw Hospital or wrote to men overseas; the volunteers who rolled bandages in the Prentiss Hall library; international issues of war and peace; and the activities of the sailors on campus. In 1944 *Clock Tower*, the student magazine, urged readers to become even more involved in the war effort; the editor admitted, however, that it was "very hard to sit by Lakum Duckum . . . and try to visualize what a beach head in the Solomon [Islands] is like."[66]

Articles in the *Pioneer*, as well as alumni recollections, reveal that the wartime years gave Whitman women a richer collegiate life. Dean of women Maureen Clow wrote: "To assist in the social activity of the Armed Forces one hundred Whitman girls go to the Naval Air Base at Pasco . . . every other Saturday night for dances with cadets stationed there."[67] Women who played hearts or sang with the patients at McCaw Hospital found it to be an emotional experience; and, as several alumni mentioned, many coeds became involved in romances with navy cadets or army officers at the air base. Some of these romances probably originated with Prentiss Hall's head resident who, working with students, arranged dates for servicemen with Whitman women. She would inquire about a serviceman's "stature, complexion, interests, background, and then tried to find through the student committee a young woman who would like to meet such a service man."[68] In 1944 the crew of a B-24 bomber came to a campus residence and asked the housemother if some of the occupants would like to accompany them to a dance at the air base; seeking fun, Delta Gammas consented, and were paired with the soldiers according to their height.

With the men so involved with the V-12 program, women had greater opportunities to be editors, varsity debaters, and student body officers; for example, for the first time in a generation a woman won election as student body president.[69] But what alumnae often remembered about wartime changes was that, because of a shortage of men, women lived in fraternity houses between 1944 and 1946. To avoid misunderstandings, the houses received new names: the Beta Theta Pi house became The Maples; the Phi Delta Theta house became Estrella House; and the Tau Kappa Epsilon house became Birch Cottage.[70] Several alumni recalled that four-motored bombers rattled dormitories and lecture halls. Jan Nye Baxter remembered that, when the women sunbathed behind Prentiss Hall, they witnessed "a great air show."[71] Trainers swooped over the building, and the pilots waved or dipped their wings to the laughing coeds.

The Second World War provided Whitman students and alumni with more travel, opportunities, danger, and excitement than any previous period in the school's history. Local newspapers, the *Whitman Alumnus*, and alumni essays reported the experiences of veterans like Eugene Fletcher, author of *Fletcher's Gang: A B-17 Combat Crew in Europe*; Baker Ferguson, a flier who spent many months in a German prison camp; Joe Jobe, a decorated naval flier; Roberta Sandoz Leveaux, a pilot in the British Royal Air Force; Tom Ichikawa, who fought with the 422nd Regimental Combat Team in France, and Robert Hosokawa, who was sent to the Minidoka relocation center in Idaho. From there he wrote to national publications about his experiences, introducing himself as "an American with a Japanese face."[72] Professor Thomas Howells wrote numerous letters that successfully helped Hosokawa find a newspaper position, so that he could escape from his internment and launch a career in journalism.[73] A few women joined the Women's Army Corps, including Shirley Frese Woods, who became a physical therapist at McCaw Hospital. Some women served in the Red Cross, including Bunt Johnson Tuttle, who wrote unusual and informative letters about assignments in New Guinea; and many did war work, including Margaret Heath Abbott, who was a social worker assigned to work with black women in the Portland shipyards. An estimated forty Whitman-trained scientists conducted "scientific research and development in a technological war."[74]

While reports of alumni in uniform and in defense work brought publicity to their alma mater, other actions produced the same result. A Portland shipbuilder launched four freighters—the SS *Marcus Whitman*, the SS *Narcissa Whitman*, the SS *Cushing Eells*, and the SS *Whitman Victory*—that honored individuals important to the college. President Anderson and students participated in the launching of the SS *Whitman Victory*.

In this same period, the historical figure of Marcus Whitman brought more publicity to the college than at any time since the 1890s. *Life* and *Reader's Digest* magazines carried stories on the hundredth anniversary of the missionary's historic 1843 ride. Justice William O. Douglas played a leading role in getting this well-illustrated story published in *Life*. According to President Anderson, Douglas convinced publisher Henry Luce to run this story, which brought unusual recognition to the college. During the war years, the jurist, who had become a Whitman overseer in June 1941, championed his alma mater because he felt "a deep sentiment and affection" for it.[75] Douglas helped in various ways: he donated money, provided autographed pictures of the Supreme Court Justices, gave books, tried to arrange a Whitman visit by Texas congressman Lyndon Johnson in 1942, and requested that President Harry Truman travel to the college in 1945 to receive an honorary doctorate.

The Whitman community knew that it had made significant contributions to the victory over the Axis powers. The *Whitman Alumnus* and a survey made by the alumni association in the mid-1990s compiled part of the record. The college had contributed to the various military branches through the V-5, V-12, and enlisted reserve

The flag over the front steps of Whitman Memorial Building honored, Pres-
ident Winslow Anderson stated, the "more than eleven hundred Whitman
men and women" who served in the Second World War.

programs. Other Whitman men and women had also served in the various theaters of war. Alumni had worked in the numerous defense industries, and some of the college's scientists had engaged in the development of weapons, including the atomic bomb. Nearly twelve hundred Whitmanites served their country, and thirty of them died. A marker recognizing their sacrifice is located in Whitman Memorial Building.

The Turbulent Post-War Transition

The college correctly anticipated a difficult time between the end of the war and the reorganization of a peacetime campus. In June 1944 Whitman overseers needlessly worried that, as the war ended, men who had matured through military service might not seek a college education, and low enrollments would mean that faculty salaries would not keep pace with inflation.[76] The significant GI Bill of Rights passed by Congress in June 1944, however, meant that veterans could attend college without any great personal financial expenditure. In March 1945 Whitman anticipated that the veterans would pursue college degrees, and predicted that their experience "and the abnormal life" they had led would give them "a maturity of personality which may mean that [their] interests will not be the same as the interests of the students who enter college directly from secondary school."[77]

The college needed a large number of veterans, because it had lost the V-5 program in August 1944 and the V-12 program had been slashed to a hundred trainees in March 1945. The summer session enrolled only those V-12 students whose program terminated in October. So, to prepare for the GIs, Whitman developed a special counseling service (based on experience with counseling the V-12 cadets), and appointed Charles Armstrong as a special veterans' counselor; it also published a bulletin with answers to questions about credit for military experience, accelerated programs, and the curriculum.

The fall 1945 trimester was unusual. It did not start until November 1, because of the V-12 program; men made up only twenty-five percent of the enrollment; women lived in Lyman House; and there was no football team. In addition, there were many faculty changes, including the appointment of Robert G. Comegys as a history instructor and William H. Bailey as a teacher of stringed instruments; classics professor and director of the V-12 program Armstrong was appointed dean of administration.

For Whitman, like its sister institutions everywhere, 1946 was a difficult year of transition. The *New York Times* on January 6, 1946, reported that colleges and universities struggled with the problems "of insufficient housing, overcrowded classrooms, and lack of instructional staff." The schools identified the shortage of student housing as the greatest difficulty.

At Whitman, too, student housing presented problems. In 1946 the college admitted a record-breaking 816 men and women. About forty percent of them were new students; the rest were either returning students from the previous year, or those whose studies had been interrupted by the war. To house this large enrollment, the administration arranged for the use of twenty apartments on the McCaw Hospital grounds for married students and four buildings at McCaw for single men, but the 115 occupants—most of whom were veterans—complained about the inconvenience of living more than a mile and a half from campus. The mixing of Greeks and independents in the Beta Theta Pi house also created discord.

Perhaps for the first time in its history, the college reported more problems with housing women than men. Though they insisted that women could not live in temporary housing at the McCaw Hospital site, school officials had difficulty controlling them in Lyman House. The dean of women reported an unusually independent spirit that prompted an "atmosphere that was reminiscent of the easy boisterous life of the freshman men who formerly lived there." The residents in Prentiss Hall and their parents resented the overcrowding. A staff member admitted that there was a "letdown in personal standards of cleanliness and order." Operating on a two-shift basis, the two dining halls were crowded and noisy and received complaints for serving inadequate meals. The Whitman Mothers' Club of Seattle, for example, protested to the trustees about the quality of food and the lack of fresh vegetables and fruits.

The administration candidly reported a decline in student morale because of crowding and unsatisfactory food. What it did not report was that numerous students expressed little confidence in the administrative abilities of President Anderson, Dean Armstrong, and

Mabel Lee, the new dean of women. None of these administrators had been at Whitman in peacetime; it seemed to many observers that they did not understand the college's culture. Some alumni recalled that, on occasion, Dean Lee would summon one or another of the senior women, note that she lacked a boyfriend, remind her that her male classmates had promising futures, and warn that this was her last opportunity to find such a man.

One of Whitman's foremost post-war problems was retaining and hiring good teachers. An unusual number of faculty resignations, including those of three very popular professors—Edith Davis, "Uncle" John Ackley, and Carroll Zimmerman—upset the students. Another loss was that of the effective head of the mathematics department, professor Irwin Stewart, who drowned in Seattle's harbor. And Maureen Clow, Mabel Lee's predecessor as dean of women and a respected leader, did not return from her leave at Stanford University. President Anderson explained the reasons for the staffing problems to the Whitman community: instructors entitled to the GI Bill were leaving for graduate school, there was a great shortage of college teachers, and Whitman's isolated location hampered their recruitment.[78]

The faculty and administration were in transition at a time when a most unusual student body—in both its size and its composition—arrived. In the fall of 1946 Whitman, like colleges everywhere, rejected scores of qualified applicants and still registered a record enrollment. The school was hardly prepared for such large numbers; furthermore, the 120 veterans held views different from those of traditional freshmen. The *New York Times* predicted: "The rising tide of veterans will tend to modify profoundly the character of the American collegiate body. Students will be older, more serious, and more seasoned."[79] Indeed, educational historian Diane Ravitch, writing in the early 1980s, noted that: "Among educators, the veterans quickly established a reputation as the hardest working, best motivated generation ever to pass through the nation's colleges. Harvard's president James B. Conant . . . concluded that the veterans at Harvard were 'the most mature and promising students Harvard has ever had.'"[80] The same was true at Whitman.

The large number of veterans, several of whom were married, brought new challenges as well as great promise. The campus had never had such an imbalance of girls fresh out of high school and experienced older men. Whitman had traditionally discouraged student marriages; now the college maintained married student housing at some buildings on the McCaw Hospital grounds, and married couples paid the college rent.

The returning GIs challenged the school's traditions and rules, especially the rules against drinking in fraternity houses. A faculty rule that the college would "not tolerate intoxication on or off campus on the part of its students," and that such intoxication could lead to expulsion,[81] prompted controversy, including disagreement over the definition of "intoxication." In the spring of 1946 a large and boisterous beer party at the Prospect Point Grange, which attracted many students aged twenty-one and over and a few faculty members, moved to the campus, where the exhuberant celebrants disturbed the sleepers. Although concerned by this event, the administration merely issued warnings to those who had participated. Drinking in the Sigma Chi house, however, resulted in the suspension of five men and a year's probation for the fraternity. Alumni recalled heavy drinking, especially at the Green Lantern.

In the fall, the veterans fought with the letterman's W Club when it tried to enforce the tradition that freshmen must wear "dinks" or submit to being thrown into Lakum Duckum. When a letterman asked one veteran why he was not wearing his beanie, the angry freshman replied, "Kid, I've killed better men than you. Get the hell out of here!"[82] Alarmed by the hostility between W Club members and veterans, Dean Armstrong arranged a special fall tug-of-war between them. By winning, the veterans ended hazing, but then honored tradition by wearing dinks on their own terms.

Administrative problems with students could not be resolved so easily. President Anderson became entangled in two significant problems, one with the majority of the student body and the other with Coach Nig Borleske. The trouble with students began early in 1944, when the trustees heard student complaints that Anderson was unfriendly and that he was reducing the size of the faculty to save money. The majority of students signed a statement charging that the "academic standards are being sacrificed to material expediency."[83] The trustees responded to these critics, declaring that the college had changed because of wartime, that faculty leaders sup-

Winslow Anderson became president in 1942 and served until his death in 1948. He saw the college through the difficult war and post-war years. During the war, the Whitman community appreciated his ability to get well-funded navy programs for the college; later, students — repelled by his stiff personality and perhaps misperceiving his goals — sought his removal from office.

ported the president, and that the board stood by him. They assured critics that Anderson was not overturning the school's "foundations or traditions."[84]

In the fall of 1946 the administration placed a senior woman on social probation. The *Pioneer* asked if the college would "punish severely all persons over 21, who take liquor socially."[85] In December, the administration and faculty received six separate petitions signed by 453 different students. Each petition came from a separate group, including Greeks, dormitory residents, and veterans. The petitioners had a variety of complaints, including charges that Whitman's academic standards had declined, that the dean of women failed to provide guidance, and that the "mal-administration of the college [was] creating ill-will among the students toward their college."[86] Some students who signed the petition against Anderson expressed reluctance about doing so; they realized he was doing his best, but felt that he lacked social skills.

Pete Reid later summarized the essential reasons for the difficulty:

most students returning from the service had matured, and there were administrative problems.[87] Dean Lee was arbitrary and unpopular, Dean Armstrong treated all students like freshmen, and President Anderson was distant. The two male administrators had found it much easier to handle V-12 trainees, who took orders, than it was to handle the veterans, who were tired of orders.

Immediately after receiving the petitions, the faculty elected a committee of inquiry chaired by Professor Sires. It interviewed fifty students and sent out a questionnaire that garnered three hundred responses. From these two sources the committee heard that the faculty was declining in quality, that the college was no longer friendly, and that President Anderson was an "inappropriate leader." Students charged that Anderson preferred to expand the physical plant and to raise money instead of seeking to attain "the educational objects of the curriculum and the acquisition and maintenance of a suitable faculty." The committee's questionnaire asked if the college's "existing conditions were essentially satisfactory." Sixty-five percent said no, and only twenty-four percent responded yes; furthermore, there was far more criticism of the administration than of the faculty. These troubling findings appeared in the final report, in which the committee pointed out inconsistencies in the student grievances and listed and evaluated ten assertions. The committee concluded with a plea for harmony between students and administrators, reminding its readers: "If the students will not stand by the name and reputation of their college, they will not spread a good report about it. A satisfied student body is one guarantee of satisfied alumni."[88] The committee, after about six months of study, reported to the faculty, which unsuccessfully recommended that the lengthy document be read to students; in fact, the final report was never made public.

Troubled by the report's findings, President Anderson asked Professor Howells about the reason for the student petitions. Howells frankly replied that people thought Anderson was "obnoxious," and confided that "he frequently wounded people's sensibilities, without seeming aware or without seeming to care."[89] Professor Ivar Highberg simply concluded that, "The student body did not like Anderson, and I cannot tell you why."[90]

President Anderson had his defenders, especially Chester Maxey and the board of trustees. In December 1946 the political scientist warned that, if the board removed the president, he would resign. He judged that Anderson "has been the best executive head the college has ever had. In my opinion Whitman is not only stronger today in every way than it has ever been, but is being far better managed" than it was under its previous three presidents.[91] Concluding that the complaints against Anderson were "pitifully weak," trustees thought it possible that "one or two influential persons" had been engaged in the "insidious work" of insisting that the administration "was overturning the ideals and traditions" of the institution. The trustees stated: "Dr. Anderson has our full support."[92]

Apparently, two changes resulted from student disaffection. Anderson became more available by scheduling hours to meet with stu-

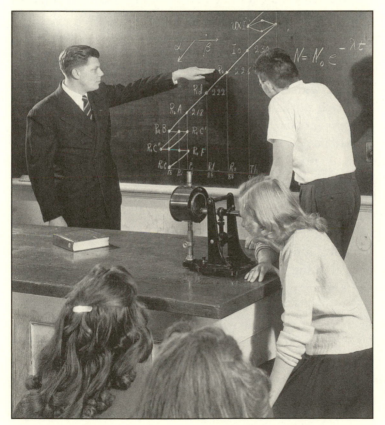

Photographed in 1947, Ivar Highberg taught physics between 1936 and 1948. Many V-12 cadets recalled his effectiveness.

dents, and a new faculty-student discipline committee was established. The petitioners expressed satisfaction that the faculty had
taken them seriously.

Student energies soon moved from complaints about administrators to more traditional concerns. For example, in 1946 the Whitman community celebrated the reinstitution of the all-college revue
and an expanded choral contest. In 1947 the handsome and popular Student Union Building (SUB) opened. In addition, many organizations had recently been reactivated and, together with debate,
athletics, and music, provided for a richer student life; in fact, some
individuals complained that there were too many extracurricular
activities. Men expressed pleasure with the administration for converting the women's annexes back to fraternity houses. Veterans
pledged the fraternities and accepted the housemothers who had
been assigned to each house when the women lived in them. Thus,
for various reasons, the complaints subsided, and very few students
transferred.

While coping with students, Anderson became embroiled in a dispute with Coach Borleske. It was risky for the president to move
against the popular coach, a Whitman institution whose reputation
and power had increased since the 1930s. A few alumni worried that
Borleske had too many responsibilities and recommended that he resign from the job of graduate manager. College leaders, including
Walter Bratton, had also complained that he was too powerful and
that he was overworked. Even Borleske confided to friends that, because of coaching three sports and serving as graduate manager, he
received only five hours of sleep a night. In 1940 he was lionized at
a banquet celebrating his twenty-five years at Whitman. Among the
five hundred celebrants were the legendary football coach Amos
Alonzo Stagg, rival Willamette University coach Roy "Spec" Keene,
and major sports writers such as George Varnell of the *Seattle Times*
and L. H. Gregory of the *Portland Oregonian*. Banquet speakers and
hundreds of letter writers—many his former players—hailed his
coaching skills, his character, and his civic spirit. Clearly, Borleske
had inspired numerous men.

But Anderson chose to reduce Borleske's influence in the 1940s,
at a time when the coach had acquired, in biographer Jack Hewins'
view, the power of a baron. Borleske took leaves from his duties in

Members of Phi Delta Theta ride a float in the 1948 Homecoming parade on a Main Street crowded with townspeople as well as students. Homecoming celebrations were major events, featuring parades, rallies, and campus signs.

1940–1941 and in 1944–1945 to carry out assignments for Rotary International. In 1944 he wrote the trustees that he was resigning because of disputes with them and with the president. He recalled that: "As a young man, I was thrilled by Whitman's traditions, its aims, and its ideals. This feeling has not diminished by the passing years. . . . So it is with the deepest regret that I am leaving the city and the college."[93] The trustees persuaded him to retract his resignation and take the second leave so that his disputes—especially with Anderson—might cool. The tactic failed. Borleske complained about "materialistic Whitman" and his salary.[94] Upon his return, the coach again denounced the president to faculty members and Phi Delta Theta brothers. Supported by the trustees, Anderson struck at the coach by insisting upon Mignon Borleske's resignation as a physical education instuctor in the spring of 1945, and in 1946 by removing Coach Borleske from his position as graduate manager. According to Franklin "Pete" Hanson, who helped coach the 1946 football team, Borleske was so distracted at this point by his dispute with Anderson that he did a poor job of coaching. He whined and cried most of the season.[95] This behavior, and a disagreement over money that the college owed Borleske, solidified the trustees against the coach.

Just after the June 1947 commencement, they terminated his long and significant career.

According to Shirley Anderson Jennings, Anderson's daughter, this long confrontation led to "systematic harrassment" of her parents. She added that letters were written to the faculty "to undermine my father's authority, and he felt this was intolerable."[96]

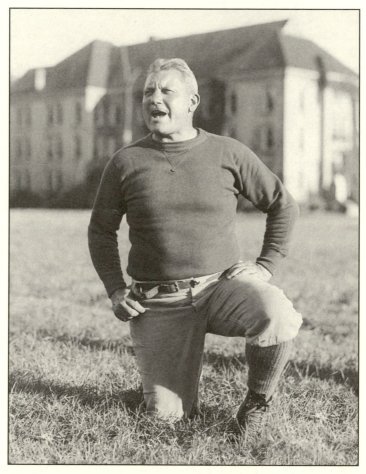

Coach Nig Borleske was the most remarkable athlete ever to graduate from the college. From 1915 to 1947 he won a regional reputation as a coach. A controversial individual, he was dismissed by President Winslow Anderson. He was immediately elected Walla Walla's mayor, and on the evening of his electoral victory Whitman students serenaded him with the college's songs.

Professor Maxey and biographer Hewins both evaluated the long-running dispute. The professor, who never supported Borleske, concluded that: "The Borleskes made it impossible for the Board of Trustees not to fire them. If these two unshrinking violets could have curbed their tongues and kept themselves out of the public eye long enough for an anti-Anderson reaction to set in, I think they would have been invulnerable. But that would have required the Borleskes not to be the Borleskes."[97] Maxey's generalizations are supported by Hewins' account. He charged that the coach's "years of unquestioned authority in athletics and student affairs had brought him a subconscious feeling of kingship which he would have denied in consternation if accused."[98]

Professor Howells assessed the matter: "Borleske was a very difficult man to deal with. . . . It was unfortunate for a thirty-year association with Whitman to end in this manner. . . . If a man who had been at the college for [so long] could be dismissed summarily, the principle of tenure would seem to be not very well established."[99]

Alumna Grace Allan Lazerson served as secretary to the president from 1929 to 1948. She thought that Borleske had been a superb coach considering his limited material, and that his removal was unfortunate. But she stressed that Borleske had regarded himself as indispensable and, in his role as graduate manager, had made critics by his allocation of student money, favoring athletic needs over others; furthermore, he had defended his wife, Mignon, whose lack of professional training and stiff personality created opposition. Maxey agreed with the secretary, asserting that student complaints about Mignon Borleske's required physical education classes had initiated conflict between the president and her husband.[100] Anderson's effort to replace her with a better-trained woman (Chloe Vicker was later appointed) increased Nig Borleske's anger with the president.[101]

With the removal of the influential coach, alumni and sports writers criticized Whitman, especially President Anderson and the trustees. Angry alumni castigated Anderson, asserting that he, not Borleske, should be dismissed; others warned that the popular coach must be retained or they would not contribute money or recruit students. One outraged writer invoked history in his reaction to the dismissal of the coach, reminding the board that the Cayuse leader Tomahas had tomahawked Marcus Whitman. He added that, a hundred years after this murder, Nig Borleske "has also been the victim of skullduggery and treachery. This time in the role of Tomahas we find Dr. Anderson."[102] There would not be another such bitter fight involving athletics until the college dropped football thirty years later. But in 1955 Borleske overcame his bitterness with his alma mater and accepted an overseer's appointment, rendering, Maxey explained, "uniquely valuable service" until his death in 1957.[103]

Alumni would disagree for decades over Borleske's dismissal; for example, Ellen Heath McNamara, who was student body president in 1945, blamed Anderson, "an arrogant and unforgiving person," for initiating confrontation with a man who had done so much for his alma mater, especially during the Great Depression.[104] But, in a 1973 interview, Maxey spoke approvingly of the removal of Borleske, because the coach had "practically issued an ultimatum to the trustees and overseers that either he went or Anderson went. Whatever the rights or wrongs of the case . . . you do not let the athletic coach issue an ultimatum to the governing boards to get rid of the president."[105] While Walla Wallans wrangled over his removal, they overwhelmingly elected "the idol of the town" as their mayor in 1947.[106] Phi Delta Theta members campaigned for him and joined their classmates in celebrating Borleske's election and political career.

The coach's dismissal in 1947 created discord at a time when the deaths of two institutional pillars—Dean William Davis and President Emeritus Stephen Penrose—grieved Whitmanites. Davis, who had been a popular professor and a fervent champion of Whitman, died at the age of sixty-nine. Penrose, about a year prior to his death at the age of eighty-two, had described his daily routine that included physical therapy, correspondence, visitors, Mary's reading to him (along with students, some of whom were paid to read to the bedridden patient), and his writing. He confided to a friend that he was "really quite alive although I would be very glad to pass on."[107] News of the great president's death brought hundreds of tributes from near and far. President Anderson gave the best summary of Penrose's pivotal career: "It can be truly said that Whitman was Penrose and Penrose was Whitman, for no man could give more of himself to a college than did Dr. Penrose."[108]

Despite the emotions and tensions of the immediate post-war period, Anderson continued to enlist support for the college, espe-

*President Emeritus Penrose in 1944. Although he had left the class-
room, he still influenced students, especially when they walked him
around the neighborhoods. He quizzed them about their studies
and futures and held forth on philosophy, religion, and college
history. Alumni well remembered these inspirational walks.*

cially seeking increased alumni giving, a larger endowment to attract
and hold a capable faculty, and several new buildings. Anderson
identified a student union as the greatest need, ranking it ahead of
a library and a women's dormitory; probably most Whitmanites
agreed with him.

The attractive Student Union Building (SUB) was built in 1947 with funds from students and alumni. The popular building was converted in 1968 to offices and classrooms; it was razed in 1975. Billings Hall is visible at right.

The best-remembered accomplishment of Anderson's presidency was the construction of the long-anticipated Student Union Building. The Cabin, which had served some of the functions of a student union when it was briefly operated by students, now had owners who seemed little interested in collegians.[109] In 1944 a faculty-student committee considered plans for building a student union and raised some money for this end. An all-college carnival and student donations provided a small building fund. In 1946 a publicity flyer stated that the union would cost $75,000, that students had pledged at least $5,000, that alumni had donated $6,000, and that the college had raised another $40,000. The facility would provide a fountain, a book store, a lounge, a post office, and other amenities. It would be a living memorial to Whitman men and women who fought in the First and Second World Wars. In May 1946 Whitman received authorization to build and the work commenced. The beautiful building along College Creek opened the following year under Vern Kinsinger's management. This was the first campus building to be

constructed since Prentiss Hall in 1926; it was unique in that it did
not exceed cost estimates. A generation of students would consider
the gracious and functional SUB to be an integral part of their Whitman experience.

There were several other notable accomplishments in the post-
war period. In November 1947 Anderson joined with faculty members in a memorial service honoring Marcus and Narcissa Whitman,
this time on the occasion of the centennial of the Whitman massacre.
Professors William Bailey and Thomas Howells composed a cantata,
"Song of the Greatly Daring," to commemorate the dedicated lives
of the two missionaries. Anderson also led the faculty in establishing a physical education major, insisting that a college "should give
as much attention to physical education as it does to the so-called
academic subjects."[110] Convinced of the merits of the Greek system
and of the need to provide fraternal groups for a student body that
numbered nearly nine hundred, Anderson joined others in bringing

*A college dance in the new SUB, about 1948. A jukebox in one corner supplied
the music, and a Coke stand in another provided refreshments. The hardwood
floor was the best dancing place that the college ever provided; the faculty chaperons also danced fox trots and waltzes with students. Various groups held meeting in this attractive room.*

Alpha Phi sorority and Delta Tau Delta fraternity to campus in 1948. The president urged all the Greeks' leaders to stress scholarship, and was pleased by the fact that about seventy percent of Whitman students affiliated with Greek organizations and maintained grades equal to those of the independents.

The president continued to work at fund raising; the financial records indicate that he raised about $312,000 in six years, matching the dollar amount that President Bratton had raised in the same amount of time. The faculty appreciated the fact that their leader improved salaries, especially those of members of the lower ranks. Those making $2,000 in 1942 jumped to $3,500 in 1948; more experienced professors earned $3,200 in 1942 and $4,000 in 1948. These salary increases helped the faculty cope with post-war inflation, but they still lived modestly. Because the Howells family of five could not afford an automobile, the parents still got around on balloon-tired bikes. The money for salary adjustments resulted from an increase in tuition. In September 1946 the annual fee climbed from $250 to $300; the next year it was increased to $350. Thus, the college simultaneously enjoyed record-breaking enrollments, veterans with GI Bill funds, and larger tuitions.

In the summer of 1948 Anderson continued to advance ambitious curricular and building plans. He proposed raising $7,500,000 for endowment and buildings during a ten-year campaign, but he became ill and died of a brain tumor late in the year. Chester Maxey concluded that the growing tumor explained why Anderson's behavior in his last two years "was so different" from that of 1941, when he had been interviewed by the selection committee.[111] Although Professor Sires chaired a committee that had found some faults with the president, in the end he nevertheless commended him for having "the insight and ability to bring about the administrative changes that were required" to meet a greatly expanded student body.[112] Anderson was certainly not one of Whitman's most popular or respected presidents, but he left the college in a stronger position than when he took office. At his memorial service in November 1948, Maxey eulogized: "His colleagues and co-workers . . . know that we are indebted to him for much that we now enjoy of material well-being and professional satisfaction."[113]

7

An Alumnus Becomes President:
The Chester Maxey Era
1948–1959

According to Robert A. Skotheim, who served as Whitman's president from 1975 to 1988, Chester Maxey was "one of the three most influential persons in Whitman's history"—Stephen Penrose and Donald Sherwood were the other two—and he was, as well, "the best known published scholar in the college's history."[1] Maxey's peers also recognized his many talents. Not since the appointment of Penrose in 1894 had the trustees had an easier time in selecting a president than they did in 1948, when they chose Maxey. Board members, as well as alumni, faculty members, and townspeople, realized that the new leader brought outstanding strengths to the office.

Maxey's remarkable career is chronicled in his frank autobiography, *The World I Lived In*. Half of this informative, entertaining book traces his life before his elevation to the Whitman presidency. Maxey, like trustee Sherwood, came from humble roots and was reared by a widow. His grandparents had moved to Ellensburg, Washington, in 1882, anticipating that this rough town would become a major rail and agricultural center. (Enthusiastic boosters even predicted that its central location would make it the state's capital.) Chester Maxey described his father, Morton Maxey, as "a born risk taker," one of those hoping that Ellensburg would flourish.[2] A farmer and laborer, the elder Maxey married Leota Collins in 1889. They had two children: Chester, born in 1890, and Aurel, born in 1891.

Morton Maxey died in 1897; Aurel died of meningitis ten years later. Chester and his mother remained in Ellensburg, a typical dusty western town of wooden buildings, privies, board sidewalks, kerosene lanterns, railroads, saloons, street fights, cowboys, brothels, disease, and primitive medicine. Maxey later accorded credit for his development to his mother, grandparents, Methodism, teachers, boyhood friends, the Normal School, the theaters, and the countryside. The boy learned the value of physical labor, acquired a love of books, and developed into an athlete and debater. His autobiography details an interesting life in a raw town; in fact, it is one of the most appealing published accounts of a Pacific Northwest boyhood.

Maxey's secondary training was weaker than Penrose's had been. A graduate of a public high school, he discovered at Whitman the value of "unlearning." In his freshman year, "Unlearning seemed to take priority over learning. History was the worst. What the college professors of history did to high school history was more than mayhem; it was total evisceration."[3]

Maxey chose Whitman College over the University of Washington because the smaller school offered him a four-year merit scholarship and a campus job. In several ways his career at the primitive Whitman was similar to Penrose's career at the sophisticated Williams. Both men attended college at a time when it was unnecessary for men to do so unless they sought professional degrees in law, medicine, or theology. Maxey stated that, in the Pacific Northwest, an individual could be successful without a B.A. "College education," he emphasized, "was the cream on the milk."[4] Both men benefited from excellent college teaching. Although Maxey did not have a famous professor like Mark Hopkins, who profoundly influenced Penrose, he nevertheless blossomed into a solid scholar under the tutelage of his professors, especially Stephen Penrose, Walter Bratton, Norman Coleman, Charles Haines, and William Lyman. Both men were at their respective colleges in critical times: Penrose observed a talented president reform Williams; Maxey was at Whitman when President Penrose and Dean Archer Hendrick advocated the ambitious "Greater Whitman" proposal. There were further similarities between the two men: both Penrose and Maxey had suffered the trauma of losing a beloved sibling; had become more liberal in their religious views; had, like their families, become Republicans (though both eventually learned to appreciate Democrats); had enjoyed extracurricular activities (sports, music, fraternities, debate, and journalism); and had their future careers shaped in college. Both educators had been trained in a classical curriculum and defended it. Maxey wrote, "Though it gave us little guidance for the future, it was not guilty of misguidance. We were not given a blueprint to follow; we were given nothing but stiff intellectual training, and that was our greatest need."[5] He added that the professors from Williams simply and successfully imitated the curriculum they had studied.

However, there were also major differences between these two influential leaders. Maxey grew up in a frontier town and did not enjoy the opportunities of urban America—as Penrose did growing up in Philadelphia—until after his college graduation. His family lacked the means to pay for his college education, so he had to work while attending classes, and in the summers he performed physical labor in Ellensburg. While Penrose's classmates were sophisticated men from wealthy eastern families, Maxey attended college with men and women who, he stated, came from "little sagebrush towns" east of the Cascades or from "the big woods" towns west of the mountains.[6] A coeducational college also gave the westerner a better chance to enjoy female companionship. In his senior year, Maxey became engaged to conservatory student Elnora Campbell.

He received a B.A. in political science in 1912, and earned an M.A. in political science at the University of Wisconsin in 1914, having the good fortune of studying under the excellent teachers John R. Commons, Edward A. Ross, and Richard T. Ely. After three years of teaching at Oregon Agricultural College (now Oregon State University), he attended Columbia University, working for a Ph.D. Again he studied under renowned scholars, including John Dewey (Maxey called him a dull lecturer), James Harvey Robinson, John Bassett Moore, and Charles A. Beard. During and after his work for his degree, Maxey was on Beard's staff at the New York Bureau of Municipal Research; he benefited professionally from this prestigious position. In 1919 Maxey received his Ph.D., and the next year accepted a professorship at Western Reserve University in Cleveland. For five years, the young scholar taught large classes and researched city government. He published two books in 1924—*An Outline of Municipal Government* and *Readings in Municipal Government*. As Maxey recalled these years: "It is difficult for me to understand how I found the time and energy to grind out books while spinning around so dizzily in the whirligig of academic and civic activity." By 1923 he and his wife, Elnora, had two daughters, Marilyn and Aurel.

Maxey did not want to spend his professional career at Western Reserve, where his independent spirit created several difficulties with "the entrenched faculty oligarchies."[7] He and Elnora concluded that they would like to return to the Pacific Northwest, which was, according to his daughter Marilyn, the only region he really enjoyed. Maxey resigned from Western Reserve, and wrote to Whitman about a position. Penrose immediately offered him the Miles C. Moore Professorship of Political Science, and his wife received an appointment in the Whitman Conservatory of Music.

Supportive of her husband, the college, and the community, Elnora Maxey became a noted townswoman. She had been born in Spokane, and had completed requirements at Pearson's Academy and the Whitman Conservatory. The young musician met Maxey in 1911 —he joked that she soon had him "fully roped and tied"—but they delayed marriage until 1915, when he was professionally established. While he attended Columbia, she enrolled in the Juilliard School of Music. When Whitman hired them in 1925, Mrs. Maxey taught vocal music at the conservatory, giving numerous private lessons. For years, her Glee Club received hearty applause across the region. Mrs. Maxey was deeply involved in music as a soloist, as the director of a church choir, and as a trainer of fraternity groups preparing for the college choral contest. In 1944 she retired from the conservatory and ended her public performances as a mezzo-soprano. Daughter Marilyn recalled that, when someone asked her why she had stopped performing, "Her response was invariably, 'I would rather you asked me why did you than why didn't you.'"[8]

At Whitman, Chester Maxey continued his unusually rich career. In 1926 the Carnegie Endowment for International Peace invited him to be among a select group of professors to enjoy an all-expense-paid tour of "the important European centers of international organization and activity." He evaluated this experience: "This Carnegie tour was one of the cardinal experiences of my life, not merely because of the European travel, but chiefly because it rewarded me with an abundance of direct information and insight relative to international affairs."[9] The Carnegie Endowment would also underwrite Maxey's expenses when he participated in programs it held in the United

States in 1928 and 1934. Maxey made some trenchant comments about the 1934 meeting, held at the University of Michigan; he thought that the invited professors of international law were "selected for their conspicuous dumbness," and that the summer heat meant that the "big big-shots let down and coasted along. . . . They couldn't even get the beer decently cool, and you know how that would handicap a man engaged in intellectual labors."[10]

In 1932 Maxey engaged in two political activities. Regionally, he unsuccessfully sought the Republican nomination for a Congressional seat; on campus, he organized students for socialist candidate Norman Thomas against Herbert Hoover and Franklin D. Roosevelt. While seeking the Republican nomination, Maxey appeared before a labor audience. Because the Democratic candidate could not appear, one of Maxey's students, William Perry, spoke in his place. Perry, who promoted left-wing politics in Walla Walla, was "sold on Maxey," but he took the floor after his professor and criticized him for talking down to an audience of working men. The student had the distinct impression that his mentor appreciated his candor; he also remembered Maxey as a "lousy campaigner" because he treated each audience as if it were a class.[11] The professor stressed a lower tariff and lower taxation by eliminating pork-barrel politics.[12] After this unsuccessful bid for office, Maxey did not run again because, "Affairs at Whitman College were approaching a grave crisis, and I wanted to be free to take a hand in working out a solution for that. I was basically more interested in trying to get Whitman . . . out of the woods than in getting myself elected to Congress."[13]

In 1934 it was necessary for Maxey to help resolve the college's financial crisis. He became chair of a special emergency fund committee to reduce the college's floating debt, explaining to alumni:

> [The college] has borrowed from the banks, borrowed from its faculty, and borrowed from mercantile firms. This indebtedness now aggregates a sum that threatens to sink the college completely. Unless, within the next year, it can be reduced to a point where it can be carried without piling up further indebtedness, there is little hope of going on. The faculty have reached the limit of their ability to carry the college, and so have the merchants and bankers.[14]

Maxey's appeals raised a small but important sum, and his experience with deficit financing would influence his policies when he became president of the college. Teaching during the Great Depression also led to his interpretation that his hard-pressed colleagues—not businessmen—carried the college through the turbulent 1930s. He judged that, "If the faculty had insisted and gone to court collecting for salaries, they could have collected because the college had the assets to pay."[15]

During his pre-presidential years at Whitman, Maxey was arguably the second most active figure on campus, next to its president (although to many people Nig Borleske's name probably would have been more familiar). For more than twenty years, he consistently taught large classes, advised numerous students, and chaired significant faculty committees. Most students enjoyed his classes because of his knowledge and his formal, organized teaching style. Winifred "Winks" Dunphy, who studied under him, and later served as his executive secretary during his presidency, summarized: "I do not believe that he exuded the warmth that many people associate with a college professor, like *Goodbye, Mr. Chips*, but he knew how to organize."[16]

His students stated that he liked to make provocative statements to arouse them, and many recalled the challenging written and oral questions he gave during senior comprehensive examinations in political science. Edward P. Morgan recalled these experiences in a letter to Maxey: "I can never quite forgive you for [the examinations]. And I can never quite thank you enough. Because somehow you managed to deflate and inflate me at the same time. The world is a wonderful and fearful place and you helped me get a little closer to the reality of it."[17] Some students, however, thought he was intimidating, and others complained about his arbitrary attendance policy: he failed students with a certain number of absences, authorized or not. Maxey recalled that the most humorous thing he did on an examination was to list books and authors, asking for additional information. He noted: "The funny part of it was that both the books and authors were phoney, but it was surprising the number of book reviews I got."[18] Penrose evaluated his lively colleague: "He is a man of very great ability, with a realistic mind which keeps him from going into the clouds or from getting away from practical human problems. He is one of our best teachers, being able to interest his students intensely in . . . his courses." [19]

Maxey was regularly engaged in administration, becoming a dean in 1931. Because of his administrative experience and popularity, several individuals recommended that he replace Rudolf Clemen as president in 1936. The political scientist maintained that he had no interest in the presidency; he preferred to teach and write. But Maxey was closely involved with college management during every administration, especially that of Winslow Anderson.

The popular and efficient professor participated in many other activities. He took time to become involved in student activities, including supporting the baseball team and serving as an adviser to Beta Theta Pi. Meanwhile, he earned a regional reputation from addresses delivered in schools and churches and to service clubs and professional associations. Many listeners would long remember his thought-provoking assessments of municipal government and the League of Nations. Maxey's writing won him a national reputation. Professor Ronald Sires accepted an appointment at Whitman in large part because of the political scientist's scholarship. Maxey's most influential book was the revised edition of *The American Problem of Government*, published in 1934, when he was "busy as a one-armed paperhanger." This book would go through several editions and would earn him "substantial royalties." [20] In 1938 he wrote another well-received book, *Political Philosophies*.

In the war years, Maxey pondered the return of "G. I. Joe" and concluded that the returnees wanted to find the school unchanged. The professor stated that a soldier on furlough told him, "If they change a single blade of grass on this campus while I am away, I am going to raise hell." Maxey feared that the "technically self-assured educators" would ensnare the bewildered veterans, and he joked about his own handicap of "knowing nothing technically about education. I know so little that I could not qualify for a teaching certificate in any state of the Union. I humbly thank God for my ignorance. I seem to remember that Plato and Aristotle and a lot of other old boys who did pretty well as educators were similarly handicapped." [21]

Despite a remarkable record, Maxey considered leaving his alma mater. In 1946 he responded to a feeler about a position at the Uni-

versity of Southern California: "I do not consider myself married
to this place. However, it happens to be a good spot. . . . Relative
to living conditions in this community, my salary is large." He added:

> My principal objection to my present position is that it has be-
> come so predominantly administrative that I have insufficient
> time for research and writing. Technically, I give one-half of
> my time to teaching and the other half to administration, but
> administration has a way of stealing much more than its share.
> I must have some talent for administration or they would not
> shove so much of it my way, but I definitely do not enjoy it
> and never have. If I were offered a position in a strong insti-
> tution which required of me nothing but teaching and would
> give me plenty of time to write, I would be greatly tempted.[22]

In 1948 the University of Washington offered him a professorship. He threatened to leave if Whitman did not match the university's salary offer. Alarmed by the possibility of losing the faculty's
most prestigious professor, Anderson and the trustees gave him the
$5,000 he requested. Maxey concluded: "Perhaps I should have been
more noble and sacrificial, but after twenty-three years of deferred
expectations at Whitman, I had no desire for more of the same."

Anderson died during the fall of 1948, and the anxious trustees
and overseers asked Maxey if he would serve as acting president. He
rejected the offer, but, like the board members, he understood that
Whitman "was confronted with a grave emergency, and it might be
that there was temporary need for a president who knew the college inside out, as I certainly did."[23] Thus the professor proposed
to the boards that they appoint him as president for a two-year term.
The trustees happily agreed to this unusual arrangement, but did not
make public the two-year limit. Chester Maxey, like Stephen Penrose, took office in the wake of an unpopular president; both faced
financial difficulties.

An Activist President

Colleges and universities experienced rapid growth following the
Great Depression and the Second World War, periods that had limited their expansion. Everywhere, private colleges in the post-war

Chester Maxey, who served as Whitman's seventh president, was one of the most important individuals in the college's history. Maxey was a published scholar, an impressive teacher, a skilled dean, and a tough-minded president. His autobiography, The World I Lived In, *is an important and sometimes controversial interpretation of the college's history.*

period reported increased student enrollments, larger endowments, and additional campus buildings; and public universities were growing even more rapidly than the private institutions. Thus, Whitman's impressive gains in the 1950s were not exceptional. Except for a brief time during the Korean War, the college was bound to grow to meet a new public demand, but the directions the school took resulted primarily from Chester Maxey's leadership. The strong-willed captain set Whitman's course.

Observers noted that Maxey was as energetic and decisive in his presidency as he had been in his classroom and in faculty meetings. He put his stamp on the college, and ranks as one of its most influential leaders; in fact, he rejuvenated the office of president. The three presidents who served between Penrose and Maxey all had short tenures, and each lacked the combination of vitality and temperament to shape the institution as these two men did. Maxey took office at the age of fifty-eight with far more experience than Penrose had had when he became president at the young age of thirty. Unlike Penrose, he grasped the administrative reins when the college was in no danger of financial collapse, but, like his illustrious predecessor, he immediately plunged into his presidential labors. While he did not teach as many classes as Penrose had, Maxey stated: "I did teach most of the time when I was president. . . . I taught one course."[24]

Unfortunately, much detail about his administration is omitted from his autobiography—only one-fifth of the book deals with this capstone of his career—and he failed to save his official correspondence for the college archives. Penrose, during his important presidency, kept nearly every letter; Maxey, although aware of the boxes of Penrose material stuffed in the tower of Memorial Hall, did not accumulate his own archives.

Fortunately, the official records of the Maxey administration have survived, providing considerable information about his tenure. His reports to the trustees, his addresses to various audiences, his authorship of *Facets* (a useful bulletin of Whitman events for alumni), and his many hours of oral interviews, particularly with Professor Robert Whitner, augment his autobiography. Furthermore, the board of trustees' minutes, recorded by Winks Dunphy, are more complete than those under most other administrations. Interviews conducted during the 1990s with alumni, faculty members, and staff members, as well as information supplied by his two daughters, also provide useful details about the man and the college in the 1950s. Regrettably, most faculty members—some of whom had voiced strong opinions about Maxey's forceful leadership—did not write about that formative decade.

In his first days Maxey confessed to students that he was bewildered by his responsibilities and that he "should be wearing a green dink," but his actions clearly demonstrated that he wielded presidential power effectively.[25] Maxey recalled that his first six weeks in office were trying, because he had to grapple with three needs: a secretary, an administrative reorganization of the faculty, and immediate fund raising to avoid an annual deficit. Although the new president failed to raise money quickly, there was no deficit, because of careful management by bursar George Marquis. In fact, the leader boasted at the end of his first year that the school was "substantially in the black."[26] Maxey also resolved the other two problems. He hired Winks Dunphy as his secretary, later recalling that "this was one of the wisest decisions I made as president."[27] She also became secretary of the board of trustees, the first woman to serve in that role. One trustee grumbled to Maxey that "women like to talk," but the president assured him that the proceedings of the trustees' meetings would be held in confidence: "You don't have to worry, she won't say anything."[28]

To provide a more efficient administration, and to permit more faculty members to serve on major administrative bodies, Maxey took the lead in creating a new administrative system, which won the faculty's full cooperation. Professors agreed with him that, under President Anderson, who had established numerous committees, there had been duplication and confusion. Under the new faculty structure—the first reorganization since 1934—the curricular divisions were increased from three to five: Division I, social sciences; Division II, literature and language; Division III, basic sciences; music and art became Division IV; and health and physical education became Division V. A new five-member faculty council, elected to a five-year term of office, served "as a preconsidering, advisory, and recommending agency of the faculty." The dean of the faculty served as its presiding officer; other administrators sat as ex-officio members. The dean of administration managed the co-curricular activities and was advisor for the administrative council, which included the office of student affairs, the student center, the infirmary, and other agencies. Maxey correctly asserted that the new two-council plan was more efficient and "more thoroughly democratic than any previous organization plan at Whitman."[29]

Maxey also created the president's council, a group consisting of the chief administrative officers and the dean of the faculty. This useful body had several functions, including making decisions in the president's absence (decisions which Maxey always sustained). The council continues to the present day, providing new presidents with valuable background information. All of Maxey's successors have used the president's council in one fashion or another.

Maxey was the first president to report detailed information about the numbers and roles of the administrative staff. When he assumed office, the college employed twenty-seven full-time and thirteen part-time individuals, most of whom worked in the business office, the library, and the student affairs office. When he resigned, there had been a small increase in full-time employees and there were an additional nine part-time employees. Maxey expressed concern about this enlarged staff, but he defended it by reminding the Whitman community that clerical and accounting workers were needed to handle the mounting paperwork required by the federal government and by various college offices. The president explained the growth of "Old Man Overhead" by asking alumni:

> Would you send your young hopeful to a college that had no health service, no infirmary, no recreational program, no organized and supervised social program, no competently staffed dormitories, no counseling service, no library service after 5:00 PM, no employment service for students and graduates, and none of the other extra-classroom appurtenances of the modern college? You definitely would not. You want your boy or girl to have higher education with all of the trimmings.

He priced the "trimmings": "This year [1955] we are putting out $381 per student for the pure quill classroom stuff and $792 per student for the trimmings, a total of $1,173. Maybe it should be the other way around, but I don't know how to get it that way."[30]

To free himself from administrative detail, Maxey reduced the number of staff officers reporting to him from fifteen to five, including the dean of administration, the dean of the faculty, and the treasurer. The president's door was not closed, but staff and faculty members knew to ask secretary Dunphy about his mood prior to making a request.

There were important changes in the administration. In 1948 the traditional positions of dean of men and dean of women were eliminated, and they became coordinated personnel officers who were

now called "director of men's affairs" and "director of women's affairs." In 1949 George Marquis, who had served as bursar for forty-
three years, retired; assistant Fritz Wilson succeeded him, bringing
experience in banking, insurance, accounting, and farm mortgaging.
As bursar, Wilson immediately helped create the farm committee
to manage Whitman's various farm properties. He also discovered
about $60,000 that his predecessor had "squirreled away in fake
accounts";[31] Marquis had hidden Whitman's money because he did
not trust any college president, considering them all to be spendthrifts.
A few years later, the offices of bursar and treasurer were merged
and Fritz Wilson became treasurer. Robert R. "Pete" Reid, also an
alumnus, became Wilson's assistant as business manager in 1952. The
Pioneer expressed approval: "There is no mistaking Pete Reid; for
his smile and personality team up to make him a friend of all."[32]

In other changes, Dean Charles Armstrong, who had originally
come to Whitman in 1943 to direct the V-12 program, was elevated
to the newly created office of vice president. Administrators appointed during this period included alumnus and faculty member

President Maxey is surrounded by key members of his administration in 1952: Ruth
Reynolds, Fritz Wilson, Pete Reid, Douglas McClane, Kenneth Hupp, and Winks
Dunphy. All were Whitman alumni and all would have long careers at the college.

David Stevens, who became dean of administration, and Paul Harvey, who became director of food services. Both men served Whitman ably for decades. An outside evaluator declared, "Dean Stevens is a man of striking personality and considerable drive and is an excellent addition to the faculty."[33] Harvey won continuing applause for providing quality food at reasonable cost.

These staff members and others commented on the fact that the new president was unhurried and punctual. He arrived at his office at 9:00 AM and left promptly at 5:00 PM. During these hours the efficient leader accomplished considerable work.

In his first eighteen months in office, Maxey set numerous objectives, including other significant organizational changes. One of his most important accomplishments, he later asserted, was the establishment of more efficient and meaningful meetings of the boards of trustees and overseers. The president charged that both boards had "become rather pedestrian and apathetic."[34] Maxey knew how to enliven a classroom, and he brought life to the boardroom through his appealing personality. He told great stories and presented interesting facts. Impatient with slow-moving committee meetings, he made board meetings pleasurable because of his tight agenda and stimulating, wide-ranging discussions of educational policy. To get the scattered overseers more involved in policy matters, Maxey called them "ambassadors" and organized them into regional groups based in Portland, Seattle, Spokane, San Francisco, and New York City. Each group—sometimes with Maxey in attendance—followed an agenda, made recommendations to the trustees, and came to the annual overseer meetings well prepared to discuss important issues.

The board of overseers, made up of about fifty individuals serving five-year terms, experienced a greater turnover in membership than did the board of trustees. A third of the members, however, remained in office during the whole period of Maxey's presidency, including Clarence Braden, Harold Crawford, William O. Douglas, and James Alger Fee, the long-time chairman of the board. The five regional overseer groups served under vice chairmen, including Ralph J. Cordiner (the Atlantic coast) and J. Ernest Knight (western Washington). The establishment of the regional overseer groups impressed Whitmanites. Alumnus Nard Jones judged: "Maxey's most brilliant stroke as president was his drawing together the key alumni by means of a system of regional overseers, a system which gives Whitman a very practical national strength."[35]

Five overseers were appointed as an executive committee, to act on behalf of the board in the intervals between its annual meetings. According to Maxey, the overseers reviewed and took final action on the college's budget, established faculty salaries, responded to reports from the trustees and from important committees, and located donors. This board also decided that the college's enrollment should be set at eight to nine hundred through selective admission, and it authorized new major studies, including speech and art. The overseers also approved combined engineering degree programs with Columbia University and the California Institute of Technology. Although the trustees actually had the final authority in all of these matters, the overseers made decisions that the trustees endorsed, under the urging of Maxey. The overseers, like the faculty, now enjoyed a more vital organization. The president boasted that he got "some sparks flying,"[36] and trustee Harper Joy agreed, praising him for his "dynamic approach."[37]

Maxey's twenty-five years on the Whitman faculty had taught him much, including the need to appoint competent and energetic trustees. To his way of thinking, the college's financial problems of the late 1920s and early 1930s had resulted from poor trustee decisions and from Penrose's inability to lead an independent-minded board. He was also aware that the trustees' confidence in President Winslow Anderson had diminished after the student petitions against him. Political scientist Maxey knew that he must lead talented and dedicated trustees in the directions that he wanted to take the college. He, not they, would set the educational goals. One of Maxey's major accomplishments was finding and retaining supportive trustees. While Maxey's book, *The World I Lived In*, does not boast about dominating the trustees, the autobiography does make it clear that his views generally prevailed. Pete Reid, who served under this strong administrator, observed: "Maxey was the leader. If he wanted to get something he went to individual trustees seeking support. He and Donald Sherwood, an influential trustee, sometimes disagreed, but the strong-willed leaders ironed out difficulties and became good friends. The board was not going to stand in the president's road. Their conservative economic views and Maxey's blended."[38]

Trustees rejoiced over the fact that the college not only avoided deficits, but actually compiled annual surpluses. They agreed with Maxey's stricture that he did "not believe in deficit financing for education any more than for business or government"; furthermore, "In these days . . . only colleges that stay out of debt can be sure of staying alive."[39] To make certain that he possessed the board's support, Maxey recalled, he had insisted that they annually vote his reappointment, as a show of confidence.[40] But the trustees' minutes contain a different story. In March 1950 they awarded him a five-year term, which he welcomed.[41] The board's minutes did not record subsequent reappointments, although Maxey served until 1959.

The trustees played a very significant role in governing Whitman. The members, who met about nine times a year, were nearly all residents of eastern Washington, including four Walla Wallans. Although the Russell report in the mid-1930s had roundly denounced the appointment of so many local trustees, the Walla Wallans in the 1950s—unlike those of the early 1930s—were extremely effective. Another important feature of this board was membership continuity. The most notable change was the 1949 retirement of Dr. Park Weed Willis, who had served as a trustee for forty-four years. There were few additions in the Maxey years: six men remained on the board throughout his tenure, including veterans Harper Joy, Dr. John Lyman, Robert "Roy" Cahill, and Herbert Ringhoffer. Maxey voiced only a mild reservation about the lack of turnover among the trustees, who tended to vote each other back into office for additional three-year terms. But there were three significant additions to the board—Seattleite Arthur T. Lee, Walla Wallan Donald Sherwood, and Spokanite Mary Cooper Jewett, the first woman trustee. Most board members were Whitman alumni with close friendships of fraternity brotherhood—Maxey and Ringhoffer were members of Beta Theta Pi; Lee, Cahill, Lyman, Joy, and Sherwood were Phi Delta Thetas. Fraternal brotherhood had much to do with the trustees' commitment to their alma mater; Stephen Penrose, who had seen this phenomenom at work at Williams College, had correctly anticipated that it would play a role at Whitman.

The trustees transacted diverse business—mostly financial—including the approval of life income contracts, the management of urban and rural properties, the negotiation of building contracts, the initiation of fund-raising programs, the fixing of tuition and room and board charges, and the approval of the budget. A variety of personnel matters came before the board, including hirings and tenure decisions. The trustees sometimes decided some inconsequential matters, such as granting a freshman the right to live in his grandfather's house rather than in Lyman House, and refusing to loan money to Mortar Board, which wanted to sell songbooks.[42] The trustees received requests to donate to the Marcus Whitman Statue Foundation, an organization that wanted to erect a statue of the missionary in the nation's capitol building; they rejected these appeals, but Whitman students raised money for the cause, judged by the *Pioneer* to be one about which "every Whitmanite can feel justly proud."[43]

Trustees and overseers served with non-board members on three productive joint committees—the finance committee, the farm committee, and the buildings and grounds committee. Chaired by Harper Joy, the modern finance committee, dating from 1937, had the task of securing "the highest return compatible with the security and stability necessary for college investments."[44] This talented and well-respected group of seven shrewdly invested the college's endowment in stocks, bonds, mortgages, and real estate.

The farm committee was established to rationalize the administration of the college's farms. Chaired by Walla Wallan Clarence Braden, a highly successful wheat farmer and dealer in farm machinery, the committee was initially composed of men chosen by him. Maxey enjoyed reporting that: "None were college men, none had even gone as far as the eighth grade, but all had minds and knew how to use them."[45] The group inspected each of the college's eight farms, arranged their leases, and reported to the boards about problems and profits. Maxey praised the farm committee: "Some of the best farm brains . . . in this county [are] working for the college."[46]

The third new group, the committee on buildings and grounds, assumed the responsibility of inspecting the physical plant and making recommendations. Maxey stated that this committee had more expertise than he did, and that it saved him time.

The members of the various boards and committees worked diligently for the institution. Under Maxey's energetic leadership, they strengthened Whitman, especially financially, setting a standard for later boards and committees. While there was far more participation

on the part of professors as well as board members under his administration than there had been previously, it was obvious in both
groups that Maxey was clearly in charge. His agenda dominated faculty and board policy. Maxey exemplified the college presidents of
the 1950s, who wielded considerable power.

In 1949 the president reported to the boards that the school enjoyed a healthy enrollment of 866, but that veterans now made up
only thirty-five percent of the student body, and that this percentage
would soon decline further. To build enrollment, Maxey strengthened the director of admissions' office by adding two assistants—one
to handle correspondence and the other to assist Douglas McClane
in his field work, especially the efforts to recruit outside the state. To
attract and retain more students, the college again needed to find
more scholarship and student-aid money. These funds had been less
important when the GIs attended Whitman, since each of them, in
effect, had possessed a government scholarship. Maxey warned that
increasing both the scholarship and aid funds meant that money
would have to come from current operating income, "thus materi-
ally reducing the amounts available for direct educational services."[47]
Once again, the professors would see money go to students rather
than to them.

In 1950 President Maxey presented additional important details
about enrollments. In April he informed alumni that, if the school
failed to maintain about 850 students, "undesirable cut-backs in faculty personnel and physical facilities" might follow.[48] In June the
president reported to the governing boards that the enrollment had
shrunk from 884 to 826 students, causing a significant loss of tuition
income. He thought, however, that the ratio of 483 men to 343 wom-
en was acceptable. Maxey expressed concern over the difficulty of
replacing two hundred graduating seniors. This was the largest senior class in the school's history, and the other three classes, with fewer
Second World War veterans attending on the GI Bill, were "abnor-
mally small."[49] He also feared, as had presidents Penrose and Bratton, that it would be difficult to recruit men. This would be a particular concern in the early 1950s, when there would be a smaller
college-age population.

Building a Stronger College

From his first days in office, Maxey mastered details of the college's
financial situation. He took seriously his presidential responsibility
to improve the school's economic standing through fund raising. In
his autobiography, he honestly admitted, "I detested fund-raising,"
but he recognized its importance and consistently worked at it.
Maxey generalized that his predecessors "chose to be occasional and
spasmodic rather than persistent and regular fund raisers" and that
Penrose had opposed persistent fund raising because "it irritated people." The former president, Maxey claimed, asked for money only
when he had a serious need, although the Penrose correspondence,
which Maxey had not read, indicated that he consistently sought
money. In his last ten years in office Penrose had hired three persons to help find donors; Maxey thought that all of these appointees
failed largely because Penrose did not involve himself in soliciting
funds until it was time for "a big push." He added, "It seemed to me
that my only chance of large success in fund raising lay in keeping
the 'big push' going all the time, and that was a job that I personally would have to spearhead. . . . There was not a single day in my
eleven-year tenure in which I did not do some work on financial promotion, and many days I did little else." He also emphasized that
he depended upon volunteer solicitors from the governing boards
and the alumni rather than upon an assistant fund raiser to make
contacts with potential donors.[50] Penrose had actually used about
the same tactics as Maxey, but, after his blindness, he employed a
series of fund raisers.

Understanding that Penrose's inability to travel during the Great
Depression had made it more difficult for him to resolve financial
problems, Maxey immediately began traveling on behalf of the college. In 1949 he traveled extensively both in the West and in the East,
meeting with alumni, overseers, and friends of the college, and hiring new faculty members. Because he knew the college as a student,
professor, and dean, the new president associated easily with alumni.
He never seemed to forget a name. Alumni often expressed great surprise at his ability to remember names and faces. He responded that
he needed to know six thousand individuals and that, "in the main,"

he did.[51] One alumnus wrote that he was "amazed at Maxey's inexhaustible knowledge of who the members of the Whitman family are, what they're doing, and what their aspirations are." He said that Maxey's interest in others resulted in their loyalty to their alma mater.[52] Encouraged by his meetings with the "Whitman family," the president reported: "The alumni, without exception, showed great interest in the college and its future, and were ready and anxious to cooperate in every way possible." [53]

Supplementing the account provided in his autobiography, Maxey's presidential reports detailed his fund raising. His 1951 report sounded like some of Penrose's earlier ones, in complaining that Walla Walla had not been generous with the college. He failed to "understand why it should ever be called upon to justify itself in its home community. From the standpoint of cold cash alone, Whitman is Walla Walla's greatest asset." Every year the college put a million dollars into the local economy, but it received less than ten percent of its income from the city; in fact, the college had not received a significant gift from a townsperson since 1937. He reminded residents that, "Were it not for Whitman, scores of people now living in Walla Walla would be residing elsewhere, and those here would be much poorer both in purse and soul." [54]

Development efforts included several fund drives (they were not called campaigns) during the Maxey presidency. The first was the Living Endowment Fund, begun in 1949. It asked alumni for donations to the annual operating budget to pay for faculty salaries, scholarships, and the costs of the alumni association. The college pushed the Living Endowment Fund throughout the early 1950s, receiving about $12,000 annually. But this amount failed to cover the whole cost of various activities in the expanded alumni office.

The results of this fund raising were dwarfed by the earnings from an unanticipated windfall—$800,000 bequeathed by Sarah Harris Johnson in 1951—that immediately earned Whitman more than $30,000 annually. This Seattleite, whose husband had operated fishing vessels, had no connection with the college, but many of her friends and their children had praised it to her. Whitman's morale soared with the receipt of this gift, the largest ever made to the college up to this time. Treasurer Fritz Wilson correctly predicted that it was the start of a bright financial future. To show their appreciation for the donor's generosity, the trustees immediately established ten scholarships in Johnson's name.

Just prior to the receipt of this magnificent gift, Maxey had bluntly warned that the college was "seriously crippled for the want of adequate funds."[55] But in 1952, because of the Johnson gift and other much more modest ones, solid earnings from the endowment, and rigid economies, the college paid off $116,000 of the bonds issued to construct Prentiss Hall, Lyman House, and the heating plant. Many Whitmanites hailed the debt's elimination; one asserted, incorrectly, that his alma mater was free from debt for the first time since 1895.[56] Regional newspapers publicized the story about the paying off of the bonds and the college's assurance that every cent donated from now on would go to better the college and not to retire old debts. Late in the year, Maxey boasted to alumni that a million dollars had been added to the endowment fund, bringing the total to about $2,400,000.[57] The euphoric president compared the value of the college in 1952 with what it had been in 1895, and said that it had grown by 12,737 percent. Few colleges had, he argued, "started with so little and gained so much."[58]

In the 1950s Whitman began a more organized approach to financial development. In 1951 eastern overseers stressed the need for an office and a staff to promote the college's financial affairs.[59] Kenneth Hupp, a former student of Maxey's, received appointment in March 1952 as assistant to the president with responsibility for "the financial development program." Maxey explained Hupp's addition to the trustees: "It would be wiser to build up a young man who is known to the college than to hire an expert in the fund-raising business."[60] In an emerging financial development program, Hupp traveled with Maxey, but the president performed the fund raising as he contacted foundations and potential donors. For example, Maxey took the lead in securing a Ford Foundation fund of $325,000. (He later recalled: "Getting money out of the foundations is like paying court to a lady. You've got to keep at it.")[61] Hupp, who sought gifts for current operations, assumed several other responsibilities as well, especially as alumni director. In mid-1952 the college announced a new development plan, which Maxey named "Ten Million in Ten Years." He stated, however, that the plan had not originated with him, but resulted from discussions among the governing boards, the faculty, and alumni. The money from this source would not be used to enlarge the student body beyond eight hundred, but it would enhance the "present plant in every way before considering expansion."[62] To give himself time to promote the long-range development of the college, Maxey persuaded the board to promote Dean Armstrong to the new position of vice president, although this office was eliminated after Armstrong resigned in 1953 to become the president of Pacific University.

In general, Maxey chose to shoulder the fund-raising responsibilities. But in 1954, sounding much like Penrose had in his last years, he admitted to the trustees that his pressing presidential duties did not give him enough time to handle the financial development program, and that some solution should be found to achieve the objective of "Ten Million in Ten Years." This campaign fizzled—Maxey does not mention it in his book—and so did his assertion that the school should "develop a permanent and experienced financial promotion staff working on a program so soundly conceived and well tested that it can be successfully carried on for the indefinite future."[63] Again in 1954, he advised the trustees that he lacked time and energy for fund raising: "Either we must employ an outside firm of professional fund-raisers or we must build up a strong fund-raising staff of our own. I urge that earnest attention be given to this problem."[64] In 1955 he repeated his plea for assistance. Later on, Maxey either changed his mind and did not push for either of his two alternatives, or—although this seems less likely—the trustees opposed them. His successors, however, would all practice what he had advocated.

In 1953 alumni were asked to donate money or to make pledges for a proposed dormitory to house 150 freshman women. In 1954 the Living Endowment Fund, which had earned about $11,000 in 1952, had attracted gifts from only about eighteen percent of the alumni. Maxey replaced it with a sustaining and development program. Donors could now select any of three funds—a salary fund, a building fund, or a student aid fund. Maxey hoped that alumni would now give in greater numbers because they could donate to a specific need.[65]

Some prestigious and unsolicited gifts improved the college's financial situation. The General Foods Corporation, for example, in

1955 gave unrestricted gifts to only three colleges—Antioch, Whitman, and Williams, because of their "high scholastic standing and records of superior administration."[66] Perhaps Bertram Warren, a 1926 graduate who had become treasurer of General Foods, made certain that his alma mater received this gift.

As the college significantly increased its endowment, the finance committee shrewdly invested this fund so that it made a healthy seven percent a year. Maxey called its chairman, Harper Joy, "an exceptionally perceptive institutional financier . . . who knew what species of monetary investment were best suited to the needs of Whitman."[67] Maxey boasted that he did not know of a "college which consistently realizes as high rates of return on invested funds as Whitman."[68] Joy humorously explained this accomplishment: "God has had His arms around Whitman College, and I have thought many times that God looks around for good investments and says, 'Those people connected with Whitman are trying to do a good job, and I am going to help them.' "[69] For ethical reasons, the trustees screened the type of stock received from donors; for example, in October 1950 they sold a distillery stock because it seemed inappropriate for the college to have investments in liquor or tobacco.

During Maxey's administration the college would develop a program of life income contracts. The president explained: "A life income contract differs from an annuity in that it does not pay a fixed return on the principal sum but pays a fixed percentage of the annual rate of return realized by the college on its whole investment portfolio."[70] He predicted that, because of the college's fine investment record, it should attract $750,000 in ten years from life income contracts. Pomona College's noted life income contract program served as a model for the one established by Whitman trustees; in 1955 one of the Pomona program's administrators came to Walla Walla to teach them about it.[71]

Maxey had to be concerned with expenditures as well as with income. Frugality became a watchword of his administration. From his long collegiate career, the new president understood the need to fund maintenance projects. Careful spending would protect structures and improve an already attractive campus. While Maxey appropriated small amounts for basic maintenance projects, he also furnished a list of new buildings, "which are almost indispensable

if the college is to continue to operate with reasonable efficiency."
The list seemed familiar: a library, a women's dormitory, and a
gymnasium. In 1949 he presented an original argument for a new
library—the greatest need—by insisting that, if the earthquake that
had struck west of the Cascades had hit Walla Walla, then Reynolds
Hall would have "tumbled to ruin."[72] The building was not only
structurally dangerous, it was also jammed with books and furniture.
Whitman also needed a new dormitory because women crammed
Prentiss Hall, and the annexes—College House, Green Cottage, and
the President's House—were ill-suited as women's residences. (Maxey preferred, as President Bratton had earlier, to live in his own home,
so women students resided in the President's House.) Unlike his predecessors, the president did not call for a separate women's gymnasium, but he favored a new structure for men and women to replace the inadequate forty-year-old building.

Maxey also wanted to find space and a staff both for the museum of natural history and for the Northwest history museum, which
had been closed because it lacked a curator. While the boards took
little interest in funding the museums, they did authorize $3,000 in
1949 to asphalt the walks and driveways. A *Pioneer* writer hailed
this improvement because it would no longer be necessary to walk
on mud, ice, "and reported areas of quick-sand."[73]

In that same year the boards also heartily approved moving four
McCaw Hospital barracks and remodeling them to meet pressing
housing needs. These wartime structures, which had served as nurses' dormitories, were brought to campus at a cost of only $54,000.[74]
Two of them—named for professors William R. Davis and Melvin
Jacobs—became women's and then men's dormitories. A third became a faculty office building and then an infirmary. The fourth
building served as the Whitman theater until it burned in 1958 (the
other three lasted until 1967, much longer than predicted). Housing the women in two of these barracks made it possible to bring the
freshmen men from the McCaw Hospital site and restore them to
Lyman House, traditionally a men's dormitory but lately occupied
by women. Assigning students to live two miles from campus had
"been bad for morale."[75]

Grappling with housing needs, the administration had rented a
section of the Odd Fellows Home, calling it "College House." But

when the Korean War slashed male enrollments there were not enough men to fill Lyman House; thus, women, who had complained about College House, moved back into the dormitory. Unhappy about the switch, the men moved to College House. Maxey also worried about the fact that the five housing annexes increased overhead costs. In 1950 the housing problem prompted the trustees to apply—unsuccessfully—for a $400,000 federal grant to build a women's dormitory.

Three years later the Odd Fellows informed Maxey that they were going to demolish College House. To meet this loss of housing, the trustees quickly approved the building of a women's dormitory south of Prentiss Hall. The need was acute, and borrowing the money from the federal government or private sources would be slow, so they sought to raise $285,000. In 1940 the heirs of Seattleite Agnes Healy Anderson (who, like Sarah Harris Johnson, had no Whitman connection) had given $165,000 for the construction of a women's dormitory; subsequently, others contributed to Whitman's Agnes Healy

In 1949 the college moved four McCaw Hospital buildings to the campus. Other Northwest colleges also used government surplus buildings for various purposes. At Whitman they served as classrooms, faculty offices, dormitories, and a theater. In 1967 they were removed to make room for Sherwood Center.

College House, built in 1896 by the Odd Fellows, was leased by Whitman for dormitory space from 1941 until 1954, the year it was razed.

Anderson Fund, which trustees earmarked for a building.[76] Maxey asked trustees to name the new dormitory,[77] and they chose to name it Anderson Hall because of the fund, although it covered less than a third of the $400,000 construction cost.[78] As with the naming of Billings Hall, a wealthy person with no Whitman connections—not a dedicated and influential professor, such as Helen Pepoon—would be honored. Many individuals reasonably assume that the dormitory honors Whitman's first president, Alexander Jay Anderson, or his family. Unfortunately, they are wrong.

Miriam Wagenschein, the dean of women, chaired a committee that planned the building, which took less than a year to finish. Some Whitmanites liked the dormitory's features, expressing pleasure with the special closets for hanging formal dresses, elevators for lifting trunks, and other amenities. But other observers faulted the dormitory's design; some also expressed shock upon seeing the telephone booth and some of the walls painted in "an intense version of the famous [Professor of art Richard] Rasmussen orange."[79] Maxey sighed, "There is only one thing I know for certain about dormitories

. . . namely, that nobody has ever been smart enough to build one that was completely satisfactory to its successive generations of occupants and administrators."[80]

While Anderson Hall's construction resulted from a pressing need, the Penrose Library was built in response to a long-standing one. For decades, the faculty, librarians, students, and alumni had joined with the college president in urging the construction of a library building to house the hundred thousand volumes that made Whitman's collection the third-largest college library in Washington.[81] In 1951 the college built an annex to the west end of the Reynolds Hall library to hold the large number of books which, stored in closets on the upper floor, had been damaging the building by their sheer weight. Constructed of cement blocks, the one-floor addition housed serials, rare books, manuscripts, and a vault. Although functional, it was, librarian Ruth Reynolds complained, "not a thing of beauty."[82] Maxey agreed, describing it as a "hideous concrete box."[83] Called only a temporary expedient, the annex actually stood for twenty-nine years, serving the college longer than

Completed in 1954, Anderson Hall was named in honor of Agnes Healy Anderson, a donor who had no direct connection with the school. The dormitory was built as a freshman women's residence, but it would later house men.

the handsome Student Union Building that had been built in 1947 and would be demolished in 1975.

Like his presidential predecessors, Maxey pleaded for a library building. "Enlightened philanthropy," he asserted, "can find no better service and no more sublime memorial than the provision of a new library building."[84] He told the alumni: "A first-rate college cannot long remain first-rate if its library is slipping downhill, and ours is." He could cite no redeeming features of Reynolds Hall as a library building and reminded everyone that, when the library moved from the old shack to its present location, "Nobody supposed that twenty years later it would still be trying to make do with an old parlor as a stack room, an old dining hall as a reading room, an old kitchen as a periodicals room, and old student quarters for every purpose from storage space to office." The president further voiced concerns about fire and limited seating.[85]

In 1955 the trustees finally agreed to construct a new library, and chose an appropriate name. Stephen and Mary Penrose had stated that, if there were to be a memorial for them, they preferred a li-

Constructed in 1902 as a women's dormitory, Reynolds Hall served as a library from 1934 until 1957. Then its first floor was used for classrooms and a faculty lounge, and the upper floors provided space for commodious faculty offices.

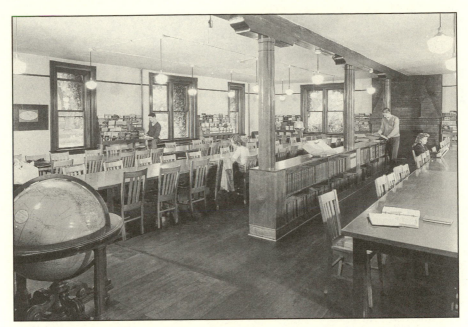

This 1948 photograph shows the reading room of the library, then housed in Reynolds Hall. The weight of the books on the upper two floors caused them to sag. To relieve the weight and to provide room for an expanding library, the annex, an unattractive structure, was added in 1951; it would be removed in 1980.

brary. Alumnus Edward D. "Ned" Baldwin, a great admirer of the Penroses, had in 1936 willed the college $60,000 for a library; this gift had been invested, so that in 1955 it was worth $200,000. The fund provided a solid foundation for a $500,000 drive for the library building. By collectively contributing $175,000, the boards made their largest gift to the college. Trustees Harper Joy and Donald Sherwood, who each generously contributed $50,000, co-chaired the solicitation campaign and successfully insisted that fund raisers seek large gifts before a general drive.[86]

Architect and overseer Harold Crawford and librarian Ruth Reynolds inspected some college libraries and drew up plans for a three-level fire-proof building with dimensions of seventy-five feet by 180 feet. In seeking donors for this critical structure the college assured the public: "The building will provide ample shelf space and reading space for more growth than there is any reason ever to expect at Whitman."[87]

In 1953 librarian Ruth Reynolds and English professor Paul Jackson examine a book on loan from the Folger Library.

At the groundbreaking ceremony, held on a rainy day in early March 1956, a buoyant Maxey said that a library building was "the first step in the fulfillment of a dream that is more than 70 years old."[88] About a year later, the leader declared a "library moving day," cancelling classes so that students could move books into the new library. A system of four organized squads, under the watchful eye of Ruth Reynolds and staff members who acted as "traffic cops," carried the books to their proper places on the new shelves. A student wrote that "Herr Santler" stood at the main entrance of the new library, "giving orders in the tone of a general at a crucial battle: 800s to the left, 300s straight ahead, 900s to the right. When a student wandered up empty-handed, Professor Santler snapped contemptuously, 'Tourist.'" The writer also emphasized that the student effort reflected solid school spirit.[89]

Librarian Ruth Reynolds was the daughter of trustee Allen Reynolds, and the granddaughter of Lettice J. Reynolds, for whom Reynolds Hall was named. Having directed one move from the library shack into Reynolds Hall in 1934 and another into the annex, she announced that this was her third and last library move. She was correct, for the move into the Stuart Wing came after her retirement.

With many members of the Penrose family attending, Dr. Gordon Wright, a Whitman alumnus who was now a distinguished professor at the University of Oregon, gave the dedication address on June 1, 1957. The historian asserted: "Creative scholarship gets its start, not in a place like the Library of Congress, but in a place like this, where potentially creative minds are turned loose for the first time in a pasture of books and periodicals—the great books of the past, the provocative and controversial articles that reflect the main trends of the present."[90] The building immediately won acclaim from the Whitman community. Chairman of the board of overseers Judge James Fee declared: "The building of the library was one of the most brilliant achievements of Whitman College."[91] Librarian Reynolds wrote: "The first complete year in the library has demonstrated the fact that pleasant surroundings and accessibility of book stacks do accelerate study habits. The tremendous increase in circulation is only a small measure of the increased activity and use of library materials and services."[92]

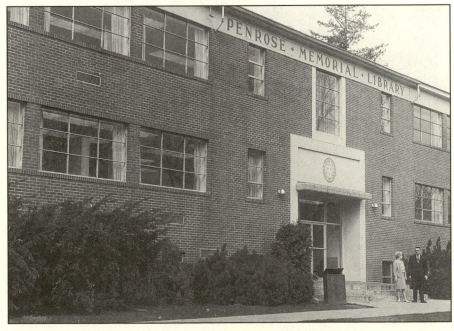

The college constructed the long-anticipated Penrose Memorial Library in 1957. It was named in honor of President Stephen Penrose and his wife, Mary.

While library construction proceeded, the college paid $50,000 for the mansion and three acres of property that had belonged to the late professor Louis F. Anderson. But the public was not aware that this acquisition followed several heated trustee meetings. In late 1952 Anderson's widow, Florence Anderson, offered her property to Whitman for $75,000. This seemed too steep for the trustees, who made a counteroffer of $30,000. A couple of board members were hesitant about buying the beautiful brick home because of uncertainty over the purpose to which it would be put. Maxey suggested that it might serve either as a women's dormitory for thirty occupants, or, gutted and rebuilt, as an administration building.

Judd Kimball, Mrs. Anderson's attorney, refused to take the board's offer to her, and stated that, if the college did not buy the house, she would implement other plans.[93] Maxey knew that this was possible, because in 1927 the Andersons had been angry with

On a memorable day in 1957, students carried books from Reynolds Hall, which had served as a library for twenty-three years, to Penrose Memorial Library.

Built in 1904 as the residence of Professor Louis Anderson and his first wife, Mabel Baker Anderson, this building was acquired by the college in 1956. Between 1968 and 1976 it was closed. Trustees gave considerable thought to how to use the historic house; in 1977 it became the Baker Faculty Center.

Whitman for not purchasing the property and turning the house into a school of fine arts. He also knew that Mrs. Anderson would not bequeath the property to Whitman.[94] After she rejected the college's offer, stories circulated about what she would do with the property. Thirty years later Donald Sherwood, who was a trustee during these negotiations, still grumbled that Florence Anderson had threatened to sell to a mortician if the college rejected her terms. Another story claimed that she was going to give the house to her husband's fraternity, Beta Theta Pi. In 1956 the owner and the trustees reached a compromise; she would sell for $50,000 and would be allowed to live in the home rent-free. The college did not announce immediate plans for the handsome twelve-room brick residence, but at least it had added an important estate, which would become the Baker Faculty Center in 1977.

To help pay for this addition, the college sold about eighteen acres of the so-called "stadium" land. In a public explanation of why the

The Whitman Theatre was built in 1958. In 1967 it was renamed the Harper Joy Theatre after distinguished alumnus Harper Joy, an active trustee, generous donor, chairman of the finance committee, and presidential advisor.

school sold to a developer, Maxey snapped that the college took "no pride in owning the lushest weed patch in Eastern Washington, and we are unable to prevent certain occurrences on this property which do not contribute to the moral welfare of the community."[95] The property became the campus of DeSales High School.

In 1957 alterations to the Student Union Building became necessary. Maxey stated: "The great initial mistake in this structure was making it too small."[96] Remodeling provided additional space for storage, for the bookstore, and for meetings; plans for a basement went unrealized because of cost.

In March 1958 the college theater burned; the local fire chief reported that the building, one of the barracks that had been moved from McCaw Hospital, "was gutted and there is little or no salvageable material."[97] Using insurance money and gifts, the college—at a cost of about $141,000—built a much larger theater on the site of the old one. The modern structure won the applause of the *Pio-*

neer, which called it "a wonderful addition . . . providing the students with enough seating space, a very good atmosphere, and excellent equipment."[98]

Maxey and the governing boards downplayed plans for a new gymnasium but sought to build a badly needed science building. In December 1957 the president unsuccessfully applied to the Olin Foundation for a grant of $1,100,000 for a building and the required science equipment.

Maxey explained that, until the college had paid off its building bonds in 1952, it had not been able to launch "a systematic program of improvement and modernization" of buildings.[99] In 1959 he reported that his administration had spent $1,160,000 for new construction and another $777,400 for repairs, improvements, and reequipment of old buildings, especially for improving the dormitories. "This is," the president boasted, "the largest outlay for plant additions and improvements in the entire history of Whitman College and has been instrumental in providing better physical facilities for the work of the college than has ever existed before."[100]

The Disruptive Impact of the Korean War

In the 1950s Whitman leaders still required most students to live on campus. All women except those from Walla Walla had to live in student housing. The college wanted to enroll at least eight hundred selected students, sixty percent of them male. Maxey saw "no special magic" in a ratio of five men to three women but generalized: "Our experience has been that both sexes adjust more satisfactorily to our type of program at about this ratio."[101]

In 1948 the school had enjoyed an enrollment of about 860; this flattering number resulted from the presence of many veterans. After the Korean War broke out in 1950, student enrollments plummeted; in the 1951–1952 school year, the college enrolled only 699 students, and not once during the next four years did it reach its goal of eight hundred. From 1956 to 1959, however, Whitman annually counted more than 850; such solid enrollments encouraged administrators to plan for a student body of one thousand. To reach this goal, it would be necessary "to break the housing bottleneck" by finding on-campus housing for three hundred additional students.

Maxey assured audiences that the institution would not grow "willy-nilly." He stressed that everyone in the college community understood that, "Whitman's special job is basic undergraduate education in the field of the humanities, the sciences, and the social studies."[102]

Student numbers and composition in the Maxey years shifted more than they had at any time since the Second World War. The GIs continued to be a significant presence through the 1951–1952 school year, with eighty-five of them enrolled. In the following year, less than half that number of GIs enrolled, but thirty-five Korean veterans joined the student body. These younger veterans were too few to dominate the college in the same way that the veterans of the Second World War had.

From 1950 to 1953 the Korean War, coupled with a change in demographics, reduced enrollments. In the first year of the war, the college suffered a fifteen-percent attrition as men enlisted or were drafted. Meanwhile, Maxey alerted the Whitman community to the realization that, "The total population of college age is less this year than at any time in the past decade, thanks to the small baby crop of the depression years."[103] The college had been aware of the population change, but, of course, it had not anticipated a short and costly hot war during the long Cold War.

Like so many other private schools fearing the loss of male students, Whitman in the fall of 1950 applied for a unit of the Reserve Officers' Training Corps (ROTC). Maxey explained to the trustees that, if the application were granted, "the advantage to the college would be the retention of men," and that he preferred an air force unit over an army one.[104] The president informed the alumni: "The only thing that would keep in college any large number of men would be some sort of military training program. We have hopes in this direction but no assurances."[105]

Whitman men worried about their ability to stay in school. On January 11, 1951, the *Pioneer* reported that they faced a grim future. "As the pressure becomes more binding, men faced with the prospect of service in the infantry will drop out of school to join the other branches of service."

In February 1951, with admissions numbers decreasing and the rate of attrition increasing, Dean Armstrong polled the faculty and students about the need for an ROTC unit; he found that eighty-

five percent of the teachers and sixty-five percent of the students favored establishing one on a permanent basis. Armstrong, who
pushed for an ROTC unit, explained: "During a national emergency
every college has an obligation to assist in every way in which it is
qualified to do it. In this instance assistance is through the training
of future officers."[106] Armstrong joined with other regional educators in seeking to convince the government to create a concurrent
military and educational program for students, and he informed
Whitmanites that the local national guard offered them an opportunity to continue in school.

In April 1951 the Department of the Air Force denied Whitman's
application, explaining that it was awarding only sixty-two units
to the 450 colleges and universities that sought them. Although
crushed by this negative news, Armstrong said hopefully, "As long
as the military and international situation do not change, large numbers of men will remain available for enrollment in college."[107] Upset
because both Willamette University and the College of Puget Sound
received coveted air force ROTC units, Whitman asked Senator Warren Magnuson to investigate the decision. The college learned that
it had not received a unit because it lacked as large a male enrollment as other regional schools. In the fall of 1952 Whitman unsuccessfully applied for an army ROTC unit.

In 1951 the failure of the college to obtain an ROTC unit prompted an unusual letter from Maxey to students and parents. He identified several rumors floating across the campus—that the college
would not have a male enrollment in the fall of 1951, that it would
not have enough students to operate in the coming year, that the college would soon be bankrupt, and that "the faculty have been notified that none of them will be employed next year." Exasperated
by these stories, the leader explained that the government's defer-
ment policy meant that those who had satisfactory class standing
or a satisfactory score on a forthcoming selective service test had
an excellent chance to remain in school until graduation. The president urged men currently at Whitman, as well as potential freshmen, to enroll in the college. "They have," he asserted, "nothing
to gain by enlisting now and much to lose." He went on to say that
these men had "a good chance to obtain draft exempt status by enlisting in reserve units, many of which are located in Walla Walla."

The writer assured his readers that, although there was a slight decline in admissions, the school would operate. He spiked the rumor that the college would close: "Shrinkage of income may require curtailment of expenditures and corresponding retrenchments . . . but there is no prospect of bankruptcy. We know that there are four or five lean years ahead, and that we shall have to adjust our financial operations." He revealed that the governing boards were presently considering a new financial development program, "which may greatly augment our resources."

To counter the rumor that faculty members would be released, Maxey stated that, "at the suggestion of the trustees," the professors were warned that "difficult times were ahead and that unforeseeable retrenchments might become necessary," but that Whitman "would make every effort to keep its faculty and staff intact." Their employer could not issue positive commitments "until there was reasonable assurance of means to carry them out." The leader bluntly declared: "Whitman is not folding." [108]

In a 1951 message to alumni, Maxey again predicted that Whitman would face five lean years, but "after that the population of college age will have grown so large that all colleges are likely to be overcrowded again." [109] The president denounced schools that were lowering their standards to attract male students and promised that his school would not take such action: "If we cannot survive without selling ourselves down the river of temporary expediency, we think it better that we should not survive." [110]

Maxey was correct on all counts—the college did not fold, it did face lean enrollments until the 1955–1956 school year, and it did not abandon its standards. But critics correctly complained that the college temporarily lowered its standards in the 1950s by creating a secretarial science department to offer courses in typing and shorthand, and by establishing a general social science department that offered some questionable courses, such as "Home Management" and "Preparation for Marriage." In introducing secretarial science the college sought to build enrollments as it had in the Penrose years. But these dubious service departments—neither offered a major— disappeared after the college's enrollment increased. During these difficult years enrollment averaged about 735, which was not nearly as low as it had fallen during the First World War. One of the important reasons for the acceptable level of enrollment was Whitman's high retention rate, annually averaging eighty percent at that time. Maxey judged that, nationally, a sixty-percent retention rate was considered satisfactory.

But to hold students, Whitman, like other schools, annually had to increase its scholarships and student aid. In 1953 Maxey reported that the school had given an average grant of $184 per student; twenty-five percent of students received assistance. He explained: "The pressure for student aid continues to grow, encouraged no doubt by intensive competition on the part of institutions fearful of losing enrollment should they not follow a liberal, if not lavish, policy of student aid." Because the college did not have enough money for student aid, it was forced to "divert tuition income to that purpose." The president was not happy about this: "Though necessary in practice, such diversions of tuition income are wrong in principle. Tuition is paid for instruction. . . . If we could devote all of our tuition income to instruction, we should have little need to worry about faculty salaries and other instructional costs."[111] Like most schools, Whitman was continuing the practice of forcing the faculty to subsidize students. Historian Frederick Rudolph has aptly summarized this historic and national situation: "The choice was a simple one: the colleges could either pay their professors to teach or they could pay their students to enroll. They chose the latter course because it was the only way they could achieve the enrollment that justified their existence."[112]

Maxey and the trustees decided in January 1953 that the college should grow to a thousand, still with about sixty percent being male. To house a larger number, the trustees requested that the city planning commission permit the building of boarding houses and fraternity houses near campus. A contrary response drew Maxey's ire, and he charged city politicians with being guilty of "political astigmatism and timidity." He also threatened that Whitman, if it could not acquire additional housing, might move all or part of its operations to another city. He elaborated: "Our students are movable, our faculty is movable, our educational equipment is movable, and our endowment is movable."[113] Apparently city leaders resolved the zoning problem in Whitman's favor, because Maxey made no mention of the issue in his presidential reports after 1954.

President Maxey's Struggles with the Faculty

During—and long after—Maxey's presidency, professors recounted his stiff treatment of them. Pete Reid recalled the faculty sitting
in the student union grumbling about their leader's attitudes and
actions. The president and the professors quarreled over three major
issues: salaries, tenure, and personnel decisions. At many other campuses in the post-war years, administrators and faculties also disputed these significant matters, with professors arguing that profes-
sionalism should replace paternalism. At Washington State College
in the late 1940s, for example, professors opposed to a paternalistic
government sought better salaries and a tenure policy, as well as
other changes.[114] At Whitman and nearly every other West Coast
school, faculties became more involved in administration.

Maxey's autobiography frankly but briefly discussed the faculty
fights at Whitman. He emphasized that, when he took office, he was
not personally close to his colleagues and that he had, from long
experience, formed generalizations about professors. He judged that
they "don't like to be coordinated, . . . don't like to comply with rules
and regulations, don't like to function as organization men"; that,
despite their protestations, they were very concerned about salaries;
and that tenure was extremely important. In general, Maxey predicted that presidential leadership would arouse resistance, especially
from "soreheads."[115]

It is much more difficult to get the Whitman faculty's side of the
disputes with Maxey, because not a one wrote publicly about the
1950s; furthermore, the faculty leaders have died, and the survivors
have forgotten the specifics of events that happened over forty years
ago. But Professor Thomas Howells, a battler for reform, kept many
of his detailed letters. This source, oral histories, and the official faculty documents present a counter-argument to Maxey's writings.

At a December 1949 faculty banquet for the new president, the
program stated that the faculty, "in honoring its president, is honoring itself."[116] Professors believed that Maxey understood their
long-standing economic plight and would therefore improve their
condition. They appreciated his reorganization of the administration
to provide a streamlined committee system and more faculty gov-

ernance. But, after two years, admiration of the leader gave way to widespread alienation. A minor grievance resulted from the president's austerity policy: he awarded meager cash payments to each teacher for supplies and student assistance. Professor Fredric Santler received $15; Howells got $10 and complained that this money would not even buy bluebooks for his classes.[117] At exactly the same time that the faculty was murmuring about the pittance allotted for classroom expenditures, there were lengthy disputes over the larger issues of salaries and tenure.

The salary disagreement was perennial; Maxey's autobiography provides a context. When he assumed office, professors immediately asked him for raises. Undoubtedly some of these pleaders referred to the 1948 salary report of the local chapter of the American Association of University Professors (AAUP). By a unanimous vote the AAUP members informed the trustees that they lived on "a marginal level of subsistence."[118]

Maxey told those who were seeking improved salaries three things: he would pay the best salaries possible; he would fix salaries on the basis of merit that he determined; and he would "never increase a salary as the result of any pressure, threat, or duress." He wrote that the faculty, upon hearing his opinions, called him "a tough nut to crack" and challenged the system.[119] At the behest of faculty acquaintances, a couple of trustees wanted the board—not the president—to set salaries. Some professors advocated that the faculty council or a special committee should determine pay. Opposed to these proposals, Maxey ruled that it was better to have one person, not a group, responsible for salary decisions. Thus, he awarded salaries within the range set by the board, a policy that rankled many recipients, especially those who complained about salary inequities, real or imagined.

Most of the major salary battles were waged by the mid-1950s and were closely related to the impact of the Korean War upon enrollments. Less than a month after the outbreak of the Korean War, Maxey wrote that college men might be drafted and the attendant loss of tuition income could mean that "the coming year may prove difficult beyond imagination." To meet this anticipated crisis, money scheduled to go into faculty salaries was shifted into a reserve to cover a decline in tuition revenue. But, even after the war ended in

1953, salaries lagged. Maxey later reflected on the situation: "I was accused, perhaps justly, of moving more slowly in respect to salaries than with other catching-up jobs."[120] Professors would concur, for his tardiness in remedying the salary crisis was one of their basic complaints. Student aid, campus maintenance, and the payment of bonds consumed large sums; some of this money could have been awarded to long-suffering faculty members and their families. In 1948 the local chapter of the AAUP had argued that the faculty was "the most important item" in the college's budget[121] but failed to persuade either the trustees or Maxey. In the president's first report to the boards, he expressed his desire to raise the salaries for associate and full professors because the compensation at this upper level was "not at all comparable with those paid in most institutions with which we like to be classed." Unfortunately, Maxey failed to convince the boards to adopt this policy; for several years they put more money into the lower ranks, not the upper ones.

In 1950 declines in both tuition and farm incomes meant that the faculty received only a $100 cost-of-living bonus. Maxey stated: "Most of our salaries are conspicuously low as compared with the salaries paid by state institutions and lower than those paid by many private institutions in this area." He hoped that it would be unnecessary to further reduce these low salaries.[122] Near the end of his term, the administration greatly improved salaries, but much of the rancor over money could have been mitigated had the president given salaries the primacy his critics desired.

In 1951 the school began providing its employees with Social Security coverage. Fearing, however, that these payments, coupled with those for the Teachers Insurance and Annuity Association retirement program, were too liberal, Maxey led the trustees in revising the college's participation in the TIAA program. Thereafter, new faculty members must wait six years instead of three to be eligible to participate.

In the winter of 1950–1951 much of the good will that flowed from the providing of even a small bonus and the Social Security coverage was lost following Maxey's gloomy speech to professors about the college's bleak prospects resulting from the Korean War. Estimating that the enrollment would slump to a number between four and five hundred, the trustees, he announced, had concluded that they would not "incur a deficit" and would close the college until there was "a demand for educational services of the type provided by Whitman."[123] The president warned his stunned listeners that they would not know until mid-summer if they would have employment in the fall. According to Howells, the speaker asserted that, if there was a major war, he would seek employment "at Boeing's as an elevator operator." Maxey also rejected the argument that additional female enrollment would make up for the loss of males. The professor judged: "Maxey's vision was of an unmitigated catastrophe."

Maxey's foreboding address troubled the faculty. When classes began again in the fall of 1951, many professors were still unhappy about this speech. Howells observed that his colleagues "are angrier over this speech than I have ever seen them. What they doubt is not only Maxey's ability to lead the college through the crisis—they doubt his inclination to do so." Many listeners assumed that their leader was encouraging faculty resignations. This seemed plausible, because the shrinking enrollment required fewer teachers. To avoid a deficit, the payroll needed to be slashed. Howells summarized the situation: "So the college enters the emergency with a self-discredited president."[124]

In response to individual concerns voiced by worried professors and to a letter from the faculty council inquiring about the college's future, the trustees wrote that they would do everything to keep the college on "as normal a basis as possible, except to incur any substantial deficit." The board also hoped that the faculty would continue "that loyalty and spirit of sacrifice that has made Whitman the great institution it is."[125]

The trustees' vague response failed to assuage the concerns of the professors, who now revived the local AAUP chapter, which they had earlier allowed to become moribund. Here, and in faculty meetings, they responded to Maxey's warning that the college might close, a possibility that received regional press coverage. (Other schools, such as Willamette, announced that they would remain open.) Howells described their meetings as "calm and reasonable." He identified Dean Armstrong, registrar McClane, and professors Ronald Sires and Frank Haigh as some of those who challenged Maxey. McClane called it "damn foolishness" to talk about closure; Haigh stressed

that, if the professors were to be effective, and if they were to encourage students to return, then they needed to believe "in the continuance of the institution." Angry with his challengers, Maxey
snapped that, if anyone thought he could do a better job as president, then he was welcome to the position; his critics responded that
they simply wanted to share his heavy burdens. Howells felt that,
in these heated confrontations, "Maxey gave a good account of himself—he had the courage of his pessimism." The professor, and perhaps other colleagues, believed that the president soon learned that
his negativism would not get the resignations he desired. Meanwhile,
the trustees, supporting Maxey, refused to meet with the faculty
council. But these icy conditions thawed when the president spoke
more optimistically about keeping the college open.[126]

In April 1951 a faculty committee—William Hutchings, Glenn
Woodward, and chairman Ronald Sires—responding to their colleagues' dissatisfaction with salaries, delivered a sweeping report to
Maxey. The faculty voted its approval of the report, which asserted
that competing colleges paid larger salaries than Whitman did. The
college paid its full professors $4,000 to $4,400, while associate
professors received $3,400 to $3,800, assistant professors $3,200
to $3,600, and instructors $2,800 to $3,300; a chart demonstrated
that several private schools, including the College of Idaho and Pacific University, provided better pay.

In truth, Whitman's teachers did not receive "remuneration sufficient for a standard of living that would enable them to keep pace
with costs in a period of rising prices or that would encourage them
to grow in their profession." Disgruntled members of the faculty
pointed out that local school teachers and recent Whitman graduates who entered the teaching profession with bachelor's degrees
were making more money than many of their professors. There was
also disaffection with the salary ranges. To retain younger teachers, the administration awarded them "the most attractive salaries."
Thus, the college had, the committee concluded, "whether by plan
or otherwise, taken advantage of the very faculty members on whom
it ought to be depending for the maintenance of its educational reputation" in the region and the nation.[127]

To meet family needs, professors had to take summer jobs in local
canneries; therefore, they lacked time for scholarship or rest. Sum-

mer employment prevented their professional development. This situation lasted for years. Professor Richard Clem, for example, in the first summer after joining the faculty in 1951 earned enough in the plum harvest to buy a new suit; every summer, he worked for Libby's in the pea harvest so that he could cover the cost of living. In 1956 his field work and his Whitman salary provided funds for a dryer and a vacuum cleaner.[128]

Faculty members also lacked the financial resources to attend professional meetings and the opportunity to keep abreast of their fields. Professors "of a first class college," the committee insisted, should have opportunities to associate with scholars.

Furthermore, "In too many cases the faculty wife finds it necessary to find employment in the community on a part-time or full-time basis, in order to balance the family budget. If the faculty wife wishes to do this for personal reasons she should feel free to do so, but she should not be forced to do so because of inadequate salaries at the college."

The report emphasized that, because of low salaries, "the more capable and productive faculty members will tend to go elsewhere and the less capable and less productive ones will tend to stay." For Whitman to retain able individuals, it would be necessary to improve their compensation.

The committee assured readers that it understood the problem of finding money for improved salaries, but stressed a basic point: "We believe also that such improvement is, along with maintenance of an adequate student body, the most important problem faced by the college today. It should be remembered that an excellent faculty, paid fully in accordance with its training and merits, is a prime drawing card for prospective students, and that a poorly paid faculty with low morale is a potential hinderance to the effective recruitment of a student body."

The committee sought a way to increase Whitman's fund raising. It urged publicizing the need for improved salaries, as other colleges were doing. Alumni should be alerted to the fact that the "greatest need . . . is the creation of an adequate salary structure for the members of the faculty." To achieve this important goal, the college should hire an individual to promote the Living Endowment Fund.[129]

Trustee minutes do not indicate that Maxey took account of this document, although he had assured the faculty that he was attempting to improve a deplorable salary scale. However, he told the board that faculty compensation was "scarcely more than a subsistence level" and that professors recommended the employment of a person to push the financial development effort.[130]

Trustees found no money for professors in the financial surplus reported for 1951, but they increased Maxey's salary to $9,000; a year later they hiked it another $1,000. In the fall, Maxey presented to the board figures on median salaries paid by colleges and universities. He acknowledged that Whitman salaries were low, but noted that they compared favorably with private schools and badly with public ones. Whitman, he advised, should narrow the gap with regional public schools.[131] In 1952 the trustees, ignoring the Sires report, froze the salary range of full professors but increased the ranges for lower ranks by an average of $500.[132]

While trustees followed this stringent salary policy at Whitman, a contrasting situation—described as harmonious by two historians —existed at Colorado College. Concerned about finding and retaining a solid faculty, a faculty-trustee committee in the 1950s continually adjusted salaries to meet the rise in living costs.[133]

Maxey often assured professors that they would eventually receive improved salaries. In 1955 he placed the ongoing salary issue into a larger context; there was, he insisted, a close relationship between the school's income and the business climate: "If the American economy has a future, then Whitman also has a future."[134]

In the early 1950s, while the salary issue smoldered, the introduction of formalized tenure regulations fanned the academic fires. Maxey's autobiography showed that he understood the sensitive nature of the issue, saying that tenure was "the most sacred of the several sacred cows worshipped by college professors." Job security, he judged, was even more important than salary, and teachers believed that "they had full rights of tenure regardless of the lack of any expressed legislation."[135]

In the fall semester of 1950 the faculty received from the trustees a revised set of bylaws, which, for the first time, contained a section on tenure. Each professor came to see Maxey and learn his status under the new tenure regulations; these conferences, the president wrote, "touched off a minor hubbub in the faculty. I was

charged with destroying academic freedom, violating long established rights of tenure, and planning wholesale dismissals from the
faculty." Certain "impassioned professors," he charged, tried and
failed to have him "indicted" by the AAUP; and some "busybody"
teacher asked trustees to support the faculty against his tenure rul-
ings. The president generalized: "The real reason the soreheads were
so sore was they had not been consulted in advance."[136]

Unfortunately, Maxey's account of this important historical event
is much too brief. Thomas Howells' letters and the official records
relate a more complex account of the lengthy tenure struggle—sometimes called "The Tenure War"—which they date from 1950 to 1953.
David Stevens and others named Howells, who had taught at Whitman since 1938, as the leader of the president's opponents; Stevens
called Howells "a gutsy fighter."[137]

In his 1950 meeting with Howells about his tenure status, Maxey
asserted that the new tenure policy had been initiated by the trustees.
Howells, for his part, thought that the president was being disin-
genuous, and that Maxey, operating on the premise that the college
had no tenure policy and that it was thus his to create, had originated the new regulations. He believed that Maxey and the deans
had decided that the president should present tenure rules to the
board of trustees, which quickly adopted them.[138]

A major conflict raged around the question of whether, in the absence of a formal policy, some individuals actually enjoyed tenure either by custom or by verbal agreement. Maxey said no to both,
claiming that nobody was tenured and that faculty members had
only annual appointments. Thus, he informed Howells that he had
merely indefinite employment "at the permanent rank of associate
professor." This was a stiff policy: at Washington State College, for
example, professors at his rank would serve only a year's probation
prior to a tenure decision. An angry Howells insisted that he and
many of his colleagues did indeed have tenure. He rejected the "provision restricting full tenure . . . to full professors and providing
that assistant and associate were to be appointed for two-year and
three-year terms respectively." Howells and many of his colleagues
believed that the new rules should be applied only to new appointments, but Maxey disagreed, saying that these rules would be applied to all.

Howells kept lengthy notes of his conversation with Maxey. He sent a telegram to AAUP headquarters asking what they knew of the college's tenure policy under the late president Anderson, and soon learned that Whitman, as far as the AAUP was aware, was "in full compliance with the 1940 Statement of Tenure, which limits the probationary period for all ranks at seven years." Howells immediately called for a meeting of the local chapter of the AAUP, where he related his disagreements with Maxey. He and others attacked the president's views of tenure in this and several other meetings of the local AAUP. Critics repeated their views at meetings of the faculty council and of the entire faculty. Howells asserted that his colleagues were "incensed over the application of the new rules to long-term members." A few teachers centered their criticism more on the trustees than on the president. Lawrence Bussard, for example, argued that the trustee action on tenure had destroyed faculty morale, and Ronald Sires added that the trustees should have discussed tenure regulations with the faculty prior to their adoption. Howells, insisting that President Anderson had tenured all of those who had been appointed as assistant professor and had subsequently served three more years, argued: "For Maxey to attempt to supplant a common-law usage system by a drastically different legal system with the argument that the previous system had no legal basis is either fantastic stupidity or the most inept piece of would-be cleverness I have ever encountered." He added, "I don't know what his reasons were—I suspect that he was clearing the ground for getting rid of some one."[139]

The AAUP chapter informed Maxey that the new tenure policy was not in accordance with the 1940 statement made by the national AAUP; that it was harming faculty morale; and that to apply it retroactively, to the detriment of professors, deserved "the strongest disapprobation."[140] The faculty council, employing more discreet language than that of the AAUP, also wanted revisions of the tenure rules, especially one providing that, after seven years of probation, an individual would be given indefinite tenure upon reappointment. The faculty protest, Howells rejoiced, had a positive effect: "The general feeling is that Maxey is a greatly chastened man." The professor concluded: "I think he knows now that the next step, for the faculty, is civil war."[141]

For many months the trustees rejected various pleas to revise the tenure regulations or to meet with the faculty council. But, in the summer of 1951, faculty persistence succeeded. Professors Thomas Howells and William Hutchings met with trustees James Johns and Arthur Lee. Howells thought it amusing that Johns, who had ardently pushed for the tenure rules, admitted that he had never met a faculty member except for one serving as a dean. The Pendleton trustee observed, "I know we have a fine faculty. I've never wanted to know the faculty as individuals; I prefer to think of them as a group." Johns also understood that the librarian had served well for twenty-five years but admitted that he did not know Ruth Reynolds' name.[142] This meeting failed to move the trustees, but the faculty protest continued. In December it voted thirty-four to four in favor of giving indefinite tenure to all those who had completed seven years of service; for all others, the crucial tenure vote was to come in the sixth year. Maxey accepted this amendment, and in February 1952 so did the trustees. With the adoption of the revision, Howells hailed the faculty's "notable victory," although professors assumed that the trustees were unhappy with them for their determined and lengthy opposition to the original rules.[143]

However, Maxey also claimed victory; he published the tenure rules in his autobiography, calling them historic. He concluded that they worked well, and that soon, "even the most virulent opponents were reconciled and satisfied."[144] His explanation was simply that the dispute had ended after two faculty members and two trustees met and revised one of the rules.

The Whitman community recognized the need for operating under formal tenure rules incorporated into the college bylaws. Previously, oral agreements with presidents had been open to various interpretations, but now the tenure rules—which could be called the Maxey rules—were clearly stated. Written rules were less vulnerable to being misunderstood, and they could be modified. Professor Stevens stated that the trustees were hostile to the idea of giving professors tenure and that Maxey had actually assisted the faculty by getting the trustees to adopt his tenure regulations.[145]

The implementation of Whitman's new tenure system—and its revision in the same semester in response to the faculty protest—had further ramifications. In 1952 Howells received tenure with the permanent rank of associate professor, which seemed to imply that he would not be advanced to full professor. This action rankled his colleagues; Pete Reid later recalled that Fredric Santler was especially angry.[146] Then the trustees denied tenure to Ruth McGeehan, an English professor, and to Robert Comegys, a history professor. Howells and others denounced the Comegys decision. It made no sense to them that the trustees, who had in February 1952 granted the competent historian a leave of absence to complete his dissertation, would, in the following June, deny him tenure. Some charged that Comegys' presidency of the local AAUP chapter during the tenure struggle, and his denunciation of state loyalty oaths, explained his dismissal. In 1951 Maxey had identified him as "one of the most successful and popular" faculty members. But the administration refused to explain its position on this tenure decision, stating that it rested largely on "personal character."[147]

Howells, however, asserted that the trustees had engaged in retaliation "and a desire to give notice to the present faculty that most of them need not expect tenure." The faculty leader also informed a colleague that the trustees would "have fired me if they had dared, but Maxey found them a formula for a suitable alternative—it would effectively discourage me and avoid an uproar. By dismissing Comegys they could be just as hasty with less trouble."[148]

In the last years of Maxey's presidency, he was less involved with tenure decisions than he was with other personnel problems. He confided that his "most disagreeable work . . . was the hiring and firing of professors." Maxey admitted that, during his presidency, there was a high rate of faculty turnover, ranging between ten and fifteen percent annually, and that some "self-appointed critics" on the faculty and in the student body blamed him for the losses.[149] Nard Jones was one of several alumni who believed that there was "a sad deterioration in the quality of the faculty" during the Maxey administration. (He also felt that it was unfortunate that the president, "a great teacher," did not find time to return to the classroom.)[150]

Concerned students, who believed a persistent rumor that Whitman was reducing its teaching staff so that it could fund a long-term building program, decried the firing of solid faculty members. A *Pioneer* editor argued in 1953 that, "When it comes to determining who is a valuable instructor . . . it should not be the views of one

Biologist Arthur Rempel instructs student Fred Santler in the mid-1950s.

. . . trustee, nor should it be the personal prejudice of 'higher-ups' ";
in fact, the students should be consulted, for they knew the good
teachers.[151]

Maxey did seek student opinion informally, especially in deciding troubling cases of contract renewal. The president laid out the
whole problem to students as well as others: "It was always easier
to put up with mediocrity than to prune it out, and a president is
often tempted to let things ride, but this is a perilous practice."
Maxey was not heartless; for example, in 1951 he recommended to
trustees that "a very poor teacher" should be retained an additional year because he had no prospects of employment and had a dependent family.

On the other hand, in defense of firings, Maxey observed that,
if the college had had enough money to hire the best available teachers, then he would not have had to weed out so many: "If I had not
been obliged to put so much money into plant rehabilitation and
financial stabilization, it would have been possible for Whitman to
match salaries with the best." The president also provided advice

to his successors: "The small college which will put most of its eggs in the basket of faculty compensation can look forward to an assured future." Some professors wished that he had been more quick to follow his own advice.

Maxey felt that Whitman lost some teachers because it was "not easy to convince the embryonic professor that he can make a great career in a small college located in a far northwestern city with an oddball name." He frankly summarized the hiring situation: "Only about a third of those I hired were good enough, by my own criteria, to reappoint."[152] The president saw that every school underwent "a turn of the cycle which marks the replacement of an old and long-tested faculty with one in which youth predominates. . . . Whitman is now passing through such a phase." He was sure that the new additions would "carry on the Whitman reputation of sound scholarship, superb teaching, and high character."[153] Many of those individuals who satisfied Maxey had long and significant careers at Whitman, including professors Walter Broman (English), Ely Chertok (sociology), Richard Clem (geology), Robert Fluno (political science), David Frasco (chemistry), Arthur Metastasio (French), Stanley Plummer (music), Richard Rasmussen (art), Harold Sims (English), William Soper (philosophy), David Stevens (economics), Robert Thomsen (physical education), Douglas Underwood (mathematics), and Robert Whitner (history); and staff members Miriam Wagenschein (dean of women; she also taught sociology) and Alta Glenny (registrar).

But Thomas Howells, who asserted that rapid faculty turnover weakened the college, took exception to Maxey's explanations for it. For example, at an AAUP meeting attended by many eager newcomers, Maxey revealed "that the trustees hate the idea of tenure and are extremely reluctant to give it to anybody." Howells judged that the president's attitude led promising young teachers to resign: "If the president had wished to encourage the new faculty to leave in the shortest possible time, he could hardly have found a better means."[154] The professor feared that a newcomer's request for a salary increase would lead to a dismissal, and that, if a tenured person made a similar request, a resignation would be requested. Howells fretted about his own future: "As far as a career is concerned, I should, of course, have left Whitman long ago. A career at Whitman is as unlikely as pregnancy in a wooden Indian. I have done and am doing some writing in the hope that it might be a pass-port out of here."

Late in 1953, however, Howells concluded that relationships be-tween the faculty and the president had improved. He wrote that Maxey made it seem that "he no longer wishes to liquidate his fac-ulty but would like to have its help in running the institution."[155] In 1956 the local AAUP chapter informed Maxey that it appreciat-ed his leadership, which had brought about new buildings and bet-ter teaching conditions.

Despite Howells' vigorous opposition on the tenure issue, Maxey admired the combative professor, and soon appointed him director of the curriculum. In his autobiography he cited Howells as one of the professors who had been of "special value" to him, and the pres-ident also chose him to be on a special committee to celebrate the college's centennial.[156] Howells was in fact advanced to the rank of full professor in 1957.

But differences still arose between a strong-willed president— with supportive trustees—and a faculty seeking better working con-ditions, professionalization, and an increased share of governance. In a May 1957 letter, Maxey once again addressed the salary ques-tion, reminding teachers that, between 1949–1950 and 1956–1957, their pay had increased at about nine percent a year—the best record in the college's history—and that Whitman salaries were higher than those at five regional private colleges, which he did not name. The weary leader assured them that he sought objectivity in salary deci-sions but lamented that it was nearly impossible to receive "full and impartial information about each individual." He frankly admitted that his knowledge came "almost entirely from hearsay." He elabo-rated: "Hearsay comes to the president from many sources—stu-dents, parents, faculty colleagues, alumni, townspeople, and many others. The president is aware of the shortcoming of such sources of information, but they are all he has." He accused the faculty of taking little interest in its "evaluation inventory"; therefore, hearsay was the basis for decisions.

Maxey observed: "Whether the non-return of a faculty member is a loss depends entirely on the replacement." He concluded by de-scribing himself as "a most reluctant college president," and reminded everyone that he would be leaving his difficult position in 1959.[157]

There was no faculty outcry in response to Maxey's letter, because soon afterwards professors received salary letters informing them of sizeable pay raises; some of them calculated that they were receiving a thirty-percent increase. Naturally, everyone recalled these unusually generous salary letters more than the letter that contained Maxey's strictures on money and description of the evaluation procedure. A series of Ford Foundation grants provided much of the money. Realizing that college professors were poorly paid, the foundation sought to call attention to this serious problem and to redress it by giving significant funds for salary endowments to schools that were not tax-supported. Whitman was among the many private institutions on the foundation list; its first grant had not been solicited by the college and came as a complete surprise. The $325,000 Whitman received made it possible to raise salaries in the late 1950s and early 1960s. The improved salaries finally reduced faculty criticism and resignations.

In the 1950s many teachers and students deplored the high rate of faculty turnover, emphasizing that it was the professors with long careers at Whitman who had made its reputation. Throughout the decade students were "more than a little disturbed about the tremendous faculty turnover."[158] Some teachers stressed that many resignations resulted from the fine job market; the expansion of a number of public institutions, especially in California, provided attractive openings.

In fact, just prior to the wonderful salary letters of 1957, student concern about faculty resignations peaked. Approximately half the student body signed a petition emphasizing their concern over the fact that nearly twenty percent of the full-time faculty had resigned. The petition also asserted that the professors were underpaid, that classes were crowded, and that there was inadequate counseling. The petitioners informed Maxey: "We feel entitled to a stable, numerically adequate faculty of excellent professors who have the time to give challenging work and personal contact to small classes."[159] At the same time, a *Pioneer* editorial evaluated the list of faculty resignations and speculated that they were prompted by low salaries rather than a dislike of Whitman students. The newspaper also carried a letter from Associate Professor Hubert E. Christenson, who said that he was leaving because "good teaching and loyal service are not rewarded financially at Whitman."[160]

Maxey responded to the petitioners by reminding them that faculty turnover had also been heavy in earlier times, by predicting that salaries would soon be improved, and by explaining frankly that "the payment of a $150,000 indebtedness and an expenditure of over $300,000 for rehabilitation and modernization of the physical plant had taken a good deal of money that might otherwise have gone toward faculty salaries."[161]

Later in 1957 a regional visitation team from the Northwest Association of Secondary and Higher Schools reported its findings to the Whitman community. It emphasized the need to pay better salaries, especially at the higher ranks; to hire more teachers; and to provide opportunities for faculty members to further their education. The visitors noted that relationships between administrators and the faculty were "unsatisfactory," or "considerably short of idyllic."[162] Surprisingly, the team did not address the issue of faculty turnover, which had troubled the campus a few months earlier. Apparently, the Whitman community believed that, with the better salaries, the issue would become less important.

Cold War Tensions at Whitman

A major issue on the nation's campuses during the Cold War era was the claim that communism influenced educational institutions. In the period of McCarthyism, conservative college trustees often distrusted liberal professors. At Pomona College, for example, the trustees criticized the political and economic views of faculty members, objected to outside speakers, and attempted to interfere with academic appointments.[163] Pomona president E. Wilson Lyon defended his faculty from these criticisms. Maxey did not write about similar interference from his trustees, but he, like Lyon, assured members of his board that they need not worry about faculty radicalism. At Whitman, the loyalty issue created few difficulties, especially when compared to the University of Washington's investigation of un-American activities, which resulted in heated hearings and a few faculty expulsions. The situation at Whitman was more like that at Washington State College: in both institutions, administrations had to require employees to take state loyalty oaths, but neither conducted a full-scale investigation. Maxey noted that, "Senator Joe McCarthy hardly created a ripple on this campus."[164]

As early as 1947, Whitman faculty members had been required by state law to swear that they would support the federal and state constitutions and the flag, and show "reverence for law and order and undivided allegiance to the government of the United States."[165] But, in both Walla Walla and Pullman, some superpatriots advocated the teaching of their own particular brand of patriotism, supported the visits of conservative speakers on campus, and questioned the loyalty of liberal instructors. In 1951 a *Pioneer* editorial denounced W. H. Harold, "a highly patriotic merchant," who offered to bring Reverend Gerald L. K. Smith to campus, where he would explain how "the Wall Street Jew bankers have led America into a countless succession of wars." In addition, Harold distributed a sheet accusing Whitman professors Gail Sheldon and Robert Comegys "of preaching the Communist Party line."[166] A few months later, a much different editorial sympathized with a California loyalty oath. Comegys spent an entire class period critiquing the editorial; in a response, the author appreciated the professor's talent to arouse indifferent students to a current problem.[167]

One professor, economist Raymond LaVallee, maintained that Maxey fired him in 1959 because he had appeared before the House Un-American Activities Committee (HUAC). La Vallee had come to Whitman with a troubled past. In 1949 Oregon State College had fired him and another untenured professor, either because of their alleged membership in the Communist Party or because of professional incompetence. Dickinson College had fired him in 1956 for being "an uncooperative witness before the HUAC." LaVallee arrived at Whitman in 1957 as an associate professor with a three-year contract.

Two recent alumni, Scott Gruber and Wayne Silzel, both of whom had been student body presidents, apparently played a key role in the decision to fire LaVallee. As students, they and classmates complained about such things as LaVallee's indifferent teaching style, his "mild contempt" for the college, his support of Marx, and his justification of "Stalin's slaughter of millions." They and other students researched AAUP *Bulletin*s and the HUAC records, discovering that

LaVallee had testified before this group, invoking the Fifth Amendment when questioned about his communist activity. In a joint letter to the faculty council, Gruber and Silzel urged the administration that the economist should immediately "be eliminated." They realized this action could cause an "eruption of public feeling . . . but," they asked, "would it not be better to eliminate him now with the ensuing consequences than to be branded as a school that would tolerate such men on its faculty, in a position to poison eager young minds?"[168] Apparently the trustees concurred; in June 1959 they bought out the economist's contract and complained to Maxey that they had wasted a $6,000 salary. Thereafter the college offered only one-year contracts to new teachers.

The LaVallee case at Whitman in 1959 was far different from a celebrated case at Reed College. In 1954 Reed's trustees fired philosophy professor Stanley Moore, a popular, tenured teacher, after he took the Fifth Amendment when questioned by the HUAC. Reed faculty members officially disagreed with the trustees, arguing that taking the Fifth Amendment was not misconduct; the Whitman faculty, by contrast, made no official response to the LaVallee firing.

While many in the Whitman community understood the administration's action in the LaVallee case, some faculty members still maintained that the president's attitude had prompted the loss of talented individuals. Sensitive to this assertion, Maxey noted in 1959 that there were seventy-five faculty changes during his administration, including thirty-two voluntary resignations and thirty-five involuntary ones—thirty-one of the latter because of professional inadequacy and four because of personal misconduct.[169]

Several professors expressed other grievances, including those who maintained that Maxey disliked them and consequently paid them less than he did his favorites. Professor Walter Broman recalled that, when he arrived in 1957 and found the faculty unhappy about Maxey's authoritarianism and the trustees' hostility, he wondered what he had joined. An unknown number of professors continually questioned Maxey's objectivity and wanted a system that provided for faculty participation in salary determinations and tenure decisions. These reforms would soon arrive.

Maxey as a Public Figure

Not since the days of Stephen Penrose had Whitman's president attracted as much public attention as Chester Maxey did. He commented on contemporary issues with certitude and competence. A recognized authority on politics, Maxey often spoke on the subject, especially city government. The scholar insisted that, although many urban reforms had been initiated, including public ownership of utilities, cities in 1950 faced as many problems as they had in 1925. He often complained that, because citizens had an over-simplified view, it would be difficult to resolve the world's political and economic problems. Maxey charged that Americans wanted "everything boiled down. We want our magazines in digest form, our newspapers as tabloids, and radio commentaries as brief as possible."[170]

Maxey's arduous duties as president and part-time teacher left him little time for writing. But, with Professor Robert Fluno, he found time to revise his textbook, *The American Problem of Government*. For a few years, college professors assigned this clear and readable text, but in the 1960s it was overtaken by competitors.

One of Maxey's speeches appeared as an essay entitled "The Work of the Teacher." In it he listed the qualities of a great teacher. The essay received wide circulation, including requests from college presidents who wanted copies to distribute to their faculties.

More important for the Whitman community were Maxey's essays on college history. He wrote *Marcus Whitman, 1802–1847: His Courage, His Deeds*, a fair-minded biography of the college's namesake. Although Maxey greatly admired the missionary, his Whitman is a lesser figure than the martyr figure Penrose portrayed. In his trenchant *Five Centennial Papers*, Maxey examined important aspects of Whitman College's past. Perhaps his essays on the college's long history of debt and its unique two-board system are the most useful. He denounced deficit spending, and defended the system of trustees and overseers against the idea of a single board.

Maxey wrote and celebrated history. At the 1955 commencement, honorary doctorates were bestowed upon six alumni who, after studying under the remarkable Professor Benjamin Brown, had gone on to earn doctorates and then had enjoyed successful scientific

*At the 1953 commencement, President Maxey posed with John Kelly,
left, publisher of the* Walla Walla Union-Bulletin, *a benefactor of the
college and a former overseer. At right is Binks Penrose, who was at
that time the president of the American University of Beirut.*

careers. Four of those honored—Walter Bleakney, Walter Brattain,
Vladimir Rojansky, and John Workman—had graduated in 1924.
Brattain was made a Nobel Laureate in physics in 1956 for co-in-
venting the transistor.

    Also in 1955 Maxey joined other community leaders in celebrating
the centennial observance of the treaty council called by Territorial
Governor Isaac I. Stevens. Leaders of the Yakama, Nez Perce, Umatilla, Cayuse, and Walla Walla tribes participated in a pageant written by Bill Gulick and directed by Professor Rodney Alexander. The
official program noted that the plaque on the campus's "treaty rock"
was "the gift of several tribes."[171]

    In 1959 Maxey led the school's centennial celebration. Governor
Albert Rosellini spoke at convocation, judging that the school was
"a sort of monument to the perserverance of some dedicated indi-
vidualists."[172] Other centennial events included banquets, special historical programs and publications, and distinguished speakers, including the renowned literary scholar Howard Mumford Jones. The
celebration created historical confusion, but not in the mind of

Maxey; he argued that, "from the standpoint both of legal and historical succession, the year 1959 is Whitman's centennial year."[173]
Although Whitman Seminary was founded in 1859, the college had
not actually been in operation until 1882; however, the centennial
of this important date would receive much less recognition than the
earlier one received at the 1959 celebration.

In addition to history, Maxey commented on fundamental educational issues. He frankly instructed alumni: "Education consists of
two processes—instruction and learning. The former is the teacher's
job, the latter the student's. Good teaching is wasted on poor learners. . . . College is no place for poor learners. Parents should not
expect a college to take them. I predict that in the not too distant
future no college will."[174]

Like Penrose, Maxey was often quoted in periodicals on the subject of education. He emphasized that only five percent of the nation's colleges and universities were independent of church or state

*Led by Professor Ken Schilling, the Whitman choir sang for the state legislature
in Olympia. This February 1959 event was part of the college's celebration of the
centennial of Whitman Seminary receiving a charter from the territorial legislature.*

control, and that Whitman was on a short list of such schools on the West Coast. He advocated the study of the liberal arts, reminding readers that business and government leaders spent most of their time meeting "a constant procession of unforeseen situations." To handle such diverse challenges, these executives needed a broad education, such as that provided by Whitman.[175] He also defended quality liberal arts colleges against larger universities. Maxey knew that his fellow citizens equated bigness with success, but he challenged this assumption: "If your sons and daughters are attending a small college which has a good faculty, a good curriculum, and good physical facilities, you may feel confident that you are giving them as big educational advantages as are to be had in the United States." He concluded: "Big puddles always float more ducks, but the important question is, 'Do they provide more food per duck?'"[176]

On another occasion he explained: "The chief value of an education is not the learning it imparts but the mental skills it develops. The most important of these are skill in learning, skill in understanding, skill in expression, skill in imagination, and skill in personal relations. It takes hard work to acquire manual skills and even harder work to acquire mental skills. That is why the means of education must be rigorous to be effective."[177]

He stated that Whitman, in his college days, had been "one of the few colleges that stood for the free enlistment of the mind on all subjects. . . . Darwinism and other concepts of evolution were freely discussed. It was at a time when reactionism dominated political thought, when such issues as the direct election of senators were thought dangerous, and the discussion of socialism was forbidden. But not at Whitman. Students were encouraged to be open-minded, to ask why, to challenge dogmas." He recalled that each student sought "a clearer, truer, and broader understanding of himself, of other persons, and of the civilization of which he is a member." He added: "This educational precept of the Whitman of my youth I would like to revitalize in the Whitman of today."[178]

Although there had been hopes that American colleges would someday be as free as grade schools or high schools, Maxey thought that these hopes would not be realized, because of the high costs of collegiate education. He identified four handicaps of youth—"speed, leisure, ease and comfort, and superficiality." The educator judged that a reputable college could help overcome the handicap of ease and comfort "by insisting on hard work under high standards."[179]

Early in the Korean War Maxey thought that, if there was a long period of "massive mobilization," then it was "certain to produce immeasurable change," and that the college student of 1950 "must live out his adult life in a world inconceivably different from all that has gone before."[180] Maxey denied that the post-war college students were degenerate,[181] and in 1951 he blamed the institutions themselves for a great athletic scandal then in the news. Maxey asserted that the "basketball scandal is only one symptom of the sickness that afflicts the entire college sports program." He urged the colleges to clean house "by doing away with special considerations for athletes. Scholarships should be awarded only on the basis of merit and need."[182]

In 1951 Maxey received an invitation to be among the small group of American leaders asked to speak for about three minutes each in the CBS series entitled *This I Believe*, a program produced by alumnus Edward Morgan. The president included this thoughtful talk in his autobiography, italicizing the sentence, "We must never kill the incentive to create."[183]

The widest distribution of Maxey's thoughts appeared in 1955, when *Life* magazine quoted a few of his sentences on teaching. He stressed the demands placed on the good teacher: "Every day of his life he must work hard, far harder than other men, to widen his knowledge, dethrone his prejudices, and rectify his judgments."[184]

Assessing the Record

In his 1959 president's report, Maxey summarized and evaluated his eleven-year administration. Although he did not stress the point, he had strengthened the college through reorganization. An orderly person, he had sought to systematize components of the college to make it more effective. Thus, he had initiated important faculty reforms, including the introduction of the five-division system, the creation of the faculty council, and the establishment of the office of dean of the faculty. These reforms—which won the backing of board members and professors—eliminated duplication, reduced committee work, and increased faculty governance. Maxey had pushed for the codification of faculty legislation and introduced tenure rules, because he recognized "faculty rights of tenure."[185]

The energetic president had also reorganized the administration by slashing the number of people who reported to him. He had appointed competent administrators to offices ranging from treasurer to food services. While finding many capable overseers, Maxey also reorganized the board of overseers, establishing regional groups and an executive board. Bert Edwards, a close observer of Maxey's Whitman and an overseer and trustee under later presidents, concluded that Maxey's greatest achievement was increasing the effectiveness of the two-board system.[186] The overseers, especially those in New York City, took a greater interest in serving the college. Although the leader did not restructure the board of trustees, he provided its membership with a well-organized and challenging agenda that won their commitment to Whitman. He also played politics to get Donald Sherwood elected a trustee; Sherwood would wield enormous influence for decades.

Maxey frequently emphasized the college's financial development during his administration. In his 1959 report, he noted that the endowment fund had increased from about $1,470,000 to $4,700,000. The income it generated in 1948–1949 was about $94,000; by 1959 this income had jumped to $222,500. The value of the campus and buildings also rose significantly, and construction and repairs totaled more than $1,600,000. The construction of Anderson Hall and Penrose Memorial Library were the most notable improvements.

Salaries for administrators and professors had finally made substantial gains: for example, in 1948 the budget for faculty salaries had been $246,000; in 1958 it was $608,000. This meant a significant rise in pay for many professors, inasmuch as there had been no increase in the faculty's size. The student-aid budget had also increased from $21,000 to $60,000, and yearly tuition rates remained modest: $350 in 1948 and $550 in 1958.

In 1959 the faculty expressed pleasure upon learning that alumni and friends had established the Benjamin H. Brown Professorship of Physics. A committee, assisted by Maxey, solicited money for this position; it hailed "the first fully endowed professorship at the college" and hoped it would lead to future chairs in other fields.

President Maxey assessed improvements and conditions in 1959:

"Many cite cogent reasons for believing that there is better teaching, better scholarship, better morale, and better ideality than in the past." He cautioned, however, that it would take twenty years to calculate "the true quality of an educational process." Although he did not mention it, he had hired a young faculty that would provide the type of teaching he desired. Maxey correctly concluded that "the material gains of the past eleven years have not merely added to the strength of Whitman College but have added strength in depth." The students were, he emphasized, the chief beneficiaries of a better faculty, increased financial aid, and an improved physical plant, particularly the Penrose Memorial Library. Maxey concluded that these improvements were appropriate ones: "The sole reason for the existence of the college is to render the best possible service to its students."[187]

The Maxey administration, however, had a negative side, as shown by faculty tensions in the early 1950s. At a time of concerns about the Korean War, McCarthyism, and runaway inflation (it was eight percent in 1950), the faculty endured a long delay in salary improvements, heard an unfortunate address about the possibility of closing the college, participated in an unnecessary fight over tenure, and felt frustration because trustees would not meet with the faculty council. A much different course was followed at Pomona College, where professors and trustees held a trustee-sponsored retreat that developed "a clearer sense of purpose and personal understanding."[188] Pomona economist Louis Perry, who would become Whitman's president in 1959, recalled that annual meetings between professors and trustees broke down barriers.

Maxey's arbitrary salary and contract-renewal decisions, as well as his questionable leadership in tenure decisions, resulted in distrust and denunciations. Compared to the writings of presidents Penrose and Bratton, Maxey's reports and publications rarely praised the faculty. In a difficult time, some public appreciation of professors' work and dedication would have improved their morale.

Another criticism of Maxey came from those who pointed out that he should have established a financial development office. Convinced that he alone should do the fund raising, Maxey simply did not have the time or energy to carry out this crucial work, including the realization of the "Ten Million in Ten Years" proposal. Maxey enjoyed some success as a fund raiser (although the large Sarah Harris Johnson trust was unsolicited), but his critics believed that he might have raised more money had he been assisted by a capable development office.

An unknown number in the Whitman community often questioned and sometimes disputed the decision of Maxey and the board members to reject deficit spending. Chastened by the Great Depression, these leaders chose not to borrow for new buildings or for any other purpose. When Donald Sherwood came on the board of trustees in 1954, he constantly warned against deficits. To record an annual surplus pleased him, his fellow board members, and the president. But not everyone hailed balanced budgets. The prestigious American Institute of Management (AIM) criticized Whitman's fundamental economic policy. The organization made a thorough audit of Whitman in 1953, emphasizing that this was the first study it had made of a college. It found much to praise, including the school's location, Maxey's scholarship and leadership, the accomplishments and loyalty of alumni, the solid liberal arts curriculum, and impressive faculty appointments.

But the AIM report faulted Whitman trustees, a group it rated no better than average. (This evaluation was marginally better than that presented in the Russell report about thirty years earlier.) The investigators, while recognizing that the trustees were men of character, judged that they were too old and too wedded to balanced budgets. AIM calculated that the average age of the trustees was more than sixty-five, and reasoned that age perhaps explained "the emphasis on balanced budgets rather than progress"; they urged the trustees to impose an age limit on their membership. The AIM report charged: "We share the opinion of others at Whitman that despite excellent financial stewardship there appears to be too much concern with immediate short-range dollar problems. The accounts payable difficulties of the 1930s seemingly have left the trustees and overseers with a penchant for a balanced budget." AIM recommended that the college borrow $100,000 and utilize it to "fund a progressive money-raising campaign."[189]

Maxey responded that this recommendation of even a one-time deficit "found no takers at Whitman [because] there were vivid memories of debt-financed drives for betterment and bitter memories of their consequences."[190] The administration clearly had been shaped by the college's debt-ridden history.

Other liberal arts colleges followed a course similar to that recommended by AIM, although comparisons among West Coast liberal arts colleges are difficult because few of them have published specific financial details. But Colorado College, another emerging liberal arts institution known to Whitman leaders, followed a different economic path. While Whitman rejected borrowing from the federal government and raised its own construction money, Colorado College, despite a very large indebtedness, in the mid-1950s borrowed more than $1,600,000 from the federal government for housing facilities.[191] In 1959 its trustees removed about $1,250,000 from its endowment to cover a long-standing indebtedness resulting from property acquisitions and operational deficits.

Although Whitman leaders would appreciate that Colorado College had erased a debt to prepare for a fund drive, they would be unimpressed with its deficit spending in the 1950s. Maxey's successors did not experience the college's long and stressful debt-filled history, but they would constantly hear the harrowing details, especially from aging board members, and Whitman's debt-free rule carried on into the 1990s. While this no-deficit policy could not be altered, presidents after Maxey would benefit from his determined administration, which had reorganized and strengthened the institution. For decades, younger leaders have hammered new policy planks onto Maxey's foundation. Whitman College has been and will be an ever-changing institution. But, in fact, much of the modern college's structure originated in the 1950s.

As Chester Maxey retired in 1959, Governor Rosellini summed up the president's record as an educator, scholar, and citizen: "Maxey has been good for Whitman and Washington. He has made this corner of North America a better place in which to live and to learn."[192]

8

The Administration of Louis B. Perry
1959 — 1967

Seeking a president who could build upon the solid foundation laid down in the 1950s, the trustees conducted the most thorough search that had ever been made in the school's eighty-six-year history. There was no internal candidate, and the trustees wanted to interview more applicants than they had when they hired Rudolf Clemen and Winslow Anderson. Dominated by its trustee members, a committtee of fourteen sought candidates from both coasts. Faculty members also served on the committee; this was a precedent according to Professor Thomas Howells, who said that, for twenty-three years, he had found news about the hiring of a new president "through the faithful reading of the *Union-Bulletin*."[1] Some committee members accumulated vital information by traveling for interviews, including one with Dr. Louis B. Perry of Pomona College.

The new president was born in March 1918, in Los Angeles. His parents were Louis H. Perry, a successful restaurateur (operating three Perry's Dairy Lunches), and Julie Irene Stoddard Perry. Neither parent had completed high school. His father had to drop out of school to work, but his mother had graduated from a music conservatory and taught piano for many years. She encouraged her two sons—Richard was six years younger than Louis—to strive for an education. Perry stated that his father had the greatest influence on him. Living among minorities, his father believed that "every man was as good as every other man." The son also admired his father's commitment to hard work.[2]

Perry attended both the Methodist church and the public schools, graduating from Los Angeles High School. He received a solid liberal arts background and pursued his interest in sports by participating on the school's track squad and by playing baseball on a city team. During the Great Depression, the teen-ager earned spending money by working for his father, and observed beggars in the restaurant and the unemployed seeking food in garbage cans.

In 1934 he enrolled at UCLA, a commuter institution located among the bean fields. Perry, who had learned to drive at his grandparents' home in South Dakota at the age of twelve, at sixteen paid $25 for a Model T Ford. He drove the thirteen miles to the university and made his automobile expenses with fares from student passengers. He majored in economics because of its several career options, including education and business, and he enjoyed the university distribution requirements. These broadened him and influenced his positive attitude about a liberal arts curriculum when he became an educator. Perry joined a regional fraternity and served as its president, but never lived in the fraternity house because it was easier to study at home. He maintained his interest in sports by lettering in cricket.

Perry completed the required two-year ROTC course and continued with the officer training program because he needed the money and because he thought that, if war should come, he would prefer to be an officer. He made a trip to Asia in 1936, when his Methodist minister had asked him to be his assistant for a tour of Japan and China. For three months the teen-ager traveled there and in Manchucko. He found Japanese soldiers to be arrogant and rural Japanese to be very curious about Caucasians.

Perry received a B.A. in economics in 1938, an M.A. in economics in 1940, and a junior-college teaching credential in 1941. He elected to pursue a Ph.D. in economics and took some courses at UCLA, but, encouraged by an advisor, transferred to Yale, enrolling with a stipend in the fall of 1941. The young scholar bade his fiancée, Genevieve "Gen" Patterson, farewell at the train depot. A native of Iowa, she had graduated from UCLA with a Phi Beta Kappa key. The two met in 1939 in a graduate school class in which their professor seated them alphabetically. Attractive and vivacious, she was one of only a few women to earn an M.A. in economics. She later recalled finding Perry attractive because he drove a Pontiac convertible with leather upholstery and super-charged pipes, but added that he "did not match the flashy car."[3]

The Japanese bombing of Pearl Harbor terminated Perry's graduate work at Yale. He was recalled to California, where he became a lieutenant in the Fortieth Division, a unit protecting the Southern California coast from possible Japanese landings. He married his sweetheart in February 1942, despite the opposition of their parents, who feared that she might become a widow with a child.

During the Second World War, Perry served in various administrative capacities, rising to the rank of major. His degrees and teaching experience in graduate schools probably explain his numerous educational assignments. For six months, he was a classification officer at Washington State College, where his wife joined him. He expressed amusement with his army career, which included "such diverse jobs as garbage disposal officer . . . and venereal disease control officer, tracking down the sources of infection."[4]

At war's end, he considered enrolling in a seminary, but returned to UCLA and, using the GI Bill, resumed study for a doctorate. To support his growing family, he became, in 1947, an instructor of economics at Pomona College. Perry remained there for twelve busy years, teaching a heavy load, receiving his doctorate in 1950, writing articles, co-authoring *Our Needy Aged*, working in the placement office, enjoying summer research fellowships, and rising quickly up the academic ranks to a full professorship in 1956. Perry, who was active in the Methodist church and the Claremont community, served for two years as an assistant to Pomona's president, E. Wilson Lyon, a distinguished medievalist and respected leader. In this capacity, he worked in the financial development office, participating in fund raising and learning about life income contracts. His wide-ranging experiences at Pomona, whose deferred giving program was superior to that of any other West Coast college, would be useful at Whitman. While a professor, he was also an investment counselor and broker, working closely with a clientele from the local retirement community. This work supplemented a modest professorial income; the economist thought that teaching and this outside business, not college administration, would be his future.

But in 1958 Lyon, who had heard about the impending vacancy

in Walla Walla, asked Perry if he would be interested in the Whitman presidency. The search committee asked him to apply; soon afterwards, trustees Harper Joy and Arthur Lee came to interview Perry and his wife. In the fall of 1958 the Perrys visited Whitman, meeting members of the college community; they made a second visit early the next year. Trustees Joy, Lee, and John Lyman encouraged Perry to accept the presidency. The candidate explained, however, that his decision would be made in close consultation with his wife. There were three reasons for their acceptance: a desire to leave the smog-bound Los Angeles area; a desire to provide their son, Bob, with the chance to exchange an urban environment for one where he could hunt and fish; and the desire to meet a new challenge. Realizing that the college had great potential, Perry also recognized the need for new buildings, campus repairs, and a development office.

Perry's selection satisfied many. Lyon summarized: "In character and professional training he possesses in high degree the qualities which make for a successful college president."[5] An editor of the *Walla Walla Union-Bulletin* noted that, while earlier the school had chosen its leadership and some of its faculty from New England, now it turned to Southern California. "From that fact," the writer judged, "it is reasonable to look for an administrative tempo characteristic of that rapidly developing part of the U.S."[6] Both commentators were correct. Perry became a successful president, and Whitman's tempo accelerated, especially in terms of adding campus buildings.

Perry's inaugural address, however, was not a discussion of the school's potential or its requirements. It was a general discussion of several topics, including the role of the modern college president. After pointing out the hazards of the office and noting the short tenure of several presidents, Perry stated that the "apparently desirable combination of educational leadership, scholarship, and business administration appropriate for the [presidential] task seems to fit in with my own background." He discussed president-faculty relations in general, and made a specific appeal to professors for cooperation in realizing the college's mission. He reminded them of their obligation in "the transmission of culture and the giving to students the opportunity to read and hear all points of view, particularly on questions of broad social policy."[7] In sum, Perry's inaugural did not indicate that the newcomer was about to launch a building program and to bring many of Pomona College's accomplishments to Whitman.

Administrators, Boards, and Buildings

The Perry family, including children Bob, Barbara, and Donna, replaced female students in the President's House. Perry soon learned about his predecessor's legacy. The college was in excellent condition: it was free of debt, it had good relationships with the city, it counted many devoted alumni, and it had effective regional alumni groups. Perry realized that Chester Maxey must have been a figure of considerable authority; some members of the faculty brought their salary and promotional grievances to Perry, complaining that his predecessor had been difficult to deal with. The new leader soon concluded that, "If we could get the financial assets, Whitman could go no place but up."[8]

Perry introduced a more democratic administration. Maxey had not recognized a need for closer faculty-board contact; his successor, however, taking from his Pomona experience, established meetings between the governing boards and the faculty. He also sought the opinions of the Whitman community, became involved in community affairs, and—unlike Maxey—consistently praised the staff and faculty for their contributions. The new president emphasized that he wanted to delegate authority, but he found resistance because administrators had looked upon Maxey as "the boss" and assumed that the president should make final decisions, large and small.[9]

But the changes in administrative style were far less obvious than the impressive expansion of both the campus and the endowment during the 1960s. According to the financial development office, "The asset base during those eight years increased from $8,000,000 to $24,000,000. The endowment and trust fund growth was from $6,600,000 to $17,000,000. The operating budget . . . doubled from $1,500,000 to $3,000,000. There were six new buildings constructed, and the faculty, which had been about 52 members in 1959, was 72 members eight years later. . . . The size of the student body had increased from 850 to 1,050."[10]

Perry retained Maxey's administrative staff, including dean of the faculty Paul Jackson and dean of administration David Stevens. The

*Considered by many to be Whitman's first modern president,
Louis B. Perry served from 1959 until 1967. His warm personality contrasted with that of his predecessor, Chester Maxey.
A thoughtful spokesman for the college, he excelled at public relations. Perry involved students and faculty in administrative matters and developed a solid fund-raising office.*

newcomer also kept Winks Dunphy as his secretary. Discreet, humorous, and well-connected in the community, she offered sage advice and warm friendship. Perry soon discovered that, "She knew
the eccentricities of the key members of the community."[11] Dunphy, who had a large circle of friends, provided valuable service in
local fund raising because she could identify the wealthy and their
interests. She also advised the president about how to relate to
strong-willed trustees. Sometimes Perry asked advice of Maxey, who
explained that, during his administration, the faculty council and the
administrative council had developed leadership that "relieved the

president of the necessity of trying to be an Argus-eyed supervisor of everything that was going on."[12] On one occasion the former president advised him: "You sit in so many committee meetings that you never want to pass a men's restroom without going in."[13]

Continuing a Whitman tradition, Perry appointed his administrative staff from within: there were no national searches, and nearly all the new officeholders were alumni. While endorsing the idea of hiring a faculty from diverse institutions, Perry seemed unconcerned about the insularity that resulted from these internal administrative promotions. The hiring in 1967 of Kenyon Knopf from Grinnell to be dean of the college broke with tradition and brought much-needed outside views and experience.

After twenty-two years of devoted service, treasurer Fritz Wilson died in 1965, and many agreed with Perry's assertion that, "There are few alumni who can claim more devoted service to and love for their alma mater than Wilson."[14] The president replaced him with business manager Pete Reid who, like Wilson, won the full confidence of the president and the boards. Alumna Almira Quinn was advanced to the position of director of placement and received praise for her commitment to her work. Representatives from employing organizations soon informed Perry that Quinn operated one of the best small-college placement services in the nation.[15] Paul Jackson, whose fair-mindedness had impressed his colleagues, returned to the English department, and Fredric Santler replaced him as dean of the faculty, a choice that would have a devastating result. In 1964 history professor Robert Whitner replaced David Stevens as dean of administration, and, when that position was eliminated soon thereafter, became the first dean of students. After a few years the historian returned to teaching, and Gordon Scribner moved into the position from the office of financial aid.

Like his predecessor, Perry enjoyed a solid relationship with the governing boards. He identified the basic qualifications for trustee membership as "work, wealth, and wisdom."[16] Owing to death and resignations, alumni Walter Minnick, Jonathan W. Edwards, and James Hill, Jr. became trustees. Dr. John Lyman, who had become a trustee in 1935 and had rendered able leadership in the depression and war periods, served as board president from 1952 to 1965. During the Perry years, members of Phi Delta Theta dominated trustee membership; if the board had been a jazz group, it could have been called "The Phi Delt Five plus two." Pomona and Reed and other colleges also had many trustees who were alumni, but Whitman's percentage of alumni was unusually high. Prior to official meetings, the Phi Delta Theta group met at Donald Sherwood's home, where they reminisced about the "old days" and discussed or even decided Whitman matters. Finding that the trustees were "a cozy little group," Perry urged the board to increase its membership from seven to the maximum of nine allowed by the charter. Portlander Donald C. Frisbee, a graduate of Pomona, joined in 1965; in the following year Walla Walla alumnus Baker Ferguson became the ninth member.

Undoubtedly the most influential and generous trustee was Sherwood. In the 1960s he played a major role in shifting endowment funds from unproductive farms and sluggish stocks to urban mortgages, government bonds, and other solid investments. Sherwood gave generously to his alma mater, was instrumental in persuading the Kellys to create the John G. and Martha M. Kelly Scholarship Fund (in 1965 the school received over $1,700,000 in this, the largest single gift to that time), negotiated a General Electric Company gift that covered one-third of the cost of Cordiner Hall, and contributed to the building fund for Sherwood Center.

Perry, Maxey, and others considered Harper Joy to be one of the most capable trustees. Energetic, positive, and personable, Joy worked to increase the endowment, stating that he wanted it "to grow like the Green Bay tree." He joked: "If it wasn't for these 'C' students who had gone on and been successful you would not have any trustees." Perry often consulted with him about administrative matters because Joy was thoughtful and discreet. Many of his friends remembered Joy's advice; for example, he encouraged everyone to travel while they were able, because he had "seen too many wives pushing their partially disabled husbands on and off steamships." When he resigned from the board in 1966, trustees honored his outstanding service by naming Whitman's theater building the Harper Joy Theatre.

Mary Jewett Gaiser was another significant trustee. The only woman on the board, she was also a trustee for both Wellesley, her alma mater, and the American University of Beirut. Perry explained that she "brought to the board a breadth of experience and maybe

Trustee Donald Sherwood was an astute Walla Walla business-man who assisted his struggling alma mater in the 1930s by serving on various financial committees. After a short period as an overseer, he became a trustee in 1954 and served until 1972. Sherwood was a conservative pragmatist; his insistence on balanced budgets and increasing the endowment, along with his personal contributions and opinions, shaped college policies.

even a certain gentility that offset that strong Phi Delt/Beta influence. The most sophisticated member of the group, she was highly respected by her fellow board members and when she spoke they listened."[17] She gave generously to Whitman and other institutions of higher education, and she took a keen interest in coeds. Gaiser asserted: "Women are wonderful. Like tea bags, they never know their strength until they get into hot water."[18]

Perry, unlike Maxey, regularly included administrators at the trustee meetings so that information would be brought to the table by somebody other than the president. He did not want trustees to make decisions without information from the appropriate college officers. This administrative style has been maintained by succeeding presidents.

The board of overseers had become more closely committed to the college's advancement in the Maxey years and maintained its loyalty throughout the Perry era. Although many on this large board had been familiar with Maxey because they were alumni—including several of his former students—or were Walla Wallans, they soon became impressed with his successor's character and competence, and voted their confidence. There were many overseers who rendered important service, including Pacific Northwest residents Ralph Edgerton, David Gaiser, Cameron Sherwood, Clark Eckart, John S. "Bud" Applegate, and Ruth Baker Kimball. Another influential and devoted group resided in New York City, including Robert H. Brome, Ralph J. Cordiner, John J. "Jack" Gurian, Richard Eells, Paul Garrett, and Ross Reid. These leaders would play a significant role in advancing the school's financial standing through their gifts and their efforts to persuade eastern individuals and foundations to assist their alma mater. The college had not enjoyed such profitable eastern connections since early in Stephen Penrose's presidency. One outstanding example was Robert Brome, who had come to Whitman from Basin, Wyoming, and majored in political science. He expressed a fervent love for his alma mater, chaired the Atlantic coast regional overseers, and, with his wife, Mary Reed Brome, a native of Waitsburg, Washington, maintained an active alumni group in New York City. He often hosted Whitman visitors. Once, he pointed out a group of leading corporation officers to Perry, and asserted that most of them were, like himself, from small towns, and that eastern "preppie guys worked for them."[19] A lawyer and high-ranking officer of Bankers Trust Company on Park Avenue, Brome introduced Maxey to the Olin Foundation; he also encouraged Paul Garrett, a ranking executive in General Motors Company, and others to make substantial gifts to their alma mater.[20] The efforts made by these New Yorkers and other committed alumni were exactly what Stephen Penrose had predicted would happen: those influenced by the college would assist it when they had the financial resources. Penrose had asserted in 1899: "The liberal arts college—founded and sustained by private philanthropy—sends its roots more deeply into American tradition and affection than any other of our institutions."[21] The college history of the 1960s seemed to bear him out.

One of the Perry administration's greatest legacies was the creation of a modern financial development office, the college's first. Penrose and Maxey had employed fund raisers; most of them had short tenures and limited responsibilities. But, under Perry, the college committed itself to an office that implemented wide-ranging activities. He brought Warren Knox, a Whittier College graduate, with him from Pomona, where Knox had become an experienced financial development officer, especially in life income and bequest programs. Perry placed the office of alumni affairs and the office of news service under Knox, explaining to overseers that he supervised "all fund-raising, publicity, alumni activities, and public relations."[22] Knox published booklets, spoke to groups about life income contracts, explained the college's needs (especially for money for a planned science building), and aroused alumni support.[23] His attractive publications, such as "The Whitman Plan: Life Income from Whitman College" and "To Give, Devise, and Bequeath," and advertisements, including those in the *Wall Street Journal*, quickly brought publicity and donations. Impressed with the immediate results of his work—$300,000 invested in the life income program in its first year—the trustees granted Knox a prestigious title, vice president for financial development.[24] Others appointed to serve under Knox were alumni Sherman Mitchell, director of public information, and Jerry Hillis, director of the alumni office.

A more significant appointment was made in 1962, when Larry Beaulaurier, a graduate of Gonzaga, a Korea veteran, and a Walla Walla businessman, joined Knox's staff to assist with raising money for the Ford Foundation challenge grant. The fact that Beaulaurier had been educated in Roman Catholic schools caused "a great resentment by one trustee."[25] But Beaulaurier would have a long and outstanding career in the financial development office. In 1964 he replaced Knox, who resigned to become president of the College of Idaho. Beaulaurier quickly put additional effort into alumni giving; he organized a parents' group, and launched the "Parents Newsletter" in an attempt to get assistance from this significant constituency.

The new development office played a major role in Perry's administration. It raised large amounts of money—especially larger donations from alumni—for a variety of campus needs, including the purchase of property, the construction of buildings, and the increase of both faculty salaries and student scholarships. The campus growth of the 1960s was the greatest increase since early in Penrose's administration, when the college had moved across Boyer Avenue, adding the Whitman Memorial Building, Billings Hall, Reynolds Hall, and the gymnasium. In the Perry years, Whitman added a dining addition to Lyman House, and constructed the Hall of Science

and Jewett Hall. But even more construction took place on land acquired west of the campus: the health center, Cordiner Hall, and
Sherwood Center. Some of these structures would not open until
soon after Perry resigned, but his administration had raised the
money for them. Perry called himself a "brick and mortar president."

While the college purchased valuable parcels of land west of the
campus, it convinced Walla Walla authorities to close a section of
Penrose Avenue to accommodate Sherwood Center. It failed, however, to gain the city's approval to close a section of Boyer Avenue,
which would have knitted together the oldest sections of the campus.

In 1960, on the eve of Whitman's expansion, it seemed necessary for board members to create a long-range planning committee. Under overseer Ruth Kimball's able leadership, the committee
quickly recommended property acquisitions, campus building sites,
and remodeling projects.

Completed in 1963, the first construction in the Perry administration was a dining addition to Lyman House to accommodate feed-
ing two hundred students. The college covered its $160,000 con-
struction costs by borrowing from the endowment and repaying it
over a fifteen-year period, at a six-percent interest rate.[26]

At about the same time that Whitman improved its dining facilities for men, it sought to construct a new dormitory for them. The
school unsuccessfully applied for a loan of $550,000 under Title IV
of the Federal Housing Act of 1950 to build such a structure.[27] Meanwhile, the president, trustees, overseers, and faculty all urged the construction of a science building, because Billings Hall, which had originally been built as a dormitory, was inadequate. Perry warned that
Whitman's "outstanding record in science is being threatened with
each passing year, so much so that the president is now meeting increased difficulty in recruiting faculty replacements in the various
basic science fields in view of inadequate facilities for research, teaching, and the operation of necessary equipment."[28]

The faculty—including many members not teaching in the science
division—urged the immediate erection of a science building, emphasizing that the college lagged behind the competition and required
a new building "if Whitman is to continue to maintain its place as
one of the better, if not the best, small liberal arts colleges in this
country."[29]

In 1960, as the Whitman community discussed the need for a new science building, the treasurer found only $150,000 to meet construction and equipment costs that would exceed $1,100,000.[30] Perry reported to trustees that the request to the Olin Foundation for a science facility was "virtually worthless" because the foundation did not know when it would ever consider Whitman's application. Other foundations also rejected the proposal.

Perry and the board members, however, elected to raise funds for the science building without a commitment from a major donor. At the 1961 Homecoming celebration, an enthusiastic crowd watched Boeing president William Allen, who donated to the building, participate in groundbreaking ceremonies. Perry predicted that construction costs would be met, and praised alumni and the governing boards for their generosity. These groups had recently responded to the financial development office's several appeals: fifteen hundred

Built in 1963, the Hall of Science replaced Billings Hall and was the first campus building to cost more than $1,000,000. While those in the science departments appreciated the building's facilities, they and others complained about its stark appearance. Landscaping has added little to the box-like structure.

alumni had contributed or pledged over $110,000 to the building fund.[31] Perry wrote in 1961: "There is little question but that Whitman alumni are not in the habit of giving to their alma mater despite the fact that the college has contributed heavily to their educational cost during their residence as students."[32] But there would be a significant increase in alumni giving in the 1960s.

Vice President Knox reported in June 1962 that the college had accumulated $1,115,000 for the science building.[33] The administration and the governing boards were demonstrating an ability to raise unprecedented sums. Because of tax laws, many donors gave stock certificates; a few local residents gave wheat. The largest gift came from overseer David Gaiser and his wife, trustee Mary Jewett Gaiser. Recognizing this Spokane couple's donation of $150,000, the college named the auditorium in the new science building Gaiser Auditorium in honor of David's parents. When the long-anticipated facility opened in 1963, the trustees borrowed $100,000 from the endowment at a five-percent rate of interest to finance some of its costs. The trustees had intended to name the structure Brown Hall after Whitman's legendary physicist, Benjamin Brown, but Perry convinced the board that, because there was support for naming it after other capable science professors, the building should be called the Hall of Science and should be jointly dedicated to Benjamin Brown, Walter Bratton, and Howard Brode.

While crews erected the science building, college leaders sought to realize other ambitious construction plans. The Whitman community insisted that the gymnasium that had been built in 1905 was, like Billings Hall, totally inadequate. In 1949 President Maxey had urged its replacement; eleven years later Perry, who reasoned that a new physical education plant was the college's second greatest capital need, complained that the gymnasium was "far inferior to those possessed by the junior high schools in Walla Walla!"[34] In 1960 there were no wealthy donors or foundations interested in underwriting part or all of the costs of this badly needed facility. With funds for the Hall of Science secured, Perry reported in 1962 that "financial development efforts must now be turned to a new physical education plant."[35] The college, however, soon shelved these plans, and the president announced that construction of a new men's dormitory ranked ahead of a new gymnasium.

Whitman was able to build a dormitory, a gymnasium, and other structures in the 1960s, however, largely because it received a prestigious Ford Foundation grant in June 1962. The leaders of this foundation, wanting to assist liberal arts colleges, asked the college to apply for a grant. The foundation required Whitman to supply a ten-year projection covering administration, instruction, enrollment, and other matters. It initially denied Whitman's feverishly prepared request, but soon changed its mind. Perry suspected that some influential eastern overseers had asked foundation officials to give their alma mater a second chance. In 1962, the school announced the gratifying news that it had been selected as one of only twenty-one institutions in the nation to receive a grant. Whitman would receive $1,500,000 if it could raise $3,000,000 in matching funds by 1965. Trustee Mary Jewett Gaiser hoped the grant would bring a golden age to the college; three decades later, long-time treasurer Pete Reid considered this grant to have been "one of the most important things in Whitman's financial history."[36]

Vice President Knox predicted that the college could raise the matching funds because it had successfully raised over a million dollars to finance the Hall of Science. In the 1962–1963 school year Whitman received an initial Ford Foundation grant of $432,000—the largest cash grant it had ever received to that time—and utilized the money for faculty salary improvements, library books, campus repairs, and new construction. Meanwhile, trustee Gaiser chaired the Whitman challenge committee, which found matching gifts from individuals, corporations, and foundations. Collaborating with the school's development office, Gaiser kept the campaign on schedule, and, by the 1965 deadline, $3,682,000 had been collected to meet the Ford Foundation challenge. The Whitman community expressed both surprise and pleasure at this gratifying accomplishment.

With the science building completed, and with the challenge committee reporting success, the optimistic trustees chose to build the men's dormitory, which they had earlier delayed. Their goal in providing more housing was to be able to accommodate additional students (in 1966 trustees set the maximum enrollment at twelve hundred), while continuing the traditional requirement that men live either on the campus in dormitories or near it in fraternity houses. The catalog for 1964–1965 offered the rationale for the residential

policy: Whitman "has concern for the entire twenty-four-hour day of its students. Life in residence halls is an essential part of the educational program."

To pay for this needed structure, the trustees appropriated $200,000 from the Ford Foundation money and allotted $200,000 from the endowment, an internal debt the trustees were willing to assume because the building would pay for itself through charges for room and board.[37] Painfully aware of the fact that the two dormitory loans made with bankers in the 1920s had meant long-lasting economic hardship, the board took financial precautions: it neither contracted outside debt nor borrowed federal money. In 1963 Perry reported to the alumni: "We are pleased . . . that all of the funds for the hall have been obtained without the necessity of government loan funds."[38]

Trustee Gaiser became actively involved in the dormitory's construction because she saw the need for attractive interiors, especially in the central lounge; and, as a result of her involvement, this aus-

Jewett Hall began operation in 1964. An undistinguished building, this dormitory is unfavorably compared with Lyman House, built in 1923, to which it is attached by the 1963 dining addition.

tere structure did provide appealing accommodations. The trustees named the building in honor of her first husband, George F. Jewett, a financial supporter of higher education, and expressed pleasure at the completion of the $550,000 dormitory, which would house two hundred men.

In 1954 the college had built Anderson Hall for freshman women; ten years later, in 1964, it opened Jewett Hall for freshman men. But neither of these dormitories was as handsome as Lyman House and Prentiss Hall, which had been constructed in the 1920s, when the college had borrowed money to build these attractive and functional buildings. In the 1950s the trustees refused to spend beyond what had been collected for a structure; thus, local architect and alumnus Harold Crawford designed the Hall of Science, Jewett Hall, and Penrose Memorial Library with minimal budgets. The tradition of building functional, unadorned buildings was broken with the erection of Cordiner Hall in the late 1960s, but resumed immediately with the construction of Sherwood Center.

Throughout the 1960s construction crews were so familiar that some faculty members joked that men in overalls, who became common campus figures, could hardly be distinguished from informally dressed students. In the mid-1960s the campus community learned that workmen would remain to construct still another facility. The General Electric Company informed Whitman in April 1964 that it would grant $500,000 to Whitman to honor Ralph J. Cordiner, who was retiring from the company.

A classmate and fraternity brother of Donald Sherwood, Cordiner had alerted him about the opportunity for the school to receive a useful gift. Reared on a wheat ranch near Walla Walla, Cordiner was another of those Whitmanites who had paid his college costs by farming in the summers and by working at various jobs during the school year. Besides waiting tables, tending furnaces, and boxing semi-professionally at the Keylor Grand Theater, he sold wooden-paddled washing machines. Deciding on a business career, he went to work for the General Electric Company, ultimately serving as the company's chief executive officer for thirteen years. Probably no Whitman graduate rose to higher prominence in manufacturing than Cordiner; in 1959 *Time* magazine recognized his importance by placing his face on its cover. Alumnus Nard Jones applauded Cordiner's business acumen, pointing out that: "Perhaps the only success of the recent [1964] Goldwater campaign [for the U.S. presidency] was the fact that it wound up in the black. None of us who know Cordiner were astonished at that, because Cordiner had undertaken to run the finances of the campaign."[39]

Cordiner acknowledged that he had been influenced by the teachings and character of President Penrose; he took little interest in endowing an academic chair, but was enthusiastic about constructing a new building. In announcing the gift, Perry stated that the facility would be both an auditorium and a physical education plant. He predicted that the new hall would enable the college "to enrich the cultural and recreational life of the college and the community."[40] Cordiner later stated that he hoped that the building would "establish an ever closer union between the students and faculty . . . and the residents of the Walla Walla Valley."[41]

Again, the college asked alumni, corporations, and board members to contribute to a badly needed facility. While this national fund-raising effort was being waged, a local committee chaired by Professor George Ball discussed the facilities that should be included. Apparently trustee Mary Jewett Gaiser played a major role in arguing against including any physical education facilities in the new building. Finally, the committee recommended that Cordiner Hall be a concert auditorium seating about fourteen hundred persons. To cover construction costs, the college added about a million dollars to the General Electric gift, including $250,000 from the Ford Foundation grant. Despite a great effort to raise money from Walla Wallans, who were told how their community would benefit from a modern auditorium, only about ten percent of the building's total cost came from local donors. In the spring of 1968 Whitman dedicated this centerpiece of the west campus. Many commented on the

Cordiner Hall was constructed in 1968. This striking building, with a seating capacity of about fifteen hundred, was named in honor of Ralph Cordiner, a classmate of Donald Sherwood. The building is used by the community and the college for a variety of functions, including lectures and concerts—and, during inclement weather, convocations and commencements.

Sherwood Center was built in 1968 to serve as a physical education and recreation center. Controversial in its appearance, it has often been called "Fort Sherwood."

auditorium's splendid acoustics, a result of alumnus Walter Brattain's efforts in obtaining the technical assistance of Bell Laboratories. While the building was being constructed in her husband's honor, Mrs. Gwen Lewis Cordiner oversaw the expenditure of $100,000 that the couple donated for campus beautification projects, including Cordiner Glen, replacement bridges over College Creek, and landscaping for Cordiner Hall.[42]

Meanwhile, other buildings emerged on the west campus. In 1967 the new health center opened, an infirmary that could accommodate twenty-four patients. But attracting far more excitement was the construction of Sherwood Center. In the early 1960s the Whitman community ridiculed its dilapidated gymnasium and urged a replacement, but college leaders questioned the likelihood of success for still another fund drive. Federal assistance seemed to be a possible answer. Perry explained to board members that other private schools, including the College of Puget Sound and Lewis & Clark College, were not, as Whitman was, wary of debts to the federal government. An overseer committee studied the implications of applying for a federal loan under the Higher Education Act of 1965. Aware that some trustees were still uncomfortable with the thought of government assistance, this committee wisely reminded them that, since 1959, the college had received over $600,000 from federal aid-to-education programs, including student loans, the National Science Foundation program, and several others. The committee then recommended that the trustees accept federal funds that would "not subject the college to regulations or conditions which will adversely restrict the college's freedom of action."[43] Undoubtedly, this advice helped convince trustees that they should seek federal assistance for the construction of a gymnasium. While the governing boards awaited a response to the college's application for federal money, Donald Sherwood gave $350,000 for the building that would be named for him. But the federal government, for the first and only time in Whitman's history making a significant contribution towards new construction, gave even more than the private benefactor. The college received a Title I higher education facilities grant of $474,000, which covered about one-third the cost of the building.[44]

Across from Cordiner Hall, the new Student Union Building also opened in 1968. (The elegant 1947 SUB was now relegated to office use.) Prodded by treasurer Pete Reid, the college had acquired the Pacific Co-operative building, including two lots that could be used for Cordiner Hall parking, at the low price of $130,000. Reid esti-

Pete Reid was one of the most popular individuals ever to work for Whitman, serving the college since his graduation in 1949. He was a fair-minded college treasurer in the lean years, and has been a loyal advocate of his alma mater, a reliable bridge between the school and the town, and a stalwart defender of the the Greek system.

mated that the well-built structure could be remodeled as a student center for $275,000.

During the Perry administration the school renovated much of the campus and paid for it from the Ford Foundation challenge grant and the end-of-the-year surpluses. Carpenters remodeled classrooms in Billings Hall, and turned the upper two floors of Reynolds Hall into faculty offices. Workmen replaced many leaky steampipes and painters freshened a score of rooms. To the delight of the library staff, the library was air-conditioned, at a cost of $169,000. The college further improved the appearance of the campus by planting trees and shrubs and installing a new sprinkler system.

In 1963 Perry discussed the acquisition of a computer. He stated that the administration, especially the registrar and the treasurer, could use it "to advantage in the work of their offices." He also stressed that professors of mathematics and the social sciences "would benefit greatly by having a computer on campus for research work."[45] Early the next year the trustees accepted the president's arguments and paid only $33,000 (borrowing again from the endowment) for an IBM 1620 computer. The administration quickly put the machine to practical use, but few faculty members worked with it. After one year of its operation, Perry identified common and traditional problems: properly staffing the equipment and determining which college programs would have priority in using this new technology. But he assured the campus that there was "little doubt that the computer is here to stay." He added: "Students have been fascinated by the computer and have even utilized it to match couples for a dance!"[46]

Perry's Relationship with the Faculty

Campus visitors saw significant changes resulting from construction and remodeling, and those who read the president's reports or heard his alumni talks could learn about significant gain in Whitman's financial strength. Fewer individuals, however, realized that the conditions of faculty life had also improved. Influenced by his Pomona experience, Perry sought to enhance the lot of the Whitman faculty. Both board members and faculty members helped him carry out his wide-ranging program.

Professors traditionally and legitimately had voiced their concerns about their salaries; in the new administration, salaries still remained an issue. Perry later recalled that his two principal objectives as president were to improve the college's physical facilities and to provide better salaries for a larger faculty.[47] Salaries steadily increased in the 1960s, but the gains were unspectacular and more modest than the faculty anticipated. When Perry first arrived some professors assumed that, because the new president had served as a faculty member for twelve years, he would forcefully push for larger salaries. Dubious professors, however, reminded their colleagues that Maxey had an even longer teaching tenure than Perry and that he had not made higher salaries a major priority. In 1960 Perry stated that there was "a need for further [salary] increases which should average, at the least, a minimum of 5 per cent a year not including fringe benefits." The president urged the trustees to increase salaries because, "The decade of the 1960s is going to bring about intense competition for first-rate faculty personnel."[48] In 1963 he wrote: "In large part, the ability to secure faculty members who will be able to chal-

The officers of the Whitman chapter of the American Association of University Professors in 1960 were Robert Bennett, Ely Chertok, Ronald Sires, and Donald Connell. The local chapter considered salary levels, tenure, and the curriculum. In the late 1960s the chapter would spend considerable time on student concerns.

lenge the ablest students continues to depend on salary and fringe
benefit issues. . . . The real question is the ability of Whitman to attract and keep the . . . persons it wants under the competitive conditions of the market place."[49] He insisted that the college wanted
to add professors "whose primary interest is teaching" and pointed out that the universities, employing a "publish or perish system,"
were granting tenure to writers, not teachers.[50]

Despite Perry's predictions about faculty compensation increases, salaries grew by five percent annually in the 1960s only if fringe
benefits were included.[51] Moreover, the inflation rate of the 1960s
limited financial progress. Looking back, Perry admitted that the
salaries were never "high enough, and we were not able to pay what
we would have liked."[52] Professor Paul Jackson sympathized: it was
"back-breaking labor for the president and his assistants to obtain
the large amounts of money to meet the needs for higher salaries in
order to get and keep a faculty which can meet the higher standards
of instruction, to say nothing of the money needed for buildings and
equipment."[53] Other experienced professors, including Arthur Rempel and Robert Whitner, agreed, and asserted that "salaries are not
a source of discontent with most of the faculty."[54] Those who had
been hired in more recent years did not have the same perspective,
however, and complained about inadequate paychecks. Some of them
expressed admiration for fund-raising efforts but grumbled that more
of the money raised by the Ford Foundation challenge grant should
have gone into the salary budget instead of into "bricks and mortar."

In the mid-1960s concerned students, such as Dick Lilly, sided
with discontented faculty members and urged competitive faculty
salaries. One *Pioneer* editor stated that faculty salaries were Whitman's most "critical problem." Feature writer Kathy Hall concluded
that there was "nothing exceptional" about Whitman's faculty salaries, after comparing them with salaries at other institutions. They
"are better than the less prestigious small colleges and state universities, and they are poorer than those of prestige colleges and most
state universities." She asserted that, in the previous decade, salary
increases had been insufficient for the college "to keep pace with
its competition."[55]

Perry consistently informed the Whitman community about market conditions, emphasizing that it was difficult to hire Ph.D.s at

entry-level salaries. The president did not name the college's competitors, but he summarized that the mean salary scale of those schools exceeded Whitman's by more than $2,000.[56] In 1963 an overseers' committee urged higher salaries, emphasizing that the college's salaries lagged behind those of such competitors as Pomona and the University of Washington. In 1966 the president of the alumni association reported that the average Whitman salary was $2,600 behind the average salary at Pomona and less than $200 ahead of that of Lewis & Clark.[57]

In his last year Perry presented a tabulation of the annual average salary, excluding fringe benefits. The figure climbed from $6,869 in 1959–1960 to $9,660 in 1966–1967. The pay scale meant, Perry explained, that Whitman could now compete for faculty members at the lower ranks; but the compensation for associates and full professors still should be improved, because the college needed to retain promising young faculty members who could challenge students and who kept abreast of their fields.[58]

The president explained that one reason for the failure to increase salaries was that additional professors had been hired; this meant more slices out of the faculty pie.[59] In Perry's administration the number of full-time faculty members increased significantly, from fifty-two to seventy-two; at the same time, the student body rose from about 850 to 1,050. The college was offering over fifty percent more classes in the 1960s than it had in the 1950s.

The notable increase in faculty size strengthened several departments, including history, English, biology, mathematics, and religion. The curriculum was enriched through the addition of competent individuals, many of whom would have long careers, including Edward Anderson (biology), George Ball (religion), Robert Blumenthal (physics), Katherine Bracher (astronomy), Frederick Breit (history), Richard Brown (biology), G. Thomas Edwards (history), John Freimann (dramatic arts), Roy Hoover (religion; he also served as religious counselor), Philip Howland (physics), Victor Keiser (mathematics), Donald King (history), Kenyon Knopf (dean of the college; he also taught economics), Donald Lehmann (biology), Joseph Maier (philosophy), James Maxfield (English), Michael McClintick (English), Corey Muse (education), James Pengra (physics), Robert Polzin (chemistry), José Rambaldi (music), James Soden (modern languages),

Richard Stuart (economics), Richard Thomassen (mathematics), Roy Thompson (physical education), James Todd (chemistry), Vernon Toews (modern languages), J. Patrick Tyson (English), J. Walter Weingart (history), and John Wilcox (physical education).

The faculty additions resulted from protracted and sometimes heated discussions by the division chairmen and the faculty council; in arranging priority lists those groups sought both to relieve pressures on popular departments and to enrich the curriculum. In making their priorities, faculty leaders made sure that every department offering a major had a minimum of two professors. The president, the dean of the faculty, and senior professors hired candidates by telephone and letters. Campus visits were not required, although efforts were made to interview candidates personally, and sometimes an alumnus served as interviewer. Perry explained that the hiring procedure was "a much more collaborative practice than had been followed by the college," but he also believed that hiring "was a presidential perogative";[60] this was the long-standing tradition at Whitman, and had been the case at Pomona when he was there. Faculty members sometimes criticized him for exercising this perogative.

Although increases did not push Whitman's faculty salaries into the top tier of salaries for liberal arts colleges—Perry reported in 1966 that they were merely at the national average—there were notable improvements in fringe benefits. In 1960 the president announced that the college would soon offer a group insurance plan. He also called for additional fringe benefits, including a group health program partially subsidized by Whitman, increased retirement benefits under the Teachers Insurance and Annuity Association, a sabbatical system, and tuition payments for faculty children attending other colleges.

Emphasizing to trustees that there was a critical shortage of Ph.D.s at a time of surging college enrollments, Perry pushed to improve faculty conditions. In 1961 he announced that children of faculty and staff members attending other colleges would receive half the Whitman tuition. He also stated that morale had recently been improved by the establishment of a travel fund, which helped members of the faculty attend professional meetings, participate in conferences, and present papers. Such activities would "prevent intellectual stagnation and offset geographical isolation." The president

Dr. Phyllis Hutchings taught astronomy from 1943 until 1965. One of the few female professors of that era, she befriended students and young colleagues. Her famous bicycle was sometimes found in Lakum Duckum or hoisted to the top of the flagpole.

boasted that professors "can now retain their professional contacts at minimum expense to themselves."[61]

Perry noted an increase in the professionalization of the faculty: more were writing books, articles, and book reviews, and attending professional meetings. The leader explained: "Even though primary emphasis is placed on teaching effectiveness, the evidence of intellectual growth on the part of the Whitman faculty is a spark that tends to stir the curiosity of students to seek the answers to disturbing questions." He added: "Professional and creative activity inevitably have their effects in terms of more inspired teaching and consequent greater student intellectual motivation."[62]

Whitman's first sabbatical system was enacted in the 1961–1962 school year. To get it adopted, Perry explained to trustees that sabbatical proposals "should include activities of professional benefit to [faculty members] and hence to Whitman and its students." He went on to say that "a sabbatical normally should be a time for a refreshment that provides for some kind of professional advancement." The plan required that applicants have tenure and have taught for six years. Perry assured doubters that "sabbaticals will not be automatic but involve the submission of a plan indicating that the sabbatical will be used productively for the professional advancement of the faculty member."[63] The president hailed the new program as "one of the most liberal of its kind," because a one-semester sabbatical paid one hundred percent of the salary, and a full-year sabbatical paid seventy-five percent.[64] Gratified by these improvements in their professional lives, all the senior professors signed a letter to Perry expressing pleasure with his work on their behalf.

Perry involved the faculty in administrative matters to a greater degree than any president since Walter Bratton. He wanted to spread participation in the school's operation so that the faculty would feel "a sense of ownership in the institution."[65] Thus, the leader appointed members of the faculty to several committees, including the long-range planning committee, the financial development advisory committee, and the Cordiner Hall planning committee. Faculty members were more involved in decisions about hiring, promoting, and granting tenure to their colleagues. The president often solicited the opinion of individual teachers about other matters. Responding to several of their requests, he supported the construction of large faculty offices in Reynolds Hall. This faculty office building, Perry reported to trustees, "improved faculty morale" and gave its inhabitants opportunities to discuss academics and other matters.[66] The Reynolds Hall faculty lounge attracted coffee drinkers, who engaged in lively academic and non-academic conversations from 8:00 AM until 4:00 PM. In retrospect, the facilities at Reynolds united the faculty as it would never be united again.

Borrowing from Pomona, Perry established biennial meetings of the faculty and the governing boards. At these conferences, faculty members, trustees, and overseers discussed such matters as the college's goals, curriculum, athletics, student body size, and residential policies. All participating groups praised the convivial meetings, agreeing with Perry, who asserted that they "furnish a most valuable means of communication and exchange of information . . . and a great deal of mutual understanding."[67] These conferences lowered the barriers between the boards and the faculty.

Perry opened up new lines of communication with students. Maxey had felt it unnecessary to explain the college's policies or its leadership. Assuming that students took an interest in college affairs and possessed useful ideas, Perry spoke to them at such special occasions as his state-of-the-college address, discussed issues at some meetings of the student congress, and communicated through the *Pioneer*. The president addressed subjects such as the goals of a liberal arts education, faculty salaries and tenure, academic freedom, residence policies, student involvement in college administration, and athletics. He referred to the college's history, its reputation for integrity, and its dependence on mature student leaders. Older members of the faculty observed that Perry was the first president since Penrose to make such an effort to inform students and solicit their views. Many students admired Perry for being approachable, and they generally understood his explanations of college policies. A few criticized his formality and conservatism, but these critics expressed surprise when he made no objections to inviting radical speakers to the campus. Some wanted Perry to oppose the Greek system and intercollegiate sports, and, especially near the end of his administration, an increasing number wanted him to renounce the practice of *in loco parentis*.

Perry recognized that the faculty and students at Whitman and elsewhere wanted "a larger share in the operation" of their schools. He cautioned that "the authority delegated to students and faculty" had limitations: "Such a limit lies in the area of fiscal responsibility." The president and the governing boards must possess the final authority in fiscal matters.[68] Probably only a few disgruntled students and professors disagreed with this interpretation.

Perry as an Educational Leader

Under Perry's leadership, Whitman grew in strength. He argued that it must improve, because state institutions, particularly those in California, were booming. They were adding new buildings, modern equipment, record enrollments, and improved salaries. Perry warned that, unless liberal arts colleges "are able to pay competitive salaries, acquire expensive equipment, and build new facilities," they faced a bleak future. He feared that, if the private schools were marginalized, it "would create a more monolithic structure of higher education with a consequent loss to our society."[69]

To bolster Whitman, Perry not only engaged in extensive fund-raising activities, but he also spent considerable time with institutional reforms. He had seen the president of Pomona build an impressive small college, and he aspired to do the same at Whitman. Furthermore, he found that Maxey had been such a strong figure that Whitman expected presidential leadership. Challenges to Perry's leadership came from trustees, not from the faculty. Perry, who had worked in a more progressive atmosphere at Pomona, did not arrive at Whitman with a blueprint in mind; instead he pushed for change only after consultation with administrators, faculty members, and students. Aware that he was receptive to their ideas, these groups voiced them in official meetings, or individuals expressed them in private conversations.

Perry frequently and clearly explained functions and goals. In 1965 he identified "his two primary functions" as further increasing the endowment fund of about $12,000,000—he called it "the largest of any private college in the West north of San Francisco"—and the acquisition of faculty members, who received "seven-thirteenths of the annual budget."[70] The president listed Whitman's two main goals. "The first is to continue to prepare students effectively to undertake graduate work. The second is to provide an undergraduate education that will equip those students who do not go beyond the undergraduate degree for effective and creative living."[71]

Perry understood that tuition and attrition issues were relevant to attaining these and other goals. In order to raise faculty and staff salaries, tuition must be increased. Reducing the rate of attrition was critical, because the school needed to retain juniors and seniors so that the faculty could offer a more balanced curriculum, so that it would not be necessary to recruit freshmen classes exceeding three hundred, and so that the college would enjoy more alumni. Although the Whitman community continually feared that increased tuition fees would price the college out of the market, and although students complained about the sharp increases in tuition, the college was not adversely affected by steady tuition increases, since other institutions also had to raise their tuition rates. At the same time, Whitman substantially increased its student aid.

The tuition in 1959 was $275 per semester; in 1962 it was $500; and in 1967 it was $750. With the tuition at $1,500 per year, one student angrily complained to his teachers that "they were all blood-suckers." The catalog, however, assured students that, through personal thrift, partial self-support, and college aid funds, they could pay the tuition as well as board and room fees, which were $810 per year in 1967. Perry explained to alumni startled by sharply increased tuition rates that there was "no such thing as inexpensive quality education," that "nearly 90 percent of the financial aid need" would be met, and that tuition did not pay the "total educational costs incurred . . . for a student."[72] Despite advancing costs, the student population increased and the institution, which had always wanted more male students than female ones, reported that men made up fifty-five percent of the student body.

Near the end of his presidency, Perry called attention to the attrition problem. In 1965 he noted that total attrition stood at nearly fifty-five percent, about the national average. He complained, however, that this percentage was too high for Whitman, and that the high rate demonstrated the college's inability to hold students—especially women—for four years. In 1967 the president said that some attrition was inevitable: "As long as Whitman is a coeducational institution it probably will have some attrition of women for marital as well as career reasons." He also acknowledged that some students transferred to institutions offering major studies in fields not to be found at a liberal arts school. Perry advised that the attrition problem needed study and stressed that there was "a distinct need for more stimulation and challenge during the freshman and sophomore years."[73]

To improve conditions for students, Perry advocated better counseling and a richer cultural environment. To strengthen non-academic counseling, the college hired religious counselor Robert McKenzie—Roy Hoover replaced him in this position in 1967—and a consulting psychiatrist. The faculty's academic advising seemed effective, but the administration helped the office of student affairs to find more time for personal advising. Perry reported to the overseers that the psychiatrist and the religious counselor had improved "preventive counseling, thus resolving some students' personal problems before they became too serious to be handled at the college."[74] The president suggested that Whitman had not experienced student suicides because an extra effort was made "to catch the floundering student who is seeking to find his or her place on the campus."[75]

The president also wanted to bring in more outside lecturers to enrich the college's cultural life, noting: "There is almost uniform agreement that a lecture series on a funded basis is badly needed."[76] Students and faculty members often grumbled about their isolation and endorsed a plan to bring in more lecturers. Perry and the student government found money for additional speakers; in the 1962–1963 school year the college community heard more than a dozen speakers, including physicist Walter Brattain, journalist Harrison Salisbury, U.S. Senator Warren Magnuson, and religious scholar and Whitman alumnus Roland Bainton. This list, and those compiled in later years, support Perry's generalization that there was "a decided increase in cultural activities."[77] In 1964 the college launched its fine-arts series with a performance by the Duke Ellington orchestra.

In addition to being concerned for the personal and cultural needs of the students, Perry was sensitive to the relationship between the college and the community. He acknowledged the vital role that the theater and the Conservatory of Music played in public relations, but he did not make the same claim for intercollegiate athletics. In fact, the leader suggested that there was "a possibility that the day of the large team sports for the small college with high academic standards may be passing."[78] He reminded readers, however, that Whitman excelled in individual sports, including tennis, track, golf, and cross-country. A rumor soon swept through the alumni that their alma mater was about to abandon intercollegiate sports. The disgusted president responded that such a rumor "often may be an excuse not to contribute to the alumni fund!"[79]

Perry reported that the college subsidized theater productions because they were "an integral part of [Whitman's] educational program," and because of their "public relations value." The theater, under the leadership of Rodney Alexander, won applause from both students and townspeople. The college also subsidized the conservatory's musical programs and staff salaries, but it received good public relations from these expenditures.[80] The president pointed out that Cordiner Hall would bring culture to Walla Walla and tie the city more closely to the college.

Walla Walla civic leader Dr. Ralph Stevens, working closely with Perry, in 1962 funded the Whitman Town-Gown Award, which would recognize the contributions of faculty members to the city with a $500 award. "It is to be given annually," Perry wrote, "to that member of the faculty, who . . . has made an outstanding constructive contribution to community, civic, and/or cultural affairs." Early winners were professors Fredric Santler, Kenneth Schilling, and Robert Whitner; in recent years staff members have sometimes received the annual award.

In serving local schools and individuals, the library, of course, had public relations value. The college, which tried to serve these diverse patrons, stressed the importance of the library to the educational mission. Perry neatly summarized the matter: "The library is the intellectual heart of the campus. It is probably the most important single instructional tool possessed by faculty members. It must continue to forge ahead in staff, acquisitions, and ease of utilization."[81] Personally interested in the library and pressured by the faculty and librarians to improve its holdings, Perry added staff and increased the minimal book budget with funds from the Ford Foundation grant and the federal government. In 1956 the budget for acquisitions was $4,700; ten years later it was $28,000.[82] But clearly this sum was inadequate. In 1962 the library held 105,500 books and 182,000 unbound documents, which was, Perry boasted, a much larger collection than the average liberal arts college library held. But he was not complacent, arguing that the library must be expanded "to meet the intellectual challenges of the future."[83] The faculty agreed, as did a professor of history who had a book budget of only $100 in 1965.

In 1962 the president took pleasure in announcing that alumnus Jerry Jesseph and others had organized the Friends of the Penrose Memorial Library. This group volunteered its labor and made a significant contribution by seeking funds, books, documents, and papers for the library and for the museum of Northwest history that was housed in the library. In 1966 librarian Ruth Reynolds retired after forty years of service. Perry recognized her dedicated career and stressed her "heartfelt loyalty to the cause of independent higher education."[84] Experienced hands hailed her efforts to expand and preserve the college archives and Northwest manuscript materials. Arley Jonish replaced her; he would oversee the significant expansion of the library.

Perry made many contacts to improve relations with Walla Walla. He was active in the Rotary Club and served as president of the Chamber of Commerce. No leader since Stephen Penrose worked harder than Perry did at explaining the role of a liberal arts college to the community. The local newspaper maintained that, "He has gained both the respect and warm regard of the community."[85] He was also involved in the Association of American Colleges and other national organizations, so that educators in other parts of the nation would know something about Whitman and recognize it "as a legitimate high-class institution."[86]

But, most important, he cultivated the loyalty of alumni, another group that marveled at Perry's ability to memorize names. He spoke to numerous alumni gatherings and wrote to them through various publications. Perry pushed for an expanded alumni magazine, which appeared in the mid-1960s. In its new incarnation, the magazine carried feature stories and considerable news about the campus and the alumni. Graduates responded favorably to the college's earnest and more frequent financial appeals: the percentage of alumni giving to the annual fund increased from thirteen percent to twenty-nine percent between 1960 and 1966. The national average of alumni giving was twenty percent; leading institutions received gifts from forty percent of their graduates. Alumni leaders set their sights on the latter figure.[87]

Alumni, faculty members, and townspeople all commented on the fact that the Perrys had made the President's House at 515 Boyer Avenue a center of college activity. Not since the Penroses departed in the mid-1930s had the house been such an important part of the Whitman community. When presidents Walter Bratton and Chester Maxey had lived in their private homes, students had resided in the President's House.

Genevieve Perry played an important role. During her husband's interview in California, she had asked trustee Harper Joy about the function of the president's wife. He responded: "The college presidents' wives are not as important as they used to be."[88] He meant that this role had diminished since the time of Mary Penrose, who had been very active on campus and in the community.

Mrs. Perry's first official task was to spend a week overseeing the renovation of the President's House, which needed considerable repair after eleven years of student residence. She turned it into a comfortable house for a family of five, with its convenient six bathrooms and outside staircase. The three Perry children consumed much of her time. This fact and the inability of the college to afford two airplane tickets meant that she only rarely traveled with her husband. But she consistently advised her husband about his various challenges.

Mrs. Perry appeared at many campus functions and participated in several Walla Walla organizations, including the Congregational church, PEO, the art club, and the PTA. Initially she did only a modest amount of entertaining of faculty members, parents, and board members. Later she hosted Sunday night dinners for graduating seniors. Inviting them sixteen at a time, she did the cooking, and college women assisted. Students as well as other college groups found her to be a delightful hostess. Townspeople enjoyed her friendliness and down-to-earth approach to life, and they knew that she took pleasure in her role as the college president's wife. Many people on and off the campus commented that the Perrys were excellent college representatives; some old-timers compared them favorably with the Penrose family.

Perry's talks and writings generally addressed either the economy or higher education. He—like educators and professors everywhere—became involved in contemporary issues, including the curriculum, the teaching of moral values, the problem of motivation, the grading system, student evaluation of professors, the growing influence of student personnel officers, and intercollegiate sports.

In "College Grading: A Case Study and Its Aftermath," Perry surveyed the troubled history of grading at Whitman. He pointed out the problems of accurate grading and quoted authorities who concluded that, "Grading is inevitable; it is, at best, inaccurate and unreliable. . . . Students would like all A's, administrators would like few F's, and the teachers would like to be left alone."[89]

In an article entitled "How to Grade the Graders," he warned faculties that students were going to evaluate them and that therefore professors should "devise effective systems before they are established for them by harried administrators or disenchanted undergraduates."[90] He recommended that able students with reputations "for balanced perspective" complete teaching evaluations and submit them to instructors, who would learn from these evaluations and could forward summaries to administrators.

In "What Should a College Teach?" written for a popular audience, Perry did not evaluate liberal arts subjects. Instead, he covered such topics as student motivation and moral values.[91] In another newspaper article, entitled "Game of Musical Chairs," Perry pointed out the shortage of professors and stressed that "responsible faculty members" had complained about "the almost hysterical bidding by institutions for staff members." This condition, he added, "may be a greater threat to effective college and university teaching than any other factor." Because of job-hopping, there was a growing lack of institutional loyalty; excessive turnover upset undergraduates.[92]

In a scholarly address, Perry discussed the importance of professional training for those entering student personnel work, especially in the small colleges. But he cautioned that a trained individual "must constantly be aware that there is no substitute for student empathy, for an understanding of the broad social problems that are bugging the current and future student generations, and for a genuine desire to be of service even under circumstances that do not seem to have been covered in the book!"[93]

In an essay entitled "Intercollegiate Sports in Academe," Perry judged that it was "high time that college and university administrators began to work more positively for the placement of intercollegiate sports in proper perspective with educational objectives." He pointed out that the students of the 1960s were better prepared for college and had "a lessened interest in sports spectaculars and a greater desire for sports participation as . . . relaxation." Perry assumed that there was a growing campus dissatisfaction with intercollegiate sports; thus, he advocated some changes necessary to continue intercollegiate sports. There should be "conference limitations on the length of seasons and the amount of time spent in practice periods," and there should be "complete elimination of post-season games, regardless of the siren calls of promoters."[94]

While Perry's publications did not have the national scope of those that came from the pen of Chester Maxey, he enjoyed a solid regional reputation. Perry received applause from the Whitman faculty because his writings and his talks reflected his involvement in issues important to their profession.

President Perry Departs

The president's many admirers worried that he would resign. They suspected that other institutions were trying to lure him from his post. They did not realize that about twenty-five institutions had requested him to be a candidate for the position of dean or president. The only one of these unsolicited contacts that he investigated was for the presidency of the University of Iowa. He considered this position because his wife was from Iowa, but finally refused it for "highly personal reasons." Perry believed that the widespread interest in him and other college administrators illustrated that the "word gets around whenever a college is progressing."[95]

In the spring of 1967 Perry took an administrative leave; he announced in late March that he had accepted Whitman overseer Garnett Cannon's offer to be a vice president of the Standard Life Insurance Company of Portland. Perry later said that he and his wife had mulled the offer over for several months. He could recall his father's observation: "Life is full of doors that await opening."[96] After electing to go through a new door, he visited Cordiner Glen with "tears in my eyes . . . because we had developed an ownership interest in Whitman, which is not necessarily good for the college, but, on the other hand, it did indicate the depths of how we felt about it." He explained to close associates that he "was tired of spending so much time in financial development as against the opportunity to participate more in the academic life of the college."[97] But in a statement to alumni he gave no explanation for his change of careers and indicated that he might return to academic life. He asserted that a change of presidents was "good for a college as well as its president. Too much longevity leads to sclerosis for both!" Perry thanked those "who have made these years so memorable," assured them that the college was in solid condition, and predicted that Whitman would "go on to greater levels of achievement."[98]

The college and the community reacted to the resignation. The *Pioneer* announced his resignation under the headline: "The Perry Years: Cautious Optimism." His decision to leave his post, he told a student reporter, was because of the potential of the position he was taking, "and the fact that it was in the Northwest."[99] Trustee

Donald Sherwood praised Perry's efforts: "During his eight years of leadership the college made outstanding progress educationally in the quality of its faculty and financial progress as indicated by increased endowment, scholarship funds, and the building of several new priority buildings." The *Walla Walla Union-Bulletin* underscored the physical improvements and added: "Perry's participation in many regional and national educational activities have added to the stature of both the president and the college." The editor noted that, in Perry's new occupation, "He will be entering a field where the details and headaches probably will be only a fraction of those of a college president."[100]

Perry later added details about his decision to resign: "I was getting a little tired of raising money and somewhat frustrated by the student unrest of that period. I suppose you could say that satisfaction was minimal."[101]

At Standard Insurance, where he practiced a style of leadership similar to the one he had demonstrated at Whitman, Perry enjoyed great success. An observer assessed his eleven years as president of the insurance company: "Perry brought a different type of leadership to Standard, which had been used to a more authoritarian style. His open style set the pace, and in his time as president he saw the company grow more than five times."[102] Perry's numerous friends in the Whitman community expressed no surprise about either his style or his success.

9

The Era of Brief Presidential Terms:
Maxey (Again), Donald Sheehan, Kenyon Knopf
1967–1975

Whitman experienced a greater turnover in its presidency between 1967 and 1975 than it has in any other period. The institution underwent major leadership changes at the same time that it and other educational institutions endured a tumultuous period. Fortunately, Chester Maxey, Donald Sheehan, and Kenyon Knopf, along with experienced faculty members, concerned trustees, and activist but reasonable students, met various challenges and instituted significant changes. While many institutions of higher learning suffered from internal problems and a diminution of their public image, some liberal arts colleges—Whitman among them—experienced an expansive period. The college changed dramatically from the late 1960s to the mid-1970s; student life in particular changed more in these years than at any other time in the college's history.

When President Louis Perry resigned late in 1967, a few members of the faculty grumbled that, although he had utilized the American Association of University Professors' rule on deadlines to block late faculty resignations, he himself had resigned so late in the year that the trustees would have to hire an interim president.

While some trustees also expressed their displeasure at Perry's late resignation, the board realized that it must appoint an acting president to serve while it conducted a national search. To fill the vacancy, the trustees asked Dr. C. Clement French, a former president of Washington State College, if he would serve temporarily. This inquiry was supposed to be confidential, but trustee Donald Sherwood groused that the appeal was well known, since the Whitman grapevine was "equal to the best in communication efficiency."[1] After French rejected the offer, the board chose former president Chester Maxey to serve for one year. In 1968, the board appointed Donald Sheehan to the presidency; unfortunately, cancer forced his resignation in 1973, and he died a year later. The trustees then advanced Dean Kenyon Knopf to the position of acting president, and, after another national search in 1975, appointed Robert A. Skotheim as president. Skotheim would serve for thirteen years in one of Whitman's longest and most influential presidencies. Thus, after three brief administrations, the college would have the benefit of an administration which endured long enough to engage in long-range planning, to conduct an impressive $50,000,000 financial campaign, and to improve teaching conditions.

Chester Maxey Returns

Acknowledging that he had been uninvolved with Whitman since retiring in 1959, Maxey expressed surprise when Sherwood asked him to serve as acting president. He later recalled that the trustee insisted "that no outsider could do that kind of trouble-shooting job as well as one of my experience." Most members of the Whitman community welcomed the former president's return, but some members of the faculty questioned the decision, stressing that Maxey was out of touch with the rapidly changing institution, especially with its activist students and its younger faculty members. They also felt that Maxey's autocratic style would be problematic after the more open administration of Louis Perry, and noted that those younger faculty members enjoyed a favorable job market that gave them more options for employment than their older colleagues had known. Finally, many felt that the old leader lacked energy; at seventy-seven years of age, Maxey claimed to be the nation's oldest college president. Not wanting a caretaker executive, some members of the faculty believed that, to maintain the Perry administration's momentum, the college needed a younger, democratic, and well-informed leader. French professor Arthur Metastasio, who enjoyed his colleagues' confidence, was an obvious choice. There was a precedent for appointing a faculty member to the position, for the trustees had successfully turned to the faculty in appointing temporary presidents in the past, including William Lyman, Louis Anderson, and Chester Maxey himself, who had begun his first presidency by accepting the office for a two-year trial.

The trustees, however, again chose to appoint Maxey, who wisely turned over the majority of administrative duties to the new dean of the college, Kenyon Knopf, and thus silenced most of the skeptics. As Maxey explained: "Dean Knopf and I virtually merged the offices of president and dean. There was an extraordinary amount of actual and proposed faculty legislation to be considered and decided. This called for wise and tactful executive guidance, and this job I intentionally left to Dean Knopf."[2]

In bringing about several fundamental changes, the faculty and students enjoyed a much greater voice in college affairs. Maxey's interim presidency was more liberal than his initial one had been. In fact, in the 1967–1968 school year he acted as a sage, providing historical information for all policy issues. For example, when the dean urged trustees to improve faculty compensation and fringe benefits, and to provide each professor with an office telephone, the president warned trustees against improvements that might result in red ink. A persistent champion of the balanced-budget principle, Maxey insisted that he would not be the first president to violate it in more than thirty years. The interim leader also brought history into a discussion of women's housing. When sororities first appeared, he recalled, they started to save money to build individual houses; with the construction of Prentiss Hall in 1926, they had agreed to drop these plans. To house senior women, the college in 1968 acquired the Riviera Motel, renaming it College House (not to be confused with the earlier College House, rented from the Odd Fellows).

Maxey's annual report compared 1908, his freshman year, with 1968, the year of his second presidency. He rejoiced over the fact that the average faculty salary had jumped from $1,200 to $10,800, but he complained that the faculty-student ratio had increased from one to seven in 1908 to one to fourteen sixty years later. Maxey blamed this unfortunate modern ratio partly on administrative expansion. In 1908 the college had employed twenty-eight faculty members, but only four administrators and a staff of seven, including five janitors. In 1968 the number of faculty members had risen to seventy-four, but there were now 121 administrators and staff members. This great addition of non-faculty employees instead of hiring more teachers meant that the ratio of students to faculty members had doubled. Concluding that other colleges had experienced a similar notable increase in non-teaching positions, Maxey asserted: "Faculty members are in large measure responsible for the administrative overgrowth. Many . . . sincerely believe they can't do their jobs without the backup of substantial administrative services. The validity of this assumption is not always unquestionable."[3] While faculty members believed that administrators and students were more responsible for the growth in staff positions than their own demands were, they agreed that Maxey had identified a real problem. An enlarged staff meant fewer teaching positions and lower salaries. As salaries improved and more teachers were added, professors became less critical of the larger staff, acknowledging that most rendered valuable service. (But President Sheehan once voiced the concern that some well-established staff members had come to think of themselves as members of a command system, rather than a support system.)

Dean Knopf Runs the College

Appointed in 1967, Kenyon Knopf was probably the most influential dean in the college's history. He actually served as acting president on three occasions—informally, in the Maxey administration from 1967 to 1968; informally again, in the Sheehan administration from 1973 to 1974; and formally, from 1974 to 1975. Born in Ohio in 1921, Knopf attended Kenyon College, graduating in 1942 with honors in economics. In the following year he joined the army air force, serving as a non-commissioned officer in the South Pacific. In 1949 he received his M.A. and Ph.D. in economics at Harvard and immediately took a teaching position at Grinnell College. There he met Siddy Trevilcock on a blind date; they were married in 1953. He taught for eighteen years at Grinnell, published significant books, and served in various administrative capacities, including chairman of the faculty. In this position, he was also acting dean for many months while the college had an acting president.

During his long tenure at Grinnell, he had gained experience from the political turmoil surrounding a controversial college president. Another president suggested that he become a dean and recommended him to Louis Perry, who was seeking a new dean of the faculty. Knopf enjoyed his early 1967 interview for the Whitman position, especially talks with senior faculty members, who informed him that Perry "was in difficulties with the faculty because he had made a number of faculty appointments without consulting the faculty or even the departments that were involved."[4] Professors appreciated Knopf's experience and accomplishments. They applauded his description of himself as a faculty man and his public assertions that professors were "the core of the college . . . and that you do not have anything unless you have an excellent faculty that feels comfortable in what they are doing." Whitman needed an outside dean who understood conditions facing a liberal arts faculty. Professors who believed that Knopf met their requirements expressed such sentiments to a sympathetic Perry and trustees.

Impressed with the Whitman faculty, Knopf was not discouraged by accounts of the school's internal problems, because he had faced somewhat similar ones at Grinnell. He observed, "I had survived and thrived. . . . And I thought I could work with Perry and I thought I could perhaps help him in his relations with faculty." In negotiating for the position, Knopf requested and received the title of "dean of the college" so that he could "be sort of second in command and in charge of the college in Perry's absence."

The president's resignation caught Knopf by surprise; he said later, "I felt that I was hanging out on a line, because presidents typically like to select their own deans." When trustee Sherwood assured Knopf that matters were under control and informed him that Maxey would serve as acting president, Knopf recalled, "I had heard just a little bit about Maxey's presidency, and I had a little trepidation about the fact that he had held things pretty close to his vest." But the acting president, Knopf added, "did something I will never forget. He said to me, 'Ken, whatever happens during this year, you are the person who is going to have to live with it. So I am going to leave all that in your hands. I am going to represent the college to the constituencies and you do the rest.' It was just exactly what I had hoped to hear . . . and I am grateful to him forever for having done that." Free from crucial administrative responsibilities,

Maxey could handle such events as the dedication of Cordiner Glen, a campus improvement project.

The 1967–1968 school year proved to be unusually productive. Normally a school under an acting president and an untested dean makes few changes. But Knopf, who had pushed faculty reform at Grinnell, assisted Whitman faculty members who supported ideas similar to his. One of the first changes accomplished by the new dean, who was "appalled by the salary level at Whitman," was to increase faculty pay scales. As had been true at Grinnell, the full professors needed the greatest increase because there was only a slender margin between green newcomers and gray veterans. Knopf also got Whitman to join eleven other liberal arts colleges that were already comparing salaries. This sharing of faculty pay scales had been practiced at Grinnell, and Knopf successfully employed it as a way to increase Whitman salaries. He also worked to improve fringe benefits, especially an increase in the college's TIAA-CREF (Teachers Insurance and Annuity Association College Retirement Equity Fund) contributions, and encouraged the faculty "to get involved professionally" by attending meetings and publishing. Knopf believed that "teaching and research, rather than being contradictory . . . are in fact necessary together. . . . I do not think a person can be an outstanding teacher unless the person is involved in doing something, whether it is ever published." More funds were allotted to the faculty for sabbaticals and research projects. In professionalizing the faculty over the next few years, the dean found that trustees Baker Ferguson and Donald Frisbee were sensitive to faculty conditions, particularly the need to increase salaries during the inflation of the early 1970s. Frisbee, a Portland businessman, and Ferguson, a local banker, had personal knowledge of the teaching profession. Frisbee's father had taught at Pomona; Ferguson had taught briefly at Whitman.

Knopf also instituted a system whereby two or three candidates for a faculty position would be brought to campus. At Grinnell, as at Whitman, teachers had been hired by the president with only minimal interviewing by the faculty or none at all. Whitman professors appreciated Knopf's making them more involved in the hiring of colleagues. Realizing the need for protection from arbitrary dismissal, the faculty eagerly followed the dean's lead in establishing AAUP dismissal procedures.

Working closely with faculty leaders, Knopf brought about significant changes, including a new academic calendar and fundamental revisions to the curriculum. He helped make psychiatric service available to students, and encouraged a new housing option for women. Although these actions of the 1967–1968 school year altered the college, student protest in this year attracted more attention.

The Brief but Influential Administration of Donald Sheehan

While the actions of the faculty—and especially those of Dean Knopf—strengthened the college, the national search for a president, conducted by an energetic committee, resulted in the appointment of fifty-year-old Donald H. Sheehan. The son of Henry and Winnifred Sheehan, he was born in New York City in 1917 and enjoyed a comfortable boyhood in Upper Montclair, New Jersey. Henry Sheehan's business career caused him to travel extensively in South America; he was able to provide his family with a good living, even during the Great Depression. Donald Sheehan attended Duke University, receiving a B.A. in economics. He thoroughly enjoyed his college experience, including service as president of the Inter-Fraternity Council and as an organizer of college dances featuring famous big bands. He wrote for the college newspaper and played intramural golf. A solid student, Sheehan enjoyed all types of classes, and earned a Phi Beta Kappa key. Returning north to study at Columbia University, he quickly earned an M.A. in English literature. To cover his school expenses, Sheehan took various jobs, including that of modeling men's clothing.

In May 1941 he married Katherine Chubb, whom he had met at a social event at Duke; she would influence him through a long marriage and during his short college presidency. She recalled: "Boy, I thought he was terrific and kind. The dog! He would get straight A's. He had a photographic memory." The daughter of Colonel Wistar M. and Edith Taft Chubb, she was born in the Philippines when her father was working on military fortifications at Corregidor. Her father left the army, and the family moved to South Orange, New Jersey. When Colonel Chubb was unable to find adequate employment during the Great Depression, his wife supplemented the family income by playing bridge for money in New York City's

Cavendish Club. In 1935 Katherine chose to attend Duke because it was far from her family and because the tuition was only $100 a semester. To cover the cost of room and board, she waited tables, but she left Duke after her sophomore year because her family could not afford even the modest tuition. She then attended Kathryn Gibbs Secretarial School in New York City.

After a brief honeymoon, the Sheehans returned to New York, where he pursued a Ph.D. in history at Columbia. Then the Second World War disrupted their lives. Following brief participation in the navy's V-12 program, he became a legal officer in the coast guard, serving between 1943 and 1945. Returning from duty in the South Pacific, Sheehan resumed his graduate work and in 1950 completed his doctorate in American history under the distinguished Allan Nevins. Although the Sheehans lived in cramped student housing, the young historian thoroughly enjoyed being the father of a son and a daughter.

Sheehan's educational career during the next eighteen years included teaching and administrative positions in several colleges and universities in the United States and Europe. His major positions were at Columbia University from 1948 to 1952, and at Smith College—which he considered to be one of the nation's premier schools—from 1952 to 1968. Lively and informed, he was a popular teacher of American studies. He enjoyed teaching at an all-women's institution, but thought it was outrageous that women knitted in his classes. He warned knitters that if anyone dropped a needle, such handiwork must stop; shortly, the clank of a needle ended the annoyance. His students recalled his wit, friendship, patience, and high academic standards. Nancy Weiss Malkiel, who became dean of the college at Princeton University, remembered Sheehan as amiable and accessible, and felt that he had influenced her professional career.[5] Sheehan once advised a foreign student that it was necessary to understand American slang, handing her a list of words, such as "buck" for "dollar."

According to his wife, Sheehan's only hobby was people, and, like Thomas Jefferson, he constantly entertained, engaging his wide variety of dinner guests in lively conversation. He golfed for recreation but, like most amateurs, failed to play as well as he wanted.

Because of his faculty leadership ability, he became an assistant to Smith's president. Sheehan became absorbed with academic planning, serving in the late 1950s as Smith's representative on a four-member committee that prepared a comprehensive educational plan for Hampshire College, an experimental school that would open in 1970. The energetic professor also chaired a faculty committee at Smith that brought major curricular changes. He was active in his profession and edited several works, notably *The Making of American History*, a widely adopted text. Sheehan served on a public school board and as a trustee of Hartford College for Women.

The historian greatly enjoyed two European sabbaticals, one to Manchester and the other to Athens, where in 1965–1966 he was acting director of the School of Liberal Studies at Pierce College. He helped establish administrative procedures, the curriculum, faculty organization, and the budget.

Upon his return to Smith, he encountered student activists seeking changes, including the recruitment of more black students and faculty members. Despite the growing turbulence in American universities and colleges, Sheehan sought a college presidency, including the one at Hampshire; he turned down an offer from Grinnell because of its cold climate and its distance from the East Coast.

In 1968 Dean Knopf called on Sheehan on behalf of Whitman College. The visitor had been impressed with Sheehan during his presidential interview at Grinnell and had submitted the historian's name as a candidate for the Whitman vacancy. According to Katherine Sheehan, her husband said, following Knopf's invitation to visit the college, "I want to see what Walla Walla is like."[6] He lacked a deep interest in the position, but the search committee, assisted by trustees, administrators, and professors, convinced him and his wife—much to their surprise—that the college and the town had a lot to offer. Upon returning to Smith College after three busy days at Whitman, Sheehan accepted the position. His Smith colleagues thought that the urbane historian was crazy for moving to a rural college in an isolated town. A newspaper published Smith president Thomas Mendenhall's response to the appointment: "Stimulating teacher of American history, leader of the faculty in the planning for the new curriculum, battle-tried administrator who loyally served as assistant to two presidents, Professor Sheehan is superbly prepared to become President Sheehan. And when one remembers that Mrs.

Sheehan goes with him, one wonders if Whitman College really knows how lucky it is."

Walla Wallans enthusiastically embraced the new leader. Trustee chairman Sherwood announced that the board was "in agreement that his background, experience, and personality ideally fitted him to serve Whitman . . . as another distinguished president." Sheehan responded: "I am proud to be associated with Whitman. It is a distinguished representative of the independent liberal arts colleges which have given our system of higher education much of its strength and uniqueness."[7]

But the summer drive to Walla Walla removed some of the Sheehans' enthusiasm for their new location. While driving through an eastern Oregon dust storm, Katherine asked her husband, "Can you turn this down if it doesn't go the first week?"[8]

It is doubtful that those who had interviewed Sheehan had read *The New College Plan: A Proposal for a Major Departure in Higher Education*, the thoughtful study that he and his three colleagues had compiled for the experimental Hampshire College. This proposal contained several controversial ideas. The writers favored the "elimination of fraternities and intercollegiate athletics in favor of more spontaneous forms of student recreation." They addressed the question of faculty research at a small school, asserting that "there need be no dichotomy between teaching and research." More controversial was their proposal "that at least a third of the Board of Trustees shall be people professionally concerned with education, so as to assure that the college develops in a way which reflects the thinking of its faculty and the larger intellectual community."[9]

Few, if any, members of the Whitman community had read of his controversial ideas, but they understood that their new leader championed reform, innovation, and the mission of the small liberal arts college. No previous Whitman president had spent more time with educational planning for a liberal arts college than Sheehan had, and his presidency provided him an opportunity to put some of his ideas and experience into action. In 1968 all components of the college anticipated his administration. The faculty, especially, desired to build upon the improvements made under Dean Knopf's leadership. Undoubtedly, that group agreed with Jeffrey Sheehan, the son of the new president, who would later state: "I can't imagine a more

Although Donald Sheehan served as president for less than six years, this sophisticated and congenial leader profoundly influenced the college in a difficult period. A superb crisis manager, he met the challenge of student activists, defended the liberal arts, won the support of the Whitman community, and reshaped the curriculum.

difficult time to take over the leadership of a college campus than in 1968."[10]

The building campaign launched by Louis Perry continued under Donald Sheehan with the construction of New Dorm, Olin Hall, and the Stuart Wing of Penrose Memorial Library. New Dorm—later named Douglas Hall in honor of William O. Douglas—was designed to house seventy-two women in nine suites, each of which had a lounge, a kitchenette, a bath, and a laundry. By the time the dormitory opened in 1970, it had been chosen as the site of the college's first coeducational living experience, embroiling it in controversy.

There was, however, no controversy over Olin Hall. In September 1969 Charles L. Horn, a director of the Olin Foundation, appeared at convocation. A packed Cordiner Hall audience anxiously waited to hear whether the college would receive a humanities building.

There was a long and interesting story behind Horn's appearance. President Maxey, President Perry, trustee Baker Ferguson, and well-placed eastern overseers had urged Horn and other Olin Foundation directors to fund a science building. Maxey reported that he had been told that Whitman's application would be buried at the bottom of the request pile. Finally, Horn announced that he would travel to Walla Walla to check out the college, which by this time was no longer requesting funds for a science building, but was instead seeking funding for a humanities building. This travel was possible only because Vice President Larry Beaulaurier, after learning that Horn refused to fly, arranged with an overseer connected with the Burlington Northern Railroad Company to provide a private railroad car. The party traveling on this special car (stocked with Horn's favorite scotch) included Horn's wife, who daily provided him with a fresh carnation for his lapel. During the journey from St. Paul to the Tri-Cities, Beaulaurier telephoned Sheehan to say that apparently Horn was not coming to campus just to visit, but he was actually going to fund Whitman's request.

The brusque Horn rode to the campus in an expensive automobile. He was introduced to members of the Whitman administration and responsed positively both to them—particularly Sherwood and Sheehan—and to the school's solid financial footing. He did not see much of the campus, because there was some concern that he should not be exposed to counterculture students, or, for that matter, to unkempt professors. Pete Reid later recalled that many Whitman leaders believed that the benefactor was intending to announce a gift to the college, "but with Horn it was very tricky because at the last minute he might get miffed at something and change his mind." Many in the Cordiner Hall crowd understood this tense situation, and rendered a standing ovation when the visitor proclaimed: "We are giving you a brand-new building and it won't cost you a penny."[11] Horn added that the old "horse-barn" would be torn down. Some feared that he was proposing that the college raze a serviceable structure, but he was referring to the antiquated gymnasium, a smelly relic that would become rubble the following year. Prior to his departure, Horn, who stated that presidents Maxey, Perry, and Sheehan had all represented Whitman to the Olin Foundation, strongly implied that the foundation might give the school a second building.

During his brief visit, Horn pontificated at length on Whitman's policies. He angrily lectured hapless division chairman Richard Clem that the college enrolled too many women, stressing that male alumni donated greater amounts of money to their alma maters than females did. Embarrassed for his colleague, division chairman Thomas Edwards noted that the agitated benefactor wore a very large Sigma Alpha Epsilon pin. After receiving Beaulaurier's encouragement, Edwards interrupted the conversation, and gave Horn the SAE handshake. The visitor then faulted Edwards for not working to establish an SAE chapter at Whitman. Horn had apparently forgotten the fact that, when former president Stephen Penrose had asked the fraternity to colonize at Whitman, Horn, in his position as a fra-

Constructed in 1972, the Olin Hall of Arts and Humanities was a gift from the Olin Foundation. The old gymnasium was removed to make room for this attractive structure.

ternity official, had refused, citing the school's small male enrollment.

Dedicated in 1972 and considered by some critics to be Whitman's last attractive building, the Olin Hall of Arts and Humanities provided the humanities division with comfortable offices and modern classrooms. It also included an art gallery that would later be named in honor of President Sheehan. Social studies professors also enjoyed teaching in this air-conditioned building, until the completion of Maxey Hall, the second Olin Foundation gift.

The connection with this organization was highly significant, for it became the major foundation donor in the college's history. Sheehan stated that former presidents and overseers had paved the way for support from the Olin Foundation, and that he was lucky to have Olin Hall donated during his administration.

Although Sheehan did not live to witness its dedication, he was largely responsible for another structure, the Elbridge Hadley Stuart Wing, an addition to Penrose Memorial Library. In announcing the gift in 1971, the president asserted that it was "one of the most exciting moments in the college's history."[12] The Stuarts had previously assisted the college through generous gifts for scholarships, religious counseling, and library acquisitions. Sheehan delighted in telling how the school acquired the Stuart Wing. Elbridge Stuart had unsuccessfully offered his fine collection of Napoleonic memorabilia to Yale University, his alma mater. Encouraged by his wife, Evelyn Clark Stuart, a 1928 graduate of Whitman, he then offered it to the college. After consultation with trustees, Sheehan told Stuart that the school had no space for his collection, but proposed that, if the Stuarts would finance a sorely needed library wing, then a beautiful room to house the collection could be part of the addition. The Stuarts agreed to a proposal that thoroughly restored the main library and added a wing that increased the size of the library by sixty percent. The Stuarts, the major contributors to the addition, donated more than $350,000. When the new wing opened in 1974, many Whitmanites hailed the library's enlargement; they congratulated Mrs. Stuart for insisting that a space be named in honor of former librarian Ruth Reynolds.

Other campus changes included a fountain dedicated in 1970 (it would be redesigned in 1991 by George Tustakawa, and rededicated in honor of President Robert Skotheim and his wife Nadine). At-

The Stuart Wing of Penrose Memorial Library, which increased the library's size by about sixty percent, came about through the skilled leadership of President Donald Sheehan. Unfortunately, he died before the wing went into operation.

tracting more comment than gushing water in the early 1970s were the leaky steam pipes which, in winter, appeared to indicate thermal activity. According to Pete Reid, a study determined that the pipes were losing thirty-nine percent of the steam in the distribution system. For several summers, work crews dug up the lawn, replacing the pipes.

In the early 1970s the trustees rejected proposals for the vacated Anderson mansion. Faculty members and students had proposed that the building be converted into either a museum or an art gallery. A townswoman sought permission to place it on the national register, and two other local women offered $5,000 to rehabilitate the grand structure. When trustees declined all these proposals, many feared that they would raze the vandalized building to make room for the construction of New Dorm.

Meanwhile, the college received and profited from Walla Walla commercial property. Alumni Al Clise and Joyce McKay Clise do-

Constructed as a men's dormitory in 1899, Billings Hall later served as a science building and then as a general-purpose academic building. After long deliberation, the college demolished the building in 1972, the same year that Olin Hall was dedicated. Many in the Whitman community opposed the destruction of Billings Hall, arguing that it was a handsome and historic structure.

nated the Walla Walla Hotel, which the college later sold. Reid assessed this ownership: "Overall we came out probably at least $200,000 ahead. And maybe more importantly saved the hotel for the downtown."[13] The Henry Copeland family donated the Copeland building; Whitman received modest annual earnings from the property and then sold it. Closer to the campus, the college received the Bennington Apartments and the Colonial Court from alumnus Virgil Bennington; for years the college benefited from rental income from these properties.

The team of President Sheehan and Vice President Beaulaurier was highly successful in raising money, especially endowment funds. Sheehan predicted that the college would grow when it acquired greater wealth. Late in 1970 the college launched an endowment drive, seeking $10,000,000 in five years. Overseer Russ McNeill chaired the effort, predicting that his committee would be successful because many people took pride in the college. Sheehan stated that the school was not in desperate straits, but sought money to strengthen academic programs. Sounding like his predecessors, he emphasized that Whitman had no deficits, insisting that "we have not and will not spend what we do not have."[14] The college reported that it had collected $6,200,000 in gifts during the 1971–1972 fiscal year, boasting that this was "the largest amount ever raised in a single year" by any Pacific Northwest school.[15] A significant increase in alumni giving also pleased fund raisers. Utilizing the class representative system, faculty speakers, and personal persuasion, alumni director F. David Hale and others—especially alumni Dr. Kenneth Fry, John S. "Bud" Applegate, and Emma Jane Kirsch Brattain— doubled the number of alumni making gifts, to about thirty-five percent. In 1974 Brattain reported that, although liberal arts colleges in general were struggling economically, Whitman had done well "through plain good management and judicious use of funds."[16]

In the late 1960s the college also received important gifts aiding students and the faculty, including the Roger and Davis Clapp Professorship of Economic Thought, the Eric and Ina Johnson Visiting Professorship, the Paul Garrett Fellows program for faculty members, and the Paul Garrett scholarships for men. Garrett explained his generosity: "I feel that I owe all of my success in business and my career to Whitman College."[17]

Larry Beaulaurier began at Whitman as a fund raiser in 1962 and went on to have an outstanding career in the financial development office. As vice-president, Beaulaurier worked closely with President Sheehan to raise substantial amounts of money for the college.

Sheehan appreciated the two-board system. He informed the overseers that "the college could not exist without points of contact and the overseers have assisted greatly in making points within their separate communities," and he noted that these "ambassadors" offered solid judgments at meetings.[18] The overseers expressed a great interest in the school; for example, Ralph Edgerton asserted: "Whitman certainly is unique in the entire Northwest. New England has a quality college at every crossroad; thus the value of any one of these fine schools is not as great as that of Whitman."[19]

At no previous time had the board of trustees been required to make so many decisions on such diverse issues and to receive such advice and criticism, especially from activist students. Averaging fifty-four years of age in 1970, the board members, including only one woman, experienced considerable turnover. The group handled traditional concerns, including the management of endowments, budgets, properties, and personnel.

But trustees also had to respond to social and political issues, which were pushed by activist students with the assistance of a few faculty members. On most American campuses during the tumult of the late 1960s and early 1970s, board members wrestled with problems raised by students and professors. Indeed, a poll conducted in June 1970 found that Americans identified campus unrest as the nation's most disturbing issue, though the pollsters went on to explain that "most student protestors are neither violent nor extremist."[20] Whitman, of course, could not escape the turmoil. The college made major changes, but did not succumb to student radicalism as some had feared.

To better understand—and to seek common ground with—the unusually questioning students enrolled in the late 1960s, the trustees, local members in particular, spent considerable time listening to them, including at meetings of the board. Some faculty members complained that, under the Sheehan administration, students, on the one hand, received considerable attention from trustees, while faculty members, on the other hand, lost contact with them, because Sheehan terminated the scheduled meetings that Perry had arranged between faculty members and the trustees. These often-fruitful meetings were never revived. The faculty posed relatively few problems for the trustees; the same could not be said of the students.

The faculty appreciated new additions to the board of trustees. Faculty chairman Arthur Metastasio observed: "The two newest members, Frisbee and Ferguson, seem to have captured the imagination of most of the faculty who have met them. They seem to be considered as welcome new blood with a more liberal viewpoint on most of the aspects of college life and planning."[21]

The faculty, of course, understood the trustees' power, and students quickly came to realize it. Some activists asked administrators and professors for significant changes in existing student rules and learned that only the trustees could grant them. Faculty members and administrators referred activists to the college catalog, which stated that the nine trustees were responsible for Whitman's "corporate concerns" and were "empowered by charter to hold all properties and to exercise all corporate affairs of the college." The trustees, who met only three times a year, delegated considerable authority to their executive committee (the members of which were Walla Wallans who could easily meet as required) and, of course, expected to manage the college through its president and subordinate officers. Furthermore, Sheehan, who did not want to isolate himself, insisted that the trustees help shape responses to students. When activists pushed for a change, Sheehan responded that it was not in his power to decide but that he would take the issue to the trustees. This course of action was mostly successful, as trustees joined him in handling unprecedented student pressure. The notable exception was the resignation of two trustees who opposed Sheehan's acceptance of coeducational housing.

Thus, Sheehan, who often brought historical precedent to current issues, put his talents to work not only for the trustees but for other members of the Whitman community as well. The popular and respected president died in March 1974, after battling cancer for many months. His had been a reassuring voice in a difficult time, and the college mourned his death. His successor, acting president Knopf, summarized the faculty's sentiments: "We all sorely miss the good-natured, imaginative leadership of Donald Sheehan."[22]

On the following pages is a map of the campus reproduced from the 1974–1975 catalog, following the building campaign of presidents Perry and Sheehan.

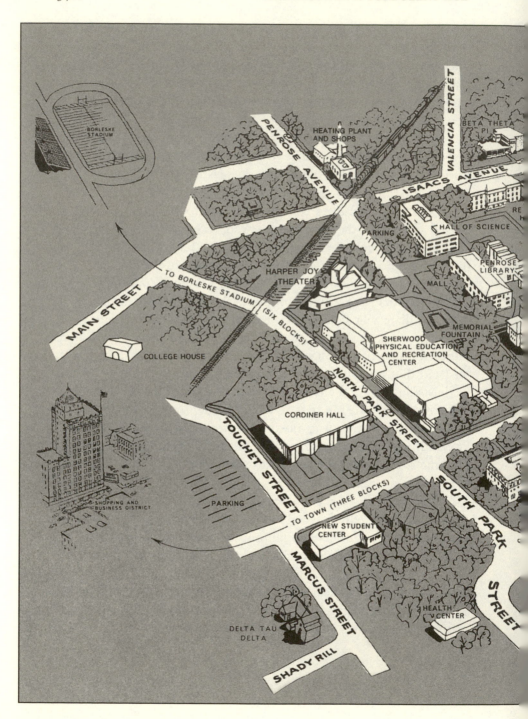

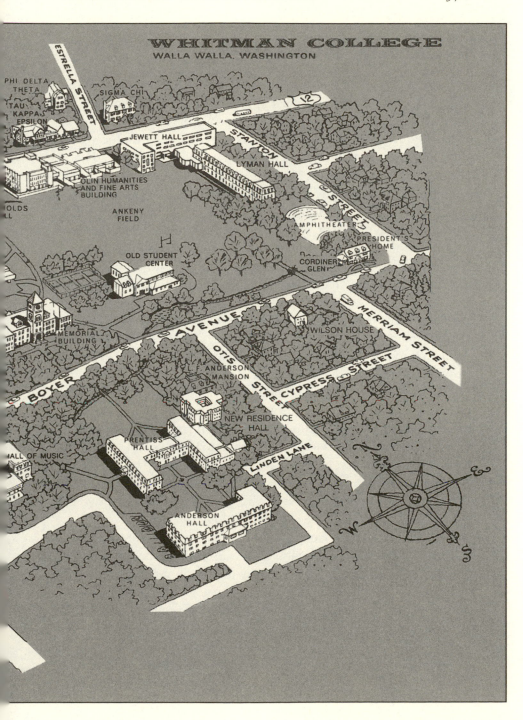

WHITMAN COLLEGE
WALLA WALLA, WASHINGTON

Kenyon Knopf Becomes Acting President

In 1970, in the middle of the Sheehan administration, dean of the college Kenyon Knopf had been appointed to the new position of provost. He began serving unofficially as acting president in 1973, when President Sheehan was hospitalized; he received the official title of "acting president" in 1974, after Sheehan's death, and served until the appointment of Robert Skotheim as president in 1975.

When Knopf took over the administrative reins, he appointed historian Robert Whitner to assist him as associate dean of the faculty. The busy acting president, who called upon professors to participate in decision making and involved faculty committees in the resolution of college problems to an unusual degree, enjoyed a number of successes. Faculty salaries improved; the Stuart Wing of the library was dedicated; a Danforth Foundation grant made possible a faculty conference at the Salishan resort on the Oregon coast; an application was made for funds for a social sciences building, which would result in the construction of Maxey Hall; and organizational reforms brought administrative efficiency.

Knopf received recognition both nationally and locally. He was elected chairman of the American Conference of Academic Deans, a national organization of deans of public and private colleges and universities. He was also awarded the Whitman Town-Gown Award for his community service, including work on behalf of the United Fund.

During Knopf's tenure, a time when the administration and faculty were grieving over the loss of Sheehan, they confronted two issues that would trouble the campus for long afterward.

As early as 1951 the campus had discussed the possibility of terminating the mediocre football progam and using its budget to build an outstanding basketball team that would "gain much more sports publicity."[23] In November 1966 football coach Keith Loper had suddenly resigned his position, predicting that the program would not succeed "under the present Whitman philosophy toward athletics."[24] Loper's action led to widespread discussions about the wisdom of continuing the program; somebody quoted Nard Jones, who stated that alumni "share the belief, that God is on the side of Whitman College except in athletic contests."[25]

In 1967 Kenyon Knopf was appointed dean of the college. An experienced teacher and former administrator at Grinnell, Knopf worked closely with President Maxey and the faculty, receiving praise from Whitman professors for improving their professional conditions. Knopf effectively ran the college on several occasions, serving officially as acting president in 1974–1975.

In 1967 Whitman had hired three new football coaches—head coach Roy Thompson and assistants John Wilcox and Jerry Anhorn —to replace Loper and Russell Monahan (Anhorn soon resigned and was replaced by Keith Jensen). Thompson, a highly successful high school coach and the principal of Roseburg High School, received the rank of associate professor—a rank, some observers grumbled, that was too high for an individual without any previous college teaching experience, although the college actually paid him less than the high school district had.

By appointing three coaches and promising needed support, the trustees, President Perry, and others were attempting to bolster the floundering program. Not only had the college added a coach, it had assured the newcomers that it wanted to maintain and improve the football team. They were promised adequate financial assistance, including more money to recruit players. Some faculty members, however, saw scant reason for optimism, figuring that, even with additional coaching staff, success would be elusive. As the college was beefing up its football program, so were its competitors improving theirs; one faculty member likened this wasteful situation to an arms race between Peru and Ecuador.

In 1974 Coach Thompson resigned in the middle of the season, asserting that the sport had little chance for success, mainly because the college—including many faculty members—did not support the program. He noted that it was more difficult to recruit after his assistant coaches, Wilcox and Jensen, had assumed additional responsibilities as the head coaches of basketball and track and thus did not have time to recruit for the football program; furthermore, conference competitors had more grant-in-aid money. Thompson's dismal assessments did not surprise those who had been pessimistic at the time of his hiring.

From 1960 through 1966 the football team had won only nine games and lost forty-seven, a sixteen-percent winning rate. After the administration proffered additional support in 1967, the record from that year through 1975 was twenty-four wins, fifty-one losses, and a tie, a thirty-two-percent winning rate. In 1969 the Missionaries posted a record of six and three, the best in thirty years, and tied for the league championship.[26] But this was the last winning season, and in the 1970s the faculty, many of whom loyally attended one-sided games and sometimes traveled with the football team to contests at other schools, increasingly condemned this floundering program. In 1969 a new student paper, the *Narrator*, provided a thorough discussion of the entire athletic program, including football. History professor Donald King concluded: "My experience in the classroom is that the athletes often have more discipline and drive than many of our students."[27] Other professors also asserted that they rarely encountered "dumb jocks" in class, but a few teachers complained about both unresponsive athletes and the football program's large budget.

In the fall of 1974 Acting President Knopf announced to professors his hope that football's future would soon be evaluated and determined.[28] Dubious about Whitman ever becoming competitive in football, some faculty members reminded their colleagues that football must belong to the current athletes, not the alumni, and that soccer currently drew more Whitman men than football did.²⁹ Referring back to the "glorious record" of former coach Nig Borleske, college constituents and alumni debated the struggling program formally and informally. Ken Woody, the new coach, failed to improve the program or to impress the faculty, whose attendance at games declined. One player reported to friends that opponents always scheduled games with the hapless Missionaries for their homecomings and parents' weekends. Whitman had played its first football game in 1893 and would play its last intercollegiate game in 1976; the decision to terminate the program, finally made in 1977, created prolonged controversy, just as professors anticipated. But most faculty members supported this decision, considering it to be long overdue.

The other major, long-lasting issue of Knopf's term as acting president revolved around biologist Donald Lehmann. In the spring of 1974 newspapers scattered across the Pacific Northwest carried a wire service story reporting that Whitman had suspended him, but the report failed to divulge the reasons for this action against a tenured professor. Distant editors did not publish many follow-up stories, but the story that the *Seattle Post-Intelligencer* published under the headline, "Whitman Suspends Top Prof," included an interview with Polly Lehmann, the professor's supportive wife. Because the professor had been advised not to speak about his dismissal, the press depended upon his wife for information. She ridiculed the charges as amounting to nothing more than "flirting with girls," and added, in defense of her husband, "One beloved old professor . . . tells his classes, 'The higher the skirts, the higher the grade.'"³⁰ Some newspapers carried the American Association of University Professors (AAUP) assessment that suspension of a faculty member was warranted only if "immediate harm to himself or others is threatened by his continuation."³¹

Across the Pacific Northwest, individuals interested in Whitman speculated about the reasons for such a harsh action and discussed Polly Lehmann's explanation of her husband's suspension and the couple's need to resist it: "It's taken the school 30 minutes . . . to annihilate 19 years of teaching. If we quit, this Gestapo treatment might run wild on other campuses."³² A University of Washington law school professor, Whitman students and alumni (several of

whom reminded readers of Lehmann's prominence in parisitology),
and other writers also challenged the college's actions, particularly
that of suspending Lehmann without an explanation. Professor
Robert Fluno defended his school, and the *Pioneer* published a special edition and in subsequent editions provided a defense and answered questions. The *Walla Walla Union-Bulletin*'s editor concluded that Lehmann was being "left dangling slowly, slowly in the
wind while the strange process of academic discipline inches toward
conclusion."[33] Acting President Knopf received anonymous, deroga-
tory, threatening letters.[34] The college's attorney, Jack Williams, said
that Whitman, because it had taken a no-publicity stance, had been
subjected to "monumental abuse."[35]

While scores of individuals speculated, the faculty investigated
and the acting president reflected. In the spring of 1973 Knopf had
met with a female student, who charged that Lehmann had made
sexual advances. Such action, Knopf explained many years later, had
since come to be called "sexual harrassment," although the term was
not then in vogue. He concluded that the student's parents would
have "fair grounds for a suit if the college learned about the problem
and then did nothing about it."[36] After long consultations with Dean
Whitner, he summoned Lehmann. Knopf informed the professor
that, if he resigned, the acting president would recommend him for
a teaching position at a men's college were he to apply for one; on
the other hand, if Lehmann refused to resign, Knopf would immediately start proceedings against him. The biologist refused to resign.

Following AAUP guidelines, which were written into the faculty
code, the five senior faculty members—acting as a "grand jury"—
recommended unanimously that several formal charges be brought
against the biologist. The ten members of the academic council,
chaired by sociologist Ely Chertok, became a hearings committee.
For about three weeks they held many closed meetings, listening to
two dozen witnesses, including students, staff members, and others.
The meetings were attended by Lehmann's lawyer, alumnus James
B. Mitchell. A court reporter recorded 1,248 pages of testimony.

The most serious charge against Lehmann, the council concluded,
was "that of sexual misconduct toward female students." The biologist responded that, if "such conduct could have occurred, . . .
it was a result of my alcoholism problem." The council's report to

Knopf concluded that students "were distressed and frightened, and the sexual advances were plainly disruptive of the educational opportunities to which they were entitled." The group judged that four other charges against Lehmann were insubstantial. The ten professors recommended either dismissal or psychiatric examination to "determine whether some course of action other than dismissal is either warranted or feasible." Some council members, impressed by the fact that a physician testified that Lehmann was an alcoholic, thought that a psychiatric assessment and a year's leave of absence might make it possible for him to rejoin the faculty.[37]

In early July 1974 the trustees, some of whom felt that the academic council had waffled in making its recommendations, chose to dismiss the biologist. On September 1 Lehmann filed a suit against the trustees and Acting President Knopf, asking for $2,000,000 in damages and reinstatement to the faculty. The suit charged that the college had violated AAUP procedural principles and that the trustees

Two dedicated and highly respected faculty leaders worked diligently to grapple with the issues presented by the charges against a colleague, Donald Lehmann. Historian Robert Whitner, left, who served as a dean during President Sheehan's illness, assisted Acting President Knopf in establishing the procedures to be used in this difficult situation. As chairman of the faculty, sociologist Ely Chertok provided thoughtful leadership as the academic council spent weeks searching for an appropriate resolution.

and Knopf had allowed to be published "libelous and defamatory material [that] subjected Lehmann to ridicule, scorn, and shame."[38] In late February 1976 a two-day trial with Lehmann as the plaintiff and Whitman as the defendant took place in Walla Walla County Superior Court. James Mitchell again represented Lehmann; Jack Williams served as the college's lawyer. Students and townspeople in attendance heard Knopf explain the background of the case. Members of the academic council testified that they had recommended Lehmann's dismissal and that the option of psychiatric treatment was merely a strong suggestion to the trustees. Judge Fred Staples stated that he needed time to render a decision because it "could set precedent nationwide for future cases involving faculty dismissal."[39] Two weeks after the trial Staples rendered a complex decision, including the crucial conclusion that the trustees' decision to dismiss the professor "was warranted."[40]

Represented by a new lawyer, Ron McAdams, Lehmann appealed the judge's decision. In April 1978 the Washington Supreme Court upheld the firing of Lehmann on the grounds that the college had properly followed the procedures of the AAUP. The *Whitman Alumnus* summarized the case and presented the complete written opinion of the high court.[41] The case had attracted the attention of college deans, many of whom had learned about it from reading the *Chronicle of Higher Education*. In February 1979 they invited Knopf to speak to the American Conference of Academic Deans at a meeting in Washington, D.C. Speaking on the subject, "Dismissal for Cause, When All Else Fails," Knopf described and evaluated the case, giving advice to deans who might find themselves having to deal with similar cases of sexual harrassment. He refused to discuss Lehmann by name, and added some humor by recalling that he had heard about "one staff wife speaking to another, asking whether the other had been propositioned by this fellow. The woman said no, and the person asking the question said, 'Neither have I. I wonder what's wrong with us.'"[42]

In May 1975 Acting President Knopf offered his thanks to the faculty for its assistance to him and Dean Whitner in making "some very complex and painful deliberations . . . [during] these past two difficult years."[43] Members of the Whitman community were likewise grateful to Knopf for his conscientious service during a trying period.

Returning to campus for their fiftieth reunion in 1974 were four distinguished physics majors trained by Professor Benjamin Brown. From left are Walter H. Brattain, 1956 winner of the Nobel Prize in Physics (who in retirement taught at his alma mater), Walter Bleakney, John Workman, and Vladimir Rojansky.

Other Campus Changes

Despite the turnover in the occupancy of the president's office during this time, much was accomplished: new buildings, Olin Hall in particular; the expanded campus, especially on lower Boyer Avenue; a growing endowment, the increase in which won considerable regional attention; changes in the curriculum and academic requirements; and increased enrollments and larger graduating classes. Some improvements tended to be overlooked, but they could be seen by even a quick reading of the campus catalogs.

Also overlooked, perhaps, was the total impact of resignations, retirements, and deaths of administrators, faculty members, and staff. Between 1967 and 1975 there were significant changes. Dean of women Miriam Wagenschein and drama professor Rodney Alexander resigned. Professors Ronald Sires, Jerry Fogarty, Paul Jackson, and Dean McSloy retired, after influential teaching careers. For various reasons, some promising younger members of the faculty re-

*Larry Dodd, Penrose Memorial
Library archivist, protected and
developed the Pacific Northwest
Collection. The archives have
become important to regional
scholars as well as to the college
community.*

signed. Several experienced administrators retired, including director of placement Almira Quinn, registrar Alta Glenny, and dean of
admissions Douglas McClane. The deaths of director of the student
center Vern Kinsinger in 1973 and lecturer in art Ruth Fluno in 1974
saddened the community. Administrators greatly regretted the retirement of Winks Dunphy, in 1975. She had been appointed secretary to Chester Maxey in 1949 and became administrative assistant
to Donald Sheehan in 1968. Her wisdom and wit proved valuable to
the school's leadership. But the college's major loss was the death
of President Sheehan in 1974.

Among many new administrators were dean of students Gordon
Scribner, dean of women Joan Hodgson, dean of admissions William Tingley, assistant deans of admissions Gene Adams and G. Ray
Warren, director of placement Robert Malde, and director of publications Eugene Thompson. Librarian Arley Jonish added alumna Marilyn McMillan Sparks, Larry Dodd, and Joe Drazan to the
library staff. Dodd and Sparks strengthened the archives, making the
records useful to an ever-increasing number of students, faculty
members, townspeople, and visitors. Thus, during the period of campus turmoil, there was a loss of long-time professors and administrators; but newcomers joined the Whitman community and helped
to cope with one of the most trying eras in the school's history.

10

Student Activism and Its Disruptions 1965–1975

The most famous college students in American history attended during the period from 1965 to 1975; the single most notable year in this period was 1968, when campuses in the United States and around the world reported great difficulties coping with student activism and political protests. The unrest originated in 1964 at the University of California; during the next few years demonstrators from one coast to the other—often shouting "Student Power!"—protested the Vietnam War, championed civil rights for blacks, denounced dormitory rules, condemned arbitrary administrations for denying free speech, faulted the existing grading system, urged the enrollment of minority students and the hiring of minority professors, and launched a new movement for women's rights. Many citizens, including alumni, excoriated these "pampered" dissidents for burning draft cards, harassing military recruiters, marring campus buildings with graffiti, dressing in unconventional ways and neglecting personal hygiene, consuming and selling illegal drugs, behaving boorishly, and engaging in casual sex.

Scholars, journalists, and politicians responded to the campus unrest. At embattled Columbia University, the distinguished historian Richard Hofstadter warned: "We are at a crisis point in the history of American education and probably in that of the western World."[1] In 1969 Congressman William Brock led a large number of his colleagues to more than fifty universities and investigated the internal and external causes of campus unrest. In a report to

President Richard Nixon the politicians stressed: "The critical urgency of the problem cannot be overstated."[2] This impressive and well-reported document identified several problems internal to campuses, including that students could not communicate with administrators and faculty, that the university curriculums failed to deal with race, poverty, and other contemporary issues, and that professors spent too much time with research and too little with teaching. Whitman professors were not surprised to learn that the Congressmen found that the smaller institutions dealt "with some problems more readily and with greater acuity than the multi-university."[3] In a discussion of external causes for campus unrest, the investigators emphasized that students often denounced "The System" as being responsible for such external problems as racism, the war in Vietnam, the draft, and materialism. Although the Congressmen did not come to Whitman, there they would also have heard criticism of "The System."

Only a minority of students participated in the campus protests, but the lack of numbers did not diminish their significance. Large universities had greater difficulties with dissident students than the small liberal arts colleges did; a distinguished historian at Stanford University, David Potter, condemned mindless student violence at his institution, and told a Whitman historian that only personalized schools like Whitman had a future. But here, as well as at the larger institutions, administrators, professors, and board members, responding to unusual student pressure, re-evaluated their decision-making processes.

Campus activists, for the most part, did not seek a political revolution; most actually sought—as did their classmates—material benefits, including rewarding jobs, stylish cars, and comfortable homes. One historian furnished his description of them: "Raised with a conviction of their own importance in indulgent, self-centered homes, they resented restrictions on their behavior and expected instant gratification and intense stimulation."[4]

Students also interpreted themselves. Whitman's Lou Boros, for example, presented the dilemma his classmates faced: "For years we have been told by our elders that we are the best generation, both in intelligence and preparation, ever to attain adulthood, [but] we are not yet ready to assume responsibilities." He emphasized that colleges nationwide practiced *in loco parentis*, and charged: "No administration can supply anything approaching the vitality of a parent. . . . At Whitman I am forced to go along with ideas and rules that my parents would laugh at as archaic—all this in the name of *in loco parentis*."[5] Although Boros saw his college's rules as oppressive, many other schools, including Willamette University, a Methodist institution, had even more stringent rules (especially with regard to the consumption of alcohol).

The rigidity of college leaders surprised incoming students, who agreed with the words of an understanding dean in 1969: "The world of higher education is just beginning to emerge from a paternalistic concern that enshrouded the students with a net of rules in which forbidden conduct was defined in general terms and enforcement procedures were almost entirely lacking in the fundamentals of due process."[6] In August 1968 *Harper's* magazine explained that school administrations everywhere played a parietal role because parents insisted that the colleges be their substitutes. "What mama and papa really feared," the writer asserted, "was premature pregnancies and shotgun marriages, so they demanded the college serve as a relentless chaperon."[7]

Whitman, of course, became involved in many of the issues besetting its sister institutions. Its protests revolved around many issues important elsewhere but did not result in serious disruptions or violence. In 1973 President Donald Sheehan boasted that, during his administration, the college "wasn't disrupted once. . . . We didn't have to endure arson, the blockading of buildings, the cancellation of classes—even final examinations." He agreed that the students' appearance might trouble alumni, but, he maintained, "They have behaved very well, and stuck to the business of getting the kind of education we want them to get at Whitman."[8]

Although the school avoided the worst aspects of the student protests, a degree of unrest accompanied changes made in regulations, the curriculum, the grading system, and student activities. The Whitman of 1975 was in many ways unlike the one of 1965: a turbulent decade had substantially affected a traditional college.

Breaking Free of *In Loco Parentis*

College students have consistently been some of society's most vocal critics. Prior to the campus revolution of the mid-1960s Whitman students, like those everywhere, had faulted rules and regulations, demanded more responsibility in the formulation of these rules, pushed for academic changes, and criticized administrators and professors. Exasperated with her critical classmates in the early 1960s, Janice Hood asked, "Why do students get such a sadistic pleasure out of tearing down their school? This school needs a few less pessimists, and a few more optimists if it wants to be on the top."[9]

Because the office of student affairs (OSA) made and enforced most campus rules—many of them written by the faculty—it would be deeply involved in the struggle to rewrite them. Formed in 1948 and composed of the director of women's affairs and the director of men's affairs, their assistants, and the religious counselor, this group directed more than fifty student organizations. It vigorously regulated students' social life; for example, it adhered to faculty legislation requiring it to compile a list of approved chaperons and to make certain that at least two of them attended every student social function. The OSA spent considerable time managing fraternities and sororities, which included nearly seventy-five percent of the student body.[10] The council of student affairs (CSA) was a faculty-student committee—composed of three professors and five students —empowered to punish rule breakers. Critics of the regulations tried to arouse the student congress, a representative body of the Associated Students of Whitman College (ASWC), and some dissatisfied women voiced their displeasure to the Associated Women of Whitman College (AWWC). But most complainers, according to the *Pioneer*, targeted the more influential OSA.

A close study of the *Pioneer* from 1955 through 1964 contains surprisingly few complaints against the school's practice of *in loco parentis*. Oral histories conducted with alumni from these years indicates that many criticisms went unreported and that students, especially the women, accepted Whitman's parietal rules. Dormitory life exasperated some occupants, who objected to rules about limited telephone usage and about turning out Anderson Hall's lights at

11:00 PM. A *Pioneer* editor in 1956 charged that dormitory inhabitants were being treated like "a group of incompetent kindergarten children."[11] Five years later a male complained that the "Whitty Family" supervised its students "as children who must come not a minute late, or receive demerits" and that the rules should not end in the "release of us into the outer world as an unreasoning flock of sheep. We have reason, let us use it for ourselves."[12] After students complained about the CSA posting the names of those it had disciplined, it ceased to do so.[13] *Pioneer* columnist Dick Lilly, spokesman for the disgruntled, charged: "Whitman only deals with its students; it rarely consults them."[14]

But, beginning in the mid-1960s, the OSA encountered students with a different attitude. According to religious counselor Roy Hoover, who spent years dealing with student activists, these young people "were determined to break the traditional patterns of being a student." They wanted a greater voice in their "out-of-classroom lives."[15]

From 1964 to 1971 at smaller colleges and universities across the nation, the practice of *in loco parentis*—especially with regard to women students—drew more attention and more involvement than any other single campus issue. A major reason for this situation was that activists could effect change more easily on their campuses than they could in Washington, D.C.; it was easier to influence a college dean than to sway Dean Rusk. The doctrine of *in loco parentis* had fewer influential defenders than did American participation in the Vietnam War, but, at Whitman, there was a longer struggle over entrenched parietal rules than there was at most schools. Student body president Alex MacLeod grumbled in 1969 that, for the previous four years, parietal rules had dominated the student protest movement.

In the early 1960s the college's rules were traditional and similar to those that were imposed at sister institutions. Men lived under a few general rules, including the prohibition of alcohol in dormitories and fraternities, and dress requirements for certain dinners. The women, however, lived under these rules as well as many others, which appeared in the annual Coed Code.

The entire campus community understood residence hours in Anderson and Prentiss halls and their vigilant enforcement. Women above freshman rank had to be in the hall by 11:00 PM on week-

In 1960 women gather around the fireside for a group sing in Prentiss Hall.

days and by 1:00 AM on weekends; freshmen women lived under
more limited hours. Rules restricted overnight stays away from campus: "A student may not spend the night in a motel or hotel without special permission from her parents or the OSA"; and faculty
legislation stated: "No woman shall take an overnight on the night
of an out-of-town dinner dance." Males could not go to any part
of Prentiss Hall "other than the social rooms off the main hall and
the chapter rooms, without permission from the residence hall staff."
Furthermore, "if a man caller is in the residence hall after closing
hours or in any unauthorized area of the building at any time without permission, he may be referred to the OSA." A judicial council
of resident women enforced regulations, giving demerits to rule
breakers, such as those who had failed to use sign-out cards properly or had returned to the hall more than ten minutes late. A resident was "expected to keep her own room neat and clean at all
times" and to be prepared for an inspection. There were fines for
illegally unlocking section doors and for removing magazines and
sports equipment from their places.

Composed of a member from each social group, the well-known standards council established and interpreted policies regarding the dress and conduct of women. Its recommendations about dress reminded women that the public judged Whitman in part by their appearance. The council emphasized: "College is one place to develop and strengthen standards of dress not only for the . . . college years but for future life. . . . It is for this reason that we stress each person's responsibility concerning her formulation of dress standards." Thus, the Coed Code prescribed the proper attire for both the campus and the city because, "The Standards Council in conjunction with the faculty has felt it is necessary for these dress standards to be rules, because it looks better and is more ladylike." Women could not wear sportswear, slacks, jeans, or sweatshirts in classrooms, in the library, or downtown; such clothing could be worn in the Student Union Building, but the code warned that jeans and sweatshirts in the SUB led "to a relaxation of manners. Also the fellows and faculty disapprove of the sloppy appearance jeans and sweatshirts give." High heels, hosiery, and gloves should be worn to church, theater, and concerts. And women must wear heels and hose to dress dinners on Sunday and Wednesday, and they were encouraged at these occasions to "wear something different from what you wore during the day to freshen up."

In the early 1960s some women, rejecting the prescribed clothing standard and wanting to look like "ordinary people," wore boots, cowboy shirts, and other similar garments, which caused the standards council to remind these "rebels" that their informal dress besmirched their sorority's reputation.

A set of dining-room policies included a provision for family-style service for six. With the host and hostess seated at the head and foot of the table, the hostess was served first; she indicated "when to begin eating by lifting her fork."[16] To improve the decorum, a new rule gave residence hall staff members and others "the authority and responsibility to ask any student to leave the dining room, who does not adhere to the standards of dress and conduct established for the dining room."[17] Besides these rules, women received advice about their behavior; there were warnings about walking on lower Main Street, a place of vile taverns and seedy, obscene men. Malinda Phillips Pankl recalled that women opposed to a scheduled execution at the penitentiary attended an airport protest against Governor Albert Rosellini. Prior to their departure from Prentiss Hall, dean of women Miriam Wagenschein inspected them, making sure that they were dressed as if for Sunday dinner, because she did not want the protestors to "embarrass Whitman by being poorly dressed."[18]

Sally Mathiasen Light remembered the dean of women's office bringing in a physician to address Prentiss and Anderson women; he blew up a condom, passed it around, and explained its use. The English major believed that her bemused classmates had never seen one before. The physician assured them that he would tell the males across campus: "Don't sleep with Whitman girls because they are good girls. If you have to have sex, you sleep with the townies."[19]

For years the enforcement of the rules rankled many women. Freshman women lived under tight regulations, while freshmen men enjoyed great freedom. Many women and dormitory men also complained about inconsistency in the enforcement of the school's liquor rules, which the fraternities seemed to violate with impunity. The OSA heard more cases arising from the discovery of alcoholic beverages in the dormitories than from similar discoveries in the fraternity houses. In one celebrated case, sorority sisters consumed frozen beer with toothbrushes; they were found guilty and were campused, and their parents were informed. Another irritation was that assistant librarian Ruth Thompson, with administrative and faculty support, rigidly maintained the library's dress code for women; this code would be liberalized in 1966, when female patrons received the right to wear pants.

Until the completion of New Dorm in 1970, many women rightfully complained about Prentiss Hall's crowded rooms. The lack of privacy and study areas were among the reasons why women sought to modify residential rules.

A *Pioneer* editorial in 1965 asserted that the *in loco parentis* approach meant that students "are cooped up in overcrowded dorms, carefully watched for the slightest sign of mental disturbance, regulated to the point of regimentation, and in general given a minimal number of choices to make." One woman recalled, "We were encapsulated in a little womb." A September 1965 editorial welcomed freshmen, but warned about the school's oppressive *in loco parentis* policy: "Students are not allowed to live in housing that is not

Tower [administration] supervised. Twenty-one-year-old girls are safely locked up in their cloister every night. In playing an overly protective mom-and-dad role the Tower stifles any attempt at total responsibility." Some Prentiss Hall residents complained about assistant dean of women Konnilyn Feig, who resided in their hall. In the evenings, she stood outside an entrance with a watch, as the women rushed to beat the deadline. Some called her "The Enforcer" and accused her of enjoying writing censure letters to parents. But some praised the strong-willed assistant dean for her intelligence, wit, feminism, and commitment to academics.[20]

Resident assistants (RAs)—upperclass students living in the dormitories—helped orient freshmen, provided them with academic and social guidance, and reported any rule breaking. Each RA received financial aid and assisted about twenty-five residents. Because there were so many more rules for women than men, the female RAs had more responsibility for their enforcement than did their male counterparts. The deans sometimes handled violations of dormitory rules, personally warning offenders or sending them letters of censure. The faculty-student council of student affairs handled disciplinary cases referred to it by the administrative office of student affairs; it also furnished advice on matters of student life. Thus, over the course of one year, the CSA's agenda covered a wide spectrum of campus issues: investigation of racial discrimination, a review of the academic schedule, and a concern for library thefts and classroom plagiarism. But the OSA minutes of the 1950s and 1960s demonstrate that it spent considerable time ruling on matters such as consumption of alcohol in the resident halls or infractions of housing rules. Occasionally, the OSA took action against pranksters, like those who bricked an office in Memorial Hall or who pried a shield from a police car. Those found guilty by the CSA often received conduct probation: for a semester they could not participate in extracurricular activities—especially college plays—or hold office on campus or in the Greek organizations; furthermore, their parents received letters describing the offense and its punishment. There was no forum for appealing the decisions of the CSA.

Whitman leaders in the late 1960s and early 1970s spent considerable time responding to activists who pushed for changes in housing policies and the method of handling rule breakers through the

CSA. Many students, not only activists, believed that they should have a major voice in writing and enforcing the rules. Administrators and trustees gave ground—sometimes reluctantly—until the early 1970s, when students, having accomplished these non-academic goals, increasingly voiced concerns over such academic issues as grades and the curriculum.

The major changes in college housing can be seen by comparing the 1964 catalog with that of 1974. In 1964 Whitman required all students to live on campus; in 1974 they only had to live on campus for two years. In 1964 Whitman offered only gender-segregated dormitories; ten years later Jewett Hall, Anderson Hall, Lyman House, and New Dorm were all coeducational. Thus, there were far more residential choices in 1974 than there had been in 1964. What the catalog does not show is that the dormitories, which no longer had housemothers, had each adopted a self-government system that wrote its own rules on visitations by the opposite sex and on the use of alcohol.

The history behind these sweeping changes is found in official records and in the pages of the *Pioneer*. It began with a controversy over housing regulations. Prior to 1964 Whitman lacked dormitory space for all of its men, so those above the freshman rank lived either in fraternities or off campus. A few men complained that the college should make the effort to house all students, men as well as women. President Louis Perry, dean of women Wagenschein, and the trustees agreed, asserting that, ideally, a residential college should house all out-of-town students. Like other colleges, Whitman operated single-sex dormitories in the early 1960s, and their locations further segregated the student body. Boyer Avenue split the sexes; men lived to the north, women to the south.

Anticipating the construction of Jewett Hall, the college announced that all students enrolled after September 1963 must live in campus housing. Such a sweeping change, of course, aroused critics. The *Pioneer* charged that, with Whitman's new plan, "the opportunities for informal privacy, formerly provided by off-campus apartments, is eliminated."[21] Some students favored liberal visiting hours allowing the mingling of men and women in dormitories and fraternities. Student body president Ben Kerkvliet believed that "the chief objection to the visiting hours plan was morality" and "the effect on the school's image."[22] Others wondered if men, under the stricter regulations, would be allowed to rent off-campus study apartments for academic and social reasons. In the fall of 1964 the issue of visiting hours dominated many campus conversations. *Pioneer* editor Dick Lilly reasoned: "The only relevant objection to any visiting hours plan is the moral one." He charged that the administration's view was: "Will open rooms be bedrooms?"[23] The philosophy major emphasized that Stanford University and Pomona College did not impose a four-year residence rule and that visiting hours —or the so-called "open dorms"—at Whitman would mitigate the effects of the new stringent residence rule. A student committee reported that it had investigated open-dorm policies at several other colleges.

Meanwhile, some women students asserted that they needed to have "study apartments" away from campus, because Prentiss Hall was too noisy and the library hours were too limited. Perry was not sympathetic to this argument; he sent a letter to students and their parents reasoning that there was no need for off-campus study apartments, stating that the rule against women renting such places still stood, and saying that the men could continue to rent these accommodations but should register them so that the students could be found in an emergency. He also anticipated that those living off campus would act in a way "compatible with the standards considered acceptable to society generally, by the local community, and by Whitman College."[24] The student body president disagreed with Perry about denying senior women or women over twenty-one the right to rent study apartments. He asserted that they were "adults and cannot forever be watched, indeed they must be permitted to be responsible people."

In December 1964 President Perry informed students of his opposition to the open-dormitory policy, arguing that the "college might be held legally responsible for any psychiatric or emotional conditions resulting from an open dormitory situation." He stated that other colleges had discovered that an open-dorm program placed a burden on women that led to their requiring psychiatric care because they "faced direct challenges to established codes of conduct before they have developed sufficient maturity to cope with them." He was not alone in voicing these concerns; at Middlebury College as late as 1966, for example, two deans insisted: "Greatly liberalized parietal hours would create social pressures in the area of sexual conduct which would encroach on individual freedom and might cause serious psychological impairment to some students."[25] Perry also said that other colleges feared that the liberal policy would result in increased pregnancies, and that he had been advised not to launch such a program. The *Pioneer* quoted him as asserting "quite forcefully that the college does not have the responsibility of providing an opportunity for pre-marital sex experimentation."[26] The faculty rejected a proposal for open housing, accepting and expanding on several of Perry's interpretations.[27] The faculty council reported that, when women visited in men's quarters, numerous problems resulted: "Increased personal difficulties and psychological problems have been reported from college after college. . . . The Faculty Council does not believe that the College should adopt policies or regulations which are known to have aggravated students' problems."[28]

Under Dean Robert Whitner's leadership, the OSA spent a year studying the college's residential system; responses from alumni to dormitory rules and conditions were diverse. Many supported—and others resented—the rules that had been and were being imposed on women. A respondent recognized the college's fear of immorality, advising that the school "would be better off to know that we were always so tired we were incapable of illicit relationships."[29] One of the results of this study was that the faculty and administration rejected open dormitories.

The students shifted their attention from the open-dorm issue to another housing question. In September 1965 Perry had announced that the trustees had granted his request to allow senior men to live off campus. He wrote: "The college recognizes that many senior men are prepared to assume responsibility for a certain kind of independence that they may not easily find possible in a residence hall or a fraternity house." Immediately some men and women complained about the administration's double standard; many senior women insisted that they were as mature as the men and should enjoy the same privileges. The *Pioneer* gloomily predicted that it would be difficult to revise this new ruling: "The tradition of keeping under-age women locked and cloistered is so well cemented as to render it immovable." An angry male accused the college of treating its women "like silly, wishy-washy scatterbrained children who must be kept for their own protection in the doll houses."

In October women petitioners to the faculty requested permission for senior women and those who were twenty-one to live in off-campus housing. They believed that professors would be more lenient than the trustees and assumed that the faculty possessed the power to make housing regulations. A thoughtful editorial by student Kathy Hall defended the petition, hoping that it would "stimulate a debate between the trustees, faculty, and students concerning under whose jurisdiction should fall the major policy decisions on student welfare."

The housing rules triggered considerable attention. *Pioneer* writer Thomas Roesler wrote a solid summary of the residence policy, including a defense by Miriam Wagenschein. The dean of women explained that locked dormitory doors were not a part of the *in loco parentis* doctrine; locks kept people out, not in. She strongly favored imposing a universal policy of on-campus residency, because "the only advantage of a small school over a large university is the community life it affords," and "the community of scholars is the salvation of the small college." Wagenschein described housing near the college as being either substandard or expensive. She assessed the fraternities, insisting that senior men should live in them because of the leadership the seniors could provide. "These mature members are essential," she emphasized, "if the houses are not to become mere drinking clubs." Roesler judged that Whitman was "caught between a desire to expand and a residence philosophy that requires that adequate housing be available for each student that is accepted." The philosophy major added that the trustees wanted an enrollment of twelve hundred but provided housing for only 965.

A new dormitory issue arose at the end of spring semester 1966, when some students and faculty members complained about the OSA policy of maintaining personal files containing reports written by resident assistants in Anderson and Prentiss halls. Deans Whitner and Wagenschein defended the system, noting that this practice had been followed for fifteen years. Wagenschein explained to critics that information from these files had helped her in writing as many as two hundred recommendations annually, and added that such details were especially useful when women applied to graduate school. "There is," she reminded them, "more often prejudice against wom-

en applying to graduate school than men."[30] Calling the procedure
a "spy system," critics expressed pleasure when women were given
the right to reject the compilation of confidential reports.[31]

In June 1966 the faculty voted in favor of a petition allowing senior women or those at least twenty-one years of age to live off campus. At the same time the CSA released a questionnaire distributed
to women. Respondents favored older women being allowed to live
off campus, but a majority still agreed that residence halls and regulations were reasonable and necessary.

The attack on traditional rules increased in the fall of 1966,
brought on in part by Professor David Stevens' provocative convocation address. The respected economist and former dean recommended several significant changes. First, he urged a "Whitman Revolution" that would include the repeal of hours and residence rules.
Then the speaker criticized independent study as often being merely a cover for "intellectual malingering."[32] He also proposed a
breath-taking hundred-percent increase in faculty salaries, but what
people remembered from his speech was his denunciation of the numerous rules imposed upon women.

A few students went further than the professor had, urging coeds
to rebel against tyrannical rules and the overcrowded conditions in
Prentiss Hall. One disgusted male judged that "many independent
minded girls" transferred away from Whitman, and that "weak-
willed, rule-abiders remained." He urged a slogan: "Organize dis-
obedience."[33] According to student Nancy Jerrick, when the college instituted bed checks in late 1966 it thereby turned Prentiss Hall
into a prison. She explained that most women did not rebel against
rules because they didn't care enough; furthermore, activist women
feared the administration would respond with "social probation,
withdrawal of scholarships, and expulsion."[34] Jerrick gave up her
struggle against Whitman's rigidity and, students reported, transferred to the University of California. Meanwhile, the student congress unanimously voted in favor of a letter to trustees requesting
them to grant senior women or those over age twenty-one the same
rights as senior men, including the right to live off campus or maintain study apartments. Senior women petitioning for study apartments stated that they wanted them "partially for study purposes
but primarily for personal reasons, including an opportunity to en-

tertain, decorate, sew, cook, and study." They further stated that the use of such an accommodation should be available only to those whose parents gave their approval. Two trustees met with these concerned students, explaining that, because the question of women living off campus had financial implications, the board must render housing decisions. The *Pioneer* supported the action of the student congress, urged patience, and favored a continuing dialogue with trustees. It also reported that other schools were adopting liberal social regulations; for example, Smith College women could entertain men on Sunday afternoon, but "doors had to be open six inches, and three feet must be on the floor."[35]

In early 1967 the CSA proposed that senior women and those twenty-one years old have the right to sign out overnight. Favoring the action, a writer accused the trustees of making decisions based on financial considerations and contended that professors were closer "to the students and their needs" and were "in a better position to govern students than board members who are scattered . . . and whose knowledge of student needs is often based on their experiences in college twenty years ago."[36] The faculty, supporting the CSA recommendation and testing its authority in matters of housing, adopted a two-year experiment in which senior women could choose their housing. Because the decision had financial implications and because it could change the residential nature of the college, the trustees rejected the action.[37] Disagreeing with the trustees' decision, the student newspaper again requested the elimination of hours for senior women and permission for them to rent study apartments. The women soon received the right to have such apartments.[38] The student congress and the ASWC now sought expanded rights: senior women should be allowed to sign out overnight to any destination.[39]

The departures in 1967 of President Perry and deans Wagenschein and Feig, the resignation of Professor Whitner as dean of students, and the appointments of President Donald Sheehan, dean of students Gordon Scribner, dean of women Joan Hodgson, and religious counselor Roy Hoover dramatically changed the administration's approach to rule making and rule enforcing.

Wagenschein had feared that traditional rules would be eliminated. During her seventeen years at Whitman, she had strongly advocated the residential college and rigid rules for women; and in 1966

*The departure of dean of women Miriam Wag-
enschein in 1967 and the appointment of dean
of women Joan Hodgson and dean of students
Gordon Scribner heralded a change in the administration's attitude toward parietal rules.
Wagenschein had been a strong defender of the
traditional rules; Hodgson and Scribner favored
efforts to liberalize them.*

Miriam Wagenschein

she was troubled by organized student protests against these rules. In
her opinion, younger male faculty members failed to appreciate the
college's traditional concern for the student outside the classroom and
instead favored the impersonalization that characterized universities.
In her last semester, she opposed the faculty vote to allow senior
women to live off-campus on a trial basis, and charged that professors failed "to understand the facts of our operation, yet they feel
free to legislate and criticize without investigation or consultation."
She warned that the OSA "must articulate more clearly the educational purposes and refute more certainly the fallacious assumption
that residence halls exist for control and *in loco parentis* reasons."[40]

Fresh from graduate schools, male teachers considered the dean
of women to be another authoritarian figure. Such rigid and old-
fashioned administrators should surrender power either to students
or to the faculty, or to both. Joined by many experienced members
of the faculty, the younger members hailed the sweeping changes in
the OSA staff, hoping that the new administrators would terminate
the oppressive rules that irritated students.

Pointing out that high school graduates lived on their own, Scribner, the new dean of students, charged that Whitman's rules were
"just ridiculous."[41] In September 1967 the *Pioneer* praised him and
dean of the faculty Kenyon Knopf for their willingness to discuss

Joan Hodgson   *Gordon Scribner*

women's living conditions, and concluded that the college was no longer "racked with a series of internecine quarrels."[42] Early in the fall an AWWC survey revealed that respondents favored regulated hours for freshmen women but not for juniors and seniors.[43] This poll influenced administrators and faculty members as the college community discussed residence requirements. "Student Power," a slogan adopted from other campuses, was increasingly voiced by dissidents insisting on a greater role in determining housing and other policies.

The residents of Jewett Hall voted for open dorms, an action that widened debate on residential rules. The president's council ignored this issue, but decided that the faculty, not the trustees, should rule on a proposal to impose curfew hours on freshman women only and to implement a different security system, replacing card-keys with a house matron.[44] OSA representatives defended the proposal at a faculty meeting. The *Pioneer* reported that, "Despite the debate about the legal age of women and the future of academics at Whitman College, the faculty put up no strong objections to the program" and overwhelmingly supported it.[45]

With most women now free from the requirement to spend certain hours in their dormitories, there was increased pressure on the OSA to allow dormitory visitation, including a plea that senior women be allowed to have male visitors on Friday and Saturday nights. To the surprise of many critics, Dean Hodgson broadened the request by stating that all Prentiss women—not just seniors—should be granted this privilege, because there was no way to restrict it to senior women. But some of the seniors informed her that their younger classmates were too immature to handle male callers.

Additional and significant changes followed the appointment of President Donald Sheehan in 1968. From his experience at Smith, he understood that colleges everywhere were debating the traditional rules. He stressed to his new campus community that dissent was vital: "Conflict between orthodoxy and free thinkers is inevitable in a free society's institutions of higher learning."[46] Quickly grasping specific disputes over housing regulations, Sheehan arranged his appearance at a student congress meeting and stressed, "Let us communicate reasonably."[47] As a result, members of the student congress, Sheehan, and the faculty agreed to the creation of an ad hoc committee composed of six students, three faculty members, and three administrators. The committee would "define the extent of group autonomy and investigate the rule-making machinery which presently exists, with the object of reforming it."[48] Sheehan convinced the committee to make him its chair and assured student skeptics that he would take action. Student body president Peter Snow concluded: "The Ad Hoc Committee is the realization of what the college has always stood for yet often failed to practice. . . . Regardless of the outcome, the committee's very existence represents an important precedent for cooperative action in the future."[49]

The lengthy and influential ad hoc committee report of February 1969 liberalized dormitory visitation hours if approved by three-quarters of the residents, permitted alcohol if two-thirds of the residents agreed, and extended curfew hours for freshmen women. The document's writers admitted, "The experience of many years has demonstrated that the long standing regulation of total prohibition of alcoholic consumption on the campus has been substantially unsuccessful."[50] The ad hoc committee required that each living group elect members to a group council that would enforce the rules, and the committee also required a student review board of five members to investigate the regulations drawn up by living groups and to review judicial decisions made by the group council for fairness.[51]

The Coed Code for 1969–1970 reflected the significant changes in the womens' halls: demerits, dress codes, fines, and sign-out cards disappeared, as did some some dining-room regulations.

At an emotional meeting, trustees accepted both the report and the resignation of trustee Edward McMillan, who departed because the changes violated his Christian principles. Prior to that gathering, trustee Donald Sherwood had sent his fellow board members a newspaper clipping reporting that a judge feared that the silly "new boy-girl visiting regulations at Indiana University dormitories put the taxpayers in the position of maintaining a free love nest."[52]

In 1972 the dress standards for women were much different from what had been mandated just a few years earlier. Casual attire such as overalls was worn to class as well as for doing weekend chores.

Students reacted differently to the ad hoc committee report: some found the alcohol policy too conservative; others believed that it was too liberal. Most dormitory residents appreciated the opportunity to make their own rules. Some activists criticized apathetic classmates for taking little interest in the committee's proceedings and were unhappy about Sheehan's influence. "Platitudes, pacification, and expert politics," one critic predicted, "will keep the students from having any say in Whitman policy."[53] A new student newspaper, the *Narrator*, edited by Jack Riehl, brought additional attention to the ad hoc committee and other campus issues during the spring of 1969.

Professor Patrick Tyson, a member of the ad hoc committee, emphasized what the committee had accomplished. It had gathered together and addressed all of the OSA and faculty rules regarding student conduct, had placed the students on an equal basis with professors in writing regulations, and had provided for student participation in the enforcement process. Because of the report, the faculty changed the procedures of the CSA in considering infractions of college regulations, insisting that it respect the due process of law. Sheehan often stressed the changes to various audiences, and he especially reminded students that they now had increased control of their daily lives.

In the *Walla Walla Union-Bulletin*'s interview of Sheehan after his first year in office, the leader emphasized the importance of campus communication. He pointed out that, at a small college, it was possible to communicate with every constituency, and that it was his responsibility to bridge any generation gaps.[54] In his 1969 annual report, Sheehan briefly discussed the ad hoc committee, stating that the policy of combining "larger areas for group decision with increased student responsibility appears to have met with considerable success."[55] In effect, a century of traditional rule making had ended.

A year after the enactment of these relaxed residential policies Sheehan asked those responsible for the living groups to assess conditions. A respondent stated that, if one accepted the "premise that dating was good, then in this respect Ad Hoc has aided and encouraged it."[56] A head resident in Anderson Hall thought that some "freshman girls were bewildered by all this freedom."[57] Lois Gatewood, a fraternity housemother, concluded that her "mother's intuition" told her that the men appreciated her helping them enforce the new rules. She added that alcohol was "a necessary evil" but that she would prefer having the men drinking in the house rather "than out in a car getting themselves killed or maimed."[58]

Meanwhile, the deans' titles, which had been used for a short time, were changed from "dean of men" and "dean of women" to "dean of students" and "associate dean of students"; new appointments as associates in student affairs, including that of Floyd Bunt, strengthened the OSA. Sheehan explained that "the reason for restructuring the OSA is in part to get rid of the stereotype of the classic dean of men and women as wardens." Both dean of students Scribner and associate dean of students Hodgson, who many observers called progressive and savvy, hailed the efforts to liberalize rules, but some students still feared the power of the trustees, who, they emphasized, had "final say over all campus procedures and changes."[59]

Because of these fears, campus activists successfully called for regular meetings between the trustees and students. In the fall of 1969 a student committee wrote a forty-two-page report to the trustees, arguing, among other things, that it was not good for men and women students to reside in separate areas of the campus, and that students had too little contact with each other outside of the classroom. The committee, which was preparing for the college's first "Interim" session, wanted to try coeducational living. The OSA, of course, had been studying this new and controversial living scheme, one that Scribner endorsed. Roy Hoover stated that a new policy had to be invented, for there were no guide books on how to make an intelligent decision. The OSA's support of change was, he recalled, "a step into the brave new world of student rights."[60] Impressed with the favorable information supplied by the Interim committee and the dean's office, the trustees, who had originally designed New Dorm for older women, approved a trial plan allowing women and men to reside on separate floors when the building opened in January 1970.

Having already liberalized housing rules, and finding that the ad hoc committee would consider additional proposals, activists emphasized the need for more coed dorms. Mary Ellen Hudgins reminded the campus that: "There is a sexual revolution going on— meaning not that students are sleeping together, they've been doing that for years—but meaning that men are beginning to regard wom-

en as companions, confidantes, pals; and that women are beginning
to regard men in the same light." Observing that the only contact
men and women had with each other was in classes or in formal dating, the drama major argued that open dorms would give everyone
a better chance to become acquainted. Her classmates would not feel
"easy and natural with each other" until there was casual contact
"facilitated by coed dorms, coed dining situations, and some degree
of self-determination on the part of students concerning their living situation on campus and off."[61] Student government made a coed
proposal based on similar arguments.

With the opening of New Dorm, coed living was launched during Interim, at the beginning of 1970. Men and women were separated by floors. One observer, noting that women were on the first
two floors, joked: "The stronger, or stair-climbing, sex is on the
third."[62] Many, including Professor David Deal and his wife, Judy,

*Called New Dorm when it opened in 1970, this dormitory was designed to ac-
commodate groups of eight residents, each group occupying a cluster of rooms.
As the college's first coeducational dormitory, it immediately prompted controversy. In 1980 some people, including a few alumni, expressed dissatisfaction when
its name was changed to Douglas Hall to honor Justice William O. Douglas.*

who resided on the first floor, declared this experiment in coeducational living a success. A freshman woman noted that some "startling discoveries were made: members of the opposite gender are human beings, not just dates, sex objects, or potential marital mates!"[63] There was a brief confrontation at New Dorm when the college installed plywood panels to limit access to the women's floors. These obstructions, which met fire-code standards, had been put in place to appease parents, donors, and trustees; students removed the panels.

More notable housing changes came in the spring of 1970. Some students requested the right to live off campus; among them was a group of women and men who had formed a local fraternity permitting coeducational living. The radical proposal failed, and so did a later idea from a few members of Phi Delta Theta that the fraternity should become a coed residence. After several controversial votes, Prentiss Hall residents voted an end to mandatory dress dinners. In April the trustees finally extended to senior and twenty-one-year-old women the right to live off campus "provided that the exercise of the option can be done without substantial impact on the revenues of the college due to vacancies in on-campus housing," and provided that those senior women under twenty-one received parental consent prior to moving off campus.

Another sweeping change regarded the employment of housemothers in fraternities. Housemothers had been mandated in 1948 and, over the years, numerous fraternity men had expressed friendship with these cultivated ladies, who seemed to be like caring grandmothers. In 1970 housemothers were made optional, and as they retired they were not replaced. Perhaps some Greeks agreed with a student editor, who reasoned that housemothers had served a need for the "post-depression students" who needed a "mom to turn to" because they could not afford long-distance phone calls, or an automobile or airplane ticket to visit home; the much more affluent students of the late 1960s no longer required housemothers, because they could afford to stay in closer contact with their families.[64] Meanwhile, the college hired young faculty families—as well as some families who had no other connection with the college—to live in the dorms, a practice which proved successful.

In the fall of 1970, citing the potential loss of income from housing, the trustees again upset students by limiting to twenty-nine the number of senior women granted the option of living off campus. An angry editorial in the *Pioneer* championed the discontented seniors: "You do not have to be liberated and bra-less to realize that these women are being discriminated against solely because of sex." The editor stressed the obvious point that senior men did not have similar restrictions placed on them when they moved from Lyman House.[65] At a time when feminism was beginning to gain ground nationally and locally, the college's sexist policy was an obvious target.

In 1970 President Sheehan shared with the faculty his concerns about residence policy. He reminded them: "All over the country, extreme pressure is being put on the residence system—to permit off-campus options; to enlarge privileges in on-campus living situations. We are trying to make on-campus living more varied with more options. . . . I suppose our goal would be to make on-campus living sufficiently attractive that a great majority of all students would wish to live on-campus, even if they had the free option to live off."[66]

Sheehan also informed the faculty that he had to "act in such a way that the majority does not join the minority."[67] The president anticipated more activist pressure, which would "involve considerable strain and tension." He concluded: "The extreme student position offers the two alternatives of total freedom or total administration suppression. The view of the United States, Mr. Scribner, and myself is that neither of these is acceptable."[68]

Sheehan explained to alumni that authority had been delegated from his office and from the faculty to the ad hoc committee, and that the committee had been created to revise non-academic regulations because students wanted "more say in matters affecting the character and quality of student life."[69] In 1969 and 1970 the administration sent a few students and faculty members to alumni and parent meetings to explain the sweeping changes on campus, including the methods and conclusions of the ad hoc committee. Historian Thomas Edwards informed Oregon groups that the doctrine of *in loco parentis* had sustained a heavy attack from activist students, but was still alive; however, the form of *in loco parentis* was evolving as Whitman moved from a restrictive approach to a supportive one. Civil authorities arrested some students suspected of being drug users, and their sympathizers urged college administrators to render assistance; some women successfully argued that the school's health service should supply them with birth control pills. After reassuring questioning alumni, Edwards noted that students remained friendly, reasonable, and studious. The professor predicted that the college would remain successful, "even though some students had more hair, more whiskers, fewer shoes, more work clothes, fewer dress clothes, fewer ribbons, more leg, fewer nylons, more animals, and fewer furs."[70]

In March 1971 the trustees expanded coed dorm living to one-third of the campus, including rooms in Jewett Hall, Lyman House, and New Dorm. The OSA had studied the residential policies of all of the four-year colleges in the Pacific Northwest as well as those of the private colleges that shared salary information. Whitman trailed nearly every other school in establishing coeducational dormitories, but Sheehan thought it necessary to explain these different types of residences to parents, friends, and alumni. He assured them that coeducational dormitories did not mean cohabitation, and pointed out that a considerable amount of information about this new type of housing appeared in both the popular and professional press. The president had read Martha W. Lear's article, "How the New Coed Dorms Curb Promiscuity," which appeared in the *Ladies' Home Journal*. The writer emphasized that "segregation by sex is considered irrelevant and unnatural by today's students." A contributing professor pointed out that coeducational living put an end to panty raids. One investigator concluded that, in coed dorms, "Manners and appearances improved. . . . There are no food fights." Sheehan repeated some of these assertions, explained that Whitman had investigated residential policies at fifty schools, and confessed that he "was astonished to learn how very widespread the practice [of coeducational living] had become." Only two schools had rejected this housing reform. Administrators wrote that this new housing arrangement had not increased immorality; in fact, one respondent noted that "students tend to seek dates less within their own residence than outside it." Despite this positive evidence, Sheehan confessed that it was difficult to adopt coeducational living, "not because we were indifferent to the moral implications, but because we cared about them."[71]

Many administrators favored moving female students into sections of Lyman House to counter the behavior of its male malcon-

tents; its conditions had deteriorated to such a point that the residence was commonly referred to as the "zoo." Soon the OSA rejoiced
over the fact that, when women moved in, this dormitory became
manageable and popular. Its creative women occupants planted flowers in the urinals and watered them with scheduled flushes. Meanwhile, men moved into Anderson Hall, increasing the male presence
on the campus's south side.

These significant housing changes came only after a thorough investigation and considerable discussion. Jeffrey Sheehan, the president's son, described his father's thinking about housing practices:

> He was of the old school when it comes to mores, and the idea
> was frankly shocking to him. . . . The evidence astounded him
> and changed his mind completely—students in co-ed dorms
> had better grade-point averages, were better adjusted, dropped
> out at a lower rate, and by empirical standards were no more
> promiscuous than students in single sex dorms. . . . There were
> very few areas in his cosmology where reason did not prevail.[72]

But not everyone came to the same positive conclusion as Sheehan. Trustee Walter Minnick, an emotional man devoted to his alma
mater, resigned from the board. Reminding the campus community
that his fellow trustee Edward McMillan had resigned in 1969 in
response to the ad hoc committee decisions, Minnick explained that
he opposed the policy of coeducational dorms because it would cost
money to renovate the halls; because Whitman's friends would oppose liberal dormitory rules; and because the Greeks would lose
members to competition from coeducational dormitories, where pre-
marital sex would increase.

Eugene Thompson, editor of the *Whitman Alumnus*, reported
Minnick's resignation and answered questions raised by alumni. He
asserted that the "discussion of the out-of-classroom life of the American student has become an overblown national preoccupation."
Thompson explained: "Co-educational dormitories and dining halls,
in addition to letting the women-civilizing-the-frontier theory go to
work, perhaps provide a better neighborhood, where social contact
can be conducted unplanned at leisure, and informally, as it was at
home . . . and there is also an elemental integrity in modern boy-
girl relationships that is very powerful."[73]

By 1970 it was clear that students, the faculty, the president, and the OSA favored further change in the rules. According to campus opinion, the powerful trustees favored the status quo and were opposed to reform, but they too had come to realize that tradition must give way to realism. Trustee Donald Frisbee concluded that the college "could not buck such powerful social trends."[74] Trustee Baker Ferguson, describing himself as the board's "ringleader in the revolution," later recalled that the trustees had finally supported housing changes for several reasons. The information compiled by the OSA demonstrated that schools everywhere had done away with traditional dormitory rules. This fact, coupled with market arguments, impressed Donald Sherwood, a conservative and influential trustee. If Whitman did not liberalize its rules, he reasoned, it would not attract the quality of young men and women it sought; Whitman would suffer by having the same strict rules as Whitworth College and other denominational schools. Ferguson concluded that the dormitory changes were "inevitable, appropriate, and in keeping with modern America." Because of such views and because he was available for conversations at his banking office, he often met with dissident students, assuring them that conditions would improve.

Baker Ferguson served as a trustee from 1966 to 1978. He had graduated from Whitman in 1939, flew combat missions in the Second World War, and taught at Whitman from 1946 to 1948. A Walla Walla banker, he was considered by professors and students to be a progressive and reasonable trustee.

Meanwhile, mothers of Whitman daughters—and mothers of daughters thinking of applying—told the banker that "they were very doubtful that moral, religious, or stringent college rules had any genuine meaning."[75]

Recognizing that rules must reflect a new reality, the board advised college officials that there was no use in having rules that could not be maintained. They emphasized, for example, that strict visitation hours were unenforceable, and recommended that the students should set their own hours, taking into account the rights of others.

In the fall of 1971 the realistic trustees, like governing boards everywhere, accepted "A Statement on the Rights and Freedoms of Students." The document had originated with the National Students' Association in 1970, and it received the blessing of Whitman's student congress, the faculty, and the trustees. In July 1970 the OSA distributed a document entitled "Student Social Regulations." Based upon the widely endorsed "Student Bill of Rights," it recognized the right of students to participate in the writing of social regulations. The OSA reminded readers that rules resulted from a consensus reached by the ad hoc committee.[76] This significant document provided for procedural due process, including the right of a student to be informed in writing of the nature of charges against him.

But the adoption of this document failed to satisfy some activists, who convinced the student congress to establish a students' rights board. This group would investigate and publicize administrative and faculty policies that might infringe upon student rights. The student board unsuccessfully sought permission from President Sheehan to see the college's financial statements and from Dean Knopf to study the athletic budget. One frustrated and ill-informed activist accused the school of trying to "keep us in a position of niggers."[77] The students' rights board, however, concluded that the school's student filing system was fair. Administrators and students had established guidelines about the types of material forming a student's record, including separating academic and disciplinary records, and limiting access to student personnel files.

After 1971 the number and intensity of student complaints about housing regulations diminished. The *Pioneer*, which by this time was publishing four-letter words that would have offended earlier generations of students, stressed academic problems rather than social ones. The ASWC arranged bi-annual meetings with trustees, where social regulations now received less emphasis than academic issues, including student concerns about curricular matters, grading procedures, and comprehensive examinations.[78]

During the long struggle over liberalized housing regulations, only a minority of students participated. There were many women who did not find the rules oppressive and who enjoyed living in Prentiss Hall. Margaret Ershler, who chose to live in women's dormitories every year, appreciated the opportunity to engage in wide-ranging discussions, and the fact that at wee hours in the morning there was always somebody seeking conversation. The history major concluded: "It was those hours in the dorm that I think were as important as if not more so" than classes.[79] Alumni remembered that their classmates were either apathetic about change or supportive of the rules. Some residents, however, chose off-campus housing. Pooling their resources, they would rent a study apartment where they read or entertained; each evening, of course, they had to hurry back to Prentiss by curfew. Sally Mathiasen rarely utilized her apartment, preferring to study in the library. Many women could not afford such accommodations; others thought them a waste of money since they must leave their apartments to sleep in Prentiss Hall.

In the early 1970s many assessed the great changes in dormitory management that had taken place in the past few years. Dean Scribner observed in late 1973 that Whitman had avoided the disruptive conditions that had occurred at other schools, and boasted: "We were fortunate in having reasonable people that wanted to talk things through and move things" in a reasonable manner.[80] Student Peter Van Oppen reflected that the students on Sheehan's ad hoc committee on social regulations could always look to the president for a fair hearing and most often they received his whole-hearted support. "Unlike many administrators he did not say everything was rosy when he knew it was not, nor was he ever pessimistic about a good idea whatever the odds against it. If one brought in a suggestion, as countless students felt free to do, he could count on an honest appraisal from Dr. Sheehan."[81] Student leaders who worked closely with the president admired his commitment to academics, his ability to listen, and his eagerness to resolve problems. Jim Waldo recalled that his classmates, experiencing Sheehan's uncanny ability to control conditions, referred to him as "the fox." Sheehan was, like other successful college administrators, a skilled crisis manager, and faculty members appreciated their leader's ability to keep abreast of campus conditions nationally through reading or research, to listen to and converse with everyone, and to finesse touchy situations. But some teachers, noting increased class absences, complained that activists ignored academic responsibilities while protesting campus regulations and that Sheehan, like the trustees, spent too much time with student concerns and not enough time with those of the faculty. Occasionally faculty members felt that he was too high-handed, and one professor privately referred to the strong-willed president as "Zeus."

Older professors agreed with Mabel Dillard's assessment of the changes. Retiring in 1969 after twenty years as Lyman's popular housemother, she observed that residents no longer found fun in campus traditions—such as May Fete—and often behaved "as if rules do not exist."[82] Under the new rule-making procedure it sometimes proved difficult to maintain orderly residences. That same year three capable resident assistants in Jewett Hall resigned because their attempts to control noise and prohibit alcoholic beverages were unsuccessful. School authorities, these men regretted, had simply told them to look the other way. Often, individuals who found that conditions made it difficult to study in their rooms spoke of their frustration to sympathetic teachers.

With the relaxation of the rules, the OSA in the 1970s heard far fewer cases, and those coming to it tended to deal with serious infractions. Alleged rule breakers had more opportunities to defend themselves because of the recent adoption of the "Student Social Regulations."

The student pressure for change diminished in the early 1970s. President Sheehan's 1972 annual report made no mention of student activism; instead, his report concerned such traditional collegiate issues as expenditures and endowments. Responding to pleas, the trustees in 1974 allowed males to have New Dorm suites on the same floor as females. But the most remarkable change came the following spring, when trustees allowed juniors as well as seniors to live off campus. The decision hardly created a ripple, and neither did the on-going discussion about enacting twenty-four-hour visitation.

Seated before the Lyman House fireplace, Mabel Dillard converses with "her boys." She was one of several beloved and well-respected housemothers who took a great interest in students and brought a concern for good manners and a measure of decorum to the college residences. It was said that "being a little hard of hearing helped her carry our her duties."

The drastic changes at Whitman were typical of those at most colleges and universities. Instead of continuing to try to protect students through a restrictive concept of *in loco parentis*, schools, as one historian concluded, adopted "policies and programs that helped the students deal with the possible consequences of their newly liberated behavior."[83]

The Issues Raised by the Black Minority

Some campus issues, on the other hand, still troubled the Whitman community. The school enrolled only a very few black students prior to 1967, including a few exchange students from Howard and Fisk universities. Seeking to add to this minority, the college recruited blacks as far away as Los Angeles, California. The fourteen new black students formed the Black Student Union (BSU) in 1968, pressured the ASWC and the faculty to become more engaged in the struggle for civil rights, and taught white classmates about racial problems. The BSU, especially under the vigorous leadership of Phil

Boss, insisted upon the college admitting more minority students, hiring black professors, and adding a black studies program. The group convinced the school to underwrite the cost of bringing the radical Black Panthers to the campus to speak; but, at the last moment, a dean urged cancellation of the meeting, reminding the faculty member who was to introduce the speakers that the state had a concealed-gun law. It was, however, too late to comply with the desires of the anxious administration, and the well-attended event went on as scheduled, with the two Black Panthers leading a spirited discussion about racism and the oppression of poor whites and blacks.

Despite its small numbers, the BSU became a major force on the campus. It received a mixed reputation in the Walla Walla Valley: some citizens disliked Afro hairstyles; even more were opposed to interracial dating. Early in 1969 the BSU, joined by some white students, formed the Coalition, receiving sympathy and advice from a few faculty members. The Coalition insisted that Whitman hire at least two black professors and initiate a black studies program, though Dean Knopf, Professor George Ball, and others pointed out the difficulties in finding black teachers, and student leader Peter Snow cautioned that such an instructor would be lonely in a city with virtually no other black residents. On the steps of Memorial Hall, the Coalition formally handed Knopf a set of demands, including the establishment both of a black culture course taught by a black professor and of a course in "Afro History." A few students watched as Knopf promised the activists that he would take action.

Polls of the student body demonstrated that there was considerable support for the Coalition's demands. Although many members of the faculty objected to the word "demands," they recognized the need to hire a black professor and reminded everyone that the college's sister institutions also sought minority professors. In 1969 Whitman sent a professor to a conference of representatives from nineteen regional colleges and universities. Delegates and speakers discussed the need for and the problems of implementing black studies programs, especially the difficulty of finding qualified teachers.

In 1970 Whitman's BSU repeatedly requested that the trustees recruit ethnic minority students. Donald Sherwood, the president of the board of trustees, appreciated the "courteous and dispassionate approach of the BSU," assured them that the college wanted to recruit

In 1971 Art Mitchell, Phil Boss, and Fred Mitchell prepare for a trip to California to recruit other black students for Whitman.

minority students, explained that it lacked the financial resources to make "substantial increases in deep-need financial assistance cases," and asserted: "The recently announced $10 million endowment campaign was a direct response by overseers and trustees to the BSU position as well as to the general situation of the college."[84]

In early February 1971 white students took the lead in organizing a town meeting—attended by four hundred students, twelve faculty members, and several administrators—to discuss the issues raised by the BSU. At this tense meeting several concerns brought responses from around the room. Angry critics, pointing out that the student body included only fourteen blacks and one Mexican-American, insisted that the school was not doing enough to recruit minority students. Many speakers, including some from the student admission advisory committee, judged that a complete educational experience at Whitman should involve contact with various ethnic groups.

While the issues pushed by the BSU under the leadership of Phil Boss received considerable attention, so did Boss himself. Articles published in the *Pioneer* document the student leader's becoming well-known—and controversial—in the city. He had recently taught a course called "Problems of Black America" at DeSales, the community's Catholic high school, and had delivered talks elsewhere employing the terms "pigs" and "racists." High school students reported his style and language to their alarmed parents, some of whom were already discomfited by the visibility and rhetoric of black Whitman students. DeSales cancelled the black activist's assignment as a student teacher, fearing that, if Boss taught, many students would leave. Brother Richard Britton concluded, "In view of our precarious financial situation, I felt it would be unwise to have him here."[85]

In August 1970 Boss was assigned to be a student teacher at Walla Walla High School, but principal (and Whitman alumnus) Richard Neher, in a faculty orientation meeting, made a reference to Lester Maddox, the avowedly racist governor of Alabama, to which Boss took exception. The resulting verbal exchange, during which Boss was asked to leave the meeting, was investigated by the Washington State Board Against Discrimination. The board's investigator conducted a hearing, made "a finding of probable cause for believing that a discriminatory practice was committed," and concluded

During the 1970s G. Ray Warren, left, served as associate director of admissions and as advisor to minority students, including the Black Student Union. William D. Tingley came to the admissions office in 1969 and was appointed director of admissions in 1971; he brought vitality to the office and implemented a variety of policies designed to diversify the student body.

with the edict that: "All teachers and administrators in the Walla Walla school system will attend a human relations seminar, especially directed toward racism with its detrimental effects."[86] But such a sweeping requirement was not imposed. School superintendent and Whitman alumnus Franklin "Pete" Hanson recalled that an affable and effective black state official came to the city and offered voluntary classes to local educators, but that these classes were not required. Boss completed his student teaching at Walla Walla High School and received encouragement from many members of the Whitman community.

The efforts of the BSU played a significant role in improving the college's efforts to attract more minority students and to counsel them. In 1971 the school hired its first black administrator, assistant director of admissions G. Ray Warren, as a recruiter and advisor of minority students. In 1971–1972 the office of admissions, led by William D. Tingley, spent more than twenty-five percent of its time visiting high schools with predominantly minority enrollment. To recruit additional West Coast minority students, black students from Whitman had their travel costs financed by the ASWC and the admissions offices.[87] Whitman also employed Henry Ollee and a black man, Vincent Lombard, both of whom assisted Whitman's ethnic minority students with part-time counseling.

In February 1971 alumni received a sound summary of minority recruitment and ethnic studies in an editorial in the *Whitman Alumnus*, "Black and White and Whitman," by Eugene Thompson. He observed: "The central student argument [was] that the college is pretty well off and could take some risks in the name of progress, could spend whatever it costs to get more black students, more black faculty members and/or a visiting professorship for a black."

The effort to increase significantly the number of minority students fell below expectations. Attempts to curb discrimination on campus also fell short, according to a panel of students and professors reported by the *Pioneer* on March 13, 1975. The panelists charged that their professors and classmates often demonstrated a lack of sensitivity. Carla Brinkley explained one aspect of this problem: "I've never met more people in my life who have never ever come in contact with a member of another race." Her classmate Michele Pitts wrote a sensitive and sensible account of the black experience at Whitman. She explained to white readers that, "Because most blacks don't feel quite comfortable with most of the white students, they soon gravitate together, their common bond being blackness."[88]

To some degree, all of the region's independent colleges struggled to increase their minority enrollments and to deal with racial issues. At Willamette University, for example, a few blacks formed a Black Student Union in 1968 that pushed an agenda similar to the one the BSU voiced at Whitman. At both institutions, the admissions office increased efforts to recruit more minority students, the administration sought to improve campus conditions for non-whites, and the BSU and others sought to establish a minority program. Alumni publications at both schools sought to explain racial issues. But Willamette in 1971 had a ten-session seminar series entitled "Black-White Uptight," which attracted about thirty faculty members and administrators and several blacks; no similar event occurred at Whitman. Moreover, being closer to a metropolitan area—Portland—and thus to a larger black population, Willamette was able to call upon more outside black leaders in an attempt to increase racial awareness.[89]

The concerns voiced by college communities, especially in the early 1970s, about the need for minority professors and students brought some progress. Responding to various pressures, Whitman, like other regional schools, continued to seek ways to become more diverse. Because of the efforts by minority students, professors, and others, racial attitudes at Whitman, as in the nation, slowly improved. In 1948 independent women had sponsored a formal dance with the theme of "In de Evenin'." Figures of "a Negro banjo player and his girl friend were hung from the wall on gay pink streamers"; a smiling black face was on the cover of the dance program.[90] In more recent times some Greek organizations conducted "slave auctions." The end of such insensitive practices demonstrated that the campus had become more sympathetic to the feelings of the school's racial minority.

Conservative Whitman and a Controversial War

In the 1960s opposition to Whitman's parietal rules attracted more student involvement than did the opposition to the Vietnam War. But the war's opponents played a significant role on the campus and in the community. Across the nation, much of the organized opposition to the Vietnam War originated on college campuses and spread to urban centers. This was the local situation as well, a fact that the *Pioneer* noted in 1969: "Whitman College was the center of [anti-war] activity in Walla Walla."[91] A tiny minority of the college's professors and students denounced the war as early as 1965, but a close reading of the *Pioneer* indicates that most of the opposition occurred between 1967 and 1970.

During these years of greatest activity against the Vietnam War and the Selective Service System (SSS), at no point were the majority of the campus community in the opposition ranks. Many students, professors, and administrators supported the war, and even more were apathetic. But the war's opponents included campus leaders, who spoke, wrote, and organized, a consistent reminder of their cause.

The majority of Walla Wallans supported the war, and their negative reaction to Whitman's anti-war activists had important consequences. In no other period was there so much local opposition to the college as during the period from 1965 to 1975. Campus anti-war sentiments were a major factor explaining the city's hostility, but so were the appearance and practice of a counterculture: the students' unconventional dress, foul language, marijuana smoking, relaxed sexual code, and vocal support for such radicals as Malcolm X and the Black Panthers. Some townspeople, especially those who read certain editions of the *Pioneer*, often expressed discontent with the college and sometimes published their criticism in the *Walla Walla Union-Bulletin*; for example, one patriotic and religious critic of a Whitman-led anti-war march in late 1965 wondered what the professors were teaching. An outraged businessman urged the community to join him in refusing to advertise in the *Pioneer* because it was "the biggest piece of junk."[92] Townspeople, who blamed Whitman students for introducing radicalism and marijuana to Walla Walla High School, were outspoken in their objections to campus radicals—faculty members and students—and urged the trustees to discipline them. Members of the campus community responded by denouncing Walla Wallans for their conservatism and intolerance.

During this period of hard feelings, a few professors observed that the strained relationship between town and gown seemed similar to the noted long-standing hostility between Portland and Reed College. But even those Walla Wallans most hostile to student activism found Whitman students in general to be likable and appreciated the fact that campus buildings, unlike those at many other institutions, were not marred with graffiti.

At Whitman, as at most campuses, opposition to the Vietnam War developed slowly. In 1965 a faculty panel discussion of the conflict drew only a small audience, most of whom supported the American military effort. In late December of that year, Whitman's Committee for Peace in Vietnam organized a march from the campus to the courthouse. Observers counted only eighty marchers moving silently along Main Street. Because the deans watched the ceremonies at the courthouse, a rumor quickly arose that these administrators supplied the names of the marchers to the FBI. Five years later a Chicago newspaper checked the validity of the story and learned that no names had been taken. The deans explained that they had watched the demonstration because of a campus rumor that other students, opposed to the marchers, would harrass them.[93]

Whitman's limited interest in anti-war speakers and marches was a typical reaction, for across the country most age groups supported President Lyndon B. Johnson's pursuit of the war in Vietnam. In 1967 his administration removed the automatic exemption of college students from the draft, a decision that only slightly increased campus anti-war sentiment. The SSS now conducted a draft like the one it had administered during the Korean War. Resourceful Whitman men, like those on other campuses, found ways to avoid induction into the army; for example, many joined the Peace Corps following graduation, and even more attended graduate school. While few students were drafted, a larger number enlisted, mostly in the navy or air force. Older professors commented that there was less enthusiasm for military service in the Vietnam War than there had been for service in the Korean War.

At many liberal arts schools, including Pomona, Willamette, and Middlebury, some students challenged the presence of the Reserve Officers' Training Corps (ROTC). Having failed to obtain an ROTC unit during the Korean War, Whitman was spared such a struggle over a military unit on campus. Furthermore, it did not lose large numbers of males to the military in the 1960s as it had in the 1950s, so there was no economic reason for it to seek an ROTC program.

During the late 1960s a minority of Whitman students marched against the war, held peace vigils, attended a rally where a few either burned or seemed to burn their draft cards, boycotted classes, listened to presentations by conscientious objectors, and signed anti-war petitions offered by faculty members and classmates. Whitman activists hosted David Harris, a Stanford student who was a leader of the national struggle against the draft. In 1965 a few students joined the radical Students for a Democratic Society, a group strongly opposing the war and the draft. Students established the Moratorium Committee, which sponsored panel discussions and town meetings. Sympathetic with the goals of the anti-war groups, a growing minority of professors spoke against the war.

There were more campus protests in 1968 than in any other single year; in the spring of that year the *Pioneer* described the sophomore class as "hyperactive."[94] Activists most mentioned in the school newspaper were: Mike Miller, Michael de Grasse, Charles Lawrence, Ian Lind, Kadi Sprengle, Richard Zahler, Meda Chesney, Michael McChesney, Phil Boss, and Davey Current.

Ultimately, the war in Vietnam, America's longest, would split the nation; only the Civil War had been more divisive. In January 1968 the Tet offensive proved that the North Vietnamese had the capacity to attack points all over South Vietnam. American enthusiasm for the war diminished. This was also the case in Walla Walla, but the ramifications of the Tet offensive created less local excitement than an April confontation in which Whitman students blocked navy recruiters from gaining access to the SUB. The sit-in tactic employed by students against military or industrial recruiters was similar to that used by students at other institutions.

The college's sit-in originated in response to a statement made by SSS director General Lewis B. Hershey in October 1967, announcing that local draft boards "may reopen the classification of anyone involved in disruptive demonstrations interfering with recruitment into the armed forces." His ill-advised pronouncement created discord at many campuses; Whitman was no exception. In January 1968 the school's student congress unanimously passed a forceful resolution: "In order to protect the constitutional rights of [Whitman] students, the ASWC Student Congress request that military recruiters henceforth be banned from the campus until recission of the Hershey statement is made."[95]

The faculty and the administration opposed Hershey's policy as well, but rejected the student resolution. In March the faculty's academic council, President Chester Maxey, and Dean Kenyon Knopf stressed the "principle of the open campus": recruiters should not be banned because the campus should be open to all points of view. The academic council warned, however, that if military recruiters reported any Whitman students to their draft boards in accordance with Hershey's statement, it would then favor closing the campus to the recruiters. At the same time, Knopf assured students that the college would not interfere "with a lawful demonstration against recruiters" and that the recruiters' schedule would be public knowledge.[96] Some activists planned to confront military recruiters if they appeared, and rumors about what would happen when activists met servicemen swept the excited campus.

In early April the college held an emotional memorial service in Cordiner Hall in honor of Dr. Martin Luther King, who had been assassinated on April 4. To a surprisingly small audience, the featured speaker—a local black minister—expressed outrage over the murder of the great civil rights leader. At the conclusion of the ceremony, about two hundred persons from the campus and the community marched to the courthouse, where speakers again honored Dr. King. Back on campus, King's opposition to the Vietnam War and the non-violent boycotts and sit-ins employed by his organization entered into numerous campus conversations.

Within a week after this event about twenty-five seated students blocked the driveway leading to the SUB against navy recruiters. Dean Scribner told the sit-in participants, who had carefully planned this action, that many in the Whitman community sympathized with their goals but opposed their tactics. If they did not move, he warned, they faced dismissal or suspension. All of the students moved from the driveway, except for Michael de Grasse and Charles Lawrence. News of the sit-in brought curious onlookers from all parts of the campus. Meanwhile, the council on student affairs, which had anticipated the sit-in, held an emergency meeting and prepared a statement, emphasizing that those blocking the recruiters "had contravened the college policy regarding the principle of the open campus." After the sit-in was more than two hours old, Dean Knopf informed the two men blocking the driveway, as well as other students standing nearby, that anyone blocking the recruiters would be suspended until he or she submitted a statement of willingness to comply with the open-campus policy. Thirteen students defied the dean and joined the two protesters. The college then summoned the Walla Walla police, parked nearby. Chief of Police A. L. Watts warned the protesters to move or be arrested; all departed except for Lawrence and de Grasse. The police arrested the two men, escorted them to a patrol car, and charged them with "unlawful assembly and disobeying an order to disperse after ordered by a police officer." Both de Grasse and Lawrence were released that same afternoon on $100 bail. Meanwhile, the recruiters entered the SUB and found about thirty student protestors reclining in front of the recruiters' table, leaving only an eighteen-inch passage.

All fifteen of the students who had blocked the driveway soon informed the administration of their willingness to comply with the open-campus policy. County prosecuting attorney Arthur Eggers summarized the event for the Whitman trustees, noting that he had received letters suggesting that he permit the two arrested offend-

Michael de Grasse and Charles Lawrence were arrested soon after this photograph was taken. Both the sit-in and the police involvement were highly controversial issues on the Whitman campus.

ers "to forfeit bail and thereby avoid having to fingerprint them, which would give them a permanent record in the FBI files." He wrote that he was also under "a great deal of pressure to prosecute them, and ask the court to impose lengthy jail sentences." He recommended that the trustees write guidelines for the faculty and students. Eggers also submitted a letter from the local police chief, who stated that ten on-duty officers and seven off-duty officers had been assigned to handle the student demonstration. In fact, the entire police force either had come to the edge of the campus or had been placed on standby. The police department's activities had cost the city nearly $340.[97]

Many campus voices responded to the controversial sit-in. The trustees rejected Eggers' appeal to write restrictions. The *Pioneer* denounced the decision to call the police "to deal with problems between students and administration" and charged that this action was "an indictment of the college's inability or unwillingness to deal with the problem in a less extreme, more constructive manner."[98] Some endorsed this criticism, but those favoring the open-campus principle supported the administration's action. Walter Brattain, who had returned to his alma mater to teach half-time, expressed disgust with the protestors for "interfering with the rights of other students." He stated that in the 1920s his classmates had not put up with non-conforming students; in those days "we would have dunked in the campus lake those lying in front of the car to cool them off!"[99] President Maxey believed that most of those who took action against the recruiters were members of the Students for a Democratic Society (SDS). In his autobiography, he emphasized that this group had not received "the requisite official permission to operate at Whitman, and for that reason I was pressured to some extent to suppress it. This I declined to do. I believed that suppression might work in reverse, and give the SDS a holy cause to espouse. Doing battle against authority might provide a rallying point for extremist students and also some of the hotheads on the faculty."[100] The council of students, seeking to avoid another confrontation when marine recruiters arrived in May, assigned them to the placement office in Memorial Hall.

Shortly after the event in which the police were summoned to the Whitman campus, Columbia University called the police to clear five buildings occupied by about a thousand individuals, most of whom were following the leadership of the SDS. The protest at Whitman had been mild compared to that at Columbia, where 150 students and police were injured, and where an SDS-led student strike ended the semester. In the fall, radical students at Columbia and elsewhere disrupted classes; Whitman did not experience such behavior and its faculty, like most professors nationally, disapproved of disruptive tactics.

The Whitman faculty, responding to the Selective Service System, held a special meeting in May 1968. Professor Robert Fluno emotionally pointed both to the events at Columbia and to student unrest around the world; he argued the need to keep Whitman operating, insisted that the college be under traditional control and not be run by the students, and encouraged his colleagues to cooperate with students when they had legitimate grievances. His speech played a major role in getting faculty approval of a letter addressed to President Johnson, General Hershey, and others. It opposed Hershey's October statement and endorsed the open-campus principle. A minority of the faculty members voted against the letter, which was signed by the chairman of the faculty, President Chester Maxey, and student body president Peter Snow. The college had officially taken a stand on a significant issue arising from the Vietnam War.

During the remaining month of the spring semester, a few students conducted a fast and vigil, and a larger number of students and professors discussed the sit-in and the use of police. Activists pointed to the bitter confrontation at Columbia University, and worried that Whitman's leaders had set a bad precedent for their campus by calling upon the police.

Opposition to the war continued into 1968. In March students and faculty members made an extensive effort to get signatures on a resolution opposing the country's policy in Vietnam; to their displeasure only twenty-five percent of the student body and only thirty-three percent of the faculty signed the document. Student activists criticized their apathetic classmates and professors, and campaigned on the campus and in the city for the nomination of Senator Eugene McCarthy, an anti-war presidential candidate. The champions of this Democrat enjoyed some success; at the least, they made national politics more prominent on the Whitman campus than at any time since 1960, when John F. Kennedy had won the presidency.

In the fall of 1968 the Whitman Resistance, an organization with a membership of about thirty men and women, vigorously opposed the draft. It held a major rally in November, in which speakers, including Phil Boss, heatedly denounced the SSS and the war.

Arriving at Walla Walla High School to distribute anti-war and draft resistance materials to students, a dozen members of the Resistance, including Meda Chesney, were met by three school administrators who screamed at the activists, demanding that they get off of their sidewalk. Policemen in two cruisers had been summoned and heard the principal instruct them to control the Whitman group. A school administrator judged that the college students were "hippies masquerading as average teenagers" and were "exposing the kids to trash." Chesney reported that some high school students took the leaflets, and concluded that the "principal, seeing the leafleters as threats to his sovereignty over the minds of the students, was unwilling to ask why the Resistance was there."[101]

High school teachers and administrators levied charges that Whitman was radical and unpatriotic, expressing fear that the college activists would demonstrate against the sophomores' springtime ROTC parade. Although Whitman lacked its own ROTC unit, the required ROTC unit at the high school came under attack from both militant students and Whitman faculty members. First-year high school social science teacher Dean Shoemaker, a recent Whitman alumnus, later recalled that, to prevent possible action against the parade, the high school administration called in the police to block nearby roads.

The war continued to be a major campus issue. Students in 1968 frequently discussed the war and the draft, although a *Pioneer* editor wrote, on September 25, 1969, that the war had not yet come to the college: "Few Whitman men have been drafted and few have died in Vietnam." Furthermore, the deaths of local young men created little notice because the college was "far away from the Walla Walla community." But opposition to the war was building. At one point the Viet Cong flag even floated over the steps of Cordiner Hall.

Richard Nixon had been elected president of the United States in November of 1968, and when his administration changed the draft to a lottery system, more Whitman men joined the anti-war move-

Whitman students participated in the national Moratorium Day in the fall of 1969. Students opposed to the Vietnam War handed out leaflets in the city; an estimated two hundred members of the Whitman community, joined by townspeople, marched to the courthouse for a rally.

ment. The college, the faculty, and the local chapter of the SDS continued to provide draft counseling. Professors wrote to draft boards in efforts to assist students in avoiding induction.

"Moratorium Day," October 15, 1969, was a major national protest against the war. At Whitman, the ASWC supported a program featuring faculty and student speakers. Senior Bill Mitchell saw little purpose in the war, saying: "If we must die then let us nobly die." He charged the United States with being inconsistent because it had been inactive when Soviet troops invaded Czechoslovakia in August 1968.[102]

On this occasion, as at other times during this period, the Moratorium Committee and others sponsored a march from the campus to the courthouse. A few professors and townspeople participated, and occasionally sidewalk observers booed or cursed the marchers.

W. W. Switzer, a retired Methodist minister, attended some Whitman classes and often spoke against the war, winning the admiration of many students and professors.

One outraged citizen on Main Street proclaimed that, if he had a gun, he would shoot the "unpatriotic sons-of-bitches." At the courthouse, several marchers, including Professor George Ball and an elderly Walla Wallan, Judge W. W. Switzer, denounced the war and urged peace. Popular with campus reformers, Switzer, a former Methodist minister in his eighties, attended Whitman classes. A defender of the Wobblies in his youth, he was a featured speaker at courthouse rallies, praising the demonstrators and condemning racism, elitism, ignorance, and war. Inspired by their elderly and activist classmate, a few students created "Switzer Park" on the campus, but the college soon paved it into a parking lot.

President Donald Sheehan refused to join other national leaders in signing anti-war declarations prepared for Moratorium Day. While the campus understood his opposition to any official political statement by the college, it did not know that Sheehan wrote to President Nixon about the national protest, repeating the point that "educational institutions should not become politicized" and reminding Nixon of the "divisive . . . effects of the war." He stated his desire not to be "associated with a demonstration whose mean-

ing will for many extend beyond the issue of withdrawal and which
will offer the opportunity to ascribe sordid and false motives to
American foreign policy, indeed, to voice a denunciation of American government and society in general." He worried about a precipi-
tous military withdrawal and concluded: "My purpose is only to
offer you the small comfort . . . of my support and confidence."[103]

On the other hand, a 1928 graduate noted that prestigious colleges protested the war and believed that Whitman belonged in that
rank. She would even be inclined to give a larger financial gift to
the alumni fund if she heard about a few anti-war demonstrations
at her alma mater.[104]

In the spring semester of 1970 the anti-war movement received
nearly as much attention at Whitman as it had two years earlier. In
February Todd Boley led a group of his classmates that harrassed
military recruiters. Some administrators warned that the police might
be summoned to end the disruption, but most participants considered this to be only a threat.

In 1971 protestors against the war in Vietnam leave the campus for a march to the
county courthouse.

Two events in May 1970 increased the anti-war protest at the nation's campuses: Nixon ordered U.S. troops into Cambodia; and, soon after, the National Guard killed four students at Kent State University in Ohio. These actions brought more Whitman students into the anti-war ranks than any previous events had. Religious counselor Roy Hoover heard angry students discussing a march "in which they would smash store windows and do other kinds of property damage in an attempt to gain the media's attention."[105] Some others wanted to apply yellow paint to the tanks parked at the local armory.

Students who were more constructively inclined joined faculty members in protesting the two May events. Late in the month they raised money to send a delegation of four students, two faculty members, and a townsman to Washington, D.C., where the group communicated the growing campus outrage to members of Congress and Justice William O. Douglas. Whitman's distinguished alumnus advised his visitors to get involved locally against the conflict; Congresswoman Catherine May rejected the delegation's mission; and Senator Henry "Scoop" Jackson expressed his support for the war.

In late September 1971 former student body president Alex MacLeod, now working for Whitman as director of the campus news service, learned that President Nixon was coming to the Walla Walla airport to transfer from a jet to a helicopter for a visit to the nuclear facility at Hanford.[106] Entertained by the possibilities, MacLeod telephoned the White House and asked if Nixon would like to receive a Whitman football jersey. Surprisingly, White House aides responded favorably, perhaps because Nixon was generally unpopular on college campuses, particularly since the U.S. incursion into Cambodia and the Kent State killings. MacLeod then asked the football team, just prior to a Saturday night game, if they would like to give Nixon a jersey. Again to his surprise, the team agreed; he quickly purchased a jersey and got a woman to sew "Nixon" and a large number "1" on the garment.

Nixon's visit brought two diametrically opposed responses. On campus, anti-war protestors flew the American flag backwards in protest, while at the airport, thousands of cheering spectators greeted the president. The crowd watched as the team captains presented the jersey to Nixon, explaining that they were making him an honorary captain and awarding him the jersey because of their es-

One of the most famous Whitman photographs shows President Nixon in 1971 receiving a homemade football jersey from co-captains John Davis, Bob Crabb, Steve Washburn, and Bob Reisig.

teem for him and his support of football. After engaging in small talk with the captains, the president graciously responded: "It's the closest I ever came to making the team. It's the greatest compliment I've ever received on one of these trips." He added: "I deeply believe in the small, independent college." Meanwhile, some Whitman students belonging to the Young Americans for Freedom picketed him because of his forthcoming visit to China.[107]

From New York to San Francisco, major newspapers carried the photograph of Nixon accepting the jersey. Probably no picture ever published brought more attention to the college. But this was not the end to the story. Many in the Whitman community expressed delight with the gift to the president and the resulting publicity, but those who disapproved of Nixon thought that the students had disgraced the college. Two activists opposed to Nixon and the Vietnam War, Doug Eglington and Eric Pryne, urged the student body officers to take this opportunity to express, in a creative way, their outrage with the escalation of the war. On May 1, 1972, the four officers did so, passing a resolution that, because the president had "not acted on his campaign promise to end American involvement in Indochina," it was therefore "resolved that we request that Richard Nixon return the Whitman football jersey bestowed in his honor last fall." [108]

This story created considerable excitement. Many people, especially alumni, unfairly denounced the entire college community for insisting that the jersey be returned. An excited student congress, by a vote of sixteen to five, censured the student body officers "for gross misrepresentation of the student body in a knowing and secretive manner." An attempt to censure the football team failed. The players and coaches immediately wrote Nixon that the student body disavowed the plea for the return of the jersey, noted that he had received the jersey because of his interest in football, and added: "Your decisions in other areas, although we might disagree with them, do not affect your enthusiasm for football." They remained "honored and proud" to have him as an honorary co-captain. The local newspaper editorialized on April 30, 1972, that the student body officers did not speak for the student body and had engaged in a "sophomoric act." Many thought the whole matter was hilarious. The White House responded to the clamor over the jersey by stating that "there would be no official comment." [109]

As the war slowly wound down in the 1970s, so did the protest movement. Whitman students did not strike against the war, nor did they block a major street through the campus as happened at Colorado College and on other campuses; and the college did not make any official resolution against the war. President Sheehan's oft-repeated assertion that "Whitman did not have a foreign policy" generally pleased most members of the community. But a disgruntled minority disagreed, recalling the precedent set by the letter that the faculty, President Maxey, and the ASWC had jointly sent in opposition to General Hershey's statement, and insisting that institutions had a responsibility to speak out against an immoral and senseless war. Those opposed to Nixon's conduct of the war cheered the resignation in 1973 of Vice President Spiro Agnew—who had vigorously denounced the nation's anti-war students—and the resignation in 1974 of Nixon himself. Many expressed relief in 1975 when the American government withdrew its military presence from South Vietnam. Thus, one of the most divisive international events in American history ended; the healing process began everywhere, including within the Whitman community.

The next issue that would arouse students to protest was that they were not consulted in the decision to discontinue the college's intercollegiate football program in 1976. Watching the students block Memorial Hall and criticize the college's president in the jammed Cordiner Hall foyer, a few faculty members were dismayed that the football decision created a greater uproar than the Kent State killings had, and that students seemed more concerned about a beleaguered sport than they were with crucial national affairs. To some experienced student-watchers, this over-reaction to the football decision seemed to indicate a return to normal campus life.

Emerging Feminism in the Early 1970s

One of the important national and campus movements in the 1970s was the effort to bring about equality between the sexes. The background of this ongoing struggle at Whitman is difficult to trace. Parts of this story can be found in the school's publications, but a thorough history will only be possible after oral interviews are conducted. Although the struggle for equality was slow—and therefore frustrating to feminists—the available evidence indicates that a foundation for reform had been established by 1975.

In the mid-1950s the purpose of the Associated Women of Whitman College (AWWC), which included every woman student, was to initiate and promote "regulations designed for the best interests of women students" and for "maintaining high standards of conduct in dormitories and among students."[110] Until the great changes affecting women in the late 1960s, the AWWC appointed boards and councils to carry out its mandates, including regulations of members set forth in the Coed Code. A different attitude was expressed in 1967, when Dean Joan Hodgson urged leaders of the AWWC (and others) to read Betty Friedan's *The Feminine Mystique*. After the organization lost its judicial role in the 1970s, it lacked a definite purpose. The 1975 catalog simply stated that the AWWC sought ways "to develop mature social attitudes and responsibilities." But in the early 1970s it would help launch the women's movement at Whitman by initiating programs that brought attention to relevant issues.

In 1970 Mortar Board sponsored a panel discussion of women's liberation. Participant Sally Underwood, a faculty wife, lamented that the mass media portrayed housewives as taking "great pride in having a shining toilet bowl when the bridge club visited."[111] Other groups, including the YW–YMCA, would continue to push the "humanist goals of the women's movement."[112]

Male domination slowly began to decrease. This significant change was in part owing to the evolution and eventual elimination of the traditional policy of *in loco parentis*, with its implicit sex discrimination. But other factors played a role as well, including the national feminist movement—exemplified by the National Organization for Women (NOW), organized in 1966—and well-publicized Congressional hearings on discrimination in education conducted by Oregon congresswoman Edith Green in 1970.

Radical feminism failed to be a significant force at Whitman or other small campuses, but moderate feminists at Whitman, like those at other liberal arts institutions, advocated political and legal changes in the status of American women. Many students and faculty members endorsed the Equal Rights Amendment to the U.S. Constitution, and rejoiced when it received large majorities in the House of Representatives in 1971 and in the Senate in 1972. The amendment's inability to win ratification by three-quarters of the states rankled those Whitman supporters who had thought that the ERA would become the law of the land.

The *Whitman Alumnus* of November 1974 took note of three "new phenomena of campus life," identifying and summarizing "the Women's Center, the women's sports program, and the academic study of women and their changing personal view of their worth to themselves and to society." Located in Reynolds Hall, the women's center attracted twenty-five women volunteers. Professor Deborah DuNann taught classes on "the psychology of love and sexuality." The women's movement had arrived at Whitman: "Women's questions are in the air."[113]

In the 1970s feminist books and periodicals were added to the library and were sold in the bookstore. Influenced by the national movement, Whitman women pushed for the addition of more female professors. During the administration of Robert Skotheim, several women would be added to the faculty—in part because there were now more women with advanced degrees—and would have a much greater voice in shaping college policy.

Other Political Concerns

In the early 1970s opposition to the Vietnam War had waned at Whitman, as at other campuses, and students of various political persuasions put their energy into the environmental movement. Newspapers published at Pacific Northwest liberal arts colleges carried more material on regional pollution than they did on the controversial war in Southeast Asia. But enthusiastic Whitman conservationists limited their activity to campus; they did not march through town to express their convictions to the public as had the school's advocates of civil rights and opponents of the war.

In 1969 Congress passed the National Environmental Policy Act, and in the following year it established the Environmental Protection Agency to enforce environmental regulations passed in the late 1960s. College students everywhere praised laws such as those protecting endangered species, limiting pesticide use, and establishing maximum levels for the emission of pollutants into the air. Whitman students, like their counterparts at other schools, observed Earth Day, supported the work of advocate Ralph Nader, and endorsed recycling, organic gardening, and solar power. Students and sympathetic professors pushed to include environmental issues in history, sociology, and geology courses.

Professor Deborah DuNann was a leading campus feminist who worked within the system for change. Because of her and likeminded members of the Whitman community, male domination slowly gave way.

Survival, a campus-based ecology action group formed in 1970 and spearheaded by student John Markoff, urged the campus and the community to boycott certain consumer goods detrimental to the environment, including detergents stocked in the SUB. Sensitive to local as well as national issues, the group urged green spaces around the campus, rather than parking lots. The *Narrator* criticized the city for removing old trees on Isaacs Avenue to provide additional traffic lanes.

The students of the early 1970s showed increasing awareness about hunger as well as ecology. In November 1971 four hundred students fasted and raised $600 for refugees of war-torn East Pakistan. Concerned about rural poverty in eastern Washington, the campus YW–YMCA conducted a conference entitled "The Faces of Poverty," emphasizing the poor conditions of farm workers; acknowledging the efforts of César Chavez, they advocated a boycott of table grapes.

Assessing the period, Professor George Ball observed that "students felt a strong call to public service" and that "the campus was definitely more involved in public issues, including fears of overpopulation, perhaps more than at any time since."[114]

Because the state penitentiary is located in Walla Walla, students have been stimulated to reflect on capital punishment and to participate in the institution's reform programs. Intermittently, students have written about and protested against capital punishment; Jeff Moore argued that its practice was "a product of ignorance, conservatism, and emotion."[115] Some students vigorously protested the executions of Don White in 1964 and Tom Music in 1972. An opponent of capital punishment, John Lewallen, debated Governor Albert Rosellini on television and received considerable support from the Whitman community.

In the early 1970s prison reform attracted students and faculty members. Sociologist Lee Bowker responded to the public concern of warden Bobby Rhay, a 1947 Whitman graduate, about drug abuse at the prison's hospital. Bowker, who had taken a lead role in investigating drug activities at Whitman, urged his sociology students to volunteer in a prison program. French professor Dale Cosper and physics professor Craig Gunsul succeeded Bowker as leaders of a program that took scores of students to the institution for sessions with volunteer inmates based on William Glasser's "reality therapy"

Professor George Ball, who taught Biblical literature and served as a religious counselor, was a thoughtful proponent of peace during the Vietman War. With his wife, Nancy, he created the "cell group" program, in which professors met weekly with small groups of students for vigorous discussions of social and collegiate issues.

approach. Speaking for many student volunteers, Mike Rona stated: "My basic motivation for getting involved in this was to help these guys and help myself. It's a two-way street."[116] Professors recalled that the students were motivated by curiosity and a desire to help inmates learn life skills.[117]

The Decline of the Greek System

Many in the Whitman community judged that the criticism of the Greek system on campus was nearly as intense as the protest over a distant war. Between 1966 and 1973 this system, which had been such a significant part of the college's history, lost influence. At small colleges nationally, fraternities and sororities had traditionally provided nearly all of the schools' social life and dominated campus politics. But at a time when individualism seemed highly desirable, students often thought that the fraternal experience was irrelevant.

Ever since its establishment at Whitman, the Greek system had been criticized by those who argued that fraternities and sororities were frivolous, elitist, undemocratic, or anti-intellectual, and did not mesh with the college's mission. The faculty and administration periodically deplored the immaturity of "hell week." To improve campus conditions, detractors urged the elimination of the Greeks, and if that were impossible, then at least the elimination of hell week and the delay of rush so that freshmen could get a better understanding of the system and make wiser pledgeships (or remain independent).

During the late 1960s the Greek system came under the greatest criticism it had encountered in Whitman's history. Many independent students and some members of the faculty predicted—and worked for—the death of all of the Greek chapters. The intense attack reduced Greek membership. In 1966 seventy-seven percent of the women and sixty-nine percent of the men had been affiliated; in 1973 those percentages had declined to forty-eight percent of the women and forty-two percent of the men. Other liberal arts colleges reported similar decreases in Greek affiliation. For example, at Willamette University, where the Greek system was nearly as old as Whitman's, the fraternities and sororities heard the same types of criticism that were expressed at Whitman. Greek membership slipped to fifty-three percent of the 1969 Willamette student body. An editor at Willamette explained: "Perhaps it is obvious that the Greek system as it is now constituted is not meeting the needs or desires of as many students as it used to."[118]

Everywhere, detractors raised traditional arguments against the Greeks. Although some individuals admitted that they had joined chapters solely to enjoy collegiate social life, young people in the late 1960s showed less interest in conforming to a fraternal group, and colleges were providing an enriched social life that made Greek membership less significant. Another factor in the decline, the national civil rights movement, drew attention to the practice of discrimination in many American institutions. The fight for racial equality shed light on the questionable membership practices of fraternal groups, and those fraternities and sororities with restrictions based on race and religion were widely condemned. At many schools these practices came under investigation, especially the way that some national organizations restricted the ability of their local chapters to pledge Jews, blacks, Asians, and Latinos. Whitman students would be among those who sought to rectify this unfortunate situation, locally and nationally.

While many worked to reform the system, others sought to terminate it. Writing for the *Pioneer* or holding student body offices, independent students, like student body president Alex MacLeod, urged students not to participate in rush. A few sorority members published negative letters about the Greek system in the *Pioneer*.

In the 1960s the campus newspaper paid more attention to the racial practices of fraternal organizations than it did to the anti-war protests. Next to the struggle over the parietal rules, students gave more time to racial clauses imposed by national headquarters on fraternities and sororities than they did to any other campus issue.

The faculty and students of Whitman did not begin their denunciation of discrimination in the 1960s. A decade earlier, some students and faculty members had decried the restrictive practices of some Greek organizations. These restrictions were not uniformly applied. Phi Delta Theta, for example, pledged a Jewish student who became the chapter's president; Robb Ball recalled that "the chapter was so strong nationally that it was able to disregard" the racial clause.[119]

But the local Sigma Chi chapter reported difficulties in its extended efforts to revise its racial clause. Early in 1961 the chapter informed the faculty that it had been "opposing national regulations that have forced us to exclude certain groups from membership." The letter continued: "We still maintain that modern sociology, biology, and psychology have destroyed theories of racial inequality upon which the so-called 'white clause' is based."[120] The chapter feared that Whitman might ban the fraternity because of the restrictive clause.

Professor Robert Whitner, who wanted to save the fraternity system, praised students for joining the national movement to end religious and racial discrimination. He judged that, by not assisting students, the "faculty and officers of the college have tacitly approved . . . of discrimination."[121] In March 1961 the faculty passed legislation warning that groups must not discriminate on racial or religious grounds but, acknowledging that local Greek delegates worked to end discriminatory rules at their national conventions, took no action against any group. Student government also refused to challenge discrimination by Greek chapters. Local alumni advisers of fraternal organizations, however, feared that this mild faculty action about discrimination might "penalize the local chapters who have been making real efforts to remove these clauses."[122]

In 1964 a Stanford University official wrote to Whitman leaders, urging them to follow his school and cooperate with groups seeking to remove the discriminatory clauses rather than banning the

Greek organizations. The Whitman community learned that public colleges and universities in California were under a state ruling requiring them to end discrimination clauses in 1964. This information had an impact.

In 1965 the attack on the discrimination clauses intensified. In March Professor Robert McKenzie and student Bruce Jones, chairman of the campus friends of the Student Non-Violent Coordinating Committee (SNCC), led a march in sympathy with those who were struggling for racial equality in Selma, Alabama. This march attracted about three hundred participants, some of whom, outraged by racial conditions in the American South, complained that Whitman was permitting its Greek groups to discriminate. At about the same time, President Louis Perry warned the Greeks to end discrimination, predicting that the faculty would probably pressure them to attain this goal.

In the fall semester the faculty identified Sigma Chi and Phi Delta Theta as two fraternities that had not succeeded in removing "discriminatory procedures in the selection of their members." The faculty insisted that the college be informed of any changes resulting from the fraternities' next national meetings, which the faculty would then review.[123]

Student body president Bob Wallace, a member of Phi Delta Theta, pointed out that his fraternity and Sigma Chi were not allowed to pledge blacks, a situation that, he judged, classmates and teachers found to be intolerable. Wallace revealed that "each chapter is still forced to discriminate," but he assured the college that both groups were working to remove these offensive clauses.[124] Wallace wanted Whitman to cooperate with other schools in ending fraternal discrimination. Dean Whitner also continued to support the efforts of local chapters to end discriminatory practices.[125]

In October, the student congress—following Wallace's leadership—by a vote of twelve to two sent letters to student body presidents of all schools listing Phi Delta Theta and Sigma Chi chapters. Wallace explained: "The purpose was to get these schools to join in a collective attack on the discriminatory policies of the two national fraternities."[126] In November, the student congress asked the faculty to set the fall of 1968 for Phi Delta Theta and the following fall for Sigma Chi "as the dates after which discrimination must be ended."

Thus, each group was given a period of time spanning two national conventions in which to remove its discriminatory policies. Bruce Jones praised his classmates for taking a "moral step," and asserted that they had an opportunity "to clean up discrimination in [their] own back yard."[127] At the same time, the faculty formed a committee to study discriminatory policies of local Greek chapters. Professors wanted to discover how much freedom these groups had in choosing their own members.

Wallace's attempt to have Whitman be a national leader in ending Greek discrimination found little support from other institutions; only twelve of the 182 schools receiving his letter offered to cooperate. Eventually, forty-seven schools responded to Wallace; eleven student governments replied that they lacked interest in changing membership practices because their institutions enrolled only a few blacks. For example, one respondent replied, "The anti-discrimination movement has not hit the U. of Montana yet."[128]

More encouraging to those who sought change was that the Whitman faculty unanimously decided "to outlaw the existence of any student social organizations . . . unable to take into membership particular students of their choice because of those students' race, color, or religion." Further, in February 1966 the faculty adopted a resolution calling for the end "to discrimination practices" by September 1969.[129] The faculty identified Phi Delta Theta and Sigma Chi and three sororities—Delta Delta Delta, Kappa Alpha Theta, and Kappa Kappa Gamma—as not being in compliance with its new rule.

The major problem for the sorority chapters, professors discovered, was the limitation which their recommendation system placed on membership. Each of these three groups was not allowed to pledge any girl who did not have a recommendation from a former active member of that sorority. This recommendation system received considerable campus discussion, including a devastating critique in a 1968 letter to the *Pioneer* by Robin Kendrick.[130]

Alarmed by the ASWC's letter to other colleges and universities seeking to organize a reform and by the faculty's actions, a few national or regional leaders of the sororities came to Whitman to consult with administrators about the faculty deadline. These women charged that intolerant professors and the "radical student government" opposed sororities. Wallace's letter had given Whitman "a radical tag"; sorority visitors and letter writers maintained that this negative label made it more difficult for representatives from local sororities to bring about reform at national conventions.[131] Such sentiment influenced the eight-to-seven vote against the ASWC sending a second letter, which would have offered that a Whitman student committee serve as a clearing house for cooperative colleges.

Craig Lesley, the new student body president, whose vote broke the tie against sending a second letter, explained that the original letter had been "misinterpreted by some other colleges as the attempt of a radical student body to overthrow the fraternity system. Whitman sororities were associated with this 'radical' movement despite the fact they were not mentioned in the letter." Fearing that a second letter would be harmful to the three sororities seeking reform, the ASWC opposed it.[132] Alex MacLeod's *Pioneer* editorial disagreed, arguing that the students were retreating from the high ground. Lesley, however, wrote to the national Sigma Chi and Phi Delta Theta organizations, asking for a waiver that "would allow the local chapters to give full membership to minority students."[133]

While the students spent long hours with the local discrimination clauses, they also got involved with distant minority issues. Whitman had its own chapter of the Southern Christian Leadership Conference (SCLC), and raised money for the national organization. In 1965 Jim Owens and another student drove to Americus, Georgia, where they worked to register black voters under the auspices of the SCLC. Some Whitmanites and townspeople sent Owens supportive letters and contributions; others heard him describe his harrowing experiences after he returned. Many of these supporters expressed disgust with conditions in the South and became more deeply committed to the civil rights movement. The ASWC allotted small amounts of money to SNCC, another group battling for black rights, and to César Chavez, an organizer of Latino farm laborers. Student leaders made the choice to assist these groups; they were not reacting to pressure from minority classmates, as the Whitman student body probably had no Latino students at this time and as yet counted only a very few blacks.

In the fall of 1966 the discrimination issue took a more dramatic turn when the campus learned that Reid Yamamoto, a Sigma Chi pledge, could not be initiated because a Spokane attorney had re-

jected his pledge form. Other West Coast Sigma Chi chapters encountered similar difficulties; the one at Stanford broke with the
national organization. Early in 1967 nine Whitman Sigma Chi members, including Rhodes scholar Baker Stocking, disaffiliated. Additional members dropped out, and in late November the local chapter voted to withdraw from the national fraternity after it failed to
obtain a waiver granting "local autonomy in membership selection."[134] In a letter to the faculty signed by fifty-four members explaining why they were disaffiliating, they reported that "Sigma Chi
is structured such that no chapter has the right to initiate whom it
pleases. Each chapter alumnus has absolute veto over membership
selection."[135] These men formed Nu Sigma Chi, dropped the discrimination clause, and received faculty recognition.

Reid Yamamoto's unfortunate story needs retelling. As a freshman, he discovered that Whitman enrolled fewer minority students
than he had known at his rural high school in the Yakima Valley.
And, as a Sigma Chi pledge, Yamamoto learned about the fraternity's racial clause. Informed that he would not be initiated, Yamamoto
recalled that he took it "stoically," but that "it hurt deeply."[136] His
father, who had been interned at Minidoka in the 1940s, had warned
him not to have expectations about Greek membership. Yamamoto expressed pleasure that many Sigma Chi members were angered
by his inability to be initiated, dropped their membership, and
formed Nu Sigma Chi. He understood that this new group did not
have a racial clause, but he did not join it. Yamamoto remained at
Whitman and graduated with a degree in sociology, but he did not
return to his alma mater for twenty-nine years.

The faculty committee on membership selection in fraternities and
sororities, chaired by physics professor Phillip Howland, consulted
with representatives of the five Greek groups that were not in compliance with the 1966 faculty resolution. The so-called "Howland
committee" urged the groups to continue pressuring their nationals to drop their discrimination policies. The delegates from these
five chapters pushed reform. For example, a Whitman professor visiting at Emory University in 1967 was asked by a member of Kappa
Kappa Gamma if his college were "a 'negra' institution." When he
asked why she thought it might be, she snapped that, at a recent
national convention, Whitman delegates had lobbied against the rec-

ommendation system.[137] For many months Greek leaders and alumni testified to the Howland committee—sometimes in a defensive manner—about membership practices and their efforts to bring the groups into compliance with the faculty legislation.

In February 1968 Katherine Levinson wrote to the Washington State Board Against Discrimination that she believed that Kappa Kappa Gamma wanted to pledge her but could not do so because an alumni member refused to grant her a recommendation. She added that she was aware "that there is a past history of anti-Semitism within KKG."[138] Several Whitman students strongly supported her claim of discrimination. Sorority president Liz Tweeddale, however, vigorously denied the charge, emphasizing that her chapter did not practice religious discrimination. Dean Joan Hodgson stated that the sorority had received confirmation of the refusal to recommend Levinson, but the dean insisted that this refusal was not based on religion: a former sorority member had simply refused to endorse Levinson. Professor Howland immediately convened the special committee, which interviewed several individuals and concluded that it "found no evidence that outside influence prevented the sorority from bidding the girl."[139] However, a field representative of the Washington State Board Against Discrimination made an informal report, which—while acknowledging that it had "no jurisdiction since fraternal organizations are exempt from the provisions of the Washington State Law Against Discrimination"—added that, if the case were covered by the law, then the investigator "would recommend a finding of probable cause to believe that Miss Levinson was discriminated against on [the basis of] her religion by . . . the sorority." Howland disagreed with this interpretation.[140]

With the divisive Levinson case in the background, the Howland committee reported in the spring of 1968 that the five fraternities and sororities were probably in compliance with the faculty's resolution, but recommended that "faculty influence" be maintained to make certain that the groups had control over their membership.[141] President Maxey praised the committee's work. In April 1969 the committee now found all of the Greek groups to be in full compliance with the faculty resolution; the faculty voted to accept the committee's finding. The ASWC, however, by a vote of thirteen to zero strongly disagreed with the faculty finding of compliance, passing resolutions asserting that Sigma Chi was allowed to remain on campus despite the facts that it had made "no substantive changes" and that the three sororities had not "meaningfully altered" their recommendation systems. Student body president MacLeod denounced the faculty's vote, suggesting that students, not professors, should sanction student groups. For reasons that aren't clear, the ASWC immediately tempered its resolutions on the faculty's action; two sororities wrote sympathetically to the faculty, calling the ASWC resolutions abrasive.[142]

An unusual attack on the Greek system came in the summer of 1969. Two recent graduates, Jay Broze and Peter Snow, urged freshmen not to participate in rush but to support Greeks seeking to reform their groups. The two former Greeks, who had been campus activists, maintained that the Greeks "show a conspicuous disregard for the welfare of the campus as a whole."[143] The Panhellenic Council's summer letter, however, countered the letter of Broze and Snow, urging all freshmen women to participate in rush. In the opening week of 1969 administrators and student body president MacLeod met with freshmen. MacLeod, who believed that he had won his election "largely on the race issue with fraternities and sororities," condemned the faculty's acceptance of the Howland committee report finding the Greek groups in compliance. The student body president accused the faculty and administration of "institutional moral bankruptcy." He urged the freshman audience not to participate in rush because the Greeks had not accepted responsibility. Many freshmen followed his advice, but there was an "illegal" incident when Greek representatives went through the dormitories urging freshmen to participate in rush. Believing that President Sheehan had sanctioned this pro-Greek action, MacLeod resigned his office in frustration.[144]

Early in 1970 the *Pioneer* reported that twenty-eight Greeks had dropped their membership and wondered "whether this is to be termed as the beginning of the end for Greek organization at Whitman, or merely as the reaction to a transitional period."[145] From scattered corners of the campus came gleeful predictions that the Greek system was in its death throes.

The debate about racism in the Greek system brought about a change on Isaacs Avenue. In 1970 Nu Sigma Chi members, partly in response to alumni pressure, voted to return to Sigma Chi. But a minority of the membership, moving to another house, remained as Nu Sigma Chi; the group expired in 1974 because of declining membership. In the same year, the *Pioneer* attacks on the Greek system diminished. The campus community generally concluded that all the fraternities and sororities now controlled their own membership and that restrictions imposed by the national organizations had ended. Faculty and student concern about the Greek system declined in the early 1970s. The anti-Greek voice was not stilled—it probably never will be—but it lacked the power it had wielded in the 1960s.

In 1975 about fifty percent of the school's men and women students were Greeks; never again would the percentage for either the fraternities or the sororities reach as high as sixty percent. Whitman, like colleges everywhere, was returning to more normal times, but the turmoil of the 1960s had diminished Greek practices and strength forever. A chance for a diverse social life and the opportunity to be elected to student office no longer depended upon having a Greek affiliation.

Assessing the Generation of Student Activists

Although some Whitman students were called radical, this term actually fit only a very few. There was, however, an influential minority of students—sometimes referred to as reformers, protestors, or dissenters, but perhaps best described as activists—who, like no previous student generation, were politically involved. These students spoke, wrote, voted, and organized to bring change. Of course, their degree of political involvement varied enormously: some of them were leaders or otherwise very committed; some of them put in attendance at meetings or rallies or marches; others were generally conservative but moved to action by a particular issue.

To a considerable degree the activists at Whitman, like those at other schools, were focused on ending long-standing regulations such as those concerning housing and dress, and on being appointed to college committees. But, like their fellows across the country, they also became involved in protesting the war in Vietnam, racism, materialism, and environmental degradation. Because of their concern about these and other societal problems, as well as their involvement

in campus issues, the college community recognized that these activists were unique, serious, and influential.

Nearly all Whitman activists worked within the system; for example, they discovered that trustees and administrators, not the faculty, had the power to enact reforms, and they sometimes consulted with sympathetic professors about the best way to achieve their
goals. The activists almost always avoided direct confrontation with
administrators; they correctly assumed that a reasonable request
would procure them a fair hearing.

Trustees, administrators, professors, students, alumni, and townspeople all voiced opinions about the student activists. All these
groups acknowledged that this minority, often joined by sympathetic
faculty, had brought remarkable change to the institution. In fact,
the students of the late 1960s and early 1970s had a greater impact
upon the institution than any other group of students. Perhaps the
only other generation that had brought a notable degree of change
were the military veterans of the late 1940s and early 1950s, but that
earlier group, which primarily emphasized better management and
the end of some immature traditions, did not have the same lasting
influence. After the generation of critical veterans graduated, they
were followed by the so-called "silent generation," which rarely disturbed the status quo. In the 1950s President Maxey ran the college, a situation that nearly all students and faculty members accepted. The activists of the later period made enormous changes;
in their era, an administration like the one over which Maxey had
presided from 1948 to 1959 would not be tolerated.

Societal conditions of the late 1960s and early 1970s had an enormous impact upon college students. The situation was ripe for
change, but effort was still required to bring it about. Assisted by
some of their professors, the activists had by the early 1970s ended
the traditional practice of *in loco parentis*, insisted that the campus
end racist practices and seek minority students, protested the Vietnam War, participated in regional and national politics, helped
launch the women's and environmental movements, insisted upon
expanding the curriculum, and convinced the administration to listen to students and to appoint them to meaningful committees. A
minority of concerned students had challenged the way that the
trustees, the administrators, and the faculty had managed the insti-

tution, and these groups responded by taking a keen interest in student opinion. No longer were students taken for granted. And they now had a much greater voice in their education.

The actions and words of activists, of course, prompted a wide variety of responses. Some Whitmanites—as well as Walla Wallans—called them impatient, ignorant, arrogant, boorish, disruptive, self-centered, immoral, and scruffy. On the other hand, many in the college community appreciated their attack on parietal rules, their rejection of fraternities and sororities, the activists' efforts to improve the traditional curriculum and grading system, their interest in equality for minorities and women, and their environmental concerns. Their questioning spirit was brought into the classroom, often stimulating professors. Whatever their degree of political involvement, nearly all of the activists gave academics priority. They generally accepted a rigorous grading system (grade inflation would be the problem of a later era). It is fair to say that the activists were, for the most part, competent and reasonable students who challenged and motivated their teachers.

The activists knew that they were making a difference and asked respected professors what they thought of them. Some responded that they hoped that this generation's spirit of reform and concern would be taken beyond the campus, and that these students would, as alumni, work to improve America's economic, educational, health, and social conditions. Thus, the faculty applauded those students—activists or not—who joined the Peace Corps upon graduation, and professors were pleased to learn of those alumni—activists or not—who sought to improve the condition of the poor, championed public education, insisted upon equality, pushed the environmental movement, and worked on behalf of many other meaningful causes.

The activists, for the most part, became thoughtful citizens as well as productive ones. Some teachers and many former activists expressed disappointment with those of the dissenters who lost their reformist spirit and joined the apathetic majority in seeking material comforts. But, no matter what they did after graduation, the activists could look back with pride upon their efforts to make their alma mater a better college. Their aging professors generally forgave the excesses of this generation and remembered the activists—individually and collectively—for making teaching rewarding.

II

Patterns of Traditional Student Life

1955–1975

Historians discussing the nation's students in the 1960s have tended to emphasize the dissidents and neglect the traditionalists; historians, like journalists, have emphasized conflict over continuity. At Whitman, nobody took a count of the activists, although everybody considered them to be an influential minority. But the activists pushing numerous reforms were fewer than those who took up only one or two of them; many students, for example, complained about parietal rules or academic regulations but expressed little or no interest in national issues such as racial or sexual equality. It also should be noted that Whitmanites, like Americans in general, only gradually came to oppose the Vietnam War. Military historian Larry Addington has concluded: "Probably the anti-war movement was less influential in changing minds than were the rising toll of American casualties; the inability of the administration to win the war at an acceptable cost of blood, time, and money; and the war's deleterious effects on the nation's economy."[1] Members of the Whitman community made reference to each of these factors.

Thus, although the militant students who commanded considerable attention are important to institutional history, it is necessary to provide some accounting of the lives of more traditional students. Both the ordinary and the extraordinary students were historical actors. Indeed, alumni have stressed that participation in traditional activities—including Greek life, athletics, and the song contest—continued to be the norm during this period of great turbulence.

A summary of conventional college life presents difficulties, because thousands of students had a considerable range of out-of-class
experiences. But some retelling of their variety is essential to understanding the period from 1955 to 1975.

The Academic Side

The vast majority of freshmen who selected Whitman had an interest in academics; rarely did students come to the college because it
was perceived to be a "party" or sports school. There is no comprehensive study of why young women and men chose Whitman
from 1955 to 1975, but perhaps a response to such a question by
the class of 1956 is typical. Ten years after its members graduated,
they recalled three basic reasons for selecting Whitman: "broad liberal arts offerings, high academic standards, or balance of social and
intellectual opportunities." Some respondents wrote further about
their selection; for example, one stressed "the small classes with individual attention and close association with senior faculty members."[2]
      Many have generalized about the qualities of the student body,
including its academic ability. According to a graduate of 1969, who
undoubtedly spoke for many, the student population tended to be
"fairly conservative, middle or upper-middle classes, quiet men and
women from the Pacific Northwest. Good students. Bright people
and fairly conventional in their goals. Most of them were going to
go into business or an established profession, as opposed to becoming artists or writers or even academicians."[3] Marsh Lee, who
graduated in 1967, recalled that students understood the value of the
liberal arts and were not "narrow career types."[4] Because of solid
teaching, hundreds of students developed interest and even competence in subjects that had failed to hold their attention in high school.
      Whitman, like other institutions, published its aspirations; al-
though, of course, not everyone agreed with its official language. But
all Whitman professors had goals, expressed in class or in a syllabus.
During the opening week of 1973 the college offered a panel dis-
cussiion of the faculty's expectations. One panelist read from the current catalog: "Whitman aspires to stimulate in its students curiosity, confidence, and the capacity to understand and relate. It hopes to
produce graduates who are equipped with the intellectual ability to

cope with any condition, and to help them secure a basis free of prejudice, on which they can build a lifetime of learning and service."

To achieve such lofty aims, professors required solid work. Most were conventional teachers, employing the lecture method described by Professor Thomas Howells as "a dialogue in which one side is more audible than the other."[5] During the period from 1955 to 1975, students and alumni generally insisted that they had been challenged academically. Richard Elmore and Ginger Porter, graduates from the late 1960s who went on to become educators at Harvard University and Guam Community College respectively, stressed that their courses at Whitman had been uniformly demanding and that those courses continued to influence their own teaching for decades. Teachers required extensive readings and gave challenging examinations. Many freshmen entered with sterling academic records and quickly discovered that they must spend far more time studying than they had anticipated. Parents sometimes wrote to administrators that their children, who had had impressive grades in high school, were getting much lower ones in college; one mother in 1964 complained that her daughter had a 3.7 grade-point average as a high school senior and received only a 1.5 average in her first semester at Whitman. Michael de Grasse concluded: "I think the availability of a really high quality instruction on this campus then was very high, and if you were willing to take advantage of it, it was there to be had. No question about that."[6] Students sometimes discovered an easy course and spread the word to friends.

Students appreciated the fact that their mentors introduced them —often with passion—to the liberal arts. Alumni frequently stressed that their alma mater had provided a solid general education, and were grateful that they had learned how to learn.

There were many able professors identified by students and by the college. Collectively, these professors established Whitman's solid teaching reputation. Surely every teacher influenced, for one reason or another, many students. Effective teachers have been credited by the administration, by an alumni survey compiled in 1992, and by numerous oral interviews. These sources list the names of dozens of successful teachers. Considering those who had taught for at least ten years by 1975, the twenty-five most effective or popular teachers were Rodney Alexander, George Ball, Walter Broman, Ely Chertok,

William Hutchings

Douglas Underwood

David Stevens

William Soper

Exceptional teachers during the 1960s and early 1970s included mathematics professors William Hutchings and Douglas Underwood, geology professor Richard Clem, economics professors

Richard Clem, Thomas Edwards, Robert Fluno, David Frasco, John Freimann, Thomas Howells, William Hutchings, Paul Jackson, Corey Muse, James Pengra, Arthur Rempel, Fredric Santler, Harold Sims, Ronald Sires, William Soper, David Stevens, Richard Stuart, James

Richard Clem

Richard Stuart

Walter Broman

Patrick Tyson

Richard Stuart and David Stevens, philosophy professor William Soper, and English professors Walter Broman and Patrick Tyson. All of them would teach at Whitman for twenty years or more.

Todd, J. Patrick Tyson, Douglas Underwood, and Robert Whitner.[7] Certainly this list would not please everyone; alumni would add to or subtract from it, according to their personal experience. Some subjects were more difficult to teach, and those teaching classes with low enrollments would necessarily have fewer positive responses from alumni. And, of course, an impressive number of professors who had served less than ten years were playing and would play a vital role; they should be acknowledged in a future college history. There were also ineffective teachers: some "burned out" and some lacked personal or teaching skills. One alumnus remembered "clinkers" as well as "challengers."

Alumni repeatedly mentioned that several classes improved their skills in writing, speaking, and thinking. Teachers frequently mentored and advised scores of individuals, and in consequence of this close contact, solid friendships developed between professors and students. Although faculty members insisted that they be respected, there was free interchange between them and the students. One alumna recalled: "I never felt like there was a huge division between the faculty and the students. They didn't think they were so holy you couldn't talk to them."[8] Appreciating their underpaid mentors, the classes of 1967 through 1970 established an endowment fund for faculty salaries or benefits instead of purchasing an object for the campus. This was gratifying to professors who taught during this period of activism.

John Stanton and Linda Kurfurst are shown participating in a class conducted in the home of Robert Fluno. Students enjoyed classes and dinners held in the homes of faculty members.

In general, teachers respected their students as individuals; the young people responded favorably, and many alumni assured the college that it had fully prepared them for graduate and professional training. They often emphasized that the dreaded oral examinations in their senior year were especially helpful. Some reported, however, that a liberal arts degree did not necessarily immediately result in meaningful employment. Perhaps Greg Thomas said it best: "A Whitman degree may not get you your first job, but it will get you your first promotion."

A member of the class of 1957 stated that the faculty "gave me an education that well prepared me for community life and parenthood."[9] These were the aims advocated by Stephen Penrose during his entire career, from the 1890s on: education for self and others.

Students were aware that some professors had published articles and books that influenced their teaching and their academic fields. Many times students assisted professors with their research, a practice that was mutually beneficial. Among the researchers and publishers were Edward Anderson, George Castile, Jay Eacker, Thomas Edwards, Robert Fluno, David Frasco, Donald Lehmann, Gordon Philpot, James Shepherd, David Stevens, and Robert Whitner.

Members of the faculty remembered favorably the students of the 1960s and early 1970s. Professors recalled not only the excesses of a few activists but the solid scholarship of the majority. Historian Whitner stated in 1964 that students were more serious and competent than they had been in the 1950s.[10] Professor Underwood noted that these students were "interested and interesting"; historian Frederick Breit found most students to be serious and motivated. Professor Pengra concluded that his students of the late 1960s and early 1970s were among the "best and most inventive." In this period before noticeable grade inflation, students were rigorously evaluated in numerous classes. Typically students disliked but accepted the "C" grade. This attitude would change.

At commencement weekend, the college recognized alumni who had earned honors in their professions. Undoubtedly, the most significant recognition between 1955 and 1975 was granted to Johnnie Dennis, a member of the class of 1960. A science teacher at Walla Walla High School, he was named the National Teacher of the Year in 1970. At the White House, he and his family posed with President

and Mrs. Richard Nixon. Perhaps this happy occasion was one reason why Nixon eagerly accepted a Whitman football jersey in 1971.

At every commencement the college recognized meritorious
achievement with its honors awards—in scholarship, music, drama,
athletics, and forensics. Besides institutional awards, seniors won numerous scholarships. Unfortunately, there is no available list naming all those who won scholarships, grants, and fellowships, but the
Whitman Alumnus and the *Pioneer* mentioned some recipients:
Baker Stocking III (Rhodes scholarship); Nagle Jackson, Vicky Cordova, and John Lewallen (Fulbright scholarships); Dean Lambe
(Woodrow Wilson fellowship); Randall Nelson, Jim De Meules, and
David Pinkham, (Noble Foundation leadership grants); Molly Mc-
Namara (Kodaly fellowship); and Carol Hastings (Rockfeller theological fellowship). It is impossible to tabulate the number of grad-
uates who received admittance to professional and graduate schools,
but many successes were noted in the alumni magazine's class notes.
Professor Glenn Woodward said he did not know of a single Whitman graduate who had "ever failed to succeed in medical school."[11]

Outsiders also appreciated the ability of Whitman students. For
example, the Norton book representative stated that the Whitman
bookstore sold more non-textbook titles per capita than any other
college or university bookstore in the Northwest except the one at
Reed College. Visiting professors frequently complimented students
for their motivation, seriousness, and friendliness.

Students realized that Whitman was in transition. Many voiced
concern about the increasing costs of annual tuitions: 1955, $430;
1965, $1,200; and 1975, $2,710. To meet these sharp increases, the
school offered many more scholarships, loans, and prizes. Nevertheless, seniors left campus with ever-larger debts.

On the other hand, students became increasingly satisfied with
the library and the faculty. Complaints that the library's holdings
were inferior gradually faded from the columns of the *Pioneer*. In
addition, the Whitman community and alumni readily acknowledged
that the faculty was larger and better trained. In 1955 there were fifty-
six professors; in 1975 there were ninety-two. These additions filled
major gaps in the curriculum, offering new courses in anthropology,
art history, Spanish, Greek, and creative writing. Many departments,
especially the larger ones like biology, English, and history, enriched

their programs. Overseas study, particularly through enrollment in the Institute of European Studies, became increasingly popular.

Some members of the Whitman community have speculated as to the reasons why those who were students during the revolutionary period of the late 1960s and early 1970s have been less involved with the college as alumni than were those who graduated during more traditional times. The figures from the 1997–1998 drive for financial contributions from alumni reveal that sixty-six percent of those who graduated in the decade from 1955 to 1964 gave money to the school, while just fifty-two percent of those who graduated in the period from 1965 to 1975 made contributions. Furthermore, records indicate that one-third of those who graduated between 1961 and 1964 returned for their twenty-fifth college reunions; one-fourth of those who graduated between 1965 and 1971 returned for theirs. Perhaps these differences indicate that the later graduates were less satisfied with their total Whitman experience.

But attendance at Whitman certainly did not deter students from seeking postgraduate education. A 1997 college study revealed that "the attainment of advanced education appears greatest among those graduating between 1967 and 1976," the school's most turbulent years.[12] About forty-five percent of all the school's graduates reported attaining some level of post-Whitman degree, and over sixty-one percent of those graduating between 1967 and 1976 obtained advanced education. One senior eagerly sought a graduate program in history because he wanted to be a professor and be paid to read. After 1967 increasing numbers of Whitman women entered professional or graduate schools.[13] The higher percentage of women and men enrolled in postgraduate education resulted from several factors, including the Vietnam War, professional opportunities, and the encouragement of professors. The fact that more women were entering the professions attracted considerable attention. From the class of 1967, eleven men and no women attended law school, but a few years later Professor Fluno identified a few women who had graduated from law school, including Nancy Wynstra, Marilyn Muench, and Karen Glover. Three women who entered college teaching also received recognition in the *Whitman Alumnus*: Donna Gerstenberger, Trova Hutchins, and Susan Salladay.

Walla Walla

Every college is influenced by its environment. In Whitman's case both the size of Walla Walla and the town's location have affected professors and students. The latter, who sometimes have complained of boredom, have consistently criticized the city's remoteness, size, restaurants, motels, movie theaters, and political conservatism. But many of these critics, who initially disliked the small town, came to enjoy it; in fact, a significant number of them returned to Walla Walla to escape urban life. Those who enjoyed the town appreciated its residents, houses, parks, taverns, culture, nearby wheat ranches, and proximity to the Blue Mountains, where they hiked, fished, hunted, skied, camped, and partied.

Many alumni emphasized that Walla Walla's remoteness and lack of social amenities made them create their own entertainment. By spending so much time on campus, members of the Whitman community became very well acquainted. Alumni often stated that they got to know their classmates and professors far better than did graduates from other colleges and universities. This positive effect was exactly what President Penrose and his successors had anticipated. Whitman clearly would be a vastly different institution if it were located in an urban center, which is one reason why Penrose refused to relocate it to Spokane.

Residence

Whitman has always stressed its residential nature; thus, the administration has taken great interest in student housing. The 1975 catalog, for example, asserted: "Residence on the campus is one of the focal points of the collegiate experience. Close association with fellow students provides the opportunity to explore informally the intellectual questions which arise in the classroom and in the residence hall." The catalog added that it was important for residents to govern their own halls.

Pressured by students, the college, like its sister schools, liberalized housing and dining rules in the late 1960s. But one important rule remained unchanged: sororities must be housed in Prentiss Hall.

Stephen Penrose had established this requirement because he sought to encourage bonding among women students and to discourage snobbery. The educator wanted women to feel loyalty to their group, to their classmates, and to the college. After more than six decades it seems that his objectives were still being achieved, for many expressed sentiments like those of Linda Weihmann Brown: "People were friendly. We got to know each other as freshmen and we stayed mixed, regardless of whether we pledged or what we pledged."[14]

Alumni often forgot many of their classroom experiences, but they generally recalled their living conditions—on or off the campus. They had, of course, spent more hours in living rooms than in classrooms. Indeed, some alumni even maintained that the residential experience was as important as the educational one. Although young women and men enjoyed living conditions that would have appalled Penrose, the positive results of campus residential life during this period were those that he had fostered and cherished from the beginning of his presidency, nearly a century earlier. Penrose had made lifelong friends as a student at Williams College; Whitman alumni generally had the same experience at their alma mater. Perhaps Susan Campbell Pratt's summary was typical: "I think the people and friends at Whitman were the best."[15] The positive experiences were a major reason why alumni generously contributed money and time to the college.

Mothers of students have asserted that one of the nation's most difficult jobs is to cook for critical college-age eaters. Probably Whitman came closest to satisfying dormitory residents when Paul Harvey was the director of food services. He arrived in the mid-1950s and remained for about twenty years, impressing the community with his skills both culinary and personal. President Donald Sheehan praised his enthusiasm and his cooperation. Many alumni agreed, fondly recalling formal dinners—complete with candles and table cloths—served on Wednesdays and Sundays, and his baking birthday and specialty cakes. By teaching table manners, Harvey carried on the tradition of Mary Penrose.

Housemothers had maintained a degree of decorum in the dining halls and assisted in preparing fraternity menus; and they had eaten meals that ranged from appetizing to appalling. Students living in apartments and houses often served meals that guests variously described as original, satisfying, or dubious.

Many students appreciated Paul Harvey's food service in Prentiss Hall and his willingness to prepare special desserts on special occasions. He served in this demanding position from 1954 to 1977.

Decades later, the college on one occasion hired an outsider to teach upperclassmen how to eat a six-course meal so that they would avoid embarrassment. This event brought smiles to those who remembered the civility of earlier dining rooms, along with hopes that this form of *in loco parentis* might be reinstated.

Organizations

There were several national honorary societies in 1955, including Phi Beta Kappa, Mu Phi Epsilon (music); Delta Sigma Rho (forensics); Mortar Board (senior women); Spurs (sophomore women); and the Order of Waiilatpu (senior men). These groups, as well as others established later, such as Signet Table (junior women), recognized student accomplishments—especially in academics—and carried out programs.

The Greeks have always played a major role on campus. Although their membership sharply diminished starting in the late 1960s, there was no decline in the number of chapters. In 1975, as in 1955, there were five fraternities and six sororities—the only change was that Kappa Alpha Theta replaced Phi Mu. Despite a declining influence in these decades, the Greeks still provided a large measure of social life and campus leadership. The Greek experience proved meaningful for hundreds of students: the friendships, activities, late-night conversations, parties, dances, pledge sneaks, "prefunction functions," serenades, choral contests, "hell weeks," Homecomings, leadership opportunities, and intramural sports enriched their lives. Whitman's leaders continually recognized these positive aspects, pointing to the Phi Delta Theta house, which yearly between 1952 and 1964 received from its national office either a first- or second-place trophy for being an outstanding chapter. In the spring of 1966, before its difficulties over the Reid Yamamoto case, the Sigma Chi chapter also received a prestigious award from its national headquarters. The college agreed with former president Penrose's 1945 assessment: "Fraternities and sororities were originally admitted to Whitman in the hope that they would contribute effectively to the process of socialization."[16] Many alumni remembered such socialization in their chapters and beyond, into marriages with other Greeks.

An unusual, revealing, and readable description of Greek life is the journal of the 1957 fall semester by Paul Knostman. A pledge of Beta Theta Pi, he recounted fraternal events—including rush, social activities, a pledge sneak to Pullman, and a pinning serenade—that united the brotherhood. He concluded his account: "With the first ten weeks or so having been so neat, how much more so the rest of the year, and for that matter, the next three?"[17] Unfortunately, Knostman did not write about those years.

To some degree the fraternities engaged in "self-policing." Upperclassmen curbed the behavior of those who caused disturbances in the house or embarrassments on campus. The college appreciated these efforts and expected the Greeks not only to provide socialization and leadership, but also to push scholarship. Through the use of study tables, room assignments, advising, test files, and tutoring, the Greeks achieved grade-point averages superior to those of the independents. The groups competed for scholarship as well as for other trophies.

The college chose to play down the system's negative aspects, including painful rejections experienced during rush, pranks, rivalries between fraternities, anti-intellectualism, and "beer busts." Periodically, critics on and off the campus denounced the whole fraternal system. The Greeks had been criticized upon their establishment, just prior to the First World War, and a similar attack came during the Vietnam War, when some at Whitman thought that the groups were in terminal decline. Detractors, who realized that the Greek system could not be terminated, wanted to limit its influence by deferring rush until the second semester and thus affording freshmen the opportunity for greater reflection before pledging. The issue of deferred rush often challenged the Panhellenic Council and the Inter-Fraternity Council. Some antagonists even hoped that the 1968 founding of French House—Whitman's first interest house—would lead to the creation of various houses based upon "common intellectual interests," which would replace the Greek system.[18]

In the turmoil of the late 1960s only a few faculty members advocated the removal of fraternities and sororities, but the perception, especially among alumni, was that the percentage of anti-Greek faculty members had increased, thus threatening to take hasty and severe action against the chapters. To keep the faculty from voting

This is a pinning ceremony in the 1950s. A sorority member receives a fraternity pin, flowers, and a fraternity serenade. The photographer's lights assist the excited observers in the windows of Prentiss Hall.

to abolish the Greek system or to change its practices, some fraternal leaders built bridges to professors by inviting them to the various chapters for dinner, dances, and programs.

Although, as this history is written, the Greeks lack the influence that they had in the period from 1955 to 1965, they no longer feel as threatened as they did in 1970, and they continue to have administrative support. Oral histories indicate that some Greek alumni now favor the elimination of the fraternal system for various reasons, including that fraternities and sororities lack the cohesiveness that was so evident in their heyday.

Student Government

Students at Whitman automatically belonged to the Associated Students of Whitman College. The student government, generally known by the acronym ASWC, was a major organization, comprising a student body president, an executive council, and a student congress with representatives from the living groups. The ASWC managed dances, publications, the campus radio station, Homecoming, and much more. It handled a large budget ($40,000 in 1964) collected from student fees. It became even more influential in expenditures after the elimination of the position of graduate manager, a position that had been held by a faculty member. The ASWC sometimes expended funds for various off-campus activities; for example, in 1961 it sponsored a drive "to help finance intelligent and talented Negroes in high school and college."[19] It sometimes authorized student investigations; for example, in 1966 a sports investigatory committee examined the school's "athletic dilemma," reporting that the college should strengthen its intercollegiate athletic program.[20] The ASWC also conducted forums, including one that explored the role of the small liberal arts college in an era of rapidly expanding public universities, entitled "Does Whitman Have a Right to Exist?"

Student leaders were generally mature and reflective, but the campus community occasionally complained about apathetic executive councils. This was an issue of particular concern in 1973–1974. An especially harsh evaluation of "negligent" student government was written by the *Pioneer* editor on February 1, 1973; this piece triggered various replies.

Undoubtedly, those involved in student government enjoyed opportunities to develop leadership and political skills, as well as some
freedom from administrative dictates. Interviews with alumni indicated that most of those who had participated in governance had
found it rewarding.

The Student Union Building

After 1947 the Student Union Building (SUB) enriched student life.
In fact, a new group developed: the so-called "sub rats," students
who spent an unusual amount of time socializing in the lounges and
booths. Manager Vern Kinsinger explained that the SUB provided
a co-curricular adjunct to the college's academic life. The beautiful
but cramped building included a fountain, a bookstore, a post office, a snack bar, and a dance floor. It offered art exhibitions, bridge
tournaments, coffee forums, lectures, and special entertainments.

Students in the 1950s and 1960s often crowded the SUB, a popular place with its
bookstore, fountain, and mail boxes. Here they greeted each other and faculty
members, especially at mail time.

Vern Kinsinger, manager of the Student Union Building for a quarter of a century, was a popular figure on the Whitman campus. He was one of many devoted staff members who made major contributions to the college community.

Friendly and cooperative with students in managing the SUB, Kinsinger continued his management when the SUB was moved to an inappropriate building in an unsatisfactory location on lower Boyer Avenue. Although the new location provided more space, the warmth and friendliness of the old building were never recaptured by either Kinsinger or his congenial successor, Vern Solbach.

Social and Political Participation

Students frequently served as valuable community volunteers, assisting at the Blue Mountain Boys Ranch (a home for disturbed boys), tutoring black adults at the Negro Baptist Church, helping at the Lillie Rice Center for physically and emotionally handicapped persons, hosting parties for low-income children, tutoring in local schools, and assisting many city and county agencies.

Politics, especially at the national level, has always attracted a measure of student interest; a poll taken in 1962 found that only a quarter of Whitman students took no interest in politics.[21] Among those who doubted this statistic was a sarcastic woman who wondered whether a Russian declaration of war on the United States would prompt Whitman students to take "time from their studies to discuss or build an interest in it."[22] But *Pioneer* articles as well as faculty and alumni recollections indicate that the 1960s were a decade when an unusually high percentage of students expressed

an interest in politics; this percentage would decline considerably
in the 1970s. John Stanton, for example, unsuccessful in attempting to initiate a debate over impeaching President Nixon in 1973,
was distressed by "the apathy on this campus."[23]

The assassination of President John F. Kennedy ten years earlier,
an event that shocked college students everywhere, was the most important political event of the period and was vividly recalled by
Whitman alumni who were students in the fall of 1963. Stunned by
the murder and unable to make sense of it, weeping students sat
glued to their television sets during a dreary November.

To unite and foster political opinion and activity, Young Republicans and Young Democrats recruited the faithful. According to Professor Whitner, both groups were far more active in the 1960s than
they had been earlier. Party affiliation was meaningful, and alumnus
Robb Ball recalled that, in the middle of that decade, Republicans
were more numerous and Democrats were more active. At various
points in time there was an international club, a chapter of the Young
Americans for Freedom, and a chapter of the Students for a Democratic Society. In 1969, one alumnus remembered, a wide spectrum

of political views could be heard; another recalled that Jeff Kane was appointed as state chairman of the Young Americans for Freedom.

Professor Fluno was a major reason for political activity and interest; for example, he was the driving force behind the Political Union. He chose its student members—limited to sixteen men and women—and they, in turn, elected its chair. This organization joined other groups in sponsoring mock political conventions in 1960 and 1964, in which scores of Whitman students served on committees or as delegates. The Political Union, which received outside funding, also hosted seminars featuring outside speakers. Non-members received invitations to attend. Fluno took students to the state capitals, Olympia and Salem, for case studies.

The presidential elections held between 1960 and 1972 provided considerable excitement. In the 1960 race, John Kennedy, an unusual candidate, stimulated campus interest. Four years later, concerned faculty members placed paid advertisements in the *Walla Walla Union-Bulletin* for either Lyndon Johnson or Barry Goldwater, actions that helped promote student participation. The election of

During the 1960s students were unusually interested in politics. Shown in 1962 at left, the Young Democrats included, standing, Sharon Johnson, Rick Odegard, and Shirley Caldwell; and, seated, Lynn DeFrees, Nancy Wynstra, and Vicky Cordova. The Young Republicans in 1962, above, included Robb Ball, Nancy Kreuter, Walter "Skeeter" Minnick, and Jack Wheeler.

1968 won even more campus attention, because of Eugene Mc-Carthy's anti-war stance and Robert F. Kennedy's assassination. In 1972 many students supported George McGovern, primarily because he campaigned for the immediate withdrawal of American troops from Vietnam. Meanwhile, faculty members, students, and alumni campaigned vigorously for Republican governor Dan Evans, whose wife, Nancy Bell Evans, had graduated from Whitman in 1954.

Several national political figures visited the campus, including Washington's U.S. senators Warren Magnuson and Scoop Jackson, and Supreme Court Justice William O. Douglas. There was a low-key but steady campus effort by students and others to name New Dorm for the controversial Douglas; this would be accomplished in 1980, after his death and after many of his regional critics had either mellowed or died.

In the early 1960s, campus leaders stressed that Whitman should be "a place of free inquiry."[24] Thus, students sought a variety of speakers, including Communist Party member Gus Hall. President Louis Perry, championing the free discussion of ideas, supported the invitation to Hall but advised that a more effective communist could be invited. Although such a speaker did not appear during the long Cold War, students wrote to the *Pioneer* about communism in the world and heard a variety of campus speakers assess the communist menace. Senator Jackson warned about the Soviet threat, especially the need for citizens to resist Nikita Khrushchev's "fear psychology."[25] Several speakers addressed national and international politics, including political scientist Richard Fontera of Whitman and historian Giovanni Costigan of the University of Washington. Professor Breit later recalled that in the late 1960s and early 1970s he had large enrollments in his modern European history classes, and that interested students faithfully read demanding books on international politics.

The arms race and the threat of nuclear war consistently prompted a degree of student concern, but specific crises during the Cold War attracted even more attention. One of these was the Hungarian uprising, which triggered an unusual student response in late 1956: wearing their student body cards on their lapels, an estimated eighty participants canvassed the city to raise about $1,300 for Hungarian students who had fled "from the Communist tormented country."[26]

The Cuban missile crisis of 1962, according to the *Pioneer*, meant that anxious students were "talking about the international situation and expressing opinions which have been dormant";[27] Whitman students stood loyally by President Kennedy in this dangerous affair. They also joined the Peace Corps—a program initiated by Kennedy—from its inception; this organization has consistently attracted a significant percentage of Whitman graduates.

Publications and Radio

Publications were extremely important to campus life. Comprehensive and well-written, the *Pioneer* won several journalism awards in the 1950s; its publication was anticipated with enthusiasm. Its quality, of course, depended entirely upon student dedication. Many capable individuals edited and wrote for the newpaper, and no faculty advisor censored their contributions. Narrowing their focus by the early 1970s, editors, who often grumbled about the lack of contributors, took less interest in broad coverage. The *Pioneer* gradually declined and lost respect on and off the campus. Like other college newspapers, it became an outlet for personal statements, and its language deteriorated, reflecting a sharp change in taste.

President Chester Maxey had once warned that, if the *Pioneer* continued to carry smutty material, those who wrote such items would have that fact noted in their permanent files.[28] The writers protested but apparently became more careful. In the 1970s the *Pioneer* contained offensive language that upset readers, especially parents and alumni. The decline of campus journalism was commonplace and tended to follow that of national newspapers. In 1971 editor Chris Pence acknowledged a degree of mediocrity in the *Pioneer* and complained about apathetic classmates: "Creating the paper is becoming increasingly less interesting and enjoyable when so few care what we're doing and care to do it with us."[29] A sexual parody appearing in a 1972 issue, according to two student critics, was "the worst example in a continuing string of tasteless, witless, and worthless journalism."[30]

In the spring of 1969, students—some of whom expressed disgust with the *Pioneer*—wanted to provide in-depth reporting of campus issues from "a slightly left of center" viewpoint, and began publishing the weekly *Narrator*. According to Greg Brown, Jack Riehl, one of the founders of the new newspaper, said, "sort of like the old Judy Garland and Mickey Rooney movie—'Hey guys, let's go put on a newspaper.'"[31] Under Riehl's editorship the *Narrator* operated without a student government subsidy and achieved its purpose.

To the disappointment of many in the Whitman community, the editions of the *Waiilatpu* yearbook produced after 1970 declined in quality and coverage. Unlike earlier volumes, which provided useful details about a college year, those produced between 1971 and 1975 were, like the *Pioneer*, highly personalized and incomplete. No yearbook was published in 1973.

Students produced other publications. *Clock Tower*, the student magazine, had ceased its existence in 1955; it was succeeded in 1957 by *Masque*, which contained fiction, art, and poetry. Maxey hoped that *Masque* would be a valuable outlet for creative writers, but noted: "Over the years literary or pseudo-literary magazines have come and gone with predictable regularity."[32] This one appeared intermittently until 1970; *Faire*, offering similar material, replaced it.

Radio station KWCW–FM has influenced hundreds of student lives since it went on the air in January 1971. In the late 1960s students expressed an interest in operating a radio station and received assistance from Professor Craig Gunsul. Funds from the graduate manager's savings account paid for new equipment. Located in the SUB, the station began with four disk jockeys, calling themselves "The Front Four," after the defensive line of the Los Angeles Rams football team. The radio station was unusual, for it lacked a faculty manager—it was as independent as the *Pioneer*. The disk jockeys generally played their favorite popular music, but in the early 1970s the "Bullshoot" program provided opportunities for them to interview faculty members, visiting speakers, and townspeople. Still, those who recalled that the station, when it was proposed, was going to offer an education and editorial forum, voiced disappointment with the limited programming.[33] KWCW provided an alternative to the monotonous country music played on local stations; program director Alan Chow correctly concluded that the station was "heavy on rock music, broadly defined."[34] From its birth, KWCW was enjoyed by a large Whitman audience, as well as local residents, including high schoolers and penitentiary inmates.

Sports

Intercollegiate and intramural athletics, especially for men, continued to attract a following on and off the campus. Coach Robert Burgess, who knew every Whitman president from the 1950s through the 1970s, emphasized that they stressed academics as being far more important than athletics, that they wanted respectability in men's intercollegiate athletics (only in the Sheehan years was this goal consistently attained), and that they attended the school's games. Students also understood that the college's presidents were concerned about Whitman's ability to be competitive in intercollegiate athletics. During his presidency, Perry, for example, told them that "as far as major team sports have been concerned, Whitman has more often than not over the past quarter of a century been an easy mark for too many conference teams, even though such has not as consistently been the case in individual sports."[35] It is interesting to note that, during the time of student activism, the college enjoyed several successful seasons in both major and minor sports.

The football program attracted some talented athletes. According to student sportswriters, coaches, and players, this list would include George Sullivan, Robert Schembs, Glen Grodem, Jerry Hillis, Phillip Tjelle, Gary Jones, Bob Coon, Mike Levins, and Eric Johnson.

The *Walla Walla Union-Bulletin* reported on November 9, 1969: "Man on the moon. Jets win Super Bowl. Mets reign supreme in baseball. Whitman won at least a share of the Northwest Conference football championship." Around this time the squads included several large linemen, who, to the surprise of football critics, were positive influences in the classroom as well as on the team. Former coaches and players cite Mike Henniger, Chuck Treneer, and Chris Helton as examples.

In 1958 the *Waiilatpu* maintained that Whitman was "never known as a basketball power," but, under Coach John Wilcox, teams between 1971 and 1974 enjoyed three consecutive winning seasons for the first time in thirty-five years. This meant that fans had moved "from the doldrums to near-delirium."[36] During two decades some of the leading scorers were Don Robinson, Del Klicker, Max Johnson, David Snow, Don Woodworth, Bruce Bennett, and Scott Miille.

In this 1969 huddle, quarterback Eric Johnson faces crouched linemen, from right to left, Jim Dow, Steve Whitman, Steve Hubbard, Chris Helton, and Mike Henniger; and receivers and running backs, from right to left, Chipps Whipple, Chuck Treneer, Bob Reisig, Art Mitchell, and Bob Coon.

William Martin, an interesting campus figure, coached track until 1970. After attending the college with teammate Nig Borleske, he coached in the East before returning to the Walla Walla Valley, where he took up ranching; he became a part-time Whitman coach in 1934. Gary Fowler, David Klicker, Terry Pancoast, Bob Perry, Evan Smith, and John Leier were some of the outstanding trackmen. Dean Shoemaker and other trackmen remembered that their opponents teased them at meets because they were studying between events.

Baseball teams also posted winning records between 1973 and 1975, and several players—Doug Allen, Cleve Larson, Bob Reisig, Jim Volz, and Randy Wooten—won the Vincent Borleske Trophy awarded annually to the outstanding male athlete.

Robert Burgess "had a long tradition of quality men's tennis teams." Professor George Ball wrote that the 1963 championship team was impressive because of its dedication and discipline. He noted that, in winning all of its tournaments, it posted a record of eighty-one wins and nine losses in individual matches and more than sixty wins with only four losses in doubles matches. The squads of the 1960s included Steve Ronfeldt, James Feutz, Thomas McCoy, Randy Jacobs, Bill Schoen, Ron Witten, Rob Lesser, Erick Baer, and Tony Barkauskas. Jacobs considered the 1965 team the best of that era; crowds as large as eight hundred turned out to watch the matches. In 1975 the team, led by Tom Wenzel and Mark Sconyers, won the conference and placed fifteenth in the NAIA nationals.[37]

Coach Robert Thomsen's golf teams enjoyed considerable success, including several league championships in the 1960s. Golfers George Anderson, Chris Varley, Rick Klobucher, Del Rankin, and Mark Lodine were all-conference in either 1966 or 1967.

Intercollegiate soccer, swimming, cross country, and wrestling started as club sports and attracted significant followings. The soccer program sprang from the great popularity that the game enjoyed in the Puget Sound region; Coach Floyd Bunt's squads in the 1970s included Ellen Harbold and other women members and enjoyed success over large school rivals. Wrestling, which replaced skiing in 1961, had some success, but ended largely because it lacked a coach. Skiing would return much later as a competitive, high-profile sport.

Organized Walla Walla boosters sought to promote the major intercollegiate sports. In the fall of 1949 only 158 individuals purchased tickets for a football game. Reacting to this lack of support, downtown boosters, calling themselves the 158 Club, sold tickets to Whitman games and raised money for athletic scholarships. Many in the Whitman community chided students for not attending games; for example, in 1960 student body president Doug Cole charged that, at a home basketball game, more students attended from the visiting school than from Whitman.[38] The rule of thumb that only winning teams attract fans was unfortunately borne out at Whitman.

On the other hand, intramural sports were extremely important for men, including those players who left the intercollegiate teams, which took too much time from academics. Intramural teams practiced and took the games—especially championships—very seriously; the *Pioneer* publicized the contests, and fans cheered, particularly at flag football games.

Women engaged in various intramural sports, including tennis, badminton, ping-pong, basketball, and skiing. Considered to be a novelty, the powder-puff football games attracted considerable attention. Perhaps the rise of women's intercollegiate sports at Whitman began in 1969 with the undefeated tennis team. In 1970 regional colleges formed a women's league, and Whitman's volleyball, swimming, and tennis teams enjoyed success by 1975. The *Pioneer* teased the basketball teams as being shy of players, size, and skill. Wearied by coaching five sports, Scottye Lewis complained that "many women come to college specifically to get married, and turning out for sports is not the way."[39]

Nearly every student generation attempts to replace the "Missionaries" nickname with a more appropriate one. Some outsiders thought that the nickname meant that the college offered missionary training, and sports writers complained about the nickname's length. Some suggested adopting a different name: "Wheaties" and "Bears," as well as others, were suggested, and in 1973 staff mem-

The physical education faculty in 1974 included, in the front row, Robert Thomsen, Keith Jensen, and Palmer Muench; in the back row, John Wilcox, Floyd Bunt, Robert Burgess, secretary Margaret Johnson, Scottye Lewis, and director of the news service Tim Marsh.

Many in the Whitman community comment upon the enormous changes over the years in the activities of women. Athletic opportunities for women expanded greatly in the late 1960s. This is an intramural flag football game in 1968.

ber Tim Marsh led an attempt to adopt the name "Shockers."[40] This nickname did not stick, but the term "Fighting Missionaries" came into use—pleasing some individuals and disgusting others. The search for another name still continues.

To some degree, athletics played a unifying role on campus in the late 1960s and early 1970s. Whitman's intercollegiate program in this period was stronger than it had been a decade earlier. Cleve Larson, a letterman in football and baseball, recalled that athletics knitted together students and faculty members during a divisive time. In a period when the counterculture—with its long hair, bib overalls, and drugs—appeared on the campus, athletics brought together those who approved of radical change with those who did not. But others thought that athletics were unimportant during a time of war and change; Greg Brown was one of those who considered football to be only a "sidebar."[41] Tom Williams expressed a different view. He concluded that Whitman put too much effort into foot-

ball, and that the school could not compete in a league in which its
opponents exhibited less interest in academics than Whitman did,
and had athletes who majored in physical education.[42]

Many professors, appreciating the academic ability and commitment of student-athletes, supported them by attending tennis
matches and baseball games played on Ankeny Field. But even if
the athletic programs did not achieve all that Larson and others believed they did, there is no doubt that sports—intramural as well
as intercollegiate—were a significant part of campus life in the college's most turbulent period.

*The Hall of Music has one of the most attractive interiors on the campus. The
sounds from the studios are ever-remembered by the Whitman community, many
of whom referred to it as the "House of Many Noises." Financed by noted benefactor D. K. Pearsons, the building was constructed in 1910.*

Professors in the music department in 1972 were William Bailey, Stanley Plummer, José Rambaldi, Kensey Stewart, and Kenneth Schilling.

Music and Drama

For many students, music lessons and performances added an important dimension to their educations. Professors William Bailey and José Rambaldi, both also conductors of the Walla Walla Symphony, taught and auditioned Whitman students for membership in the musical group, which grew in quality and recognition. The department sponsored both pep bands and larger ones. By 1971 Professor Kenneth Schilling had participated in twenty-seven annual concert tours, important to the college as well as to the singers; the *Pioneer* asserted that the tours' main purpose was to advertise the college to potential applicants in the region.[43] The choir performed the *Messiah* about every four years, and, in association with the drama department, produced musicals, including a very successful production of *South Pacific* in 1957. The music department promoted Whitman's "Fine Art" series, scheduling classical musical groups, such as the Moscow Chamber Orchestra in 1966. At commencements between 1959 and 1975 music majors who had given outstanding recitals received soloists' diplomas. In 1960 senior Marlene Carpenter was the sole winner; in 1975 ten musicians, many of them Rambaldi's piano students, won diplomas.

Professors Rodney Alexander, left, and John Freimann were major contributors to the development of the Whitman theater program.

The college and the community consistently applauded the productions of the theater department. Professor Rodney Alexander came to Whitman in 1948; during his tenure he established a drama major and produced about a hundred plays, including those of the "Summer Circle" (plays produced off campus). He ran the theater program in one of the old barracks buildings that had been moved from McCaw Hospital, until it burned in 1958 (just as he was preparing a production of *Guys and Dolls*, which had to move to another location for its performances); he then designed the new theater building, which would be named the Harper Joy Theatre. Alexander's efforts were praised by many, including one observer who explained that the productions incorporated "the talents of drama students, of art students in stage and costume design, of dance students in choreography, and of music students in singing roles and orchestral accompaniment."[44] Many theater-goers anticipated the reviews written by Professor Thomas Howells. In 1955 he judged: "In the amateur theatre . . . it is notorious that first nights often show the petticoat of achievement drooping some inches below the skirtline of potentiality."[45]

Alexander resigned from Whitman and moved to Dartmouth College in 1967. John Freimann and Nancy Simon maintained the theater's regional reputation, involving numerous students in producing a wide range of plays, including some written by Whitman faculty members and students. The department produced one-acts, children's plays, and—assisted by the music department—popular spring musicals. For example, in 1972 they offered *Mame*, called by a critic "a fast-paced, engaging romp."[46] Students who contributed to successful shows included Carl Clark, Nagle Jackson, Maureen O'Reilly, Dirk Niewoehner, Gene Engene, Kathryn Shaw, Duncan Mackenzie, Margie Boulé, and Steve Carlson.

Forensics

Whitman had a winning tradition in debate. Speech professor Dean McSloy came to campus in 1954 and stayed until 1969. During that time he established effective intramural and varsity debate programs; in 1965 thirty-two men and women were on the varsity squad. His debaters won many tournaments and received invitations to participate in prestigious eastern tournaments. Among the college's outstanding debaters were Othal Lakey and Walter "Skeeter" Minnick. Although numerous successful debate tournaments could be recalled,

Jeanne Eagleson, Dirk Niewoerhner, and Joy Schick play in The Cat and the Canary. *Nieowerhner, who took the stage name Dirk Benedict, went on to become well-known in television.*

perhaps the Pi Kappa Delta tournament at Gearhart, Oregon, in 1966 was representative. Among those receiving the highest ratings were talented juniors—Jim De Meules, Dave Wyckoff, Mal Higgins, John Silko, Kathy Shelton, and Nancy McCornack.[47] Seven years later Coach Remy Wilcox's speech team won its first sweepstakes award in fourteen years in the Boise State College tournament.

Issues Old and New

The costs of a private college have required many students to seek jobs. Thus, numerous young men and women took advantage of the placement service, directed by Almira Quinn. Her office assisted students in securing part-time employment during the school year and vacations. She also provided seniors with information about career choices and brought many employers to campus. Quinn's efficiency and ability to carry out many activities impressed the entire Whitman community.

Every campus employs staff members who influence numerous students. In the period from 1955 to 1975 several alumni identified two such individuals, Karl Schwarz and Genevieve Rasmussen. Schwarz took employment in 1935, became superintendent of buildings and grounds in 1950, and retired in 1968. During many summers, faculty members worked on the grounds under his supervision, but he hired far more students, who appreciated his conversation and German foods. Responding to his support of their activities, students in 1956 made him an honorary member of the ASWC. Both Schwarz and his successor, the resourceful Jay McClure, worked hard to beautify the campus. Rasmussen, known to hundreds as "Miss R," came to Whitman as a nurse with the navy program in 1943, and became director of the health center. According to patients, she was tyrannical, favored men, and sympathized with and aided those with hangovers. In 1971 the college made an award in her name to "an outstanding senior girl."

Insisting that automobiles were essential in remote Walla Walla, students drove them to campus. George Anderson spoke for many, asserting: "I would have gone crazy if I did not have a car in Walla Walla."[48] But, late in Chester Maxey's first presidency, car owners learned that they would not receive financial aid. Maxey explained,

During a visit to Whitman, poet Allen Ginsberg autographed a book for Professor Steve Rubin. Ginsberg's appearance was an instance of the college bringing a controversial speaker to campus.

"If a student cannot pay his bills in full he cannot justly expect Whitman to give him enough financial aid to permit him the luxury of a car." The president added that "students of the horse-and-buggy days would not have thought themselves entitled to financial aid if they could afford to whirl around in a surrey with the fringe on top."[49] Maxey's restriction on automobile use received favorable recognition in *Time* magazine and the *New York Times*, from radio networks, and in numerous supportive letters.

Students had often complained that, since Whitman was out of the mainstream, they missed opportunities to hear popular figures and scholars available at urban campuses. In response to this criticism, groups received additional funds to bring more events and guest artists to the campus, and beginning in 1971 these were publicized in the college catalog. In one brief period, between October 1974 and January 1975, Whitman hosted comedian Bill Cosby, poet Allen Ginsberg, and novelist Ken Kesey.

Drugs troubled American college communities in the 1960s. In the early part of the decade, drug use was minimal and underground. Malinda Phillips Pankl recalled that her classmates were "extremely fortunate" because they did not "get caught into that huge drug mess" which occurred at other campuses and which would soon enough come to Whitman.[50] But by 1967 students were talking openly about various drugs and consuming them on campus. The faculty warned that drug users could be expelled, but added that "in some situations the college will rely on its counseling resources in preference to either legal action, separation, or other college disciplinary actions." The statement went on to say that the college would not intervene when student "involvement in drug usage comes to the attention of civil authorities."[51]

The faculty's policy, of course, could not limit drug use in the 1960s any more effectively than it had been able to limit the use of alcohol in the 1950s. Walla Wallans worried about drugs, and a few charged that Lyman House was the center of the city's drug activity. On June 27, 1969, President Donald Sheehan deemed it necessary to write to the community through the *Walla Walla Union-Bulletin* that the school prohibited "the use, possession, or distribution of narcotic or dangerous drugs, such as marijuana and LSD." He added that the college had recently instituted action against two students who had run afoul of the regulations. But, because they faced court action, the school dropped its proceedings and the accused departed.

It was impossible to know how many students used drugs. Perhaps John Coleman gave the best summary in 1971: "There's a large percentage of students who have tried marijuana. I don't think that there's any serious drug problem, like heroin freaks or a lot of psychedelic drugs, but I do think that there is a large percentage of students who have experimented." Sandra Gassner assured the community that if a person declined to use drugs it did not end "social relationships."[52] Probably the situation at Whitman was similar to the one at Middlebury College: "People dealt drugs, people bought drugs, and people did drugs—some professors included."[53] At Whitman as at numerous other schools, the college joined the local community in providing education and clinical service in response to the drug problem.

Some members of the Whitman community advocated the legalization of marijuana. When Washington gubernatorial candidate Dan Evans came to the campus in 1972, he heard such an argument. Surely he also heard an administrator or a professor explain that alcohol remained the students' drug of choice.

At about the same time that illicit drugs impacted student life, so did the birth-control pill. Whitman students, of course, participated in the sexual revolution, but many denied sexual promiscuity. However, stories circulated that there was a significant increase in pregnancies and abortions. Alumni who had attended the college in the mid-to-late-1960s recalled a marked increase in sexual activity, a fact that they attributed to the pill. In 1970 Margaret Chesney, a leading activist, wrote about the problems of birth control facing her classmates. She asserted that "birth control is no longer a parlor topic at Whitman, it is a reality." Chesney discussed the difficulty in acquiring the pill, insisting that some women borrowed them, an "extremely dangerous" practice, and concluded that, in Walla Walla, "male contraceptives are much easier and less expensive to obtain than are female contraceptives."[54]

Traditions Old and New

Alumni recalled various reactions to campus rules. For example, in the 1950s, instead of wearing nylons to dress-up dinners, residents of Prentiss Hall used eyebrow pencils to draw "seams" down the backs of their legs. Pranks were part of the oral tradition passed along by fraternity men. Panty raids provided excitement, but, as had been predicted, they ended after the opening of coeducational dormatories. Students engaged in various antics, including placing a drawing of Mickey Mouse on the face of the clock on the Memorial Hall tower, stacking tires—or hoisting Professor Phyllis Hutchings' bicycle—on the flag pole, removing the table tops from the library, and taking the outfield fence from Ankeny Field and wrapping it around Memorial Hall. Because a concrete lining had been placed in Lakum Duckum, the freshmen-sophomore tug-of-war ended, and the practice of dunking fraternity pledges or victims of a kangaroo court gradually terminated.

While most pranks amused everyone, a student incident on May 30, 1964, angered the community. Following an "unsuccessful and destructive raid" on the women's dormitories, about fifty men, most of them freshmen, staged a "sit-in" on Isaacs Avenue, explaining that they were seeking relief from the tensions of final examinations. President Louis Perry rushed to the scene and put an end to the disrup-

In 1970 Mickey Mouse appeared on the Memorial Hall tower. Over the years student pranks diminished in originality and frequency.

tion. The *Pioneer*, joined by townspeople, denounced these immature participants; but the editor sympathized with them: "Walla
Walla is obviously a town of little excitement for the urbanized or
'tension-filled' student. At times the Whitman family must provide
and generate its own excitement and entertainment."[55]

More recent students look back with indifference on these inci-
dents. They seem as removed from their Whitman experience as
housemothers are. In general, as the college discarded its rules, the
students engaged in fewer pranks.

Traditional groups and activities, including the rally squad, the
lettermen's club, Back-to-Marc (its skits, picnic, dance, and costumes
were popular in the 1950s), May Fete (a pageant with a royal court),
and class government had disappeared by 1975. A much less elaborate version of Homecoming remained in the fall; a tuba festival,
however, made for a unique Homecoming in 1974. Created in 1971,
Renaissance Faire provided a springtime break from academics. Reflecting the renewed interest in hiking and camping, students revived
the outing club (one had existed in the late 1950s), an organization
that attracted increased support from the administration and stu-

dents. The leader of the organization was Andy Dappen, who wanted classmates to capitalize on Walla Walla's "good location."[56]

In the mid-1970s "streaking" attracted male participants, some of whom assembled at Anderson Hall, played the *1812 Overture*, fired the Delta Tau Delta cannon, and ran naked across the darkened campus, amusing the coeds. Baffled by this new tradition, which appeared on campuses nation-wide, members of the Whitman community wondered what would come next.

It is fair to conclude that those attending Whitman at various times during the period from 1955 to 1975 experienced different campus cultures, but surely the majority earning their degrees in these twenty years benefited from both academic and non-academic conditions. Many would agree with Don Jones, who thought he was lucky to attend college from 1967 to 1971. The liberal arts experience provided his classmates with "the impetus to think about things

One of the significant changes in spring traditions was the abandonment of the historic May Fete and the adoption of Renaissance Faire in the early 1970s. May Fete included the election of a queen as well as other ceremonies. Here ASWC president Craig Lesley presents the royal cape to Queen Louise Wilkinson in 1966, as the young sons of faculty members demonstrate minimal interest.

The Renaissance Faire of 1973 included Professor Katherine Bracher and student musicians.

they would not have thought about otherwise, and to broaden their horizons."[57]

And in 1975 the new president, Robert Skotheim, put the college community into context:

> One of the most remarkable aspects of a small college such as Whitman is the sense of community shared by students, faculty, and administration. In an earlier day, most Americans had a meaningful communal experience in their backgrounds, but big cities have fragmented communities for millions of American families, just as large universities have done for most students. The idea that a community exists to give support to its members is lost today to most of our contemporaries. One of the best aspects of your time at Whitman, I think, will be the concern others have for your welfare.[58]

These sentiments about community are exactly what Stephen Penrose expressed when he took the college presidency in 1894. It is to be hoped that the college president in 2094 can relate a similar message about the ever-changing Whitman community.

12

The Faculty and a Changing Whitman
1955–1975

The faculty minutes for the years from 1955 to 1975 portray two contrasting periods: during the first ten years professors enjoyed a period of relative calm; the second ten years, however, was a time in which they experienced great activity and unusual stress. In both decades, of course, the faculty had similar aspirations, including a livable salary structure, comprehensive fringe benefits, tenure, sabbaticals, good students, well-equipped laboratories, a high-quality library, a meaningful voice in college administration, and some relationship with the trustees. A study of faculty minutes demonstrates that, in periods of peace or of passion, professors showed a consistent concern about the curriculum, graduation and majors requirements, the faculty code, the discipline of students, the grading system, and the academic calendar, as well as several routine matters.

Presidential leadership, of course, continued to influence faculty careers. From 1955 through 1958 President Chester Maxey gave increasingly optimistic reports to the faculty about the financial status of the college, including their salaries. In January 1955 professors responded positively to his recitation of improvements: during the past five years the endowment had increased by eighty-seven percent, the amount paid for salaries had climbed by thirty-six percent, over $400,000 had been expended for new construction, and, most notably, the retirement of $115,000 in bonds finally freed the school of a debt nearly three decades old. Maxey stressed that operational reserves of $230,000 guaranteed that, "in case something unforeseen happened and no income was collected," faculty salaries would be paid for six months.[1]

Throughout the late 1950s the faculty congratulated Maxey for raising funds for the library building, scholarships, and the endowment, which had risen to about $3,800,000 by 1956. He assured professors that Whitman could offer them as "fine a professional future as any college of similar character."[2] Maxey, as always, tempered his optimism by cautioning them that the school was dependent upon the ability of the students to pay their bills, but said: "If the American economy has a future, then Whitman College also has a future."[3]

In 1956 Maxey presented to the faculty another set of flattering financial numbers, and the leader must have startled his listeners— many of whom took summer jobs in the canneries in order to survive financially—by predicting "that the time is not distant when the salary schedule of Whitman will be the best anywhere in the United States."[4] In 1957 the president informed professors that, because of the school's improving financial position, a new salary range of $5,000 for instructors to $10,000 for full professors was possible. This new salary structure would not yet make Whitman the leader— salaries at public schools were still higher—but it would make the school "comparable to the best Pacific Coast colleges."[5]

Few faculty wives worked outside the home at this time; they stayed home and reared their children. Many faculty families struggled to pay their bills, and to provide music lessons and ski equipment for their children. Thus, in the summer many professors worked in the canneries during pea harvest, or later in the wheat harvest.[6] Historian Ronald Sires boasted that he now had a position at a grain elevator, which allowed him to read on the job. Discontented with their meager salaries, faculty members told each other that they deserved improved salaries. A few individuals, lacking Maxey's blessing, received markedly smaller paychecks than those awarded to his favorites. Professors seeking salary adjustments rarely convinced Maxey that they had a legitimate case. When Louis Perry became president, faculty members either grumbled to him about low salaries and his predecessor's hollow predictions about increased compensation, or they accepted Maxey's view that the president simply could not raise the overall salary level.

Teachers sought not only to increase their pay but also to enlarge their numbers, so that the curriculum could be enriched and teaching loads reduced. Every semester, most of them taught five classes and consulted with many advisees about courses and major fields of study. Seeking relief, some professors advocated additions to the faculty. Such pleas brought a sharp rebuke from Maxey, who fervently warned against unnecessary expansion. The president judged that the existing curriculum could be divided into three lists: "necessary or indispensable courses, useful but not indispensable courses, and superfluous courses." Maxey concluded, "What shall it profiteth a man to have a snug academic empire and thus sell himself down the river of salary attrition?"[7]

Without financial resources, the faculty in the late 1950s could add only a few courses to its bare-bones curriculum. This factor helped explain why faculty meetings tended to be routine and short—many of them were only thirty to forty minutes long. Another major reason for brevity was that the five men on the faculty council thoroughly preconsidered issues, particularly revisions of the faculty code, prior to their introduction at faculty meetings. Thus, professors rarely rejected the council's recommendations. The five academic divisions also brought well-considered motions, mostly for course changes, to the faculty floor. In 1956 professors made a major decision when they accepted a proposal from the social sciences division to transfer religion and philosophy to the humanities division. Historian Robert Whitner's motion to terminate the social science major, because it was, he felt, "becoming a soft berth for those who wish to slip by without notice or work," failed; however, his colleagues soon reversed themselves and discarded this hodge-podge major. Among the few resolutions passed by the faculty, one congratulated board members, emphasizing that the new library had stimulated reading and thought.

According to Pete Reid, professors often gathered in their lounge in the Student Union Building and grumbled about President Maxey's domineering leadership. When economist Richard Stuart arrived in 1960 he found his colleagues in a "sort of euphoria with Perry"; others agreed that morale improved once Maxey departed.[8] Even his critics, however, acknowledged Maxey's impressive scholarship and his accomplishments, including new alumni support and construction of the long-awaited library building.

After the strong-willed Maxey left the presidency in 1959, the faculty made some significant changes. Foremost, they terminated a controversial grading system, which he had authored and defended. Initiated in the spring of 1948, this unusual collegiate grading system awarded "highest honors" in place of an "A" and "high honors" in place of a "B," and included a "P" for a passing grade; it lacked the equivalent of a "D," but did include an "F." Opponents of the system argued that it created problems when students transferred or applied to graduate schools. Calling it "a novel and experimental grading system," Professor William Hutchings pushed for a change; in 1961 his colleagues happily adopted the "A" through "F" system, traditional and familiar since 1933.

Insisting that it lacked both facilities and student interest, the physical education department easily convinced the faculty in 1961 to drop its major. At the same time, professors began ranking students by grade-point average, a debatable decision because the difficulty of students' course loads varied greatly.

During the Perry administration, teaching conditions improved. Upon taking the presidency, Perry informed professors that he was "interested in people rather than buildings and would work for the improvement of faculty welfare first and bricks and mortar second."[9] Early in his presidency, he impressed some members of the faculty with his openness and his ability to raise even more money than Maxey had. After five years of leadership, Perry reported significant progress: the faculty had increased by thirty percent and "many material benefits have accrued to the college—a 90% increase in the number of library volumes, a computer center, increased funds [for] visiting professors, a faculty travel fund, a major medical insurance program, a group life insurance program, a tuition plan for faculty children attending other colleges, and a faculty-designed sabbatical program."[10] Professors recognized these presidential accomplishments; they also appreciated both Perry's active encouragement of participatory faculty governance and his achieving the prestigious $1,500,000 Ford Foundation grant in 1962.

Professors joined with their low-key president in bringing about such notable improvements as course reductions and a sabbatical program—inaugurated in 1963—designed to "advance the applicant professionally."[11] Only a portion of the faculty initially enjoyed these improvements, but Perry hoped that reducing teaching loads to three classes a semester would provide teachers with an opportunity to "keep on the frontiers of their fields."[12] Further, the faculty clarified tenure rules, reduced the number of teaching divisions from five to three, created a challenge examination opportunity, debated and rejected replacing the traditional semester system with a three-three plan (courses taken in three blocks of three), and adopted a calendar that ended the first semester prior to Christmas.

Professor Richard Stuart, who emphasized that Whitman had eliminated business administration courses, sought additional revisions in the curriculum. He stressed that Whitman "is not and simply cannot be a small university. A small university would be a midget. Whitman College will not be a midget; I believe it will be a giant among small colleges."[13]

In 1966, late in the Perry administration, the faculty adopted the "pass-fail" grading option, similar to systems adopted by other schools at about the same time. According to the catalog for that year, "The Pass-Fail plan enables students to enter areas of study comparatively unfamiliar to them without the potential of lowering their over-all grade point average." In 1970 the faculty revised the option to "pass-D-fail" in order to ensure that students receiving a passing grade under this option would be working at least at a "C" level.

During the Perry years, the faculty identified persistent and serious problems: turnover among the teaching staff, a need for faculty additions, inadequate library and laboratory budgets, minimal salary increases, and the attrition of students. The Whitman chapter of the American Association of University Professors (AAUP) and other faculty members expressed great concern about attrition, especially of able students who transferred after their sophomore year to the University of Washington, causing some faculty members to lament that Whitman actually served as a junior college for the university. The loss of upperclassmen meant that dean of admissions Douglas McClane—who enjoyed a regional reputation for his professional expertise—and his staff had to spend long hours recruiting freshmen.

The AAUP chapter as well as individual teachers expressed concern about minimal salary increases. Perry insisted that improvements in compensation had brought Whitman's minimum salary within $1,000 of the highest minimum salary paid by other institutions surveyed; the teachers, however, countered that the construction of buildings should be delayed until their salaries could be "raised substantially."[14]

Finally, there was the long-lasting problem of the tenure system. Presidents Louis Perry and Donald Sheehan, joined by professors, faulted the tenure evaluation system of ad hoc committees appointed by the dean, but this system would remain in place for decades.

An Evolving Faculty

The faculty profile in 1965 was a traditional one. According to catalog figures, of eighty-one individuals on the faculty payroll, twenty-five percent were full professors, fifty-eight percent had Ph.D.s, and males predominated. Twelve women comprised fifteen percent of the faculty, and seven of them served at the rank of instructors or lecturers. No woman was a full professor; only two had attained the rank of associate professor. Few in the Whitman community complained about this inequity. In the next ten years, some departments made an effort to hire women but discovered that few had Ph.D.s; furthermore, in this generally favorable job market, single women, fearing a deadly social scene, often refused to apply for positions in remote Walla Walla.

By 1975 the faculty profile had changed slightly. In a faculty of ninety-seven, twenty-seven percent were full professors, fifty percent had Ph.D.s, and only seventeen, or eighteen percent, were females. None of the women served as full professors; sixty-six percent of them worked as lecturers or at a lower rank, and most had only part-time appointments. In the early 1970s a few female students, influenced by the women's rights movement, complained about the gender disparity within the faculty and the consequent lack of female role models. But the call for more women professors was less shrill than the call for the addition of racial minority faculty members. The college's extensive attempts to hire minorities were detailed to the community in Dean Kenyon Knopf's report of 1971. No similar effort was made to hire women.

During the 1960s and much of the 1970s the predominantly male faculty enjoyed commodious offices in Reynolds Hall, featuring windows that opened, large oak desks, big bookcases, and wooden file cases. Some of this equipment had been supplied by the V-12 program, and other pieces came from a much earlier period. After a person resigned, newcomers to the faculty scrounged his office, seeking additional furnishings. As men increased in seniority, they moved to the larger offices in the middle of the building. The sagging second and third floors of Reynolds Hall housed workrooms, a single telephone, a couple of worn, manual typewriters, and a ditto machine. There were no photocopiers, but a sluggish Savin machine, requiring chemically treated paper, provided minimal copying. When the student assistant was off duty, the telephone rang incessantly, because no professor hurried down the hall to answer it; thus, students learned that it was easier to come to a Reynolds Hall office than it was to reach a professor on the telephone. Some faculty members used personal typewriters, and a scant few had college-owned machines. Each division employed only one secretary, who served about twenty-five individuals; therefore, professors waited for their work, did it themselves, or employed a student assistant. Writers either took manuscripts to the central stenographic office—operated by an efficient but officious woman—or to other female typists, who received payment from the college's modest summer grants program.

Reynolds Hall housed some noisy, hot, and cramped classrooms. Margaret Ershler recalled that, while seated in them, one often felt as though "Marcus and Narcissa Whitman were going to wander through at any minute."[15]

Many of the Reynolds Hall faculty had to cross the campus to teaching stations located in Memorial Hall or Billings Hall. These rooms, also noisy and cramped, had marred blackboards, carved desk chairs, and clanking radiators. The classrooms ranked far below those in new buildings at state universities or even high schools.

Faculty members from across the campus sought their morning mail in the Student Union Building, where the campus community jostled for access to mailboxes. This daily activity meant that the community engaged in short greetings or extended conversations over coffee.

While visitors to Reynolds Hall often commented about its austere conditions, they also saw the importance of the first-floor lounge, a place reeking with pipe smoke. From early morning to late afternoon, professors from all three divisions sat in comfortable, over-stuffed chairs and engaged in light or serious conversations. In this lively place, or in upstair offices, the professors became friendly with each other, conversing about students, scholarship, books, families, social news, and campus politics. Young faculty members soon learned "the Whitman tradition" from the veterans housed in Reynolds Hall, a place that demonstrated the usefulness of a faculty office building. Professors also became acquainted through various meetings, including their clubs, evening seminars where professional papers were presented, the annual fall picnic, and private dinners. Even the newest appointees noted that faculty wives served the best meals in Walla Walla. The faculty wives' club—it became the Whitman Women's Club—did much to integrate newcomers into the community and to provide a measure of social life, including a reception dinner for new families, potlucks, and small fund-raising projects for campus improvements. While all faculty members had the opportunity to engage in the school's social life, the occupants of Reynolds Hall, until the early 1970s, lacked the fine teaching facilities that the scientists enjoyed. Constructed in 1956, the science building provided air conditioning, modern classrooms, and suitable laboratories, which had been improved by grants from the National Science Foundation and other sources. But the members of divisions I and II enjoyed better physical facilities after Olin Hall's construction in 1972. Division II chairman Roy Hoover spoke for many when he asserted that this structure "impressively testifies to the excitement and enjoyment which a building can offer."[16] The new audio-visual specialist, Lawrence Paynter, whose office was in Olin Hall, introduced the college to new equipment and produced instructional materials.

By the mid-1970s teaching conditions also improved, partly because of an increased library book budget and the addition of the Stuart Wing to Penrose Memorial Library. The handsome Napoleon room, with its expensive artifacts, brought culture to the community.

While faculty members in the 1960s sometimes complained about physical conditions, especially inadequate classrooms, they brought more serious professional complaints to President Perry, who, in turn, arranged an annual meeting between trustees and senior faculty members—eventually junior members also participated—to discuss many relevant issues. No previous president had tried as hard to open a dialogue between these two groups as Perry did. Participants openly—and sometimes heatedly—discussed the liberal arts, a maximum student body size of twelve hundred, salaries, fringe benefits, faculty additions, and even the need for tenure. Although some teachers grumbled that these exchanges failed to improve professional conditions, many participants thanked Perry for these give-and-take sessions, which provided the faculty a chance to engage in long-range planning. A few of them later unsuccessfully urged President Sheehan to resume these meetings with trustees.

In the summer of 1966 Dean Donald Lehmann chaired a committee that met several times and developed a plan to reorganize the faculty system of governance. A somewhat surprised Professor Thomas Howells discovered that the new dean actively supported this reform. "Lehmann definitely favors giving the faculty a strong voice in the formulation of college policy, including budgetary policy."[17] Lehmann even suggested housing the dean of the faculty in a classroom building, rather than in Memorial Hall. At a meeting in September, teachers voted to replace the old faculty council, which had only five members, with a new system—a chairman of the faculty, who would preside over the business part of faculty meetings; a three-member policy committee; and a board of review with six members, including the three division chairmen. This change gave the faculty a greater voice in administration, extended participation to ten professors instead of just five, and provided a more efficient means of handling an ever-increasing amount of faculty business. Experienced teachers informed their younger colleagues that, under the old system, President Maxey had dominated the faculty; they hailed this progressive and democratic reform. After more than three decades this system of faculty governance remains in place.

The Nadir of Faculty Morale

In 1960 President Perry stated that he "was not assuming full responsibility for hiring and promoting the faculty," but was calling on faculty leaders to assist him.[18] He irritated many of them, however, by making three appointments either without adequate faculty approval or with none at all: Sir Richard Allen in history, Dr. Reynaldo Arciniegas in Spanish, and John Burns in English. The chairman of the history department expressed surprise that Allen, a career British diplomat, received a second-year appointment without the chairman's knowledge; furthermore, several teachers with low salaries felt that Sir Richard did not deserve the rank of full professor. But most of the complaints about Perry's appointments came from members of the humanities division, who passed a resolution in March 1966 disapproving of the hiring of Arciniegas—a former politician from Colombia—because it led "to the creation de facto of a new department of study without prior opportunity for the division faculty" to consider the need for such a program. President Perry and dean of the faculty Fredric Santler responded that Division II had plans to add Spanish in the future, and that Arciniegas possessed solid qualifications.

Professor Paul Jackson reported that his English department opposed the hiring of Professor Burns, who was currently teaching at Walla Walla College. According to Jackson, because Whitman professors had not seen Burn's credentials, Perry had "violated proper academic procedures." The president frankly admitted making the "appointment against the recommendation of the department, acting in what I felt to be the best interest of the college, because I felt that the man's credentials and years of teaching experience do speak for him."[19]

Many professors were unhappy about Perry's appointments. A few defenders of faculty rights warned that the school was returning to the autocratic style of the Maxey era, when the faculty had only a muted voice in administrative matters. But Dean Santler later complained that these faculty appointments brought more criticism of him than they did of Perry.

The appointment, in 1963, of Professor Santler as dean of the faculty resulted in a divisive faculty revolt three years later. Dean Paul Jackson had resigned the administrative position to resume teaching in the English department. Perry then appointed Whitman alumnus Himy B. Kirshen, an experienced dean at an eastern institution, as Jackson's replacement. But the trustees opposed this appointment, pressuring the president to select another person. Perry had to tell his appointee that he had been rejected; fortunately, Kirshen was able to regain his previous position. Angry with the trustees' decision,

Perry considered resigning, and complained that he was "forced to eat crow."[20] Some trustees and faculty members then assured the president that Santler, who sought the position, would make a fine dean, because he was a loyal, popular, and experienced member of the faculty, he understood Whitman's administrative structure, and he enjoyed good relationships with townspeople. Santler had many faculty friends who appreciated his close examination of problems and enjoyed his story telling. At an orientation session, for example, Santler said that he had heard people express displeasure with "boring" Walla Walla Saturday nights; he quipped that they should go to the Safeway during these evenings and watch the new electric meat-slicer.

Well-acquainted with Santler, Professor Howells, joined by some colleagues, judged that the German professor was unsuitable for the administrative post. Howells warned Perry that his appointment would create dissension and that a failure would bruise Santler's ego; despite this warning, Perry appointed him. Many teachers soon compared the new dean unfavorably with his predecessor. Jackson had been fair, soft-spoken, and democratic; Santler, by contrast, was arbitrary, officious, and authoritarian. As dean, Santler supported President Perry's controversial appointments. He refused to give teachers the student evaluations compiled by the senior class and in general turned a deaf ear to his colleagues; indeed, he told one young faculty member that, although he did not care if the teacher liked him, he wanted his respect. His blustery manner discouraged candidates interviewing for teaching positions. After nearly three years in office, he had offended many faculty members, and they voiced strong objections. Moreover, Santler had failed to earn advanced academic degrees. Whitman had awarded him a B.A. in 1941 and an honorary M.A. in 1942; a growing number of faculty members had Ph.D.s or were working on their dissertations, and they charged that Santler, who had never pursued any original scholarship, refused to acknowledge the importance of advanced degrees. Some faculty members, especially younger ones, complained that their dean should have, at least, an earned M.A., and should be a productive scholar. But perhaps an old friend of Santler's, Winks Dunphy, the president's executive secretary, gave the best explanation for his difficulties when she emphasized his verbosity and "Teutonic temperament."[21]

Frustrated with Santler, some professors, at AAUP meetings and at special gatherings, expressed their grievances. But there was no unanimity: a minority of faculty members insisted that Santler should remain in office and that everyone should be loyal to leaders. Among the discontented, economist Jonas Horvath, who had fled Hungary during the uprising in that country, urged his colleagues to unite and battle an "autocrat." On the other hand, biologist Richard Brown, a former navy officer, advised that the faculty should obey its commander. Historian Ronald Sires retorted, "I shall have you remember that this is not the U.S. Navy!" Economist Richard Stuart, one of the leaders of the revolt, stressed that, prior to his appointment, Santler had been a reasonable committee man, but, as dean of the faculty, he dominated meetings at Whitman (and even did so while serving on a committee at another campus). Political scientist Robert Fluno cautioned the trustees that, "because of lack of confidence in the Dean," even senior faculty members might resign.[22] Following a few meetings where emotions punctuated talks, forty professors signed a document that listed grievances accumulated over three years and urged the trustees to remove Santler. Professor Howells explained this unusual political action to an inquiring *Pioneer* editor: "We believe that the faculty and administration cannot work together when a significant number of the faculty lack confidence in the dean."

Dean Santler fought back, maintaining that his opponents had not brought their grievances to him: "I have received not one word of advice, not one word of warning, criticism, or helpfulness."[23] He found allies: about seventeen professors, including historian Robert Whitner and biologists Donald Lehmann and Arthur Rempel, supported him. Several administrators and townspeople wrote to the trustees, most in support of the embattled dean. Somebody alerted a Tri-City television station about the faculty revolt; its negative coverage angered all the disputants. Remarkably, the *Walla Walla Union-Bulletin* downplayed the story, providing only some quotations from the *Pioneer*.

Some trustees met with selected leaders of the disgruntled faculty contingent, accusing them of lacking institutional loyalty and leaking their protest to the television station. Professor Thomas Howells and others heatedly denied these charges. During this rancorous

For many years Fredric Santler was a successful German teacher, but his service as dean of the faculty prompted a faculty revolt. He was eventually forced to resign this position but was then made vice president for administration in 1967.

meeting, professors readily agreed with trustees that Santler was a respected teacher devoted to Whitman, but unanimously insisted that he lacked the temperament to serve as dean. The immediate result of the confrontation was Santler's forced resignation from the post in May 1966. He was then made vice president for administration, a new position.

The "Santler Revolt" had several consequences: some board members criticized Perry for "not being sufficiently authoritarian,"[24] while many professors blamed the trustees for having forced the appointment of Santler as their dean. The event fractured the teaching staff; for several years, some individuals were barely on speaking terms.

To the dismay of those who had opposed the dean, President Perry, who lacked time to find a qualified replacement from elsewhere, appointed biologist Donald Lehmann as dean of the faculty for one year. The Whitman community recognized Lehmann's academic credentials and his biological research. But the fact that he had championed Santler's retention, calling the dean's foes "revolutionaries" seeking administrative power, made him an unlikely successor.

Discouraged by this appointment, many of the forty protestors concluded that no one who had played such a conspicuous role in the "Santler Revolt" should have been appointed. Critics believed that Lehmann lacked personal skills, was authoritarian, and was a specialist too devoted to biology at the expense of the liberal arts. Professor Stuart concluded that Lehmann lacked "political instincts."[25] The fight over Santler had demoralized administrators and faculty members, and his replacement could not or would not heal the breach. Because of the low faculty morale—and finding jobs to be available elsewhere—several young professors resigned. Older, experienced teachers, such as Arthur Metastasio, who were devoted to the institution, decided to stay.[26] Between 1966 and 1968 about forty percent of the assistant professors departed; a significant percentage of the instructors also left. The Whitman community, including students, worried about the departure of so many individuals and insisted that the college must recruit and retain able men and women. Long-time, competent faculty members had established the college's reputation for solid teaching; similar individuals must be hired and retained to see the college through the next decades.

In earlier periods professors had worked to remove presidents Stephen Penrose and Rudolf Clemen; their participation, however, had attracted scant attention. But the faculty's action against Dean Santler was publicized, both locally and among the alumni. Although the *Pioneer* presented details about the "Santler Revolt," most student readers expressed little interest in it. Still, a few later remembered the basic details. For example, one activist reminded a faculty mentor that, when students denounced the administration, they were simply following the faculty's example. While students did not comprehend the legacy of the emotional struggle over the deanship, professors certainly did. Divided and depressed by it, the combatants agreed with Perry that such a battle over a dean should not occur more than "once in a lifetime."[27]

To heal the breach and to bring professional leadership, several faculty members during the 1966–1967 school year urged Perry to appoint an outsider as dean, insisting that he find someone who had administrative experience and solid academic credentials. Perry had understood this reasoning back in 1963, when he had tried to hire Kirshen, only to be overruled by the trustees. This time, however, he prevailed; the result was the hiring of Dean Kenyon Knopf, a man who met the major requirements. Meanwhile, faculty chairman Metastasio, through personal persuasion, labored at mending the

Long-time French professor Arthur Metastasio was well-liked by both students and colleagues; in 1966 he was the consensus choice when the faculty, for the first time, elected a chairman. Devoted to Whitman, he labored hard to repair divisions within the faculty in the late 1960s.

fractures within the faculty; but the stressful conflict over the dean initiated a difficult decade for the faculty.

In 1967 Fredric Santler, now the vice president for administration, assembled evidence about some of the recent changes for an official accreditation visit. While the evaluators praised the school, giving it their highest rating, Santler cautioned that "no college could lay claim to perfection." His conclusion impressed some of the disaffected professors: "We need from time to time, to be reminded that our institution, too, is in danger of stagnation because human beings frequently adjust equally as well to bad conditions as they do to good."[28]

In 1968 Donald Sheehan, newly appointed president but not yet in office, informed trustees that he would not accept Santler in the position that had been created for him, but Santler might again serve as a full-time German professor. Chester Maxey later evaluated this situation, which he had grappled with at the end of his second presidency: "With Santler the problem was to abolish his job and reconcile him to a return to something like his pre-dean and pre-vice-president promotions." The final agreement terminated the office of vice president of administration but awarded Santler a vice president's salary and promotion to the status of "distinguished professor of modern languages." Maxey justified the enhanced salary and professorial title as "a just recognition of what he had been for many years—an outstandingly great teacher,"[29] but some faculty members bemoaned the creation of this new rank of "distinguished professor"; they would have been further agitated had they known about Santler's unusual pay raise.

While the battle over Santler was taking place—and for a period of time afterwards—junior members of the faculty found themselves involved in another struggle, this one with several of the senior faculty members over economic issues and professional aspirations—including for example, the desire to attend meetings and conferences away from Walla Walla. The older professors had themselves constantly wrestled with low salaries and limited administrative influence; some had little sympathy with the economic plight of the younger professors and were reluctant to share their limited and hard-won power with their junior colleagues. In the late 1960s the latter group improved their situation by electing some of their rank to influential positions and committees.

Meeting Student Challenges to Academic Practices

A wise and experienced professor and dean, Paul Jackson, warned his colleagues and others in 1966 that there was a revolution underway at the college. "Having seen the social and intellectual impact upon Whitman in the last fifteen years, I cannot but believe that future changes will be greater than those we have so far experienced." He judged that students were brighter and more dedicated, and that "the students' perceptions of value are more complex and sophisticated." Jackson explained: "It is difficult for an older faculty member to realize the intense concern of the present college generation in problems of ethics."[30] Although he correctly anticipated a period of unusual change, the professor could not predict its breadth and power.

After the mid-1960s faculty difficulties were less with the administration and more with the student activists concerned about the civil rights movement, the Vietnam War, and the practice of *in loco parentis*. The faculty had met challenges from the 1930s to the mid-1960s, including those associated with the Great Depression, the Second World War, the Korean War, and the early Cold War. But in each

Members of the history department posed for a yearbook photograph in 1972. Seated are Robert Whitner, Walter Weingart, David Deal, and Thomas Edwards; standing are Frederick Breit and Donald King.

of these cases, the faculty had tried to meet the needs of students. For example, professors had revised the curriculum to serve student needs; similarly, they had accepted low tuition fees to accommodate needy students, knowing that low tuitions kept their salaries low as well. Between 1966 and 1975, however, professors and activist students were often at odds about how the college should react to campus and non-campus issues, including relaxed dormitory rules, the war in Vietnam, the curriculum, and grades. It is hard to find another period in which professors and students criticized each other so much. President Sheehan pointed out that faculties nationally "were unaccustomed to contentions in which their views of what was right were challenged not by administrators and governing boards, but by students and other faculty members. They began often as partisans of student extremism; many ended as its victims."[31]

Whitman counted a very few faculty "victims" who consistently sided with the student protestors; such types were called "hippie professors" in the press.[32] Pro-student, anti-society teachers rankled many alumni, as well as some veteran professors, who accused their colleagues of placating thoughtless young people who sought power beyond their capability. The so-called "hippie professors" lost the respect of many colleagues when, for example, they joined students

like student body president Mike Malone in arguing for the elimination of the "F" grade, or, indeed, of all grades. Malone said he
could "definitely foresee an end to majors by the completion of his
term in 1974." He and many other students thought that there was
an excellent chance that the grading system would be restructured
to "an A, B, C, No Credit grading system."[33] But the majority of
the faculty rejected such sweeping changes.

In the 1970s many in the Whitman community feared that activist and traditionalist teachers would engage in a sharp disagreement over the curriculum. In the spring of 1969 a group of dissident whites joined with the Black Student Union to form the
Coalition, which advocated, among other things, a degree of "student power." Responding to the pressure of these activists, Professor Fluno took action. On May 1, 1969, the political scientist ex-
citedly authored a resolution emphasizing that: "The location of
the authority and responsibility for the development and administration of curricular and teaching policy . . . lies with the faculty."
To the surprise of the traditionalists, this resolution passed by only
a narrow margin of nineteen to sixteen.[34]

Although dissident students—sometimes joined by others—criticized the faculty for opposing a black studies major, for allowing
the Greek system to continue, and for simply being too unresponsive to student proposals, confrontation between vocal students and
the faculty did not dominate campus life. In fact, there were several instances, such as the controversy over Greek racial clauses, the
search to find "disadvantaged students," or the relaxation of rules
about alcoholic beverages, when concerned teachers and students
reached an accommodation.

Two types of contact brought faculty members and students into
mutual understanding. The groups served on several recently created joint committees that gave students an awareness of educational
problems, including admissions and financial aid. The so-called "student life" or "cell group" program initiated by Dr. George Ball and
his wife, Nancy, also brought understanding. Each cell group con-
sisted of eight to twelve students (participation was voluntary) and
a teacher, and met weekly for ninety minutes in the professor's home.
Vigorous discussions of national issues, such as civil rights or Vietnam, and collegiate issues, such as *in loco parentis* or the curricu-

lum, were among the many topics covered in weekly meetings. Although there were disagreements over controversial issues, friendship and respect emerged. Participants treated professors and their families with respect; for example, the participants called their hosts by their formal titles, not by their first names, and thanked them for their hospitality. Some of these cell groups continued for years; others failed to generate much interest and died after a semester or two. But, whatever their duration, they did much to build trust, understanding, and friendship. Many alumni recalled that the cell groups were among the highlights of their collegiate experience. They also expressed fond memories of dinners served in faculty homes, including those auctioned by the World University Service, a popular organization that provided financial assistance for foreign students.

From the mid-1960s through the mid-1970s the faculty would make tremendous changes in its governance, in the curriculum, and in the regulation of students. The administration often took the lead in pushing programs; students, too, advocated what they often called "reforms," and the faculty itself sometimes took the lead in trans-

In 1972 the language faculty posed on a new campus bridge: Martin Kopf, Dale Cosper, Celia Richmond Weller, Vernon Toews, Arthur Metastasio, and Roy Hoover.

forming the institution. Activist students at Whitman, like similar groups at other schools, pressured the faculty to revise curricular as well as extra-curricular regulations. Thus, it was difficult to know what group was the catalyst for various changes or investigations, but the significant fact is that the faculty took action on many issues. The college catalog of 1975, a document that reflects faculty action, was a much different publication than the 1965 version. Some in the Whitman community thought that the institution had simply evolved; others, especially alumni, maintained that it had experienced a revolution. But no matter what the decade is called, it is hard to find an earlier period in which the faculty had acted more boldly in response to pressing societal and collegiate concerns.

The Changing Circumstances of the Faculty

In responding to various pressures, professors sometimes improved their own working conditions. Some changes pleased everyone; for example, they terminated the traditional and required chaperonage because the students did not desire faculty presence at dances and because faculty guests could not tolerate the unfamiliar loud music and untraditional dancing. Teachers terminated academic processions at baccalaureate, but they faithfully attended traditional graduation ceremonies. Attendance at faculty meetings declined. It had never been required, but traditionally a high percentage of the faculty had participated. Absenteeism became such a problem in 1971 that President Sheehan took the unusual and successful step of asking everyone to attend faculty meetings.

Professors acknowledged many significant changes in the period from 1965 to 1975. There was probably less complaint about salaries during this decade than at any other previous time, due to an improved pay scale. Professors knew that Dean Knopf was pushing to establish a salary scale that would place Whitman in "a middling position" among twelve noted liberal arts colleges.[35] Although it did not achieve the level Knopf sought, in 1974 and 1975 the college compared more favorably with the other schools. The faculty, struggling with inflationary pressures, generally appreciated Knopf's efforts. An exception was in January 1975, when Knopf (now acting president), seeking "to reduce some expenditures," asked the fac-

In 1972 the economics faculty included James Shepherd, David Stevens, Gordon Philpot, and Richard Stuart.

ulty to "please restrict the use of blue books to final examinations" and noted that "ditto paper may be reasonably satisfactory to use for quizzes and hour examinations at noticeably reduced costs."[36] Faculty members expressed both annoyance and amusement.

Improved salaries and fringe benefits contributed to the decline and death of the local AAUP chapter. In 1967 the AAUP boasted that it had played an important role in obtaining a tenure system, fair procedures used in faculty appointments and promotions, the sabbatical program, summer research grants, and travel allowances.[37] The sketchy surviving minutes of the AAUP indicate that its members—who comprised more than half the faculty—discussed such campus issues as student attrition. Some faculty members dropped their membership in the AAUP because they lacked time, because they thought it was too militant, or because they concluded that the national organization was indifferent to the needs of a liberal arts faculty. Many members, especially long-time AAUP leader Thomas Howells, expressed concern that this once-valuable organization had weakened and was nearing death by the mid-1970s.

Other changes were more obvious than the dean's pursuit of improved faculty compensation. These resulted from the recommendations offered by the faculty's standing committees or by several in-

vestigative committees that often introduced either proposals or ideas
that merited action or at least discussion. In 1965 a committee sought
"the facts and problems involved in the attraction, retention, and attrition of good students." The committee members reported that
their colleagues must comprehend that their decisions, especially
about curriculum, would attract and retain students. Such knowledge had some impact on faculty actions. Meanwhile, another committee examined the library's budget and expenditures, emphasizing that the library required more books and journals for student
use; faculty chairman Arthur Metastasio reported that the present
library facilities restricted faculty research as well. Still another
committee explored "innovative ideas in teaching [and] course and
curriculum design," and Howells wrote its lengthy report, which
prompted discussion.[38] For several years faculty committees spent
long hours, many of them with local Greek alumni, investigating the
fraternal groups' racial clauses. Subsequently, another committee—
which included student members—heard complaints about Greek
membership practices and sought ways to increase racial minority
enrollment.

In 1970 the college's joint faculty-student committee on ethnic
studies reported its findings, including a list of courses that contained
information on ethnic groups and courses that directly focused on
ethnic minority studies. In 1971 the faculty welcomed the appointment of G. Ray Warren, the first black person to become a member of the college staff, as the assistant director of admissions. The
1971 college catalog stated that "it was important in a time characterized by attempts of minority groups to realize in full the guarantees of citizenship and the rights of human beings, that the college's curriculum should include courses which help a student body
—predominantly white—understand cultures and societies which are
not Western in origin, and to appreciate the experiences of non-
white, non-Western peoples in American society."[39] Whitman, for
the first time, now listed courses in ethnic and non-Western studies, including "The History of the Negro in the United States" and
"Race and Ethnic Group Relations." Such courses initially received
respectable enrollments.

While the faculty would increase the number of classes dealing
with minorities, it steadfastly refused to offer a major in black stud-

Members of the biology department in 1974 were Edward Anderson, student lab assistant Betty Eidemiller, Donald Lehmann, Arthur Rempel, and Richard Brown.

ies. Further, the faculty rejected the Black Student Union's demands of September 14, 1970, that Whitman immediately enroll a hundred minority students—seventy-five blacks, twelve Indians, and thirteen Chicanos. On the other hand, professors, who agreed with the trustees that the word "proposals" should be substituted for the word "demands," sympathized with the BSU's request for the employment of a black counselor and the addition of "a black viewpoint" in subject matter.[40] Teachers advocating campus diversity praised the exchange program with Fisk and Howard universities, two outstanding schools that had predominantly black enrollments. Although only a handful of students from these eastern institutions came to Whitman, they provided a significant measure of diversity in and out of the classrooms. Unfortunately, these fine exchange programs collapsed in the mid-1970s.

Many faculty actions supported by the administration and various numbers of students enriched the curriculum. In 1969 students originated a two-week period between semesters—"Interim"—and often cooperated with professors in establishing noncredit courses and projects. Altering the academic calendar to accommodate Interim, teachers hoped that its varied programs would give students an opportunity to increase their "responsibility for self-direction in education."[41] Interim depended upon student leaders both for a program and for an involved audience. After four years the policy committee reviewed Interim, praising it for attracting about 450 participants annually. For several years after this review, Interim, with faculty members as invited participants, reached some degree of its early potential; then it gradually lost focus.

Sometimes, a joint committee of students and faculty members expanded or investigated academic practices. In the late 1960s students served on the student advisory committee on financial development and the student admissions advisory committee. Meanwhile, Whitman and other schools had anticipated that, after the students had successfully dismantled the parietal rules, they would take aim at the academic rules. In the early 1970s this prediction proved correct, as students everywhere sought a much larger role in administration. But, as faculty chairman Robert Whitner emphasized in 1971, students seeking various academic changes were calm, reasonable, and helpful. Few were defiant, and most expressed a concern for the college's well-being. Whitner believed that Whitman's small size made it much easier to work with students, especially the fair-minded student body leaders.[42] The result was that students were appointed to numerous committees. Some students expressed concerns about the curriculum; so, during the 1970 school year, the faculty and students established a permanent student-faculty curriculum advisory board. This new group explained to students the complexities of adding new departments or new courses, but alumnus Doug Eglington stressed another point. He stated that the committee got the college "away from a kind of Euro-centric view of the world to one that was much more open to the history of people of color." Thus, the seeds planted in the early 1970s led to the more "universal approach" of two decades later.[43]

Another joint committee thoroughly investigated the grading systems employed by other schools. Driven by its student co-chairman Michael Rona, the so-called "grade reform committee" issued a report that alerted its readers to a few unconventional grading systems, including the one at the University of California at Santa Cruz. But, reminded by old-timers of the controversial grading system that they had discarded in 1961, faculty members were not willing to adopt another untraditional system. Indeed, they altered the pass-fail grading option to include a "D" and cautioned that graduate schools might react negatively to students who over-used this option.

In May 1974 yet another joint committee investigated Whitman's long-standing comprehensive examination system, wherein senior students underwent comprehensive examinations in their major field of study. Starting in the late 1960s there had been heightened student complaints about "comprehensives," including accusations that some departments gave more demanding examinations than others, that students did not know what the examiners expected, and that this testing placed seniors under undue stress. The complaints came from more students than just the activist ones, but Whitman faculty members, unlike their colleagues at Willamette University, weathered the criticism and maintained the traditional comprehensive examination system. Reacting to the lively discussion of these tests, some departments modified their requirements.

At Willamette, the faculty reacted in a different way to student pressure. It lifted "the traditional ordeal of oral comprehensive ex-

In 1972 science and math professors gathered around the buffalo in the museum. In the front row are James Pengra, Larry Anderson, Richard Thomassen, and Katherine Bracher; in the back row are Craig Gunsul, William Hutchings, Walter Brattain, Robert Blumenthal, Richard Clem, Victor Keiser, and Douglas Underwood.

aminations before graduation." Furthermore, the departments would decide "as to whether a senior must pass a senior evaluation or whether he must merely be subjected to such evaluation."[44]

Responding to a variety of pressures, especially from students, a Whitman faculty committee on academic matters concerning minority students made efforts to add to the number of such students and to increase the number of classes about minorities and non-Western subjects. Seeking to enrich the curriculum, the faculty pushed to add new fields of study: art history (a subject enthusiastically supported by President Sheehan), Asian studies, and anthropology. Feeble attempts to add geography and journalism and to reintroduce a major in physical education received scant support. In 1972 the faculty added four new majors: history–American studies; history–Asian studies; sociology–plural societies; and environmental studies. In 1973 professors offered another option: combined majors. For a combined major a student, along with faculty members from the relevant subject areas, planned a course of study that required the concurrence of the board of review. This program allowed smaller departments (such as religion and astronomy) that did not offer a major an opportunity to join larger departments in creating a personalized one.

In 1975 the faculty offered still another new program—freshman seminars. The catalog listed several advantages of such courses, including an opportunity "to work with mature scholars on topics of their special interest" and "to increase student's facility in reading, writing, speaking, and discussion."[45]

Beginning in 1968 many of the academic departments increased class credits from three to four—the "modified four-course system"—in an effort to limit class sizes, to reduce the number of courses that students carried, and to provide more depth. Older members of the faculty praised this significant change, partly because it reduced the number of classes that students took. But many in the Whitman community complained about a lack of consistency: numerous courses still only granted three credits but required as much effort as those awarding four credits.

Late in the 1960s, as the faculty implemented so many curricular changes, they also—partly in response to student pressure for more freedom—significantly altered requirements, including some

Members of the chemistry department in 1974 were Charles Templeton, David Frasco, Glenn Woodward, and James Todd.

that had been in place for decades. In 1967 a divided faculty terminated the long-standing freshman English requirement. More important, they dropped the distribution requirements, which had mandated fifteen credit hours in each of the three divisions—social sciences, humanities, and basic sciences—for graduation. Students praised "the new spirit of the faculty," which led to this change as well as to liberalized dormitory rules, observing that professors "often took as much or more of a lead in sponsoring and supporting innovation as the students. . . . The administration played its traditional cautionary role."[46] Under this new system, which would last until the early 1980s, students took about a third of their credit hours in their major field, about a third in courses supporting the major, and about a third in "breadth of study." To make this system work effectively, teachers had to spend more time advising students about course distributions that would fulfill their four-year course plan. A committee conscientiously reviewed each plan for compliance with the new graduation guidelines. (At first this committee was known as the "committee reviewing academic progress," but because of the acronym—CRAP—its name was changed to the student academic progress committee.) This review process absorbed considerable faculty energy, and faculty advisors discovered that the new system necessitated a closer working arrangement with students. One final re-

quirement, swimming, caused a wag to joke that Whitman required
only 124 credits and the ability to swim fifty yards.

In the early 1970s the Whitman faculty greatly expanded foreign-
study programs. This action brought unforeseen and significant
changes, especially late in the century, when a high percentage of
juniors studied abroad. In the late 1960s the college participated in
the Experiment in International Living, a program that lacked
structure and drew only limited faculty interest. In 1973 the faculty
approved Professor Corey Muse's unusual exchange program for
student teachers between Whitman and St. Luke's College at the University of Exeter in England. In the same year Dean Knopf, an ardent supporter of foreign study, worked with other concerned individuals in affiliating the college with the Institute of European
Studies. Professors also approved participation in the Independent
Liberal Arts Colleges Abroad.

Professional Concerns of the Early 1970s

Of the predominantly male faculty in the early 1970s, only a few
members had been hired prior to 1960. Thus, most professors were
young, serving in the lower academic ranks. Several of them had publication plans, but learned that they were under no pressure to publish. Reed College took the same position as Whitman: publication
was not a requisite for promotion.[47] On the other hand, pressure
to have a Ph.D., which had begun in the 1960s, was intensifying, and
would continue to increase over the next thirty years.

President Louis Perry praised those who were active in their professions, but seasoned faculty members worried that the quality of
teaching might decline if professors spent too much time with research and writing. One young professor informed his colleagues
that he had published an essay in a prominent journal and was
shocked to hear two experienced professors state that he should not
publish until after retirement. Alumni, too, feared the principle of
"publish or perish," arguing that solid teaching had made the college successful. Alumnus Nard Jones pitched into the discussion,
insisting that Whitman's William Davis had been "one of the best
teachers of Shakespeare ever to appear in the Northwest . . . but had
published nothing, nor had the time or money to get a doctorate."[48]

English professor Thomas Howells lectures from his famous black books. Reflecting upon his long career, he stated, "I have taught many Whitman students. Others I have known in campus activities and friendships. To all of them I am grateful for the sharing of our time, the sharing of our lives."

Committed to teaching, the faculty spent long hours in class preparation, grading, and advising and mentoring young colleagues; for example, historian Ronald Sires jokingly informed recent additions to his division that to write a lecture from one book was plagiarism, but to write it from two books was scholarship. For years, the college catalog stated that professors "are encouraged to do scholarly work with a view to publication or to the improvement of their institution, but they are selected, retained, and promoted chiefly on the basis of their promise and their demonstrated effectiveness as teachers and advisers."[49] Some of Whitman's best professors published little or not at all. Professor Howells, for example, was a superb teacher, an ardent defender of the liberal arts, and a persistent advocate of faculty rights. He preferred teaching, advising students, and committee work to publishing. Professor Stuart believed that President Sheehan did not support "publish or perish," but that he had created and maintained "an environment of encouragement."[50] Political scientist Robert Fluno opposed required publication but observed: "People who say they are going to publish when they retire never do. The time to do it is when stimulated by classes."[51] After the arrival of President Robert Skotheim, more emphasis would be put on professional activity, including publications, and the disagreement over required publications would continue. The younger faculty members published much more than their predecessors because they have more time, support, and interest than their predecessors. Several of their essays and books made an impact on their disciplines and added to the school's reputation. Still, Professor George Castile's essay, "Publish or Putrify," argued for more faculty publication, reporting that between 1973 and 1975 the faculty had published five books, seven book chapters, and eight-two articles; had read forty-three meeting papers; and had reviewed sixty-three books. He found that slightly less than one-third of the faculty published books, book chapters, or articles during this period.[52]

In the decade between 1965 and 1975, professors put more time and energy into committees and regular and special faculty meetings than ever before or ever since; at the same time, the administration urged them to become more effective advisors. Those who sought to engage in research and writing complained that committee work, added to teaching and advising responsibilities, drained their energy. At the same time, faculty members recognized the fact that, more than their predecessors, they had responded to pressing contemporary issues, including race, poverty, war, and the environment.

In the 1970s a few visiting professors, funded either by the Johnston Foundation or through the Edward F. Arnold Visiting Professorship, added expertise and diversity to the curriculum. However, the Paul Garrett Fellows program had far greater impact upon the faculty than the Arnold appointments did, since it financially assisted those at the assistant and associate level who possessed—according to the catalog—"scholarly qualifications and a high degree of demonstrated competence in teaching."

In 1974 Acting President Kenyon Knopf, speaking about concerns that were also voiced by informed faculty members, emphasized the problems of financial inflation and a decline in the college-age population. He added that Whitman could not offer "no-need scholar-ships because our classrooms and student residences are full, and we would lose revenue rather than gain it." Some faculty members dis-agreed, arguing that other colleges with endowments smaller than Whitman's, including Reed College, were offering no-need scholar-ships as a means to attract better students and to reward those who had excelled in secondary schools. Knopf received greater faculty support when he emphasized, as had President Sheehan in the 1970s, that too many Americans denied the career value of liberal arts and that "the world's problems of minorities, war, poverty, and envi-ronmental deterioration led students in higher education to cry for relevance in their studies." The liberal arts had been defended by Stephen Penrose and his faculty; their successors would uphold them long after 1975, as they watched Whitman's sister institutions offer "relevant programs" on and off their campuses.

Epilogue:
Uplifting Gatherings
1975

On March 23, 1975, an Oregon State police cruiser, operating on the I-84 freeway near The Dalles, pulled over a brown and yellow bus marked "Walla Walla Padres," a vehicle used by the Class A baseball team. The patrolman boarded the bus and saw pipe-smoking sociology professor Ely Chertok seated in the front, with several middle-aged passengers located behind him. The surprised officer exclaimed, "This is no baseball team!" Actually, "this" was a large proportion of the Whitman faculty, riding the rented bus to a faculty conference scheduled at Salishan, a resort on the Oregon coast. This incident greatly amused the riders. Later, at the Salishan registration desk, a young Whitman couple—intent on spending their honeymoon in a pleasing environment—blanched, upon seeing numerous members of their faculty saunter into the office. Professors made some wisecracks to the baffled seniors, including the explanation that they had journeyed to the coast to serve as chaperons. The newlyweds, dismayed by the fact that nearly the whole faculty was coming to Salishan, cancelled their reservations. This incident increased the faculty members' fun.

The professors were attending the "Whitman Conference on Learning Theories and Teaching Practices," scheduled for March 23–26 and funded by the Ford Foundation. A committee co-chaired by professors Jay Eacker and Philip Howland had arranged a program that registered fifty-one full-time faculty members and fifteen others, including administrators, trustee Baker Ferguson, and Whitman's newly appointed president, Robert A. Skotheim. Spouses and children were invited to the conference, but, to the regret of some, they were denied attendance at the sessions. The committee explained its ruling: "It feared that if the conference was open to a general audience, then the program would tend to lose its focus . . . and become less productive for Whitman."[1]

Larry Paynter videotaped the conference sessions for those who were denied attendance and for anyone who wanted to review the proceedings. According to Paynter, nobody ever requested his eleven tapes. The four invited speakers spoke on a variety of theoretical and practical approaches to teaching and learning. Following the presentations, the professors commented upon them. At a session held without the four authorities, the participants generally concluded that the speakers had little to offer and that their colleagues could have presented more practical papers. Professor Eacker concluded that "some participants felt that questions about learning as well as teaching practices could probably be dealt with by resident experts on these issues within the faculty." The presenters were evaluated in private conversations during the conference and long afterward; Professor Robert Fluno's criticisms of the speakers brought laughter.

Scheduled evening sessions competed with gatherings in private rooms with free wine or beer furnished by the conference or purchased locally by conference coordinator Floyd Bunt, who made periodic runs to local grocers. Between sessions, the professors enjoyed tennis, a hot tub, golf, the beach, delicious meals, and fine wines from Salishan's well-stocked cellar. The diners consumed the most expensive wines that had been recommended by trustee Baker Ferguson and economist David Stevens.

In formal and informal settings, the professors discussed a variety of challenging topics, including the rise of careerism on campuses, the problem of student retention, the faculty evaluation process, and the ever-troublesome football program. The report by director of admissions William Tingley that in 1975 applications had dropped to 805, the lowest figure since 1968, prompted sober discussions. In 1969 and into the early 1970s Whitman had enjoyed good admission numbers, including many Californians who preferred the comparative tranquility of a small college to the turmoil besetting the universities. Professors contemplated the reasons for the sharp decline in applications, including that many high school seniors were selecting colleges nearer to their homes because of the energy crisis following the Arab oil embargo of 1973, that skyrocketing inflation was driving up college expenses in general, and that the state of Washington and the Seattle area in particular were suffering from a serious economic downturn. The faculty understood that once again distant factors, in this case a volatile economy, was influencing their personal and professional lives at remote Whitman College.

Although most participants agreed with mathematician Douglas Underwood that none of the speakers was memorable, they readily acknowledged that the conference provided a store of anecdotes and memories. Eacker concluded that the professors discovered "that they had many things in common with their colleagues but had never taken the time, nor had the opportunity occurred to find out what they were."[2] The so-called "Salishan I" knit the faculty. Perhaps the word "bonding" is too strong, but participants emphasized that a closeness developed that they had not previously experienced. Younger faculty members stressed, at one session, that Whitman lacked a sense of community, and, for a brief time after Salishan, the school provided the community that they had urged. For example, the "Faculty Forum" program, in which a professor would speak to colleagues about his special interest, temporarily gained in popularity; and, for many Friday afternoons, professors gathered for a social hour at Professor Fluno's home. Several participants recalled that the faculty in the late 1970s was closer than it would be in succeeding decades.

The 1975 conference provided some release after a stressful decade. The professors had worked hard at teaching, advising students, and serving on committees. Some had squeezed in time for professional activity—presenting papers and writing books, articles, and reviews. Professors had recently been saddened by the critical illness of faculty leader Arthur Metastasio (who died later in the year), and by the recent deaths of several colleagues and friends, including President Donald Sheehan; geologist Richard Clem, a steady colleague; Anna Eacker, wife of Jay Eacker; Ruth Fluno, wife of Robert Fluno; and Vern Kinsinger, the popular director of the Student Union Building.

The conference served as an opportunity to wind down from a difficult time and to gear up for a promising new presidency. Under President Skotheim's administration, the college would become noticeably stronger. And, during this time, professors who had attended "Salishan I" would recall the conference not for what had been said about learning theory, but for what they had learned about each other. Although there would be other faculty conferences, none would have the impact of this first one.

A New Presidency Begins

On September 14, 1975, a large audience crowded into Cordiner Hall auditorium, anticipating the inaugural address of President Skotheim. The title of the address, "Dreams of Success: Whitman and the World," gave the crowd no hint of his message. But members of the presidential selection committee, who had met with him in New York City the previous October, realized that Skotheim understood and respected both the college's history and its current condition. They appreciated the contrast between historians Donald Sheehan and Robert Skotheim: the members of the selection committee had had to sell the college to Sheehan, but Skotheim was already sold when he met with them.

The young speaker—at the age of forty-one, he was the youngest Whitman president since Stephen Penrose—began his inaugural address by stating that most of the audience knew "infinitely more" about Whitman than he did. Skotheim then gave a thoughtful summary of the college's history in the context of national history, quoting from the books by Penrose and Chester Maxey; few in the audience had read either. The new president emphasized that Whitman was "one of the most financially secure [colleges] in the country" and observed that, "as befits its origin, the college's consumption has not been conspicuous, but its relative wealth is nonetheless significant." He then asked: "What is one to make of this tale of piety, self-sacrifice, hard work, and eventual success?"

Looking to the future, as a historian should, Skotheim pointed out two areas of special concern. He judged that the first was "curricular and raises the question whether Whitman, and other liberal arts colleges, will be able to adopt a body of academic study that will

Robert Skotheim served as president between 1975 and 1988. He came to office demonstrating a solid under-standing of Whitman's history and the condition of its faculty and students. His inaugural address indicated that he would be a devoted spokesman for the school and that he would build upon the college's firm foun-dation. His important presidency is the starting point for any future history of the college.

be intellectually coherent and addressed to the world which students will inhabit after they graduate." The second concern he raised was "the quality of student life, or the overall human development of stu-dents." The speaker reminded his audience: "The shelter has been largely removed, and life for students on a college campus is more like life for other Americans." Skotheim concluded, "There is still a challenge for Whitman, and that is to create an environment in which greater intellectual vitality can exist in conjunction with max-imum personal and social development."

In this speech—and until the day he resigned in 1988—President Skotheim would use his understanding and appreciation of Whitman's history in his successful effort to advance the college, particularly during an ambitious and successful fund drive in the 1980s. Winks Dunphy, who worked closely with Skotheim, noted that no president since Maxey had been so interested in the Penrose legacy. Experienced faculty members agreed.

When asked why he came to Whitman, Skotheim explained that he had chosen the college because of its tradition, its $28,000,000 endowment, its loyal alumni, its dedicated faculty, and the adequate physical plant. In sum, the school had its "head screwed on right." An intellectual historian, Skotheim had become keenly interested in institution building, for which he left a highly successful professional career of teaching and writing. And there was another reason for his selecting Whitman: its location in the Pacific Northwest. He and Maxey were the only Whitman presidents to have been born in the region; both men wanted to build a liberal arts college in the region they loved.

A Seattle native, Skotheim had earned his history degrees at the University of Washington. He had taught in universities and had served three years—1972 to 1975—as dean and provost at Hobart and William Smith Colleges in upstate New York. His first contact with Whitman had been in 1960, when he came to Walla Walla to visit historian Ronald Sires and his family. He was struck by the difference between the condition of the faculty at the University of Washington and that at Whitman. Skotheim's father, a high school educator, had worked roofing houses in the summer; Professor Sires had only recently been able to escape work in the wheat harvest.

But it was his time in New York that first introduced Skotheim to the liberal arts college, which he found to be strikingly unlike the large, public research universities, especially in the differences between the concerns of the faculties. For example, as a dean, Skotheim had learned that a liberal arts college treated undergraduates differently from the way that he had observed while teaching at the University of Colorado. Engaged by the challenge of building a liberal arts institution, Skotheim sought a college presidency in the Pacific Northwest. He judged that, of the regional colleges, Whitman and Reed had the greatest potential.

In the fall of 1975, assisted by his conscientious and personable wife, Nadine, the energetic president began his thirteen-year endeavor to lift Whitman to a higher level. In his efforts, he never forgot those who had sacrificed to place the school in a very respectable position by the time he assumed the reins, a point he had emphasized in his inaugural address. How Skotheim and many others—faculty members, administrators, staff members, students, alumni, board members, and, of course, donors large and small—advanced the college late in the twentieth century is a subject for another history. Such a study should include the fact that in 1975 the trustees revised the school's constitution by deleting the requirement that "a majority of the Trustees shall be members of Christian churches" and that "the president shall be a member of a Christian church."[3] Penrose had separated the college from the Congregational Church; now the trustees relieved it from Christian requirements.

The sharp-eyed Chester Maxey evaluated Whitman's favorable circumstances in 1975: the school "had no dead horses to pay for, no losses to offset, no entanglements to undo."[4] Fully aware of this positive situation, Skotheim informed the Whitman community that the first requirement in building the institution was an increased endowment. He approached the need for a larger academic budget as a professor would. Agreeing with teachers who had long argued that such a budget would help diversify the curriculum and would allow professional development, the new president sought to bring about this necessary reform. Supporting professional development would enhance faculty members' individual reputations as well as the reputation of the college. At the beginning of his presidency, Skotheim "wondered why the faculty was not worn out" from its heavy teaching, advising, and committee service. He observed that, at Whitman and other small colleges, the "faculty governed with great care but lacked time for an intellectual life;" by contrast, the faculty of a large university "emphasized intellectual life and spent little time in campus governance." Curriculum reform and the physical plant concerned him less than the need to improve the faculty's situation.[5] Building a better Whitman depended upon securing a much larger endowment, which would strengthen the faculty and lead to a string of improvements, including the recruitment of more and better students and additional library materials.

During the last quarter of the twentieth century, the nation would experience a growing economy and much less turmoil than it had during the previous fifty years. The college would continue to develop during years that were relatively unencumbered by severe economic depression and wild inflation, or by terrible wars, or by student activists pushing various causes (the major exception would be the negative reaction against the decision to end football in 1977). Thus, during a period of comparative tranquility and increasing prosperity, the school would build upon what had been accomplished in a long period of turbulence. Nobody appreciated that fact more than historian Skotheim and the many individuals who had served Whitman College since the Great Depression.

Notes

Abbreviations

The collections in which some cited materials are found are referred to in these notes by the following acronyms:

CMC Chester Maxey Collection, Whitman College Archives

THC Thomas Howells Collection, Whitman College Archives

RCC Rudolf Clemen Collection, Whitman College Archives

SPC Stephen Penrose Collection, Whitman College Archives

WBC Walter Bratton Collection, Whitman College Archives

WCA Whitman College Archives

Prologue

1. Stephen Penrose to Thomas Burke, October 6, 1925, SPC.
2. Penrose to George M. Ryker, October 27, 1927, SPC.
3. President's Report, 1930, 4, WCA.
4. Penrose to Frank Atherton, February 1, 1927, SPC.
5. Penrose to Calvin Kirchen, May 6, 1933, SPC.
6. *Whitman College Pioneer*, September 29, 1933.
7. *R. L. Polk's Walla Walla City & County Directory*, 1925–1926, 6.
8. *Up-To-The-Times Magazine*, July 1925, 6363; Penrose to Elizabeth Prague Coolidge, February 2, 1932, SPC.

9. *Up-To-The-Times Magazine*, January 1925, 6034.
10. Penrose to Edward Baldwin, May 4, 1934, SPC.
11. *Whitman College Pioneer*, November 30, 1933; *Walla Walla Union-Bulletin*, November 25, 1933.

Chapter One

1. Stephen Penrose to Otto Rupp, June 14, 1927, Otto Rupp Collection, WCA.
2. Penrose to Arthur Smith, January 25, 1927, SPC.
3. Interview with Markham Harris, November 15, 1995, WCA.
4. Ibid.
5. H. B. Goodrich, *Origins of American Scientists*, 180.
6. Lorna DeFoe, "Gin, Joy, or Solid Work," *Washingtonian*, November 1928, n.p.
7. Penrose to Robert S. MacClenahan, December 14, 1926, SPC.
8. Penrose to Norton Johnson, October 25, 1927, SPC.
9. Interview with Markham Harris, November 15, 1995, WCA.
10. Penrose to MacClenahan, December 14, 1926; Penrose to Robert S. Carnochan, December 4, 1926, SPC.
11. Penrose to William Sidley, November 9, 1925, SPC.
12. Ibid.
13. Penrose to Edward Ruby, December 8, 1925, SPC.
14. Penrose to Miss Evelyn Johnson, March 8, 1929, SPC.
15. Penrose to William E. Carnochan, December 4, 1926, SPC.
16. Penrose to John H. Finley, December 4, 1926, SPC.
17. Penrose to Arthur Smith, January 25, 1927, SPC.
18. Penrose to John Brining, February 13, 1926, SPC.
19. Penrose to Susan Cooper, December 5, 1930, SPC.
20. Penrose to Mitchell Stewart, April 5, 1928, SPC.
21. Penrose to Edward Parsons, October 8, 1928, SPC.
22. Penrose to Charles Barton, June 17, 1926, SPC.
23. Penrose to Parsons, October 8, 1928, SPC.
24. Penrose to Barton, June 17, 1926, SPC; Penrose to W. A. Ashbrook, October 5, 1929, SPC.
25. Penrose to Melvin Brannon, October 27, 1925, SPC.
26. President's Report, 1925, 22, WCA.
27. Penrose, "Possible Modifications in the Deanship," 3, SPC.

28. "Description of Whitman College, 1930," 29, SPC.
29. Penrose to Mitchell Stewart, May 15, 1928, SPC.
30. Ibid.
31. Penrose to Bishop Robert Paddock, June 12, 1928, SPC.
32. Penrose to Wellington Pegg, November 3, 1928, SPC.
33. "Description of Whitman College, 1930," 30, SPC.
34. Penrose to Mrs. David Honeyman, September 20, 1926, SPC.
35. President's Report, 1925, 4.
36. President's Report, 1925, 6, WCA; Penrose to Brannon, March 17, 1926, SPC.
37. President's Report, 1925, 8-9, WCA.
38. President's Report, 1926, 6, WCA.
39. President's Report, 1927, 16, WCA.
40. Penrose to James E. Babb, March 3, 1926, SPC; Penrose to W. H. Cowles, March 3, 1926, SPC.
41. Penrose to Kent Cooper, April 26, 1926, SPC.
42. Penrose to Jackson Elliott, May 15, 1926, SPC.
43. Penrose to George H. Rummens, May 24, 1926, SPC.
44. Ibid.
45. Penrose to Josephine Corliss Preston, December 7, 1927, SPC.
46. Penrose to Howard Pratt, February 6, 1928, SPC.
47. Penrose to Rosella Woodward, June 10, 1927, and June 25, 1928, SPC.
48. President's Report, 1925, 26, WCA.
49. Penrose to Louise Fitch, June 18, 1925, SPC.
50. Fitch to Penrose, June 24, 1925, SPC.
51. Penrose to Reverend Lucius O. Baird, September 30, 1925, SPC.
52. *Whitman College Pioneer*, September 17, 1926.
53. Penrose to John Stone, September 4, 1926, SPC.
54. President's Report, 1927, 1, WCA,
55. Stadium File, n.d., SPC.
56. *Walla Walla Union-Bulletin*, October 28, 1926.
57. President's Report, 1927, 3, WCA.
58. President's Report, 1925, 31, WCA.
59. President's Report, 1926, 21, WCA.
60. President's Report, 1929, 20, WCA.
61. President's Report, 1925, 20, WCA.
62. Penrose to R. L. Ringer, February 9, 1926, SPC.

63. Penrose to Fitch, June 24, 1926, SPC.
64. Penrose to Jean McMorran, February 24, 1928, SPC.
65. Penrose letter of recommendation for Ruth E. Wenstrom, April 7, 1927; Penrose to Wenstrom, May 2, 1928, SPC.
66. Penrose to Howell Cheney, December 19, 1923, SPC.
67. Penrose to Mark Harris, February 11, 1931, WCA.
68. President's Report, 1926, 23, WCA.
69. President's Report, 1927, 8, 10, WCA.
70. President's Report, 1928, 24, WCA.
71. President's Report, 1926, 11-12, WCA.
72. President's Report, 1927, 9, WCA.
73. President's Report, 1929, 14.
74. Penrose to Oscar A. Fechter, January 6, 1925, SPC.
75. Mildred Winship to Penrose, February 2, 1925, SPC.
76. Penrose to Winship, January 22, 1925, SPC.
77. Winship to Penrose, February 9, 1925, SPC.
78. Winship to Penrose, January 26, 1925, SPC.
79. Winship to Penrose, February 5, 1925, SPC.
80. Winship to Penrose, April 13, 1925, SPC.
81. Penrose to Winship, May 21, 1925, SPC.
82. Penrose to George O. Tamblyn, June 16, 1925, SPC.
83. Penrose to Winship, September 10, 1925, SPC.
84. Penrose to Winship, September 22, 1925, SPC.
85. Winship to Penrose, May 21, 1928, SPC.
86. Penrose to William Howard, October 27, 1925, SPC.
87. Burke to Penrose, September 21, 1925, SPC.
88. President's Report, 1925, 37, WCA.
89. Penrose to Brannon, October 27, 1925, SPC.
90. President's Report, 1928, 9, WCA.
91. Penrose to Colonel Robert Burton, June 14, 1927, SPC; Penrose to Hugh Elmer Brown, April 27, 1927, SPC.
92. President's Report, 1928, 11, WCA.
93. Penrose to Mrs. W. H. Cowles, November 4, 1927, SPC.
94. Burton to Penrose, January 26, 1928, SPC.
95. Penrose to Edward Pease, April 16, 1928, SPC.
96. President's Report, 1928, 10, WCA.
97. Penrose to Allen Reynolds, April 25, 1928, SPC.
98. Penrose to Mrs. S. B. Hopkins, November 13, 1928, SPC.

99. Penrose to Mrs. Robert Burton, October 15, 1928, SPC.
100. Burton to Penrose, October 1, 1928, SPC.
101. Burton to Penrose, October 19, 1928, SPC.
102. Penrose to Burton, October 27, 1928, SPC.
103. Penrose to Burton, July 25, 1929, SPC.
104. Penrose to William Worthington, November 8, 1928, SPC.
105. Penrose to Wellington Pegg, November 3, 1928, SPC.
106. Penrose to Worthington, November 24, 1928, SPC.
107. Penrose to Clarence Morrow, March 25, 1929, SPC.
108. Morrow to Penrose, April 4, 1929, SPC.
109. Worthington to Penrose, July 22, 1929, SPC.
110. Penrose to Worthington, July 15, 1929, SPC.
111. President's Report, 1929, 24, WCA.
112. John L. Rand to Penrose, May 23, 1929, SPC.
113. Penrose, "Education At Less Than Cost," 3, Administrative Publications File, WCA.
114. Penrose to Caroline Kamm, January 4, 1928, SPC.
115. Penrose to Archer W. Hendrick, September 9, 1932, SPC.
116. Penrose to Genevieve Bonner, March 11, 1926, SPC.
117. Penrose to Rabbi Koch, October 13, 1928, SPC.
118. Penrose to H. J. Thorkelson, November 23, 1926, SPC.
119. Penrose to Thorkelson, February 21, 1928, SPC.
120. Penrose to Charles C. May, May 15, 1926, SPC.
121. Penrose to Harper Joy, March 29, 1927, SPC.
122. Penrose to Mrs. John P. Weyerhauser, October 7, 1927, SPC; Penrose to Mrs. William H. Baltzell, November 8, 1929, SPC.
123. Penrose to Bishop Frank Touret, February 11, 1928, SPC; *Whitman Alumnus*, May 1934, 11.
124. In the 1920s several Whitman graduates attended the Prince School of Store Service Education in Boston. These women studied a curriculum that centered around selling in department stores. The graduates took employment in department stores and taught sales people how to teach. Lucinda Prince, director of the school, praised her Whitman students, including Frances Penrose and Martha Douglas, and hoped that her school would always have at least one Whitman representative. Interview with Frances Penrose Owen, October 13, 1991, WCA; Lucinda W. Prince to Penrose, November 10, 1927, SPC.

125. Penrose to Howell Cheney, February 22, 1927, SPC.
126. Penrose to Rev. Charles E. Tyuke, November 15, 1927, SPC.
127. Penrose to Dr. Albert W. Staub, February 28, 1928, SPC.
128. Penrose to Marie Felthouse, September 14, 1928, SPC.
129. Penrose to M. W. Wilson, February 6, 1929, SPC.
130. Penrose to Daniel Reed, April 19, 1928, SPC.
131. *Walla Walla Bulletin*, January 5, 1926.
132. Penrose, "What the State Needs Most," Washington Press Association Publication, December 1930, SPC.
133. Penrose to Bessie Locke, June 12, 1928, SPC; Penrose to George H. Palmer, April 11, 1927, SPC.
134. Penrose to Vaughn MacCaughey, October 21, 1926, SPC.
135. Penrose to F. M. Padelford, March 31, 1927 and April 9, 1927, SPC.
136. Penrose to Mr. Harding, September 10, 1928, SPC.
137. Penrose to J. H. Horner, May 26, 1929, SPC.
138. Penrose to William Proctor, February 14, 1928, SPC.
139. Penrose to Harding, September 10, 1928, SPC.
140. Interview with Chester Maxey, June 18, 1979, WCA.
141. Penrose to Joseph Griggs, March 26, 1928, SPC.
142. Penrose to Francis Dodge, October 12, 1925, SPC.
143. Penrose to J. R. Bullock, January 16, 1929, SPC.
144. Penrose to Lucius Baird, November 7, 1927, SPC.
145. Penrose to C. H. Harrison, April 26, 1928, SPC.
146. Penrose to E. Mowbray Tate, January 28, 1928, SPC.
147. Penrose to Hon. Daniel A. Reed, April 19, 1928, SPC.
148. Penrose to Ralph Hanson, September 18, 1929, SPC.
149. Stephen Penrose, "Child Labor," Penrose Pamphlet File, WCA.
150. Penrose to Burton, November 9, 1928, SPC.
151. Penrose to William D. Mitchell, November 8, 1930, SPC.
152. Tom Copeland, *The Centralia Tragedy of 1919: Elmer Smith and the Wobblies*, 77.
153. Penrose to Hubert N. Dukes, February 16, 1926, SPC.
154. Penrose to Governor Roland Hartley, November 25, 1930, SPC.
155. John McClelland, Jr., *Wobbly War: The Centralia Story*, 205.
156. Penrose to Harry Warner, March 17, 1926, SPC.
157. Penrose to Governor Gifford Pinchot, December 17, 1928, SPC; Pinchot to Penrose, January 2, 1929, SPC.

158. Penrose to Elihu Root, October 4, 1928, SPC.

159. Penrose to Nicholas Murray Butler, July 30, 1928, SPC.

160. Penrose to George Wickersham, February 1, 1927, SPC.

161. Penrose to Senator C. C. Dill, December 10, 1929, SPC; Penrose to Senator Wesley L. Jones, June 13, 1930, SPC.

162. *Spokane Spokesman-Review*, April 7, 1930.

163. Penrose to A. E. Holden, January 3, 1930, SPC.

164. Penrose to Reverend William Hawthorne, June 14, 1927, SPC.

165. Penrose to Hawthorne, June 14, 1927, SPC.

166. Penrose to Clara Crane, June 20, 1928, SPC.

167. L. V. McWorter to Penrose, May 17, 1926, SPC.

168. Alvin M. Josephy, Jr., *The Nez Perce Indians and the Opening of the Northwest*, 322.

169. Penrose to James E. Babb, April 1, 1930, SPC.

170. *Washington Historical Quarterly*, April 1930, 158.

171. A. W. Laird to Penrose, April 21, 1930, SPC.

172. Corbett Lawyer to Penrose, February 3, 1930, SPC.

173. James E. Babb to Penrose, March 27, 1930, SPC.

174. Penrose to Babb, April 1, 1930, SPC.

175. *Seattle Times*, June 2, 1930.

176. Penrose to O. C. Upchurch, April 2, 1930, SPC; Penrose letter to the *Walla Walla Union-Bulletin*, April 30, 1930, SPC.

177. Penrose to Laird, May 23, 1930, SPC.

178. *Walla Walla Union-Bulletin*, June 3, 1930. The *Pioneer* on September 19, 1930, evaluated these critics, concluding that they argued that Lawyer "was a friend to neither his own people nor Stevens, but rather an opportunist who sought his own personal advantage at every turn."

179. *Walla Walla Union*, June 4, 1930.

180. Winship to W. H. Cowles, January 13, 1925, SPC.

181. Penrose to Oscar M. Voorhees, October 18, 1930, SPC.

182. Penrose to Charles Reid, March 1, 1927, SPC.

183. Penrose to Cowles, February 28, 1929, SPC.

184. Penrose to Baldwin, February 27, 1930, SPC.

185. "Inquiry Club Constitution and By-Laws, December 1894," Inquiry Club File, WCA.

186. Penrose to James R. Garfield, February 8, 1927, SPC.

187. Penrose to John F. Sinclair, March 8, 1929, SPC.

188. Penrose to Frank Pratt, February 27, 1929, SPC.

189. Penrose to Winship, April 24, 1925, SPC.

190. Penrose to Lewis Mills, February 1, 1928, SPC.

191. Stephen Penrose, "Evolution of Pendleton," Stephen Penrose File, WCA.

192. Penrose to Carroll L. Maxcy, January 21, 1931, SPC.

193. Penrose to Baldwin, September 4, 1926, SPC; Penrose to Marie Felthouse, September 4, 1928, SPC.

Chapter Two

1. Stephen Penrose to W. R. Kedzie, January 2, 1934, SPC.

2. Charles M. Gates, *The First Century at the University of Washington, 1861–1961*, 180; George A. Frykman, *Creating the Peoples University: Washington State University, 1890–1990*, 97-99; *Willamette University Bulletin*, April 1927, 18, and Reports of the President and Other Officials, Willamette University, 1932–1933, 6, Willamette University Archives; *Pacific University Register*, April 1929, 3, and *Pacific University Register*, May 1933, 4, Pacific University Archives.

3. Chester Maxey, *The World I Lived In*, 322.

4. Mildred Uehlinger to John F. Dobbs, January 14, 1926, SPC.

5. Stephen Penrose, *Whitman: An Unfinished Story*, 197.

6. Chester Maxey, *Five Centennial Papers*, 15.

7. Penrose to Dobbs, January 18, 1926, SPC.

8. Penrose to R. A. Penrose, May 12, 1930, SPC.

9. Penrose to W. W. Robertson, January 23, 1930, SPC.

10. President's Report, 1928, 6, WCA.

11. See G. Thomas Edwards, *The Triumph of Tradition: The Emergence of Whitman College, 1859–1924*, especially Appendix A, for a fuller discussion of D. K. Pearsons and his role as Whitman's benefactor.

12. President's Report, 1926, 7, WCA.

13. Penrose to Mrs. Joyner, February 21, 1928, SPC.

14. See Edwards, *The Triumph of Tradition*, 284-367.

15. Whitman College Application to the State Advisory Board, Federal Emergency Relief Administration, September 3, 1933, SPC.

16. President's Report, 1925, 33, WCA.
17. Penrose to Worrall Wilson, November 19, 1926, SPC.
18. Penrose to Wilson, December 1, 1926, SPC.
19. W. H. Cowles to Penrose, January 10, 1927, SPC.
20. Penrose to Wilson, October 21, 1926, SPC.
21. Penrose to Cowles, January 24, 1927, SPC.
22. Penrose to Dorsey Hill, February 1, 1927, SPC.
23. Penrose to Cowles, December 6, 1927, SPC.
24. Hill to Penrose, February 2, 1927, SPC.
25. Penrose to H. J. Thorkelson, February 21, 1928, SPC.
26. Penrose to W. W. Robertson, January 23, 1930, SPC.
27. Board of Overseers Special Finance Committee Report, June 16, 1928, Board of Overseers Minutes, WCA.
28. Penrose to Oscar A. Fechter, June 19, 1928, SPC.
29. President's Report, 1928, 6, WCA.
30. Penrose to Hill, April 17, 1929, SPC.
31. Penrose to Harper Joy, May 4, 1929, SPC.
32. Penrose to Mrs. Josephine Corliss Preston, November 26, 1929, SPC; Penrose to Cowles, December 11, 1929, SPC.
33. Penrose to Cowles, June 16, 1931, SPC.
34. *Whitman Alumnus*, February 1930, 3.
35. Penrose to Joy, September 23, 1931, SPC.
36. Penrose to Rudolf Clemen, April 11, 1934, SPC.
37. President's Report, 1932, 4-5, 10-11, WCA.
38. Penrose to George T. Welsh, February 12, 1926, SPC.
39. Penrose to Otto Rupp, April 8, 1932, Otto Rupp Collection, WCA.
40. President's Report, 1933, 2, WCA.
41. Maxey, *The World I Lived In*, 321-22.
42. Penrose to John D. Rockefeller, December 6, 1930, SPC; Whitman College reprint of the *Atlantic Monthly* articles, n.d., 10, Penrose Pamphlet File, WCA.
43. Donald Sherwood, "Forty Years of Balanced Budgets," 11, WCA.
44. Penrose to Cowles, November 18, 1931, SPC.
45. Penrose to Paul Garrett, January 21, 1931, SPC.
46. Penrose to George Tamblyn, December 8, 1931, SPC.
47. Penrose to Clemen, April 17, 1934, SPC.
48. Penrose to Tamblyn, March 3, 1932, SPC.

49. Penrose to Tamblyn, March 17, 1932, SPC.

50. Penrose to Tamblyn, February 16, 1932, SPC.

51. Tamblyn to Penrose, February 20, 1932, SPC.

52. Walter Bratton to Trustees, March 17, 1932, SPC.

53. Penrose to F. P. Keppel, March 30, 1926, SPC.

54. Penrose to Keppel, September 17, 1932, SPC.

55. Penrose to Keppel, October 3, 1932, SPC.

56. Penrose to Keppel, December 9, 1932, SPC.

57. Penrose to Park Weed Willis, October 12, 1932, SPC.

58. Penrose to Willis, November 18, 1932, SPC.

59. Penrose to Keppel, April 28, 1932, SPC.

60. Penrose to Keppel, November 8, 1933, SPC.

61. Board of Trustees to Carnegie Corporation, February 16, 1934, SPC.

62. Henry Pritchett to Penrose, February 16, 1934, SPC.

63. Maxey to Edward Foster, August 24, 1982, CMC.

64. Penrose to D. Newton Barney, April 2, 1932, SPC; Penrose to Professor R. S. Osgood, June 14, 1932, SPC.

65. Interview with Chester Maxey, May 22, 1974, WCA.

66. Penrose to Homer A. Post, December 18, 1930, SPC.

67. Allen H. Reynolds and Dorsey M. Hill, "The Financial Condition of Whitman College, October 10, 1933," SPC.

68. Interview with Fredric Santler, January 30, 1980, WCA.

69. Penrose to Mildred Winship, March 18, 1933, SPC.

70. Penrose to Hugh Elmer Brown, August 16, 1933, SPC.

71. Board of Overseers Minutes, June 18, 1934, WCA.

72. Penrose to Professor Howard R. Driggs, September 27, 1929, SPC.

73. "Projects for Walla Walla City and County," Centennial Celebration File, SPC.

74. Penrose to Lena M. Phillips, February 26, 1932, SPC.

75. Penrose to Guy A. Turner, February 24, 1932, SPC.

76. Penrose to George H. Penrose, February 5, 1932, SPC.

77. Penrose to Manson F. Backus, February 24, 1932, SPC; Backus to Penrose, February 27, 1932, SPC.

78. Penrose, "The Three Spokanes," 1931, 10, Stephen Penrose File, WCA.

79. Penrose to Baldwin, March 25, 1933, SPC.

80. Penrose to H. Jurgenson, February 15, 1934, SPC.
81. Penrose to F. Bartow Fite, December 17, 1932, SPC.
82. Penrose to Secretary of the Interior Ray L. Wilbur, March 4, 1931, SPC.
83. Penrose to Baldwin, April 10, 1933, SPC.
84. Penrose to James E. Babb, June 21, 1933, SPC.
85. Penrose to Babb, June 21, 1933, SPC.
86. Penrose to Rupp, April 7, 1933, SPC.
87. *Walla Walla Bulletin*, July 23, 1933.
88. Norman Clark, *The Dry Years: Prohibition and Social Change in Washington*, 238.
89. Penrose to W. W. Connor, October 23, 1933, SPC.

Chapter Three

1. Stephen Penrose to William Cowles, December 8, 1933, SPC.
2. Penrose to Hugh Elmer Brown, August 6, 1933, SPC.
3. Brown to Penrose, September 9, 1933, SPC.
4. Penrose to Brown, September 18, 1933, SPC.
5. Brown to Penrose, September 24, 1933, SPC.
6. Henry S. Pritchett to Penrose, January 16, 1934, SPC.
7. Penrose to Pritchett, January 22, 1934, SPC.
8. Penrose to William Proctor, January 24, 1934, SPC.
9. Brown to Penrose, January 29, 1934, SPC.
10. Penrose to Brown, August 16, 1933, SPC.
11. Penrose to Cowles, December 8, 1933, SPC.
12. Arnold W. Palmer to Proctor, February 13, 1934, SPC.
13. Penrose to Cowles, February 23, 1934, SPC.
14. Penrose to Edward Baldwin, March 9, 1934, SPC.
15. Maxey to Albert Garretson, May 10, 1934, CMC.
16. Penrose to Eugene Buchanan, March 21, 1934, SPC.
17. Penrose to Ruth Pontius, February 27, 1934, SPC.
18. Penrose to Rudolf Clemen, March 3, 1934, SPC.
19. Chester Maxey, *The World I Lived In*, 324.
20. Penrose to Arthur Morgan, November 3, 1933, SPC.
21. Penrose to Pritchett, February 9, 1934, SPC.
22. Clemen to Penrose, May 16, 1934, SPC.
23. Clemen to Penrose, April 15, 1934, SPC.

24. Clemen to Penrose, March 8, 1934, SPC.

25. Clemen to Penrose, April 25, 1934, SPC.

26. Penrose to Clemen, April 30, 1934, SPC.

27. Penrose to Clemen, April 6, 1934, SPC.

28. Clemen to Penrose, April 10, 1934, SPC.

29. Clemen to Penrose, April 25, 1934, SPC.

30. Penrose to Clemen, March 14, 1934, SPC.

31. Penrose to Clemen, April 13, 1934, SPC.

32. Penrose to Violet Hughes, December 7, 1933, SPC.

33. Penrose to John Safford, April 13, 1934, SPC; Penrose to John Hoyt, May 24, 1934, SPC.

34. Herbert Ringhoffer to Penrose, February 16, 1934, SPC.

35. Penrose to Park Weed Willis, January 1, 1934, SPC.

36. Maxey, *The World I Lived In*, 332.

37. Penrose to Henry Lefavour, February 14, 1934, SPC.

38. *Whitman Alumnus*, June 1934, 4-7.

39. Presentation speech by Robert L. Ringer, June 17, 1934, SPC.

40. Rudolf Clemen, "Youth and Tomorrow," RCC.

41. Robert Skotheim, "Dreams of Success: Whitman and the World," *Whitman Alumnus*, November, 1975, 18.

42. Penrose to Harry Garfield, April 23, 1934, SPC.

43. Clemen to Dorsey Hill, March 24, 1934, RCC.

44. Clemen to Frank Haigh, April 2, 1934, Frank Haigh File, WCA.

45. Clemen to My New Friends, July 30, 1934, Frank Haigh File, WCA.

46. Clemen to Dear Colleagues, August 3, 1934, Frank Haigh File, WCA.

47. Clemen Report to Board of Trustees, July 1934, Board of Trustees Minutes, WCA.

48. Clemen to John G. Kelly, December 18, 1935, RCC.

49. Ibid.

50. Clemen Report to Board of Trustees, August 1934, Board of Trustees Minutes, WCA.

51. Maxey, *The World I Lived In*, 327.

52. Board of Trustees Minutes, August 23, 1934, WCA.

53. John Dale Russell, "Report of a Financial Survey of Whitman College, September 1934," 2-3, 5, 20, 38, 61, WCA.

54. Maxey, *The World I Lived In*, 328-30.

55. Interview with Donald Sherwood, August 14, 1990, WCA.

56. Maxey, *The World I Lived In*, 329.

57. Russell, "Report of a Financial Survey," 15, WCA.

58. Reginald Parsons to Penrose, December 30, 1936, in Donald Sherwood, "Forty Years of Balanced Budgets," 36, WCA.

59. Penrose to Clemen, April 6, 1934, SPC.

60. Clemen Report to Trustees, November 1934, Board of Trustees Minutes, WCA.

61. Clemen Report to Trustees, January 1935, Board of Trustees Minutes, 2, 3, 9, 11, 13, WCA.

62. Clemen to Kelley, December 18, 1935, RCC.

63. Board of Overseers Minutes, March 30, 1935, WCA.

64. *Whitman Alumnus*, May 1935, 5.

65. Rudolf Clemen, "Higher Education in 1934," 5, speech to Spokane Chamber of Commerce, July 17, 1934, RCC.

66. *Whitman Alumnus*, October 1934, 3.

67. Rudolf Clemen, "Freedom to Learn," *Whitman Alumnus*, October 1935, 3.

68. *Whitman Alumnus*, December 1934, 4.

69. *Walla Walla Union-Bulletin*, April 16, 1936.

70. W. W. Baker to Overseers and Trustees, March 29, 1935, Trustees Correspondence, WCA.

71. Board of Overseers Minutes, June 8, 1935, WCA.

72. Clemen to Kelly, December 18, 1935, RCC.

73. Clemen to Allen Reynolds, October 31, 1935, RCC.

74. Interview with Fredric Santler, February 20, 1980, WCA.

75. Maxey, *The World I Lived In*, 330; interview with Chester Maxey, June 21, 1979, WCA.

76. Board of Trustees to Board of Overseers, unsigned letter, n.d., Board of Trustees Minutes, WCA.

77. Interview with Philip Ashby, February 8, 1990, WCA.

78. Reginald Parsons to Allan Reynolds, April 16, 1936, Board of Trustees Minutes, WCA.

79. Reynolds to Parsons, April 18, 1936, Board of Trustees Minutes, WCA.

80. *Whitman College Pioneer*, April 17, 1936.

81. Reynolds, Bennington, and Maxey to Alumni, n.d., RCC.

82. *Whitman Alumnus*, June 1935, 10.

83. Nard Jones to Maxey, n.d., CMC.

84. Winlock Miller to Penrose, May 29, 1936, RCC.

85. Penrose to Miller, June 2, 1936, RCC.

86. Maxey, *The World I Lived In*, 325-26.

87. Walter Bratton to William O. Douglas, July 27, 1937, Security and Exchange Commission Papers, William O. Douglas Collection, Library of Congress.

88. Interview with Philip Ashby, February 8, 1990, WCA.

89. Interview with Keith Soper, May 4, 1990, WCA.

90. Bratton to Douglas, July 27, 1937, Security and Exchange Commission Papers, William O. Douglas Collection, Library of Congress.

91. Interview with Philip Ashby, February 8, 1990, WCA.

92. Rudolf Clemen, Jr. to the author, June 29, 1993, author's possession.

93. Rudolf Clemen, Sr. to the author, June 21, 1993, author's possession.

94. Maxey, *The World I Lived In*, 326.

95. Clemen to Kelly, December 18, 1935, RCC.

96. John G. Kelly to Penrose, June 6, 1936, RCC.

97. Clemen to Kelly, December 18, 1935, RCC.

98. Interview with Chester Maxey, June 21, 1979, WCA.

99. G. Thomas Edwards, *The Triumph of Tradition: The Emergence of Whitman College, 1859–1924*, 121.

100. Maxey, *The World I Lived In*, 332.

101. Walter Bratton, "Reminiscences of Whitman in 1895," WBC.

102. Stephen Penrose, "A Great Teacher and Leader," Walter Bratton File, WCA.

103. Otto Harbach to Bratton, "Whitman College Honors Walter A. Bratton, May 30, 1942," Walter Bratton File, WCA.

104. Interview with Ivar Highberg, February 8, 1995, author's possession.

105. Interview with Zelma Conway Williams, March 18, 1991, WCA.

106. Bratton to Penrose, 1928, SPC.

107. *Whitman Alumnus*, June 1935, 7.

108. President's Report, 1936, 35, 15, 18, WCA.

109. Board of Overseers Minutes, June 15, 1936, 46, 47, 43, WCA.

110. Sherwood to Haigh, January 4, 1937, Frank Haigh File, WCA.
111. Donald Sherwood, "Whitman College, 1936–1976: 40 Years of Balanced Budgets Without Deficit Financing," 4, 6, 7, 9, 14, 20, 36, WCA.
112. Board of Overseers Minutes, June 7, 1937, 68, WCA.
113. Committee on Selection of a New President to Board of Trustees, December 29, 1937, WBC.
114. John C. Lyman to Dean Frank L. Haigh, January 26, 1951, Faculty Council Minutes, WCA.
115. President's Report, 1938, 17, WCA.
116. President's Report, 1937, 9-10, WCA.
117. President's Report, 1940, 3-4, WCA.
118. President's Report, 1941, 4, WCA.
119. President's Report, 1939, 5, WCA.
120. President's Report, 1938, 22, WCA.
121. Board of Overseers Minutes, June 13, 1938, 94, WCA.
122. Board of Overseers Minutes, June 5, 1937, 3, WCA.
123. Board of Overseers Minutes, June 1, 1940, 3, WCA.
124. Frank H. Bowles to Bratton, November 7, 1938, WBC.
125. President's Report, 1941, 15, WCA.
126. *New York Times*, May 16, 1926.
127. Edith Quimby, "For Doctor Bratton," n.d., Walter Bratton File, WCA.
128. Douglas to Bratton, May 8, 1942, Security and Exchange Commission Papers, William O. Douglas Collection, Library of Congress.

Chapter Four

1. James Bryce, *The American Commonwealth*, Volume II, 549.
2. Stephen Penrose to Arthur Wright, September 25, 1925, SPC.
3. Walter Bratton, Chester Maxey, and William Proctor, "The Educational Development and Influence of Whitman College," October 1933, 8, SPC.
4. Penrose to Warren Arnquist, February 22, 1929, SPC.
5. Penrose to William Proctor, November 9, 1925, SPC.
6. Penrose to Wright, September 25, 1925, SPC.
7. Penrose to Louis A. Parsons, April 16, 1926, SPC.

8. Penrose to Rowena Ludwig, May 29, 1928, SPC.
9. Penrose to J. Harold Dubios, January 23, 1931, SPC; Penrose to Philip Von Lubken, January 20, 1928, SPC.
10. Penrose to Henry Ward, January 20, 1926, SPC.
11. Penrose to Proctor, October 22, 1925, SPC.
12. W. C. Eells, "Teaching Load of Whitman College Faculty," 1926, SPC.
13. Penrose to Rees E. Tulloss, June 19, 1929, SPC.
14. Penrose to George M. Ramsey, June 16, 1927 and February 15,1930, SPC.
15. Stephen Penrose, *Whitman, An Unfinished Story*, 227-28.
16. Penrose to Mary Bausch, February 15, 1930, SPC.
17. John Miller to Penrose, September 3, 1929, SPC.
18. Penrose, *Whitman: An Unfinished Story*, 224.
19. Interview with Markham Harris, November 15, 1995, WCA.
20. Penrose to J. E. Ransom, September 26, 1929, SPC.
21. W. C. Eells, "Teaching Load," 1926, SPC.
22. Penrose to William Galbraith, February 21, 1929, SPC.
23. Penrose, for the Committee on Plans for Celebration of the Seventy-fifth Anniversary of Whitman College, to the Faculty, January 10, 1930, SPC.
24. Penrose to Charles H. Clarke, May 21, 1930, SPC.
25. Penrose to Omen Bishop, October 24, 1929, SPC.
26. Penrose to Robert L. Grant, February 28, 1928, SPC.
27. Faculty Petition, Board of Overseers Minutes, June 16, 1928, WCA.
28. Chester Maxey, *The World I Lived In*, 251.
29. Benjamin Brown to Penrose, December 9, 1925, SPC.
30. Penrose to Howell Cheney, November 13, 1928, SPC.
31. Howard Brode to Mary Ringer, April 16, 1931, Howard Brode Collection, WCA.
32. Interview with Markham Harris, November 15, 1995, WCA.
33. Penrose to Emory Hoover, March 2, 1932, SPC.
34. Brode, Bratton, and Maxey to the Trustees and Overseers, February 21, 1932, WCA.
35. Penrose to Mary Butterfield, June 22, 1932, SPC.
36. "Faculty Salaries," December 23, 1936, Frank Haigh File, WCA.
37. Maxey, *The World I Lived In*, 261.

38. Board of Overseers Minutes, Douglas McClane, Secretary of the Faculty, "To Whom It May Concern," December 6, 1932, WCA.
39. Penrose to the Faculty, 1933, SPC.
40. Penrose to Worthington, April 28, 1932, SPC.
41. Penrose to the Faculty, 1933, SPC.
42. Penrose to Betty Cameron, April 14, 1933, SPC.
43. Maxey, *The World I Lived In*, 322; Maxey, "Whitman's Diamond Jubilee," Chester Maxey File, WCA.
44. Interview with Fredric Santler, February 20, 1980, WCA.
45. *Whitman Alumnus*, September 1933, 5.
46. Penrose to John L. Rand, April 25, 1933, SPC; Penrose to Calvin Kirchen, May 6, 1933, SPC.
47. Penrose to Rudolf Clemen, March 10, 1934, SPC.
48. Maxey, *The World I Lived In*, 326.
49. Board of Overseers Minutes, August 23, 1934, WCA.
50. Report of Rudolf Clemen, Board of Trustees Minutes, January 16, 1935, 7, WCA.
51. Maxey, *The World I Lived In*, 327.
52. John Dale Russell, "Report of a Financial Survey of Whitman College, September 1934," 45-46, 48, 51, 63, WCA.
53. Ibid.
54. Maxey, *The World I Lived In*, 323; Russell Blankenship to Penrose, March 25, 1932, SPC.
55. Fredric Santler, Founders Day Address, February 16, 1984, Oral History File, WCA.
56. Maxey, *The World I Lived In*, 331.
57. President's Report, 1937, 13-14, WCA.
58. Maxey, *The World I Lived In*, 332.
59. G. B. Marquis to Haigh, January 17, 1938, Frank Haigh File, WCA.
60. Dorsey Hill to Haigh, May 20, 1932, and Bratton to Haigh, June 25, 1941, Frank Haigh File, WCA.
61. President's Report, 1942, 8, WCA.
62. President's Report, 1939, 5-6, WCA.
63. Penrose to Bratton, January 11, 1929, SPC.
64. Penrose to Wayne Darlington, December 14, 1929, SPC.
65. *Whitman College Catalog*, 1938, 43.
66. Penrose to Proctor, November 9, 1925, SPC.

67. President's Report, 1939, 5, WCA.
68. Bratton, Maxey, and Proctor, "Educational Development and Influence," October 1933, 5, SPC.
69. President's Report, 1940, 16, WCA.
70. Board of Trustees Minutes, October 18, 1934, WCA.
71. "Twenty-Five Years at Whitman, 1924–1949," Biographical File, WCA.
72. President's Report, 1937, 29, WCA.
73. President's Report, 1940, 6, WCA.
74. Brown to Penrose, December 9, 1925, SPC.
75. Penrose to Brown, December 14, 1925, SPC.
76. Penrose to Henry Pritchett, December 14, 1925, SPC.
77. Brown to Penrose, February 15, 1926, SPC.
78. Howard S. Brode and Catherine Bingham Brode, Golden Wedding Celebration, 1943, WCA.
79. Maxey, *The World I Lived In*, 150.
80. Russell Blankenship to Penrose, February 9, 1933, SPC.
81. H. L. Mencken, "The Library," *The American Mercury*, December 1931, 507-08.
82. Bratton, Maxey, and Proctor, "Educational Development and Influence," October 1933, 5, SPC.
83. *Whitman College Pioneer*, September 29, 1933.
84. Interview with Melvin "Jake" Jacobs, March 19, 1990, WCA.
85. Interview with John Haigh, February 23, 1990, WCA.

Chapter Five

1. Edward Ruby to Stephen Penrose, November 10, 1925, SPC.
2. Penrose to W. E. Belleau, May 14, 1929, SPC.
3. Penrose to Ruby, February 16, 1928, SPC.
4. *Whitman College Catalog*, 1927, 89; Penrose to Joseph Tewinkel, January 29, 1931, SPC.
5. Board of Trustees Minutes, November 4, 1926, WCA.
6. Ibid; *Whitman College Catalog*, 1926, 47.
7. William Worthington to Douglas McClane, October 21, 1932, SPC.
8. Board of Trustees Minutes, April 25, 1929, WCA.
9. *Whitman College Catalog*, 1933, 23.

10. Dean Walter Bratton's Report to President Rudolf Clemen, June 5, 1935, RCC.
11. *Whitman College Catalog,* 1937, 95.
12. Penrose to W. F. Begelow, Nov 3, 1927, SPC.
13. Penrose to R. W. Ogan, July 15, 1929, SPC.
14. Bernard Peach, "Mr. and Mrs. Penrose: A Memorial," n. d., Penrose Recollections File, SPC.
15. Penrose to F. T. Post, December 16, 1931, SPC.
16. Interview with Margo Collins Hoth, July 28, 1994, WCA.
17. Interview with D. Herbert Armstrong, March 9, 1990, WCA.
18. Interview with William Harris, May 9, 1974, WCA.
19. Interview with Dwelley Jones, n.d., 1973, WCA.
20. Bernard Peach, "Student Life at Whitman College," author's possession.
21. Interview with Margo Collins Hoth, July 28, 1994, WCA.
22. *Whitman College Pioneer,* March 8, 1935.
23. Interview with Thomas McNeill, July 12, 1994, WCA.
24. *Whitman College Pioneer,* March 9, 1934.
25. *Whitman College Pioneer,* September 27, November 1, and November 22, 1935.
26. *Whitman College Pioneer,* March 20, 1936.
27. *Whitman College Catalog,* 1935, 98.
28. Telephone interview with Franklin "Pete" Hanson, July 15, 1995.
29. *Facets,* December 1956, CMC.
30. Interview with Janette Moses Armstrong, March 9, 1990, WCA.
31. Interview with William Harris, July 27, 1995, WCA.
32. Interview with D. Herbert Armstrong, March 9, 1990, WCA.
33. Interview with John Richards, August 11, 1994, WCA.
34. Interview with Iris Little Myers, February 24, 1990, WCA.
35. *The Blue Moon,* November 1931, 7, WCA.
36. *Yeast,* 1936, 7, WCA.
37. Penrose to Colonel Robert Burton, April 12,1928, SPC.
38. Penrose to Leonard Koos, June 2, 1931, SPC.
39. *Whitman College Catalog,* 1934, 27.
40. *Whitman College Pioneer,* September 21, 1934.
41. *Whitman College Pioneer,* May 3, 1935.
42. William O. Douglas, "Commencement Address," *Whitman Alumnus,* October 1938, 2.

43. Interview with Dwelley Jones, n.d., 1973, WCA.

44. Interview with Kenneth Garner, February 8, 1990, WCA.

45. Interview with D. Herbert Armstrong, March 9, 1990, WCA.

46. Interview with Frankie Ladley Wakefield, February 26, 1990, WCA.

47. Interview with Jake Jacobs, March 19, 1990, WCA.

48. Penrose to Howell Cheney, November 21, 1932, SPC.

49. Penrose to Evelyn Johnson, January 24, 1929, SPC.

50. Alice Hogue True, in *50th Reunion Booklet, Class of 1934*, WCA.

51. Interview with Iris Little Myers, February 24, 1990, WCA.

52. Almira Quinn, "Memories of Dr. Stephen B. L. Penrose," n.d., Penrose Recollections File, SPC.

53. Interview with Dorothy Robinson West, July 24, 1994, WCA.

54. Interview with William Harris, July 27, 1995, WCA.

55. Penrose to Clyde Bridger, March 10, 1930, SPC.

56. Helen Barrett Woodroofe, "Memories of Dr. Penrose," n. d., Penrose Recollections File, SPC.

57. Joe Davis, "Memories of Life with the Penrose Family," n.d., Penrose Recollections File, SPC.

58. Mary Johnson Koch, Untitled paper on Penrose, n. d., Penrose Recollections File, SPC.

59. Interview with Dorothy Robinson West, July 24, 1994, WCA.

60. Interview with Kenneth Garner, February 8, 1990, WCA.

61. Interview with Iris Little Myers, February 24, 1990, WCA.

62. Interviews with Ralph Edgerton, June 19, 1993, and June 9–10, 1995, WCA.

63. Interview with Richard Eells, May 19, 1990, WCA.

64. Interview with Lucile Lomen, October 12, 1994, WCA.

65. Elizabeth Johnson to Mrs. C. W. Johnson, January 26, 1937, in the possession of Elizabeth Johnson Tuttle.

66. Interview with Margo Collins Hoth, July 28, 1994, WCA.

67. Telephone interview with Bert Edwards, July 23, 1995.

68. Interview with Merlin Young, April 25, 1990, WCA.

69. Interview with D. Herbert Armstrong, March 9, 1990, WCA.

70. Interview with Almira Quinn, n.d., WCA.

71. Interview with Dorothy Robinson West, July 24, 1994, WCA.

72. Interview with Edith Pope Patten, March 15, 1990, WCA.

73. Interview with Rod Alexander, May 17, 1991, WCA.

74. Interview with Kenneth Garner, February 8, 1990, WCA.

75. Interview with Almira Quinn, n.d., WCA.

76. Interview with Hattie Gordon Fry, February 14, 1990, WCA; interview with Margo Collins Hoth, July 28, 1994, WCA.

77. Interview with Vivian Cochran Garner, February 8, 1990, WCA.

78. Interview with Zelma Conway Williams, March 18, 1991, WCA.

79. Brode to Arthur Parker, July 30, 1940, Howard Brode Collection.

80. Interview with Margo Collins Hoth, July 28, 1994, WCA.

81. Interview with William L. Kelly, October 9, 1978, WCA.

82. "A Golden Age of Physics at Whitman," *Whitman*, Spring 1995, 11.

83. Interview with Thomas McNeill, July 12, 1994, WCA.

84. Interview with Georgia Mae Wilkins Gallivan, May 21, 1990, WCA.

85. Interview with Russ McNeill, June 9, 1995, WCA.

86. Interview with Thomas McNeill, July 12, 1994, WCA.

87. Peach, "Student Life."

88. Elizabeth Johnson to Mrs. C. W. Johnson, October 3, 1937, in the possession of Elizabeth Johnson Tuttle.

89. Penrose to Marjorie Lewis, March 19,1925, SPC.

90. Ruth McBirney to parents, May 28, 1937, McBirney Letters, WCA.

91. Interview with Lola Sims Snyder, March 2, 1990, WCA.

92. Interview with Almira Quinn, n.d., WCA.

93. Interview with Bert Edwards, July 26, 1995, author's possession.

94. Penrose to Stephen "Binks" Penrose, Jr., October 3 1932, SPC.

95. Penrose to J. R. Bullock, January 16, 1929, SPC.

96. Penrose to John Dyer, November 13, 1929, SPC.

97. Penrose to Earle A. Rowell, January 6, 1928, SPC.

98. Penrose to Lewis Bates, November 1, 1928, SPC.

99. Penrose to President C. C. Mierow, March 5, 1926, SPC.

100. Penrose to Binks Penrose, *Fifty Year Plus*, Spring 1991, 13, WCA; *Whitman College Pioneer*, March 5, 1926.

101. Penrose to Richard Springer, November 29, 1932, SPC.

102. Telephone interview with Pete Hanson, July 23, 1995.

103. Interviews with Gordon Scribner, May 4 and 10, 1991, WCA.

104. *Seattle Times*, August 25, 1930.
105. Interview with Iris Little Myers, February 24, 1990, WCA.
106. McBirney to parents, October 25, 1936, McBirney Letters, WCA.
107. Penrose to Ray Lowman, March 9, 1934, SPC.
108. Interview with Thomas McNeill, July 12, 1994, WCA.
109. "Guide to Whitman Life for Women Students," 1941–1942, 26, Whitman Publications File, WCA.
110. Penrose to Roger Folgate, February 26, 1929, SPC.
111. Louise Blomquist to Penrose, July 26, 1929, SPC.
112. "The Constitution of the Women's Organizations," 1928, 2, 9, 14, Whitman Publications File, WCA.
113. Interview with Georgia Mae Wilkins Gallivan, May 21, 1990, WCA.
114. McBirney to parents, December 3, 1936, McBirney Letters, WCA.
115. Interview with Margo Collins Hoth, July 28, 1994, WCA.
116. Penrose to John Barber, January 9, 1933, SPC.
117. Interview with Margo Collins Hoth, July 28, 1994, WCA; *Waiilatpu*, 1933, 92; *Whitman College Pioneer*, March 13, 1941.
118. Interviews with Gordon Scribner, May 4 and 10, 1991, WCA.
119. Interview with Lucile Lomen, October 12, 1994, WCA.
120. Interview with John Richards, August 11, 1994, WCA.
121. Penrose to Crane Walker, April 10, 1934, SPC.
122. Penrose to Jasper Morrison, June 22, 1927, SPC.
123. *Whitman College Pioneer*, January 25, 1932.
124. Interview with Edward McMillan, June 19, 1993, WCA.
125. Grace Robertson, "Health Service Report," 1926–1927, 2, WCA.
126. Penrose to Alex McDonell, December 13, 1927, SPC; Penrose to Herman Goodman, December 15, 1927, SPC.
127. McClane to Board of Trustees, Board of Trustees Minutes, February 12, 1932, WCA.
128. *Whitman College Pioneer*, January 17, 1936.
129. Interview with V. Purdy Cornelison, April 10, 1991, WCA.
130. Interview with Vivian Cochran Garner, February 8, 1990, WCA.
131. McBirney to parents, September 24 and 27, 1936, McBirney Letters, WCA.
132. *Yeast*, April 1934, 7, WCA.
133. *Whitman College Pioneer*, April 19, 1929.

134. *Waiilatpu*, 1936, 99.
135. Penrose to H. N. Wright, January 11, 1928, SPC.
136. Penrose to H. W. Reherd, January 27, 1926, SPC.
137. *Whitman College Pioneer*, February 24, 1928.
138. Penrose to Francis Shepardson, March 30, 1925, SPC.
139. Bernard Molohon, *Sons of Marcus Whitman*, 101-09, WCA.
140. Shepardson to Penrose, November 20, 1930, SPC.
141. *Whitman College Pioneer*, November 2, 1939; *Walla Walla Union-Bulletin*, November 2, 1939.
142. *Whitman College Pioneer*, May 16, 1930.
143. Interview with Hattie Gordon Fry, February 14, 1990, WCA.
144. Interview with Thomas McNeill, July 12, 1994, WCA.
145. Board of Deans Minutes, June 6, 1927, WCA.
146. Board of Deans Minutes, May 22, 1939, WCA.
147. Walter Bratton to Harold Piper, May 26, 1942, WBC.
148. Mrs. K. E. Mathieson to Penrose, October 11, 1929, SPC.
149. Interview with Margo Collins Hoth, July 28, 1994, WCA; Elizabeth Johnson to Mrs. C. W. Johnson, November 9, 1935, in possession of Elizabeth Johnson Tuttle.
150. Carlin Aden, in *50th Reunion Booklet, Class of 1934*, WCA.
151. Penrose to William Galbraith, February 21, 1929, SPC.
152. Penrose to Fred S. Wiman, February 17, 1932, SPC.
153. Interview with James Hill, Jr., March 16, 1990, WCA.
154. McBirney to parents, October 3, 1936, McBirney Letters, WCA.
155. Penrose to H. L. Bowman, January 12, 1928, SPC.
156. *Whitman College Pioneer*, March 9, 1928.
157. McBirney to parents, March 2–10, 1937, McBirney Letters, WCA.
158. *Waiilatpu*, 1937. 54.
159. Interviews with Gordon Scribner, May 4 and 10, 1991, WCA.
160. *Whitman College Pioneer*, April 24, 1931.
161. *The Blue Moon*, November 1931, 7, WCA.
162. *Whitman College Pioneer*, Jan 20, 1928; *The Blue Moon*, 1927, 28.
163. *Clock Tower*, January 1950, 11
164. Interview with Dorothy Robinson West, July 24, 1994, WCA.
165. Jack Hewins, *Borleske: Never Far From Hope*, Foreword.
166. *Whitman Alumnus*, January 1925, 11.

167. Leo C. Humphrey, "A Study of Athletics and Scholarship at Whitman College," May 1928, SPC.

168. *Whitman College Pioneer*, October 24, 1940.

169. Concerns about sports, scholarships, and commitment to sports can be found in letters from William F. Howard to Penrose, October 7, 1925, SPC, and from R. L. Ringer to Borleske, April 20, 1927, SPC; interview with Baker Ferguson, August 17, 1995, author's possession.

170. Jim Morrill, *Clock Tower*, January 1940, 7.

171. Penrose to F. J. Finucane, October 11, 1930, SPC.

172. *Seattle Post-Intelligencer*, March 2, 1986.

173. Penrose to Malcolm C. Morrow, February 17, 1927, SPC.

Chapter Six

1. Chester Maxey, *The World I Lived In*, 334.

2. Frank Baker to Binks Penrose, February 22, 1940, Stephen Penrose, Jr. Collection, WCA.

3. Stephen Penrose to Binks Penrose, November 21, 1941, Stephen Penrose, Jr. Collection, WCA.

4. Binks Penrose to D. F. Baker, December 1, 1941, Stephen Penrose, Jr. Collection, WCA.

5. Stephen Penrose to Professor Livingstone Porter, October 13, 1927, SPC.

6. Penrose to Hubert Herring, May 23, 1934, SPC.

7. *Whitman College Pioneer*, March 8, 1935.

8. *Whitman College Pioneer*, April 19, 1935.

9. Donald W. Whisenhunt, "The Veterans of Future Wars in the Pacific Northwest," *Pacific Northwest Quarterly*, October 1994, 134.

10. *Whitman College Pioneer*, April 24, 1936.

11. *Whitman College Pioneer*, April 15, 1940.

12. *Whitman College Pioneer*, December 11, 1941.

13. *Whitman College Pioneer*, April 2, 1942.

14. *Whitman College Pioneer*, May 21, 1942.

15. *Portland Oregonian*, April 12, 1942.

16. *Whitman College Pioneer*, February 5, 1942.

17. Board of Overseers Minutes, May 30, 1942, WCA.

18. Douglas McClane, "A Bulletin Concerning You and Uncle Sam," August 7, 1942, one addressed "to young men" and one "to young women," World War II Collection, WCA.

19. *Whitman Alumnus*, November 1943, 5.

20. "A War Program," *Whitman College Bulletin*, September 1944, 8; *Whitman College Pioneer*, October 22, 1942 and November 5, 1942.

21. *Whitman College Pioneer*, January 7, 1943.

22. W. S. Anderson to William O. Douglas, October 15, 1942, William O. Douglas Collection, Library of Congress.

23. Anderson to Douglas, November 20, 1942, William O. Douglas Collection, Library of Congress.

24. Anderson to Bratton, March 20, 1943, WBC.

25. Anderson to Douglas, April 21, 1943, William O. Douglas Collection, Library of Congress.

26. Douglas to Anderson, April 27, 1943.

27. President's Report, 1943, 25-27, WCA.

28. "A War Program," *Whitman College Bulletin*, September 1944, 23.

29. President's Report, 1944, 10, WCA.

30. Charles Armstrong, "Historical Report," March 20, 1945, 1, World War II Collection, WCA.

31. President's Report, 1944, 8, WCA.

32. "A War Program," *Whitman College Bulletin*, September 1944, 27.

33. *1944 Supplement to the War Issue Catalog of Whitman College*, 45.

34. "Problems of War," *Whitman College Bulletin*, September 1944, 28.

35. *Career Planning for Whitman Women*, 3, Whitman Publications File, WCA.

36. Chester Maxey to Charles Martin, January 4, 1944, CMC.

37. President's Report, 1945, 1, WCA.

38. Maxey to Howard Jay Graham, December 5, 1944, CMC.

39. *Whitman Alumnus*, July 1945, 7.

40. *New York Times*, March 26, 1945.

41. Stephen Penrose, *Whitman, An Unfinished Story*, 192.

42. Maxey, *The World I Lived In*, 338.

43. *Whitman College Pioneer*, November 19, 1948.

44. Robert D. Gregg, *Chronicles of Willamette: Those Eventful Years of the President Smith Era*, 16; J. Juan Reid, *Colorado College: The First Century, 1874–1974*, 160.

45. *Whitman Alumnus*, December 1944, 3.

46. Interview with Arthur Rempel, June 16, 1995, WCA.

47. *Whitman Alumnus*, October 1945, 2.

48. Interview with Maxine Sires, August 22, 1995, WCA.

49. Sires to the author, December 13, 1995, author's possession.

50. Walla Walla Interracial Committee to Penrose, January 30, 1946, SPC.

51. *Whitman College Pioneer*, December 20, 1945.

52. "Little Theater Articles of Incorporation," Little Theater File, WCA.

53. *Whitman College Pioneer*, December 3, 1942.

54. *Whitman College Pioneer*, May 21, 1942.

55. *Whitman College Pioneer*, November 12, 1942.

56. *Whitman College Pioneer*, May 21, 1942 and October 8, 1942.

57. Geoffrey Perrett, *Days of Sadness, Years of Triumph: The American People, 1939–1945*, 373.

58. *Whitman Alumnus*, November 1943, 4.

59. President's Report, 1944, 9, WCA.

60. Interview with Donald Pickering, April 26, 1990, WCA.

61. *Whitman College Pioneer*, January 25, 1945.

62. *Waiilatpu*, 1945, n.p.

63. Interview with Donald Pickering, April 26, 1990, WCA.

64. President's Report, 1945, 11, WCA.

65. Interview with Ken Bendure, April 26, 1991, WCA.

66. *Clock Tower*, April 1944, 25.

67. Informal Address of Dean Maureen Clow, "Colleges are Called to the Colors," April 1, 1943, World War II Collection, WCA.

68. President's Report, 1945, 15, WCA.

69. *Waiilatpu*, 1945, n. p.

70. *Whitman Alumnus*, December 1944, 3.

71. Interview with Jan Nye Baxter, August 14, 1997, WCA.

72. *Whitman Alumnus*, April 1943, 5-6.

73. Bob Hosakawa, "Under Heaven's Kindly Blue," Phi Beta Kappa Address, May 19, 1990, WCA.

74. *Whitman Alumnus,* July 1946, 14; October 1946, 10.
75. Douglas to Bratton, November 9, 1940, WBC.
76. Board of Overseers Minutes, June 17, 1944, WCA.
77. *Whitman Alumnus,* March 1945, 2.
78. President's Report, 1946, 12, WCA.
79. *New York Times,* January 7, 1946.
80. Diane Ravitch, *The Troubled Crusade: American Education, 1945–1980,* 14.
81. Faculty Minutes, March 12, 1946, WCA.
82. Ed Stokes to David Maxwell, January 31, 1990, WCA.
83. "Statement of Opinion," June 16, 1944, Trustees Correspondence, WCA.
84. Frank Baker to S. B. Fairbank, October 9,1944, Trustees Correspondence, WCA.
85. *Whitman College Pioneer,* November 21, 1946.
86. *Whitman College Pioneer,* December 19, 1946.
87. Interview with Robert R. "Pete" Reid, November 13, 1995, author's possession.
88. Report of the Committee of Inquiry, 1947, 23, THC.
89. Thomas Howells to Paul Jackson, July 9, 1947, THC.
90. Interview with Ivar Highberg, October 20, 1998, WCA.
91. Maxey to D. F. Baker, December 12, 1946, Trustees Correspondence, WCA.
92. D. F. Baker to Robert Bratton, March 11, 1947, Trustees Correspondence, WCA.
93. Nig Borleske to Frank Baker, September 22, 1944, Trustees Correspondence, WCA.
94. Frank Baker to Borleske, April 21, 1945, Trustees Correspondence, WCA.
95. Interview with Pete Hanson, November 30, 1995, author's possession.
96. Interview with Shirley Anderson Jennings, July 24, 1990, WCA.
97. Maxey, *The World I Lived In,* 339.
98. Jack Hewins, *Borleske: Never Far From Hope,* 133.
99. Howells to Jackson, July 9, 1947, THC.
100. Interview with Chester Maxey, May 14, 1973, WCA.
101. Interview with Grace Allan Lazerson, May 7, 1973, WCA.

102. Robert G. Tugman to Frank Baker, August 7, 1947, Trustees Correspondence, WCA.
103. President's Report, 1957, 2, WCA.
104. Interview with Ellen Heath McNamara, April 28, 1990, WCA.
105. Interview with Chester Maxey, May 14, 1973, WCA.
106. Hewins, *Borleske*, 140.
107. Penrose to Lesters, January 26, 1946, SPC.
108. *Whitman Alumnus*, April 1947, 1.
109. *Whitman College Pioneer*, November 16, 1944.
110. *Whitman College Pioneer*, May 21, 1948.
111. Maxey, *The World I Lived In*, 343.
112. *Whitman College Pioneer*, November 19, 1948.
113. Maxey, *The World I Lived In*, 346.

Chapter Seven

1. Interview with Robert Skotheim, July 30, 1999, author's possession.
2. Chester Maxey, *The World I Lived In*, 33.
3. *Whitman Alumnus*, October 1951, 5.
4. Interview with Chester Maxey, August 7, 1980, WCA.
5. *Walla Walla Union-Bulletin*, September 19, 1958.
6. Interview with Chester Maxey, May 22, 1974, WCA.
7. Chester Maxey, *The World I Lived In*, 230, 242.
8. Marilyn Alexander to the author, June 5, 1996, author's possession.
9. Maxey, *The World I Lived In*, 281.
10. Chester Maxey to "Shube," August 15, 1934, CMC.
11. Interview with William Perry, December 4, 1995, author's possession.
12. *Whitman Alumnus*, October 1932, 15.
13. Maxey, *The World I Lived In*, 308.
14. *Whitman Alumnus*, September 1933, 5.
15. Interview with Chester Maxey, August 7, 1980, WCA.
16. Interview with Winifred "Winks" Dunphy, March 15, 1993, WCA.
17. Edward P. Morgan to Maxey, April 27, 1950, CMC.
18. *Whitman College Pioneer*, November 24, 1938.

19. Penrose to H. L. Talkington, October 23, 1933, SPC.

20. Maxey, *The World I Lived In*, 274.

21. Maxey to James Alger Fee, July 14, 1944, CMC.

22. Maxey to W. H. Freeman, December 3, 1946, CMC.

23. Maxey, *The World I Lived In*, 342, 345.

24. Interview with Chester Maxey, May 22, 1974, WCA.

25. *Whitman College Pioneer*, December 3, 1948.

26. President's Report, 1949, 6, WCA.

27. Maxey, *The World I Lived In*, 352.

28. Interview with Winks Dunphy, February 22, 1993, WCA.

29. Maxey, *The World I Lived In*, 35, 357.

30. *Facets*, March 1955, CMC.

31. Interview with Chester Maxey, June 22, 1979, WCA.

32. *Whitman College Pioneer*, May 1, 1958.

33. "Report of the Higher Commission of the Northwest Association of Secondary and Higher Schools on the Visitation to Whitman College," November 2–7, 1957, 25, Administrative Publications File, WCA.

34. Maxey, *The World I Lived In*, 406.

35. *Seattle Post-Intelligencer*, August 21, 1966.

36. Interview with Chester Maxey, June 21, 1979, WCA.

37. Harper Joy to Maxey, April 19, 1950, Maxey Letter Book, CMC.

38. Interview with Pete Reid, June 18, 1996, author's possession.

39. *Walla Walla Union-Bulletin*, May 29, 1949; President's Report, 1951, 7, WCA.

40. Maxey, *The World I Lived In*, 358.

41. Board of Trustees Minutes, March 24, 1950, WCA.

42. Board of Trustees Minutes, July 15, 1949, and August 25, 1950, WCA.

43. Board of Trustees Minutes, December 1952, WCA; *Whitman College Pioneer*, November 9, 1950.

44. President's Report, 1951, 2, WCA.

45. Chester Maxey, "Whitman's Expertise Committees," September 26, 1983, CMC.

46. Interview with Chester Maxey, June 22, 1979, WCA.

47. President's Report, 1949, 7, WCA.

48. *Whitman Alumnus*, April 1950, 5.

49. President's Report, 1950, 7, WCA.

50. Maxey, *The World I Lived In*, 361, 362.
51. *Facets*, December 1956, CMC.
52. Frederick McMillen to Maxey, April 17, 1950, Maxey Letter Book, CMC.
53. *Whitman Alumnus*, October 1949, 2.
54. President's Report, 1951, 8, WCA.
55. President's Report, 1951, 8, WCA.
56. *Whitman Alumnus*, October 1952, 6.
57. *Spokane Chronicle*, November 6, 1952.
58. President's Report, 1952, 10, WCA.
59. Board of Trustees Minutes, April 28, 1951, WCA.
60. Board of Trustees Minutes, February 23, 1952, WCA.
61. Interview with Chester Maxey, January 16, 1976, WCA.
62. *Whitman Alumnus*, July 1952, 7.
63. President's Report, 1952, 12, WCA.
64. President's Report, 1954, 14, WCA.
65. Maxey to "Loyal Whitman People," December 1, 1954, Administrative Publications File, WCA; *Whitman Alumnus*, July 1954, 5.
66. *Facets*, January 1955, 1, CMC.
67. Chester Maxey, "Whitman's Expertise Committees," September 26, 1983, CMC.
68. President's Report, 1954, 10, WCA.
69. *Whitman Alumnus*, December 1952, 6.
70. President's Report, 1951, 10, WCA.
71. Board of Trustees Minutes, April 30 and May 27, 1955, WCA.
72. President's Report, 1949, 8, WCA.
73. *Whitman College Pioneer*, September 22, 1949.
74. President's Report, 1956, 15, WCA.
75. *Whitman Alumnus*, February 1949, 7.
76. *Walla Walla Union-Bulletin*, September 12, 1954.
77. Board of Trustees Minutes, December 12, 1953, WCA.
78. Board of Trustees Minutes, August 13, 1954, WCA.
79. *Whitman College Pioneer*, September 23, 1954.
80. Maxey, *The World I Lived In*, 377.
81. *Whitman College Pioneer*, May 20, 1954.
82. *Whitman College Pioneer*, October 4, 1951.
83. Maxey, *The World I Lived In*, 374.

84. President's Report, 1952, 6, WCA.

85. *Facets*, March 1955, CMC.

86. Donald Sherwood to John Lyman, July 20, 1955, Board of Trustees Minutes, WCA.

87. Chester Maxey, Penrose Library booklet, Administrative Publications File, WCA.

88. *Whitman College Pioneer*, March 8, 1956.

89. "Operation Book-Lift," Buildings File, WCA.

90. *Whitman Alumnus*, July 1957, 5.

91. *Walla Walla Union-Bulletin*, September 8, 1957.

92. President's Report, 1958, 5, WCA.

93. Board of Trustees Minutes, December 1952, WCA.

94. Maxey, *The World I Lived In*, 384.

95. *Walla Walla Union-Bulletin*, August 19, 1956.

96. President's Report, 1956, 9, WCA.

97. *Whitman College Pioneer*, March 19, 1958.

98. *Whitman College Pioneer*, January 22, 1959.

99. President's Report, 1957, 14, WCA.

100. Chester Maxey, *Whitman College: A Summation, 1948–1959*, 8, WCA.

101. President's Report, 1956, 6, WCA.

102. *Whitman Alumnus*, October 1952 and December 1952, 7.

103. President's Reports, 1951 and 1952, WCA.

104. Board of Trustees Minutes, September 29, 1950, WCA.

105. *Whitman Alumnus*, February 1951, 5.

106. *Whitman College Pioneer*, February 15, 1951.

107. *Whitman College Pioneer*, April 26, 1951.

108. Maxey to Whitman students and their parents, May 5, 1951, CMC.

109. *Whitman Alumnus*, April 1951, 5.

110. *Olympia Olympian*, February 1951, Newspaper Clipping File, CMC.

111. President's Report, 1953, 4, WCA.

112. Frederick Rudolph, *The American College and University: A History*, 197.

113. President's Report, 1953, 17, WCA.

114. George Frykman, *Creating the People's University*, 144.

115. Maxey, *The World I Lived In*, 385.

116. "Banquet Program," December 1, 1949, Chester Maxey File, WCA.
117. Thomas Howells to Paul Jackson, November 24, 1950, THC.
118. William O. Pugh to the Board of Trustees, April 9, 1948, Board of Trustees Minutes, WCA.
119. Maxey, *The World I Lived In*, 387.
120. Maxey to Pete Reid, July 20, 1950, author's possession.
121. Pugh to the Board of Trustees, April 9, 1948, Board of Trustees Minutes, WCA.
122. President's Report, 1949, 34, 35, WCA.
123. Frank Haigh to the Board of Trustees, January 17, 1951, Board of Trustees Minutes, WCA.
124. Howells to Jackson, December 29, 1950, THC.
125. Board of Trustees to Frank Haigh, January 26, 1951, Board of Trustees Minutes, WCA.
126. Howells to Jackson, January 15, 1951, and February 4, 1951, THC.
127. Professors Ronald Sires, William Hutchings, and Glenn Woodward to Maxey, April 30, 1951, Faculty Minutes, WCA.
128. Interview with Shirley Clem Farmer, July 22, 1996, author's possession.
129. Professors Sires, Hutchings, and Woodward to Maxey, April 30, 1951, Faculty Minutes, WCA.
130. President's Report, 1951, 7, 9, WCA.
131. Board of Overseers Minutes, May 24, 1952, WCA.
132. Report and Recommendations on the Faculty, Board of Trustees Minutes, May 25, 1951 and May 23, 1952, WCA.
133. J. Juan Reid, *Colorado College: The First Century, 1874–1974*, 170; Charlie Brown Hershey, *Colorado College, 1874–1947*, 133.
134. Faculty Minutes, November 3, 1955, WCA.
135. Maxey, *The World I Lived In*, 392.
136. Thomas Howells, "Report on a Conversation with Maxey," October 31, 1950, THC.
137. Maxey, *The World I Lived In*, 394, 395.
138. Interview with David Stevens, July 30, 1996, author's possession.
139. Howells to Jackson, November 24, 1950, THC.

140. Thomas Howells, President of the AAUP to Maxey, November 10, 1950, THC.
141. Howells to Jackson, February 4, 1951, THC.
142. Howells to Jackson, July 7, 1951, THC.
143. Howells to Sires, January 27, 1952 and March 1, 1952, THC.
144. Maxey, *The World I Lived In*, 399.
145. Interview with David Stevens, July 30, 1996, author's possession.
146. Telephone interview with Pete Reid, April 24, 2000.
147. Robert Comegys File, February 27, 1951, WCA.
148. Howells to Sires, June 8, 1952, THC.
149. Maxey, *The World I Lived In*, 399.
150. *Whitman College Pioneer*, September 17, 1966.
151. *Whitman College Pioneer*, May 14, 1953.
152. Maxey, *The World I Lived In*, 401.
153. President's Report, 1951, 7, WCA.
154. Howells to Gail Sheldon, April 11, 1953, THC.
155. Howells to Robert Comegys, June 28, 1953 and November 27, 1953, THC.
156. Maxey, *The World I Lived In*, 441.
157. Chester Maxey, "A Statement to the Faculty," May 31, 1957, CMC.
158. *Whitman College Pioneer*, May 21, 1953.
159. Faculty Council Minutes, May 21, 1957, WCA.
160. *Whitman College Pioneer*, May 23, 1957.
161. Faculty Council Minutes, May 21, 1957, WCA.
162. "Report of the Higher Commission," November 2–7, 1957, 4, 26, Administrative Publications File, WCA.
163. E. Wilson Lyon, *The History of Pomona College, 1887–1969*, 410.
164. Interview with Chester Maxey, May 22, 1974, WCA.
165. "Oath of Chester C. Maxey", April 12, 1947, CMC.
166. *Whitman College Pioneer*, March 8, 1951.
167. *Whitman College Pioneer*, April 26, 1951, and May 3, 1951.
168. Scott Gruber and Wayne Silzel to the Faculty Council, September 11, 1958, Faculty Council Minutes, WCA.
169. President's Report, 1959, 11, WCA.
170. *Walla Walla Union-Bulletin*, January 22, 1949.

171. "Centennial Observance Program, Stevens Treaty Council, 1855–1955," 5, WCA.
172. Address by Governor Albert Rosellini, February 23, 1959, Chronological File, WCA.
173. Chester Maxey, "One Hundred Years," Chronological File, WCA.
174. *Facets*, April 1957, CMC.
175. Newspaper Clipping File, December 3, 1950, CMC.
176. Chester Maxey, "A New Look at Bigness," *Whitman College Bulletin*, September 1949, 3, Administrative Publications File, WCA.
177. *Facets*, August 1958.
178. Newspaper Clipping File, n.d., CMC.
179. *Walla Walla Union-Bulletin*, October 21, 1956.
180. Newspaper Clipping File, September 9, 1950, CMC.
181. *Spokane Chronicle*, January 17, 1949.
182. Newspaper Clipping File, February 4, 1951, CMC.
183. Maxey, *The World I Lived In*, 429.
184. "Last Words on the Campus," *Life*, June 20, 1955.
185. Maxey, *Whitman College: A Summation, 1948–1959*, 15, WCA.
186. Interview with Bert Edwards, August 1, 1996, author's possession.
187. Maxey, *A Summation*, 21.
188. Lyon, *The History of Pomona College*, 411.
189. American Institute of Management, "Management Audit: Whitman College," December 1953, Administrative Publications File, WCA.
190. Chester Maxey, *Five Centennial Papers*, 13.
191. J. Juan Reid, *Colorado College*, 191-92.
192. Address by Governor Rosellini, February 23, 1959, Chronological File, WCA.

Chapter Eight

1. *Whitman College Pioneer*, January 23, 1975.
2. *Portland Oregonian*, April 17, 1983.
3. Interview with Louis Perry, December 3, 1996, WCA.
4. *Portland Oregonian*, April 17, 1983.

5. *Walla Walla Union-Bulletin*, February 3, 1959.

6. *Walla Walla Union-Bulletin*, February 12, 1959.

7. "Inauguration of Louis Perry, October 18, 1959," 9 and 11, WCA.

8. Interview with Louis Perry, December 7, 1996, WCA.

9. Interview with Louis Perry, December 3, 1996, WCA.

10. Interview with Louis Perry, October 1, 1992, WCA.

11. Interview with Louis Perry, December 3, 1996, WCA.

12. Chester Maxey, *The World I Lived In*, 357.

13. Interview with Louis Perry, June 25, 1992, WCA.

14. President's Report, 1965, 22, WCA.

15. President's Report, 1963, 25, WCA.

16. President's Report, 1960, WCA.

17. Interview with Louis Perry, December 3, 1996.

18. *New York Times*, December 19, 1996.

19. Interview with Louis Perry, December 3, 1996, WCA.

20. Interview with Larry Beaulaurier, December 4, 1996, WCA.

21. *Whitman College Quarterly*, June 1899.

22. Board of Overseers Minutes, 1960, 8, WCA.

23. Board of Trustees Minutes, December 8, 1960, WCA.

24. Board of Trustees Minutes, April 14, 1961, WCA.

25. Interview with Larry Beaulaurier, December 4, 1996, WCA.

26. Board of Trustees Minutes, October 27, 1961, WCA.

27. Board of Overseers Minutes, 1960, 6, WCA.

28. President's Report, 1960, 7, WCA.

29. Board of Overseers Minutes, 1961, 12, WCA.

30. President's Report, 1960, 17, WCA.

31. President's Report, 1962, 25, WCA.

32. President's Report, 1961, 22, WCA.

33. Board of Overseers Minutes, 1962, 6, WCA.

34. President's Report, 1960, 14, WCA.

35. President's Report, 1962, 7, 10, WCA.

36. Interview with Pete Reid, October 1, 1992, WCA.

37. Board of Overseers Minutes, June 6, 1964, 5, WCA.

38. *Whitman Alumnus*, December 1963.

39. *Whitman College Pioneer*, March 11, 1965.

40. *Whitman Alumnus*, April 1964, 5.

41. *Whitman College Bulletin*, May 1968, 2.

42. Ralph Cordiner to Donald Sherwood, June 9, 1965; Board of Trustees Minutes, June 1965.
43. Board of Overseers Minutes, June 4, 1966, WCA.
44. Board of Overseers Minutes, 1968, WCA.
45. Board of Trustees Minutes, September 20, 1963, 4, WCA.
46. President's Report, 1965, 13, WCA.
47. Interview with Louis Perry, June 25, 1992, WCA.
48. President's Report, 1960, 6, WCA.
49. President's Report, 1963, 7, WCA.
50. *Whitman College Pioneer*, March 11, 1965.
51. President's Report, 1965, 6, WCA.
52. Interview with Louis Perry, June 25, 1992, WCA.
53. *Whitman College Bulletin*, May 1966, 8.
54. *Whitman College Pioneer*, April 23, 1964.
55. *Whitman College Pioneer*, March 31, 1966.
56. President's Report, 1965, 6, WCA.
57. *Whitman College Bulletin*, August 1966, 3.
58. Interview with Louis Perry, June 25, 1992, WCA.
59. President's Report, 1965, 17, WCA.
60. Interview with Louis Perry, June 25, 1992, WCA.
61. President's Report, 1961, 5, WCA.
62. President's Report, 1962, 6, WCA.
63. President's Report, 1961, 7, WCA.
64. President's Report, 1962, 6, WCA.
65. Interview with Perry, June 25, 1992, WCA.
66. President's Report, 1962, 7, WCA.
67. President's Report, 1967, 5, WCA.
68. *Whitman College Pioneer*, February 24, 1966.
69. *Whitman College Bulletin*, November 1964, 3.
70. *Spokane Spokesman-Review*, October 17, 1965.
71. *Whitman College Pioneer*, April 21, 1966.
72. *Whitman College Bulletin*, February 1967, 2.
73. President's Report, 1967, 18, WCA.
74. President's Report, 1963, 8, WCA.
75. President's Report, 1967, 20, WCA.
76. President's Report, 1960, 6-7, WCA.
77. President's Report, 1966, 3, WCA.
78. President's Report, 1962, 22, WCA.

79. President's Report, 1965, 7, WCA.

80. President's Report, 1961, 18, WCA.

81. President's Report, 1962, 11, WCA.

82. *Whitman College Bulletin*, February 1967, 8.

83. President's Report, 1962, 13, WCA.

84. *Whitman College Bulletin*, May 1966, 2.

85. *Walla Walla Union-Bulletin*, March 29, 1967.

86. Interview with Louis Perry, June 25, 1992, WCA.

87. *Whitman College Bulletin*, August 1966, 2.

88. "Women of 515 Boyer," 1994 Senior Alumni College, video-tape, June 14, 1994, WCA.

89. Louis Perry, "College Grading: A Case Study and Its After-math," *Educational Record*, Winter 1968, 84.

90. Louis Perry, *College and University Business*, June 1967, 33.

91. Louis Perry, "What Should a College Teach?" *Spokane Spokes-man-Review*, January 8, 1967.

92. *Seattle Post-Intelligencer*, October 10, 1965.

93. Louis Perry, "The Profession and Its Future: The Views of a College President," *Journal of Student Personnel Workers*, Summer 1966, Louis Perry File, WCA.

94. Louis Perry, "Intercollegiate Sports in Academe," *Liberal Education*, October 1963, 1-7.

95. Interviews with Louis Perry, June 25 and October 1, 1992, WCA.

96. Newspaper clipping, September 19, 1974, Louis Perry File, WCA.

97. Interview with Louis Perry, June 25, 1992, WCA.

98. *Whitman College Bulletin*, May 1967, 2.

99. *Whitman College Pioneer*, April 10, 1967.

100. *Walla Walla Union-Bulletin*, March 29, 1967.

101. Interview with Louis Perry, December 6, 1996.

102. *Portland Oregonian*, April 17, 1983.

Chapter Nine

1. Donald Sherwood to Kenyon Knopf, May 6, 1997, Kenyon Knopf Collection, WCA.

2. Chester Maxey, "The View from Ninety-One, A Supplement to *The World I Lived In*," 10, WCA.

3. President's Report, 1968, 3, WCA.

4. This and the subsequent quotations are from an interview with Kenyon Knopf, May 6–7, 1997, WCA.

5. Nancy Weiss Malkiel to the author, June 14, 1998, Donald Sheehan Collection, WCA.

6. Interview with Katherine Sheehan, July 28, 1997, WCA.

7. *Daily Hampshire Gazette*, April 1, 1968.

8. Interview with Katherine Sheehan, July 28, 1997, WCA.

9. "The New College Plan," Amherst, Massachusetts, 1965, 5, 13, 35, Donald Sheehan File, WCA

10. Conversation between Katherine and Jeffrey Sheehan, 1997, Donald Sheehan Collection, 2, WCA.

11. Interview with Pete Reid, August 1997, WCA.

12. *Whitman Alumnus*, August 1971, 3.

13. Interview with Pete Reid, August 1997, WCA.

14. *Whitman Alumnus*, November 1970.

15. *Whitman Alumnus*, November 1972.

16. *Whitman Alumnus*, August 1975.

17. *Whitman Alumnus*, November 1969.

18. Board of Overseers Minutes, May 24, and June 17, 1969.

19. Ralph Edgerton to Loren E. Baldwin, June 1969, Board of Overseers Minutes.

20. *Academe*, October 1970.

21. Arthur Metastasio to Knopf, February 20, 1967, Knopf's possession.

22. President's Report, 1974, 2, 3, WCA.

23. *Whitman College Pioneer*, February 22, 1951.

24. *Whitman College Pioneer*, November 10, 1966.

25. *Whitman College Pioneer*, September 17, 1966.

26. *Whitman College Pioneer*, November 13, 20, 1969.

27. *Narrator*, March 5, 1969.

28. Faculty Minutes, December 5, 1974, WCA.

29. Author's letters, September 30, 1975.

30. *Seattle Post-Intelligencer*, April 12, 1974.

31. *Walla Walla Union-Bulletin*, April 16, 1974.

32. *Walla Walla Union-Bulletin*, April 12, 1974.

33. *Walla Walla Union-Bulletin*, April 15, 1974.

34. Interview with Kenyon Knopf, May 6–7, 1997, WCA.

35. *Walla Walla Union-Bulletin*, March 19, 1976.
36. Interview with Kenyon Knopf, May 6–7, 1997, WCA.
37. *Whitman College Pioneer*, February 21, 1975.
38. *Walla Walla Union-Bulletin*, October 27, 1974.
39. *Whitman College Pioneer*, March 4, 1976.
40. *Walla Walla Union-Bulletin*, March 19, 1976.
41. *Whitman Alumnus*, May 1978, 20-21.
42. "Comments by Kenyon A. Knopf," American Conference of Academic Deans Conference, February 3, 1979, 10, WCA.
43. Faculty Minutes, May 8, 1975, WCA.

Chapter Ten

1. Quoted in "Crisis on the Campus," *Americana Annual*, 1969, 15.
2. *AAUP Bulletin*, Autumn 1969, 327. The full report was republished in this issue of the *Bulletin*.
3. Ibid., 332.
4. Paul S. Boyer, et. al., *The Enduring Vision: A History of the American People*, 992.
5. *Narrator*, February 12, 1969.
6. Robert B. McKay, "A Proposed Bill of Rights for Students," *Americana Annual*, 1969, 32.
7. John Discher, "The Case for the Rebellious Students and their Counterrevolution," *Harper's*, August 1968, 12.
8. Jeffrey A. Sheehan, compiler, *Selected Speeches of Donald H. Sheehan*, 108.
9. *Whitman College Pioneer*, April 26, 1962.
10. Whitman College *Handbook for Faculty and Staff*, 1963, 22.
11. *Whitman College Pioneer*, November 10, 1956.
12. *Whitman College Pioneer*, December 14, 1961.
13. *Whitman College Pioneer*, December 20, 1962; February 14, 1963.
14. *Whitman College Pioneer*, Febrary 21, 1963.
15. Interview with Roy Hoover, August 23, 1995, WCA.
16. *Whitman College Coed Code*, 1962–1963, 12.
17. *Whitman College Coed Code*, 1963–1964, 14.
18. Interview with Malinda Phillips Pankl, August 28, 1997, WCA.

19. Interview with Sally Mathiasen Light, June 30, 1997, WCA.
20. *Whitman College Pioneer*, September 18, 1965.
21. *Whitman College Pioneer*, April 30, 1964.
22. *Whitman College Pioneer*, May 14, 1964.
23. *Whitman College Pioneer*, October 6, 1964.
24. *Whitman College Pioneer*, October 22, 1964.
25. Quoted in David M. Stameshkin, *The Strength of the Hills: Middlebury College, 1915–1990*, 298.
26. *Whitman College Pioneer*, October 29, 1964.
27. *Whitman College Pioneer*, January 14, 1965.
28. Faculty Council to Student Congress, January 5, 1965, Ad Hoc Committee File, Office of Student Affairs Collection, WCA.
29. "Comments on Some Women Graduates," Dean of Students' Report, 1966, WCA.
30. *Whitman College Pioneer*, October 7 and October 28, 1965.
31. *Whitman College Pioneer*, March 8, 1966.
32. *Whitman College Pioneer*, September 29, 1966.
33. *Whitman College Pioneer*, October 26, 1967.
34. *Whitman College Pioneer*, September 29, 1966.
35. *Whitman College Pioneer*, November 10, 1966.
36. Letter from AWWC officers to Perry, November 10, 1966, Office of Student Affairs Collection, WCA.
37. *Whitman College Pioneer*, December 8, 1966.
38. *Whitman College Pioneer*, February 16, 1967.
39. *Whitman College Pioneer*, March 3, 1967.
40. Miriam Wagenschein to Dean of Students, May 13, 1966 and Wagenschein to Robert Whitner, April 26, 1967, Office of Student Affairs Collection, WCA.
41. Interview with Gordon Scribner, September 25, 1997, WCA.
42. *Whitman College Pioneer*, September 16, 1967.
43. *Whitman College Pioneer*, October 5, 1967.
44. *Whitman College Pioneer*, December 7, 1967.
45. *Whitman College Pioneer*, December 14, 1967.
46. *Whitman College Pioneer*, September 12, 1969.
47. Donald Sheehan to Student Body President Peter Snow, October 3, 1968, Office of Student Affairs Collection, WCA.
48. *Whitman College Pioneer*, October 10, 1968.
49. *Whitman College Pioneer*, November 7, 1968.

50. *Whitman College Pioneer*, March 6, 1969.
51. *Whitman College Pioneer*, September 11, 1969.
52. Donald Sherwood to Trustees, December 16, 1968, Office of Student Affairs Collection, WCA.
53. *Whitman College Pioneer*, March 20, 1970.
54. *Walla Walla Union-Bulletin*, April 13, 1969.
55. President's Report, 1969, 3, WCA.
56. David Carr to Sheehan, February 2, 1970, Office of Student Affairs Collection, WCA.
57. Joyce Briggs to Sheehan, February 11, 1970, Dean of Students File, WCA.
58. Lois Gatewood to Sheehan, February 16, 1970, Office of Student Affairs Collection, WCA.
59. *Whitman College Pioneer*, September 4, 1969.
60. Interview with Roy Hoover, August 23, 1995, WCA.
61. *Whitman College Pioneer*, November 6, 1969.
62. *Whitman Alumnus*, February 1970, 13.
63. *Whitman College Pioneer*, November 19, 1970.
64. *Narrator*, March 5, 1969.
65. *Whitman College Pioneer*, November 19, 1970.
66. *Selected Speeches of Donald H. Sheehan*, 69.
67. Walter Brattain, "The University in a Troubled Society," 1974, 3, Walter Brattain Collection, WCA.
68. *Selected Speeches of Donald H. Sheehan*, 70.
69. President's Report, 1970, 5, WCA.
70. G. Thomas Edwards, "A Professor's Perspective on a Changing Campus, May 23, 1970, author's possession.
71. President's Report, 1971, 6, WCA.
72. *Selected Speeches of Donald H. Sheehan*, xi.
73. *Whitman Alumnus*, May 1971, 1.
74. Telephone interview with Donald Frisbee, December 19, 1997, author's possession.
75. Interview with Baker Ferguson, October 8, 1997, WCA.
76. "Student Social Regulations," July 1970, Chronological File, WCA.
77. *Whitman College Pioneer*, February 24, 1971.
78. *Whitman College Pioneer*, October 18, 1973.
79. Interview with Margaret Ershler, June 25, 1997, WCA.

80. *Whitman College Pioneer*, November 8, 1973.
81. *Whitman College Pioneer*, March 14, 1974.
82. *Whitman Alumnus*, July 1969, 33.
83. Robert D. Loevy, *Colorado College: A Place of Learning, 1874–1999*, 202.
84. *Whitman College Pioneer*, February 4, 1971.
85. *Whitman College Pioneer*, December 3, 1970.
86. "Findings of Investigator," September 11, 1970, Black Student Union File, WCA.
87. "Report of Current State of Ethnic Studies at Whitman College," Faculty Minutes, April 1970, WCA.
88. *Whitman College Pioneer*, March 7, 1974.
89. *Willamette Scene*, April 1971.
90. *Independent Women Scrapbook*, 1947–1948, WCA.
91. *Whitman College Pioneer*, October 16, 1969.
92. *Whitman College Pioneer*, September 17, 1970.
93. Robert Thomsen, memorandum, January 27, 1971, Robert Thomsen File, WCA.
94. *Whitman College Pioneer*, November 14, 1968.
95. *Whitman College Pioneer*, February 15, 1968.
96. *Whitman College Pioneer*, March 7, 1968.
97. Arthur Eggers, Prosecuting Attorney to Donald Sherwood, Board of Trustees, May 31, 1968, Board of Trustees Minutes.
98. *Whitman College Pioneer*, April 18, 1968.
99. Walter Brattain, "The University in a Troubled Society," 2, Walter Brattain Collection, WCA.
100. Chester Maxey, "The View from Ninety-One, A Supplement to *The World I Lived In*," 7, WCA.
101. *Whitman College Pioneer*, October 17, 1968.
102. *Whitman College Pioneer*, October 23, 1969.
103. Sheehan to Richard Nixon, October 14, 1969, Donald Sheehan Collection, WCA.
104. *Whitman Alumnus*, July 1970, 33.
105. Interview with Roy Hoover, August 23, 1995, WCA.
106. Interview with Alex MacLeod, August 17, 1997, WCA.
107. *Whitman Alumnus*, November, 1971, 3.
108. Interview with Eric Pryne, August 18, 1997, WCA.
109. *Whitman Alumnus*, May 1972, 1-2.

110. *Whitman College Catalog*, 1954–1955, 7.
111. *Whitman College Pioneer*, November 5, 1970.
112. *Whitman College Pioneer*, February 15, 1973.
113. *Whitman Alumnus*, November, 1974, 3.
114. George Ball to the author, May 18, 1999, author's possession.
115. *Whitman College Pioneer*, February 23, 1961.
116. *Whitman Alumnus*, May 1972, 13.
117. Interview with Craig Gunsul, January 28, 1999, author's possession; interview with Dale Cosper, January 28, 1999, author's possession.
118. Willamette University *Alumnus*, May 1969, 5.
119. Robb Ball to the author, August 24, 1998, author's possession.
120. Ronald Norris to Whitman Faculty, February 21, 1961, Faculty Minutes.
121. *Whitman College Pioneer*, February 21, 1961.
122. Mrs. J. A. Haase and twelve other signers to the Whitman Faculty, March 23, 1961, Faculty Minutes, WCA.
123. *Whitman College Pioneer*, October 7, 1965.
124. *Whitman College Pioneer*, October 14, 1965.
125. *Whitman College Pioneer*, April 1, 1965.
126. *Whitman College Pioneer*, October 28, 1965.
127. *Whitman College Pioneer*, November 11, 1965.
128. *Whitman College Pioneer*, December 9, 1965.
129. *Whitman College Pioneer*, February 17, 1966.
130. *Whitman College Pioneer*, March 21, 1968.
131. *Whitman College Pioneer*, June 3, 1966.
132. *Whitman College Pioneer*, March 8, 1966.
133. Interview with Craig Lesley, September 5, 1997, WCA.
134. *Whitman College Pioneer*, December 14, 1967.
135. Sigma Chi Fraternity to L. P. Howland, December 6, 1967, Faculty Minutes, WCA.
136. Interview with Reid Yamamoto, October 3, 1998, WCA.
137. Recollection of the author.
138. *Whitman College Pioneer*, September 4, 1969.
139. *Whitman College Pioneer*, March 7, 1968.
140. *Whitman College Pioneer*, September 4, 1969.
141. *Whitman College Pioneer*, September 12, 1968.
142. *Whitman College Pioneer*, April 24, 1969.

143. *Whitman College Pioneer*, September 4, 1969.
144. Interview with Alex MacLeod, August 17, 1997, WCA.
145. *Whitman College Pioneer*, February 12, 1970.

Chapter Eleven

1. Larry H. Addington, *America's War in Vietnam*, 112.
2. *Whitman Alumnus*, May 1966, 25.
3. Interview with Michael de Grasse, August 29, 1997, WCA.
4. Interview with Marsh Lee, December 1, 1991, WCA.
5. *Whitman Alumnus*, May 1975, 1.
6. Interview with Michael de Grasse, August 29, 1997, WCA.
7. "Profile of Whitman College," Administrative Publications File, WCA, 1971; *Whitman College Pioneer*, 1968; and Development Office database.
8. Interview with Malinda Phillips Pankl, August 28, 1997, WCA.
9. *Whitman Alumnus*, May 1970, 21.
10. Robert Whitner talk to Seattle Mother's Club, March 1964, Robert Whitner File, WCA.
11. *Whitman Alumnus*, February 1973, 2.
12. Ronald Urban, "Educational Attainment Among Whitman College Alumni, 1913–1991," June 1997, WCA.
13. *Whitman Alumnus*, November,1973, 8.
14. Interview with Linda Weihmann Brown, January 22, 1999, WCA.
15. "25th Reunion Class of 1966," WCA.
16. *Clock Tower*, April 1945, 2.
17. Paul Knostman, "Journal," 1957, WCA.
18. *Whitman Alumnus*, November, 1969, 18.
19. *Waiilatpu*, 1961, 21.
20. *Whitman College Pioneer*, April 21, 1966.
21. *Whitman College Pioneer*, February 8, 1962.
22. *Whitman College Pioneer*, March 1, 1962.
23. *Whitman Alumnus*, November, 1973, 21.
24. *Whitman College Pioneer*, April 26, 1962.
25. *Whitman College Pioneer*, November 16, 1961.
26. *Whitman College Pioneer*, December 6, 1956.

27. *Whitman College Pioneer*, October 25, 1962.
28. Maxey to Jack Pearson, February 12, 1951, Fredric Santler File, WCA.
29. *Whitman College Pioneer*, April 22, 1971.
30. *Whitman College Pioneer*, November 16, 1972.
31. Interview with Greg Brown, January 22, 1999, WCA.
32. *Masque*, Winter 1959, 2.
33. *Whitman Alumnus*, May 1970, 11.
34. *Whitman Alumnus*, February 1972, 6.
35. *Whitman Alumnus*, November, 1966, 3.
36. *Whitman Alumnus*, February 1973, 7; and August 1975, 9.
37. *Whitman Alumnus*, August 1975, 3-4.
38. *Whitman College Pioneer*, February 11, 1960.
39. *Whitman College Pioneer*, February 28, 1974.
40. *Whitman College Pioneer*, October 25, 1973.
41. Interview with Greg Brown, January 22, 1999.
42. Interview with Tom Williams, April 24, 1999, author's possession.
43. *Whitman College Pioneer*, April 11, 1963.
44. *Walla Walla Union-Bulletin*, February 19, 1956.
45. *Independent Women Scrapbook 1952–1960*, WCA.
46. *Walla Walla Union-Bulletin*, April 26, 1972.
47. *Whitman College Pioneer*, April 21, 1966.
48. Interview with George Anderson, August 21, 1997, WCA.
49. *New York Times*, March 11, 1958.
50. Interview with Malinda Phillips Pankl, August 28, 1997, WCA.
51. Faculty Minutes, December 7, 1967.
52. *Whitman Alumnus*, May 1971.
53. David M. Stameshkin, *The Strength of the Hills: Middlebury College, 1915–1990*, 262.
54. *Whitman College Pioneer*, February 19, 1970.
55. *Whitman College Pioneer*, June 6, 1964.
56. *Whitman Alumnus*, November, 1975, 3.
57. Interview with Donald Patrick Jones, December 6, 1998, WCA.
58. *New Student's Handbook*, 1975, 3.

Chapter Twelve

1. Faculty Minutes, December 9, 1954, WCA.
2. Faculty Minutes, October 6, 1955, WCA.
3. Faculty Minutes, November 3, 1955, WCA.
4. Faculty Minutes, October 4, 1956, WCA.
5. Faculty Minutes, October 3, 1957; May 30, 1958, WCA.
6. Interview with Maxine Sires, August 22, 1995, WCA.
7. Faculty Minutes, January 12, 1956, WCA.
8. Interview with Richard Stuart, December 6, 1998, WCA.
9. Faculty Minutes, September 1959, WCA.
10. Faculty Minutes, March 19 and 24, 1964, WCA.
11. Faculty Minutes, December 14, 1961, WCA.
12. Faculty Minutes, March 8, 1962, WCA.
13. *Whitman Forum*, Spring 1963, n.p.
14. Faculty Minutes, March 19, 1964, and March 25, 1965, WCA.
15. Interview with Margaret Ershler, June 25, 1997, WCA.
16. President's Report, 1973, 11.
17. Thomas Howells to James Story, September 13, 1966, Thomas Howells Collection, WCA.
18. Faculty Minutes, April 7, 1960, WCA.
19. *Whitman College Pioneer*, May 19, 1966.
20. Interview with Louis Perry, June 20, 1995, WCA.
21. Interview with Winks Dunphy, June 8, 1990, WCA.
22. Robert Fluno to Trustee Sherwood, May 16, 1966, Board of Trustees Minutes, WCA.
23. *Whitman College Pioneer*, May 16, 1966.
24. Louis Perry, remarks to trustees, Board of Trustees Minutes, August 5, 1966, 2, WCA.
25. Interview with Richard Stuart, December 6, 1998, WCA.
26. Interview with Peggy Metastasio, January 11, 1999, WCA.
27. Faculty Minutes, June 2, 1967, WCA.
28. *Whitman Alumnus*, May 1966, 7-8.
29. Chester Maxey, "The View from Ninety-One, A Supplement to *The World I Lived In*," 6.
30. *Whitman Alumnus*, May 1966, 7-8.
31. President's Report, 1973, 9, WCA.

32. Irving Kristol, "The Strange Death of Liberal Education," *Fortune*, May 1968, 256.
33. *Whitman College Pioneer*, March 1, 1973.
34. Faculty Minutes, May 1, 1969, WCA.
35. President's Report, 1973, 14, WCA.
36. Acting President Kenyon Knopf to Faculty and Administrative Staff, January 9, 1975, author's possession.
37. AAUP President Howells letter, October 11, 1967, Whitman College AAUP Minutes, WCA.
38. Thomas Howells, "Whitman History," n.d., Thomas Howells File, WCA.
39. *Whitman Catalog*, 1971–1972, 65.
40. BSU to Whitman Community, September 14, 1970, Black Student Union File, WCA.
41. *Whitman Catalog*, 1970–1971, 14.
42. Report of the Chairman of the Faculty, 1970-1971, Faculty Minutes, May 1971, 3, WCA.
43. Interview with Doug Eglington, August 15, 1997, WCA.
44. *Willamette Scene*, December 1967, 12.
45. *Whitman Catalog*, 1975, 94-95.
46. *Waiilatpu*, 1968, 23.
47. Nelson Bryce, "Reed College: Hunting for Money, a President, and a Mission," *Science*, September 15, 1967, 1283.
48. *Seattle Post-Intelligencer*, May 4, 1964.
49. *Whitman College Bulletin*, 1975, 16.
50. Interview with Richard Stuart, December 6, 1998, WCA.
51. *Whitman College Pioneer*, November 14, 1974.
52. George Castile, "Publish or Putrefy," 1976, George Castile File, WCA.

Epilogue

1. Jay Eacker, "Salishan Conference Memo," March 12, 1975, WCA.
2. Jay Eacker, "Whitman Conference," Jay Eacker File, WCA
3. Board of Trustees Minutes, October 17, 1975.
4. Chester Maxey, "The View from Ninety-One, A Supplement to *The World I Lived In*," 16, WCA.
5. Telephone interview with Robert Skotheim, January 30, 1999.

Sources

Bibliographical Note

In the early 1990s several Pacific Northwest colleges and universities published centennial histories. Because there were so few modern college studies to utilize, these new histories depended almost entirely upon primary source materials found in their school's archives. Some of these histories lack crucial detail because of inadequate archival resources, or because the institution favored a celebratory account rather than an analytical one. Scholars who utilized such primary sources as trustee minutes, faculty minutes, and student body records soon discovered that these sources are almost always incomplete. Motions, amendments, and votes are recorded very simply; the arguments surrounding issues—significant or not—are generally unrecorded. On the other hand, reports by presidents, deans, professors, and students can be extremely helpful because of their depth of detail and analysis.

Unfortunately, too few administrators, faculty members, and students have kept written records. Professors, for example, rarely realize how important their personal or official documents are to those writing institutional histories. Official college publications, including catalogs and alumni magazines, are rarely analytical, and, like some college histories, smack of boosterism. But these sources demonstrate the fact that colleges respond to societal changes; even a casual investigation of catalogs at various time periods is instructive. Institutional publications describe conditions that often are at variance with those described in the college newspaper, yearbooks, or oral histories taken from alumni.

The decline of college journalism complicates the scholar's ability to write institutional history. Over the past fifty years college newspaper editors became less interested in reporting details about campus events and more interested in controversy and personal concerns. Indeed, the decline in the quality of national and college newspapers happened simultaneously. The decline or disappearance of traditional yearbooks also make it more difficult to write about the student's social life. Oral histories also present problems: those interviewed are sometimes not asked the correct questions, and the responses are sometimes incomplete or inaccurate.

Despite the problems with all of these primary sources, it is still possible to write a reliable history of a college. An objective scholar must utilize all of these primary and secondary sources, especially histories of higher education and histories of American society. Fortunately, Whitman has rich resources, including books by presidents Penrose and Maxey and an extensive and well organized archives. Furthermore, its impressive oral history collection and personal files are more extensive than those at other regional institutions. Any shortcomings of this college history cannot be attributed either to inadequate sources or to administrative interference.

Manuscript Collections

Pacific University Archives, Forest Grove, Oregon.

Whitman College Archives, Penrose Memorial Library, Walla Walla, Washington: Ad Hoc Committee File, Administrative Publications File, Biographical File, Black Student Union File, Board of Deans Minutes, Board of Overseers Minutes, Board of Trustees Minutes, Walter Brattain Collection, Walter Bratton Collection, Buildings File, George Castile File, Centennial Celebration File, Chronological File, Rudolf Clemen Collection, Robert Comegys File, Dean of Students File, Dean of Students Reports, Faculty Council Minutes, Faculty Minutes, Frank Haigh File, Thomas Howells Collection, *Independent Women Scrapbook*, Inquiry Club File, Kenyon Knopf Collection, Little Theater File, Chester Maxey Collection, Office of Student Affairs Collection, Oral History File, Penrose Pamphlet File, Penrose Recollections File, Stephen Penrose Collection, Stephen Penrose, Jr. Collection, Louis Perry File, Presidents' Reports, Otto Rupp Collection, Fredric Santler File, Donald Sheehan Collection, Stadium File, Robert Thomsen File, Trustees Correspondence, Whitman College AAUP Minutes, Whitman Publications File, Robert Whitner File, World War II Collection.

Willamette University Archives, Salem, Oregon.

William O. Douglas Collection, Library of Congress, Washington, D.C.

Original Sources, Special Studies, Articles, and Reports

Academe, October 1970.

AAUP Bulletin, Autumn 1969.

Bryce, Nelson. "Reed College: Hunting for Money, a President, and a Mission." *Science*, September 15, 1967.

Clemen, Rudolf. "Freedom to Learn." *Whitman Alumnus*, October 1935.

"Crisis on the Campus." *Americana Annual*, 1969.

DeFoe, Lorna, "Gin, Joy, or Solid Work." *Washingtonian*, November 1, 1928.

Discher, John. "The Case for the Rebellious Students and their Counterrevolution." *Harper's*, August 1968.

Douglas, William O. "Commencement Address." *Whitman Alumnus*, October 1938.

Kristol, Irving. "The Strange Death of Liberal Education." *Fortune*, May 1968.

"Last Words on the Campus." *Life*, June 20, 1955.

Maxey, Chester C. *Five Centennial Papers*. Walla Walla: Whitman College, 1959.

———. "A New Look at Bigness." *Whitman College Bulletin*, September 1949.

———. "The View from Ninety-One, A Supplement to *The World I Lived In*." Walla Walla: Whitman College, 1981.

———. *Whitman College: A Summation, 1948–1959*. Walla Walla: Whitman College, 1959.

McKay, Robert B. "A Proposed Bill of Rights for Students." *Americana Annual*, 1969.

Perry, Louis. "College Grading: A Case Study and Its Aftermath."
    Educational Record, Winter 1968.
———. "Intercollegiate Sports in Academe." *Liberal Education*, Oc-
    tober 1963.
———. "The Profession and Its Future: The Views of a College Pres-
    ident." *Journal of Student Personnel Workers*, Summer 1966.
———. "What Should a College Teach?" *Spokane Spokesman-
    Review*, January 8, 1967.
R. L. Polk's Walla Walla City & County Directory. 1925–1926.
"Report of the Higher Commission of the Northwest Association
    of Secondary and Higher Schools on the Visitation to Whitman
    College." 1957.
Russell, John Dale. "Report of a Financial Survey of Whitman
    College, September 1934."
Skotheim, Robert. "Dreams of Success: Whitman and the World."
    Whitman Alumnus, November, 1975.
Whisenhunt, Donald W. "The Veterans of Future Wars in the Pacific
    Northwest." *Pacific Northwest Quarterly*, October 1994.

Interviews and Oral Histories, Whitman College Archives

Rodney Alexander, May 17, 1991
George Anderson, August 21, 1997
D. Herbert Armstrong, March 9, 1990
Janette Moses Armstrong, March 9, 1990
Philip Ashby, February 8, 1990
Jan Nye Baxter, August 14, 1997
Larry Beaulaurier, December 4, 1996
Ken Bendure, April 26, 1991
Greg Brown, January 22, 1999
Linda Weihmann Brown, January 22, 1999
V. Purdy Cornelison, April 10, 1991
Michael de Grasse, August 29, 1997
Winifred "Winks" Dunphy, June 8, 1990; February 22, 1993; March
    15, 1993
Ralph Edgerton, June 19, 1993; June 9–10, 1995
Doug Eglington, August 15, 1997
Richard Eells, May 19, 1990

Margaret Ershler, June 25, 1997
Baker Ferguson, October 8, 1997
Hattie Gordon Fry, February 14, 1990
Georgia Mae Wilkins Gallivan, May 21, 1990
Kenneth Garner, February 8, 1990
Vivian Cochran Garner, February 8, 1990
John Haigh, February 23, 1990
Markham Harris, November 15, 1995
William Harris, May 9, 1974; July 27, 1995
Ivar Highberg, October 20, 1998
James Hill, Jr., March 16, 1990
Roy Hoover, August 23, 1995
Margo Collins Hoth, July 28, 1994
Melvin "Jake" Jacobs, March 19, 1990
Shirley Anderson Jennings, July 24, 1990
Donald Patrick Jones, December 6, 1998
Dwelley Jones, n.d., 1973
William L. Kelly, October 9, 1978
Kenyon Knopf, May 6–7, 1997
Grace Allan Lazerson, May 7, 1973
Marsh Lee, December 1, 1991
Craig Lesley, September 5, 1997
Sally Mathiasen Light, June 30, 1997
Lucile Lomen, October 12, 1994
Alex MacLeod, August 17, 1997
Chester Maxey, May 14, 1973; May 22, 1974; January 16, 1976; June
    18, 1979; June 21, 1979; June 22, 1979; August 7, 1980
Edward McMillan, June 19, 1993
Ellen Heath McNamara, April 28, 1990
Russ McNeill, June 9, 1995
Thomas McNeill, July 12, 1994
Peggy Metastasio, January 11, 1999
Iris Little Myers, February 24, 1990
Frances Penrose Owen, October 13, 1991
Malinda Phillips Pankl, August 28, 1997
Edith Pope Patten, March 15, 1990
Louis B. Perry, June 25, 1992; October 1, 1992; June 20, 1995; De-
    cember 3, 1996; December 6, 1996; December 7, 1996

Donald Pickering, April 26, 1990
Eric Pryne, August 18, 1997
Almira Quinn, n.d.
Robert R. "Pete" Reid, October 1, 1992; August 1997
Arthur Rempel, June 16, 1995
John Richards, August 11, 1994
Fredric Santler, January 30, 1980; February 20, 1980
Gordon Scribner, May 4, 1991; May 10, 1991; September 25, 1997
Katherine Sheehan, July 28, 1997
Donald Sherwood, August 14, 1990
Dean Shoemaker, October 13, 1998
Maxine Sires, August 22, 1995
Lola Sims Snyder, March 2, 1990
Keith Soper, May 4, 1990
Richard Stuart, December 6, 1998
Frankie Ladley Wakefield, February 26, 1990
Dorothy Robinson West, July 24, 1994
Zelma Conway Williams, March 18, 1991
Reid Yamamoto, October 3, 1998
Merlin Young, April 25, 1990

Interviews and Oral Histories, Author's Possession

Dale Cosper, January 28, 1999
Bert Edwards, July 23, 1995 (telephone); July 26, 1995; August 1, 1996
Shirley Clem Farmer, July 22, 1996
Baker Ferguson, August 17, 1995
Donald Frisbee, December 19, 1997 (telephone)
Craig Gunsul, January 28, 1999
Franklin "Pete" Hanson, July 15, 1995 (telephone); July 23, 1995
    (telephone); November 30, 1995
Ivar Highberg, February 8, 1995
William Perry, December 4, 1995
Robert R. "Pete" Reid, November 13, 1995; June 18, 1996; April 24,
    2000 (telephone)
Robert Skotheim, January 30, 1999 (telephone); July 30, 1999
David Stevens, July 30, 1996
Tom Williams, April 24, 1999

Newspapers

New York Times
Portland Oregonian
Olympia Olympian
Seattle Post-Intelligencer
Seattle Times
Spokane Chronicle
Spokane Spokesman-Review.
Walla Walla Bulletin
Walla Walla Union
Walla Walla Union-Bulletin

College and University Publications

The Blue Moon (Whitman student publication)
Clock Tower (Whitman student publication)
Daily Hampshire Gazette
Facets (Whitman alumni publication)
Masque (Whitman student publication)
Narrator (Whitman student publication)
Pacific University Register
Waiilatpu (Whitman student yearbook)
Whitman, the Quarterly Publication of Whitman College
Whitman Alumnus
Whitman College Bulletin
Whitman College Catalog
Whitman College Coed Code
Whitman College *Handbook for Faculty and Staff*
Whitman College *New Student's Handbook*
Whitman College Pioneer
Whitman College Quarterly
Whitman Forum
Willamette Scene
Willamette University *Alumnus*
Willamette University Bulletin
Yeast (Whitman student publication)

Books

Addington, Larry H. *America's War in Vietnam*. Bloominton: Indiana University Press, 2000.

Attebery, Louie W. *The College of Idaho, 1891–1991: A Centenneial History*. Caldwell: The College of Idaho, 1991.

Boyer, Paul S., et. al. *The Enduring Vision: A History of the American People*. Lexington, Massachusetts: D. C. Heath, 1996.

Bryce, James. *The American Commonwealth*, Volume II. London: Macmillan, 1888.

Chafe, William H. *The Unfinished Journey: America Since World War II*. New York: Oxford University Press, 1999.

Clark, Norman H. *The Dry Years: Prohibition and Social Change in Washington*. Seattle: University of Washington Press, 1988.

Copeland, Tom. *The Centralia Tragedy of 1919: Elmer Smith and the Wobblies*. Seattle: University of Washington Press, 1993.

Dodds, Gordon B. *The College That Would Not Die: The First Fifty Years of Portland State University, 1946–1996*. Portland: Oregon Historical Society Press, 2000.

Edwards, G. Thomas. *The Triumph of Tradition: The Emergence of Whitman College, 1859–1924*. Walla Walla: Whitman College, 1992.

Fletcher, Eugene. *Fletcher's Gang: A B-17 Crew in Europe, 1944–1945*. Seattle: University of Washington Press, 1988.

Frykman, George A. *Creating the Peoples University: Washington State University, 1890–1990*. Pullman: Washington University Press, 1990.

Gates, Charles M. *The First Century at the University of Washington, 1861–1961*. Seattle, University of Washington Press, 1961.

Goodrich, H. B., and R. H. Knapp. *Origins of American Scientists*. Chicago: University of Chicago Press, 1952.

Gregg, Robert D. *Chronicles of Willamette: Those Eventful Years of the President Smith Era*. Salem, Oregon: Willamette University, 1970.

Hershey, Charlie Brown. *Colorado College, 1874–1947*. Colorado Springs: Colorado College, 1952.

Hewins, Jack. *Borleske: Never Far From Hope*. Seattle: Superior Publishing Co., 1966.

Josephy, Alvin M. Jr. *The Nez Perce Indians and the Opening of the Northwest*. New Haven: Yale University Press, 1965.

Loevy, Robert D. *Colorado College: A Place of Learning, 1874–1999*. Colorado Springs: Colorado College, 1999.

Lyon, E. Wilson. *The History of Pomona College, 1887–1969*. Claremont, California: Pomona College, 1977.

Maxey, Chester C. *The World I Lived In*. Philadelphia: Dorrance & Co., 1966.

McClelland, John Jr., *Wobbly War: The Centralia Story*. Tacoma: Washington State Historical Society, 1987.

Molohon, Bernard. *Sons of Marcus Whitman*. Seattle: Sterling Publishinc Company, 1952.

Penrose, Stephen B. L. *Whitman: An Unfinished Story*. Walla Walla: Whitman Publishing Company, 1935.

Perrett, Geoffrey. *Days of Sadness, Years of Triumph: The American People, 1939–1945*. Madison: Wisconsin University Press, 1985.

———. *A Dream of Greatness: The American People, 1945–1963*. New York: Coward, McCann & Geoghegan, 1979.

Petersen, Keith. *Educating in the American West: One Hundred Years at Lewis-Clark State College, 1893–1993*. Lewiston, Idaho: Confluence Press, 1993.

Ravitch, Diane. *The Troubled Crusade: American Education, 1945–1980*. New York: Basic Books, 1983.

Reid, J. Juan. *Colorado College: The First Century, 1874–1974*. Colorado Springs: The Colorado College, 1979.

Rorabaugh, W. J. *Berkeley at War: The 1960s*. New York: Oxford University Press, 1989.

Rudolph, Frederick. *The American College and University: A History*. New York: Vintage Books, 1962.

Schwantes, Carlos Arnaldo. *The Pacific Northwest: An Interpretive History*. Lincoln: University of Nebraska Press, 1999.

Sheehan, Jeffrey A., compiler. *Selected Speeches of Donald H. Sheehan*. Peterborough, New Hampshire: Windy Row Press, 1974.

Soden, Dale E. *A Venture of Mind and Spirit: An Illustrated History of Whitworth College*. Spokane: Whitworth College, 1990.

Stameshkin, David M. *The Strength of the Hills: Middlebury College, 1915–1990*. Hanover, New Hampshire: University Press of New England, 1996.

Index

Following the names of those who graduated from Whitman, and/or who served as faculty or board members, are the dates of graduation and/or service, in parentheses; dates of service for staff members are included when they are known with some degree of certainty. For example, Baker Ferguson graduated from Whitman in 1939, was a member of the faculty from 1946 to 1948, and served as an overseer from 1957 to 1966 and a trustee from 1966 to 1989, and is listed thus:

Ferguson, Baker (1939; 1946–1948; 1957–1989)

G. Thomas Edwards

A native of Oregon, G. Thomas Edwards received his B.A. in history at Willamette University and his M.A. and Ph.D. in history at the University of Oregon. In 1964 he came to Whitman College, where he taught a wide variety of classes in American history, especially the Civil War and the American West. He received a teaching award from the senior class of 1968, a Burlington Northern Teaching Award in 1988, and the Robert Y. Fluno Teaching Award in 1996, and was appointed William Kirkman Professor of History in 1986. In 1998 his former students established the G. Thomas Edwards Faculty Award for Excellence in Teaching and Scholarship; that same year Willamette University awarded him the Distinguished Alumni Citation for Achievement in Education.

During his long career at Whitman Edwards served on numerous committees and was elected chair of the division and chair of the faculty. He has spoken widely on behalf of the college and in 1996 he received the Alumni Faculty Award for Service. He has published numerous book reviews and many articles on reformers, women, promoters, politicians, soldiers, and educators. Edwards co-edited *Experiences in a Promised Land* and authored *Sowing Good Seeds: The Northwest Suffrage Campaigns of Susan B. Anthony*, and *The Triumph of Tradition: The Emergence of Whitman College, 1859–1924*, for which he received a Governor's Writing Award in 1994.

In 1998 he retired; he and his wife, Nannette, who taught in Walla Walla public schools for many years, moved to Portland in 2000.

Tradition in a Turbulent Age has been designed and produced by John Laursen at Press-22 in Portland, Oregon. The type is Sabon, and the paper is acid-free Glatfelter Sebago. Printing and binding are by Publishers Press, Salt Lake City, Utah.

One hundred copies of *Tradition in a Turbulent Age* have been bound in leather and numbered and signed by the author.

This is number *78*